ENCOUNTERS WITH WORLD AF

CW01021564

Encounters with World Affairs

An Introduction to International Relations

EDITED BY
Emilian Kavalski
Australian Catholic University, Australia

Routledge
Taylor & Francis Group

LONDON AND NEW YORK

First published 2015 by Ashgate Publishing

Published 2016 by Routledge
2 Park Square, Milton Park, Abingdon, Oxon OX14 4RN
711 Third Avenue, New York, NY 10017, USA

Routledge is an imprint of the Taylor & Francis Group, an informa business

British Library Cataloguing in Publication Data
A catalogue record for this book is available from the British Library

Library of Congress Cataloging-in-Publication Data
Kavalski, Emilian.
  Encounters with world affairs : an introduction to international relations / by Emilian Kavalski.
    pages cm
  Includes bibliographical references and index.
  ISBN 978-1-4724-1115-0 (hardback) -- ISBN 978-1-4724-1116-7 (pbk) – ISBN 978-1-4724-1117-4 (ebook) – ISBN 978-1-4724-1118-1 (epub) 1. International relations – Case studies. I. Title.
  JZ1305.K3785 2015
  327–dc23

                                                                                    2014031729

ISBN 13: 978-1-4724-1116-7 (pbk)
ISBN 13: 978-1-4724-1115-0 (hbk)

Contents

Detailed Contents

List of Figures and Tables

Figures

Tables

List of Contributors

Anne Ally – Early Career Research Fellow at Curtin University (Australia). Her research interests are in the areas of terrorism studies and counterterrorism with a focus on the public and policy responses to terrorism. Anne has a professional background in policy having worked as a Senior Policy Officer and Manager within the Western Australian Government. She is the author of *Terrorism and Global Security: Historical and Contemporary Approaches* (Palgrave Macmillan, 2011).

Greg Anderson – Associate Professor of Political Science at the University of Alberta (Canada). Greg's research is oriented around the political economy of international trade relations and North American integration. He is currently working on (with Chris Kukucha, University of Lethbridge) a new textbook on *International Political Economy* to be published by Oxford University Press (Canada) in 2015 and just completed a volume (with Brian Bow, Dalhousie University) focused on multilevel governance in post-9/11 North America (Routledge). Greg's current research involves the dynamics of asymmetrical power in North American integration, exploring power's hierarchical nature in the context of different forms of pooled sovereignty.

Alex Balch – Senior Lecturer in Politics at Liverpool University (UK). His research focuses upon state responses to international mobility and security, the politics of hospitality in Europe and rights-based approaches to problems of forced labour and human trafficking. Dr Balch has published extensively on the policy process, the role of expertise and the ethics of immigration politics in the UK, Spain and the EU. He has also worked with – and for – a number of public and third sector organisations at national and international levels on these topics.

Theresa Callan – Principal Lecturer in International Relations at the University of Portsmouth (UK). Her research interests include state- and nation-building in post-conflict societies as well as security-building after violent conflict. She has researched the decommissioning of armaments in the Balkans and Northern Ireland. She is the author of (with Lisa Harrison and Jamie Munn) *Key Research Concepts in Politics and International Relations* (Sage, 2013) and (with Fergus Carr) *Managing Conflict in the New Europe: The Role of International Institutions* (Palgrave Macmillan, 2002)

Mark Chou – Lecturer in Global Studies at the Australian Catholic University (Melbourne). His research lies at the intersection of international relations, democratic theory and cultural politics. Mark's most recent work has been exploring how national and global democratic configurations collapse.

Eunyoung Ha – Assistant Professor of Politics at Claremont Graduate University (USA). Her research areas include comparative politics, political economy and political institutions. Her primary research interest involves the impact of globalization and domestic political institutions on domestic political economy, in particularly as manifested in the following areas: inequality, poverty, growth, unemployment, inflation, welfare spending and taxation. Her research is published in major political science journals such as the *Journal of Politics*, *Comparative Political Studies*, *European Political Science Review* and *International Interactions*. She currently investigates the impact of globalization and government ideology on aspects of economic performance such as economic growth, unemployment and inflation and the differentiation between these impacts on developed and less developed countries.

Lui Hebron – Associate Dean for the the College of Business and Management and the Keller Graduate School of Management at the San Francisco Bay Metro of DeVry University (USA). His research focuses on the areas of political economy (Globalization), international relations (ethnicity, conflict and war) and Asian studies (Pacific Rim and China). Dr Hebron's publications include *Globalization: Debunking the Myths* (Pearson Prentice Hall, 2008, 2010; co-authored with John Stack) and *The Ethnic Entanglement* (Praeger Publishers, 1999; co-edited with John Stack). His current book-project, *Globalization and China: Political Economy's Odd-Couple* is under contract with CQ Press. He has also published several chapters in edited volumes as well as numerous journal articles.

Stephen Hobden – Senior Lecturer in International Politics at the University of East London (UK) where he teaches courses on international relations theory and China in world politics. His previous research project involved examining the links between international relations and historical sociology and included the publications *Historical Sociology and International Relations* (Routledge, 1998) and a volume edited with John Hobson, *Historical Sociology of International Relations* (Cambridge University Press, 2002). More recently he has been involved in a project with his UEL colleague Erika Cudworth on complexity thinking, ecology and international relations, which has included the publication *Posthuman International Relations: Complexity, Ecologism and Global Politics* (Zed Books, 2011).

Emilian Kavalski – Associate Professor of Global Studies at the Institute for Social Justice, Australian Catholic University (Sydney). Emilian's research has focused on International Theory, Security Studies and Asian Affairs. He is currently working on (i) the encounter of International Relations with life in the Anthropocene, especially the conceptualization of and engagement with non-human actors; and (ii) the nascent Asian normative orders and the ways in which they confront, compliment and transform established traditions, norms and institutions. Emilian contends that in both these areas the application of Complexity Thinking has important implications for the way global life is approached, explained and understood.

Julia Hyeyong Kim – Assistant Professor at the Department of Political Science and International Studies, Incheon National University (South Korea). Julia's research interests are on institutions, globalization, welfare state, economic crisis, neoliberalism and poverty alleviation. She is currently working on (i) welfare spending in developing countries after economic crisis; and (ii) welfare state development and democratization in authoritarian regimes. Julia is examining whether welfare state development can help alleviate poverty in developing countries.

Brian R. King – Associate Professor of Political Science at Muskingum University (USA). His academic areas of interest reside mainly in American politics, with a focus on political institutions such as the presidency, Congress and the Supreme Court. Brian also studies judicial politics, constitutional law and American foreign policy. Apart from these American areas, he also studies international relations, with a focus on international crisis and crisis decision-making. He coordinates the pre-law program, advises the American Studies program, manages the University's association with American University's Washington Semester program and is advisor to various student organizations.

Lavina Lee – Lecturer in the Department of Modern History, Politics and International Relations at Macquarie University (Australia). Lavina's research has focused on the role of norms in international relations, legitimacy and US hegemony, US foreign policy, international law on the use of force, nuclear non-proliferation and Indian foreign and security policy. She is currently working on a series of articles focused on India's foreign policy identity as expressed in its attitude to democracy promotion and the nuclear non-proliferation regime.

Kevin Marsh – Visiting Assistant Professor of Political Science at the College of Wooster (USA). His research and teaching interests include US foreign policy, national security policy and defense strategy. Kevin has published articles analysing the politics of the US foreign policy-making process, including the decisions to adopt troop surges in the Iraq and Afghanistan wars, and the decision to intervene in Libya in 2011. Kevin is currently working on research projects examining AirSea Battle, the impact and influence of the Tea Party in US foreign policy and the future of US defense strategy in the post-counterinsurgency era.

David Muchlinski – Adjunct Professor of Political Science at the University of Nebraska, Omaha (USA). David's research interests lie primarily in two areas: (i) studies of conflict including ethnic, religious and civil conflicts, and (ii) the ability of non-state actors to develop systems of governance and public goods provision in weak and failed states. David's current research focuses on Israeli state-building from 1920–48 and examines the implications that Jewish agricultural settlements had on Israeli military strategy and economic development during that time period.

Avery Poole – Lecturer in International Relations at the University of Melbourne (Australia). Her research focuses on institutional change in regional organisations, particularly in regard to human rights in the Association of Southeast Asian Nations (ASEAN). She also examines the changing role of Indonesia in the region and the world, and Australian foreign relations in the context of Asia Pacific regional architecture.

Sandra Popiden – Assistant Professor of Political Science at Bridgewater State University (USA). Sandra's research lies at the intersection of International Relations, Comparative Politics and

Economic Development. She specializes in the causes and consequences of civil and separatist wars, the internationalization of separatist and ethno-religious conflicts and the role of globalization, economic development and natural resources in fragile states. Her other research areas include the politics of identity, conflict management, democratization and trans-national security challenges.

Nilay Saiya – Assistant Professor of Political Science and Director of International Studies at the State University of New York, Brockport (USA). His research focuses on the intersection of religion and international relations, especially religious violence and the role of religion in foreign policy-making.

David Siroky – Assistant Professor of Political Science at Arizona State University (USA), where he is a core faculty member of the Center for Social Dynamics and Complexity and a faculty affiliate of the Center for the Study of Religion and Conflict and the Melikian Center for Russian, Eurasian and East European Studies. He received his Ph.D. in Political Science and M.A. in Economics from Duke University and was then the Henry Hart Rice Postdoctoral Fellow at Yale University before arriving at ASU. His research has appeared or is forthcoming in *Comparative Political Studies, Comparative Sociology, Defence and Peace Economics, Democratization, Ethnopolitics, International Organization, Nationalities Papers, Polity, Post-Soviet Affairs, Security Studies, Statistics Surveys* and *Yale Journal of International Affairs*.

Taku Tamaki – Lecturer in International Relations at Loughborough University (UK). He is interested in the intersection between International Relations Theory and Social Theory, focusing particularly on the role of identity and constructions of reality in international politics. Applying this theoretical framework, his current research investigates the contemporary constructions of Asian Otherness in Japanese foreign policy discourse. Also, he is looking into the efficacy of Japan's soft power in winning the hearts and minds of the international community in the era of growing competition from China. He has published articles in academic journals such as *International Relations, International Relations of the Asia-Pacific* and *East Asia: An International Quarterly*.

David Walton – Senior Lecturer in Asian Studies and International Relations at the University of Western Sydney (Australia). David's research focuses on foreign policy in the Asia-Pacific, Security Studies and Diplomatic History. He is a Visiting Professor at the University of Seoul and a 2014 Japan Foundation Fellow at the University of Tokyo. David is currently working on (1) a co-edited book project dealing with the rise of China and power transition in the Asia-Pacific; and (2) a book-project examining Australian foreign policy approaches towards Japan and China over the past three decades.

Chris Wilson – Lecturer in Politics and International Relations at the University of Auckland (New Zealand). His research focuses on violent intra-state conflict in the Asia-Pacific region, particularly Indonesia and India. Chris is currently writing a book examining why large-scale human migration sometimes leads to conflict, while in other cases, migrants and local communities coexist peacefully. He also researches the politics of Southeast Asia, with a focus on the prevalence and practice of illiberal democracy and semi-authoritarianism.

Prologue
Observing and Encountering Global Life

EMILIAN KAVALSKI

In a now well-known response to the question how can he define the disciplinary domain of International Relations, the Danish scholar Ole Wæver famously quipped, 'IR = observing ir' (Wæver 2007, 288). In this statement, 'IR' – with capital letters – stands for the discipline of International Relations (which, just like any other field of knowledge, has its own proponents, theories, subfields and so on), while 'ir' – with small letters – stands for the actual practices and occurrences of international relations (in this sense, 'ir' is very often used interchangeably with phrases such as 'international/world/global affairs' and 'international/world/global politics'). Wæver's suggestion is that the main intent of the disciplinary inquiry into the dynamics of world affairs is to develop appropriate lenses through which to observe the practices of 'ir' – that is, recognize and account for the processes, events and dynamics of international politics. While not necessarily disagreeing with Wæver's observation, the contention proffered in this textbook is that IR is not merely about observing, but also *encountering* world affairs.

In other words, the claim is that *IR=observing and encountering ir.* Encounters do not imply impartiality and in fact demand that you form (as well as express) an opinion on what is going on. The American IR scholar Donald J. Puchala has suggested that by allowing themselves to encounter world politics, students of international relations rather than 'distancing [themselves] from the object under investigation to *observe* it' are able to 'empathetically approach the object, or "live into it", in order to understand it' (Puchala 2003, 222). Depending on the situation, encounters suggest that you are present, engaged and considering what is the appropriate course of action. For instance, imagine bumping into a friend that you have not seen for a long while – you do not merely meet this person, you encounter him/her, you are emotionally engaged by coming face-to-face with that person (most likely you are very happy), and deciding whether you should go on with your pre-planned schedule for the day or just scrap everything and catch up with your friend. Encounters are intense, involved and not necessarily pleasant experiences (for instance, encountering a letter from the tax office that you owe them money is anything but a happy experience). *Encounters usually imply some form of (or the potential for) change* – even if you are not always aware of it.

You will be surprised how common these encounters with world affairs are. In fact, they are so ingrained in our daily practice that we have seized to pay attention to them. Usually, when we think of global politics, we have in mind meetings between heads of state and government, major international conferences, military conflicts between states and so on. However, the encounters with world affairs do not have to be as dramatic as being near the World Trade Center in New York on 11 September 2001. In fact, our daily practices – such as shopping, going to work or surfing the internet – are all instances of individual encounters with world affairs.

For instance, something as simple as buying a chocolate bar from your local corner store offers an encounter with the patterns of world affairs, where a substantial part of the coco that goes into the making of chocolate is being sourced through child slave labour. In this respect, our innocent act of indulgence contributes to the suffering others. Owing to this quotidian nature of our encounters with world affairs, Karl W. Deutsch, one of the grandees of the discipline, has argued that 'international relations and foreign policy are far too important to be left to specialists. Many young men have thought that world affairs need not concern them, until their draft boards told them otherwise. If our lives are so deeply affected by, and our responses so essential to international affairs, then we must increase our capacity to understand, to decide, and to act' (Deutsch 1968, viii).

While this textbook aims to draw your attention to the various encounters with world affairs, it has to be acknowledged that such encounters are not unaffected by your own personal assumptions, perceptions and views. In other words, the events, persons and things that you encounter are not independent of the outlook that you have imbibed at home, that you have acquired through participating in communal and cultural practices, that you have learnt at school. In this respect, our individual and subjective mode of observation frames the encounters with world affairs that we have. For instance, consider the experience of what some have called the 'age of discovery' – the nearly five centuries (from the fifteenth all the way to the beginning of the twentieth century) of intense (and mostly ruthless and violent) European colonization and exploitation of the peoples and resources of Africa, Asia, the Americas and the Antipodes (Australia, New Zealand, the South Pacific islands).

As you know, the 1492 voyage of Christopher Columbus set in motion the period of European conquest – often referred in Western scholarship as the 'age of discovery' and by indigenous communities as a period of 'invasion and dispossession'. However, Columbus himself failed to recognize the newness of the 'New World' that he encountered because of his particular worldview. To begin with, he did not think that he had reached a new continent, but that he had hit the eastern shores of Asia. More importantly, his encounter of the various Amerindian peoples was prejudiced (and some might even argue that it has effectively been prevented) by his own cultural, religious and ideological expectations. It might be puzzling today, but initially Columbus refused to recognize that the Amerindians spoke a different language from him. In a well-known study of the discovery of the Americas, the French scholar Tzvetan Todorov shows that Columbus merely assumed that the indigenous populations were unable to speak. For this reason, he took several Amerindians to teach them how to speak (a European language). Reading the journals and letters of Columbus, Todorov uncovers that 'Columbus's failure to recognize the diversity of languages permits him, when he confronts a foreign tongue, only two possible, and complementary, forms of behaviour: to acknowledge it as a language but to refuse to believe it is different; or to acknowledge its difference but to refuse to admit it is a language' (Todorov 1982, 30). In this respect, Columbus carried with him a set of schemes and representations of the world that informed a mindset making it impossible for him – perhaps, the best known of discoverers – to encounter the Amerindians. Instead, Columbus 'knows in advance what he will find' (Todorov 1982, 17) and acknowledges only the things that fits his preconceived model, while ignoring all the aspects that were incongruent. In fact, Columbus went as far as to suppress any alternative explanations by requiring every member of his expedition to swear an oath that subscribed to his own version of the nature of the voyage. The penalty for decentres was quite severe: 'A fine of ten thousand *maravedis* [Spanish currency] is imposed on anyone who subsequently says the contrary of what he now said, and on each occasion at whatever time this occurred; a punishment also of having the tongue cut off, and for the ship's boys and such people, that in such cases they would be given a hundred lashes of the cat-o'-nine-tails, and their tongue be cut off' (Todorov 1982, 22).

Those following in Columbus's footsteps appeared to comprehend better that the new world was different, yet they were likewise unable to overcome the Eurocentric mindset that framed their encounter. The memoirs of Bernal Díaz del Castillo probably offer one of the most graphic illustrations of the type of encounter that will come to dominate most of world politics in subsequent centuries. Bernal Díaz was one of the participants in the expedition of Hérnan Cortés that conquered the Aztec Empire (1519–21). His description of the fate of the Aztec capital is particularly poignant:

> And when we saw all those cities and villages built in the water, and other great towns on dry land, and that straight and level causeway leading to Mexico, we were astounded. Gazing on such wonderful sights, we did not know what to say, or whether what appeared before us was real. These great towns and cues [temples] and buildings rising from the water, all made of stone, seemed like an enchanted vision. Indeed, some of our soldiers asked whether it was not all a dream. It is not surprising therefore that I should write in this vein. It was all so wonderful that I do not know how to describe this first glimpse of things never heard of, seen, or dreamed of before ... I say again that I stood looking at it, and thought that no land like it would ever be discovered in the whole world ... But today all that I then saw is overthrown and destroyed; nothing is left standing. (Díaz 1963, 216–20)

This passage clearly demonstrates that Díaz and his companions were able to encounter both the Aztecs difference and achievements 'never heard of, seen, or dreamed of'; yet, such acknowledgement did not prevent them to pillage and ultimately destroy this 'enchanted vision'. Thus, the pattern of international affairs that was ushered in by the experience of European conquest is probably best described as a period of 'the understanding-that-kills' (Todorov 1982, 127). The encounters of world affairs should therefore not be assumed to be just a record of particular occurrences. These encounters are underpinned by specific aims and preconceptions of those that tell us about them. For instance, we have no accounts of the Amerindian 'encounter' with Columbus and, generally, very little in terms of the indigenous experience of European colonization. In this respect, when we think of the various encounters with world politics, it is very important to consider who tells the story of what happened. For instance, whenever two of your closest friends have a quarrel, you can always talk to both of them and hear each of their versions of the reasons for the particular conflict. In the history and study of world politics, we rarely have that.

Instated, more often than not, we have only the version told by one of the participants. Or if there is an alternative version of events, it is usually related in a language other than English that does not make it onto the pages of 'our' history books and foreign policy manuals. While this is not unique to the discipline of IR, its domain of analysis marks it as a particular and distinct 'Anglosphere' that has consistently silenced non English accounts of international relations (Vucetic 2011). This not least reflects that first the British Empire and then the United States have been the dominant actors on the world stage during the birth and growth of the discipline of IR. In fact, in the post-World War II period, IR began to be increasingly perceived as an 'American

What is International Relations?

Consider the similarities/differences between the following statements and think in what way they reflect/challenge your own understanding of the nature of international relations – both as a discipline and as a pattern of interactions.

The aim of [international relations] is to help towards forming the habit of mind that is required for appreciating questions of foreign policy ... There is no smooth and easy path for the conduct of international policy; nor for its study. The fortunes of nations should not be left to the hazards of the unforeseen. Those who are responsible for guiding the relations between states need a vast equipment in knowledge and in aptitude. They must know the resources, the constitution and the manner of government, the treaty obligations, the character of the dominant personalities, the national temperament and national objects, both of their own state and of its connexions – sometimes unruly and suspicious connexions – in the family of nations. They must well consider the relations of means to ends. Here, without any doubt, there is need of eyes for the past, the present, and the future – need of the three eyes of prudence: memory, intelligence, providence. By these Fortuna is won. Of all the regions of politics there is no other of which it is so strictly true as of the international, that only the most complete knowledge and command available of all the factors should be allowed to count, whether for those who direct or for those in a succeeding age who try to judge them. There is often in history and politics some 'one thing unknown' that is required as the key to all. Especially has that been true of relations between state and state ... Thus, the student of international relations needs precise as well as vast equipment in knowledge but, not less, he needs equipment in habits of mind.

D.P. Heatley (1919, 48, 87–8)

It is, of course, a truism to say that these relations are extremely complicated and that they cover the widest possible field. They are relations, by definition, political in character between states as such. They are also relations between states and private individuals, and those relations can become political if the home state of the individual takes sufficient interest in the matter. On the other hand, the relations may be of a rather technical nature, for instance between government administrations; in this case, being apolitical, I do not think they would easily give rise to international conflicts. Finally, there are – at least, I should like to consider them as part of international relations – relations between private citizens in different countries.

M. Åke Hammarskjöld (1930, 468)

Historical international relations therefore have been overwhelmingly an exercise of one or more state organisms against others ... International relations are now a definite addition to what has been referred to as the concentric circles of society – states coming into external contact rapidly develop forms of cooperation, of working together for the common end of their own aggrendizement.

Denys P. Myers (1937, 437–8)

The study of international relations ... is an introduction to the art and science of the survival of mankind. If civilization is killed within the next thirty years, it will not be killed by famine or plague, but by foreign policy and international relations. We can cope with hunger and pestilence, but we cannot yet deal with the power of our own weapons and with our behaviour as nation-states ... International relations is that area of human action where inescapable interdependence meets with inadequate control. We can neither escape from world affairs nor wholly shape them to our will. We can only try to adjust the world while adjusting to it. Within this limited scope, we must retain and, where possible, enhance our most deeply held values.

Karl W. Deutsch (1968, vii)

International politics seems more and more like politics in general; and politics in general is becoming synonymous with man's efforts to carve out a pattern of coexistence with his biological and physical environment. International politics becomes ecopolitics. No wonder things are complex ... International complexity already exists because there are many interconnected parts. The environmental crisis, the North-South gap, rising unemployment, unplanned urbanization, new dependencies upon raw materials, new vulnerabilities to terrorism, and the food shortage constitute the interconnected parts. But the existence of this complexity is not matched with a political recognition of the problem. The knowledge to bring about recognition exists. But the political institutions for acting on the knowledge do not. Hence, we are headed toward ecological catastrophe.

Ernst Haas (1975, 853)

Death stinks. Left unattended, it finds many ways to make its presence felt. Jogging on the college grounds, it is not unusual to be suddenly assailed by the stench of a dead animal in the bushes. I take notice, maybe make a passing comment to my jogging companion, and continue running. I imagine dead humans stink too. I say imagine because, unlike the stench of dead animals, or of rotting potatoes, or of slimy mushrooms, I cannot recall any strong sensory evidence of that stench ... But I suspect I shouldn't have trouble imagining that stench, especially given the nature of what I study: international relations. International relations is a field littered with dead and dying bodies. But the dead never seem to rot or stink, whether portrayed discretely or starkly, sketched crudely or stylistically. Qana, Haditha, Fallujah. International relations overflows with corpses. I see them every day. Trained primarily to conceptualize some piles of corpses as a sign of 'power' and others as 'crimes against humanity', other languages of the body pass me by silently.

Himadeep Muppidi (2012, 3)

social science' both as a result of the growth in US superpower and because of the growing influence of US-based IR scholars, academic journals and funding agencies (Hoffmann 1977). Thus, the study and the narratives of encountering world affairs reveal important power relations that define the content and practices of international interactions. Edward Said has famously ascertained that these patterns reflect an underlying narrative of *orientalism*. According to him, orientalism is a dominant Western ideology 'to control, manipulate, even to incorporate, what is a manifestly different (or alternative and novel) world'. This orientalist ideology 'conceives of the difference between cultures, first, as a battlefront that separates them and, second, as inviting the West to control, contain, and otherwise govern (through superior knowledge and accommodating power) the Other' (Said 1978, 12, 47–8).

As you will see in the following chapters, borne out of prejudice, ignorance and the pursuit of hegemony such a profound and complete disregard for non-Western experience and practices has come to define quite a few of the encounters in world affairs. In many ways, the prioritization of Western experience and mode of explanation has also marked the very study of international affairs. For instance, consider the statement of Alfred Thayer Mahan, deemed to be one of the most influential American strategists of the nineteenth century, who advocated that the West had an obligation to spread its 'civilization' (if necessary by force):

> *The tendency to efficient organization is a faculty wholly distinct from the personal qualities of the individual members of certain races which do not show the same capacity for organization; such as the Chinese or the Turks. To right what is amiss, to convert, to improve, to develop, is of the essence of the Christian ideal ... This fundamental proposition is not impaired by the fact that force is best exercised through law, when adequate law exists. Except as the expression of right, law is an incubus. Hence, much of the present magnification of law is the mere worship of a fetish. To such a view aggression, in the primary sense of onward movement, is inevitable. Those who will not move must be swept aside. They may be drawn into the movement of moral forces, as Japan has; but if not, they must be brought despite themselves into external conditions favourable to their welfare and the general good, as has been done in India, in Egypt, and in the Philippines. (Mahan 1912, 116–17)*

In fact, just like Columbus failed to recognize the diversity of languages and cultures that he encountered during his voyage of 'discovery', the study of world affairs has consciously and purposefully tended to exclude the political experience and form of organization that did not fit the Western template. Living in nineteenth-century Cairo (Egypt), the British legal scholar Sheldon Amos ascertained the ubiquity of the Eurocentric view emphatically:

It might be asked why the accidental re-arrangements of the countries of Europe which followed on the fall of the Roman Empire should dictate, for ever, the notion of a true state. To this it may be replied that the geographical area to which the science of politics extends at present is limited to the countries of Europe and North America and to those countries that are directly subjugated to the influence and dominating control of Europe and the United States. Thus it is not saying too much to allege that, for all purposes of practical politics and, therefore, of that science on which all sound practice must rest, the state is that integral unity which has been discovered by the accidents of European development. (Amos 1890, 66)

Less than half a century later, the influential American political scientist John W. Burgess echoed these sentiments in his proclamation that 'only Europe and North America have succeeded in developing such political organizations to furnish the material for scientific treatment' (Burgess 1933, 7). As the British philosopher and theologian Alfred Caldecott explained, these attitudes reflect a deep-seated conviction that owing to the presumed 'weakness of "people of colour"', 'the higher races of [Europe and North America]' have a 'responsibility to [act] as Trustees, Guardians, and Elder brothers of the lower races'. As Caldecott put it, 'the very fact that this protective function [of the higher races] has brought so many backward peoples out of isolation into the graduated scheme of international life cannot be overrated as a presage of future good' (Caldecott 1910, 17–21). While the crass racism underpinning these sentiments has long been expunged from the discipline of IR, the 'colonial signs' (Muppidi 2012) of its intellectual foundations can hardly be overlooked.

For instance, Kenneth Waltz – probably the most influential IR scholar in the post-World War II period – has ascertained that the 'theory of international politics is written in terms of the great powers of an era. It would be … ridiculous to construct a theory of international politics based on Malaysia and Costa Rica' (Waltz 1979, 73). Bearing in mind its intellectual foundations and subject matter, it should not be surprising that there is 'no non-Western International Relations theory' (Acharya and Buzan 2007). For the last 300 or so years, the rivalry over structural power in world politics has been 'the great game' of Western actors. Thus, the so-called Oriental/Third World/developing nations have been the plaything of Western whims – either as mere observers (at best) or as victims (at worst). In both instances, however, *agency* (especially, global agency) was not a feature of their international identity. Instead they were assumed to be passive recipients of the Western gaze/rule/aid/securitization as scripted by the templates of colonialism, the Cold War order, democratization and the war on terror. As a result, 'students of world politics have not been socialized into being curious about the "non-West" but have been encouraged to explain away non-Western dynamics by superimposing Western categories' (Bilgin 2008, 11). The outcome has been an overwhelming tendency to produce 'crude and caricatured understanding of … the varying forms of life of "non-Western peoples"', whose difference is 'almost pre-consciously treated as simultaneous with disorder, fear, suspicion, and condescension' (Inayatullah and Blaney 2004, 123). At the same time, the Eurocentric preoccupations of the discipline have tended to prioritize topics and issues that concern the West (such as 'the struggle for/balance of power'), while those preoccupying the non-West have tended to be ignored (such as malnutrition and disease).

Thus, it is only with the nascent rise of Asia to global prominence that scholars, policymakers and publics have begun to confront be need to 'reOrient' (Frank 1998) the language and outlook of the study of world affairs. The call for a new vocabulary that will account for the dynamism

Should there be a discipline of International Relations?

Consider which side of this conversation do you support and why.

While there is a general agreement that International Relations (IR) constitutes a separate field of knowledge with subfields such as Foreign Policy Analysis, Security Studies, International Political Economy, etc. (hence, the multitude of textbooks on the topic), there is an emergent debate whether there should be such a discipline. For instance, the British academic Chris Brown (2001: 218), taking into account the parochial Eurocentric and Anglophone nature of the discipline, has recommended that 'if we truly wish to promote diversity in international thought, it may be that a crucial first step will be to contribute to the work of dismantling "International Relations" as an academic discipline'. His rationale is that 'the very idea that one actually needs a discipline of IR may be tied with a particular worldview'. According to another British scholar, John M. Hobson (2012, 344) the key normative purpose of the discipline of IR has been that of 'defending and celebrating the idea of the West in world politics'. In this respect, much of the support for 'the end International Relations' originates in the understanding that the discipline as a whole is premised on 'a thinly disguised parochialism masquerading as a global field of study' (Griffiths and O'Callaghan 2001, 188). Other scholars, while accepting the Western character of IR, have argued for the 'decentring' of the discipline. Such decentring entails an active and committed project of 'interrogating, disturbing, engaging, reframing, challenging, mocking, or even undoing mainstream, privileged ways of viewing the world' (Nayak and Selbin 2010, 8). Such a project will profoundly alter the identity and operational codes of the discipline but not lead to its demise. The aim of this is to develop diverse forms of non-Western IR (Inayatullah and Blaney 2004; Schilliam 2011). Thus, rather than dismantling the discipline, the intention is to make possible 'other ways of becoming otherwise in worlds that do not end where we have learnt to draw the line with such elegance, and with such violence' (Walker 2009, 258).

and turbulence of global life has to address two deep-seated tendencies in IR – (i) to think-in-paradigms and (ii) to return to familiar concepts. This is a perplexing trend, bearing in mind that the topography of the theory and practice of IR – especially following the end of the Cold War – has developed into a multi-coloured matrix of perspectives and frameworks on the appropriate ways for studying world affairs. Motivated by the failure to anticipate the demise of Soviet superpower, the discipline embarked on an unprecedented widening and deepening of its outlook. It appears, however, that two-and-a-half decades later the innovative spark that invigorated this proliferation of views has petered out. Instead, what used to be a liberating tearing up of conceptual straitjackets seems itself to have oscillated into the very 'paradigmatic imperialism' that it sought to displace. As the American IR scholar J. Samuel Barkin cogently demonstrates, the discipline is plagued by a 'castle syndrome' – proponents of different IR schools engage in defending and reinforcing the bulwarks of their analytical castles, while bombarding the claims of everybody else (Barkin 2010).

The contention is that the discipline has increasingly immersed itself in debates on the substantiation of particular paradigms rather than encountering the reality of global life. To put it bluntly, the turbulence of world affairs appears to have relevance (primarily) to the extent that it can validate (or disprove) the proposition of a particular IR school. Such contention should not be misunderstood as a condemnation of the field, or as a suggestion that it lacks sophistication. On the contrary, post-Cold War developments have challenged the discipline to venture into intellectual terrains that it previously did not deem either necessary, or important or worthwhile. The contention here is that while this has been going on, IR scholars failed to break from the leftover mode of thinking-in-paradigms – probably one of the most palpable Cold War legacies of the discipline. Thus, despite the 'new challenges', IR has not abandoned its 'old habits' (Waltz 2002). Such a proclivity has recently been termed as 'returnism' – IR's predilection for traditional conceptual signposts that provide intellectual comfort zones – but are 'simply images of old concepts' de-contextualized from (and, therefore, inapplicable to) current realities (Heng 2010).

This textbook is intended to assist you in your individual journeys to encounter the diverse and fascinating realities of world affairs in the full spectrum of their unabridged complexity, contingency and contradictions. The first part of the textbook introduces you to the key perspectives on and frameworks for the explanation and understanding of international relations. In particular, this section familiarizes you with the history and theories of global politics. At the same time, it also outlines the ethical and moral considerations accompanying the patterns and practices of international affairs as well as the levels of analysis from which they can be perceived. The second part of the volume details the central actors on the world stage. While the significance of states, individuals and international organizations has long been recognized in the study of IR, this textbook offers the first ever consideration of nature as a meaningful actor in the dynamics of world affairs. The final, third part of the textbook discusses a number of topics and issues that inform the study and practice of international politics. While the third section does not pertain to be exhaustive in its treatment of 'all' the topics and issues, it nevertheless addresses those that are considered to have the greatest bearing on the study and practice of world affairs. The contention underpinning the analyses provided in the following chapters is that if IR is to maintain its relevance, it has to get comfortable with the inevitability of ongoing change – that is, abandon existing assumptions and 'adjust to the unexpected in creative and appropriate ways' (Rosenau 2001, 149). The hope is that the studies included in this textbook make a small, but meaningful step in this direction.

BIBLIOGRAPHY

Acharya, A. and Buzan, B. (2007) 'Why is there no Non-Western IR Theory', *International Relations of the Asia-Pacific* 7(3), 287–312.

Amos, S. (1890) *The Science of Politics* (London: Kegan Paul, Trench, Trübner & Co).

Barkin, J.S. (2010), *Realist Constructivism: Rethinking International Relations Theory* (Cambridge: Cambridge University Press).

Bilgin. P. (2008) 'Thinking Past Western IR', *Third World Quarterly* 29(1), 5–23.

Burgess, J.W. (1933) *The Foundations of Political Science* (New York: Columbia University Press).

Caldecott, A. (1910) 'International and Inter-Racial Relations', *The Sociological Review* 3(1), 13–23.

Deutsch, K.W. (1968) *The Analysis of International Relations* (Englewood Cliffs, NJ: Prentice Hall).

Díaz, B. (1963) *The Conquest of New Spain* (London: Penguin Books).

Frank, A.G. (1998) *ReOrient: Global Economy in the Asian Age* (Berkeley, CA: University of California Press).

Haas, Ernst (1975) 'Is There a Hole in the Whole? Knowledge, Technology, Interdependency, and the Construction of International Regimes', *International Organization* 29(3), 827–76.

Hammarskjöld, M.Å. (1930) 'The Permanent Court of International Justice and Its Place in International Relations', *Journal of the Royal Institute of International Affairs* 9(4), 467–97.

Heatley, D.P. (1919) *Diplomacy and the Study of International Relations* (Oxford: Clarendon Press).

Heng, Y-K. (2010) 'Ghosts in the Machine: Is IR Eternally Haunted by the Specter of Old Concepts', *International Relations* 47(5), 535–56.

Hoffmann, S. (1977) 'An American Social Science: International Relations', *Daedalus* 106(2), 41–60.

Inayatullah, N. and Blaney, D.L. (2004) *International Relations and the Problem of Difference* (London: Routledge).

Mahan, A.T. (1912) *Armaments and Arbitration: The Place of Force in the International Relations of States* (New York: Harper & Bros).

Muppidi, H. (2012) *The Colonial Signs of International Relations* (London: Hurst).

Myers, D.P. (1937) 'The Bases of International Relations', *American Journal of International Law* 31(1), 431–48.

Nayak, M. and Selbin, E. (2010) *Decentering International Relations* (London: Zed Books).

Puchala, D.J. (2003) *Theory and History in International Relations* (London: Routledge).

Rosenau, J.N. (2001) 'Stability, Stasis and Change: A Fragmenting World'. In R.L. Kugler and E.L. Frost (eds), *The Global Century: Globalization and National Security* (Washington, DC: National Defence University Press), 127–53.

Said, E.W. (1978) *Orientalism* (London: Routledge and Kegan Paul).

Shilliam, R. (ed.) (2010) *International Relations and Non-Western Thought: Imperialism, Colonialism and Investigations of Global Modernity* (Abingdon: Routledge).

Todorov, T. (1982) *The Conquest of America: The Question of the Other* (Norman, OK: University of Oklahoma Press).

Vucetic, S. (2011) *The Anglosphere: A Genealogy of Racialized Identity in International Relations* (Berkeley, CA: Stanford University Press).

Walker, R.B.J. (2009) *After the Globe, Before the World* (Abingdon: Routledge).

Waltz, K. (1979) *Theory of International Politics* (Reading, MA: Addison-Wesley).

Waltz, K. (2002) 'The Continuity of International Politics'. In K. Booth and T. Dunne (eds), *Worlds in Collision* (Basingstoke: Palgrave Macmillan), 348–54.

Wæver, O. (2007) 'Still a Discipline after All These Debates?' In T. Dunne, M. Kurki and S. Smith (eds), *International Relations Theories: Discipline and Diversity* (Oxford: Oxford University Press), 288–308.

PART I:
Perspectives and Frameworks

Chapter 1
The History of Global Politics

KEVIN MARSH

This chapter reviews the history of the international system from the beginnings of the Westphalian order through the present day. The chapter introduces key terms and concepts of global affairs, including the balance of power, sovereignty, globalization, security, arms races, and the state, among others. Additionally, this chapter is intended to provide students with an overview of the development of the international system since 1648 and how the Westphalian order is changing. Scholars have traditionally ignored or underemphasized the role of the East in international relations, and in particular have minimized or glossed over the importance of India, China and other Eastern powers in global affairs. As the international system is changing and wealth and power flow to the East, it is necessary to review the origins and influence of a Eurocentric dominant perspective in global affairs and how the changing world order is challenging this traditional view. In this chapter, students will learn about the creation of the nation-state system, the changing notion of sovereignty, the development of the balance of power and how the international system has evolved over the past 400 years. Students will read about important eras and events in global affairs, including the rise of the nation-state, the Napoleonic Wars and subsequent Concert of Europe system, imperialism and the Industrial Revolution, the emergence of the United States as a great power, the World Wars, the Cold War, globalization, ethnic conflict and the challenges and features of the post-9/11 world.

Key Words: Sovereignty, Balance of Power, Treaty of Westphalia, Thucydides, Nation-State, Concert of Europe, Treaty of Versailles, Nuclear Proliferation, Deterrence, Eastphalia.

Chapter 1

The History of Global Politics

KEVIN MARSH

INTRODUCTION

The contemporary international system marks the latest stage of the continued evolution of international relations. Issues such as terrorism, economic inequality, interstate conflict and cooperation, among others, are all rooted in history. Studying history, then, allows for students of international relations to develop a contextually sophisticated understanding of the contemporary international system. People often look to the past when trying to make sense of current events or major transitions in politics and international relations. It is in that vein that this chapter seeks to explain the central events, periods and trends of history and how these factors shaped and guided the development of the current international system.

This chapter will provide an overview of the significant historical periods and events of international relations from the Peace of Westphalia in 1648 through to the rise of China and the Asia-Pacific in the present. This chapter is intended to familiarize the student with important international relations concepts such as **sovereignty**, **the balance of power, nation-state, Nationalism, deterrence** and **the Peace of Westphalia**. The chapter will also review the development of the modern international system and outline the emergence of the nation-state system, the establishment and progression of sovereignty and fluctuations of the international balance of power. Admittedly, this chapter provides a traditional, Eurocentric account of the history of global affairs. While the standard history of global affairs does bear the hallmark of a Eurocentric or Anglophone view of international relations, it is the intent of the author to explore the underlying reasons for the dominance of this perspective and also analyse the implications of recent challenges to the Westphalian interpretation of international relations.

> **Sovereignty** – a state that has defined boundaries, political control over that territory and has the power to exert taxes from its population.
>
> **The Balance of Power** – how power is distributed within the international system.
>
> **Nation-state** – basic unit of organization in the international system. A sovereign state organized around a common national characteristic.
>
> **Nationalism** – a sense of common allegiance that binds people together. It may be the result of common ethnic, racial, cultural, linguistic, religious or civic ties.
>
> **Deterrence** – the ability to prevent an attack or make it too costly for an adversary to attack.
>
> **Peace of Westphalia** – the system of treaties ending the Thirty Years' War and establishing the modern international system.

EUROCENTRISM AND THE HISTORY OF INTERNATIONAL RELATIONS

The discipline of international relations has traditionally been dominated by a Eurocentric or Anglophone interpretation and account of global affairs. Beginning with Thucydides and *The History of the Peloponnesian War* and reinforced by the emergence of the Westphalian system, Western definitions of power, diplomacy, sovereignty, law and the balance of power were promoted by scholars and policymakers. Traditional histories of international relations focus almost exclusively on the Treaty of Westphalia, the development of the nation-state system and balance of power in Europe, and then proceed to assess the evolution of these concepts largely from a Western perspective.

For more information on the tradition Eurocentrism in accounts of the history of the international system, see Hobson (2012), Vucetic (2011), Kayaoglu (2010), Kim, Fidler and Ganguly (2009). Also, Kayaoglu (2010) provides an overview of scholars who discuss Eurocentrism, including Osiander (2001), Beaulac (2004) and Teschke (2003). Some scholars have gone so far as to reject the Westphalian interpretation of international relations as inaccurate, Eurocentric and one that artificially imposes Western ideas and values on the international system.

In a valuable summary of the counterarguments to the Westphalian interpretation of international relations, Kayaoglu (2010) argues:

> The Westphalian narrative allows scholars to reinvent a framework of normative hierarchy depending on where Western and non-Western societies are placed in the narrative. Western states produce norms, principles, and institutions of international society and non-Western states lack these until they are socialized into the norms, principles, and institutions of international society. In this perspective, international society is a normative hierarchy assumed to reflect the natural division of labor in international relations.

Furthermore, the traditional discussion of the pre-Westphalian era of international relations also reflects a Western-dominated perspective as ancient Greece and Rome feature heavily in accounts of the beginnings of the international system. Scant attention is paid to the role of China and India in the pre-Westphalian order, and the East's role in international relations is then analysed according to Westphalian terms as well. This chapter will conclude with an analysis of the implications of Eurocentrism for the history of international relations.

THE ENDURING LEGACY OF THUCYDIDES IN INTERNATIONAL RELATIONS

The Greek historian Thucydides is generally credited with creating the field of international relations. Thucydides wrote *The History of the Peloponnesian War*, a truly magisterial work recounting the events of the war for dominance over Greece between the city-states of Athens and Sparta. Thucydides cast a long shadow over international relations and continues to influence the discipline to this day. *The History of the Peloponnesian War* discussed core features of international relations, including the distribution of power, alliances, competition, security, diplomacy, public opinion and war. Thucydides also provided the basic framework for the development of international relations theory as he reflected on human nature, politics, justice, power and role and nature of diplomacy.

In addition to inspiring the emergence of international relations as a distinct discipline, Thucydides contributed to the Eurocentric narrative of the history of the international system. Thucydides was the first of a series of Greek and Roman historians who wrote about the key events of international relations in the ancient world. These texts continue to form the basis for much of international relations scholarship, and The History of the Peloponnesian War in particular has strongly influenced the course of international relations theory. European and US historians continued this pattern of dominance and have interpreted the history of international relations from a distinctly Eurocentric or Anglophone perspective. In short, Thucydides continues to influence the history of international relations and theory of international relations. His legacy, as stated before, still looms over the discipline.

THE WESTPHALIAN SYSTEM AND THE DAWN OF MODERN INTERNATIONAL RELATIONS

Almost two centuries of unremitting religious conflict between Catholics and Protestants in Europe came to a climax in the Thirty Years' War from 1618–48. The war was fought mainly in Germany and Central Europe and was the culmination of the religious wars between Protestantism and Catholicism. Northern Europe, including England, Scotland, Scandinavia and much of Germany, sided with Protestantism while France, Spain and Austria led the Catholic coalition. One common aspect of this era of religious warfare in Europe was the doctrine of foreign intervention in the domestic politics of states. European monarchs believed that they were justified (and in some cases, commanded by God) in intervening in their neighbours' domestic affairs and, if necessary, going to war to impose a particular religion on their adversaries.

The Thirty Years' War broke out in 1618 and produced unprecedented levels of violence, carnage and destruction. Various armies ravaged the countryside of Central Europe and little distinction was made between civilians and combatants (Mingst 2004). Germany was particularly devastated by the war and suffered massive population losses. All of the great powers in Europe intervened in the war and employed religious pretexts to settle old scores with enemies, recover lost territory or conquer new lands (D'Anieri 2014; Kissinger 2014). The war also saw widespread employment of mercenaries and other private armies and militias (Mingst 2004). By 1648, with the continent exhausted from warfare, the warring countries commenced peace negotiations and eventually produced a series of treaties leading to the Peace of Westphalia.

The Peace of Westphalia ended the war and also established the foundations of the modern international system and international relations. The Peace of Westphalia established the modern conception of sovereignty, ended religious warfare in Europe and ushered in the nation-state system (Kissinger 2014). Modern international relations, albeit Eurocentric in scope, therefore, can be traced back to the Peace of Westphalia in 1648. Sovereignty dictated that states had clearly defined and accepted borders, and were free to determine their own domestic policies without foreign interference. The European great powers recognized each other's territorial boundaries and also accepted the principle of non-interference in domestic politics (Mingst 2004).

Recognition of the supremacy of state authority resolved the complex system of overlapping loyalties and blending of Church and state that had framed European politics for centuries (Mingst 2004). Westphalia also ended the era of religious warfare in Europe and enshrined the right of monarchs to decide the official religion of their subjects. States agreed to extend the principle of non-interference in domestic affairs to religion, thus removing one of the causes of much of the wars in Europe for the preceding centuries.

Perhaps the single most significant aspect of the Peace of Westphalia was the inception of the modern nation-state system in Europe. The nation-state remains the most significant political unit in the contemporary international system and has dominated international relations for hundreds of years. Prior to the Westphalian system, Europe (and indeed, much of the world) was a confused system of feudal kingdoms with multiple overlapping avenues of authority and empires featuring considerable local autonomy and weak central governments. The Catholic Church also exerted substantial political authority over the lands of the Holy Roman Empire (modern-day Germany) and in Italy.

These feudal kingdoms, while loosely organized around a measure of nationhood, failed to meet the definition of a *state*. For example, the monarchs of these feudal states did not command standing, professional state armies. Instead, monarchs were dependent upon lords to raise levies on behalf of the king and also collect and distribute tax revenue (Mingst 2004). These lords retained significant autonomy and often challenged the central monarch over succession and other political issues.

The Westphalian system contributed directly to the rise of the modern nation-state as the old feudal order collapsed. States with strong central government and bureaucracies replaced the multiple levels of lords and competing jurisdictions of Feudalism. The monarch commanded a standing state military, governed with the assistance of an expanded and more capable bureaucracy, asserted central government control over a defined, recognized territory and, perhaps most importantly, controlled the collection and dissemination of tax revenue (Mingst 2004). Local armies were disbanded, as was the reliance on mercenaries and other non-state military actors. Westphalia, then, gave rise to the modern nation-state system as collections of people with similar ethnic, linguistic, religious or other characteristics formed political units led by a strong central government controlling professional militaries and possessing sovereignty over a clearly defined and recognized territory.

FROM NAPOLEON TO WORLD WAR I: THE INTERNATIONAL SYSTEM IN TRANSITION

The rise of Napoleon Bonaparte as the leader of post-revolutionary France and the series of wars that resulted from his attempts to establish French hegemony over Europe signalled a new era of international relations. Napoleon, an officer in the French army, seized control of the country as the revolutionary regime collapsed at the end of the 1790s. Bonaparte was eventually named Emperor of France in 1804 and sought to conquer Europe. Napoleon then exploited French Nationalism to develop a massive citizen army that he wielded with ruthless efficiency in conquering much of Europe (D'Anieri 2014). An alliance of Britain, Russia and Prussia eventually defeated the French at Waterloo in 1815 and Napoleon was exiled to the island of St Helena where he lived out the rest of his days and died in 1821. While Napoleon was ultimately unsuccessful in imposing French hegemony on Europe, his wars would inspire the creation of a new order in Europe that would impose a measure of great power, peace and stability for the next 100 years.

The victorious powers in Europe met in Vienna in 1815 to create a new postwar system for Europe. This order, which became known as the **Concert of Europe**, sought to prevent war and stabilize the relationship between the great powers. The great powers of Europe, including Britain, Russia, Prussia, Austria and France, instituted multiple meetings in order to conduct diplomacy and resolve interstate disputes peacefully. The Concert system maintained relative peace and stability among the great

> **The Concert of Europe** – a system of conferences held by the European great powers to resolve conflicts after the end of the Napoleonic Wars.

powers in Europe over the next 100 years. Mingst (2004, 29) describes the impact of the Concert on international relations in Europe, stating; meeting over thirty times before World War I, the group became a club of like-minded leaders, and through these meetings they legitimized both the independence of new European states and the division of Africa by colonial powers'. The Concert established a distribution of power where no member sought hegemony and where stability and the *status quo* were valued (Kissinger 1994).

However, while preventing the sort of continental-wide wars of the Napoleonic Era, the Concert system failed to stop several major wars from breaking out during the second half of the nineteenth century. The Concert system began to erode starting with the Crimean War and also struggled to accommodate German and Italian unification in the 1860s. A series of wars instituted by Prussia against Denmark, Austria and France established a unified German Empire led by the Prussian *Kaiser* by 1871. Italy also fought wars of independence against Austria and emerged as a unified state with Rome as its capital by 1870. This series of wars redrew the map of Europe and shifted the distribution of power to the new German *Reich*. The rise of a powerful united Germany dramatically altered the balance of power in Europe and played a large role in the eventual collapse of the Concert system in the years preceding the outbreak of World War I. Indeed, the rise of Germany upset the balance of power and produced a new round of alliance formation and jockeying for position in Europe.

The Concert of Europe era coincided with the Enlightenment and the rise of Liberalism and Nationalism (Mingst 2004; D'Anieri 2014). The Enlightenment unleashed powerful ideas and philosophies of government that would transform politics in Europe and throughout the international system. The principles of **Liberalism** and Nationalism blossomed during this period as the American colonies declared independence from Britain and established the United States of America. The new

> **Liberalism** – a political philosophy stressing individual rights and freedoms.

nation instituted a democratic form of government and espoused the values of Liberalism and individual rights. Liberalism, championed by philosophers such as John Locke, argued that the individual had inalienable rights to life, liberty and property and that the function of the state was to protect those rights (Mingst 2004). Liberalism also supported the right of the people to participate in governance and argued that absolute power concentrated in the hands of monarchs represented tyranny. Liberalism swept through Europe in the 1800s, culminating in the series of revolutions in 1848 that threatened the traditional power and privileges of absolute monarchies (Kissinger 2014).

France's revolution, while eventually succumbing to radical tyranny and the rise of Napoleon, contributed to the rise of Nationalism as a political force. Nationalism proffered that people developed a shared sense of identity through common language, history, ethnicity or religion (Mingst 2004; D'Anieri 2014). European states employed Nationalism to create mass standing armed forces, large centralized government bureaucracies and further solidify the political control of the central state government. Nationalism also directly led to the unification of Germany and Italy and would also pose major political challenges to the viability of the Austro-Hungarian, Russian and Ottoman Empires (D'Anieri 2014). Nationalism would later prove a powerful political force in Asia and Africa as European colonies sought independence following World War II.

INDUSTRIALIZATION AND THE AGE OF IMPERIALISM

During the Concert era, two other developments revolutionized the international system and, by extension, international relations. First, industrialization in Europe and North America dramatically transformed economics, politics and daily life. Industrialization greatly expanded economic activity and trade throughout the world and contributed to urbanization as millions sought to leave the drudgery of agricultural work for the promise of jobs in cities (Mingst 2004). The Industrial Revolution and urbanization also resulted in the invention of modern sanitation systems, the telegraph and telephone and advanced transportation technology including the railroad, steamships and, eventually, automobiles. Industrialization also unleashed powerful political forces within European and North American states as workers sought more rights and higher salaries and struggled against entrenched class interests.

The Age of Imperialism began in earnest in the second half of the nineteenth century as European powers scrambled to seize control of Africa and Asia. Britain, France and Spain all were major imperial powers by the 1700s and had established colonies in North and South America. The Age of Imperialism reached its zenith with the race for Africa. European powers, including Britain, France, Belgium, Italy, Germany and the Netherlands, divided the continent of Africa amongst themselves. The European imperial powers agreed to a set of rules and procedures for establishing colonies in sub-Saharan Africa and dividing the continent in a manner aimed at preventing the outbreak of great power war at the Conference of Berlin in 1884–85 (Mingst 2004). In effect, the European colonial powers drew lines on the map of Africa in order to divide their imperial spheres. This division of the continent was accomplished without consideration of the tribal and ethnic divisions in Africa. Contemporary Africa continues to struggle with the legacy of the European colonization and division of the continent.

European powers seized control of much of Asia during the Age of Imperialism as well. Perhaps most famously, the Indian subcontinent formed the 'crown jewel' of the British Empire. France joined Britain as a colonial power in Asia by seizing Indochina in the 1800s and the Netherlands entered the fray as well by colonizing Indonesia. Britain expanded its Asian holdings to include Hong Kong, Malaysia, Singapore, and also founded colonies in Australia and New Zealand. European domination of Asia became so entrenched that even the great

Chinese Empire granted substantial territorial and political concessions to Britain, France and Germany in the late 1800s.

The expansion of European Empires into Africa and Asia would prove to be particularly significant events in the history of international relations. European Imperialism directly influenced the course of both World Wars and helped transform those conflicts from inter-European to truly global in nature. The Age of Imperialism also set the foundations for the rise of modern Nationalism and ethnic conflict, unstable and failed states and reinforced economic inequality between the Global North and South. Even as the locus of power in the international system shifts to the Asia-Pacific, the legacy of the Age of Imperialism continues to impact international relations in the twenty-first century.

THE RISE OF THE UNITED STATES AS A GREAT POWER

After declaring independence from Great Britain the United States was initially a weak country most concerned with expanding and consolidating its hold on the North American continent. The United States was an active participant in global trade but remained a minor military power throughout most of the nineteenth century. The US did not enter into European power politics, preferring to remain on the sidelines unless European imperial powers threatened to expand into the Western Hemisphere. While not a strong military power and without imperial ambitions of its own, the US steadily grew in economic power throughout the 1800s and asserted its control over the centre of North America from the Atlantic to the Pacific Oceans. Following the carnage and destruction of the Civil War, the US fully industrialized and quickly became one of the most powerful economies in the world by the 1890s.

However, the US did not become a great power until the Spanish-American War of 1898. Using the suspicious destruction of the USS *Maine* battleship in the harbour of Havana, Cuba, as a pretext, the US declared war on Spain and proceeded to quickly defeat the declining European imperial power. The US found itself in possession of numerous former Spanish colonies, including the Philippines, Guam and Puerto Rico. In short, the US was now a great power. During this time period the US also established a powerful navy and expanded the peacetime standing army. While the US armed forces were not in the same league as their equivalents in the European great powers, the United States by 1914 had acquired all of the characteristics of a major power in international relations.

THE WORLD WARS AND THE DEMISE OF THE OLD ORDER IN INTERNATIONAL RELATIONS

World War I

World War I marked the final collapse of the old order of the Concert of Europe system. The unification of Germany fundamentally altered the balance of power in Europe as a united, militarily powerful German Empire inherently threatened other great powers, notably France and Russia (D'Anieri 2014). France and Russia, following the pattern of balance of power politics in international relations, formed a military **alliance** in order to balance rising German power and also contain their mutual enemy in Austria-Hungary. Germany and Austria-

> **Alliance** – a formal military agreement between states to aid one another in case of war.

Hungary then established the Central Powers military alliance in response, thereby dividing Europe into two opposing coalitions.

Britain also warily observed the growth of German military and economic power. The British regarded any potential continental hegemon that could threaten its access to Channel ports as a primary security threat. Germany fitted that description in the first decade of the twentieth century as its industrial output outpaced the British economy and the German army became the largest and most capable in Europe. Anglo-German relations steadily declined in the decade leading up to World War I and helped precipitate a naval **arms race** between the two powers. Britain launched the first modern battleship, the HMS *Dreadnought*, in 1906 and sought to counter a subsequent massive German

> **Arms Race** – when two or more states compete against each other to increase their respective quantity and/ or quality of weapons.

naval expansion program throughout the remainder of the decade. The arms race coupled with expanding German military and economic power led to Britain eventually aligning with France and Russia in the Triple Entente alliance.

World War I was sparked by the assassination of Austrian Archduke Franz Ferdinand on 28 June 1914 in Sarajevo, Bosnia. The assassin, Bosnian Serb nationalist Gavrilo Princip, had received support from the Black Hand, a terrorist organization with links to the Serbian military. The assassination of the Archduke led to a month-long diplomatic crisis that engulfed the great powers of Europe and resulted in the final collapse of the balance of power amidst the outbreak of continental war between the Central Powers and Triple Entente. Austria-Hungary responded to the assassination by issuing a set of demands via a formal ultimatum to Serbia. The Serbs refused to accede to the full list of demands and Austria-Hungary declared war on 28 July 1914. Russia responded to the declaration of war by ordering mobilization of its armed forces in order to protect its Serbian ally and declared war on Austria-Hungary. Germany, fearing the consequences of defeat of its principal ally, ordered mobilization on 30 July and prepared to fight a two-front war against France and Russia. Germany then declared war on France and Russia on 2 August and invaded neutral Belgium in advance of its efforts to first knock France out of the war and then devote its full resources to defeating Russia. Britain issued an ultimatum demanding that Germany withdraw from Belgium and then declared war on Germany on 4 August following the refusal of that ultimatum.

Four brutal years of war followed in which tens of millions of people perished and war spread across the whole of Europe, the Middle East, Africa, the Atlantic and Pacific oceans and Asia. The war featured trench warfare, poison gas, submarines, tanks, aerial combat and shocked the belligerent powers in terms of its cost and length. The war also became a prolonged stalemate as the various armies discovered that machine guns, modern artillery, barbed wire, outmoded tactics and trench systems made advances extraordinarily costly (D'Anieri 2014). Germany employed its submarines or U-Boats against Allied merchant shipping in an effort to starve Britain and force it out of the war.

1917 saw two critical developments that changed the course of the war and also had long-range implications for the history of the international system. First, Russia, wracked by internal political instability and revolution, withdrew from the war as Czar Nicholas II abdicated and a communist government eventually took power led by Vladimir Lenin. Second, the German submarine campaign against Allied shipping contributed to the United States entering the war on the Allied side in April. US troops began to arrive in France in large numbers in 1918 and helped exhaust Germany, who sued for peace in November 1918.

The Aftermath of World War I

The end of World War I dramatically transformed the map and politics of Europe. The dissolution of the German, Russian, Austro-Hungarian and Ottoman Empires resulted in the creation of a score of new states (Mingst 2004; D'Anieri 2014). These states included Poland, Czechoslovakia, Austria, Hungary, Yugoslavia, Estonia, Latvia and Lithuania in Europe. The collapse of the Ottoman Empire resulted in British and French colonization of the Middle East and the formation of Iraq, Lebanon, Syria, Palestine and Kuwait. British and French colonization of the Middle East would have profound implications for international relations and its legacy continues to affect the region today.

World War I also unleashed a new wave of Nationalism throughout Europe as former provinces of the great continental Empires sought to form independent states based around common ethnic and linguistic characteristics (Mingst 2004). This wave of Nationalism soon spread beyond Europe, however, as the European Empires in Asia and Africa confronted growing resistance to foreign occupation. Nationalism was fully embraced by US President Woodrow Wilson, who endorsed the concept of **self-determination** (Mingst 2004; D'Anieri 2014). In sum, the Age of Empires was over in international relations. This new wave of Nationalism would return following the end of World War II and contribute to the European powers divesting themselves of their colonies in Africa and Asia.

> **Self-determination** – the principle that national groups should have the right to create their own nation-states.

Following the armistice in November 1918, the belligerents met at the French town of Versailles to negotiate a formal peace treaty. The **Treaty of Versailles** placed extraordinarily harsh terms on Germany, including the imposition of a 'war guilt' clause, and ordered Germany to pay massive reparations to the Allies. The punitive nature of the treaty, particularly the 'war guilt' clause and the crushing economic disruption caused by the reparations, led to widespread resentment towards the treaty by the German public (D'Anieri 2014). Extremist political groups capitalized on the weakness and instability of the postwar German government and exploited popular opposition to the Treaty of Versailles, eventually leading to the rise of Adolf Hitler and the Nazi Party (Mingst 2004).

> **The Treaty of Versailles** – adopted in 1919, this Treaty officially ended World War I and imposed strict restrictions on German military and economic power.

A second noteworthy resultant of the end of World War I and the Treaty of Versailles was the creation of the **League of Nations**. The League of Nations, championed

> **The League of Nations** – an international organization founded after World War I in an attempt to eliminate aggressive war in international relations.

by US President Wilson, sought to establish an international community that would prevent war and resolve interstate disputes in a peaceful and judicial manner. Wilson envisioned the League effectively outlawing war through instituting the doctrine of **collective security** where the entire international community would unite to defeat aggressive states (D'Anieri 2014). The League was fundamentally undermined as the United States (the US Senate refused to ratify the Treaty of Versailles) and Russia refused to join, and enforcement mechanisms for League decisions were non-existent (Mingst 2004). The League of Nations would prove totally ineffective and collapsed by the beginning of World War II in 1939.

> **Collective Security** – states seek to eliminate aggressive war through uniting together to punish the aggressor state.

Following the Treaty of Versailles, a semblance of stability returned to international relations during the 1920s. Europe was thoroughly exhausted by World War I and Germany and the Soviet Union were too weak and consumed with internal problems to become aggressive. The United States retreated to its familiar isolationist foreign policy and resolved to never again become involved in a European war. However, this period of relative stability would be short-lived.

In 1929, the US stock market crashed, causing massive economic disruptions throughout the world. Global economic activity regressed, unemployment rates in the industrialized nations reached 25 per cent or higher and trade came to a standstill as well as the Great Depression paralysed the economies of Europe and North America. The Depression quickly crippled the European economy and struck Germany particularly hard. Societal tensions, political instability and extremism and persistent resentment over the Treaty of Versailles fatally weakened the German Weimar Republic, paving the way for the rise of Adolf Hitler (D'Anieri 2014).

Adolf Hitler and the Nazi Party took advantage of the chronic instability in Germany and built a growing political movement that eventually rose to power as Hitler was named Chancellor in 1933. Hitler quickly proceeded to consolidate complete control over Germany and instituted a totalitarian state. Hitler then withdrew from the Treaty of Versailles, engineered a massive military build-up, and began to assert territorial claims against Germany's neighbours, including Austria, Czechoslovakia and Poland. British and French efforts to appease the German dictator at the 1938 Munich Conference failed to dissuade Hitler from continuing to demand territorial concessions from Poland and other German neighbours.

The rise of Nazi Germany coincided with two other significant developments in the international system. First, Imperial Japan emerged as an aggressive great power in Asia and sought to create a Japanese-dominated Empire in the Pacific that would displace the United States and the European colonial powers from Asia. Japan also envisioned dominating China and proceeded to deploy troops to Manchuria (a northeastern province of China in 1931) before mounting a full-scale invasion of China in 1937. The Japanese invasion of China caused relations between Japan and the United States to quickly deteriorate, with the United States gradually escalating diplomatic and economic pressure on Japan, including imposing an oil embargo in July 1941. Japan's government was dominated by an ultranationalist wing of the military who believed that Japan needed to conquer much of Southeast Asia in order to secure vital natural resources. This confluence of events set the stage for the eventual Japanese attack on the US naval base at Pearl Harbor in Hawaii in advance of unleashing a massive assault against the Philippines, Indonesia, Indochina, Malaysia and various Pacific islands including Wake and Guam.

Second, the Soviet Union arose as a major new power in Europe following the consolidation of a totalitarian communist state under the dictator Josef Stalin. Stalin succeeded Lenin and imposed complete communist party control over virtually all aspects of Soviet society. Stalin purged the Soviet military and government of perceived traitors and enemies of the state, instituted a program of forced collectivization of agriculture, oversaw the rapid industrialization of the Soviet economy and engineered a famine in the Ukraine that killed millions. The Soviet Union encompassed the whole of the former Russian Empire and maintained the largest military in Europe. As the 1930s came to a close, it appeared that Europe would be divided between two totalitarian superpowers, with the Soviet state standing as the clear totalitarian rival to Nazi Germany.

World War II

The appeasement of the Munich Conference in 1938 failed to dissuade Hitler's lust for territory and dreams of a massive German superstate dominating central and Eastern Europe. Nazi Germany issued an ultimatum to the Polish government in 1939 demanding that Poland concede the Danzig corridor (a strip of land separating Germany proper from East Prussia). The Polish government refused, and on 1 September 1939, German troops invaded Poland. In response, Britain and France declared war on Germany. World War II had begun in Europe. German forces expertly employed combined arms warfare and **blitzkrieg** tactics to quickly defeat the Polish military and force the surrender of Poland. The Soviet Union also invaded Poland from the east and split the now-occupied country with Germany. German forces then invaded Belgium, Holland and France in May 1940 and

> **Blitzkrieg** – a style of warfare emphasizing speed and combining tanks, infantry, artillery, and aircraft to quickly defeat an opponent.

defeated the Western Allies in a surprisingly quick victory. Following the French surrender in June 1940, Britain stood alone against Germany and endured months of fierce bombing raids in what became known as the Battle of Britain. German armies then invaded the Balkan countries in southeastern Europe, conquering Yugoslavia and Greece by the end of spring 1941.

1941 was one of the most critical years of the war as Germany invaded the Soviet Union on 22 June, the Japanese attacked the US naval base at Pearl Harbor on 7 December, thereby expanding the war to the Asia-Pacific, and Germany and Italy declared war on the US. The war which had begun in Europe was now a fully global struggle that would ultimately result in the deaths of between 50–60 million people and usher in the nuclear era. The German invasion of the Soviet Union, while initially spectacularly successful, eventually bogged down within sight of Moscow and descended into a war of attrition. Initial rapid Japanese victories and advances through the Asia-Pacific were rebuffed at the Battle of Midway in June 1942. The Soviets then turned the tide on the Eastern front at the Battle of Stalingrad and put German forces on the defensive. Allied forces landed in North Africa in the fall of 1942 and proceeded to defeat German and Italian troops seeking to conquer the Middle East. 1943 saw American forces gradually grind away at the Japanese-occupied zone in the Pacific while Allied forces invaded Sicily and Italy. Soviet armies steadily pushed back their German counterparts from European Russia, Belarus and the Ukraine throughout 1943 as well.

The course of the war swung irrevocably in favour of the Allies in 1944 as the Soviet Union expelled German troops from Soviet territory and then invaded occupied Poland, American forces inflicted a series of major defeats on Japan in the Pacific theatre and the British, Americans and Canadians opened a second front in Europe with the invasion of Normandy. German and Japanese forces continued to stubbornly resist the Allied advances, however, exerting a terrible price for territory seized. The British and American advance on Germany from the West, despite a temporary setback at the Battle of the Bulge, wore away at the German military as the Soviet army relentlessly slogged forward in the East. Soviet and American forces met at the Elbe River in spring 1945, and Soviet troops captured Berlin in May 1945. Germany unconditionally surrendered on 8 May 1945, thus ending the war in Europe.

Japan could not stop the American and British drives across the Pacific throughout 1944 and 1945 and the home islands soon came under unremitting strategic bombing from the US Army Air Force. American forces suffered heavy losses in their island-hopping campaign across the Pacific and incurred massive casualties in the costly and hard-fought invasions of Iwo Jima and Okinawa in spring and summer 1945. US President Harry Truman, who had assumed office following the death of Franklin Roosevelt, decided to go forward with the Manhattan Project, which was the codename for the US research program on atomic weapons. Following a successful test of an atomic bomb at Alamogordo, New Mexico, on 16 July 1945, Truman decided to use atomic bombs against Japanese cities in an effort to convince Japan to surrender and prevent the planned invasion of the Japanese home islands. The US dropped atomic bombs on Hiroshima and Nagasaki in August 1945 and secured the unconditional surrender of Japan on 2 September 1945. The most destructive war in history was over, as was the multipolar balance of power in the international system. The Soviet Union and the United States now stood as the two superpowers in international relations. The nuclear era had begun, and the Cold War would soon follow.

THE COLD WAR AND INTERNATIONAL RELATIONS

Origins

The end of World War II marked an epochal shift in the international system. The traditional multipolar distribution of power structuring international relations for several centuries was replaced by a bipolar system where two ideologically opposed rival superpowers would confront one another across the globe for the next 46 years. Following the defeat of Nazi Germany, Europe was divided between the Western Allies and the Soviet Union. Germany became the border between Western, non-communist Europe and the Soviet-dominated communist East and was itself divided into a democratic, capitalist West Germany and an authoritarian, communist East Germany. Tensions over how to proceed with dividing Germany led to the Soviet blockade of West Berlin in 1948 and the resultant US-British airlift of food and other essential supplies to the beleaguered population. The United States and its allies in Western Europe formed the North Atlantic Treaty Organization (NATO) in 1949 to protect against potential Soviet aggression, and the Soviets and their allies in Eastern Europe countered with the formation of the Warsaw Pact military alliance. The Cold War had begun in earnest and the conflict between the United States and Soviet Union would dominate the international system for the next 50 years.

What are the reasons for the outbreak of the Cold War? One underlying explanation is a conflict over competing interests, ideologies, and visions for the postwar order (Mingst 2004). First, the ideological orientations of the two states were incompatible as the United States championed democracy and Capitalism while the Soviet Union espoused Marxist-Leninist doctrine and Communism (Mingst 2004). Second, each side believed that the other maintained aggressive intentions and planned to seize control of the other's respective sphere of influence in Europe. Third, the Soviet Union, reeling from the cataclysmic destruction unleashed by the 1941 German invasion, wanted to establish a buffer zone of friendly communist states in Central and Eastern Europe that would guard against future German militarism and any potential invasion (Mingst 2004). Fourth, the United States was afraid that the Soviet Union, having refused to demobilize its massive armies after the end of the war, was planning on invading Western Europe.

A second explanation for the Cold War is rooted in the international relations theory of structural Realism which maintains that state foreign policy is predicated on the distribution of power in the international system. Structural Realism was created by Kenneth Waltz (1979) in his seminal work *Theory of International Politics*. As the Soviet Union and United States were the two superpowers, it became a near-certainty that the two states would compete and come into conflict with one another. In a bipolar system, any gain by one side would be interpreted as a loss by the other. Therefore, the Soviet Union and United States were effectively predestined to view each other as their mutual primary geopolitical adversaries.

The Cold War Goes Hot In Asia

The Cold War quickly spread to Asia. In 1949 the Chinese Civil War ended as the Chinese communists under the leadership of Mao Zedong defeated the Nationalist government of Chiang Kai-Shek. Mao immediately declared China to be a communist state, renamed it the People's Republic of China and officially allied with the Soviet Union. China's alignment with the communist bloc dramatically altered the global balance of power and officially brought Asia into the field of competition between the US and Soviet Union.

The dominoes then continued to fall in Asia as North Korea, a communist state, invaded South Korea in July 1950. Korea had been divided along the 38th parallel following the end of World War II as the Soviet Union occupied the northern half and the United States occupied the southern part of the peninsula. The Soviets installed Kim Il-Sung as the leader of North Korea and provided military equipment and advisers for the North Korean army. The United States, in turn, established a non-communist regime in South Korea and provided direct military assistance to the fledgling Republic of Korea. The North Korean invasion caught the US by surprise and quickly overwhelmed the South Korean army and the small number of US troops in support. US reinforcements and air power helped stop the North Korean advance at Pusan and a daring amphibious invasion led by US general Douglas MacArthur at Inchon then routed the North Koreans. China intervened in the war as US forces approached the Yalu River and pushed US troops back into South Korea. The war then became a stalemate for the next three years until an armistice agreement was reached in 1953 which resulted in the division of the peninsula and a highly tense security situation that persists to the present day.

Vietnam served as another central Asian flashpoint during the Cold War. Vietnam was part of the overall French colony of Indochina and had been occupied by Japan during World War II. France then sought to reassert its control over Indochina following the Japanese surrender and soon became embroiled in a full-scale guerrilla war with Vietnamese rebels. French forces were defeated at the Battle of Dien Bien Phu in 1954 and withdrew soon afterwards. Like Korea, Vietnam was divided between a communist North and a non-communist South. And as in the case of Korea, war almost immediately broke out between North and South Vietnam as the North supported communist Viet Cong guerrillas and eventually sent troops into South Vietnam.

Following the Gulf of Tonkin incident in 1964, the United States, which had provided substantial military assistance and large numbers of advisers to South Vietnam, directly intervened in the war. US involvement gradually escalated over the next five years and grew to include over 500,000 troops fighting in South Vietnam, massive conventional bombing raids of North Vietnam and incursions into Cambodia. The Vietnam War engendered serious social divisions in the United States and turned into a quagmire. US President Richard Nixon withdrew US troops from Vietnam by 1973 and agreed to a cease-fire and then signed the Paris Peace Accords, officially ending US involvement in Vietnam. War quickly resumed, however, and North Vietnam conquered South Vietnam on 30 April 1975 as North Vietnamese troops seized the South's capital of Saigon.

The Nuclear Arms Race and Cuban Missile Crisis

One of the most important features of the Cold War was the nuclear arms race between the United States and the Soviet Union. The United States enjoyed a brief monopoly in nuclear weapons until the Soviets detonated their first atomic bomb in 1949. Britain and France developed their own nuclear arsenals in the 1950s and China tested its first bomb in 1964. Israel attained nuclear capability in the 1960s with India and Pakistan then following in the 1970s. North Korea became the newest member of the nuclear club in 2006 when it officially tested an atomic device.

The arms race between the United States and Soviet Union led to the deployment of over 50,000 nuclear weapons at the height of the Cold War in the mid-1980s. Both countries maintained the ability to absorb a full nuclear strike and respond with an equally devastating counterattack. The shared vulnerability of the two superpowers to nuclear attack resulted in mutually assured destruction (MAD). MAD referred to the ability of the US and Soviet Union to absorb a nuclear attack and respond in kind. Essentially, it would be suicidal for either superpower to use nuclear weapons as that would ensure the destruction of both countries. MAD produced a tenuous level of stability throughout the Cold War and also reinforced the concept of deterrence. Deterrence refers to the ability of a state to prevent an adversary from attacking it either through possessing the capabilities to defend against the attack or convincing the adversary that the costs of an attack are prohibitive.

The single greatest crisis of the Cold War was a direct result of the arms race. In 1962, the Soviet Union deployed nuclear weapons and substantial numbers of troops to Cuba. The nuclear weapons on Cuba could reach targets in the United States in as little as four minutes and could hit anywhere in the US outside of the Pacific Northwest. Upon discovering the nuclear missiles, the Kennedy administration imposed a blockade on Cuba and prepared to launch air strikes and mount a full-scale invasion. The crisis was resolved when the Soviet Union agreed to withdraw the missiles in exchange for a public assurance by the Kennedy administration that the US would not attack or invade Cuba and a private guarantee that the US would remove its Jupiter nuclear missiles from Turkey.

Decolonization in Asia and Africa and the Arab-Israel Conflict

The Cold War coincided with two other critically important events in the history of international relations. First, the great European empires in Asia and Africa dissolved, creating scores of new independent states. Decolonization remade the maps of Asia and Africa and had long-ranging implications for the international system. While most colonies were granted independence peacefully, major colonial wars broke out in Algeria and Vietnam as France fought to retain control of its empire. The British partition of the Indian subcontinent resulted in independent and mutually hostile India and Pakistan. India and Pakistan would go on to fight three wars with one another and develop nuclear weapons. Decolonization also resulted in the creation of the State of Israel in 1948 and the subsequent Arab-Israeli conflict.

Following British withdrawal from Palestine, Jews living in the former mandate declared independence in 1948 and established the Jewish State of Israel. Israel secured its independence by defeating an invasion by the neighbouring Arab states. Israel would go on to fight three more major wars with Arab coalitions in 1956, 1967, and 1973. The 1967 Six-Day War was particularly consequential in international relations as Israel occupied the Palestinian territories of the West Bank and Gaza Strip and asserted full control over Jerusalem. The Israeli occupation of these territories provided the foundation for the ongoing Israeli-Palestinian conflict. Israel and its principal Arab adversary, Egypt, signed a peace treaty at the Camp David Accords in 1978 that reduced the threat of regional war in the Middle East. The Middle East remains one of the most unstable regions in international relations and, as this chapter will address later, is in the throes of a new round of political instability and transformation.

Endings: the Collapse of Communism in Europe and the Dissolution of the Soviet Union

Significant internal problems plagued the communist states of Europe by the 1980s. The Soviet Union and its satellites were unable to implement economic policies that could meet consumer demand and compete with the capitalist West. In addition, the Soviet Union, despite spending some 25 per cent of its annual gross domestic product (GDP) on defense, lagged behind the United States in terms of military technological capabilities. Soviet leader Mikhail Gorbachev instituted economic and political reforms in the USSR in an effort to modify but ultimately preserve the communist system (Mingst 2004). Gorbachev also announced that the Soviet Union would no longer use force to maintain communist governments in the Warsaw Pact states. Gorbachev unleashed a tidal wave of pent-up opposition to the communist governments of Eastern Europe that would lead to a massive transformation of Europe and presage a new era of international relations.

The East German government unsealed its border with West Germany in November 1989 and also opened the Berlin Wall which had divided East and West Berlin since 1961. By the end of 1989, the communist governments of Eastern Europe had all fallen, and the Warsaw Pact dissolved soon thereafter. Gorbachev limped on in power in the Soviet Union and defeated a coup attempt in August 1991. However, the attempted coup sealed the fate of the Soviet Union, and on 25 December 1991 the Soviet Union officially dissolved. It was the first time in history that a superpower had simply decided to peacefully cease to exist. The Cold War, the nuclear arms race and the bipolar international system were finished.

THE POST-COLD WAR ERA: CHANGE AND CONTINUITY IN INTERNATIONAL RELATIONS

Hope for a New Era 1991–2001

The end of the Cold War unleashed a wave of optimism in international relations. The threat of global nuclear war had receded, the tense competition and conflict between the United States and Soviet Union was finished and the last great totalitarian ideology of Communism had been defeated. Francis Fukuyama (1989, 1992) argued that the 'end of history' was at hand; meaning that the era of ideological conflict was over. Capitalism and democracy had triumphed against authoritarianism and command economies. Reflecting liberal international relations theory, Fukuyama and like-minded scholars, as well as policymakers, believed that the spread of democracy and Capitalism in the international system would result in a greater level of global peace, stability and prosperity.

Scholars and policymakers pointed to **democratization** and **globalization** as two forces that were fundamentally transforming the international system, economics, politics and international relations. Many authoritarian states throughout the world democratized during this period, including the former communist states in Europe, Russia, as well as dozens of countries in Latin America, Africa and Asia. The number of democratic states was at its highest in world history in this period of the post-Cold War era. This latest wave

> **Democratization** – the process by which states transition from non-democratic forms of government to democracy.
>
> **Globalization** – the integration of the global economic, trade, communications and financial systems.

of democratization would be challenged in the post-9/11 era as some nascent democracies regressed back into authoritarianism (Gat 2007).

The global economic integration unleashed by globalization deepened as states removed trade barriers and liberalized their economic policies. Globalization included massive increases in international financial and capital flows, rapid economic development and industrialization in the Global South, the erosion of manufacturing and other heavy industries in the Global North, freer movement of capital and labour and the ability of consumers and producers to trade goods and services over vast distances cheaply and quickly. In addition to its economic aspects, globalization spread US and Western cultural norms and values throughout the world. For example, US fast food chains and other corporate icons such as Starbucks, Apple and Microsoft, and US popular culture became widespread and part of an emerging global culture. The proliferation of advanced communications technology such as mobile phones, personal computers and the internet revolutionized trade, finance and economics as well as further entrenched global economic integration and the penetration of US brands and popular culture into markets around the world. The world economy boomed throughout the 1990s and the international system enjoyed a period of relative peace and stability.

In another noteworthy development in the history of global affairs, the United States, as the victor of the Cold War, achieved unparalleled dominance in international relations. The United States entered its unipolar moment as the Soviet Union ceased to exist, leaving a dramatically weakened Russia in its wake. Commentators such as Charles Krauthammer (1990, 2002) argued that the United States effectively possessed the power to remake the international system. US economic and military power far outstripped any potential rivals during the 1990s as well. American dominance of the international system was further solidified by a lack of balancing against the United States by rival great powers.

International organizations became important players in the post-Cold War era as well. The European Union was founded in 1992 and proceeded to implement political and economic integration of its members and would eventually grow to include the former communist states in Central and Eastern Europe. NATO transformed from an anti-Soviet military alliance into a security organization that enforced the peace in the Balkans and promoted democracy. Finally, the United Nations Security Council sought to play a larger role in international relations, reduce conflict and war and resolve pressing issues such as global poverty, human rights, environmental protection and nuclear proliferation.

Economic power began to shift in earnest to the Asia-Pacific during the 1990s as globalization proceeded. China reformed its economic policies, liberalizing its system and joining the international trade and financial system. China's rapid and consistent economic growth transformed the state into a true economic powerhouse in the twenty-first century. China soon coupled its impressive economic development with military modernization, thereby firmly establishing itself as a great power.

However, while the 1990s was an era of relative peace, prosperity and stability in the international system, trouble lurked on the horizon. Ethnic conflict in Africa and the former Yugoslavia resulted in atrocities in Rwanda, Sudan, Bosnia and Kosovo (Mingst 2004). Terrorism became truly transnational as Al Qaeda emerged and carried out an escalating series of attacks against US interests. Russia regressed into authoritarianism, the Israel-Palestinian conflict continued unabated and tensions remained high on the Korean peninsula, the Taiwan Straits and on the Indian subcontinent. AIDS and other infectious diseases continued to afflict millions, and climate change, resource depletion, famine, poverty and economic inequality each emerged as significant international relations problems. Then, on a clear late summer day in September 2001, the international system suffered a tremendous shock at the hands of non-state actors.

The Post-9/11 World 2001–Present

The 9/11 terrorist attacks mark a critical transition point in the post-Cold War era of international relations. The United States responded with an invasion of Afghanistan in October 2001 and a mounted a global campaign against Al Qaeda and related Islamic fundamentalist terrorists. Terrorism emerged as one of the central security problems in contemporary international relations in the post-9/11 era as major terrorist attacks occurred in Pakistan, Britain, Russia,

India, Spain and Indonesia, among other countries. The relative peace and stability of the 1990s had been shattered as non-state actors demonstrated their ability to dramatically impact the international system.

Following the invasion of Iraq in 2003, the unipolar moment came to an end for the United States. Indeed, the distribution of power in the international system experienced marked shifts in this decade as the United States entered a period of relative decline, China displaced Japan as the second-largest economy in the world, Russia re-emerged as an assertive great power, the Middle East experienced profound political instability and change as a result of the Arab Spring and the European Union wrestled with political integration and the effects of fiscal and economic crisis. The US suffered military overstretch as it struggled to conduct gruelling counterinsurgency operations in Iraq and Afghanistan. The Global Financial Crisis beginning in the fall of 2008 nearly collapsed the international financial system and resulted in a severe recession that crippled the economies of the United States and Europe. Fiscal crises compounded the impact of military overstretch for the US and also threatened to scuttle the European Union and its common currency.

The locus of power in the international system had clearly transferred to the Asia-Pacific by 2014. The rise of China and other great powers coupled with the commensurate relative power decline of the United States is expected to usher in a new balance of power in the international system. A multipolar system of several great powers appears to be, at the time of writing, emerging in the international system. China, Russia, India, Brazil and Iran have all achieved regional great power status. These states have enjoyed considerable economic growth over the past decade and possess abundant **latent power**. China is at the precipice of attaining global superpower status and is expected to imminently overtake the United States as the world's largest economy (Chan 2014). While the United States does not currently face a hostile coalition of great powers balancing against it, the era of unipolar dominance for the US is clearly finished.

> **Latent Power** – states with latent power have highly advanced economies and have the ability to develop significant military power.

Finally, non-traditional security issues, including the impact of climate change and other environmental problems, energy security, transnational crime, health care and disease, poverty and development, and continued economic uncertainty, have also become substantial features of the contemporary international system. Contemporary international relations is more complex and non-state actors, multinational corporations, regional and international organizations are now established players in global affairs. Traditional interstate power politics may still dominate international relations, but the international system has clearly evolved past the traditional strictures of the Westphalian system. In sum, international relations in the twenty-first century remains a paradox of continuity and change.

CONCLUSION: THE RISE OF 'EASTPHALIA' IN INTERNATIONAL RELATIONS?

The dramatic shift of power to the Asia-Pacific may represent a fundamental change in the foundations of the practice and study of international relations. Scholars and policymakers have noted how the transforming distribution of power is affecting international relations and that traditional Westphalian concepts and interpretations of sovereignty, the nation-state and power politics are increasingly challenged by the rise of the Asia-Pacific. In effect, the rise of a new 'Eastphalian' order in the international system may presage the end of Eurocentric Westphalian dominance of international relations. Kim, Fidler and Ganguly (2009) reflected on the dawn of 'Eastphalia':

> With power shifting towards the East, Asian preferences and ideas have a greater opportunity than ever before to affect world politics, potentially supplanting Western dominance and universal principles, known for centuries as 'Westphalian' and 'post-Westphalian' concepts, with a new 'Eastphalian' alternative. Effectively, an Eastphalian international order would reinvigorate the concepts of national sovereignty and non-intervention in the domestic affairs of states, first set forth in the Peace of Westphalia in 1648, and back these principles with increased material power and an Asian perspective.

The rise of the Asia-Pacific is an opportunity for a fundamental reordering of the basic concepts of international relations. Core issues such as sovereignty, the nation-state, diplomacy, the permissible use of force, the right to intervene in another state's domestic affairs and soft security have essentially been defined by the West and its interpretation and adherence to the Westphalian order. An Eastphalian international order directly challenges the basic foundations, definitions and interpretations of modern international relations. How these potentially competing perspectives on international relations are reconciled will frame the practice and study of international relations in the twenty-first century.

QUESTIONS FOR REFLECTION

1. How did the Treaty of Westphalia contribute to the development of the modern international relations concepts of sovereignty and the nation-state?
2. What is the role of the balance of power in international relations?
3. How did World War I transform the international system?
4. Why did the Cold War develop between the United States and Soviet Union?
5. How has the international system changed since the 9/11 attacks?

REVISION QUIZ

1. The Peace of Westphalia ended which war?

    a. World War I
    b. World War II
    c. The Thirty Years' War
    d. The Franco-Prussian war

2. _____ wrote *The History of the Peloponnesian War.*

   a. Pericles
   b. Thucydides
   c. Marcus Aurelius
   d. Livy

3. The European great powers established _____ following the end of the Napoleonic Wars.

   a. The League of Nations
   b. The Hanseatic League
   c. NATO
   d. The Concert of Europe

4. European colonial powers divided the continent of _____ at the Congress of Berlin in 1884–85.

   a. Africa
   b. Asia
   c. South America
   d. Australia

5. World War I was caused in large part by the assassination of the Archduke of what European empire?

   a. German
   b. Russian
   c. British
   d. Austro-Hungarian

6. World War II began with the German invasion of _____.

   a. Czechoslovakia
   b. Soviet Union
   c. Poland
   d. France

7. The balance of power in the international system during the Cold War was _____.

   a. Unipolar
   b. Bipolar
   c. Multipolar
   d. Tripolar

8. The Soviet Union dissolved in what year?

    a. 1990
    b. 1989
    c. 1992
    d. 1991

9. Western Europe, Canada, and the United States formed what military alliance in 1949?

    a. Warsaw Pact
    b. Tripartite Agreement
    c. Central Powers
    d. NATO

10. _____ recently became the second-largest economy in the world.

    a. China
    b. Japan
    c. India
    d. Russia

Answers: 1: c; 2: b; 3: d; 4: a; 5: d; 6: c; 7: b; 8: d; 9: d; 10: a.

BIBLIOGRAPHY

Beaulac, S. (2004) 'The Westphalian model in defining international law: challenging the myth', *Australian Journal of Legal History*, 8(2), 181–213.

Chan, S. (2014) 'China Overtakes US to be Biggest Economy by 2024', *The Telegraph* 7 September. Available at: <http://www.telegraph.co.uk/finance/economics/11078885/China-overtakes-US-to-be-biggest-economy-by-2024.html>.

D'Anieri, P. (2014) *International Politics: Power and Purpose in Global Affairs* (Boston, MA: Cengage).

Fukuyama, F. (1989) 'The end of history?', *The National Interest*, Summer 1989.

Fukuyama, F. (1992) *The End of History and the Last Man* (New York: Free Press).

Gat, A. (July/August 2007) 'The Return of Authoritarian Great Powers', *Foreign Affairs*, July/August 2007.

Hobson, J. (2012) *The Eurocentric Conception of World Politics* (Cambridge: Cambridge University Press).

Kayaoglu, T. (2010) 'Westphalian eurocentrism in international relations theory', *International Studies Review*, 12, 193–217.

Kim, S.W., Fidler, D.P. and Ganguly, S. (2009) 'Eastphalia rising? Asian influence and the fate of human Security', *World Policy Journal*, 26(53), 53–64.

Kissinger, H. (1994) *Diplomacy* (New York: Simon & Schuster).

Kissinger, H. (2014) *World Order* (New York: Penguin Press).

Krauthammer, C. (1990/91) 'The unipolar moment', *Foreign Affairs*, 70(1).

Krauthammer, C. (2002/03) 'The unipolar moment revisited', *The National Interest*, Winter.

Mingst, K.A. (2004) *Essentials of International Relations*, 3rd edition (New York: W.W. Norton).

Osiander, A. (2001) 'Sovereignty, international relations, and the Westphalian myth', *International Organization*, 55(2), 251–88.

Teschke, B. (2003) *The Myth of 1648: Class, Geopolitics, and the Making of Modern International Relations*, (London: Verso).

Vucetic, S. (2011) *The Anglosphere: A Genealogy of Racialized Identity in International Relations* (Palo Alto: Stanford University Press).

Waltz, K. (1979) *Theory of International Politics* (Boston, MA: McGraw Hill).

Chapter 2
Theories of World Affairs

MARK CHOU AND AVERY DOROTHY HOWARD POOLE

This chapter demonstrates the importance of theory in the study of International Relations. The suggestion is that that the nature of the international system – how and why it came to be – cannot be fully understood without first understanding the system's conceptual building blocks. Thus, we challenge the commonplace dichotomy that is thought to exist between 'theory' and 'practice' in International Relations. This chapter looks broadly at some of the most prominent theories of International Relations that have gone on to not only alter the debates within the discipline, but also fundamentally impact the course of twentieth-century world affairs. First, we develop this discussion by saying a few words about the role and significance of theory. We argue that theory helps us to interpret facts and make sense of reality; it helps us to categorize, give significance to and predict phenomena that may otherwise seem unintelligible. Second, we review the so-called Great Debates that have influenced the theoretical trajectory of International Relations since the discipline's establishment in the wake of World War I. Third, we explore some of the more prominent theoretical perspectives which have influenced International Relations scholars and practitioners. We focus on familiarizing students with the two mainstream theories of Liberalism and Realism, and their so-called 'neo' variants. We also consider Constructivism and Feminism – theoretical perspectives which have set out to critique many of the liberal and realist assumptions entrenched within contemporary International Relations.

Key Words: International Relations Theory, the Great Debates, Liberalism, Realism, Constructivism, Feminism.

Chapter 2

Theories of World Affairs

MARK CHOU AND AVERY POOLE

INTRODUCTION

International Relations Theory was by far the most enriching course we took as undergraduate students in Political Science. Challenging yet rewarding, the subject matter radically opened our eyes to seeing how different the world could look depending on what conceptual tools one chose to view the world with. Using a variety of theoretical filters to tell the story of International Relations, the professors we had demonstrated to us that reality in International Relations, as elsewhere, can be more complex than it might seem. This is why it is not just myths and opinions about world affairs that deserve our critical scrutiny, but also facts about reality and taken-for-granted political truths. Having had to reappraise our political beliefs and conceptions of reality more than once, we walked away from the course, seeing International Relations very differently.

> **Realism** – a collection of theoretical perspectives based on the notion that fundamental truths can be observed in the international system, which is inherently competitive.
>
> **Constructivism** – a set of approaches to the study of international relations which have in common the notion that reality is socially constructed.
>
> **Feminism** – a set of approaches to the study of international relations which have in common the notion that mainstream theory in the discipline is gendered.

But today many students of International Relations either seem indifferent to theory or sceptical of its practical utility. The often-heard gripe is that course readings are too dense and classroom discussions too abstract. Some even see the course as a waste of their time, particularly when the focus shifts to the more critical theories and concern with reality, it seems, is jettisoned for purely philosophical inquiries. Given that the world is now engulfed with such pressing issues as famine, war, terrorism, financial crises and environmental devastation, some students therefore ask whether their time is best used engaging in theoretical discussions that appear far removed from the reality of world affairs.

This discord between theory and practice, or theorizing and policy-making, is a familiar one in the discipline of International Relations more broadly (Zalewski 1996). And it is not just students, but also scholars and policymakers, who sometimes question the purpose of theory and theorizing. Indeed, for those who accept the value of theory, the view is that the nature of the international system – how and why it came to be – cannot be fully understood without first understanding the system's conceptual building blocks. As a result, theorists like to point out that those who denigrate theory run the risk of understanding neither why theory is important nor how intimately theorists are engaged in political reality. At the other end of the spectrum, there are scholars, policymakers and statespeople who are sceptical of theory's utility. For them, theorists do little else but theorize in university departments removed from the pressures of political decision-making and leadership. In the real world, they argue, where threats to national security are ever-present, there is little time and place for such idealistic theorizations of world affairs.

Both perspectives are justified and based on different calculations of what best serves the discipline of International Relations. However, the apparently simple dichotomy between theory and practice betrays a deeper complexity. No matter what the student, scholar or practitioner of International Relations says, theory is a crucial part of what they do. This is because theory helps us interpret facts and make sense of reality. Without conceptual assumptions of some sort, facts and reality – no matter how objective and obvious they might otherwise seem – are fundamentally meaningless. States, warfare, alliances, the international-domestic divide and other such seemingly natural lynchpins of our current international system will become no more significant than any other grouping, relationship or issue. Theories help us categorize, give significance to and predict phenomena that may otherwise appear unintelligible and random to us. They give us the capacity to think logically about what we observe empirically, thus enabling us to act decisively.

In this way, theory is not divorced from practice in International Relations. In fact, the 'practice' of International Relations is, more often than not, a direct result of established theoretical outlooks. Theory *constitutes* reality in International Relations to the extent that unquestionable facts about reality in the international realm and taken-for-granted political truths owe their existence to those theories of International Relations which have become particularly dominant or commonsensical. That is why when International Relations scholars and practitioners want to understand why a certain event or decision took place, and how best to respond, they implicitly draw on theoretical explanations in the formulation of their answers (Knutsen 1997).

In this chapter, we look broadly at some of the most prominent theories of International Relations that not only have altered the debates within the discipline, but also fundamentally impacted the course of twentieth-century world affairs. The conventional way to do this is to review the so-called **Great Debates** that have influenced the theoretical trajectory of International Relations since the discipline was founded in the wake of World War I. For some, International Relations has been a fundamentally theoretical discipline from the outset (Burchill and Linklater 2009), in that these great theoretical disputes generated among notable scholars and practitioners of International Relations spoke to – but also then altered – real-life political events: from World War I and World War II through to the beginnings and conclusion of the Cold War. The first of these Great Debates, which occurred in the interwar years of the 1920s and 30s, centred on a series of exchanges between **idealists** (liberal internationalists) and **realists**. At stake in this debate

> **International Relations theory** – a range of propositions or ideas which seek to explain phenomena observed in the international system. These have developed particularly since the end of World War I.
>
> **The Great Debates** – four theoretical 'debates' or major points of difference among International Relations scholars which took place during the twentieth century.
>
> **Liberalism** – a collection of theoretical perspectives based on liberal ideas such as the possibility of progress in human relations, and that cooperation can mitigate the risk of conflict.

was whether and by what means international warfare – specifically the horrifying events of World War I – could be avoided. The Second Great Debate, taking place in the 1960s, was largely based around a dispute over whether the discipline (and the social sciences more generally) can or should be modernized to include the best of the methodological innovations being founded at the time in the natural sciences. As a debate that primarily involved traditionalists and **behaviouralists**, the key point of difference revolved around the question of whether theories of International Relations would benefit from being made more scientific. The third or so-called **interparadigm** debate took place during the course of the 1970s and 80s, and concerned not so much a dispute over methodology as theory choice. As Realism, Marxism and pluralism vied for theoretical dominance, theorists were forced to ask which paradigm should International Relations adopt to best serve its objectives. Finally, the fourth and most recent theoretical debate to have consumed International Relations is the quarrel between positivism and **post-positivism** in International Relations theory, something which emerged in response to the less certain international environment of the post-Cold War world. In this chapter, we will examine each of these Great Debates in turn before exploring briefly some of the key theoretical perspectives that have influenced International Relations in the twentieth and twenty-first centuries: Liberalism, Realism, Constructivism and Feminism.

THEORY AND THEORIZING IN INTERNATIONAL RELATIONS

Before we discuss the Great Debates and the key theoretical outlooks in International Relations though, we should consider further the role of theory and theorizing in International Relations. What is theory? Why is theorizing important in International Relations? And how does theory relate to real-world political events?

Of course, theory and theorizing can be understood in numerous ways, some more complex than others. But at its core, theory is simply about illumination. As Torbjørn Knutsen (1997), a historian and theorist of International Relations, once observed: 'Theories enlighten'. That is, they bring to light phenomena that may have previously been invisible and, by doing so, enable us to better comprehend its nature. More importantly, argues Knutsen, '[a] theory is an abstract, conjectural or speculative representation of reality'. It is reality – by means abstract, conjectural and speculative – that theory addresses. Thus, students of International Relations who are suspicious that theory has anything to do with reality should remember that it is reality – or the 'real world' – that is the focus of theory.

> Theories help us categorize and predict phenomena that may otherwise appear unintelligible.
>
> They give us the capacity to think logically about what we observe empirically, thus enabling us to act decisively.
>
> **Theory constitutes reality** in International Relations to the extent that unquestionable facts about reality in the international realm and taken-for-granted political truths owe their existence to those theories of International Relations which have become particularly dominant or commonsensical.

By seeing theory this way, two important implications follow. The first is that the often assumed separation of theory and reality is actually false or, at the very least, overdrawn. And the second is that theory, specifically in International Relations, responds to and impacts upon the way political events play out in reality. Nothing vindicates these two points better than how intimately connected the foundation of the discipline of International Relations was with the horrific events of World War I. The creation of the former was a direct corollary of the ferocity of the latter. Indeed, it was the total destructiveness of war, the new mechanized ways of killing and the unfathomable human cost that gave rise to the first great theoretical school of the twentieth century: International Relations. In struggling to comprehend how devastation on such a global scale was possible, the first theorists of International Relations sought a more conceptual explanation of why war was possible and, more crucially, how it could be avoided in future.

In this sense, the overarching aim of theory during the discipline's infancy was the prevention of international hostility and warfare, such that the mass murder which had taken place between 1914 and 1918 would never again be repeated. And while students of international history would know this endeavour to be a failed one, it does not diminish the point that '[a] close connection existed between theory and practice: theory was not disconnected from the actual world of international politics' (Burchill and Linklater 2009).

That said, it is vital here to emphasize the temporal lag that frequently separates theory from practice. According to Steve Smith, who was a leading intellectual protagonist in the fourth Great Debate, it is a truism that '[i]nternational theory underpins and informs international practice, even if there is a lengthy lag between the high-point of theories and their gradual absorption into political debate' (Smith 1996). It takes time for theories to acquire political power and become widely accepted outside the often small intellectual circles in which they were formed. But when they do, theories can have the potential to speak to and sometimes speak on behalf of individuals, organizations, states and global alliances in the 'real world'.

Such is the importance of representing if not mirroring reality that International Relations theories have tended to acquire (and lose) their political prominence based on the capacity to map and predict global events. As their proponents like to emphasize, the theories that became orthodox during the two World Wars and the Cold War demonstrated this capacity. They were observations, increasingly scientific in their nature, that professed to capture the underlying motivations and dynamics of international actors and the international system more broadly. But as they filtered their way down into the policy initiatives and military responses of state leaders, something fascinating also occurred: these theories began to acquire the status of common sense. When this happens, 'theories become increasingly powerful since they delineate not simply what can be known by also what it is sensible to talk about or suggest' (Smith 1996). They become synonymous with reality itself in International Relations – even though they initially began life as mere abstractions, conjectures and speculations about reality. This is the power that theories can have in practice.

Yet in order for theories to reflect reality, theorists have to first use certain conceptual tools to help them distinguish the significant facts and phenomena from the insignificant ones. It is here that students of International Relations theory will likely encounter terms such as **ontology**, **epistemology** and **methodology**. Increasingly, debates about these matters dictate theorizing in International Relations. So while it is unnecessary for students to be experts in philosophy to engage with these concepts, a basic knowledge of their meaning is required to navigate the waters of International Relations theory.

There is much that could be said about ontology, epistemology and methodology, much of which is complex, confusing and technical. Yet for newcomers to the field, the best way to introduce these concepts is perhaps through the analogy of a conceptual 'toolkit'.

> **Ontology** – revolves around the notion of being.
>
> **Epistemology** – denotes theory of knowledge.
>
> **Methodology** – touches on analytical approaches and methods.

Ontology, which revolves around the notion of being, helps theorists tackle questions such as: what or who makes up the world; who are the key actors in International Relations; and how are they constituted? Epistemology, on the other hand, simply denotes theory of knowledge: how do we acquire knowledge about the world and those who inhabit it; what are legitimate or illegitimate ways of knowing a certain topic? Finally, methodology concerns the analytical approaches or methods we use, and the reasons we have for using them, to collect our evidence and gather our data about International Relations.

How these concepts get deployed by theorists is both complicated and diverse. Just as a screwdriver can be used in different ways to create different objects, so theorists can deploy these conceptual tools in various ways to understand International Relations differently. 'On the basis of these assumptions', write Milja Kurki and Colin Wight in the highly regarded volume, *International Relations Theories: Discipline and Diversity*, 'researchers may literally come to "see" the world in different ways: ontologically in terms of seeing different object domains, epistemologically in terms of accepting or rejecting particular knowledge claims, and methodologically in terms of choosing particular methods of study' (Dunne, Kurki and Smith 2010). Fittingly, the cover art for this volume contains a set of lenses of varying colours. Depending on what one studies ontologically, how one studies it epistemologically and why one studies it methodologically, different shades and different images may appear. Much like Benjamin Franklin's multi-coloured spectacles in *National Treasure* (the otherwise forgettable film starring Nicholas Cage and Diane Kruger), if one flicks between the lenses different and even hidden features of the same image will emerge or vanish. In International Relations, the analogy implies that, depending on what ontology, epistemology and methodology we use to theorize, the predominant image of the international sphere – the state, war and power politics – can quickly transform: into other, clashing images comprised of sub- and supra-national entities, of famine and disease, women and children and of subaltern or non-Western actors and rationalities.

This, in large part, brings us finally to the crucial demarcation drawn by scholars between so-called **problem-solving theories** and **critical theories**. Less concrete conceptual dichotomies than fluid categories that change with time and place, these two groups of theories are important because they focus their analyses on different, often opposing, sets of ontological, epistemological and methodological concerns. The more conventional problem-solving theories can simply be understood as an umbrella term for all those theoretical contributions that seek to *explain*, in an objective manner, the world 'out there'. Their purpose is not so much to question and change as to reflect, categorize and fix what exists in the world today. Identifying causal links, general trends and patterns of behaviour in the international sphere is thus central to the task performed by problem-solving theories in International Relations. What rates as success, in this regard, is not fundamentally *changing* the world in which we live but offering a better understanding of the way the world currently works.

> **Problem-solving Theories** seek to explain the world out there in an objective manner. They reflect, categorize, and fix what exists in the world today.
>
> **Critical Theories** challenge the status quo representations of reality. Having done this, critical theories also seek to change pre-existing power structures in the international sphere.

But the issue with problem-solving theories, as advocates of critical theories like to point out, is that they work within and, as such, work to reinforce the *status quo*. Purely reflecting the world 'out there' does nothing to identify and rectify the existing inequalities, rifts and oversights of the international system. It does nothing to publicize the distorting, subjective and imperfect nature of theories, which are never perfect, objective reflections of reality. Theories highlight specific ontologies, prefer particular epistemologies and utilize certain methodologies to generate a particular worldview or viewpoint of real-world politics. They are never a complete representation. Instead, they are always influenced by such factors as gender, ethnicity, language, class and geography. This is why one of the intellectual forefathers of critical

International Relations theory, Robert Cox, once noted that 'theory is always *for* someone and *for* some purpose' (Cox 1981). It is the task of critical theories to expose who that 'someone' behind the objective theory is and what their 'purposes' are. Yet the point of critique is not only negative but also positive to the extent that many critical theories seek *change*, or emancipation, from pre-existing power structures in the international sphere. By elevating a variety of erstwhile marginalized ontologies, epistemologies and methodologies, critical theories therefore seek to make visible those aspects of international reality that have been hidden and obscured by the more mainstream problem-solving theories.

Understood this way, we can begin to realize why theory can be both an instrument used to *reflect* reality and a means through which to mount a *critique* of that reality. The long and short of it, then, is that theory is important in International Relations. Without theoretical assumptions, the reality that surrounds us would be meaningless and even frightening. Only through theoretical insight – flawed and as imperfect as they are – can we come to know the world, act in the world and be mindful of our place and the place of others within the world.

INTERNATIONAL RELATIONS THEORY AND THE GREAT DEBATES

As should be clear by now, theories are products and reflections of their times. International Relations theories are no exception. And nowhere is this more apparent than in the so-called **Great Debates** that have marked out the discipline's short 90-year history.

The label 'Great Debates' is a misnomer of sorts. As a number of scholars have pointed out since, there was no debate in the sense of different protagonists converging to discuss the discipline's key theoretical differences. Rather, the label was more a retrospective moniker given by scholars to delineate the discipline's main theoretical rifts. And while no student of International Relations should consider their education complete without at least a working knowledge of the Great Debates, it has been noted that a telling of the discipline's theoretical development in this way tends to encourage 'navel-gazing' rather than introspection (Brown and Ainley 2005). Still, an overview of International Relations theory would not be complete without briefly introducing students to the main claims of these Great Debates.

The First Great Debate

To make sense of the discipline's first great theoretical debate, one needs to understand something of the global political environment during the 1920s and 30s. The horrors of World War I had driven a number of Western statesmen and intellectuals to despair. Many vowed to themselves and to their citizens that war on such scale should never again be repeated in the history of humankind. It was in the aftermath of this war that efforts to establish a new academic discipline dedicated to the study of the causes of war and the creation of peace took hold. But for all the despair and the lives that had been lost, it was ironic that the new discipline was actually founded upon a hope that humankind could co-exist, that nations could cooperate politically without the need for war and aggression. It was, of course, an immensely idealistic aspiration – something which would be pointed out during the course of this first theoretical debate – but **idealism** was perhaps what was needed to rally leaders and citizens behind a vision for the world that was as removed from bloodshed and violence.

Spearheaded by such notaries as then-US President Woodrow Wilson, British philanthropists David Davies and Montague Burton and leading intellectuals like Alfred Zimmern and Norman Angell, the new discipline of International Relations was driven largely by a broad-based liberal disposition. There are two main reasons for the prominence of **Liberalism** in the discipline's early years. The first is a theoretical one: Liberalism provided an answer to the perceived oversights in notions like the **balance of power** and the **alliance** system which, the proponents of liberal internationalism argued, actually caused aggressors like Germany and Austria to take the path they did. The focus on power and egoism was a fundamental reason why war became inevitable. In its stead, **liberal internationalism** tried to get around this by accentuating international cooperation, diplomacy and democracy as a way to overcome the more basic and violent urges that flourished during World War I. The second reason for Liberalism's prominence in International Relations had more to do with the personal political views of Woodrow Wilson, who oversaw the late entry of the US into World War I to decisively bring an end to hostilities. As a political science academic before he entered politics, Wilson had been influenced by liberal ideas for some time and wanted to spread Liberalism through Europe as a way to prevent future warfare. Given his political influence on both the war's conclusion and the postwar international order, his theoretical worldview became orthodox in International Relations by proxy.

We will discuss the key claims of Liberalism explicitly in the chapter's final section. For now, though, we will outline briefly the key premise of Liberalism. Based on two cornerstones – democracy promotion abroad and the creation of an overarching international organization to regulate the relations among states – the ideas of Liberalism were internationalized with the aim of establishing rule of law, collective security and open diplomacy in the international sphere. Articulated most famously in Wilson's **'The Fourteen Points' speech**, which he delivered in 1918, the idea was that world affairs would be made more transparent and less hostile through two developments in particular. The first was the **promotion of democratic politics** in countries led by militaristic autocrats. The liberal assumption here was that the people, on the whole, neither want nor benefit from war. As such, if political power is handed over to the people – rather than autocratic leaders or military elites – the likelihood of war would be diminished. Democracies do not go to war with democracies, or so the thinking went. The second liberal development which Wilson spearheaded was the creation of an **authoritative international organization** that would rid politics among states of secret diplomatic dealings and alliances for something more structured, open and democratic. This was the basis for the creation of the League of Nations (the precursor to the United Nations) after World War I, an institution that many hoped would nurture international cooperation, rule of law and collective security. The League, with its mission to eradicate the zero-sum mentality that had previously dictated world affairs, would be bolstered by the subsequent creation of the Permanent Court of International Justice in 1921 and the ratification of Kellogg-Briand Pact of 1928, signed by all countries to outlaw war in all but the most extreme cases.

> Wilson's **Fourteen Points Speech** envisioned a liberal world order premised on democracy promotion abroad and the creation of an authoritative international organization to regulate the relations among states.

Regrettably, as the 1920s gave way to the 1930s, optimism for lasting peace began to deteriorate. Not helped by the worsening economic situation and deepening depression, many newly formed democracies slid back into their former, authoritarian moulds as a new wave of aggression swept through parts of Asia, Europe and Africa. Neither the League nor the Kellogg-Briand Pact seemed able to halt the slide into what, with time, would become a truly globalized war of worlds. Wilson's prediction of peace through Liberalism simply did not eventuate.

These 'real-world' political developments had a profound impact on Liberalism's credibility in the theoretical world. In spite of liberal ideas and institutions, the world rushed headlong into another war. Scholars who had long been wary of Liberalism's veracity pounced on this state of affairs to mount their critique.

In what would become the discipline's second orthodox theoretical school of thought, **Realism** emerged to countenance the many idealistic promises of Liberalism. As a worldview, Realism was predicated on the belief that power and self-interest could not be removed from the political equation. At best, it can only be checked or balanced by other powers and self-interests. In his now legendary diagnoses of what had gone wrong during *The Twenty Years' Crisis, 1919–1939*, the British diplomat and historian E.H. Carr argued that liberals had been far too idealistic (or utopian) and not 'realistic' (or

> The theoretical critique mounted by realists such as E.H. Carr and Hans Morgenthau exposed the flaws of Liberalism and its inability to truly grasp the reality of world affairs: that states, driven by self-interest, lust for power in an anarchic international sphere lacking in any authoritative body capable of stamping out aggression.
>
> In this way, even though Realism would become one of the orthodox schools of international relations theory, it first emerged as a critical theory.

scientific) enough in their analyses. With his argument centred on the inescapable fact of world scarcity, Carr observed that the 'haves' and 'have-nots' in the world will never learn to cooperate but, rather, be consumed by hostility. This is how the world really works, argued Carr; something which the naïve liberals had fundamentally misunderstood. As a result, by wasting their energies on creating international organizations and promoting democracies, they had effectively manufactured a 20-year crisis that finally erupted with the onset of hostilities in World War II.

These thoughts were echoed by the German-Jewish intellectual Hans Morgenthau. Writing in what remains one of the discipline's canonical texts, *Politics Among Nations*, Morgenthau maintained that human nature – the sinful nature of man – impregnates all politics with power-seeking and self-interest. This is why states are driven by their national interests, something which was an objective law of International Relations for Morgenthau. Fundamentally, then, the theoretical critiques mounted by Carr and Morgenthau, among others, exposed the flaws of Liberalism and its inability to truly grasp the reality of world affairs: that states, driven by self-interest, lust for power in an anarchic international sphere lacking in any authoritative body capable of stamping out aggression. The aptly named realists argued that these important features of the international system must be recognized rather than wished away. Their arguments became key to how International Relations was theorized during and in the aftermath of World War II.

The Second Great Debate

Reality, then, or the dispute over what is reality, defined the discipline's First Great Debate. The political developments that saw the world powers embroil themselves in another war vindicated the realist take on reality. In so doing, they are universally considered to have been the victors of the First Debate.

Reality, or rather how best to capture and represent reality methodologically, was again fundamental to the discipline's second Great Debate. Having awarded themselves the mantle of the most 'realistic' theory of International Relations, Realism was considered by scholars and policymakers to possess the most methodologically astute observations about world affairs. Yet, ironically, as the discipline expanded and Realism became more widely practiced, particularly in the US, concerns arose as to whether the observations made by theorists such as Carr and Morgenthau were in fact realistic enough. It is important to remember, as a new breed of scholars began to point out during the 1950s and 60s, few of the early generation of International Relations scholars had actually been trained as proper social scientists. Carr, for example, was a historian by trade while Morgenthau was an international lawyer. Both experienced firsthand aspects of the realist reality they would theorize about. And though their theoretical takes were largely accurate, the conclusions they reached were neither scientific enough nor sufficiently empirical.

Influenced by the rising prominence of **behaviouralism** in the natural sciences (physics, chemistry, biology), many new generation scholars, such as Morton Kaplan and David Singer, argued that the social science of International Relations had to be revised to reflect the latest scientific developments in how to study the physical world. Extensive debates have not resolved what precisely behaviouralism is and how it impacted on the social sciences. As such, all we can do here is to provide a brief summary of its main claims. Beginning with the premise that facts about reality can only be known

> Drawn from the natural sciences, **behaviouralism** was premised on the notion that the reality could be scientifically understood by collecting, analysing and quantifying data to identify the key patterns and universal laws.
>
> What matters are facts about reality (which are universal), not values (which are subjective).
>
> For behaviouralists, realists erred because they emphasized values over facts in their theorizations.

accurately by using methods generated in the natural sciences, behaviouralism revolved around the notion of **positivism** which, it contended, was the only legitimate knowledge form with which to study the world around us. What made positivism superior to other epistemologies was its claim of mirroring reality, something which it could do because of the behaviouralist methodology it employed: the collection, analysis and quantification of data to identify key patterns and formulate universal laws about reality. The thinking behind these theoretical claims was that the social sciences, including International Relations, should seek to grasp and categorize the objective laws about social reality in much the same way that the natural sciences had, by then, been able to do with the physical universe. Importantly, as a method of studying the social world, behaviouralism made the distinction between facts (which are universal) and values (which are subjective). International Relations theories should focus on the former, not the latter.

Influenced by these ideas, behaviouralists in International Relations criticized their realist forebears for emphasizing values over facts in their theorizations. They charged that their

[handwritten note: Both behav. + Trad. realists believe there's a 'solution'. but dispute the means of finding it.]

'traditionalist' realist counterparts over-relied on philosophy, history, morality, and literature, and argued that they were unable to measure and thus know with definitive accuracy how power and the national interest operated in the international sphere. All they could do was conjecture, and this was simply insufficient as a basis to articulate the objective laws about International Relations. In response, the traditionalists pointed out that try as one might, no amount of scientific observation and quantification will ever lead to the creation of such things as an objective law or laws about International Relations. A good case in point is Morgenthau's *Politics Among Nations*. Though the book clearly states sets out to create a 'rational theory' of international politics capable of reflecting the 'objective laws' of world affairs, the Morgenthau does not turn method into madness (Morgenthau 1985). *Politics Among Nations* is full of so-called objective laws but it is also full of anecdotes, philosophical insights and value judgements. Hedley Bull, author of *The Anarchical Society* and a proponent of the English School of international theory, concurs, particularly in regard to value judgements. One may strive for objective, universal knowledge about world affairs. Yet such knowledge, according to Bull (1966), would be meaningless without an 'explicit reliance upon the exercising of judgment'.

> The **'traditionalist'** realists rebutted, arguing that that scientific observation and quantification would never lead to a definitive law of International Relations.
>
> As Hedley Bull argued, objective and universal knowledge about the world is meaningless without an 'explicit reliance on the exercising of judgment'.

In the end, behaviouralism can be said to have won this Second Debate – particularly in North America. Contemporary students of International Relations who wonder why statistics and game theory is part of their curriculum can thank the behaviourialist victory for this. More fundamentally, the second Great Debate is memorable to this day because it brought to the discipline's attention the significance of knowledge and how best to acquire it. What is 'real' and how we recognize it when we see it are very pressing concerns with which all theories and theorists need to grapple.

The Third and Fourth Great Debates

To all but a smaller cross-section of the discipline's theorists and scholars, the first two debates were by far the most theoretically influential. It is for this reason that we have dedicated more space to them in this chapter. Nevertheless, the Third and Fourth Debates have much to offer, particularly for those left unconvinced by the wisdom of Liberalism, Realism and behaviouralism.

Often described as the **'interparadigm' debate**, International Relations' third Great Debate took place largely during the 1970s and 80s. By this time, particularly in North America, behaviouralism had already left an indelible mark on International Relations scholarship and practice. Given this, theoretical debates of the 1970s and 80s were dictated less by questions of methodology and more by concerns over how best to judge and choose between competing theories. At stake was the issue of commensurability or, more accurately, **incommensurability**. For more than 50 years, the

> At stake in the interparadigm debate was the issue of **incommensurability** between different theoretical conceptions of world affairs. Despite the behaviouralist claim that a scientific approach to studying International Relations would lead to a set of universal laws about the world, none emerged. In fact, as different theories developed so did different and incommensurable paradigms.

discipline of International Relations had been amassing new theoretical conceptions of how the world worked and how international actors interacted. But though competing theories had become more sophisticated, driven in large part by the behavourialist revolution, they had not necessarily reached a general consensus about the key characteristics and universal patterns of the international system. If anything, as different theories developed, different and incommensurable paradigms about world affairs emerged. There was little to no commonality shared between the diverging conceptions and assumptions in International Relations. Despite the behaviouralist claim that adopting a scientific approach to the study of world affairs would lead to the articulation of a set of universal laws, no such laws or none that were universally agreed upon had emerged.

The inability to reconcile and even compare the main tenets of theories worried scholars, particularly those who subscribed to the Kuhnian notion that the advancement in understanding required some sort of dominant, unified paradigm. But despite the concern, this debate more or less ended in much the same way it began: with little agreement among scholars as to what amounted to the best paradigm through which to understand International Relations. To this day, theoretical perspectives espouse fundamentally different worldviews which, in some cases, cannot be easily reconciled or compared.

The issues of reality, science and irreconcilable paradigms, found in the second and third debates, were hardly resolved. They still lingered, often implicitly, within the broad debates which consumed the discipline. As the 1980s gave way to the 1990s, and as the seemingly intractable Cold War between the US and the Soviet Union ended as few within the discipline had imagined it could, new global realities seemed to appear almost instantly and often in defiance of what the established wisdom of scientific analyses held was possible. 'Reality', writes Jim George (1994) in his now classic contribution to the discipline's fourth Great Debate, *Discourses of Global Politics*, 'is not what it used to be in International Relations'. In fact, reality was never just what the mainstream theories of Liberalism and Realism said they were. Reality is much more than can be contained within any one grand theory of world affairs. It defies as much as it affirms the tenets of positivism. For scholars of the Fourth Debate, the end of the Cold War, the emergence new sub- and supra-state actors and the prominence of individuals, women and non-traditional security issues on the international stage all vindicated their criticisms and confirmed the need to recognize **post-positivist** epistemologies and methodologies in International Relations.

> The fourth great debate moved the discipline in a **post-positivist** direction by examining previously ignored phenomena. From sub- and supra-state actors, the prominence and individuals to non-traditional security issues, theorists began to challenge the orthodox epistemologies, ontologies and methodologies in International Relations.

In this way, the Fourth Debate is significant because it recast the esteemed place that science – positivist epistemologies and behaviouralist methodologies – had held in International Relations theorizing to date. It celebrated the incommensurability of theories and their competing conceptions of reality – which had previously been thought of as undesirable. And it began to shift its ontological focus – from states and international organizations – to previously invisible entities and peoples. Into this more open space came theoretical innovations inspired by such traditions as postmodernism, critical theory, Feminism, Constructivism, social theory and green theory. As the discipline's voices of dissent – its 'language[s] of exile' (Ashley and Walker 1990) –

these are the avenues to which students looking for alternatives to the mainstream conceptions of International Relations should turn.

LIBERALISM, REALISM, CONSTRUCTIVISM AND FEMINISM

In the final section of this chapter, we want to continue our discussion by providing a more in-depth examination of some of the more prominent theoretical positions which have influenced International Relations scholars and practitioners. Here, we will focus our attention on familiarizing students with the two mainstream theories of Liberalism and Realism – and their so-called 'neo' variants. We will also consider Constructivism and Feminism – theoretical perspectives which have set out to critique many of the liberal and realist assumptions entrenched within contemporary International Relations.

Liberalism

At its core, Liberalism is based on the assumption that progress is possible in human relations. In this respect, conflict is not inevitable but can be overcome or at least mitigated. Of course, it must be noted that Liberalism is not one unified theory but has several different strands and areas of enquiry. What we want to emphasize here is just one particular aspect of Liberalism in International Relations: its post-Cold War revival through liberal democratic peace theory and neoliberal institutionalism.

The superpower rivalry of the Cold War lent weight to realist arguments about power, security, the ineffectiveness of international institutions like the United Nations and the pre-eminence of the state (to be discussed below). However, with conclusion of the Cold War and the subsequent collapse of the Soviet Union in 1991, debate began to shift to what world affairs would look like in future. Some saw the end of the Cold War as signifying the triumph of Capitalism and democracy. In 1992, Francis Fukuyama famously predicted 'The End of History', by which he meant that the 'end point of mankind's ideological evolution'. He

> **Liberal Democratic Peace Theory** – a theory which holds that liberal democracies do not go to war with each other.

believed that the 'ideal state' – democratic and capitalist – had triumphed, and that there was a consensus with regard to the legitimacy of liberal democracy. The implication was that the spread of liberal democratic polities would lead to the end of conflict.

Relatedly, the end of the Cold War seemed to give credence to liberal democratic peace theory, which holds that liberal democracies do not go to war with one another. It is often described as neo-Kantian, as it builds on Immanuel Kant's argument in the late eighteenth century that a 'perpetual peace' was possible if a federation of liberal republics was created. In these liberal republics, he argued, individual rights would be respected and rulers would be held accountable. These arguments reflect classical liberal ideas (advanced by seventeenth-century thinkers such as John Locke) about individual freedom, liberty and equality before the law – rights which underpin the principles of limited government and the consent of the people.

The proponents of liberal democratic peace theory, most notably Michael Doyle (1986) and Bruce Russett (1993), argued that the spread of liberal democracy would create and enlarge a 'separate zone of peace'. This theory reflects the underlying liberal assumption that war is not a normal state of affairs. Conflicts occur due to the selfish interests of (unrepresentative) rulers; however, humans have the capacity to overcome this through liberal democracy, which is characterized by rule of law and restraint in international relations. The checks and balances within democratic polities provide a system of 'constitutional caution' that will influence world affairs.

Liberal democracies are also thought to promote peace because they give rise to a situation of global economic interdependence, whereby it no longer becomes in the states' interests to fight each other. Again, this reflects Kant's view that trade between republics would help to develop common interests and mutual identification, thus reducing the likelihood of conflict. In the post-Cold War period, the increasing volume of trade is frequently interpreted as an incentive for states to resolve disputes and tensions before they erupt into violence. After all, war is costly.

However, liberal democratic peace theory has some methodological problems. First, it can be argued that it is based on correlation rather than causation. In other words, while scholars have observed that liberal democracies do not go to war with each other, this does not *in itself* prove that liberal democracy 'causes' peace. There may be other factors which explain the absence of war. For example, one can consider several reasons why the US and Canada do not fight with each other, apart from the fact that 'they are both liberal democracies'. They have strong trade ties, a long history of diplomatic relations and interpersonal relations among political elites and share a very long border. Democratic rule no doubt *facilitates* the peaceful relationship, but it is difficult to demonstrate convincingly that it is *in itself* the explanation.

Relatedly, it is difficult to present a 'theory' which is based on the *absence* of a certain phenomenon; this is sometimes described as the 'dogs that didn't bark' problem (using an analogy from a Sherlock Holmes story). Finally, liberal democratic peace is not statistically significant; *liberal* democracies (that is, 'consolidated' democracies that respect civil liberties and other individual rights) are in the minority in the international system. This renders the observation of a 'liberal democratic peace' less significant. The theory has also been criticized due to its implication that policymakers and the so-called 'international community' should seek to promote the spread of liberal democracy. The notion that democratic rule can be introduced by external actors is controversial; moreover, democratic transition is often conducive to *instability*, which may make violence and even war more likely.

The core liberal ideas about common interests and transactions such as trade mitigating the risk of conflict persist in another strand of Liberalism to which we now turn: **neoliberal institutionalism**. However, neoliberal institutionalists are less focused on regime type or political values in the domestic realm, and more interested in the possibility of cooperation in the context of international institutions. Importantly, they do not deny the realist premise (to be discussed) that states are the primary actors in international relations. However, they recognize the importance of other actors, such as international organizations. And, like the liberal internationalists and liberal idealists, they believe in the value of international law, cooperation and diplomacy.

> **Neoliberal Institutionalism** – a theoretical perspective which holds that the effects of anarchy can be mitigated (to some degree) by cooperation among actors under the auspices of international institutions.

Given that neoliberal institutionalists recognize the primacy of states in the international system, they also recognize the condition of **anarchy**. As mentioned, this is the notion that there is no 'world government'; in other words, there is no higher political entity than the state. However, they differ from realists in terms of how they interpret the *effects* of anarchy. From a neoliberal institutionalist perspective, the effects of anarchy can be (at least somewhat) ameliorated. Rather than being destined to be perpetually suspicious of each other in the anarchic international system, states may be willing and/or able to **cooperate**. And this cooperation (which may be defined simply as policy coordination) is expected to take place in an institutional context – that is in an environment in which institutions (the 'rules of the game') provide a code of conduct for interstate relations.

While neoliberal institutionalists agree that states see their own interests as paramount, they argue that states also recognize that these may coincide with the interests of other states. As such, they can mutually benefit from cooperation – in other words, they can play a **'positive-sum' game** in which absolute gains are possible. Moreover, membership of international organizations may actually *shape* and perhaps broaden state interests, in turn widening the scope for cooperation (Keohane and Nye 1977). (This depends, of course, on respect for the rules and for diplomacy in an international organization.) Despite the condition of anarchy, international organizations can provide forums for interaction and dialogue, and reduce uncertainty. They also reduce 'transaction costs', by providing these (usually permanent) forums with established rules which underpin a code of conduct among member states. Thus, for neoliberal institutionalists, it may not be such a bleak and insecure self-help world as the realists make out; mistrust and suspicion can be mitigated over time through interaction in pursuit of mutual benefits.

The World Trade Organization (WTO) provides an example of the neoliberal institutionalist viewpoint. The WTO facilitates cooperation among states on trade and investment. Though negotiation and formal agreements, states agree to reduce the barriers to trade in certain goods and services (such as agriculture or textiles). The WTO provides the framework of rules and regulations (that is, institutions) within which states coordinate their policies. Thus, states can benefit from participating in WTO dialogue and agreements.

Realism

Realists are often regarded as pessimists. However, they do not tend to see themselves this way. To the contrary, realists believe they see the world 'as it is', identifying fundamental truths about the way the international system works; they eschew idealism and what they see as utopian perspectives. Indeed, modern Realism in International Relations emerged as a response to the idealism of the interwar years. As discussed earlier in this chapter, for early realists such as Carr and Morgenthau, the outbreak of World War II proved that it was not possible to achieve peace through international cooperation and diplomacy. States are mistrustful and perpetually expect conflict; they are driven by self-interest in a 'self-help' anarchic system.

Like Liberalism, Realism is not one unified theory but has several variants. We will concentrate in particular on classical Realism and NeoRealism (also referred to as 'structural' Realism). Classical realists (such as Morgenthau) emphasized the pursuit of power as an end in itself. Their work was influenced by prominent early thinkers such as Niccoló Machiavelli, whose sixteenth-century work, *The Prince*, became something of a handbook for statesmen, and Thomas Hobbes, whose seventeenth-century work, *The Leviathan*, argued that a strong central authority is needed to avoid war.

Classical realists tend to focus on individuals rather than states; individuals are regarded as innately selfish and power-seeking. This means that the pursuit of national power is a *natural* drive; as Morgenthau (1948) wrote, politics is "governed by objective laws that have their roots in human nature." National interest is defined as power. Thus, classical realists expect that conflict is always possible. They believe that foreign policy advisers must be cognizant of this, and should avoid utopian or idealist inclinations.

> **Classical Realism** – a theoretical perspective which focuses on individuals and their selfish nature.
>
> **Structural Realism** – a theoretical perspective which focuses on the structure of the international system.

Neo- or **structural realists** are influenced by classical realist ideas, but focus less on human nature and more on interstate relations. Kenneth Waltz, the most prominent neorealist, sets out in his *Theory of International Politics* (1979) an analysis of the *structure* of the international system, which he sees as dictating the behaviour of states. States are perceived 'like units', which behave in similar ways, despite domestic differences. While realists do not necessarily deny that such differences exist (for example, in regard to regime type, electoral systems, and political and economic ties), they see them as not fundamentally important when it comes to interstate relations. The crucial factor is states' relative positions in the international system.

The condition of anarchy means that states cannot rely on a world government or other 'supranational' authority to mediate interstate relations. Given the structure of the international states system, states can hope only for *relative* (not absolute) gains – a **'zero-sum' game**. In other words, one state's gain (for example, in terms of power) necessarily means another state's loss. This gives rise to a 'self-help' world in which states are mistrustful and expect that conflict is always possible. In this system, states' ultimate goal is **security,** in order to survive. They seek power (traditionally defined in terms of military capability) in order to achieve security. Thus, power is the *means* to an end (of security) – in contrast with the aforementioned view of classical realists that power is an end in itself. Realists thus see their perspective as explaining the recurrence of conflict throughout history.

Moreover, as will by now be clear, realists do not expect cooperation among (self-interested) states. The only exception is the case of military **alliances** – short-term arrangements which are formed in response to a common threat. They are created by treaties among states in accordance with the **balance of power** principle; if one state or a group of states increases in power and poses a threat to the stability of the international system, an alliance may redress this imbalance. However, no state can ever be sure of another state's intentions, and only expect other states' interests to temporarily coincide with their own. Thus, alliances are expected to last only as long as the threat exists, and we see alliances between different combinations of states over time. For example, during World War II the United States and Soviet Union were allied against Nazi Germany; they later became adversaries during the Cold War, and the United States entered an alliance with Canada, the United Kingdom and several Western European states to balance against the Soviet threat (the North Atlantic Treaty Organization, or NATO).

> *An example of an alliance which persisted beyond the dissipation of the threat is the North Atlantic Treaty Organization (NATO), which was formed in 1949 in response to the threat posed by the Soviet Union, but it still exists today despite the dissolution of its erstwhile enemy. One could argue, however, that NATO has transformed in form and substance and is now a security organization rather than an alliance; its mandate has broadened well beyond the original treaty and it has a physical presence and bureaucracy. Thus, to the extent that NATO has an important role in international security today, one could argue that its existence is best explained through a neoliberal institutionalist lens.*

Realism, particularly NeoRealism, is often described as 'parsimonious' – it is economical, focusing on (what are perceived as) fundamental truths of international relations, rather than less important details such as domestic characteristics of states. Realism thus has a high degree of *explanatory* power – and indeed, to return to earlier discussions, realists see themselves as explaining the world as it is, rather than how it 'should be'. This parsimony inevitably leads to criticisms. Realists are sometimes charged with neglecting the complexities of empirical reality, and instead providing an overly simplified view of international relations. Relatedly, they tend to be seen by other scholars (including liberals and constructivists) as taking an overly state-centric view; they overlook the role of other actors, such as international (governmental and nongovernmental) organizations and transnational corporations.

Other sources of criticism focus on the ontological orientation of Realism. For example, realists tend to see states as 'black boxes' – their identities and interests are treated as fixed and trans-historical. However, one could argue that we cannot overlook the differences between, say, China and the United States in terms of identities, regime types, histories and so on. Realists also do not recognize the possibility of moral or humanitarian motivations for state behaviour; they see initiatives such as foreign aid and overseas humanitarian assistance as attributable to states' strategic interests. Jack Donnelly, a prominent human rights scholar, criticizes this perspective: 'States often can and do act out of moral concerns' (Donnelly 2009: 50). In actuality, there are probably always a multiplicity of reasons why states formulate such foreign policies; as with many other empirical observations, they are difficult to explain entirely through only one theoretical lens.

Scholars often refer to the so-called 'mainstream debate' between neorealists and neoliberal institutionalists. These have been the predominant theoretical perspectives in international relations since the end of World War II. As explained, they agree that states are the principal actors in the international system, and that anarchy exists. However, neorealists are sceptical about the value of institutions, arguing that they have a minimal influence on state behaviour (for example, Mearsheimer 1994/95). They see international organizations as merely arenas in which states pursue their interests; they were (in most cases) created by states, and operate in states' interests.

Neoliberal institutionalists disagree, seeing organizations as important actors in world affairs. They see neorealists as unable to explain the rise of cooperation between states, particularly in the areas of trade and investment. Relatedly, as discussed, neorealists hold that states are concerned with relative gains, whereas neoliberal institutionalists argue that states may obtain *absolute* gains through cooperation. These 'mainstream' perspectives have been dominant in International Relations theoretical debates for some time, but in recent years have faced challenges from alternative approaches, including Constructivism.

Constructivism

The core observation of constructivist approaches is the social construction of reality. As Michael Barnett (2011) notes, 'reality does not exist out there waiting to be discovered'. Rather, humans 'construct and give meaning to reality' through shared knowledge. For example, constructivists challenge the assumption of anarchy as an inevitable condition of international relations. They see anarchy as constructed, rather than a 'reality'; in the words of Alexander Wendt (1999) 'anarchy is what states make of it'. It exists because in the political order constructed by humans, 'states' have been created and are the highest form of political entity. Relatedly, constructivist scholarship brings attention to the *social* aspects of world affairs. It has drawn on insights from sociology, and in so doing directly challenges the notion of states as 'units' or 'billiard balls'. Rather than making assumptions about state behaviour based on their interests imposed by the structure of the international system, constructivists ask 'how are states' interests constituted in the first place?' They argue that states' interests should not simply be taken as fixed and given, but in fact are dynamic and change over time *as a result of interaction* with other states. Interests are 'mutually constituted' (for example, Hopf 1998).

> **Constructivism** – a theoretical perspective which contends that reality is a social construction. Instead of making assumptions about state behaviour based on their interests, constructivists question how are states' interests constituted in the first place.
>
> **Critical Constructivism** – a theoretical perspective which challenges mainstream assumptions about the international system. Critical constructivists argue that the system was constructed by powerful actors, while other groups were marginalized.

Moreover, constructivist approaches recognize the different **identities** of states, which are shaped by factors such as historical and cultural experiences and also by social interaction with other states. The distinct identities of, say, Australia and Indonesia *do* matter in interstate relations, and help analysts to understand how relations between these two states differs from, say, relations between Australia and New Zealand.

Before going further we should distinguish among the quite different constructivist approaches. One way to do so is to distinguish 'conventional' from 'critical' constructivists (Hopf 1998). We will concentrate here on the former. **'Conventional' constructivists** respond to and engage with the 'mainstream' debate. They see mainstream approaches as too focused on **material** power and as neglecting ideas and **ideational** power. From a constructivist perspective, ideas are very important in world affairs – they shape the identities and interests of states.

For example, ideas about freedom and democracy have been long reiterated and reinforced in US foreign policy, and are used to justify initiatives such as 'Operation Iraqi Freedom' in 2003 and the subsequent occupation by the so-called 'coalition of the willing'. Australia's successful bid for a UN Security Council seat in 2013–14 drew on ideas about Australia as a 'middle power' which played an important role in world affairs. At the time of writing, there are competing ideas about whether China is a rising (and possibly threatening) power, or a developing, *status quo* state. Constructivists argue that ideational debates permeate world affairs and shape the context in which decisions about *material* power are made.

International politics is social and dynamic, rather than static. This means that, from the constructivist point of view, there are possibilities for global change. This contrasts most markedly from the neorealist view that there are fundamental truths in international relations – that self-interested states behave in a predictable way in the international system and that conflict is perpetually possible. For constructivists, the notion that states exist in a *social* world and interact over time in ways which *shape* their interests and identities means that world affairs are *not* predictable, and may change quite significantly over time.

Constructivist perspectives gained prominence after the end of the Cold War. The mainstream approaches did not predict and could not explain the collapse of the Soviet Union; from a neorealist perspective, a bipolar system is quite stable and should persist unless one 'pole' (in this case, one of the superpower adversaries) manages to defeat the other militarily. The implosion of the Soviet Union, in the absence of 'hot' conflict with the US, did not fit with such a perspective. In contrast, constructivist approaches were better able to explain the end of the Cold War with reference to the role of ideas and ideology. They could analyse the failure of communist ideas to sustain and enhance the international standing of the Soviet Union (and, relatedly, its economic fortunes).

Thus, in the 1990s, constructivist scholarship proliferated as scholars not only developed the conceptual and theoretical aspects of Constructivism, but demonstrated the important contribution it could make in empirical research. As prominent constructivist scholar Christian Reus-Smit (2009) puts it, a new generation of scholars 'saw potential for innovation in conceptual elaboration and empirically informed theoretical development' (219). For example, constructivist scholars have conducted studies in areas such as chemical and nuclear weapons taboos (for example Price 1997; Tannenwald 1999) and the moral aspects of state behaviuor (for example, Reus-Smit, 1999). These studies demonstrate the importance of recognizing ideational factors in international relations research.

In this way, (conventional) constructivists hold that they make an important contribution to social science research. They do not necessarily seek to overhaul or undermine the 'mainstream' approaches, but rather to challenge them – by broadening the definition of 'power' (to include ideational as well as material power) and by highlighting the social aspects of world affairs, in which interests and identities are dynamic and 'mutually constituted' rather than static and trans-historical. Moreover, conventional constructivists acknowledge the importance of structures in international relations, but consider ideational structures to be as important as material structures. As Reus-Smit (2009) points out, 'systems of shared ideas, beliefs and values also have structural characteristics, and … exert a powerful influence on social and political action' (220).

Modern-day Europe provides an empirical example which can be analysed through a constructivist lens, in regard to the significance of identity, ideational power and dynamic relations in world affairs. In Europe today, there is a level of cooperation and sacrifice of sovereignty to a supranational authority (the European Union) that one could not have imagined at the end of World War II. Germany has become an economic power and diplomatic leader which plays a significant role in Europe and worldwide; other European Union members look to Germany to provide leadership in a difficult economic period, assisting other economies such as Greece and Spain. A constructivist explanation would emphasize the role of ideas and identity in these changing relationships; for example, Germany's identity today is fundamentally different from the Nazi era.

'Critical' constructivists, on the other hand, pose a much more fundamental challenge to mainstream theoretical perspectives. Drawing on insights from critical theory, they question the basic premises upon which mainstream international relations theories are based. Critical constructivists agree with conventional constructivists in regard to the notion of a 'social' world and the argument that institutions, identities and practices are not 'given' but are constructed

*the extreme unwillingness to use money and resources

by humans. However, they go further by challenging mainstream assumptions about the 'international system', and drawing attention to the way this system was constructed by powerful actors, while other groups were marginalized. Thus, critical constructivists tend to have a more **normative** approach – they seek to highlight the hierarchy and subordination in world affairs, and also to bring about *change*. Their outlook reflects the emancipatory agenda of critical theory.

Like the other theoretical perspectives, Constructivism can be criticized on ontological and methodological grounds. The obvious objection from the 'mainstream' perspectives is that it is difficult to 'measure' concepts such as ideas and identity. In terms of an empirical research agenda, then, constructivist approaches may seem somewhat nebulous, taking into account many factors which pose methodological challenges (in contrast to the parsimony* of Realism). However, Constructivism contributes important insights into world affairs, where other approaches are limited. Students of International Relations should be driven in their engagement with theoretical perspectives by empirical puzzles, and consider which explanations best explain them.

Feminism

Finally, we turn our attention to Feminism, one example of the now many so-called critical theories to influence how world affairs are conceptualized and practiced. Though there is more that separates than unites these numerous **critical theories**, many who participate in the critical project share the view that Liberalism, Realism and, to some extent, even Constructivism are all articulated by and from a similar cultural and gendered perspective. Their focus on the state and the system, on warfare and trade and on the sovereign individual have, for critical theory scholars, meant a corresponding neglect of other voices and subjects. In our multifaceted world, where religion, ethnicity and gender are also crucial determinants and barriers to political action, theorists and theories must therefore look farther afield if they truly want to do justice to the competing realities that exist globally.

Having gained its prominence in the discipline during the 1990s, Feminism is one such theoretical innovation which saw the need for scholars and practitioners to become more conscious of the gendered undertones of mainstream International Relations theorizing. The relative absence of women in positions of political power when compared to men and their systematic marginalization in the mainstream discourses of International Relations needed to be addressed. Filling this void have been a number of pioneering feminist International Relations theorists, including here J. Ann Tickner, Jan Jindy Pettman, Cynthia Enloe, Christine Sylvester, V. Spike Peterson, Jacqui True and Katrina Lee-Koo, who have brought their concerns about gender to areas of inquiry in International Relations such as international political economy, security and warfare, peacebuilding and of course violence against women.

Though there have been numerous waves of Feminism and various schools of feminist thought in International Relations, making it thus very difficult to essentialize Feminism in any neat way, we can perhaps say that at their core feminists have primarily focused on gendered relations and oversights in world affairs. **Gender**, as such, is the lens which feminists employ to view the politics among nations. Ontologically, Feminism highlights the plight of women and other subjugated individuals who, because of their gender orientation, are persecuted or repressed by others in positions of power, including here 'man', 'the state' and 'the international system'. Defining gender 'as a set of socially constructed characteristics describing what men and women ought to be', J. Ann Tickner and Laura Sjoberg (2010) characterize feminist critiques by their objective to expose and undo the privilege accorded in International Relations to **masculine traits** like 'strength, rationality, independence, protector, and public'. Where an individual, organization, state or alliance displays such traits, they are perceived as powerful. But where feminine characteristics such as 'weakness, emotionality, relational, protected, and private' are displayed in political affairs, it is powerlessness that is ascribed to the actor. Ignored, belittled or pitied, they are thus rarely taken seriously. Feminist scholarship goes against the grain of conventional wisdom by taking these voices and subjects seriously. Through gendered lenses, unfamiliar viewpoints, concerns and realities can thus flood into the international political realm, challenging the discipline's boundaries as it does so.

But it is important to emphasize that just as there is no one universal conception of gender, there is not one but many feminisms. To support this claim, let us briefly look at the main claims and differences of two influential variants of Feminism in International Relations: liberal Feminism and post-colonial Feminism.

> **Feminism** – a set of theoretical perspectives which focus on gendered relations and oversights in International Relations. Using gender as a lens to examine world affairs, feminists have challenged the orthodoxy of the state, the man and war in International Relations theorizing.

Arguably the most politically influential strand of Feminism, **liberal Feminism** asks the important but overlooked question of 'where are the women?' in International Relations (Enloe 1989). Often subordinated to men, women are paid less and more frequently discriminated against if they are not altogether rendered invisible in the public realm. At home in the private realm, women's concerns are thus considered personal not political. Extrapolated to the international sphere, the consequences of women's marginalization has resulted in their habitual political oppression – whether as exploited slaves in sweatshops, the victims of sex trafficking, targets of war crimes and human rights abuses or those excluded from positions of power, there is no equality for women in world affairs. This first wave of feminists questioned why this is so: why has women's subordination and suppression become thought of as 'natural' in International Relations, and what would the consequences be if women were treated equally along with men? Would the way in which world affairs are conducted change? Would the focus of policymakers shift increasingly away from wars between states to initiatives for social justice and cooperation?

Post-colonial feminists often critique the oversights of their liberal counterparts. They argue that, though they are not wrong to call for equal political, economic and human rights for women, liberal feminist theorizations primarily stem from Western women drawing from Western conceptions of sex, equality and rights. Implicitly, they universalize a particular subset of women's claims and conceptions of gender without realizing how culturally, economically and ethnically determined they are. Many of the women – and men – in non-Western countries who have little concern for rights and equality will not benefit from liberal calls for women's right and equality. What is more, those whose existence in the Global South is predetermined by the logic of neoliberal economic globalization may desire less a 'liberal' form of Feminism than a non-liberal, non-Western realization of gender empowerment. Because of this, post-colonial feminists like to point out that too often feminists from the West speak of their experience as if it is the experience of all feminists in all places and at all times. This clearly is not the case. Those who see world affairs through a liberal feminist lens, for example, would thus do well to realize the ease with which they can unthinkingly colonize the realities of subaltern feminist realities as their own.

> Feminist scholarship in International Relations has brought to the fore many previously neglected realms of inquiry. A good example of this is the now classic text, Let the Good Times Roll: Prostitution and the U.S. Military in Asia, by Saundra Pollock Sturdevant and Brenda Stoltzfus (1992). Though by no means the only study to delve into the relationship between **gender and warfare**, Sturdevant and Stoltzfus' book was one the earliest to highlight the sexualized nature of international conflict. As they note, in military towns like Uijongbu in South Korea, prostitutes and 'mixed-blood' children would have lined the streets. Downtime from active service meant R&R for servicemen (and women) and that inevitably meant partaking in some form of I&I (intoxication and intercourse). For Sturdevant and Stoltzfus, though stories of genuine cross-cultural bonds formed between foreign soldiers and the local women whose jobs it was to pleasure them did exist, they certainly numbered in the minority. For every one of the more positive stories, there were thousands more that tell of the mechanical and institutional abuse of women, whose bodies were used by military personnel in the same way that they had used a machine.

CONCLUSION

In this chapter we have sought to provide an introduction to theory and theorizing in International Relations, to the discipline's Great Debates and, finally, to a number of influential theoretical positions. What has informed this endeavour is our shared belief that theory is fundamental to understanding International Relations in any meaningful way. No student, as such, should think their education complete without at least familiarizing themselves with some of the basic theoretical articulations of world affairs. Given how much the world has changed, and is still changing, nuanced theoretical understandings are now imperative for students to discern why states act the way they do, and why some statespeople are incapable of grasping the motivations behind such things as terrorism, climate change, the plight of refugees and nuclear proliferation. A student of theory will be better prepared than others to answer questions of who gets what and why. And a student of theory may be better placed to appreciate, if not agree with, some of the theoretical assumptions motivating their antagonists than one who has simply studied current affairs. This is the impact and virtue of theory. We hope that by introducing theory in straightforward language we will have demystified the topic at least in part, making students a little less apprehensive about what it means to theorize and think theoretically about world affairs.

QUESTIONS FOR REFLECTION

1. How does Knutsen explain theory? What are the practical implications?
2. What's the best way to understand ontology, epistemology and methodology?
3. What's a problem-solving theory? What's a critical theory?
4. What was the First Great Debate about?
5. What was the Second Great Debate about?
6. What were the Third and Fourth Great Debates about?
7. In a nutshell, what picture does
   - Liberalism paint of the world?
   - Realism paint of the world?
   - Constructivism paint of the world?
   - Feminism paint of the world?

REVISION QUIZ

1. What were the first International Relations theorists trying to prevent?

   a. The establishment of a new international society
   b. The rise of Hitler
   c. Nuclear warfare between the US and USSR
   d. International hostility and warfare on the scale seen in World War I

2. Which of the following is *not* generally considered to be a purpose of theory in International Relations?

   a. To help us to understand empirical observations, that is, phenomena we observe in the 'real world'
   b. To provide an abstract representation of reality
   c. To inform policymakers and helps them to make wise decisions
   d. To contribute to the body of knowledge about world affairs

3. According to the theorist Steve Smith, what occurs when theories acquire the status of common sense?

   a. Everybody becomes aware of them
   b. They begin to delineate not simply what can be known but also what is sensible to talk about
   c. They become easier to understand
   d. They begin to dictate political actors and actions in the way that Liberalism dictated policy options during the interwar years

4. According to the theorist Robert Cox, 'theory is …'

   a. 'an incisive methodology with which to understand ontology'
   b. 'always *for* someone and *for* some purpose'
   c. 'a tool for explaining the world out there'
   d. 'a scientific way to analyze historical events'

5. Which of the following is *not* a premise of Liberalism?

   a. Global economic interdependence may reduce the chances of conflict
   b. Humans are capable of progress and change
   c. States are inevitably mistrustful of one another
   d. The condition of anarchy can be mitigated to some degree through cooperation

6. Which statement best describes the reason that proponents of liberal democratic peace theory believe that liberal democracies do not go to war with each other?

   a. Liberal democracies do not usually have large military expenditures
   b. The leaders of liberal democracies generally do not wish to become involved in international conflict
   c. Liberal democracies do not see war as a normal state of affairs
   d. Liberal democracies are characterized by rule of law and their governments depend on consent of the people, who do not tend to approve going to war

7. According to neo- or structural realists, why do states always recognize the possibility of conflict?

   a. Heads of state are usually seeking to acquire more territory through conquest
   b. There is no world government to oversee world affairs, i.e. states exist in an anarchic, self-help system
   c. International organizations make conflict more likely because states cannot cooperate
   d. Ideas and ideology can be dangerous and become the basis for conflict

8. Which statement best describes the way in which constructivists view the role of state interests in world affairs?

   a. State interests can change over time as a result of interaction with other states
   b. State interests are more or less fixed and are focused on security and survival
   c. State interests are dictated by the structure of the international system
   d. State interests determine the outcome of negotiations in international organizations

9. Which of the following is *not* a common criticism of the realist perspective?

   a. It risks neglecting the complexities of the 'real world'
   b. It focuses too much on states as the important actors in world affairs
   c. It is an overly complex theory which incorporates too many factors
   d. It tends to neglect the role of non-state actors, such as international organizations

10. Ontologically, what have feminist theories tended to highlight the most?

   a. The plight of women and other subjugated individuals who, because of their gender orientation, have been disadvantaged in the international realm
   b. The plight of women who are disenfranchised in the international realm
   c. Those who are not men
   d. Those who are weak and powerless

Answers: 1: d; 2: c; 3: b; 4: b; 5: c; 6: d; 7: b; 8: a; 9: c; 10: a.

BIBLIOGRAPHY

Ashley, R. and Walker, R.B.J. (1990) 'Introduction: Speaking the Language of Exile: Dissident Thought in International Studies', *International Studies Quarterly*, 34(3), 259–68.

Brown, C. and Ainley, K. (2005) *Understanding International Relations*, 3rd edition (Basingstoke: Palgrave).

Bull, H. (1966) *The Anarchical Society: A Study of Order in World Politics* (New York: Columbia University Press).

Burchill, S. and Linklater, A. (2009) 'Introduction'. In S. Burchill et al., *Theories of International Relations* (New York: Palgrave Macmillan), 1–30.

Carr, E.H. (1939) *The Twenty Years' Crisis, 1919–1939* (London: Macmillan).

Donnelly, J. (2009) 'Realism'. In S. Burchill et al., *Theories of International Relations* (New York: Palgrave Macmillan), 31–56.

Doyle, M. (1986) 'Liberalism and World Politics', *American Political Science Review*, 80(4), 1151–69.

Dunne, T., Kurki, M. and Smith, S. (2010) *International Relations Theories: Discipline and Diversity* (Oxford: Oxford University Press).

Enloe, C. (1989) *Bananas, Beaches and Bases: Making Feminist Sense of International Politics* (London: Pandora).

Fukuyama, F. (1992) *The End of History and the Last Man* (New York: Free Press).

George, J. (1994) *Discourses of Global Politics: A Critical (Re)Introduction to International Relations* (Boulder, CO: Lynne Rienner).

Hopf, T. (1998) 'The Promise of Constructivism in International Relations Theory', *International Security*, 23(1), 171–200.

Keohane, R. and Nye, J. (1977) *Power and Interdependence: World Politics in Transition* (Boston, MA: Little, Brown).

Knutsen, T. (1997) *A History of International Relations Theory* (Manchester: Manchester University Press).

Kurki, M. and Wight, C. (2010) 'International Relations and Social Science'. In T. Dunne et al., *International Relations Theories: Discipline and Diversity* (Oxford: Oxford University Press), 14–35.

Mearsheimer, J. (1994/95) 'The False Promise of International Institutions', *International Security*, 19(3), 5–49.

Morgenthau, H. (1948) *Politics Among Nations: The Struggle for Power and Peace* (New York: Alfred A. Knopf).

Price, R. (1997) *The Chemical Weapons Taboo* (Ithaca, NY: Cornell).

Reus-Smit, C. (2009) 'Constructivism'. In Scott Burchill et al., *Theories of International Relations* (New York: Palgrave Macmillan), 212–36.

Reus-Smit, C. (1999) *The Moral Purpose of the State: Culture, Social Identity and Institutional Rationality in International Relations* (Princeton, NJ: Princeton University Press).

Russett, B. (1993) *Grasping the Democratic Peace* (Princeton, NJ: Princeton University Press).

Smith, S., Booth, K. and Zalewski, M. (eds) (1996) *International Theory: Positivism and Beyond* (Cambridge: Cambridge University Press).

Sturdevant, S. and Stoltzfus, B. (1992) *Let the Good Times Roll: Prostitution and the U.S. Military in Asia* (New York: New Press).

Tannenwald, N. (1999) 'The Nuclear Taboo: The United States and the Normative Basis of Nuclear Non-Use', *International Organization*, 53(3), 433–68.

Tickner, J.A. and Sjoberg, L. (2010) 'Feminism'. In T. Dunne et al., *International Relations Theories: Discipline and Diversity* (Oxford: Oxford University Press).

Waltz, K. (1979) *Theory of International Politics* (New York: McGraw-Hill).

Wendt, A. (1999) *Constructing International Politics* (Cambridge: Cambridge University Press).

Zalewski, M. (1996) '"All these theories yet the bodies keep piling up": Theory, theorists, theorising'. In Smith et al., *International Theory: Positivism and Beyond* (Cambridge: Cambridge University Press).

Chapter 3
Ethics and Morality in International Relations

LAVINA LEE

In this chapter our aim is to understand how particular theories of international relations approach the issue of ethics and morality in interstate conduct. These issues are often marginalized in the discipline because of a desire to produce research that is practically useful to policymakers, on the assumption that ethical and moral questions are of little relevance to problem-solving. What is often not recognized is how particular international relations theories are styled as scientific, objective and descriptive, claiming to divorce ethics from politics, whilst in reality advocating practices that are prescriptive with ethical implications. What should be clear at the end of the chapter is that the two dominant political approaches in international relations we will focus upon – Realism and Liberalism – are not devoid of ethical implications and that these should be discussed and debated. In the chapter to follow we will differentiate between the terms morality and ethics, identify categories of ethical action drawn from moral philosophy, discover the realist, Liberal and Just War theory approaches to questions about the values and principles that ought to govern relations between states and the possible duties owed to individuals beyond state boundaries. We will show how realist approaches are far from purely descriptive of the reality of international politics, but in fact contain normative assumptions about how national interests ought to be defined and which privilege conceptions of 'necessity' and prudence as having primacy over moral considerations. We will also discuss how the universal morality espoused by Liberal approaches to international relations contain their own moral dilemmas. Specifically, this includes contestation over how universal human rights actually are, and whether the promotion of liberal values by force could endanger international stability, and is ultimately counterproductive to the wellbeing of individual human beings in other states. This is followed by an explanation of the ethical principles governing the use of force developed under the Just War tradition. Finally, we then examine how ethical and moral arguments are used to evaluate and assess the use of force in international relations using the Iraq War of 2003 as a case study.

Key Words: Moral Norms; Ethical Norms; Cosmopolitanism; Pluralism; Utilitarianism; Realism; *Raison d'état*; Prudence; Ethic of Responsibility; Liberalism; Categorical imperative; Harmony of Interests; Perpetual Peace; Democratic Peace Theory; Liberal Institutionalism; Defensive Liberalism; Offensive Liberalism; Just War Theory; Iraq War 2003.

Chapter 3

Ethics and Morality in International Relations

LAVINA LEE

INTRODUCTION

In this chapter our aim is to understand how particular theories of international relations approach the issue of ethics and morality in interstate conduct. The study of ethics and morality in international relations is often marginalized, or treated as an interesting side issue that would be relevant if the world were more perfectible. What is often not recognized is how particular international relations theories are styled as scientific, objective and descriptive, claiming to divorce ethics from politics, whilst in reality advocating practices that are prescriptive with ethical implications. Moral and ethical questions are also often neglected because of a desire for the discipline to be practically useful to policymakers, the assumption being that such questions are of marginal relevance to problem-solving. What should be clear at the end of the chapter is that the two dominant political approaches in international relations we will focus upon – Realism and Liberalism – are not devoid of ethical implications and these should be discussed and debated. We then examine how ethical and moral arguments are used to evaluate and assess the use of force in international relations using the Iraq War of 2003 as a case study.

But first, we need to define precisely how the terms ethics and morality will be used in this chapter. What we are primarily concerned with are arguments about the role ethical and moral values ought to play in interstate conduct and how much of a role they actually do play in particular case studies. Morality is a broader concept than ethics, but both are a type of norm, that is, collective expectations of proper behaviour for an actor with a given identity. **Moral norms** are principles of behaviour based on shared conceptions of right and wrong within a particular society, with the source often attributed to religious belief, natural law or the application of human reason. **Ethical norms** are not equivalent to moral norms. They are similar to moral norms in that they specify standards of right and wrong, but do so in a confined context of social relations – a given field of human activity or thought – for a particular group of actors. The *Collins English Dictionary* for example provides a number

> **Moral Norms** are principles of behaviour based on shared conceptions of right and wrong within a society drawn from religion, natural law or human reason.
>
> **Ethical Norms** are a subset of moral norms that specify standards of right and wrong but in a confined context of social relations for a particular group of actors. Theories of IR put forward codes of ethics applicable to international politics.

of definitions of ethics (3rd edition, 1991) including: '2. Plural "a social, religious or civil code of behavior considered correct, esp. that of a particular group, profession, or individual"'.

For example, professional groups such as lawyers, doctors and accountants develop codes of practice that define legitimate behaviour for members of the profession in pursuit of their goals. Ethical codes do not necessarily conform to wider moral codes held by society in general. For example, under most common codes of legal ethics a lawyer is under an ethical obligation to defend the right of an individual to be treated as innocent until proven guilty. As such they ought not to refuse to defend a potential client, even if their own personal moral beliefs may make them uncomfortable about agreeing to defend an accused paedophile or murderer, in a particular case.

Similarly, scholars of international relations have attempted to develop ethical codes of practice that apply to the context of international politics to guide political decision-makers in answering questions about: the formation of national interests, how these interests ought to be pursued, what duties are owed to a state's own citizens and what duties are owed to individuals outside of the state, if any. These ethical codes may be derived from higher order moral conceptions of right or wrong held within particular nation-states. The development of an ethic of international politics must grapple with the fact that the world is presently divided into separate territorial entities, each composed of societies with often very different cultural and religious values. The formation of shared ethical norms becomes much more difficult in these circumstances. The political division of the world among formally equal entities also creates a decentralized system without an overarching authority capable of guaranteeing that such ethical values will be upheld. This uncertainty opens up an element of risk and provides greater incentives for self-regarding rather than other-regarding behaviour.

Ethical approaches to international relations often draw on conceptual categories developed from moral philosophy, particularly **Cosmopolitanism**, **Pluralism** and **Utilitarianism**. A cosmopolitan believes that all of us are citizens of the world first, rather than merely citizens of the states in which we are born, and following from this that 'all natural or man-made borders are morally contingent' (Beardsworth 2001, 17). State boundaries should therefore be irrelevant in deciding questions of moral duties owed to human beings. This forms the basis of liberal ideas about the inherent equality and dignity of all human beings and a commitment to the promotion and protection of universal values expressed as rights 'which hold for any and every culture, irrespective of whether a particular culture subscribes to them or not'(Graeme 2008, 192).

> **Cosmopolitans** believe that we are citizens of the world first and foremost and that ethical duties are therefore universal.
>
> **Pluralists** believe that value systems are specific to particular cultures, societies and identities. No one value system should be viewed as universal or superior to another.

Pluralists, in contrast, do not subscribe to the existence of universal values that apply to all human beings everywhere. Rather, they argue that throughout the world a plurality of value systems have developed within particular societies, cultures and ethno/national groups and that 'none of them can any longer be thought of as superior, or subscription to them held to be paramount'(Graeme 2008, 190). In international relations theory, some strands of the **English School** argue that citizens of states owe more extensive moral duties to others within those territorial boundaries than to individuals residing outside them. The English School theorist, Hedley Bull, cautioned against attempts to expand the goals of international society beyond striving for peaceful co-existence – such as to protect the human rights of individuals everywhere – without consensus about what 'justice' would entail. Given the plurality of value systems among states this would lead to conflict and undermine the existence of an international society. He argued that whilst maintaining order did not always trump questions of justice, it was 'prior' in that without order other human goods such as security, the ability to make and keep promises 'and the stabilization of possession by rules of property' could not be achieved (Bull 1995, 18 and 93). Other pluralists defend the continued existence of a states system as the best means of ensuring the freedom of individuals within them to express their identity, values and culture free from outside interference (Walzer 1977). Realists are to an extent also pluralists but come to this view on the basis of an assessment of what is morally possible in an anarchic system, where states are not reliably punished for failing to observe normative imperatives.

Utilitarianism is a type of consequentialist ethics with the unit of value being the individual. Utilitarians argue that an 'agent is morally obliged to perform any action, no matter what, if and only if it has the best consequences or ... if and only if it maximizes the good [i.e. well-being] ... all of our moral duties can be reduced to one: that we should try to maximize well-being or utility' of all (Ellis 1992, 158). A utilitarian approach can be seen to be reflected in Just War principles such as the use of force only in circumstances where there is a reasonable chance of success, and the weighing up of the proportional benefits and costs of war. Some cautious liberal views that question the prudence of humanitarian intervention into states with scant experience of liberal-democratic values have utilitarian premises. They ask whether the export of Liberalism would create more harm than good both in relation to the people being 'liberated' and those doing the liberating. Realism too can be thought of as a type of consequentialist ethics. However, realist approaches reckon 'the value of consequences in terms of the survival and well-being of particular communities', whilst Utilitarianism does so 'in terms of the well-being of humanity at large' (Mapel and Nardin 1992, 298).

> **Utilitarians** are consequentialist and define morality in terms of maximizing the utility of humanity at large.

REALISM

Realist theoretical approaches to international relations are largely viewed as being skeptical about the influence of moral or ethical principles on interstate conduct. This flows from assumptions made about the nature of human beings, and/or the anarchic structure of the international system. These factors, it is argued, limit the possibilities for ethical action and, rather, it is national interest, defined largely in terms of the pursuit of power, that truly guides the foreign policy of states, or *should* do so. There are many realist approaches to understanding international relations and here we will discuss the work of three scholars – Niccoló Machiavelli, Hans Morgenthau and Kenneth Waltz – who are considered to be highly influential in the field. Each vary in relation to the implications for foreign policy attributed to human nature and international anarchy and therefore the role they believe ethics can and should play in international politics. We will start with Machiavelli, whose ideas form part of the foundation of Realism in Western political theory.

> **Realist** approaches are **skeptical** about the influence of moral or ethical principles on interstate behaviour stemming from assumptions about human nature and/or the anarchic structure of the international system.

Machiavelli

Niccoló Machiavelli (1469–1527) is famous for his elaboration of a particular brand of realist political ethics, centring on the concept of *raison d'état*, or reason of the state, based on his own experiences as a politician and diplomat in Florence during the time of the Italian city-states in around 1500, and his own interpretation of the history of the Roman Republics. Machiavelli firmly believed that there was a perpetual tension between politics and morality, and that ultimately political leaders should not be limited by the ethics of ordinary citizens, but by different ethical standards that must prioritise *raison d'état*.

> *raison d'état* – or reason of the state. Machiavelli argued that leaders of states must subscribe to a different ethical code to ordinary people with the preservation of the security of the state as the highest form of morality.

Before explaining this concept of *raison d'état*, it is necessary to explain that the privileging of the state within Machiavellian thought is derived from a dim view of the essential nature of man from which the famous maxim that 'it is safer [for a ruler] to be feared than loved' is drawn:

> For this may be said of men generally: they are ungrateful, fickle, feiners and dissemblers, avoider of danger, eager for gain. While you benefit them they are all devoted to you … but when you are hard pressed, they turn a way … Men are less hesitant about offending or harming a ruler who makes himself loved than one who inspires fear. For love is sustained by a bond of gratitude which, because men are excessively self-interested, is broken whenever they see a chance to benefit themselves. But fear is sustained by a dread of punishment that is always effective. (The Prince, Chapter XVII, 59)

Political leaders can temper these traits and 'make men good and virtuous by subjecting them to good laws and institutions' (Boucher 1998, 94). It is only through the establishment of order and stability by strong leadership of the state that ideas about justice and morality are at all possible and citizens are therefore able to flourish. Thus, for Machiavelli, the Prince must subscribe to a different ethical code to ordinary men, by which the promotion and preservation of the state is itself the highest form of morality, and necessity may require the rights of individuals be overridden for the common good of the state. In Chapter 15 of *The Prince* he writes:

> … how men live is so different from how they should live that a ruler who does not do what is generally done, but persists in doing what ought to be done, will undermine his power rather than maintain it. If a ruler who wants always to act honourably is surrounded by many unscrupulous men his downfall is inevitable. Therefore, a ruler who wishes to maintain his power must be prepared to act immorally when this becomes necessary.

Machiavelli also subscribes to a pluralist rather than cosmopolitan ethical code by which understandings of morality are only made meaningful within the state by the establishment of a stable and strong system of government. It therefore does not make sense to speak of the existence of a universal moral code.

In terms of relations between states, Machiavelli's experiences and interpretation of history also led him to the conviction that the leaders of states are driven by ambition and the pursuit of glory. As a result, international relations are riven by conflict, and to ensure survival each state must be prepared to advance the common good of the state at the expense of foreigners, or else suffer the same fate. War is just if compelled by necessity, with perceptions of necessity driven by fear of other states' intentions, or the quest for security:

> *For when the safety of one's country wholly depends on the decision to be taken, no attention should be paid either to justice or injustice, to kindness or cruelty, or to its being praiseworthy or ignominious. On the contrary, every other consideration being set aside, that alternative should be wholeheartedly adopted which will save the life and preserve freedom of one's country.*
> (Discourses, III.41, p. 515)

What is ethical behaviour for a state in its international relations is to privilege the survival of the state over ordinary moral compunctions, which may in fact leave the state and its people in danger. Given the ambition of other states, the Prince is compelled by necessity not merely to defend but to expand or else be the subject of other states' expansionist plans. This logic justifies the pre-emptive or preventive use of force. The only real restraint on territorial expansion is prudence, that is, that such plans are credible and feasible given the state's capabilities (Boucher 1998, 126). Machiavellian political ethics are thus highly open-ended. Subjective perceptions of what is necessary in pursuit of the common good of the state are only tempered by the limits of a state's resources, and can be used to justify expansionary foreign policy and war (Boucher 1998, 133).

Morgenthau → centred around pessimism about PEOPLE

Hans Morgenthau is considered to be the foremost proponent of modern day classical Realism. He wanted to establish international politics as an independent area of study – like science or economics – with its own system of ethics adapted to conditions found in the international system. Morgenthau's most famous work, *Politics Among Nations: The Struggle for Power and Peace*, was written as a direct antidote to idealist thought in the interwar years as well as the perceived tendency of US foreign policy to promote cosmopolitan values abroad through military intervention. Morgenthau's six principles of political Realism begin with the claim that politics is 'governed by objective laws that have their roots in human nature' (Morgenthau 1978, 4). Like Machiavelli and Hobbes before him, Morgenthau takes a pessimistic view of human nature described as consisting of the 'bio-psychological drives … to live, to propagate, and to dominate' (Morgenthau 1978, 36–7). From this essential human desire to dominate comes a deep-seated 'lust for power' (Morgenthau 1962, 42), which in turn defines all politics – domestic and international – as a struggle for power. His second principle of political Realism thus states that 'all statesmen think and act in terms of interest defined as power, and the evidence of history bears that assumption out' (Morgenthau 1978, 5). Whilst hierarchic political organization with the capacity for the enforcement of law can temper power politics within the state, in an anarchic international realm states must pursue power resources to increase the chance of survival. What room is there then for morality in the pursuit of national interest?

Morgenthau's Realism puts forward the consequentialist view that in 'a world of opposing interests and of conflict among them, moral principles can never be fully realized' and the best that can be realized is the 'lesser evil' rather than the 'absolute good' (Morgenthau 1978,: 3–4). The universality of moral principles is not denied, however,

> … while the individual has a moral right to sacrifice himself in defense of such a moral principle, the state has no right to let its moral disapprobation of the infringement of liberty get in the way of successful political action, itself inspired by the moral principle of national survival. There can be no political morality without prudence; that is, without consideration of the political consequences of seemingly moral action. Realism, then, considers **prudence** – the weighing of the consequences of alternative political actions – to be the supreme virtue in politics. Ethics in the abstract judges action by its conformity with the moral law; political ethics judges action by its political consequences. (Morgenthau 1978, 10–11)

That is, a political statesman ought to first be guided by universal moral principles in the practice of politics, but where national survival is at stake, pure ethical conduct must give way to the higher moral duty to protect one's own nation. Where the nation's survival is at stake a prudent statesman is not absolved from his universal moral obligations, but must choose 'among several expedient actions the least evil one' (Morgenthau 1946, 203). This puts Morgenthau at odds with 'the Machiavellian logic of *raison d'état*, according to which promoting

> **Prudence** – the weighing of the consequences of alternative political actions.

the good of the state always justifies infringements on ordinary morality by the statesman' (Recchia 2007, 537). Thus, Morgenthau's Realism does have a substantial moral element, outside of the extreme cases where a state's survival is at risk.

Having answered the question of whether and in what circumstances states ought to follow universal moral imperatives, he then turns to the question of whether in fact they do put these into practice. Whilst states often cloak politically expedient behaviour in moral terms, he acknowledges that some moral principles are so well entrenched in international relations that statesmen and diplomats 'refuse to consider certain ends and to use certain means, either altogether or under certain conditions, not because in light of expediency they appear impractical or unwise but because certain moral rules interpose an absolute barrier' (Morgenthau 1978, 237). These include the assassination of rival political leaders in peacetime, mass exterminations of civilians as a means to achieve

> **Prudence and moral action** – Morgenthau argued that where a nation's survival is at stake a prudent statesman must choose the least evil action possible to defend it. He viewed the promotion of moral values in foreign policy as potentially irresponsible if it exposed the state to strategic vulnerability.

a political end, protections of civilians and combatants unwilling or unable to fight in wartime and the shared moral belief that modern war is an evil that should be avoided rather than used as a regular instrument of foreign policy.

Finally, consistent in Morgenthau's scholarship is a caution against the tendency of nation-states to embark on what he would describe as moral crusades in the practice of foreign policy, particularly military intervention into other states to uphold or defend moral values (Recchia 2007, 539). Here he was particularly wary of the tendency of liberal democratic states (specifically the United States) to promote those values abroad on the basis that they are

*fear of ideology and ethics;
a 'pragmatic' approach.*

71

universal, rather than nationalistic. By implication it can only be concluded that Morgenthau would argue that it is not possible for a political leader to objectively tell the difference between the two. In these circumstances, to prevent the 'blindness of crusading frenzy [which] destroys nations and civilizations – in the name of moral principle' Morgenthau appeals to the concept of interest defined in terms of power

> **Morgenthau's Ethic of Responsibility –** in a world where states define their national interests in terms of the pursuit of power, the primary moral responsibility of a political leader is to ensure the survival of their own state and citizens.

as a moderating influence on the tendency toward 'moral excess' (Morgenthau 1978, 11). That is, the concept of the national interest defined in terms of power – or what he might term an **ethic of responsibility** for the state – provides a prudent limit on military action in pursuit of moral values.

In his view, without an ethics of responsibility, political action based on moral values would have no limit. So, for example, Morgenthau viewed US intervention in Vietnam as imprudent, because the communist threat there was remote to the direct US national interests and unconnected to sponsorship by the Soviet Union. Where resources are scarce, **prudence** required that the United States concentrate only on direct threats to the nation's security, namely the spread of Communism in Europe rather than any moral defense of liberal values (Morgenthau 1967). Morality therefore imposes a negative constraint on political action – ruling out particular means to achieve national interests, or ruling out some national objectives altogether – but does not impose positive duties on human beings in general, outside the nation-state to which we belong.

Waltz   → *Emphasis on the agency of STATE over People*

A discussion of Realism and morality would be incomplete without also mentioning neoRealism or structural Realism. Our discussion can be brief, however, because structural Realism views the influence of norms – ethical norms being a subset of wider social norms – as derivative of the underlying distribution of power within the international system. Structural realists put aside arguments based on human nature in an attempt to introduce a more scientific approach to international relations using a positivist methodology, which they believe is descriptive or empirical, rather than normative. Assumptions about inherent characteristics of human beings are unprovable and potentially variable and therefore provide shaky foundations for building a scientific and objective theory of international politics. Structural realists focus not on the attributes of the units in the international system (states) – such as ideology, political leadership and cultural, social and political institutions – but on the principle that orders the arrangement of units. In the international system this is anarchy.

Kenneth Waltz's structural Realism argues that in an anarchic or decentralized system structure, the primary units of the system, states, are forced to acquire material power in order to ensure survival, as the minimum national interest. Moral or ethical preferences must always give way to this instinct of survival. Whilst rules and norms do have a role in international relations, they are at best derivative of the distribution of power between states in the international system and have little independent effect. That is, international law and institutions reflect the interests of the most powerful states at any particular time. Moral, ethical or normative values do not ultimately drive interstate politics because a rational state must place considerations of power and survival ahead of all other preferences in an anarchic system. States are ultimately like units, in that they must perform the same essential function of ensuring survival. Promises – legal or ethical – will be disregarded in circumstances where compliance may leave a state in a disadvantageous relative power position to other states.

> **Waltz and norms** – structural realists believe that norms – legal, moral or ethical – are at best secondary drivers of state behaviour. The absence of a central authority in the international system causes states to pursue power above all other values.

For Waltz, this is a description of international politics in anarchy, rather than a prescription for how things ought to be. States may not conform to this model by choosing other preferences than survival and security – moral or ethical considerations for example – however, the imperatives of anarchy will 'reward or punish behavior that conforms more or less nearly to what is required of one who wishes to succeed in the system' (Waltz 1979, 92 and Chapter 5). Like Adam Smith's abstraction of the market, states behaving rationally in their self-interest will conform to this model, and those that do not will expose themselves to vulnerability.

LIBERALISM

Whilst realist theories of international relations purport to describe the world of politics as it is, Liberal theories of international relations are self-consciously prescriptive, meaning that they place morality at the centre of inquiry and seek to put forward a set of ideas to create a world that it is consistent with these moral imperatives. The starting point of theorization for Liberals is the individual human being with theory built upon what is morally required to allow human beings to achieve their intrinsic potential. Human beings are posited as free, equal and morally autonomous and as are subject to universal morality. According to Immanuel Kant, the central moral duty or **categorical imperative** (Paton 1991, 67) is a duty to respect the freedom of others by treating them as ends in themselves rather than as means to an ends (Boucher 1998, 272). All human beings everywhere are said to share a '**harmony of interests**', the two most fundamental being interests in self-preservation and material wellbeing (Owen 1994, 94). Liberal

> **Categorical Imperative** – a duty to respect the freedom of others by treating them as ends in themselves rather than as means to an ends.
>
> **Harmony of Interests** – liberals believe all human beings share two fundamental interests, self-preservation and material wellbeing.

theorists then develop a theory of human rights and propose political institutional frameworks applicable within the state and between states that protect human freedom and equality and enable individuals to freely pursue their preferences. The establishment of liberal institutions and values domestically and internationally is thus morally required as the only means by which individuals are able to express their true nature.

Within the state a moral political order must uphold core human rights of citizens. This includes a set of rights designed to defend the freedom of the individual from the arbitrary use of power by the state, as well as to ensure that the government reflects the will of the people. This includes the right to freedom of speech, religion, association, of the press, to participate in elections and to hold, acquire and dispose of property without the threat of arbitrary governmental seizure. Positive rights such as economic and social rights to education and healthcare must also be guaranteed by the state to ensure that individuals are in fact able to freely pursue their interests. Economic freedom is guaranteed by the right to private property, minimal state interference and a market economy based on supply and demand (Doyle 1997, 207). Institutionally, the accountability of the government to the will of the people is protected by periodic democratic elections, the rule of law and a separation of powers between the legislature, executive and judiciary. This institutional mix underpins the moral basis of the state, that is, to promote and protect the fundamental interests of human beings.

How then do Liberals conceive of relations between states? If peace and order can be constructed within states in such a way as to protect the rights and interests of individual human beings, ethically we must attempt to create the conditions for peace between states. As we have seen above, realists are skeptical about whether this is possible on the basis that the anarchic structure of the international system cannot be transcended. The only escape is through the establishment of an international leviathan, a world state, which is far from likely. As such, international relations are marked by deep insecurity among states about others' intentions leading to conflict, war and security dilemmas, with periods of relative stability dependent upon the formation of a balance of power. Liberal states, like any other states, are forced to compete on these terms, leaving little room for ethical conduct where such conduct would leave the state vulnerable to predation.

Liberals have a different view of what life in an anarchic system entails. International relations are not marked by a war of all against all as a consequence of human nature, and/or anarchic structural conditions. Rather, Liberals argue that the character of individual states must impact upon how they behave and respond to others in their international relations. The international state of nature is characterized as a mix of peaceful and sometimes warlike interactions, with the possibility that peace can in fact become the norm under certain conditions. Importantly for liberals, peace will become the norm if liberal prescriptions are followed within all states and, therefore, they ought to be followed to deliver the most moral outcomes for individual human beings (Doyle 1997, 210).

Immanuel Kant first proposed the liberal prescription for peace between nations in his work *Perpetual Peace* written in 1795. Kant predicts peace between liberal states based on an acceptance of three 'definitive articles of peace' establishing a formal 'pacific federation' among them, which will eventually spread to encompass all states and create perpetual peace in the international system as a whole. The first article requires that the prospective members of the federation have a Republican constitution

Perpetual Peace – Immanuel Kant postulated the formation of perpetual peace between liberal democratic states through an agreement to form a pacific federation outlawing war among them.

supported by liberal institutions such as the separation of powers and legal equality for all, to protect individual freedom and equality. Only states with a republican constitution can attain a perpetual peace because citizens would be unlikely to consent to their governments leading them into war because the costs of war are personally felt:

> For this would mean calling down on themselves all the miseries of war, such as doing the
> fighting themselves, supplying the costs of war from their own resources, painfully making good

the ensuing devastation, and, as the crowning evil, having to take upon themselves a burden of debt which will embitter peace itself and which can never be paid off on account of the constant threat of new wars. (Kant 2002, 437)

In contrast, for a monarch it is 'the simplest thing in the world to go to war' which will 'not force him to make the lightest sacrifice' (Kant 2002, 437). The second article specifies the conditions for a pacific union to be formed among republican states, based on a federation rather than a world state, with the rights of individual states maintained, and which legally outlaws war among them. Whilst there are likely to be many backward steps, Kant's faith in human reason and progress underpinned his view that the creation of such a federation was indeed possible and would inevitably spread to 'encompass all states … leading to perpetual peace':

For if by good fortune one powerful and enlightened nation can form a republic (which is by its nature inclined to seek perpetual peace), this will provide a focal point for federal association among other states. These will join up with the first one, thus securing the freedom of each state in accordance with the idea of international right, and the whole will gradually spread further and further by a series of alliances of this kind. (Kant 2002, 440)

Because it is only under conditions of peace that the rights of man can be truly expressed, the spread of republican government then becomes a moral duty. Modern day **democratic peace theorists** such as Michael Doyle point to the empirical observation of an absence of war among 'constitutionally secure' liberal democratic states between 1816 and 1980 (Doyle 1997,10) as vindication

> **Democratic Peace Theory**: attempts to explain the empirical observation of an absence of war between liberal democratic states between 1816 and 1980.

of Kant's perpetual peace thesis. In addition to the Kantian explanation for peace between liberal states, democratic peace theorists also point to the pacifying effects of Capitalism and free trade based on the law of comparative advantage. Free access to markets, capital and goods is argued to create mutual dependencies among trading economies at all levels that would be directly threatened by war. Schumpeter also argued that free trade eliminated the incentives for imperialist expansion because 'foreign raw materials and food stuffs are as accessible to each nation as though they were in its own territory' (Schumpeter 1955, 75–6; Doyle 1986, 1153). Democratic peace theorists also argue that increased people-to-people contacts as a result of trade stimulates deeper understanding of interests and values between cultures and encourages mutual empathy. Finally, the institutionalization of the peaceful settlement of disputes within liberal states is said to spill over into relations between liberal states, delegitimizing the use of violence to settle disputes between them.

Other liberals use a **domestic analogy** to argue that the same institutional formula for creating peace and protecting human values and interests can be utilized to pacify relations between all states. In the interwar years the **liberal institutionalist** experiment included the establishment of the first collective security institution, the League of Nations, based on the principle that a threat to the

> **Liberal Institutionalists** use a **domestic analogy** to argue that interstate peace and human rights can be promoted through the establishment of liberal institutions and practices in the international realm. This underpins their support for international law, the creation of international courts and collective security institutions.

K-B Pact: A treaty signed in 1928 by western powers "renouncing war as an instrument of national policy."

security of one state threatened the security of all. It was hoped that collective security would reduce incentives for states to build up their own armaments for defence and to relinquish their faith in maintaining a balance of power as a guarantor of peace. In the interwar period there was a greater push for the codification of international law, the first attempts to ban the use of force under the Kellogg-Briand Pact, and to establish peaceful dispute settlement mechanisms via the League of Nations Council as well as the establishment of a Permanent Court of International Justice.

Despite the fact that this institutional remedy did not prevent the outbreak of a second world war, since then states have placed even greater emphasis on the establishment of international law and institutions as a means of resolving disputes peacefully as well as enabling deeper cooperation on a range of issues. Modern liberal institutionalists – **neoliberal institutionalists** – argue that institutions can play a functional role for states by encouraging them to cooperate in areas of common interest by providing in-built mechanisms to clarify the scope of agreements, monitoring and verifying compliance, publicizing cheaters, providing dispute settlement mechanisms and enforcing agreements which ameliorate the distrust caused by anarchy. Whilst the results may be imperfect, these mechanisms are found in institutions such as the United Nations, the World Trade Organization

> **Neoliberal Institutionalists** argue that institutions help states to cooperate by performing important functions that allow them to build trust that promises will be kept.

and the Nuclear Non-Proliferation Treaty, whilst the enforcement of international law has been enhanced by the creation of *ad hoc* Tribunals in Rwanda, Yugoslavia and now the International Criminal Court.

Liberal ideas about moral or ethical foreign policy have also found expression in the promotion of human rights around the world. From a liberal perspective without a guarantee of respect for social and political rights by the state, the ability of individuals to express their core moral natures as free and equal beings would be under threat. In the words of Jack Donnelly, '[a] list of human rights can be seen as a political specification of what it means to treat all human beings as ends' in line with Kant's principle categorical imperative (1993, 23). Given that human rights are universal, the question then arises as to whether liberal states have a duty to export their values and institutions to other states. Do they have a duty to protect citizens of other states whose governments fail to respect their human rights? Would this duty extend to a duty to use political and military resources to overthrow governments of other states that grossly abuse their citizens – who treat citizens within the state as means rather than ends?

Such questions come against the entrenched political principle of sovereignty, which itself has a moral dimension. The traditional meaning of sovereignty acknowledged by the European society of states adhered strictly to the view that it represented a reciprocal obligation of non-interference in the internal affairs of other states. This effectively guaranteed a level of Pluralism in international society, acknowledging a toleration of cultural, religious and political differences that would in turn support a core interest of all states – maintaining system stability by reducing potential causes of political and military conflicts. From this perspective, international efforts to uphold the human rights of individuals everywhere would involve impermissible intervention into the internal affairs of states, and potentially become the cause of war. Thus protection of human rights pits a statist worldview – backed by realists – against a cosmopolitan worldview where individual human beings are the core moral and political units.

Even among Liberals, there is continuing division about whether human rights should be protected or exported forcefully. Under the leadership of Presidents George H.W. Bush and Bill Clinton, the United States practiced a form of **defensive Liberalism**, which accepted the democratic peace thesis, that is, the 'use of "soft power" in a multilateral manner for promoting democracy, free-market economies, [free trade] and international institutions' (Miller 2010, 33, 41). Where force was used it was used to pursue limited goals to end mass violations of human rights and conducted mostly through multilateral

> **Defensive Liberalism** – the use of liberal 'soft power' in a multilateral manner for the promotion of democracy, free-market economics and international institutions. The use of force is acceptable, multilaterally, in extreme cases to prevent mass human rights violations.
>
> **Offensive Liberalism** – advocates the use of force, unilaterally where necessary, to create a liberal zone of peace in the world.

institutions (with the exception of the Kosovo intervention) in accordance with the liberal institutionalist principle that 'security should be achieved interdependently (multilaterally) rather than unilaterally' (Miller 2010, 34). This more cautious approach to creating a liberal zone of peace has been ascribed to the ideas of Immanuel Kant. Whilst Kant was optimistic about human beings' ability to use reason to ensure progress, he believed that the creation of the conditions for perpetual peace would occur very gradually. He opposed military intervention to spread democracy, arguing that a commitment to liberal values is difficult to impose from the outside. Rather it must evolve indigenously because 'reason does not itself work instinctively, for it requires trial, practice, and instruction' (Kant 1991, 42). The removal of illiberal regimes by force could lead to worse outcomes for the population if intervention created anarchy (Walker 2008, 462).

On the other side of the spectrum fall **offensive liberals** who advocate the use of force, unilaterally where necessary, to create a liberal zone of peace. This approach is exemplified in US foreign policy after 9/11 under the Bush administration in the war on Iraq in 2003. Here, advocates argued that regime change in Iraq would create a domino effect in the Middle East by demonstrating 'that democracy is preferable to tyranny … [which would] inspire and encourage other peoples in the region to topple their own dictators and establish democratic regimes'. Thus a zone of peace would be created in the region, 'drain[ing] the swamp' from which international terrorists were able to hide and multiply (Walker 2008, 49, 56). Offensive Liberalism is inspired by the revolutionary Liberalism espoused by Thomas Paine in the 1790s who approved the use of force to spread democracy, based on the view that man's essential harmony of interests were obstructed by illegitimate governments. Paine was optimistic that once these regimes were removed, liberal forces within a country would be able to tap into these natural interests of women and men and establish liberal democracy rapidly. Debate continues between these two strands of Liberalism, however the outcome of the Iraq War has injected a more cautious approach about the spread of liberal democratic values by force.

ETHICS AND THE USE OF FORCE: THE CASE OF THE IRAQ WAR

One of the most difficult ethical questions in international relations is the question of the ethics of going to war, known as *jus ad bellum* in the Just War tradition. Under what circumstances might the decision to go to war by a state's leaders be morally justified? **Just War theory** begins with the premise that killing and injuring people is immoral and should be avoided. However, war and the destruction of life and property may not always be able to be avoided. There may be competing duties that require the general presumption against war be displaced. Just War theory represents an attempt to decipher general principles of ethical action that ought to guide political leaders as to when killing in the name of the state may be justified. Thinking on Just War has moved away from its natural law and religious origins toward a secular approach based on positivist international law i.e. a focus on what states actually recognize as restraints on war in their practices and as expressed through consent.

> **Just War Theory** – puts forward general ethical principles to guide political leaders in making decisions about when killing in the name of the state may be justified.

There are six ethical criteria used to judge the decision to go to war in a particular case drawn from the Just War tradition. A Just War must be fought: for a just cause; under the sanction of a rightful or legitimate authority; for the right intentions; as a last resort; and where there is a reasonable chance of success. It must also demonstrate that 'the moral cost of a war must not be out of proportion (or disproportionate or excessive) in relation to the moral cost the war would avoid' (Lee 2012, 85 and chapter 3). In the current international order international law has circumscribed significantly what are considered permissible or just causes for the resort to war, primarily as a result of the sheer destruction of modern weaponry and technology demonstrated in World War I and II. Under the UN Charter the threat or use of force is prohibited under Article 2(4), with two exceptions: the use of force in individual or collective self-defence (Article 51), and in circumstances where the Security Council deems that a threat to international peace and security exists – effectively a threat to order and stability – in accordance with the powers granted to it in Chapter VII. A legitimate authority in this context therefore may be an individual state when acting in self-defence, or a group of states assisting another that is the victim of aggression in particular circumstances or the UN Security Council using its powers under Chapter VII of the UN Charter.

The criteria of rightful intention is linked to that of just cause, that is, the purpose pursued in going to war must be to correct the wrong, giving rise to the just cause for war. That is, the claim to act under a just cause must be the primary motive for war, rather than for revenge or territorial conquest. The criterion of last resort speaks for itself, namely that because the results of war are so destructive, all effective and timely peaceful means of resolving the dispute in question should be exhausted before considering the use of force. The use of force must also have a reasonable chance of success, 'unless the war is for the very survival of the members of the state or group making the fight' (Lee 2012, 97). Finally, the proportionality principle sets limits on what can morally be done to right the wrong that supports the claim of a just cause for war: that 'greater evils do not arise out of the war than the war would avert' (Vitoria 1990, 315; Lee 2012, 85). These Just War criteria provide a useful background for the discussion of one of the most controversial episodes relating to the use of military force by states in recent times – the US war on Iraq in 2003 and the doctrine of pre-emptive self-defence.

The Iraq War 2003

After Iraq's invasion of Kuwait was reversed by a UN endorsed military action in 1991, under the terms of the cease-fire agreement (UNSCR 687 of 3 April 1991) Iraq was placed under a weapons inspection regime designed to disarm it of all ballistic missiles with a range over 150 km, chemical, biological and nuclear stockpiles and the means to produce them. By 1997 the Hussein regime had begun to systematically block access of UN Special Commission and IAEA inspectors to suspected weapons sites and by December 2002, with Russia, China and France refusing to take military action against Iraq, all inspectors were forced to withdraw from the country. By late 2002, Iraq had gone without international monitoring of its possible WMD capabilities for four years and momentum had further shifted within the UNSC towards an easing of the sanctions regime. Iraq would have likely broken free of the international sanctions and inspection regime if not for US pressure. This resulted in UNSC Resolution 1441 (7 November 2002) under which a weapons inspections regime was reinstated with 'serious consequences' being threatened if Iraq failed to adequately declare its stockpiles and cooperate 'immediately, unconditionally and actively' with the inspectors from UNMOVIC and the IAEA.

In the ensuing months UNMOVIC reported that it was highly critical of Iraq's substantive compliance with Resolution 1441 (UNMOVIC 2003; Rajendram Lee 2010, 89), with the US, UK and Spain advocating that Iraq should now face the 'serious consequences' alluded to in Resolution 1441, namely the use of force to effect regime change. The UNSC did not endorse this position, and in March 2003 the United States and a 'coalition of the willing' waged war on Iraq unilaterally. In terms of the Just War criteria, was the use of force by the US and its allies ethical? Arguments can be made against this view based primarily on the absence of a just cause, the sanction of a legitimate authority and the failure to exhaust all peaceful remedies.

The first question to ask is whether the US had a just cause. In September 2002, the US Bush administration released its first *National Security Strategy* (NSS), a year after the September 11 terrorist attacks. In it the administration stated that the possibility of an alliance between 'rogue states' and transnational terrorist groups posed a core threat to US national security. Particularly, the US argued that rogue states – including Iraq – had shown themselves to be inherently aggressive, disregarded the norms of international order and would doggedly pursue WMD. If successful in acquiring WMD capabilities, the US argued that rogue states had an incentive to share this technology with international terrorist groups, who would have no hesitation in using these weapons against the United States and others. Importantly the administration argued that neither rogue states nor terrorist groups could be deterred from either acquiring or using WMD, and in these circumstances it was imperative to prevent them from successfully acquiring WMD, if necessary through the use of force.

This line of reasoning required a shift in international law on self-defence. In these circumstances, states could no longer afford to wait 'until an armed attack occurs' as per the terms of Article 51 of the UN Charter. There is some support among states for the view that customary international law does allow the use of force in self-defence where there is clear evidence that an attack is 'imminent'. However, the US contended that where a state was likely to face a terrorist attack using WMD, 'weapons that can be easily concealed, delivered covertly, and used without warning', it would be impossible to determine whether an attack was imminent. Given the catastrophic consequences of a successful attack using WMD, in these circumstances states 'would have no choice but to act where an attack is not necessarily imminent, but highly likely to occur in the near future' (Rajendram Lee 2010, 81). This reasoning provided the justification for the use of force under a new doctrine of pre-emptive self-defence or preventive war.

The Bush administration's justification for war did not provide a just cause for war in the view of a strong majority of states. As mentioned above, the international community has over time worked to reduce the permissible just causes for war to eliminate as far as possible the use of force as an ordinary political tool. The scope of the new doctrine of pre-emptive self-defence, allowing for the use of force not only where an attack is clearly imminent but also where merely forseeable according to a state's own subjective assessment, dangerously blurred the boundary between self-defence and aggression. In this case, the US had not yet suffered any wrong which would ground a case for just cause. If the case for self-defence could not be supported, then the only legitimate authority that could sanction the use of force was the UN Security Council under Chapter VII of the Charter. In this instance, whilst Iraq's failure to disarm was viewed as a threat to international order, the US failed to obtain agreement for a second resolution specifically giving the green light to military force. Rather, the majority of the Council favoured an approach which gave Iraq further time to demonstrate cooperation with the inspections teams. In other words, whilst all options for the peaceful settlement of the dispute had not yet been resolved, the US could not argue that war was a last resort.

The rationale for the Iraq War also did not accord with the ethics of both realist and Liberal approaches to the use of force in international relations. Prominent realists such as Stephen Walt and John Mearsheimer branded the war as 'unnecessary' without a 'compelling strategic rationale' (Mearsheimer and Walt 2003). In direct contradiction to the administration's case for war, both argued that the Hussein regime was in fact highly deterrable – even if it acquired WMD – and could be contained. Whilst Hussein had waged aggressive wars against his neighbours Iran and Kuwait, in both cases the decision to go to war was made on the basis of a rational calculation of strategic advantage and threat: 'Both times he [Hussein] attacked because Iraq was vulnerable and because he believed his targets were weak and isolated'. The regime had also been deterred from using WMD against the US and Israel during and after the first Gulf War as a result of credible threats of retaliation, and had only used chemical weapons against Iran and Iraq's own Kurdish population because they could 'not respond in kind'.

If Saddam were to acquire WMD, Walt and Mearsheimer argued that any threat Iraq posed could be contained through a deterrence strategy, whilst they found it highly unlikely that the regime would transfer nuclear weapons to terrorist groups like al-Qaeda because the regime would not be able to control against whom and how those weapons would be used. Given the risk that such a transfer would be suspected or traced back to the regime, in the event of the use of WMD against the US targets, Hussein would fear overwhelming retaliation, potentially using tactical nuclear weaponry.

In Walt and Mearsheimer's view therefore, war was not in America's national interest because the US was not under any direct existential threat. The choice of war was simply not based on a rational calculation of national interest. Rather, the US was again falling into the trap of placing universal moral considerations ahead of the national interest, and rather should have placed the highest moral value on the survival of the state and its people. On this point, realists like Schmidt and Williams (2008) warned against the pursuit of a moralistic foreign policy crusade aimed at the spread of democracy in similar terms to those used by Hans Morgenthau in his opposition to the US war on Vietnam in 1965 (Morgenthau 1965). Alternative strategies, short of regime change by force in a country with no history of democracy and deep nationalistic divisions, were available. These strategies would use scarce resources more effectively and efficiently whilst war could lead to an increase in terrorist threats to US national security (Walt 2012).

Liberal perspectives on the ethics of the Iraq War were broadly split among three camps. The Bush administration exemplified an offensive liberal approach, that is, a wholehearted belief in the democratic peace thesis, the spread of democracy by force and an optimistic view about the ease by which societies can be transformed. Importantly, for this group the potential alliance between rogue states and international terrorists posed a direct threat not only to US national security, but also to the whole liberal project of extending the zone of peace internationally by advocating a fundamentalist ideology directly at odds with human rights and liberal governance. Among the dissenting liberal voices were those liberal institutionalists who warned against the effects of unilateral military action because it directly undermined the UN as a collective security institution. US unilateralism, backed up by a legal doctrine justifying preventive war, took away any faith states may have had in establishing peace through voluntary institutional and legal restraint, compromise, collective action and trust and encouraged states to place reliance on self-help. The creation of the conditions for peace in international relations should itself be considered a moral duty, given that without peace the respect for human rights within states could not be realized. In light of the consequences for the credibility of the UN, and the voluntary restraint of power embodied in the Charter, these liberals viewed the use of force as premature and that a collective solution could still have been brokered. Finally, there were those liberals in the Kantian vein that were skeptical about the possibility of exporting democracy through force to a country with no real history of liberal democracy and strong ethnic divisions. In this respect both liberals and realists have much in common and the proven difficulties of establishing resilient liberal democracy in Iraq are seen to have vindicated their positions.

CONCLUSION

In this chapter we have differentiated between the terms morality and ethics, identified categories of ethical action drawn from moral philosophy and focused upon realist, Liberal and Just War theory approaches to questions about the values and principles that ought to govern relations between states, and the possible duties owed to individuals beyond state boundaries. We have found that realist approaches are far from purely descriptive of the reality of international politics, but in fact contain normative assumptions about how national interests ought to be defined and which privilege conceptions of 'necessity' and prudence as having primacy over moral considerations. We have also seen that the universal morality espoused by Liberal approaches to international relations contains its own moral dilemmas, specifically contestation over how universal human rights actually are, and whether the promotion of liberal values by force endangers international stability and is ultimately counterproductive to the wellbeing of individual human beings in other states. As the Iraq War case demonstrates, grappling with ethical questions form an integral part of the practice of international relations. As such, the study of ethics should not be thought of as merely a sub-field within the discipline, but is in fact at the centre of it.

QUESTIONS FOR REFLECTION

1. What is the difference between the terms ethics and morality? What kinds of issues would an ethical code of international politics focus upon?
2. What are the differences between cosmopolitan, pluralist and utilitarian ethical approaches? Do liberal and realist approaches to international relations fit within any of these categories?
3. What is the role of *raison d'état* and 'necessity' in Machiavellian ethics of IR?
4. Does Morgenthau recognize the existence of universal morals? What role does 'prudence' play in his approach to ethics? Why does he view the pursuit of moral values in foreign policy as dangerous?
5. Is there a significant role for morality or ethics in neoRealism?
6. Who are the core moral subjects of liberal theories of international relations? How do liberal institutions protect the values of these subjects? Why are liberal-democratic states argued to be inherently pacific? What is meant by the 'domestic analogy' in liberal institutionalist thought? Do all liberals believe that liberal values can or should be promoted by force?
7. Was the decision to go to war in Iraq viewed as just under the Just War principles? Did realists or liberals approve of the use of force by the United States? What ethical principles influenced their evaluations?

REVISION QUIZ

1. What is the main difference between moral and ethical norms?

   a. There is no difference between the two terms. Both can be used interchangeably.
   b. Ethical norms specify conceptions of right and wrong applicable in a particular society. Moral norms also specify standards of right and wrong but do so in a very confined context of social relations for a particular group of actors.
   c. Moral norms specify conceptions of right and wrong applicable in a particular society. Ethical norms also specify standards of right and wrong but do so in a very confined context of social relations for a particular group of actors.
   d. Ethical norms apply to a narrower group of subjects and in narrower circumstances than moral norms do.
   e. Both (c) and (d) are correct.

2. What is Cosmopolitanism?

   a. Cosmopolitanism argues that we are citizens of states first and foremost and owe moral duties only to those within a state's boundaries.
   b. Cosmopolitanism argues that no one moral value system is superior to another.
   c. Cosmopolitanism argues that there is no such thing as universal morality. All value systems are culturally specific to a particular community.
   d. Cosmopolitanism argues that we are all world citizens and that moral duties owed to other human beings are universal.

3. What is Utilitarianism?

    a. Utilitarianism is a type of consequentialist ethics with the unit of value being particular identity groups.

    b. Utilitarianism is a type of consequentialist ethics that measures the moral value of a course of action according to whether it achieves the maximum wellbeing for a state.

    c. Utilitarianism is a type of consequentialist ethics that measures the moral value of a course of action according to whether it achieves the maximum wellbeing of humanity as a whole.

    d. Utilitarianism argues that it is universal principles rather than consequences that should guide moral action.

4. Which of the following statements is true in relation to Machiavellian ethics?

    a. Machiavelli acknowledged the tension between politics and morality but ultimately argued that moral leadership of the state was most likely to promote the survival of the state.

    b. Machiavelli subscribed to a cosmopolitan ethical code.

    c. Machiavelli subscribed to a utilitarian ethical code.

    d. Machiavelli believed that without strong leadership of the state capable of imposing order, ideas about justice and morality could not realized.

    e. Both A) and B).

5. Which of the following is most correct in relation to Hans Morgenthau's political ethics?

    a. Morgenthau believed that the promotion of the interests of the state always justified the disregard of ordinary moral standards.

    b. Morgenthau believed in an ethics of responsibility that privileged the national interest – defined in terms of power – over and above the pursuit of moral values.

    c. Morgenthau believed that in an anarchic environment states merely masked their pursuit of material interest with moral rhetoric. State's leaders are unaffected by moral or ethical beliefs in deciding on national goals and the means to achieve them.

    d. The political ethics of Morgenthau and Machiavelli are essentially identical.

6. What is Kant's central categorical imperative?

    a. human beings are free, morally autonomous and equal in possessing an inherent worth and dignity. They should never be treated as means to an ends.

    b. human beings are free, morally autonomous, and equal in possessing an inherent worth and dignity. They should be treated as means to an ends.

    c. Human beings are free, morally autonomous and equal and share a 'harmony of interests', especially interests in material wellbeing and self-preservation.

    d. Both b) and c).

7. Which of the following are used as arguments to explain the democratic peace thesis?

   a. liberal democratic institutions ensure the accountability of government to the will of the people. Ordinary people suffer most from conflict and are less likely to give their consent to war.
   b. Capitalism and free trade create mutual dependencies between states and increased people-to-people contacts. Ordinary people would have the most to lose from conflict and are less likely to give their consent to war.
   c. International institutions can play a functional role for states by providing mechanisms that build trust between states.
   d. Both a) and c).
   e. Both a) and b).

8. Which of the following is correct?

   a. Kant believed that liberal states should forcibly spread liberal values and institutions to other countries and that foreign populations would accept such values and institutions readily.
   b. Kant believed that liberal states should not forcibly spread liberal values and institutions to other countries because the commitment to liberal values was difficult to impose from the outside and needed to occur indigenously.
   c. Thomas Paine believed that liberal states should forcibly spread liberal values and institutions to other countries and that foreign populations would accept such values and institutions readily.
   d. Thomas Paine believed that liberal states should not forcibly spread liberal values and institutions to other countries because the commitment to liberal values was difficult to impose from the outside and needed to occur indigenously.
   e. Both a) and d).
   f. Both b) and c).

9. Which of the following ethical criteria form part of the Just War Principles?

   a. Where the survival of the state is jeopardy, the ends justify the means.
   b. The use of force must be based on a just cause for war such as for the purposes of retribution.
   c. The use of force must be based on a just cause for war such as self-defence.
   d. The use of force must be based on a just cause for war such as territorial conquest.

10. Which of the following statements is true in relation to the 2003 Iraq War?

   a. Realists approved of the use of force in Iraq because it furthered the national security of the United States by removing a confirmed enemy of the state – Saddam Hussein – from power.
   b. Realists disapproved of the use of force in Iraq because they believed that the Hussein regime did not pose a direct existential threat to the United States and that a containment

strategy rather than regime change would have served the national interest whilst more effectively using scarce resources.

c. Realists approved of the use of force in Iraq because they believed that Saddam Hussein could not be deterred from acquiring WMD and therefore removing him from power was the best means of ensuring national security.

d. Realists disapproved of the use of force against Iraq because the Bush administration did not obtain the approval of the UN Security Council and this undermined the credibility of collective security.

Answers: 1: e; 2: d; 3: c; 4: d; 5: b; 6: a; 7: e; 8: f; 9: c; 10: b.

BIBLIOGRAPHY

Beardsworth, R. (2001) *Cosmopolitanism and International Relations Theory* (Cambridge: Polity Press).

Boucher, D. (1998) *Political Theories of International Relations* (Oxford: Oxford University Press).

Bull, H. (1995) *The Anarchical Society: A Study of Order in World Politics*, 2nd edition (London: Macmillan Press).

Donnelly, J. (1993) *International Human Rights* (Boulder, CO: Westview Press).

Doyle, M.W. (December 1986) 'Liberalism and World Politics', *American Political Science Review* 80(4), 1151–69.

Doyle, M.W. (1997) *The Ways of War and Peace* (New York: W.W. Norton & Company, Inc.).

Doyle, M. (Summer and Fall 1983) 'Kant, Liberal Legacies, and Foreign Affairs', *Philosophy and Public Affairs* 12(3 & 4), reprinted in M.E. Brown, S.M. Lynn-Jones and S.E. Miller (1997) *Debating the Democratic Peace* (Cambridge, MA: The MIT Press).

Ellis, A. (1992) 'Utilitarianism and international ethics'. In T. Nardin and D.R. Mapel (eds), *Traditions of International Ethics* (Cambridge: Cambridge University Press).

Graeme, G. (2008) *Ethics and International Relations*, 2nd edition (Malden, MA: Blackwell Publishing).

Kant, I. (1991) 'An Idea for a Universal History With a Cosmopolitan Purpose'. In H. Reiss (ed.), *Kant's Political Writings* (Cambridge: Cambridge University Press).

Kant, I. (2002) 'From Perpetual Peace: A Philosophical Sketch'. In C. Brown, T. Nardin and N. Rengger, *International Relations in Political Thought: Texts from the Ancient Greeks to the First World War* (Cambridge: Cambridge University Press).

Lee, S.P. (2012) *Ethics and War: An Introduction* (Cambridge: Cambridge University Press).

Machiavelli, N. (1990) *The Prince*, edited by Q. Skinner and R. Price (Cambridge: Cambridge University Press).

Mapel, D.R. and Nardin, T. (1992) 'Convergence and Divergence in International Ethics'. In T. Nardin and D.R. Mapel (eds), *Traditions of International Ethics* (Cambridge: Cambridge University Press).

Mearsheimer, J.J. and S. Walt (Jan/Feb 2003) 'An unnecessary war', *Foreign Policy*.

Miller, B. (2010) 'Explaining Changes in US Grand Strategy: 9/11, the Rise of Offensive Liberalism and the War in Iraq', *Security Studies* (19), 26–65.

Morgenthau, H.J. (April 1967) 'To Intervene or Not to Intervene', *Foreign Affairs* 45(3), 425–36.

Morgenthau, H.J. (1978) *Politics Among Nations: The Struggle for Power and Peace*, 5th edition (New York: Alfred A. Knopf).

Morgenthau, H.J. (1962) *Politics in the 20th Century, vol. 1: The Decline of Democratic Politics* (Chicago, IL: University of Chicago Press).

Morgenthau, H.J. (1946) *Scientific Man vs. Power Politics* (Chicago, IL: University of Chicago Press).

Morgenthau, H.J. (April 1965) 'We are Deluding ourselves in Vietnam', *The New York Times*, 18 April.

Owen, J.M. (Fall 1994) 'How Liberalism Produces Democratic Peace', *International Security* 19(2), 87–125.

Paton, H.J. (1991) 'Analysis of Argument'. In H.J. Paton (ed.), *The Moral Law: Kant's Groundwork of the Metaphysics of Morals* (London: Routledge).

Rajendram Lee, L. (21010) *US Hegemony and International Legitimacy: Norms, Power and Followership in the Wars on Iraq* (London and New York: Routledge).

Recchia, S. (2007) 'Restraining Imperial Hubris: The Ethical Bases of Realist International Relations Theory', *Constellations* 14(4), 531–56.

Schmidt, B.C. and Williams, M.C. (2008) 'The Bush Doctrine and the Iraq War: Neoconservatives versus Realists', *Security Studies* 17(2), 191–220.

Schumpeter, J. (1955) *Imperialism and Social Classes* (Cleveland, OH: World Publishing Co.).

UNMOVIC (2003) 'An update on Inspection – Executive Chairman of UNMOVIC, Dr Hans Blix', 27 January.

Vitoria, F. (1990) 'On the law of War'. In A. Pagden and J. Lawrence (eds), *Vitoria: Political Writings* (Cambridge, Cambridge University Press).

Walker, T.C. (2008) 'Two Faces of Liberalism: Kant, Paine, and the Question of Intervention', *International Studies Quarterly* (52), 449–68.

Walt, S.M. (2012) 'What if realists were in charge of US foreign policy?', *Foreign Policy Online*, 30 April.

Waltz, K. (1979) *Theory of International Politics* (Massachusetts: Addison-Wesley Publishing).

Walzer, M. (1977) *Just and Unjust Wars*, 2nd edition (New York: Basic Books).

Chapter 4

The Levels of Analysis of the International System

TAKU TAMAKI

What is the best way to study the international system? We can utilize the 'level of analysis' approach as a conceptual tool in trying to understand how state actors formulate foreign policies. We can observe what the individual policymaker is saying; we can try to decipher the domestic rivalries between and among the bureaucracies; or we can 'black box' the state and focus solely on the foreign policy outcome of the state as a unitary actor. But what about the international system itself, if it is comprised of various state actors, along with international institutions and non-state actors such as Multinational Corporations? Perhaps we can use levels of analysis to understand how each state in the international system formulates its own foreign policy and aggregate the result. However, this chapter suggests that there is a better way to try to understand the complexities inherent in the international system.

This chapter makes sense of the levels of analysis of the international system by trying to 'tell stories' about how we might begin to conceptualize them. We explore four stories that provide different perspectives on how the international system 'works'. The first story takes a holistic view of the international system and assumes that international actors are power maximizers who seek to balance power amongst themselves. At the same time, this story recognizes states as the only relevant actors in the international system, effectively 'black boxing' the state. The second story shares similarities with the first story, by taking a holistic approach, and focusing on the system level. However, it also suggests that actors are able to take a longer term view and engage in cooperative behaviour, creating international institutions – such as the UN – in the process. This story recognizes that the international system is comprised of not only states, but also non-state actors. The third story considers the international system to be a complex web of social relations in which perceptions, ideas and symbols matter – just as human society revolves around such intangible factors. For this story, not only the state, but bureaucracy and individual policymakers are relevant actors. Finally, the fourth story takes a radically different approach, using metaphor to suggest that our understanding of the international system – and the international life in general – are nothing but stories in and of themselves.

The aim of this chapter is not to identify the 'correct' story; but rather, to make ourselves aware of the various ways through which we can begin to make sense of the complex international system. The debates in IR theory often revolve around thinkers exchanging their own stories about how the international system 'works'. The four stories should make debates more accessible. The task for us – as students of International Relations – is to try to tell the most convincing story about the complexities of the international system.

Key Words: International System; Levels of Analysis; Actors; States *versus* Individuals; Stories.

Chapter 4

The Levels of Analysis of the International System

TAKU TAMAKI

INTRODUCTION

The international system is complex. It might be seen as a constellation of states interacting with one another. Or, it might be a macro-level social interaction involving actors at multiple levels: the individual decision-makers, the bureaucracy and the interest groups. Given that humans are involved – both individually and collectively – in international politics, analysis at various social levels needs to be considered, just as these factors are important in explaining social life in general.

So far, we have seen the historical evolution of global politics (Chapter 1), along with the various theories that seek to explain international politics (Chapter 2). Now we will analyse the complexities of the international system. One useful 'tool' for doing this is the **levels of analysis** approach, seeking to divide complex international politics into smaller, bite-sized, 'chunks'. The levels of analysis tell several 'stories' about the way the international system works. For instance, the approach allows us to appreciate the various interactions between and among the individuals and the larger political environment. It also equips us with a framework for analysing the interplay between domestic and international factors. In short, the levels of analysis provide stories about the way the world 'works'. This chapter starts out with the discussion of the stories told by the levels of analysis approach. Then we explore other stories people tell about the way the international system 'works'. The aim of this chapter is to show that there are many stories out there, and as students of International Relations (IR), we need to be mindful of the benefits and disadvantages of such stories.

> **Levels of Analysis** – ways of analysing how foreign policy decisions are made at various levels of the state – individual policymaker; the bureaucracy; or the state as a collective.

THE LEVELS OF ANALYSIS: STORIES WE TELL

One useful, conceptual, tool in analysing international politics is the levels of analysis approach. As the name suggests, we divide the complex reality of international politics into smaller chunks – or 'levels' – so that studying it becomes easier, enabling us to determine *what* decisions are made by *whom*, and under *what* constraints. As such, the issue is partly methodological: *how* we might go about exploring international affairs. Frederick Frey (1985, 127) makes an important point when he says that,

> *Politics and political science [including IR] are indubitably about people, but in rather special sense, not in the most common intuitive sense. Political science usually does not deal with people in either their individuality or their totality.*

Hence, it is the notion of **actor designation** that lies at the heart of the levels of analysis approach: designating 'actors' – whether be it individuals, the bureaucracy or the state – at various overlapping levels that effect an outcome on the international stage. As Frey (1985, 147) notes, this actor designation, 'though largely taken for granted, is a crucial feature of political analysis'. This is also the case in IR: *who* our actors will determine *what* we can discuss, and *how*.

> **Actor Designation** – deciding who/what the main focus of analysis is going to be.

One approach is to follow the **Three Images** identified by Kenneth Waltz. He suggests that there are three levels of analysis that can be utilized in the study of how wars occur. In the First Image, the assumption is that the egotistical human nature causes wars. This level of analysis suggests that we do not need to go further than the personal attributes of policymakers to appreciate the causes of wars.

Waltz's Three Images:

- First Image: human behaviour (Waltz, 1959, Chapter 2);
- Second Image: the internal structure of states (Waltz, 1959, Chapter 4); and
- Third Image: international anarchy; or the constraints of the international system (Waltz, 1959, Chapter 6).

Waltz (1959, 16) argues that,

> *According to the first image of international relations, the locus of the important causes of war is found in the nature and behaviour of man. Wars result from selfishness, from misdirected impulses, from stupidity.*

Therefore, the First Image provides us with one level of analysis: in order to appreciate international events, we need to look at individuals.

The Second Image, on the other hand, focuses on the internal constitution of the state, such as its ideological underpinnings. Arguments such as whether or not democracies are more peaceful than autocratic states determine the way we explain international events. Waltz (1959, 81) points out that,

> *One explanation of the second-image type is illustrated as follows. War most often promotes the internal unity of each state involved. The state plagued by internal strife may then, instead of waiting for accidental attack, seek the war that will bring internal peace.*

Thus, we see a shift from an individual level to a more collective level. Yet, as we move onto the Third Image, we go 'up' another level: the anarchic nature of the international system. Waltz (1959, 159) argues that,

> With many sovereign states, with no system of law enforceable among them, with each state judging its grievances and ambition according to the dictates of its own reason or desire – conflict, sometimes leading to war, is bound to occur.

At this level, the main concern is less to do with *who* the actors are, as it is to do with *how* the international system is structured. Waltz himself is sympathetic towards the Third Image, and the story he tells about the way the international system 'works' will be discussed later.

In a similar vein to Waltz, Robert Jervis (1976, 16–17) argues that perceptions and misperceptions that drive international political dynamics need to be studied with the above levels in mind. He posits that, in order for us to explain how international actors make decisions, we need to be mindful of the interplay of international, national, and bureaucratic levels; and deciding on which level 'is the most important may be determined by how rich and detailed an answer we are seeking'. Similarly, in order for us to fully understand the factors involved in foreign policy decision-making, Graham Allison (1971) argues that we need to move back and forth between and among the various levels: the state as a whole; bureaucracies and their constraints; as well as politics between and among the individuals within government.

Levels of Analysis in US Foreign Policy towards the Middle East

- When exploring the US policies towards the Middle East, there are various levels from which we can explore the topic, including:
- The personal 'chemistry' between the US president and the prime minister of Israel;
- The effects of Jewish lobby on US politics;
- The politics of United Nations (UN) – particularly the UN Security Council – in determining whether or not to sanction Syria; and
- Perceptions and misperceptions in US-Iranian diplomatic relations (*The Economist*, 15 December 2012, 48–9).

While discussing US policies towards the entire Middle East would lack focus, dividing them up into pieces allows us to make a better sense of what is happening.

Hence, paying attention to multiple levels is beneficial, as it makes it easier for us to understand the complexities of the international system. However, there are several issues with the levels of analysis approach. Are individuals really bad, as in the First Image? How then can we explain international cooperation (Waltz 1959, 28)? And are states sharing an ideology apt to be peaceful to one another, just as the Second Image might predict (Waltz 1959, 121)? Also, is it really the case that democracies do not fight one another? Bruce Russett (2009) argues that the findings are inconclusive, suggesting that we need to pay close attention to other systemic factors – just as in the Third Image.

Telling Stories about the International System

The Three Images, as well as other iterations of the levels of analysis, provide us with a useful tool for analysing international *politics*, but how about the international *system* itself? We need to bear in mind that the international system itself is usually one of the three levels of analysis. Each level of analysis can be construed as stories people tell about decision-making, instances of war and other aspects of international politics in general. Indeed, this is what many IR theorists do (see Chapter 2). Just as in the levels of analysis approach, we can start telling stories about the international system, taking into consideration different actors, focal points and concerns. Therefore, we can also tell stories about the international system: some stories are more amenable towards the levels of analysis approach, while other stories are less so. But just as the levels of analysis provide us with a variety of explanations about international affairs, the following stories also provide us with multiple explanations of the international system.

STORY ONE: THE *HOMO ECONOMICUS* VIEW OF THE INTERNATIONAL SYSTEM

The First Story is that of the *Homo Economicus* view of the international system. By *Homo Economicus*, we mean a rational actor whose sole interest lies in the maximization of his/her wellbeing. This is the view that is most prevalent in Economics and Business Studies, but traditional IR theories, such as Neorealism and Neoliberal-Institutionalism, also follow this approach. Similar to economic presumptions about the actors and what they do, this particular story makes the following assumptions:

> **Homo Economicus** – A philosophical depiction of humans as benefit-maximizers. In Economics, it means that humans and corporations seek to maximize profit; while in IR, it indicates that states are in constant struggle to maximize power.

- Actors are *rational*, meaning they are capable of making informed decisions when faced with choices; and
- Actors are *unitary*, meaning that the proponents of this story are concerned less with what happens inside a state than what happens when a state collectively formulates a policy. In other words, what goes on inside the state is often left out of the story.

So, when economists discuss the behaviour of corporations, they are primarily concerned with how companies make decisions as though they are individuals. Similarly, some IR theorists consider main actors to be states coping in an anarchical international system, with Waltz being one of the main proponents of this story. In his seminal book, *Theory of International Politics*, he draws lessons from Economics to make the point that international politics needs to be studied in the way economists analyse the economy. For him, domestic factors might be important; but systemic factors play an even more crucial role, such that the focus should be firmly on the behaviour of states as unitary, rational actors, rather than what goes on inside them (Waltz 1979, 62–3).

Therefore, this story makes several working assumptions about how the international system 'works':

- Actors in this story refer solely to states. While neorealists recognize other potential actors on the international stage, given that it is the states who enjoy legitimate monopoly of violence, non-state actors such as Multinational Corporations (MNCs) become less significant.
- As mentioned above, states are considered as unitary actors, meaning they are to be treated as 'things'. Again, while neorealists recognize the role of groups, such as bureaucracies and interest groups, as well as those of charismatic individuals, such as John Kennedy during the Cuban Missile Crisis in October 1962, these factors are considered less significant.
- This story also takes for granted that the international system is anarchic, meaning there is no world government or world police. While 'anarchy' sounds as if the international system is chaotic, it does not have to be so.

Thus, this story provides a very simplified view of the international system. As Waltz (1979: 9) argues, the main task is to construct a model of reality, not the reality. For neorealists, this simplicity is the primary strength of this story.

In order for states to guarantee their own survival, the neorealists think that states are constantly seeking to maximize their power. *Power* in this case is defined as the ability to influence others. This includes physical ability to influence your opponent's thinking, such as possessing nuclear weapons; or it could be psychological power – the ability to change others' thinking without any physical or financial outlay on your part (Morgenthau 1985, Chapter 1). The result is a constant competition for survival. Accordingly, cooperation between and among actors might happen; but the fear of someone reneging on promises is too great, to the extent that there is a constant fear of war. And if everyone in the international system thinks this, the logical conclusion is that wars can happen at any moment. John Mearsheimer (1995) warns us that just because the European Union (EU) provides a forum for member states to negotiate their national interests, the EU is not a world government, nor is it an international police force. As such, Mearsheimer argues that EU cannot prevent war in Europe – if it ever comes to that. This pessimism is the hallmark of this particular story. The vision of the international system resembles a billiard table, where billiard balls collide and react against one another.

Waltz (1959, 227) suggests that,

> According to this [thinking], there is a constant possibility of war in a world in which there are two or more states each seeking to promote a set of interests and having no agency above them upon which they can rely for protection.

This is because the 'state in the world are like individuals in the state of nature. They are neither perfectly good nor are they controlled by law' (Waltz 1959, 163). At this level of analysis, the anarchic nature of the international system begins to resemble Rousseau's 'stag hunt'. This is a hypothetical situation in which five hungry men agree to cooperate in a joint endeavour to catch a stag. When the five slowly approach the target, one man sees a hare. Because he is hungry, he jumps for it – after all, there is no guarantee that the five can capture the stag, and he thinks that he has a good chance of catching the hare for food. As a result, the stag escapes. The lesson here is this: under anarchic conditions, cooperation becomes difficult (Waltz 1959, 167–8). Such a way of thinking provides the justification for this story: what is at stake is the way unitary state actors interact with one another. Using the stag hunt analogy, while what might be happening inside each man's head might be salient, what is more important is what happens when individuals decide to act to maximize their interests – in this case, satisfying their hunger and, therefore, the urge to survive.

This is the basic framework that the neorealists use to analyse the way the international system works. It is the anarchic structure of the international system that makes it difficult for state actors to see beyond their own, individual, self-interests (= survival). In short, wars occur because there is nothing to prevent them from happening (Waltz 1959, 232). The proponents of this story think it a waste of resources to hope that cooperation can take place, especially if there is a real danger of your friend turning into your enemy at some point. The flip side of this argument is that cooperation is seen as a rare mutual coincidence of wants, though there is no guarantee that it can be sustained. The proponents of this story assume that the possibility of conflict is always there, and postulate that actors are constantly preparing for such an event.

The Critique

As you can see, the lack of insight into domestic actors, coupled with the assumption that national interests of state actors are predefined in terms of maximizing power means that this level of analysis takes an overtly top-down, holistic view. The state actors are effectively 'black boxed' in this story to the extent that they are almost like atoms engaged in some form of a chain reaction. Despite what we might read in the newspapers – such as the preferences of US presidents colliding with those of the Congress in many American foreign policy areas including China, Iran and international trade – these factors are recognized and yet trivialized. This story provides a very simplified and accessible model of the international system; but it prevents us from asking questions such as the role of domestic coalition patterns in the formulation of foreign policies, as is usually the case in European states; or the role of religion in Iranian foreign policy, or the ideological and historical dimensions of Chinese foreign relations.

To be sure, this story provides an entry-level analysis into the study of international politics. This story is exactly the sort of description of the international system that we are familiar with in media reporting. Yet, there is no escaping that the **black boxing of states** leaves many questions unanswered. The more we think about what makes states act in the way they do, and the more we wonder about what motivates presidents and prime ministers to make decisions that they make, we need to start plying into the black box of states. This story necessarily provides a macroscopic view of the international system. It is a good start, but it begs more questions than it answers.

> **Black Boxing of States** – an assumption that considers states to be unitary actors; and that only their foreign policy outcomes matter in international politics. As such, only a cursory attention is given to domestic politics. This is an approach favoured by neorealists and neoliberal-institutionalists.

STORY TWO: POWER, COOPERATION, NORMS AND INTERDEPENDENCE

The previous story on the international system focused primarily on the *system-level* analysis. That is, state and bureaucratic levels were deemed to be less important in understanding how the world 'works'. In that story, wars occur because there is nothing to prevent them from happening. We now move onto another story which shares similar assumptions about the anarchic nature of the international system, but takes on a less pessimistic outlook compared to neorealists. This story is often told by neoliberal-institutionalists (see Chapter 2).

The Role of Institutions

The proponents of this story take **international institutions** very seriously. Here, 'institutions' include international organizations like the UN and the EU. While there are various discussions on the different meanings attached to terms such as 'institutions', 'regimes' and 'organizations', for the purposes of this chapter, we use them interchangeably (Hasenclever et al. 1997, Chapter 2).

According to Stephen Krasner (quoted in Keohane 1982, 341–2), institutions embody 'principles ("beliefs of fact, causation, and rectitude") and norms ("standards of behavior defined in terms of rights and obligations") as well as rules and decision making procedures'. Unlike the pessimism of Neorealism, this story is optimistic that actors are able to realize the longer term benefits of cooperation. This is in stark contrast to neorealists who consider international cooperation to be a mere coincidence. A very good example might be the North Atlantic Treaty Organization (NATO): the Cold War has ended with the collapse of the Soviet Union; but NATO has found new *raison d'etre* in Kosovo and Afghanistan, for instance. Now,

> **International Institution** – set of rules and norms for international behaviour. Can be both formal (for example, the UN) and informal (the so-called 'special relationship' between the US and the UK).

this does not mean that the proponents of this story consider international institutions to be a panacea. They do consider actors to be rational egotists who are 'hard-wired' into making cost-benefit calculations. Indeed, Robert Keohane (1984, 73) argues that, 'although international regimes may be valuable to their creators, *they do not necessarily improve world welfare*. They are not *ipso facto* "good"'. Yet, they also question the pessimism of Neorealism. Keohane (1984, 7) states that, '[i]f international politics were a state of war, institutionalized patterns of cooperation on the basis of shared purposes should not exist except as part of a large struggle for power'. For Keohane (1984, 51–2; emphases deleted), 'intergovernmental cooperation takes place when the policies actually followed by one government are regarded by its partners as facilitating realization of their own objectives, as the result of a process of policy coordination'. Hence, this story suggests that states are also capable of looking at the longer term benefits, as compared to the assumption that actors are short-termist, as in the stag hunt example. Hence, the neoliberals see the international system as potentially a billiard ball model, but consider that international institutions can ameliorate some of the worst excesses of international anarchy. It is precisely because the states are rational actors that they create international regimes as a way to 'establish stable mutual expectation about others' patterns of behaviour and to develop working relationships that will allow the parties to adapt their practices to new structures' (Keohane 1982, 331). One factor that makes this possible in the eyes of the neoliberals is the existence of *norms* – 'standards of behaviour defined in terms of rights and obligations' (Keohane 1984, 57). neoliberal-institutionalists allege that international regimes are akin to international 'market' for national interests: once the state actors agree to enter into that 'market', they are socialized into the particular ways of behaviour expected of them in that context. Through such a process, a notion of reciprocity emerges through which participants come to expect how others will act within that particular context (Hasenclever et al. 1997, 9–10).

This way of thinking potentially opens up the level of analysis to include non-state actors, such as MNCs, with enough economic clout to become a significant player on the world stage. Once cooperation is understood as sustainable, and not just a coincidence, then other entities can be granted actorhood. If war is seen as almost a default position within the international system, then state actors are the only entities capable of exerting influence. However, if a story allows for the institutionalization of cooperative behaviours, then other entities become more visible, due to their influence on the world stage. The global financial crisis following the Lehman Shock of September 2008 is a case in point: the idea that some banks are 'too big to fail' gains potency because they are recognized as powerful actors in the international system, either because their failures can precipitate a financial contagion or because the governments are heavily dependent on these banks to underwrite their debts.

Hence, this story is much more complex than the previous one, simply because there are more vectors of interaction between and among the state and non-state actors. To be sure, some neorealists such as Robert Gilpin (1987) recognize that non-state actors might play an important role, but they also suggest that states tramp non-state actors. But, the complexity of the neoliberal story makes an important move in the levels of analysis, because of the shift down from Waltz's Third Image towards the Second Image, if not the First Image. The potentials for complex interactions between and among the various actors and the recognition that both politics and economics play crucial roles in the way the international system works gives rise to the notion of **complex interdependence** (Keohane and Nye 1977). Furthermore, firmly within the First Image is another derivation of this story, introducing the notion of *policy entrepreneurs* – individuals who are charismatic and instrumental in bringing about change. These policy entrepreneurs provide convincing arguments and ideas that can influence the course of international outcomes, such as the negotiations leading up to the evolution of the EU

> **Complex Interdependence** – an idea in which the international system is comprised of states and non-state actors interacting cooperatively (especially economically), while maintaining a semblance of balance of power (especially militarily) (Nye and Keohane, 1977).

in the 1980s and the 1990s (Moravcsik 1999). Hence, the variations of the Second Story allow proponents to construct a variety of models that help explain the complex workings of the international system – not something that is possible with the inherent simplicity of Neorealism.

The Critique

This story is more complex than the First Story: the decision to take international cooperation seriously opens the way for discussions on international institutions, as well as potential to recognize other actors in the international arena, including MNCs and individuals. It is a story not just of balance of power but one of power and interdependence in which rational actors at various levels of analysis engage in rivalry as well as cooperation. As such, we are beginning to move away from solely focusing on Waltz's Third Image of international relations, but gradually allowing us to explore Second and First Images. It also allows us to engage better with Allison's three levels of foreign policy analysis in which decisions made at individual, group, and state levels can all impact on the workings of the international system. The model here is more complex, and is therefore more difficult to conceptualize than Neorealism; but it also allows us to appreciate the interplay of various forces that are behind world affairs (see Chapters 6 and 7).

However, it is also the case that this story shares some of the problems of the previous one. On the one hand, this story holds potential to widen the scope of enquiry, moving away from a simplistic billiard ball model. As such, there is great promise in proposing a truly systemic exploration of the international system. However, just as Neorealism effectively reduces explanation to unit-level analysis, there is an inherent danger that neoliberals might end up doing the same. Despite the promise of a story that seems to take seriously the complex nature of the international system, the entangled web of interactions remains underutilized. Put differently, if and when a proponent of this story needs to decide who the most influential actor might be, there is not much choice but to favour states over other actors. Hence, while an exploration into First and Second Images are always possible in this story, the default position remains the Third Image.

STORY THREE: THE WEB OF SOCIAL INTERACTIONS

So far we have seen two stories that are more or less focused on the role of state actors. They differ from one another in that the First Story provided very much a top-down view of the world that depicted the international system as a billiard ball model, on the one hand; while the Second Story provided a picture of the international system in which international regimes acted as a market for national interests, on the other. The First Story was less interested in domestic dynamics, focusing instead on the states as rational egotists. In contrast, the Second Story created a space for other actors, including MNCs and individuals, to be considered as influencing international affairs. However, once we take a step back, they seem to share a common trait: that states are the most influential actors on the international stage. Indeed, it is interesting to see Keohane (1988, 312) arguing that system level theories, including Neorealism and Neoliberalism, do not pay 'sufficient attention to domestic politics'. This a striking comment, as Keohane – one of the main proponents of the Second Story – is arguing to move back from the Third to Second, if not the First Image analysis.

The Third Story of the international system seeks to address Keohane's critique. While maintaining some element of systemic analysis, this story also provides a conceptual tool for IR theorists to take domestic politics into consideration. This story seeks to do this by considering the international system as a macro-level social interaction. Compared to the billiard ball analogy of the First Story, the international system in the Third Story is much more complex. Instead of considering the state to be an innate black box akin to an automaton, the Third Story treats states as intentional actors who are engaged in social interactions, comparable to individuals within human society. One major proponent of this story, Alexander Wendt (1999, 217), suggests that states and societies 'have a collective dimension that causes macro-level regularities among their elements ... over space and time'. As such, we are looking at potentially a very complex theory of the international system.

In treating the international system as a macro-level social sphere, the proponents of the Third Story, namely **constructivists**, make the following assumptions:

- Just like human interaction within communities and societies, meanings are important;
- Actors are assumed to be intentional, not just rational. This means that actors have identities and use symbolisms in their interactions;
- Actors could be states, groups or individuals, thereby opening the way for an even more complex analysis of the international system than the Second Story.

The main concern for constructivists has less to do with the appropriate levels of analysis as it is to do with the nature of the international system more generally. In other words, the Third Story is concerned about the *social context* of the international system.

Take our everyday social context. In our relationships, we have friends and foes. We sort of know how it feels to be with friends – it differs from how it feels to be with our nemeses. But the most important thing is this: friendship or foe depends

> **Constructivism** – a theoretical approach in which actors' perceptions, ideas, images and symbols are taken seriously: borrows heavily from Social Theory and Philosophy of Language.

primarily on how we interact with other individuals. In other words, friendship is one form of social context; we act towards our friends in a particular way, because that is the 'right thing' for us to do; and we expect our friends to act towards us in a particular way as well. In short, we have identities as friends; and that contextualizes the interaction (= friendship) into a particular social dynamic.

Constructivists model the international system in a similar way. Instead of friends and foes, we can substitute allies and enemies. States, for instance, have a very good idea of who the allies are, and who the potential enemies might be. Unlike the neorealist international system where everyone else is a potential enemy, the proponents of the Third Story suggest that allies and enemies are the products of socialization – how states have behaved toward one another over time. States expect allies to act in a particular way, invoking collective defence when an ally comes under fire (see Chapter 13). Wendt (1999, 97) suggests that the structure of the international system is all about ideas; and he suggests that 'history matters' because it is through history that precedents create meanings for a particular international context (Wendt 1999, 109).

The logical conclusion to this is that the constructivists consider the anarchic structure of the international system to be a **social construct**. This is in stark contrast to the neorealist assumption that anarchy is the defining feature of the international system. Wendt (1992, 395) argues that 'self-help and power politics are institutions, not essential features of anarchy. *Anarchy is what states make of it*', just as friendship relies on friends sustaining that relationship. Hence, Constructivism provides a significant corrective to the First Story: there is nothing deterministic about the international system; and that actors are not billiard

> **Social Construct** – any 'thing' which exists by virtue of humans reproducing its concept. Intangible 'things' such as 'society' and 'state' are good examples of social constructions. While social constructs might seem like figments of people's imaginations, they nevertheless impact on humans by affecting the way we behave.

balls, but, rather, intentional actors, just as individuals in society have intentions. For instance, Waltz's use of market analogy to show that actors are rational egotists is criticized for failing to appreciate that markets themselves are social constructions, relying heavily on participants' intentions (Kratochwil 1989, 47). Furthermore, there is also a critique of the Second Story. John Ruggie (1998, 63) argues that, while the neoliberals' attention to international regimes is useful, their analyses are inadequate, given that the success or failure of regimes also depends 'by the intentionality and acceptability others attribute to those acts in the contexts of an intersubjective framework of meaning'.

In this story, individual human decisions are as important as the analysis of what states do at collective levels. States might remain one of the main actors, but constructivists are ready to pay close attention to other actors such as individuals and groups. In that sense, the Third Story has moved on from the Third Image to the other images. Also, it seems as if this story is concerned with *all three levels* of decision-making. Again, there are parallels to Allison's three levels, as constructivists pay close attention to what individuals and groups do. This story recognizes that groups and other macro-level social actors such as the state, MNCs, non-governmental organizations, bureaucracies and society are all made of individuals acting in their respective roles within various levels. Put differently, the constructivists are cognizant of the fact that social actors are *layered* actors comprised of:

- Individuals with their identities and personal beliefs and backgrounds (see Chapter 6);
- These individuals come together to form groups, including various levels of decision-making in governments and other organizations; and
- These individuals and groups make individual and collective decisions in the name of the organizations that they *represent* (Wight 2006).

In other words: individuals (presidents, prime ministers, company executives) come together to form an executive branch; the executives deliberate on a policy; and particular individuals vested with particular roles and decision-making powers within the executive (President John F. Kennedy during the Cuban Missile Crisis or Steve Jobs deciding on the design of iPhones) make decisions that represent the collective decision of the organization.

To be sure, the Third Story is not fully compatible with the Three Images or the levels of analysis precisely because it is more concerned with the web of interaction between and among the individuals and groups. Put differently, Constructivism is interested in:

- How states, as complex social entities, interact with one another;
- How ideas shape the world;
- How individuals with their identities and biases come together and negotiate an outcome as a group; and
- How individuals and social entities 'think' about the world.

Hence, the Third Story is not 'structural' in that it is not only interested in states as billiard balls; nor is it necessarily interested in focusing on the groups and individuals. Instead, the Third Story tells a very complex story of the international system that is starting to resemble stories about society and our day-to-day experiences. To that extent, constructivists do not necessarily subscribe to the neat delineation of Three Images or the three levels of decision-making.

The Critique

From the perspective of the Third Story, both the first and second stories treat states and other actors as lacking intentions and, as a result, they resemble automatons. This is problematic for constructivists since there is nothing deterministic about the way the international system 'works'. Furthermore, given the constructivists' interest in identities as a source of actor interests, the neorealist and neoliberal penchant for interests as things that are predetermined by the structure of the international system becomes an issue. Simultaneously, the constructivist assumption that social actors are layered actors enables a smoother transition from one level of analysis to another.

What sets the Third Story apart from the first two is its attention to intangibles, such as ideas and intentions. On the one hand, this is a definite plus, as our daily experiences are full of intangibles, such as meanings we attach to our actions. We are able to distinguish between the subtle nuances in our daily lives; and even within the international system there are subtleties in the form of ambiguities that govern the way state actors interact with one another. The American 'pivot' back to the Asia-Pacific might be another instance of a social context full of meanings and symbolisms. Is rising China a threat? If so, then the US intentions might be to contain China. If China is not a threat, then how are we to understand US intentions? Is Washington jealously trying to maintain its hegemonic power? It is primarily a case of 'where you stand depends on where you sit'; and the constructivists take this very seriously.

However, the Third Story is extremely complex. As a model for analysing the international system, it involves guess work – guessing what the various actions mean. It does not help that one of the main proponents of this story, Wendt (1999, Chapter 3), is uncertain whether or not the international structure is comprised of 'ideas all the way down'. From the perspective of the first two stories, there is a question of how 'scientific' this story really is (Keohane 1988, 392). Perhaps this is an unfair critique, but it is an issue that needs to be addressed by those who subscribe to this story.

STORY FOUR: INTERNATIONAL SYSTEM AS A STORY

The three stories thus far shared some similarities while being distinct in their own ways. On the one hand, the first two stories focused mainly on the system-level analysis exploring how actors – both state as well as non-state – behave in an anarchic international system. On the other hand, the Third Story emphasized that the international system is akin to a macro-level social interaction in which social actors, large and small, interact with one another; and in analysing such a complex web of social interaction, we need to move up and down the various levels of analysis. As such, the three stories operate at particular points on the levels of analysis as a framework for understanding the way the international system operates.

The Fourth Story is radically different. It is highly critical of the preceding stories. Critical in a sense that it engages with the three stories, 'takes apart' the logic of these stories and seeks to unravel the 'hidden meanings'. For theorists accustomed to the three stories, the fourth one makes for a very uncomfortable reading; but these criticisms are worth exploring. As for the levels of analysis, it is seen as just one of many stories we might tell about the world. But the

Fourth Story also tells us that there are many other stories to be told about international life. It is for this reason that this story is truly critical.

The main theme of the Fourth Story is **metaphor**. What is meant here is that social reality is constituted of symbols, language, performance and other forms of representations, as opposed to the 'certainty' of the existence of the state or the international system as a 'thing' to be analysed. Put differently, the Fourth Story has problems with whatever is meant by the 'state', the 'international system', 'national interests' and so on. This story is concerned less with how to provide a 'scientific' understanding of international politics, as it is concerned primarily with the ways in which we use language and ideas to explain and represent our international experience. It is, by definition, critical:

Metaphor – a figure of speech in which a word is used to describe something it does not literally mean (Blackburn 1994, 240). The phrase, the 'Axis of Evil', used by President George W. Bush in January 2002 to describe Iraq, Iran and North Korea is an example of metaphor *in practice*. Some IR theorists consider the notion of a unitary state as a metaphor as well, given that a state is a social construct – a product of human interactions.

it is critical because this story seeks to unravel the 'common sense' that seems to permeate within the three previous stories about the need to prioritize states and their behaviours.

Hence, one of the levels of analysis, the state, ceases to be as clear-cut an entity as it was in the first two stories. Even the more complex formulation of the state as a complex social entity does not escape criticism. Iver Neumann (2004, 260) takes issues with such formulations, suggesting instead that we should treat states as discursive constructions – or metaphors – accusing Wendt and others of 'prorgrammatically reifying social phenomena'. For him, treating states as complex social entities, let alone things to be analysed, 'seems to constrain rather than to enable our inquiry into what is happening to states and their place in global politics here and now' (Neumann 2004, 267). Thus, the proponents of the fourth story are insinuating that states are not so much 'things out there', but rather a set of symbols and meanings that change from time to time. Put differently, they are arguing that states are not things we 'analyse' but they are things we 'talk about'. To say that states – and other things in international relations – are metaphors provides potentials for transformation: changes in the way we alter our interpretations about, and meanings we attach to, concepts in IR such as states potentially transform our understanding of them. Consequently, just as we are interested in the various stories we tell about the levels of analysis of the international system, the proponents of this story consider ideas *about* states to be another set of stories.

In a further critique of the constructivist depiction of the international system as a complex web of social relations, Roxanne Lynn Doty (1997, 376) argues that it should be treated not as a constellation of state actors interacting with one another in a social context, but, rather, as a set of practices. She suggests that the concern with tangible entities such as the state and the international system prevents us from telling stories that are based on meanings and practices. She argues that practice is 'inextricably

The fourth story is often told by theorists belonging to Post-structuralism or Postmodernism in IR Theory. While these labels might be inaccurate, it is important to remember their common approach to IR: the primacy of language in the way we understand the world.

connected to the production of meanings', since it is more fruitful to consider the international system as sets of practices rather than overlapping layers. For her, the international system is a set of practices that are 'embedded in discourse(s) which enable particular meaning(s) to be signified' (Doty 1997, 377). In this formulation, the international system becomes less of a structured realm where actors at various levels interact with one another, but more as a set of meanings that change over time. Doty (1997, 385) notes that, '[w]hat becomes sayable, doable, imaginable within a society results from a process of discursive repetition and dissemination'. This includes our stories about the international system: Doty (Ibid.) posits that 'the issues of agency and structure(s) cannot be adequately or critically examined without also examining representational practices'.

In a similar vein, foreign policy is treated in a significantly different manner. Instead of approaching foreign policy as sets of decision-making processes that can be analysed from various levels, the proponents of the Fourth Story identify elements of meanings and practices that are inherent in it. David Campbell (1998, 69) argues that foreign policy is the 'constant (re) construction of identity through the strategy of otherness', that it is a 'discourse of power that is global in scope yet national in legitimation' (Campbell 1998, 70). Hence, Campbell is suggesting that foreign policy is less an outcome of decision-making against which the levels of analysis approach can be applied, as it is a set of practices and meanings about national identities as well as a shared sense of danger as a result of historic practice. In short, foreign policy is about understanding 'who we are', and 'whom we are against'. For him, 'it is the objectification of the self through the representation of danger that Foreign Policy helps achieve' (Campbell 1998, 71). Hence, in addition to Doty's preoccupation with practice, Campbell is concerned about shifting worldviews that give rise to the notion of *us versus them*. The main focus of the Fourth Story ceases to revolve around how we conceptualize the relationship between the actor and the international system; but rather, the primary aim is to critique the 'language' of 'talking about' states and the international system. Subtle though this may seem, such distinction becomes crucial in appreciating the Fourth Story.

Hence, the Fourth Story is quite subversive. On the surface, this story refuses to engage with the other three. Yet, it is also the case that this story recognizes an important point: however much other stories seek to provide a more definitive tool for analysing the international system, they remain stories that one can decide whether or not to adopt. By extension, the levels of analysis considerations remain another set of stories that people tell about international relations: the choice of Waltzian First, Second, or Third Image is really about a choice of stories with which one wants to engage. The first two stories focused on the role of states within the international system; but they remain only

> The main message of the fourth story is this: the international order, as we know it today, is an accident of history. Hence, concepts such as the 'state' and the notion of 'sovereignty' are products of particular events in history.

two of many stories we can tell, however much this way of telling about the world has been the most dominant of stories (Walker 1993, 126). R.B.J. Walker (1993, 154–5) notes that, '[s]tates, it is often observed, have not disappeared. Nor have they lost their capacity to deploy violence on a frightening scale. But this says very little about the continuing capacity of states to resolve the contradiction between citizenship and humanity through claims to absolute authority'. For Walker (1993, Chapter 5), if territorial sovereignty is the defining element of the international system, it is because this is simply an accident of history. If the levels of analysis are seen to be pertinent to our understanding of how the world 'works', again, it is because we are made to think so. In essence, the Fourth Story seeks to demonstrate that there are many more stories waiting to be told about how the world 'works'.

The Critique

The Fourth Story differs significantly from the previous three stories in its approach to the international system and to the levels of analysis. This story provides a dramatic critique of the other stories, unravelling the subtle biases and exposing the inherent assumptions underlying each of the other stories. To this extent, the Fourth Story is very subversive; and its readiness to admit that we are all telling stories about the international system is revealing. This story provides us with a further set of tools to critically reassess other stories and question their underlying assumptions. In other words, this story equips us with a critical 'tool box' to deconstruct any story anyone is telling about the way the international system 'works'.

If anything, this story is inconclusive. It is one thing for us to appreciate that we are all telling stories. It is quite another for us to simply suggest that other theories are stories. While we can appreciate that we are telling stories about whatever concerns us on the international stage, this story prevents us from asking questions such as 'how would Iran respond to US sanctions?', or 'what is the role of identity politics in the Arab-Israeli conflict?' Yes, they are stories, after all, but it is not at all clear whether reducing everything down to stories might help us in exploring whatever international events make us curious. To be sure, stories are important, and we all engage in story-telling; but it is also the case that we tell stories with a particular aim of explaining or understanding the complexities of the international system. We tell stories because we have intentions to try to engage with what is happening around the world. This is an important thing that must not be overlooked.

CONCLUSION

The levels of analysis provide us with a useful starting point for the study of international politics. It is a versatile methodological tool that allows us to appreciate various factors affecting decision-making processes. The levels of analysis enable us to ask questions about how foreign policy decisions are made, or how international conflicts emerge. Furthermore, moving back and forth among the various levels enables us to understand how each of the levels interacts with one another. While the proponents of the levels of analysis approach might have preferences over which levels to prioritize, this way of looking at IR makes us more aware of the complexities of the reality of international life.

However, there are limits as to whether we can adopt the levels of analysis approach to the study of the international system. The main reason for this is that the international system itself is one of the levels of analysis – whether be it the study of international conflicts or foreign policy decision-making. Given the usefulness of this approach, having an enhanced set of tools for the study of the international system would be beneficial. As seen in previous chapters, there are many perspectives on the way world politics evolved over time and space (Chapter 1), as well as many different ways of theorizing about it (Chapter 2). Taking multiple

> Patrick Jackson (2011) is implying that the story we – as students of International Relations – decide to tell is primarily determined by how we understand our complex world. There is no 'right' or 'wrong' story; and the task for us is to try to tell a convincing story about our observations and experiences.

perspectives further enables us to think about stories we might tell about the international system. Some of the stories are amenable to the levels of analysis approach, while others might be fundamentally at odds with it. To the extent that the levels of analysis also tell stories about how foreign policy decisions are made, or how international conflicts come about, we can tell stories about the international system itself. In short, the stories we tell represent how we '**hook up to the world**' (Jackson 2011, xii; xiii), precisely because we need to tell particular stories about the complex realities of the international system due to our limited conceptual capacities (Jackson 2011, Chapter 1).

As stated above, one of the benefits of the levels of analysis approach is that they enable us to take variations in the way we can depict international actors seriously. While we do need to be mindful of their interactions with the systemic constraints of the international political environment, once we are aware of the benefits and limits of the levels of analysis approach, we can better appreciate what the actors are thinking, how they might behave within the international system and what effects their actions might have on the outcomes of world politics.

QUESTIONS FOR REFLECTION

1. What are the *pros* and *cons* of the levels of analysis approach?
2. What are the main characteristics of the First Story?
3. What is the main difference between the second and first stories?
4. What is meant by treating the international system as a macro-level social interaction?
5. What are the *pros* and *cons* of the Fourth Story?

REVISION QUIZ

1. What is Waltz's Third Image?

   a. The state
   b. Ideology
   c. Political leaders
   d. The international system

2. What is Allison's second level of analysis?

   a. The state
   b. Ideology
   c. Bureaucracy
   d. The international system

3. What role do international institutions play?

    a. Conduct wars
    b. Resolve wars
    c. Act as a 'marketplace'
    d. Not much

4. What factor is considered most important by realists?

    a. Power
    b. Cooperation
    c. International institutions
    d. Norms

5. Which level of analysis does Waltz think is most important?

    a. The state
    b. The individual
    c. Bureaucracy
    d. The international system

6. Do the proponents of Fourth Story subscribe to the levels of analysis approach?

    a. Yes
    b. No

7. Do constructivists subscribe to the levels of analysis approach?

    a. Yes, definitely
    b. Yes, to an extent that the international system is complex
    c. Yes, to the extent that it is preoccupied with foreign policy
    d. Definitely not

8. Which level of analysis does Robert Jervis say is most important?

    a. The individual
    b. The bureaucracy
    c. The international system
    d. All levels are important in international politics

9. What do the First and Second Stories agree on?

    a. The role of individuals
    b. The role of international institutions
    c. The role of states
    d. The role of MNCs

10. The Fourth Story believes in one true story

   a. True
   b. False

Answers: 1: d; 2: c; 3: c; 4: a; 5: d; 6: b; 7: b; 8: d; 9: c; 10: b.

BIBLIOGRAPHY

Allison, G.T. (1971) *Essence of Decision: Explaining the Cuban Missile Crisis* (Glenview, IL: Scott Forseman).

Blackburn, S. (1994) *Oxford Dictionary of Philosophy* (Oxford: Oxford University Press).

Campbell, D. (1998) *National Deconstruction: Violence, Identity and Justice in Bosnia* (Minneapolis, MN: University of Minnesota Press).

Doty, R.L. (1997) 'Aporia: A Critical Exploration of the Agent-Structure Problematique in International Relations Theory', *European Journal of International Relations* 3(3), 365–92.

Frey, F.W. (1985), 'The Problem of Actor Designation in Political Analysis', *Comparative Politics*, 127–52.

Gilpin, R. (1987) *The Political Economy of International Relations* (Princeton, NJ: Princeton University Press).

Hasenclever, A. et al. (1997) *Theories of International Regimes* (Cambridge: Cambridge University Press).

Jackson, P.T. (2011) *The Conduct of Inquiry in International Relations: Philosophy of Science and Its Implications for the Study of World Politics* (London: Routledge).

Jervis, R. (1976) *Perception and Misperception in International Politics* (Princeton, NJ: Princeton University Press).

Keohane, R.O. (1988) 'International Institutions: Two Approaches', *International Studies Quarterly* 32(4), 379–96.

Keohane, R.O. (1984) *After Hegemony* (Princeton, NJ: Princeton University Press).

Keohane, R.O. (1982) 'The Demand for International Regimes', *International Organization* 36(2), 325–55.

Keohane, R.O. and Nye, J.S. (1977) *Power and Interdependence* (Boston, MA: Little Brown).

Kratochwil, F. (1989) *Norms, Rules, and Decisions* (Cambridge: Cambridge University Press).

Mearsheimer, J. (1995) 'The False Promise of International Institutions', *International Security* 19(3), 5–49.

Moravcsik, A. (1999) 'A New Statecraft? Supranational Entrepreneurs and International Cooperation', *International Organization* 53(3), 267–306.

Morgenthau, H.J. (1985) *Politics Among Nations*, 5th edition (New York: Knopf).

Neumann, I.B. (2004) 'Beware of Organicism: The Narrative Self of the State', *Review of International Studies* 30(2), 259–67.

Ruggie, J.G. (1998) *Constructing the World Polity* (London: Routledge).

Russett, B.M. (2009) 'Democracy, War and Expansion through Historical Lenses', *European Journal of International Relations* 15(1), 9–36.

Walker, R.B.J. (1993) *Instde/Outside: International Relations as Political Theory* (Cambridge: Cambridge University Press).

Waltz, K.N. (1979) *Theory of International Politics* (New York: McGraw-Hill).

Waltz, K.N. (1959) *Man, the State, and War* (New York: Columbia University Press).

Wendt, A. (1999) *Social Theory of International Politics* (Cambridge: Cambridge University Press).

Wendt, A. (1992) 'Anarchy is What States Make of It: The Social Construction of Power Politics', *International Organization* 46(2), 391–425.

Wight, C. (2006) *Agents, Structures and International Relations: Politics as Ontology* (Cambridge: Cambridge University Press).

PART II:
Actors

Chapter 5
The State on the World Stage

THERESA CALLAN

This chapter introduces the state as an actor in international politics. It explains the origins of the state and how it has expanded to be a key actor on the world stage. It discusses how the state overcame competitors and embedded itself within the political fabric. It notes how states became more diverse in their functionality and came to be regarded as the 'natural' unit of political organization. The state's evolution has not always been smooth, though, and in some places it has been more testing than others. The chapter identifies and discusses the challenges that the state has faced and continues to face from globalization, the legacy of colonialism and the changing distribution of power in the international system. These processes affect the rise of non-state actors and reduce the capacity of states to unilaterally manage their own affairs. The chapter looks then at how states, especially less powerful ones, struggle to deliver security and stability to their populations and how even the more powerful states have had to adapt to change. It looks at the concept of 'failed states' in terms of their inability to supply public goods to their people and their construction as sites of insecurity for the region and the international system. The competition between state-centric views and more holistic readings of politics and security is noted in the chapter, through coverage of the debate on state sovereignty. The conditionality of state sovereignty in terms of the need for 'good governance' and the need to protect and promote human rights is noted, and tied into a wider discussion of the 'humanitarian imperative' and intervention. The view of the state as the Leviathan, the sovereign actor par excellence, is no longer accurate (if it ever was). The chapter concludes, though, that the state remains the principal form of political organization in the international system and reports of its demise are much too premature.

Key Words: The State, Internal Sovereignty, External Sovereignty, Realism, Hegemonic States, Post-Colonial State, Vertical Legitimacy, Horizontal Legitimacy, Failed States, Human Security, Humanitarian Imperative.

Chapter 5

The State on the World Stage

THERESA CALLAN

INTRODUCTION

The state is the primary actor on the world stage despite the many obituaries that have marked its passing. The state's continued presence belies claims that it no longer has a role in the drama of international affairs due to the post-territorial, post-sovereign, contemporary setting. This chapter introduces and explains the origins and the evolution of the state, notes its changing characteristics and the challenges it faces from other actors. It contends that the state remains central to international politics due to its adaptability and resilience.

THE ORIGINS AND EVOLUTION OF THE STATE

The birth of the state generally is dated to the Peace of Westphalia (1648) in Central Europe. This Peace marked the end of the bloody Thirty Years' War (1618–48) and dealt a death blow to the prevailing feudal system. The bonds of fealty which underpinned the feudal system were sundered and temporal authorities eclipsed those of a more spiritual nature. The emergence of the state marked the secularization of political life as it undermined the position of the Papacy and the Holy Roman Empire. The state attracted and sustained support because it demonstrated that it was the most effective provider and guarantor of security and safety for its people. In due course, this efficacy ensured that states saw off competitors, such as city leagues, like the Hanseatic League, and city states, such

> **The State** – the governmental apparatus in charge of a demarcated territory, providing public goods to its people.

as Florence and Venice, because 'their institutional logic gave them an advantage in mobilizing their societies' resources' (Spruyt 1994, 185). The state triumphed over rival forms of political organization because its extractive capacity allowed it to best secure the interests of the people. It was the right actor at the right time. It set about expanding its remit, embedding itself into the political, economic and societal fabric by 'abridging, destroying or absorbing rights previously lodged in other political units: manors, communities, provinces, estates. In cases like the state's seizure of control over justice from manorial lords, churches and communities, the right itself continued in more or less the same form, but under new management' (Tilly 1975, 77). By 1700, the state had established itself as the primary form of political organization.

The Peace of Westphalia (1648) comprised a series of multilateral treaties signed at Osnabrück and Münster by a variety of signatories including Ferdinand III, the Holy Roman Empire, the Kingdom of France, the Kingdom of Spain, the Swedish Empire, the Dutch republic, the Princes of the Holy Roman Empire and the rulers of the imperial cities – demonstrating the

heterogeneity of political rule at the time. At the heart of this Peace, and at the heart of the state which emanated from it, was the issue of sovereignty. The Peace established the principle of cuius regio eius religio, 'whose region, his religion'. This allowed the temporal prince of the territory the right to decide the denomination of the subjects in his realm – Lutheran or Catholic. This principle acknowledged the two sides of sovereignty as the prince was deemed sovereign within his territory, and the rule of each prince was afforded legal equality between their respective territories. Territory and sovereignty have been characteristics of the Westphalian state and its state system since their inception. The territorial requirement of the state is relatively unproblematic. The state is 'an area of "bounded space"' (Storey 2001, 1). The state has a clearly demarcated territory within which it has the exclusive right to rule. It is this 'right to rule' criterion that is more challenging – and which, in turn, can have consequences for the territorial integrity of the state. Sovereignty is comprised of two inter-related dimensions – **internal sovereignty** and **external sovereignty** – and encompasses a number of principles, such as territorial integrity, non-interference, legal equality –
all providing the parameters of the 'sovereignty game' (Jackson 1990). Internal sovereignty requires that the people within the set territory recognize and abide by the authority of the state. The state then is the ultimate power within its bordered space and is sovereign in its domestic jurisdiction. Externally, the state is one among equals as each state is, in law anyway, legally

> **Internal Sovereignty** – the writ of the state – its right to rule, is recognized by the people within its territory
>
> **External Sovereignty** – the legal equality of the state is recognized by the other states in the international system.

equal to its peers. This means that the state has the right to have its domestic jurisdiction respected by other states. Other states must observe the principle of non-interference and not meddle in one another's internal affairs.

This legal equality between states is explicitly enshrined in the United Nations Charter. Article 2 clearly states that 'The Organization is based on the principle of the sovereign equality of all its Members' and explicitly safeguards the principle of non-interference; 'Nothing contained in the present Charter shall authorize the United Nations to intervene in matters which are essentially within the domestic jurisdiction of any state'. Membership of the United Nations allows entry into the club of states and serves notice of the standing of the state, that the state is entitled to all the rights of its kind. Given what such membership bestows, it is not surprising that newly declared states seek recognition from the United Nations and a place among their peers. Recently, following its unilateral declaration of independence in 2008, Kosovo has sought recognition from the United Nations, albeit without success thus far. Although denied entry to the United Nations, the International Criminal Court, the principal judicial organ of the United Nations, has ruled that the declaration of statehood was not against international law.

Recognition of state sovereignty though is not simply a legal matter. It is a political act and has political consequences. The opposition of states such as Serbia and Russia to the recognition of Kosovo ensures it cannot become a member of the United Nations – not least as Russia is a permanent member of the United Nations Security Council. A state can only belong to a club when the other members do not 'blackball' its bid for membership. Thus Kosovo is a member of the World Bank and the International Monetary Fund. It is not, however, a member of the European Union. Indeed, the European Union's position on Kosovo's statehood is particularly conflicted – 5 of the 27 member states refuse to recognize that Kosovo is a state whilst the other 22 accept it is so. Recognition then is a political act. A would-be state can declare itself a state, look like a state, sound like a state, but, ultimately, not be a state until it is accepted as such by the other states in the international system.

Internally then – and speaking normatively, the state is in charge. Externally, however, there is no sovereign above the state. This external environment has been characterized by some political theorists, notably those of a realist persuasion, as an anarchical international system. **Realism** is one of the oldest traditions in the study of international relations, tracing its antecedents to the time of the Greek historian Thucydides. Realism constitutes a broad tradition, accommodating a range of variants

> **Realism** – a state-centric approach to International Relations which depicts the state as a rational, egotistical actor that has primacy international politics.

such as classical Realism, Neorealism, offensive Realism, defensive Realism and, more recently, neo-classical Realism. All the different variants share a set of common core assumptions: that the state is the primary actor within international politics, that the international system is anarchical and that, in this Hobbesian systemic environment, the state must seek its own security and so promote and protect its national interests over those of other states. In this anarchical system, there is no coercive power superior to that of the state. In practice, though, not all states are equal – notwithstanding liberal claims to the contrary. In the competitive and unrelenting world of international politics, legal equality is eclipsed by the inequalities of power. Strong states do what they like, and weaker states do what they are told. States are egotistical and rational actors who seek power over one another – that is their nature. They prioritize their security and help themselves to it, often at the expense of weaker states. There is then a hierarchy of states in the internal system, with the more power or **hegemonic states** at the top, then other core but secondary states, then third-level states and then weak and failing states.

> **Hegemonic States** – the most dominant states within the system, such as the 'superpowers' during the Cold War, or regional hegemons, such as India in South Asia.

Legal sovereignty – the sovereignty to be – is important for a state but it is not what really counts. What matters is power – the sovereignty to do.

As the state evolved, it did so in terms of both its remit and its geographical range. The state has never been a static actor. Its role changed significantly when Nationalism entered the scene. The American Revolution (1776) and the French Revolution (1789) brought with them the idea of the nation. Nations and Nationalism had repercussions for the state, not least because of the doctrine of popular sovereignty. Sovereignty now lay not with kings and queens and their divinely ordained right to rule but with the people. People no longer were subject *to* sovereignty but subjects *of* sovereignty, making way for calls for states to be based on popular consent and representation. In the nineteenth century especially, the *nation* became more emphatic, with the state adapting to become 'the major vehicle for creating, sustaining, and promoting the sense of a unique political community' (Holsti 2004, 47).

This singular political community expanded its geographical presence via Nationalism, not least in the wake of wars, further underscoring Tilly's aphorism that 'war made the state, and the state made war' (Tilly 1975, 42). In the wake of World War I, many 'nations', now freed from the imperial yoke of the Ottoman or the Austro-Hungarian Empires respectively, demanded their own states on the grounds of national self-determination. In accordance with President Wilson's 14 Points, underpinning the negotiations at the Paris Peace Conference (1918), nation-states were self-governing, autonomous actors in charge of their own affairs and their own destinies. Whilst the concept sounded undeniably appealing on paper, in practice it proved rather more challenging.

On paper, there is a checklist for the rather nebulous, and often contested, psycho-cultural entity that is the nation – it should have a common language, a common culture, a shared sense of identity, a shared history and a commitment to a common future. Realizing such 'imagined communities' (Andersen 1983) into nation-states was difficult. How many people constituted a nation? What was the viability threshold? What should happen when two or more nations claimed the same territory as their homeland? Despite such gritty concerns, this normative assumption that states and nations should be congruent was further revitalized after World War II and the wars of national liberation that came in its wake. Having fought a war for freedom and democracy, it was difficult for the victorious colonial states to deny such claims (albeit some tried to do so for as long as possible). The impact of decolonization can be seen in the expansion of the membership of the United Nations. In 1945, the United Nations had 51 original member states, by 1975 it had 144. As Holsti (1999, 288) puts it, 'By the 1970s, the sovereignty game has gone universal'. The game attracted still more players at the end of the Cold War. The collapse of Communism led to many of the nations in Central and Eastern Europe and in Eurasia to seek a territorial state of their own.

The state expanded not only in terms of its geographical spread but also in terms of its functionality, especially in terms of its regulatory and extractive capacities, further cementing its position as the 'natural' unit of political organization. This growing public realm of the state was such that, in the case of more developed states, 'By the twentieth century, the list of government functions expanded to include education, health, science, and technology, welfare, massive infrastructure subvention (airports, highways, and the like), economic regulation in the broadest sense, disaster relief and sports' (Holsti 2004, 47).

To contextualize further, in such states the birth of a citizen is recorded, the schooling is provided or regulated, the making and unmaking of marriages and civil partnerships noted, employment status documented, taxes and earnings registered, deaths and duties confirmed. From the cradle to the grave, the state is a constant companion. The increased functionality of the state has not been confined to the traditional public sphere as the state has increased its presence in areas traditionally regarded as being in the private realm. Some states have been more emphatically and visibly intrusive than others in terms of ruling on issues such as the amount of children permitted, the sexual orientation allowed and so on, but even those less so have advice to give on healthy eating, regular exercise and lifestyle choices. The state then has become more interventionist in the matters once considered the private preserve of the individual. The classical liberal view of the state as a night-watchman, providing and ensuring sufficient security both within the state and from external threats so that the individual citizen could go about their business without undue interference from others has retreated as states have assumed more and more functions and responsibilities: 'States are now asked to legislate and enforce moral conduct in what had been hitherto private arenas. I can no longer pollute the public environment by smoking; my dog's defecations are almost more restricted' (Mann 1999, 256). Such interventionism has led to claims that the state now is too 'bloated' and that it should be 'rolled back' thereby releasing all sorts of entrepreneurial spirit among the citizens and allowing the individual to reclaim their rightful freedoms.

There is a certain irony, however, in some of these calls, especially those made in the heat of so-called 'culture wars'. Although these wars may well take place across states, at the regional or the global level, all sides seek recourse in the state and its regulatory powers in the 'private' sphere: 'most contending actors demand *more* regulation by their own nation-state through its legal or welfare agencies: to restrict or liberalize abortion, pre-marital conception and single parenting; to clarify harassment, child abuse and rape and the evidence needed to prosecute them; to guarantee or restrict the rights of those with unorthodox sexual preferences of lifestyles' (Mann 1999, 257).

STATES AND STATENESS

The debate over the rightful realm of the state is significant but it is limited to those states which arguably have the luxury of ruminating on such matters. Other states have lacked the capacity to make meaningful their writ within their territories. This has particularly been the fate of some **post-colonial states**. Securing their nominal independence from the colonial power did not equate with meaningful and practical independence. Such states often were premised on the most generous reading of a nation – that is, there was little, if any, congruence between state borders and the distribution of the national people. Instead the people were dispersed across the boundaries of more than one state. This was part of the legacy of colonialism. The borders of the newly independent state had been drawn up by the former colonial powers, with the focus on their competing material, imperial interests rather than any concern with the ontological needs of the indigenous peoples. In many cases, these states suffered a deficit of legitimacy, both in its vertical and horizontal forms (Holsti 1996).

> **Post-colonial States** – states that were former colonies and whose 'stateness' is affected by the legacy of colonialism and imperialism.

In terms of **vertical legitimacy**, there was little sense of allegiance among the people towards the structures of the state. The state's right to rule within its sovereign space was not acknowledged by all of the citizens within its boundaries. Its authority was contested and so its institutions were weak and compromised.

> **Vertical Legitimacy** – refers to the relationship between the state and the society. High levels of vertical legitimacy denote that the people recognize the authority of the state, consent to its right to rule and are loyal to it.

In terms of **horizontal legitimacy**, there were few ties of belonging and togetherness between the people themselves. There was little or no shared understanding of societal and political norms. Often the people did not consider themselves as constituting a nation at all, instead seeking their identity and ontological security within their own sub-national groups, whether they were tribes, clans or ethnic groups. Such a retreat to groupness further weakened the social fabric of the state. The weakness was compounded when (and it usually was a case of when rather than if) leaders adopted neo-patrimonial means to strengthen their shaky grip on power. Elites engaged in corrupt practices, such as nepotism and clientelism, favouring their own power base and playing patronage politics. Such behaviour further eroded trust between

> **Horizontal Legitimacy** – refers to the shared understandings among the people about the idea, identity and role of their state. High levels of horizontal legitimacy denote a tolerant and inclusive society.

the people and the state and among 'the people' itself. These fragile states are places 'where the government cannot or will not deliver core functions to the majority of [their] people, including the poor' (Department for International Development 2005).

During the Cold War such fragile and weak states often were sustained by the patronage of external powers, notably by the hegemonic largesse of the superpowers in pursuit of perceived strategic interests in their all-encompassing bipolar contest. The universalizing dynamic of the superpower competition brought all regions and states into play, regardless of whether or not they had any impact on the global balance of power. Arguably, the superpowers aggravated state weakness. Intra-state conflicts were sustained and exacerbated 'as the superpowers sought to gain influence in the Third World by supporting groups, which in turn created a climate of instability, such as in Angola and Mozambique' (Blair and Curtis 2009, 161).

These 'quasi-states' (Jackson 1990) became still weaker in the wake of the Cold War. Elites that had been propped up by external support found that it had been withdrawn as the Soviet Union collapsed and the United States retrenched in light of the new strategic environment. Often weak and fragile states slid along the scale and became **failed states**, demonstrating that 'State failure is not, therefore, a static concept. Rather, it denotes a continuum of circumstances afflicting states with weak institutions; this continuum extends from states that do not or cannot provide basic public goods to Somalia-style collapse of governance' (Chesterman, Ignatieff and Thakur 2005, 2).

> **Failed States** – states whose internal and/or external sovereignty is severely circumscribed or non-existent.

These states may have the shell of external sovereignty but their 'stateness' is fatally compromised. They are 'juridical more than empirical entities' (Jackson 1990, 5). In such failed states, the people find themselves in a vacuum where law and order has collapsed and security is in scarce supply. The security dilemma is transposed from the state level to the intra-state level of analysis (Posen 1993). Individuals resort to their respective groups, frequently tribe, clans and ethnic groups, in their search for safety. This situation frequently proves to be conducive for the emergence of intense intra-state conflicts. Often predatory elites mobilize ethnic sentiment to maintain their position, using myths and symbols to exacerbate fears of 'the Other', and unleashing conflict behaviours that they soon cannot control (Kaufman 2006). As with Tolstoy's unhappy families – each is unhappy in its own way – so too 'failed states are not homogenous'. That said though, they tend to share a characteristic – 'more than structural or institutional weaknesses, human agency is also culpable, usually in a fatal way' (Rotberg 2006, 132).

Somalia is the archetypal failed state. In 2012, Somalia had the dubious distinction of topping the Failed States Index, compiled by the Fund for Peace, for the fifth year in a row. The Index lists 178 countries and assesses their status using 12 primary and 14 sub-indicators to measure the impact of issues such as poverty, migration, the 'brain drain', inter-group conflict, demographic pressures on resource scarcity, elite behaviour and its adverse effects on the social contract. The assessment revealed that 'At the worst end of the Index, Somalia continues to endure widespread lawlessness, ineffective government, terrorism, insurgency, crime, abysmal development and rampant piracy'. Indeed Somalia is more failed than ever as its 2012 score was 'the highest score in the history of the Index' (Messner 2012).

Weak states have always been found within the international system but in the wake of the Cold War they became increasingly securitized and a recurrent leitmotif in the security discourse of more developed states, especially in the West. In the immediate wake of the Cold

War, there had been some optimism that this 'new world order' would herald a new era of international cooperation and progress now that the bipolar competition had ended: 'A world where the United Nations, freed from cold war stalemate, is poised to fulfill the historic vision of its founders' (Bush 1991). There was triumphalism in some quarters, that such change was so momentous that it represented 'the end of history' (Fukuyama 1992). On the other hand, though, others offered much more pessimistic counsel, warning of 'the return of the repressed' (Ignatieff 1993), or, more frightening still, 'the coming anarchy' (Kaplan 1994) and a potential 'clash of civilisation' (Huntington 1996). In such a time of flux, with the disappearance of the core threat of a war between the superpowers, weak and failing states were depicted as sources of instability within the international system. The conflict paradigm had changed as interstate conflict had largely been displaced by conflict within states. Events in such 'states of concern' threatened other states, not least as people fled from conflicts into neighbouring states where their arrival could upset delicate demographic balances as well as place further demands on the destination state's resources. This was clearly illustrated when the Hutu-Tutsi conflict in Rwanda expanded into Zaire (now the Democratic Republic of the Congo) and contributed to the outbreak of civil war there. Failing states then were pathologized as sources of contagion which could undermine the stability of areas, regions and possibly the system itself. The threat was especially seen to lie in Africa, notably sub-Saharan Africa. This led to some counter claims that this securitization of weak and failing states was heavily politicized and reflected a construction of an alien 'Other' that was neither valid nor helpful. Such critics (Chandler 2006; Boas and Jennings 2007) were especially concerned that post-colonial states were being thus labelled as a prelude to intervention by Western states and other agencies.

Europe was not immune to state failure closer to home, notably that stemming from the dissolution of Yugoslavia in 1991. The consequences are still ongoing as the situation in contemporary Bosnia-Herzegovina attests. In Bosnia-Herzegovina low levels of state capacity are allied with inter-ethnic conflict. The United Nations and, increasingly, the European Union play major roles in propping up the state. Bosnia's complex constitutional architecture is a particular cause for concern. The state is split into two 'entities', the Federation of Bosnia and Herzegovina and the Republika Srpska, and the autonomous region of Brcko whose governance the entities share. Each entity has its own constitution and a significant degree of autonomy. Powersharing is evident in the Presidency of Bosnia-Herzegovina, which rotates among its three members, each representative of one of the three constituent peoples of the state: Bosniaks, Croats and Serbs. The principle of proportionality is evident in the constitutional arrangements and a proportional representation system is used to elect members to the parliament and there is a consociational government. At the apex of this complex architecture stands the High Representative for Bosnia and Herzegovina, effectively the CEO of the country and representing the core states who drew up the Dayton Peace Agreement (1995) which ended the Bosnian War. The High Representative is sovereign in the state and can overrule the parliament and remove elected representatives. The internal sovereignty of the state then is compromised. In addition, the territorial integrity of the state is frequently challenged by Serb and Croat nationalists. Bosnia-Herzegovina has weak state institutions, fractionalized political leadership, high unemployment and a poorly performing economy (International Crisis Group 2012). Arguably, the support of the international community alone is what prevents the implosion of this state, as former High Representative for Bosnia-Herzegovina, Paddy Ashdown states: 'For 10 years Bosnia was the poster boy for international relations, making steady and sometimes miraculous progress towards statehood, capable of joining the EU and NATO. For the last five years the dynamic in Bosnia has reversed itself. The centripetal forces have become centrifugal ones. The dynamic now is moving in the wrong direction' (cited in Waterfield 2011).

SECURITIZATION AND WEAK STATES

The events of 9/11 further spurred the securitization of weak and failing states. Now they were principally portrayed as hotbeds of radicalism and havens of terrorism. The security threat posed by such states was a core theme in the security strategies of core states and security actors. The United States National Security Strategy (2002) stated clearly that 'America is now threatened less by conquering states than by failing ones' (US Department of State 2002). The threat was acknowledged in the United Kingdom's National security Strategy (2008): 'In the past, most violent conflicts and significant threats to global security came from strong states. Currently most of the major threats and risks emanate from failed or fragile states' (UK NSS 2008, 14) The EU's first ever European Security Strategy (Solana 2003, 4) confirmed that 'State failure is an alarming phenomenon that undermines global governance and regional instability'. Weak and failing states were presented as anarchical, ungoverned spaces which demanded redress.

This securitization of weak and failing states was part of a wider reconceptualization of security itself. During the Cold War, realist readings of security were dominant. Security was for states and was best delivered by states using traditional politico-military means to do so. After the Cold War, this state-centric view of security was down-graded as attention shifted to other non-military forms of insecurity and threat as well as other referent objects of security rather than the state alone. Security now was seen as embracing a wider remit, including, for example, economic security, environmental security, political security and social security (Buzan, Waever and Wilde 1998). The referent object – who or what is to be made secure – expanded too. Security referents now were to be found below the level of the state, for example groups or individuals, as well as across states. Providing security was no longer seen as the preserve of states but included too institutional actors at the regional and international levels too.

This new thinking led to the concept of **human security**. Instead of the primacy of the state, this view of security stresses the centrality of the individual. People mattered more. This was not an entirely new theme in the security discourse. Ever since the close of World War II there had been developments in the realm of human rights at the expense of the state's position. The criminal tribunals at Nuremberg and Tokyo signalled that no one could hide behind the state and go unpunished for gross

> **Human Security** – a concept that stresses the multi-dimensional nature of security and sees the individual/group as the core security referent.

violations of human rights. Subsequent documents such as the United Nations Declaration (1948), the Convention on the Prevention and Punishment of the Crime of Genocide (1948) and the Geneva Convention (1949) clearly conveyed the premise that individual rights were worthy of promotion and protection. The overriding concern of human security then is to facilitate the positioning of 'the security of the individual on the same level as the security of the state' (Oberleitner 2005, 197). This positioning can be accommodated within the Westphalian system but it has implications for state sovereignty, though as Axworthy (2001) notes, such challenges to the state are nothing new as 'The world had no idea what sovereignty and the security infrastructure would look like immediately following the signing of the Treaty of Westphalia. Norms evolved through decades of debate, thought, action, conflict and compromise'.

The idea of human security appeared in a United Nations Development Programme (UNDP) Human Development Report in 1994, though its lineage can be traced through earlier reports stemming from the Brandt Commission, the Palme Commission and the Brundtland Commission respectively. Despite its salience in both academic and policy making circles, human security, like so many other concepts in international politics, is heavily contested. The Human Development Report (1994) puts people and their development at the core of security concerns. Socio-economic inequalities and under-development are seen as a multilevel source of insecurity, present within and between states and societies, as they threaten the multi-dimensional aspects of security: 'For most people today, a feeling of insecurity arises more from worries about daily life than from the dread of a cataclysmic world event. Job security, income security, health security, environmental security, security from crime – these are the emerging concerns of security all over the world' (UNDP 1994, 3). Ultimately human security 'is a concern with human life and dignity' (UNDP 1994, 229).

This expansive understanding of security attracted, and still attracts, criticism on the grounds that it includes so much that it is difficult to understand how any of it could be realized. Paris (2001) indeed went so far as to wonder whether the matter constituted a 'paradigm shift or hot air'. Despite such debate the idea of human security gained traction on the international political agenda, pushed by some academic, international institutions and 'middle-level' governments such as those of Norway and Canada. It was acknowledged that in the modern world, full of trans-sovereign challenges such as international terrorism, nuclear proliferation, environmental degradation, poverty, transnational organized crime and global health risks, states could not be effective unless they worked together and with non-state actors.

The focus then was not on defending the state, but on helping the state to better deliver security to its people in an increasingly interdependent, multi-centric world. Not only was the state now seen as struggling to meet the security needs of its people, but, in some cases, the state was seen as the chief source of their insecurity. In situations where the state has turned on its people and become the chief threat to their safety and wellbeing, then the sovereignty of that transgressor state can be abrogated and the international community can intervene in its internal affairs. This argument that there is a **humanitarian imperative** that not only allows but demands action by the international community is further evidence of the changing role of the state on the world stage. Recognition of the sovereignty of states was merited 'not because they are intrinsically good but because

> **Humanitarian Imperative** – the argument that a state unable/unwilling to protect and promote the human rights of its people has violated the right to non-intervention. The needs and security of the people trump the sovereignty of the state.

they are necessary to achieve the dignity, justice, worth and safety of their citizens' (UN 2004, 17) In cases where states default on this duty then the international community would intervene on the grounds of 'the emerging norm that there is a collective responsibility to protect … in the event of genocide and other large-scale killing, ethnic cleansing or serious violations of international humanitarian law which sovereign Governments have proved powerless or unwilling to prevent' (UN 2004, 66).

CHALLENGES TO THE STATE

State sovereignty then is not a right but a privilege that the state must continue to earn by looking after the welfare of its people. The normative environment in which states exist and act is changing. In the late 1990s, the war in Kosovo marked a turning point when the increasingly vocal rhetoric on human rights and the need for states to protect and promote them was matched by action. Yugoslav President Slobodan Milosevic was harshly repressing the ethnic Albanian campaign for independence for Kosovo. When international efforts to reach a diplomatic resolution to the conflict appeared to be failing, NATO intervened through a series of air strikes against targets in both Kosovo and Serbia. Throughout these events there was a campaign of ethnic cleansing against the Albanian Kosovars. After almost three months of bombing, Milosevic withdrew his forces and Kosovo was placed under United Nations administration. During the bombing campaign Milosevic was indicted for crimes against humanity by the International War Crimes Tribunal at The Hague – the first serving head of state to be so indicted. NATO's intervention was not authorized by the United Nations Security Council (UNSC), creating a debate over the legitimacy of its action. Whilst accepting the intervention was not legal given the absence of a UNSC mandate, its supporters claimed that it was morally justified as the international community had a duty to be in the business of 'saving strangers' (Wheeler 2000). There was a higher duty than to respect the sovereignty of the state. State sovereignty was no longer absolute – if indeed it ever had been: 'The time for absolute and exclusive sovereignty, however, has passed; its theory was never matched by reality' (Boutros-Ghali 1992). The Responsibility to Protect (R2P) norm has continued to evolve with notable articulations to be found in the respective reports of the International Commission on Intervention and State Sovereignty (ICISS) (2001), Secretary-General Annan's commissioned High-Level panel on Threats, Challenges and Change (2004) and the UN's World Summit (2005). All have endorsed this norm of 'sovereignty as responsibility'.

The pace of norm evolution is slow, however, and state sovereignty seems to be more contingent for some states than others. As ever, the more powerful states in the system have proven rather more resilient to the 'unpacking' of sovereignty, further supporting Krasner's thesis of 'organized hypocrisy' (Krasner 1999). After the 9/11 attacks, a more statist interpretation of both security and national sovereignty started to reassert itself, not least as evidenced in the actions of the unilateralist Bush administration. Its pursuit of a 'war on terror', to be executed primarily, and, at times, apparently exclusively, through the use of hard power, has arguably undermined the case for norm change and more inclusive understandings of security and its referent objects. The expansion of the war into Iraq was notable not for its primary, heavily contested, rationale of finding and destroying Weapons of Mass Destruction but for its secondary rationale concerning democratization and human rights. As the war expanded and extended, complete with continued human suffering and documented instances of human rights abuses by the intervening coalition, the credibility of the United States and the United Kingdom as 'norm carriers' has been eroded. The reassertion of state sovereignty has been expressly and strongly defended by the weaker states in the system too, reflective of their concern that they could be next in line for intervention.

The leaders of such states charge that interventions are made under the guise of humanitarian concern but, in reality, constitute the pursuit of neo-imperialist ambitions by powerful states (Ayoob 2010). Even when such interventions have UNSC authorization, there remains disquiet as such institutions are seen as dominated by the strongest states: 'We do not deny that the United Nations has the right and the duty to help suffering humanity, but we remain extremely sensitive to any undermining of our sovereignty, not only because sovereignty is the last defense [sic] against the rules of an unequal world, but because we are not taking part in the decision-making process of the Security Council' (Algerian President Abdelakia Bouteflika quoted in Newland, Patrick and Zard 2003, 37).

The international political stage is a very crowded place and states are only one member of the expanding cast of actors. They now share the limelight with non-state actors such as transnational corporations, non-governmental organizations, international institutions, regional institutions, regimes, transnational movements and so on. The realist depiction of international politics as a game of billiard balls no longer holds – if it ever did. The actorness of states occurs within a context of multilevel governance, with sites of authority and representation above and below the state.

The divide between the internal and the external realms of politics has become blurred with the rise of 'intermestic' **trans-sovereign issues** and the permeability of the state to external forces and pressures. National governments must work with other governments and non-state actors to better meet the economic, political and societal demands of their peoples. States have had to learn to 'share' or 'pool' their sovereignty on matters of common interest. This can clearly be seen in the workings of the European Union, where, in some issue areas, European law takes precedence over

> **Trans-sovereign Issues** – these are matters that cross state borders and permeate societies and cannot be effectively addressed by unilateral action. Examples of such issues are environmental degradation, global health threats and unauthorized migration.

national legislation. That said, in matters of national defence and traditional security concerns, states still jealously guard their sovereignty as can be seen by the intergovernmentalist nature of decision-making in areas such as the Common Foreign and Security Policy. Internally also the state has changed, as demands from below result in greater devolution or decentralization of power, especially in the case of the more economically developed states. Internal and external change has resulted in the 'hollowing out' of the state (Jessop 1990) in that some of its functions have passed to other political actors.

Such developments have led some to the conclusion that the state is dying away in this globalized and globalizing world. There are claims that we are witnessing 'the end of the nation-state' in this increasingly 'borderless world' (Ohmae 1995; 1999) as while 'On the political map, the boundaries between countries are as clear as ever … on the competitive map, a map showing the real flows of financial and industrial activity, those boundaries have largely disappeared' (Ohmae 1995, 7). Recent announcements of statehood by Kosovo and South Sudan respectively, and campaigns for statehood by Kurds, Basques and Palestinians, among many others, however, evidence the continuing pull of the state in the allegedly post-territorial, post-Westphalian world.

Ultimately however, the more things change, the more they stay the same. The state has never existed in a vacuum. It has never been the only actor on the world stage. The staying power of the state – its adaptability and its resilience – should not be underestimated. The state shares the world stage with other actors but it still has a central part in the drama of international politics. Indeed, many of those other actors are vehicles for states to continue to deliver their lines. Almost 40 years ago, Krasner explained that the state had been 'multinationalized, transnationalized, bureaucratized and transgovernmentalized' but still remained a powerful construct within the study of international relations (Krasner 1976, 317). In this first decade of the twenty-first century, the curtain has not yet fallen on the state: 'It is an epoch of multiple contradictions … States are changing but they are not disappearing. State sovereignty has eroded, but it is still vigorously asserted. Governments are weaker, but they can still throw their weight around … Borders still keep out intruders but they are also more porous. Landscapes are giving way to ethnoscapes, mediascapes, ideoscapes, technoscapes, and financescapes, but territoriality is still a central preoccupation to many people' (Rosenau 1998, 18).

QUESTIONS FOR REFLECTION

1. Is globalization eroding state sovereignty?
2. When can we say a state has failed?
3. Are 'humanitarian interventions' really humanitarian?
4. Should state sovereignty be conditional on good governance?
5. Has the realist approach to international politics any relevance in an age of global governance?

REVISION QUIZ

1. What is NOT a feature of a state?

   a. Demarcated territory
   b. UN recognition
   c. Government
   d. Sovereignty

2. Which treaty established the contemporary state system?

   a. The Treaty of Westphalia
   b. The Maastricht Treaty
   c. The Treaty of Rome
   d. The Treaty of Versailles

3. Which level of analysis focuses on the relative power of states and their interactions with each other?

   a. Global
   b. Interstate
   c. Regional
   d. National

4. Which of the following is NOT a core assumption of Realism?

    a. The primacy of international law
    b. International anarchy
    c. State centrism
    d. State egotism

5. Which of the following is NOT a trans-sovereign issue?

    a. Transnational organized crime
    b. Nuclear proliferation
    c. Environmental degradation
    d. Smoking policy

6. Which of the following is NOT a feature of a failed state?

    a. Internal lawlessness
    b. Diplomatic recognition
    c. A highly functioning government
    d. A monarch

7. An institution whose members are states is known as:

    a. International Governmental Organization (IGO)
    b. Transnational Corporation (TNC)
    c. Non-Governmental Organization (NGO)
    d. International Non Governmental Organization (INGO)

8. What is a post-colonial state?

    a. A state that had a colony
    b. A state that remains a colony
    c. A state that was a colony
    d. A state that wanted a colony

9. What is international anarchy?

    a. There is no sovereign above the level of the state
    b. There is no governance within the international system
    c. International chaos
    d. The primacy of human rights

10. What is vertical legitimacy?

    a. When less powerful states obey more powerful states

b. When people within a state believe that they belong together
c. When people within a state acknowledge the state's right to rule
d. When international institutions intervene in a state

Answers: 1: c; 2: a; 3: b; 4: a; 5: d; 6: c; 7: a; 8: c; 9: a; 10: c.

BIBLIOGRAPHY

Andersen, B. (1983) *Imagined Communities – Reflections on the Origin and Spread of Nationalism* (London: Verso).

Axworthy, L. (November 2001) Comments to the UBC Human Security Graduate Course (Vancouver, BC: LIU Institute for Global Issues).

Ayoob, M. (2010) 'Making Sense of Global Tensions: Dominant and Subaltern Conceptions of Order and Justice in the International System', *International Studies* 47 (2–4), 129–41.

Blair, A. and Curtis, S. (2009) *International Politics: An Introductory Guide* (Edinburgh: Edinburgh University Press).

Boas M. and Jennings, K.M. (2007) 'Failed States and State Failure: Threats or Opportunities?' *Globalizations*, 4(4), 475–85.

Boutros-Ghali, B. (1992) An Agenda for Peace – Preventative Diplomacy, Peacemaking and Peacekeeping, Report of the Secretary General. UN Doc.A/47/277-S/24111. http://www.unrol.org/files/A_47_277.pdf

Bush, G.H.W. (1991) Address Before a Joint Session of Congress on the End of the Gulf War. http://millercenter. org/president/speeches/detail/3430.

Buzan, B., Wæver, O. and de Wilde, J. (1998) *Security: A New Framework for Analysis* (Boulder, CO: Lynne Rienner Publishers).

Chandler, D. (2006) *Empire in Denial: The Politics of State-Building* (London: Pluto Press).

Chester, S., Ignatieff, M. and Thakur, R. (2005) 'Introduction: Making States Work'. In S. Chesterman, M. Ignatieff and R. Thakur (eds), *Making States Work: State Failure and the Crisis of Governance* (Tokyo: United Nations University Press), 1–10.

Department for International Development (2005) Drivers of Fragility: What Makes States Fragile? http://www.dfid.gov.uk/documents/fragile/drivers-fragility.pdf.

Fukuyama, F. (1992) *The End of History and the Last Man* (New York: The Free Press).

Holsti, K.J. (2004) *Taming the Sovereigns: Institutional Change in International Politics* (Cambridge: Cambridge University Press).

Holsti K.J. (1999) 'The Coming Chaos? Armed Conflict in the World's Periphery'. In J.A. Hall and T.V. Paul (eds), *International Order and the Future of World Politics* (Cambridge: Cambridge University Press), 283–310.

Holsti, K.J. (1996) *The State, War, and the State of War* (Cambridge: Cambridge University Press).

Huntington, S.P. (1996) *The Clash of Civilizations and the Remaking of the World Order* (New York: Simon & Schuster).

Ignatieff, M. (1993) *Blood and Belonging: Journeys into the New Nationalism* (Toronto: Viking).

International Commission on Intervention and State Sovereignty (2001) The Responsibility to Protect. Ottawa: ICISS http://responsibilitytoprotect.org/ICISS%20Report.pdf.

International Crisis Group (2012) Policy briefing: Europe Briefing No.68 Bosnia's Gordian Knot: Constitutional Reform.http://www.crisisgroup.org/~/media/Files/europe/balkans/bosnia-herzegovina/b068-bosnias-gordian-knot-constitutional-reform.pdf.

Jackson, R. (1990) *Quasi-States: Sovereignty, International Relations and the Third World* (Cambridge: Cambridge University Press).

Jessop, B. (1990) *State Theory: Putting the Capitalist State in its Place* (University Park, PA; Pennsylvania State University Press).

Kaplan, R. (1994) 'The Coming Anarchy', *The Atlantic Monthly* 273, 44–76.

Kaufman, S.J. (2006) 'Symbolic Politics or Rational Choice? Testing Theories of Extreme Ethnic Violence', *International Security* 30(4), 45–86.

Krasner, S. (1999) *Sovereignty: Organized Hypocrisy* (Princeton, NJ: Princeton University Press).

Mann, M. (1999) 'Has Globalization Ended the Rise and Rise of the Nation-State?' In J.A. Hall and T.V. Paul (eds), *International Order and the Future of World Politics* (Cambridge: Cambridge University Press), 237–61.

Messner, J.J. (2012) Failed States Index: Change is the Only Constant, http://ffp.statesindex.org/.

Newland, K., Patrick, K. and Zard, M. (2003) *No Refuge: The Challenge of Internal Displacement* (New York: United Nations University Press).

Oberleitner, G. (2005) 'Human security: A Challenge to International Law?' *Global Governance*, 11, 185–203.

Ohmae, K. (1995) *The Borderless World: Power and Strategy in an Interlinked World* (New York: HarperCollins).

Ohmae, K. (1999) *The Borderless World: Power and Strategy in an Interlinked Economy* (New York: HarperCollins).

Paris, R. (2001) 'Human Security: Paradigm Shift or Hot Air?' *International Security* 26(2), 87–102.

Posen, B.R. (1993) 'The Security Dilemma and Ethnic Conflict', *Survival* 35(1), 27–47.

Rosenau, J.N. (1998) *Along the Domestic-Foreign Frontier: Exploring Governance in a Turbulent World* (Cambridge: Cambridge University Press).

Rotberg, R.I. (2006) 'Failed States in a World of Terror'. In R.W. Mansbach and E. Rhodes (eds), *Global Politics in a Changing World: A Reader*, 3rd edition (Boston, MA: Houghton Mifflin), 131–7.

Solana, J. (2003) A Secure Europe in a Better World. European Security Strategy, http://www.consilium.europa.eu/uedocs/cmsUpload/78367.pdf.

Spruyt, H. (1994) *The Sovereign State and Its Competitors: An Analysis of Systems Change* (Princeton, NJ: Princeton University Press).

Storey, D. (2001) *Territory: The Claiming of Space* (London: Prentice Hall).

Tilly, C. (1975) *The Formation of National States in Western Europe* (Princeton, NJ: Princeton University Press).

United Kingdom National Security Strategy (2008) The National Security Strategy of the United Kingdom: Security in an Interdependent World. Norwich: Her majesty's Stationary Office.

United States Department of State (2002) The National Security Strategy of the United States of America, http://www.state.gov/documents/organization/63562.pdf.

United Nations (2004) High-level Panel on Threats, Challenges and Change, A More Secure World: Our Shared Responsibility, http://www.un.org/secureworld/report2.pdf.

United Nations (1945) Charter of the United Nations. http://www.un.org/en/documents/charter/index.shtml

United Nations Development Programme (1994) *Human Development Report* (New York: Oxford University Press).

Waterfield, B. (2011, May 27) Bloodshed to return to Bosnia, Paddy Ashdown fears. *The Telegraph*, http://www.telegraph.co.uk/news/worldnews/europe/serbia/8541578/Bloodshed-to-return-to-Bosnia-Paddy-Ashdown-fears.html.

Wheeler, N. (2000) *Saving Strangers: Humanitarian Intervention in International Society* (Oxford: Oxford University Press).

Chapter 6
Individuals in International Politics

DAVID WALTON

The role of individuals and the concept of individual agency is one of the most problematic and contentious areas in the study of global politics. A number of key questions immediately come to mind: Do individuals make a difference? If so, under what circumstances and, importantly, how do we quantify the impact of individuals on the global, domestic or local stage? How do international relations theories view the role of the individual? This chapter will address these questions and provide background information to understand and appreciate contending arguments and perspectives on the relationship between the individual and the nation-state. To assist in this process, dilemma boxes, which highlight key debates and issues, are dispersed throughout the chapter. For example, dilemmas such United States Presidential Executive Orders on assassination of foreign leaders and the impact of controversial Latin American figures Fidel Castro and Hugo Chávez in international affairs have been included. As well, a series of tables have been added to clarify and highlight the foreign policy decision-making process.

Students will gain insight into the role the environment and type of government play in determining the level and extent of influence possible by an individual. The chapter also offers examples of transformational individuals with very different backgrounds and the making of foreign policy in the post-1945 period. Accordingly, the role of leader and the decision-making process will be assessed and crucially the type of government and impact on the role of individuals and the decision-making process will be analysed. Key models explaining foreign policy decision-making such as the Rational Actor, Bureaucratic and Cognitive models are discussed. Finally, an assessment on how international relation theories used in this textbook view the individual agency will be provided. It will be argued that realist, liberalists and constructivists have contending views on the role of the individual and that critical approaches (which tend to be outside the mainstream view) tend to be more supportive of individual agency.

Key Words: Individual Agency, Arab Spring, Bureaucratic Politics, Rational Actor, Pluralistic Societies, Cognitive Model, Constructivism, Gender Neutral.

Chapter 6

Individuals in International Politics

DAVID WALTON

INTRODUCTION

The role of individuals in international politics is a fascinating area of study. There are many examples of individuals making a substantial impact on international affairs as leaders, activists and sometime unintentional triggers for worldwide transformation. Consider the following three examples.

In July 1996 South African President Nelson Mandela gave a speech to an estimated audience of one million people in central London. Mandela was (and remains) an international symbol of hope. His fight for equality and justice in Apartheid South Africa led to his imprisonment for 27 years (1963–1990). Upon release, Mandela was able to negotiate with South African President F.W. de Klerk to abolish **Apartheid** as part of a peaceful transition to full democracy for which he and de Klerk were awarded the 1993 **Nobel Peace Prize**. The following year (1994) Mandela became South Africa's first black President in the first fully democratic election held in that country. Only two years later he was in England as part of a European lecture tour. The arrival of such a significant figure created a highly charged atmosphere throughout London and his speech received a rapturous response from an adoring audience. Mandela remained a revered elder statesman for his country and for

> **Apartheid** – separation of people based on race or caste.
>
> **Nobel Peace Prize** – one of five prizes created by Swedish inventor, industrialist and armaments manufacturer Alfred Nobel.

the fight for equality worldwide until his death on 5 December 2013. Indeed towards the end of his life, Mandela's health status and visits to the hospital received global media attention. The state funeral, subsequent mourning in South Africa and the arrival of world leaders paying their last respects was a fitting end for one of the most extraordinary figures in world history.

In an extraordinary chain of events in 2010, the actions of Mohammed Bouazizi, a lowly 26-year-old market trader in Tunisia, triggered the collapse of a corrupt regime and a movement in the Arab world that has led to a chain of revolutions in Tunisia, Egypt and Libya and bloody civil war in Syria. On 17 December that year, Bouazizi claimed that an official had slapped him over a petty issue and set himself on fire in protest of what he saw was an oppressive and corrupt regime. As noted in the *Observer* newspaper, his suicide, borne out of frustration with authoritarian rule, highlighted Bouazizi as the ordinary man struggling to make a living against a uniformed symbol of a corrupt regime (Day 2011). His death led to spontaneous anti-government protests throughout the country on a massive scale. Within 28 days, the President of Tunisia had fled

> **Arab Spring** – uprisings and protests that began in December 2010 demanding greater levels of democracy and more transparency in politics across the Middle East.

to Saudi Arabia and the country started the **Arab Spring** which then swept the Arab world.

Julian Assange has been hailed as a hero of the free press and alternatively as an attention-seeking opportunist. He is the founder of WikiLeaks, which has released, and continues to release, thousands of confidential US intelligence and embassy information reports to several prominent global newspapers including *The Guardian*, *The New York Times* and *Der Spiegel*. The information, which ranges from top secret views on leaders to banal and trivial embassy reports, was passed on by US Private Bradley Manning, who is now facing **treason** charges in the United States.

> **Treason** – act of betraying one's own country

A critical issue in the Assange case has been the reason behind releasing what is regarded as the biggest leak of diplomatic correspondence in diplomatic history. Assange argues that he is an online activist advocating for freedom of the press and is passionate about fighting censorship and supporting the public right to access information. The counter argument is that Assange is a publicity-hungry individual, guilty of 'aiding the enemy and endangering lives' by organising the publication of sensitive material not meant for public distribution that can be read by anyone with an Internet connection (Harrrell 2010). At the time of writing, Assange remains a high-profile person who, since 19 June 2012, is being forced to reside in the Ecuadorian Embassy in central London to avoid facing a trial in Sweden for alleged sexual assault.

> 'The biggest misdeed Mr. Assange exposed did not concern the informational substance of the data package, but the fact that the U.S. report management system is far too integrated, allowing confidential documents to be downloaded by Bradley Manning, a 23-year-old army private'. (Richter 2011)

Should he leave the embassy, he will be arrested by British police and extradited to Sweden. Assange and his supporters are convinced that he will then face the prospect of extradition from Sweden to the United States to face trial on treason charges, which carries the possibility of the death penalty or life imprisonment.

Mandela's ability to influence events in South Africa and across the globe, Bouazazi's suicide and subsequent uprisings in the Arab world (which has global implications) and Assange's role as the founder of WikiLeaks raise some of the big questions in international politics: Is the decision-making process prone to the idiosyncrasies of individuals? Could one person have so much influence on the outcome in world history? What role do individuals play in foreign policy/international relations? How do we evaluate the role of individual agency? This chapter will examine these issues with special reference to the role of individuals in leadership positions and how international relations theories view the question of individual agency.

LEADERSHIP

Media coverage of international events tends to focus our attention on world leaders. Not a day goes by without coverage of a President, Prime Minister or Foreign Minister signing an agreement or attempting to broker a deal to resolve an international impasse. Understandably, there is a tendency to assume that all events are determined, or at the very least heavily influenced, by leaders as key actors in the decision-making process.

There are compelling reasons to focus on leaders. For example, what if Democratic Presidential candidate Al Gore won the November 2000 Presidential election instead of George

W. Bush? The election campaign between them was very close. Indeed Gore won the majority of votes but Bush just managed to receive sufficient electoral college votes to claim the presidency after the Supreme Court ruled in his favour on the disputed Florida balloting. What if Gore had become President? A key distinction on foreign policy matters between a Gore and Bush administration would have been policy towards Iraq. The invasion plan for Iraq was legitimised by the Bush administration on the basis that Iraqi leader Saddam Hussein had close links with terrorist group al-Qaeda and that the Iraqi regime was assembling nuclear weapons and other **weapons of mass destruction** and was, therefore, a threat to US and security in the region and globally. No evidence has been produced to support these claims. Unlike the George W. Bush administration, which had senior members of Cabinet and advisor who served under President George H. Bush and were involved in '**Desert Storm**'
in 1990, an Al Gore Presidency would have had no past baggage in relation to Iraq and would have been far less likely to have been influenced by the neo-conservative agenda to ensure American dominance in the Persian Gulf.

It would be reasonable to assume, therefore, that a Gore administration would most likely have had a more nuanced foreign policy approach to the **War on Terror**; with much more attention on stabilising Afghanistan and Pakistan through multilateral arrangements thereby securing international support and cooperation. The implications of the Bush 2000 election victory are quite stark. A recent study of the

> **Weapons of Mass Destruction** – weapons (nuclear, chemical, or biological) that cause indiscriminate death or injury on a large scale.
>
> **Desert Storm** – code name for a massive US-led military campaign to drive Iraqi forces out of Kuwait (1991).
>
> **War on Terror** – a campaign by the United States and allies to fight terrorist organisations aligned with al-Qaeda as a result of the September 11, 2001 attacks on the United States.
>
> **Iraq War** (2003–11) – US-led occupation of Iraq and subsequent civil war.

cost of the **Iraq War** by Barry S. Levy and Victor W. Sidel estimated that more than 116,903 Iraqi non-combatants and more than 4,800 coalition military personnel have died so far. In addition to the injuries and mental stress of the ongoing conflict on Iraqis and coalition forces, an estimated 5 million people have been displaced (Levy and Sidel 2013, 949–58). The cost of the war on the US economy is mind-boggling. Estimates, including substantial costs for veterans care up to 2053, suggest that the war will cost approximately 2.2 trillion US dollars (Watson Institute for International Studies 2013).

How do we deal with this conundrum of a very different international system and US foreign policy under a Gore administration? In a response, it is worth noting that there are fundamental issues that need to be examined when discussing these problematic issues. For example, not all leaders have the same level of influence or role in the decision-making process. As well, a leader may have the disposition but not the opportunity to pursue foreign policy as he/she desires. Or indeed the reverse: leaders may have the opportunity to pursue a particular foreign policy goal, but not the disposition to do so. It is also worth noting that hundreds of decisions are made each day within bureaucracies designed to deal with day-to-day foreign policy-related issues. In other words, only issues deemed to be of high importance will receive

> **Bureaucratic Politics** – the contest for resources and influence amongst government departments.

the attention of the senior decision-makers and subsequently head of government. This filtering process means that decisions are made on a subjective basis and subject to bureaucratic politics. In many respects it is fair to argue that the process of decision-making can be flawed as a result of human error, misunderstandings or a set of belief systems that ensure leaders follow a particular line of logic. As indicated in Table 6.1 below, history is replete with examples of foreign policy blunders and miscalculations based on bias, poor information and lack of time to come to a carefully thought through decision.

Table 6.1   Foreign policy decision-making

Foreign Policy Ideal	Foreign Policy Reality
Decisions are made with ample time for reflection and discussion among all constituents. Final decisions are based on thorough and exhaustive analysis.	Decisions are often made on the run, with insufficient time for careful discussion. There are ongoing requirements to respond to multiple issues from state and non-state actors.
A wide range of expert reports are analysed and taken into consideration during final decision-making.	Reports are requested but are selected on the basis of confirming already established beliefs. Leaders determine policy based on beliefs, values and established perceptions of the external environment.

Dilemma: Environmental Determinists vs. Hero in History

An age-old debate in the study of leadership is the role leaders play in world events. In particular, do leaders shape the environment or are they themselves a product of the environment?

Environmental determinists argue that the international and domestic environment will heavily influence foreign policy decisions. As a consequence, environmental determinists argue that world leaders are essentially responding to their political environment when they make policy. In this context, leaders are the result of their 'Zeitgeist' (world around them) and therefore rise to the occasion in time of crisis.

Supporters of the 'Hero or Villain in History' approach by contrast argue that a dynamic leader emerges and through their forceful personality, personal disposition and approach to international affairs, alters the course of history and shapes the international environment.

Consider, for example, if Adolf Hitler had never existed. How would this have affected the political landscape of Germany and Europe? Could the carnage of World War II and millions of deaths have been avoided? Certainly it can be argued that the aftermath of World War I for Germany (including a 'hard peace' settlement with reparations) and a severe global economic depression would have provided the conditions for social and political unrest in Germany and allowed the fascist movement to become a powerful political force by the late 1920s. The key question however is, would the environment have created another leader similar to Hitler? Or was Hitler's family background and experiences a critical factor in shaping his personality, idiosyncrasies and worldview? If this is the case, the role of the 'hero-in-history' deserves considerable attention. On the other hand, if the environment shapes leaders and how they deal with a crisis, there is a compelling argument that a fascist leader would have carried out similar policies to Hitler with the same consequences for Europe and world order.

One thing is for certain; the issue of whether the individual or the environment is more important is highly contentious.

FOREIGN POLICY CONSIDERATIONS

As noted by Kal Holsti, foreign policy considerations are complex and there are a number of variables that must be considered. Below are tables with key variables based on Holsti's seminal work. The concepts are a useful tool in evaluating the process of decision-making.

Factors that influence foreign policy deliberations

Orientations – Dispositions of states to the international environment
Roles – Decision-makers' views of states' main functions in international affairs
Objectives – Reflect a state's aspirations for the future in the system
Actions – Foreign policy means such as diplomacy, propaganda, economic weapons and use of military force.

Kal Holsti (1989)

To reconcile the issue of the impact of individual leaders and foreign policy, therefore, it is necessary to consider the domestic structures such as the type of government and be aware of the external environment, as states do not exist in a vacuum and respond to a variety of other state and non-state actors objectives and actions. As well, it is necessary to examine key foreign policy decision-making models to assist in determining the role leaders might play. Table 6.2 below highlights the impact the type of government has on the foreign policy process. Two main types have been chosen: constitutional democracy (representative government) and autocratic rule (authoritarian or totalitarian) to demonstrate the different responses.

Table 6.2   Type of government and foreign policy

Time to make a decision

Autocratic – typically a few elites determine policy. The process is usually fast and implemented quickly.
Constitutional Democracy – typically slower than in autocratic governments as the executive in government make decisions on behalf of the nation but needs to consult with a wide range of actors.

Range of constituencies to consult

Autocratic – few if any.
Constitutional Democracy – can be many and varied.

Level of influence of public opinion, specific interest groups and mass media

Autocratic – low level.
Constitutional Democracy – high level. All three groups may play a strong role in policy outcomes through lobbying the government and in determining who is allowed to participate.

Level of influence of key individuals in decision-making

Autocratic – high.
Constitutional Democracy – medium, leaders have influence but are subject to organised interest groups, public opinion and preferences.

KEY MODELS USED TO UNDERSTAND THE ROLE OF DECISION-MAKERS

Rational Actor Model

The rational actor model provides an explanation for decision-making, but remains highly contentious. In essence, the model outlines the sequences of foreign policy that are processed through identifiable machinery within the state. Decisions to follow one course of action rather than another are based on a cost/benefits analysis; decision-makers assess the problem and order their competing values and goals as part of the deliberation and final policy outcome. As part of this process they identify alternatives, list the consequences of these alternatives and then compare the alternatives with the goals to be achieved. The assumption the model makes is that leaders of other nation-states are 'rational actors' and as such their decisions will be based on rational choices within their states' national interests. According to this approach, decision-makers in one country can cut across political, cultural and linguistic divides to accurately anticipate how decision-makers in another country will respond to a particular foreign policy endeavour.

An underlying assumption within the model is that nations speak with one voice in terms of preferred values and goals. Clearly, this is problematic. In **pluralistic societies** (such as constitutional democracies as demonstrated in Table 6.1) for example, there are multiple interest groups articulating their interests and competing for attention. Within government, moreover, there are different organisations and individuals with views on particular issues.

> **Pluralistic Societies** – societies where political parties and multiple interest groups compete for power.

As per Table 6.1, another major flaw with the rational actor model is time limits on making a decision. Due to competing pressures, there is not always time to ponder over issues to ensure the best possible outcome. Indeed, the constant flow of information and the requirement to make policy in response to the actions of other nations or non-state actors effectively means that it is not feasible to achieve a 'model outcome'.

Scrutinising an inscrutable leader

As Secretary of State John Kerry landed in Seoul for talks with South Korean officials on Friday, his staffers were frank about the uncertainty. 'Number one, we don't really have real insights to what is going on and what we see is from our side', one official told journalists travelling with Mr Kerry from London. He continued that if you understand Korean culture, and North Koreans' regard for older leaders as well as the primary of the military in their system, 'it is difficult to believe that a 29, 30 year-old would have complete control over bureaucracy, over military, over giving orders, thinking about what those orders mean', the official said. 'And so at what level of decision making Kim Jong-un actually says this is the way to go, whether it is at the bottom or at the top, but certainly the name of Kim Jong-un is being used' as the source of decisions, he said. Lacking direct access to North Korea, American officials have depended heavily on South Korea and on China, the North's only real ally, chief trading partner and financial benefactor, for insight. But the Chinese are also having trouble getting through. A senior American official told me last week that the Chinese had described Mr Kim as immature and brash. It seems that neither Bejing, nor Mr Kim's ostensible handlers in Pyongyang, have the leader under control.

Carol Giocomo, *New York Times*, 13 April 2013

If we apply the rational actor model to tensions with North Korea in 2013, the limitations with the model become apparent. On 17 February 2013, the United Nations Security Council strongly criticised and placed sanctions on the North Korean government for conducting a nuclear missile test. The leader of North Korea, Kim Jong Un, responded by cutting ties with South Korea and threatening to launch rockets with nuclear warheads at targets in South Korea, Hawaii and mainland United States. These provocative actions by the North Korean regime have serious consequences for regional and global stability. In applying the rational actor model, it would be assumed that the belligerent announcements and threats to launch an attack would most likely suggest that leader Kim Jong Un is shoring up his domestic support base (particularly with the military elite) and wanting to receive economic concessions in return for ending the

North Korean nuclear program. Further analysis would suggest that it would not be in the national interest of North Korea to launch rockets as the response by the United States would be catastrophic and, therefore, the level of probability of rockets being launched is very low. The problem with this analysis is that we are assuming that the leadership in North Korea is operating as rational actors. The issue of rationality is problematic in a country cut off from the international community and facing serious economic hardships. The potential for the country to implode as a result of severe authoritarian rule and chronic food shortages allows for a wider range of possibilities including launching missiles as a last act of defiance as the country falls into civil war or implodes. Notably, little is known about Kim Jong-Un (unlike his father and grandfather). This uncertainty factor and lack of knowledge about the current leader dilutes the predictability of the model in anticipating a 'rational' response.

Bureaucratic Model

The bureaucratic model focuses on the government machine and the organisations and political actors involved in the decision-making process. Polices, according to this model, are based on a combination of the bargaining process among organisations/departments and the role of individuals in prominent positions to influence the final outcome. An analysis that applied this approach would involve close scrutiny of which governmental organisations are the most powerful and how competing interests are combined to produce decisions and actions.

There are several inter-related points of interest with this model that highlight the difficulty of producing effective policy free of **self-interest**. In particular, parochial priorities and perceptions affect the quality of policy produced. Notably, each organisation is focused on the narrow range of issues emanating from the central budget allocation and subsequent resource allocations, including money and people. Within this framework, it is logical for the organisation to want to showcase itself in the best light possible to decision-makers to ensure further expansion and growth. As power is viewed as the main factor to determine player impact, the most powerful departments in the bureaucracy will have substantial influence on policy outcomes.

> **Self-interest** – personal gain rather than collective gain.

As a result of this culture, departments will tend to produce reports that will protect their interests and attempt to prevent decision-makers from selecting options from other departments. In extreme cases, the department may hold up, modify and even defy directives in order to promote departmental interests. In the United States, the most celebrated example involves competition for resources and attention of the 'Presidential ear' is between the State Department and the Defence Department. During the George W. Bush presidency, Secretary of Defence, Donald Rumsfeld, wielded enormous power and as a result of the 'War on Terror' his department grew substantially. In Australia, the key bureaucratic rivalry on foreign affairs issues has been between the Department of Foreign Affairs and Trade, Department of Defence and Office of National Assessments. As a means of receiving credible and reliable information, the Prime Minister also has his own foreign policy specialists within his Department of Prime Minister and Cabinet.

A classic example of information being modified involved the case made by Secretary of State Colin Powell to the United Nations Security Council on 3 February 2003. In essence, Powell presented evidence that the Saddam Hussein regime in Iraq had weapons of mass destruction and had mobile chemical warfare laboratories as justification for a US-led intervention and removal of the Hussein regime. The evidence was used to shore up international support and led to the subsequent invasion and occupation of Iraq the following month. Yet in the following year (2004) Powell was forced to admit that the information was not correct and that had he known, he would have had second thoughts

> **US Secretary of State Colin Powell admits evidence mistake** – Mr Powell said the US intelligence officers 'indicated to me' that the information about the mobile labs was reliable, and 'I made sure it was multi-sourced'. 'Now, if the sources fell apart we need to find out how we've gotten ourselves in that position', he said. 'I have discussions with the CIA about it', he said, without providing further details. It is the first time Mr Powell has acknowledged key evidence he used to make the case for war may have been wrong. (*BBC News* 2004)

about the decision to invade Iraq (*BBC News*, 2004). Much of the evidence came from the intelligence community and in particular the CIA. The concoction of evidence to demonstrate a case for an invasion suggests that the intelligence community in the United States and US allies had the disposition to take decisive action to topple the Hussein regime and, although lacking evidence, were willing to fabricate evidence and present it to an administration wanting to take action.

Ethical dilemma: should countries sanction the assassination of leaders?

Since 1976 successive administrations in Washington have abided by Executive Order 11905. Issued by President Gerald Ford, the order stated:

'No employee of the United States Government shall engage in, or conspire to engage in, political assassination'. (Executive Order 11095, Ford Library, 1976) The executive order was a reaction to the various well-publicised and often botched attempts by US intelligence agencies to assassinate foreign leaders in the 1960s and 1970s without the sanction of anything resembling a state of war. There were, for example, several attempts on President Fidel Castro's life. President Ford wanted to ensure through the executive order a more ethical response by the United States. The caveat in the executive order, however, is that in a state of war the killing of a leader is not considered an assassination. This has allowed Presidents Bush and Obama to carry out instructions to kill Osama Bin Laden without contravening the Executive Order.

On 6 May 2011, a crack United States Navy Seals Special Operations team carried out the killing of Bin Laden in Pakistan. Viewed by a tense President Obama and key advisors in the Situation Room of the White House, the killing was considered a pivotal moment in the 'War on Terror'. Bin Laden was the mastermind behind a series of terrorist attacks throughout the world (including the '9/11' attacks) and, as such, was responsible for thousands of deaths. Did killing the leader of al-Qaeda make a difference? His death was viewed in the United States and by allies as a major victory. There is no tangible evidence, however, that Bin Laden's death has in any way diminished the terrorist group. Nonetheless, the killing substantially improved President Obama's popularity rating within the United States and enhanced his status as a 'tough guy'.

Cognitive Model

The cognitive model examines how decision-makers perceive their environment. As indicated in Table 6.1, the perception of the external environment is a critical factor in the foreign policy-making process. In essence, the model argues that the process of cognition (mental activities associated with acquiring, organising and using knowledge) affects how the external environment is perceived and subsequently how policy is formulated. How the individual perceives his/her image and role and associated set of beliefs (past, present and future reality) affects the way in which information is assessed. As well, the selective perception (wishful thinking, image of the enemy) and psychological processes (such as mirror-imaging, where each side sees the other as the enemy or as a devil and itself as moral, virile and upholding good values) play an important role in overall policy decision-making.

In 1946 George Keenan wrote the famous 'Long Telegram' on Soviet aggression and its dangers for the 'Free World'. The following year, he published an article discussing his concerns to a broader audience in the journal *Foreign Affairs* using the pseudonym Mr X. He argued that the Soviet Union's inherent aggression must be met with long-term, patient, but firm containment of Russian expansionist tendencies. The article generated considerable debate and fear in the United States about Soviet Union and assisted in solidifying a 'bad faith' model about Soviet policy among US policymakers and with the general public. In many respects the article symbolised concerns about the Soviet Union and belief in a global contestation between the 'Free World' and the 'Communist World'. ('Mr X' article in *Foreign Affairs*, July 1947 'The Sources of Soviet Conduct')

The 'Bad Faith Model' was a classic example of how the Soviet Union and United States saw each other during the height of the Cold War in the 1950s and 1960s before, and indeed after, attempts at rapprochement between the two superpowers from the 1970s. No matter what actions were initiated, the other side viewed it as an act of aggression. In the example below the Mr X article set the standard for US hostility towards the Soviet Union.

THE LEADER AND PSYCHO-ANALYTICAL STUDIES

A derivative of the cognitive model is psycho-analytical studies of leadership. This is a growth area in international relations literature that focuses on leaders and their background and psychological makeup to determine how their special traits, attributes, and leadership skills were developed and to anticipate how this might affect their judgement. Notably, the most popular material deals with character flaws such as sexual habits, alcohol or drug abuse and battles with depression. In many respects, there is substantial general interest in understanding how leaders function and a general fascination with successful people with flawed characters. The emphasis in this approach is to evaluate idiosyncrasies and psychological profiles of elite individuals and assess the direction of foreign policy and overall capacity of leaders to cope during an international crisis. This can be a highly contentious area of study.

A new area of related study is the assessment of mental illness and its impact on leaders. According to Ghaemi (2011, 17), for example, 'The best crisis leaders are either mentally ill or mentally abnormal. The worst crisis leaders are mentally healthy'. His analysis argues that leaders who had or continue to suffer from depression or mild forms of mental illness tend to make better leaders in a crisis situation due to their capacity to think creatively and ability to empathise with the enemy. Ghaemi's analysis, which includes numerous case studies of famous leaders, describes how Winston Churchill, who suffered from depression and was prone to heavy drinking during his tenure as Prime Minister of Great Britain 1940–45 and 1951–55, had courage beyond reason in 1940–41when Britain faced the real threat of German occupation. Churchill, it is argued, 'had faced death many times before 1940' and therefore was not subsumed by fear

(Ghaemi 2011, 66). In the case of George W. Bush, however, Ghaemi argues that he was mentally healthy and therefore responded in a straightforward fashion rather than with the creativity of a leader in a crisis situation with mental illness such as Ghandi or John F. Kennedy.

According to his thesis, many of the greatest leaders are often abnormal, even flat out mentally ill. For Ghaemi, 'being normal is great in a friend and a spouse and in one's daily life; but leaders of nations and armies and businesses are faced with tasks and crises that no one faces in normal life. For abnormal challenges, abnormal leaders are needed' (Ghaemi 2011, 278). Although a new area of study and problematic, it demonstrates the ever-growing fascination with leadership studies.

> **George W. Bush: '9/11' response at a time of crisis** – 'Bush showed no evidence of the complex integrative thinking that characterised the better generals of the Civil War. He did not empathise with his enemies, as Martin Luther King and Ghandi (and even Sherman) had. He did not realistically assess the dangers of Saddam Hussein's weapons of mass destruction. He did not prepare (as Kennedy had during the Cuban missile crisis) a creative response that avoided war as a last resort. Bush made all the options other than war untenable'. Ghaemi (2010, 239)

HOW DO THE THEORIES OF INTERNATIONAL RELATIONS VIEW INDIVIDUAL AGENCY?

Among the theories analysed in this book, classical Realism, Neoliberalism and Constructivism (in different ways) are perhaps the premier examples of theories emphasising the role of individuals and offering scope for individual agency. This section will analyse international politics theories discussed in Chapter 2 with the view to assessing how individual agency is perceived from a theoretical standpoint. In essence, individual agency is the capacity for individuals to break through the structural dominance of the state and exert their influence. Rather than focusing on the 'big players', individual agency has allowed small actors a role and capacity to make an impact on the international system. In the post-1945 period, there has been considerable emphasis on individual agency. We see this phenomenon in diverse ways

> **War Crime** – an act in contravention of international law or accepted conventions on behaviour during war.

such as the role of Bouazizi and Assange already mentioned, activists in the area of human rights and the environment and in prosecuting key individuals responsible for **war crimes** (such as former Serbian leader Slobodan Milošević who is being tried for war crimes committed during the Bosnian war) with the development of the International Criminal Court.

Realism

For *classical realists*, the study of leaders and their worldviews is a critical factor in the development of foreign policy As mentioned in Chapter 2, classical realists tend to focus on individuals rather than states and individuals are viewed as innately selfish and power seeking. Because of the sense of anarchy beyond national borders and the fact that conflict is perceived to be inevitable in the international system, leaders are preoccupied with the need to preserve the national interest. Notably, there is limited scope in the theory to accommodate individual agency beyond the study of leadership. Indeed the classical realist text 'The Prince' by Niccolo Machiavelli is a guide to political cunning in the Florentine Republic in the sixteenth century. The focus on individuals examines the inherent evilness of 'man' (rather than a positive examination of individual agency). Thomas Hobbes encapsulated the problem in the Leviathan. Hobbes's famous quote that 'life is short, nasty and brutish' was a reflection of Europe during a period of warfare and violence. His book discusses in detail the necessity for a bureaucracy (legal process and rules of enforcement) and a police force to protect man from man.

By contrast, neorealists have an even more reductionist view of individual agency. The theory argues that the key actor or unit in the anarchical international system is the nation-state. As the state's ultimate goals are security and maximising power, the focal point of study is understanding how the structure of the international system operates and where states fit in within the hierarchical system. As states pursue their goal of survival, the national interest of the state are in essence the same; ensuring the security of the state and economic wellbeing of its citizens. As noted in Chapter 2, Neorealism is parsimonious, with a focus on state survival and the structure of the international system and less concern with domestic characteristics of the state. This means that neorealists are not worried about a focus on leaders or key elites. The structure of the international system and the twin pillars of state survival (security and economic) according to neorealists will determine national interests and subsequent policy outcomes. Indeed neorealists, who support the rational actor model of decision-making, go further by arguing that

> **Gender Neutral** – free of explicit or implicit reference to gender or sex.

their approach is **gender neutral**; leaders and decision makers, regardless of their background and gender, will respond as 'rational actors' to preserve state interests.

Liberalism

The *idealist* tradition focuses on the inherent good of man and that progress is possible in human relations. Traditional Idealism has several streams. One major stream was embedded within the Christian faith and, as such, supported the role of individual agency to promote core beliefs of Christianity through missionary work. A major philosophical stream developed by Immanuel Kant (1724–1804) argued that international relations would result in greater human freedom (increased security, wealth and freedom of political expression) and eventually to an international cosmopolitan society freeing people from state boundaries. It is this philosophical thread that is at the core of individual agency.

The post-war developments and construction of Neoliberalism have mainly been focused on the **democratic peace** and **neoliberal Institutionalism**. Inherent in the liberalist tradition has been the belief of individual freedom, liberty and equality before the law. As noted in Chapter 2, these sentiments are closely connected to the principles of limited government and the consent of the people. The democratic peace thesis argues that democracies rarely go to war with each other, highlighting the influence of freedom and equality in international politics. Implicit in this argument is the prevailing view that individual agency is an intrinsic component of the overall peace-related initiative.

Neoliberal institutionalists, however, focus on **international law**, cooperation and diplomacy. As noted in Chapter 2, neoliberalists recognise the primacy of states and the system of international anarchy. Regimes such as the World Trade Organization (WTO) provide forums for peaceful resolution of trade disputes by presenting incentives for states to cooperate. The rights of the individual and the promotion of individual agency are implicit in many of the institutions with the United Nations and its agencies such as the International Court of Justice as premier cases. Nonetheless, the approach taken by institutionalists tends to focus primarily on the structural issues to assist in the promotion of the individual.

> **Democratic Peace** – agreement that democracies do not engage in armed conflict with other identified democracies.
>
> **Neoliberal Institutionalism** – a neoliberal view that institutions can reduce fear and uncertainty among states and thereby reduce the likelihood of conflict.
>
> **International Law** – a set of laws, rules and principles (often non-binding) that deal with the conduct of the nation-states and international organisations.

Constructivism

Constructivists are part of a re-evaluation of international politics that began in earnest in the 1990s. Unsatisfied with the liberalist/realist debates and the limitations of theoretical models that ignored social values and social constructions, constructivists have articulated the need for a fundamental rethink of international politics. For constructivists, international politics is in many respects the role of human consciousness and its role in international life (Ruggie, cited in Finnemore and Sikkink, 2001). Focusing on the agent-structure relationship, constructivists claim to be able to provide a more insightful analysis by highlighting and broadening the concepts of ideas, norms, knowledge, culture, identity and power. As such, there is a strong focus on issues such as the effectiveness of norms in the international system. The study of identity and culture in particular involves an analysis of individual agency as a core factor. Indeed all shades of constructivist thought view individual actions and agency as an integral part of understanding the social construction. The actions and beliefs of people and the social facts, that are followed because they are believed to exist and therefore followed, constitute the reality of the international system. As noted in Chapter 2, *critical constructivists* as an offshoot of critical studies reflects an emancipatory agenda as exemplified by their emphasis on inequalities and individual activism as part of possible resolution. In this context, the notion of individual agency is a central component of analysis and critical constructivists would argue that the Arab Spring phenomenon is a classic example.

THE ROLE OF INDIVIDUAL AGENCY: WHAT DOES IT ALL MEAN?

The overview of theoretical approaches to individual agency provides us with a clearer understanding of how individual agency is viewed in international politics. Despite the prominent role of individuals and the increasing acceptance of the role of individual agency having influence on nation-states and at a transnational level, attention is mainly focused on the international structure of the international system and the role of key decision-makers.

Castro and Chávez: strong personalities in Latin American Politics. Did they make a difference?

There have been many outstanding leaders in Latin America, but two extraordinary leaders are Fidel Castro and Hugo Chávez. Both were charismatic leaders who were willing to stand up to US dominance in regional politics and trade and articulated alternative paths to political and economic development.

Castro led the 1959 Cuban socialist revolution and, despite sanctions from the United States (and several assassination attempts by the CIA and associated bodies), maintained his control over Cuba until transferring power to his brother Raul in 2008. A highly controversial figure, Castro alienated the United States and sought close ties with the Soviet Union at the height of the Cold War which lead to the 1962 Cuban missile crisis. His policies and charismatic style influenced two generations of Latin American leaders. In particular, his demonstration that it is possible to stay on course with national interests while in an antagonistic relationship with a superpower only a few hundred miles away has left a profound legacy on regional politics. Opinion on Castro is divided; he is both vilified and viewed as a hero. The obituaries upon his death will be compelling reading.

The death of Venezuela's President Hugo Chávez's on 5 March 2013 received global attention. Due to his charismatic and strong-willed personality, Chávez became a champion for the developing world and transformed how politics is conducted in Latin America. While his heavy -handed (some analysts would argue 'maverick') approach to highlighting issues of injustice and development included a confrontational approach with the United States and thereby created tension with Washington and US allies, his flamboyant style, fiery political discourse, economic support for the poor and grassroots politics made him tremendously popular in Venezuela and Latin America more broadly. According to the BBC analysis, his death could alter the political balance in Latin America – dealing a blow to leftist states while favouring more centrist states. (BBC News, 2013)

The lack of attention on individual agency in theories has important implications. First, the dominance of the mainstream theories such as the neorealist school of thought (and focus on the state as the unit of analysis) in international politics means that not enough attention is placed on individuals. Neoliberalist theory moreover tends to focus on the international system, states and regime-building as a principle means to enhance democracy, human rights and the quality of life for individuals. Although the theory has more scope to examine the role of individuals, the theory seems bound by positivist discourse to demonstrate that it has credibility as a theory by being able to measure outcomes.

A second and inter-related implication is that individual agency is now a core aspect of critical studies of international politics. Mainstream theories face the prospect of becoming increasingly redundant if the role of individuals is not re-evaluated to include a more significant evaluation of how individual agency has an impact on international politics and life more generally.

QUESTIONS FOR REFLECTION

1. Is the international system shaped by 'Heroes' or 'Villains' in history? Or does the environment allow leaders with particular skills and ability to emerge and deal with particular events? What arguments and evidence can you provide to support your conclusion?

2. Consider the famous Mr X article. What would be the compelling issue in the contemporary world? What social media would a modern day Mr X use to articulate his/her foreign policy agenda?

3. The use of drones on the Pakistan/Afghanistan border has continued the US policy of targeting and killing key individuals as part of the 'War on Terror'. Although successful in hunting wanted senior members of al-Qaeda, the drones have also killed innocent

bystanders including women and children who happen to be at the wrong place at the wrong time. These deaths have strengthened the resolve of anti-US forces and indeed have been a recruiting ground for al-Qaeda. Should assassinations (either in person or by remote devices such as drones) be condoned in the twenty-first century?

4. US Secretary of State Colin Powell (who was the only person in the executive to have first-hand experience as a soldier and had served in the 1990 Desert Storm in Iraq) was not a supporter of the invasion of Iraq in 2003. Yet he accepted the prevailing view, which he has regretted upon retirement. What does this suggest about group dynamics and the role of bureaucratic politics?

5. Which theory in your opinion best explains the growth and development of individual agency in the contemporary world?

6. Is international politics really a study of elites? Should more attention be given to everyday people and efforts of individuals to change their conditions?

7. Are psycho-analytical studies of leaders a legitimate form of scholarship? To what extent do they assist in our understanding of foreign policy decision-making?

8. Latin America has produced charismatic and revolutionary leaders such as Fidel Castro and Hugo Chávez. What do they have in common and why is the relationship with the United States a defining feature of regional politics in Latin America?

9. Julian Assange is one of the iconic figures of the early twenty-first century. Why is he so well known? In your view, is Assange a ground-breaking on-line activist hero fighting for freedom?

10. Why is the reality of foreign policy decision-making different from the ideal type as demonstrated in Table 6.1? What does it suggest about competing priorities and the construction and outcomes of foreign policy?

REVISION QUIZ

1. Individual agency refers to:

    a. A government department
    b. A philosophical state of mind
    c. The ability if individuals to break through the structural dominance of the state and exert their influence
    d. A 1970s a non-violent protest movement in the United Kingdom

2. The 'Bad Faith' model refers to:

    a. Problems in Apartheid South Africa in the 1970s and 1980s
    b. The cognitive model of foreign policy decision-making in which a set of beliefs affect the way in which information is assessed. The classic example is the way the key policymakers in the United States and the Soviet Union saw each other during the height of the Cold War
    c. Unites States policy towards North Korea as a legacy of the Cold War
    d. Departmental rivalry and its impact of foreign policy decision-making

3. Neorealists argue that the role of the individual in international politics is:

   a. A core feature of the theory and central to understanding international relations
   b. Part of the social construction of society
   c. Limited as the theory is state-centric and focuses on the structure of the international system. Leaders will pursue policies that are in the national interest of the nation-state
   d. Only matters during wartime when soldiers are required

4. Environmental Determinists believe that:

   a. The international and domestic environment will heavily influence foreign policy decision-making and that leaders respond to their political environment
   b. Key individuals will shape the environment and transform the international system
   c. Climate change is real and that governments need to act now
   d. Hitler was propped up by his need to please people and had psychological problems

5. Ghaemi is a psychiatrist who contends that the best leaders of nations in a crisis are those who are:

   a. Mentally ill
   b. Conservative by nature
   c. Cool under pressure
   d. Reserved

6. In 1976 President Gerald Ford issued Executive Order 11905 to:

   a. Exonerate former President Richard Nixon
   b. Improve relations with China
   c. Allow Afro-Americans to work in the White House
   d. Ensure no employee of the United States shall engage in, or conspire to engage in political assassination

7. Julian Assange is well known for:

   a. Being arrested while interviewing the Queen of England
   b. Creating WikiLeaks and promoting freedom of information
   c. Advising the Prime Minister of Australia on Aboriginal art
   d. Starting the Arab Spring movement

8. The rational actor model argues that:

   a. Decision-makers act in a rational manner, apply a cost/benefits approach to policy-making and will pursue policies that are in their national interest
   b. We are all rational beings
   c. Rational thought is not possible while nuclear weapons exist
   d. Only leaders in democratic governments act in a rational manner

9. What did Fidel Castro attempt to do during the Cold War?

   a. Bomb New York
   b. Allow a Soviet missile base to be built in Cuba (only a few hundred miles from Florida)
   c. Create an anti Japanese bloc in Latin America
   d. Sell cigars in the United States in order to make money for his family

10. What are the three foreign policy models discussed in this chapter?

   a. Individual agency, hero-in-history and ethical dilemmas
   b. Rational Actor, Bureaucratic and Cognitive
   c. Environmental Determinism, Constructivism and Neoliberalism
   d. Arab Spring, stumbling through approach and Realism

Answers: 1: c; 2: b; 3: c; 4: a; 5: a; 6: d; 7: b; 8: a; 9: b; 10: b.

BIBLIOGRAPHY

BBC News, (2004), 'Powell admits Iraq evidence mistake'. http://news.bbc.co.uk/2/hi/middle_east/3596033. stm (accessed 13 April 2013).

BBC News; Latin America and Caribbean, (2013) 'Venezuela's Hugo Chávez dies at 58', 6 March. http://www.bbc.co.uk/news/world-latin-america-21679053 (accessed 6 March 2013).

Byman, D. (2006) 'Do Targeted killings work?', *Foreign Affairs*, April/May.

Day, E. (2011) 'The slap that sparked a revolution' *Observer*, 15 May 2011. http://www.guardian.co.uk/world/2011/may/15/arab-spring-tunisia-the-slap cited 6 April 2013).

Executive Order 11905: United States Foreign intelligence Activities, 18 February 1976. http://www.ford.utexas.edu/library/speeches/760110e.asp#Sec.5

Finnemore, M. and Sikkink, K. (2001) 'Taking Stock: The Constructivist Research Program in International Relations and Comparative politics', *Annual Review Political Science* 4, 391–416.

Floyd A. and Benkler, Y. (2013) 'Death to Whistleblowers? http://www.nytimes.com/2013/03/14/opinion/the-impact-of-the-bradley-manning-case.html?_r=0 (cited 20 March 2013).

Ghaemi, N. (2011) *A First-rate Madness: Uncovering the Links Between Leadership and Mental Illness* (New York: The Penguin Press).

Giacomo, C. (2013) 'Scrutinising an Inscrutable Leader', *New York Times*, 13 April 2013. http://takingnote.blogs.nytimes.com/2013/04/12/scrutinizing-an-inscrutable-leader/?ref=kimjongun   (cited   13 April 2013).

Harrell, E. (2010) 'WikiLeaks comes under fire from rights groups'. http://www.time.com/time/world/article/0,8599,2010309,00.html (accessed 7 April 2013).

Hermann, M. and Hermann, C. (December 1989) 'Who makes foreign policy decisions and how. An Empirical Study', *International Studies Quarterly* 22(4), 361–87.

Holsti, K. (1989) *International Politics: A Framework for Analysis* (New York: Prentice Hall). Kennan, G. (1947) 'The Sources of Soviet Conduct'. http://www.historyguide.org/europe/kennan.html (cited 8 March 2013).

Lebow, R.N. (2010) *Forbidden Fruit: Counterfactuals and International Relations* (New Jersey: Princeton University Press).

Levy, B.S. and Sidel, V.W. (2013) 'Adverse health consequences of the Iraq War'. *The Lancet* 381(9870), 949–58. http://www.thelancet.com/journals/lancet/article/PIIS0140-6736(13)60254-8/fulltext (accessed 20 March 2013).

Mainwaring. S. (December 2012) 'From Representative Democracy to Participatory Competitive Authoritarianism: Hugo Chávez and Venezuelan Politics', *Perspectives on Politics* 10(4), 955–67.

Richter, S. (2011) 'Julian Assange: Villain or Hero?' *The Globalist*, 26 July.

Stephan R. (2011) 'Julian Assange: Villain or Hero?', *The Globalist*, 26 July. http://www.theglobalist.com/storyid.aspx?StoryId=9262 (cited 8 April 2013).

'The Iraq War, Ten years on' (2013) http://www.gwu.edu/~nsarchiv/NSAEBB/NSAEBB418/ (cited 26 March 2013).

Walt, S. (2011) 'Where do bad ideas come from?' http://www.foreignpolicy.com/articles/2011/01/02/where_do_bad_ideas_come_from?page=0,3 (cited 14 April 2013).

Watson Institute for International Studies, Brown University (2013) 'Cost of War project', http://news.brown.edu/pressreleases/2013/03/warcosts (cited 18 March 2013).

Chapter 7
Transnational Actors in World Politics

BRIAN R. KING

This chapter examines the nature of transnational actors (TNAs) in contemporary international relations. Sometimes also referred to as non-state actors, TNAs represent one of the more significant changes to the international landscape in the twenty-first century. In the past decade alone, these groups – which are continually growing in both number and influence – have been at the centre of major wars, regional conflicts and civil strife; a significant reason behind the global economic crisis and a crucial player in its recovery; instrumental in fostering popular uprisings against tyranny as well as in the efforts to put them down; and a critical part of global efforts to tackle global problems such as disease, poverty, climate change and human rights abuse, just to name a few.

The wide array of transnational actors is explained, including the relative place of each type in the international system and differing views on their definition, scope and impact. Among the types of TNAs discussed are civil service organizations, international nongovernmental organizations, transnational advocacy networks and epistemic communities, multinational/transnational corporations, grassroots organizations and grassroots support organizations, transnational religious movements, non-state nationalist groups and diasporas, transnational criminal organizations, terrorist organizations and insurgent groups. Common characteristics of these different types are discussed, including considerations of size, geographic reach, organizational purpose, funding and internal structure.

Transnational actors engage in a range of activities to reach their goals, and these are explained. These activities include direct action, lobbying, raising issue awareness and fundraising. The ways in which groups differ in employing these activities is explored. Through these activities, TNAs have a significant impact on global affairs, and this impact is examined in more depth with regard to issue advocacy, international regimes, democratization efforts around the world, the struggle for human rights and political liberties, globalization and the use of soft power. This rise in relevance and in relative influence has posed a number of challenges for the current Westphalian system, two of which are examined in detail. First, the traditional concept of state sovereignty seems to be challenged by notions of responsible sovereignty and the role of international institutions on the world stage. Even small groups of people are finding ways to challenge the governments that repress them, and there is significant pressure for states and international government organizations to intervene to help those whose own governments will not. Second, as transnational actors continue to gain prominence in global affairs, how should they be viewed with regard to legitimacy, accountability and credibility? These challenges show no signs of abating, and so must be addressed as the international system moves forward. Finally, the debate over the current influence of transnational actors is explored, and their prospects for increased power and influence in the future is addressed.

Key Words: Transnational Actor, Civil Society, Nongovernmental Organization, Transnational Advocacy Network, Multinational Corporation, Grassroots Organization, Non-state Nationalist Group, Transnational Criminal Organization, Terrorism, Insurgency, Regimes, Soft Power, Responsible Sovereignty.

Chapter 7

Transnational Actors in World Politics

BRIAN KING

INTRODUCTION

The world is ever-changing, and perhaps one of the more significant changes to the international landscape over the past few decades has been the dramatic increase in the number, size, resources and overall power of transnational actors on the world stage. Their impact is undeniable, as just in the twenty-first century they have been at the centre of monumental changes in the international system, including a decade-long war on terror, a prolonged global economic crisis, more than one environmental disaster and the spread of the revolutionary spirit in an Arab Spring that has had a direct, significant effect on at least a dozen countries throughout the world.

What Is a Transnational Actor?

The term **transnational actor** (TNA) is somewhat ambiguous, in its most general sense referring to any persons or groups that work across nation-state boundaries to achieve their goals. Various scholars and practitioners use alternate terminology for this type of entity, most notably **non-state actor** (Reinalda 2011). This includes the classic definition of transnational relations as interactions between actors across state boundaries where at least one participant is a non-state actor (Nye and Keohane 1971). While the term offers slightly more precision, it is still overly general and utilized in differing ways by different actors in different contexts. For example, in the Cotonou Agreement between the EU and ACP, each ACP country may define within its own context what qualifies as a non-state actor.

> A **Transnational Actor**, sometimes referred to as a **Non-state Actor**, is a private group not directly controlled by any government organization. It is typically policy-oriented, political in nature and operates between and across state boundaries.

Regardless of how they are labelled, such groups are regarded as private actors, not directly controlled by any state or international governmental organization. Their members are volunteers, their aims are policy-oriented and their approach is generally political in nature. A great diversity exists in the types of actors that fit under this umbrella, but there are a number of common characteristics which bind them together. Before exploring these characteristics, however, it is important to explore the place of TNAs on the international stage today, and examine how the current arrangement came to be.

Historical Trends and Current Status

The Treaty of Westphalia in 1648 had a profound impact on international relations, ushering in an era of state sovereignty that has persisted into the present time. By then, a few transnational actors already operated, most notably trading companies that today might be labelled as multinational corporations. However, the number of nongovernmental entities operating in the international sphere remained relatively low until the mid- to late nineteenth century, when there was the first of three rapid expansions of transnational actor activity (Boli and Thomas 1999; Kuchinsky 2011). Humanitarian concerns, human rights causes, labour rights and religious missions were largely responsible for this growth period. Following World War I, the second expansion saw relief agencies and philanthropic organizations, among others, rise in both number and prominence on the world stage. The third growth phase began in the late 1960s and continues to the present, accounting for the vast majority of all international nongovernmental organizations currently in existence. From a few hundred in the years following World War II, the number of international nongovernmental organizations (INGOs) is estimated by the Union of International Associations to be in excess of 27,000 in the first decade of the twenty-first century. While many are global in scope and operation, much of the growth is due to the emergence of groups focusing on regional issues. As the numbers continue to grow, so does the collective influence of TNAs within and between states. Indeed, no discussion of international relations in the twenty-first century would be complete without discussing the role of TNAs.

What accounts for this explosion of TNAs over the last few decades? There are differing explanations, which may best be considered collectively in trying to answer the question. One school of thought is that the increase is due to the rise in demand for action on a widening range of global issues, including such things as civil rights, global peace, environmental awareness, democratization of newly independent states and economic development. Populations, especially in the West, felt the need to address these and a host of other transnational concerns, and felt empowered to organize and act privately to influence the policies and the actions of states and international organizations. A second school of thought posits that technological advances are responsible for the growth in TNAs. Innovations in communication and transportation have made the world a much smaller and more interactive place, and the rise of the computer age has done nothing less than revolutionize daily life for billions. This has led to an exponential growth in business opportunities, as well as a greater awareness of the differences between the haves and have-nots around the world, both of which have spurred the growth of TNAs into new areas of human civilization. Globalization can said to be a direct result of technological advancement and innovation.

Whatever the cause, it is apparent that TNAs are an ever-increasing part of global discourse, with an ever-increasing influence on the issues discussed and the actions taken on a wide range of subjects. As such, it is important to gain a better understanding of these entities, including who they are, how they operate, how they interact with other global actors, what impact they have on world affairs and what challenges they pose for the future of international relations.

TYPES OF TRANSNATIONAL ACTORS

A wide array of groups may be classified as transnational actors, each connected by a common sense of purpose and similar strategies and tactics to achieve them. Scholars differ on how to classify and organize such groups, and there is indeed significant variance with regard to both terminology and classification (Kuchinsky 2011). This chapter attempts to include much of the variety of terminology and classification utilized in policy circles, academia and mass media. What may be discovered, among other things, is that while some classifications are easily distinguished, others are not. There is certainly a good deal of overlap between types, in terms of goals, activities and other parameters. Furthermore, terms such as civil society, non-state actor and nongovernmental organization are sometimes used in ways that make them difficult to distinguish from one another without the benefit of the author's intent as found in the context of his/her writing. In fact, there are times when these terms seem to be interchangeable in their usage by different people and organizations, only serving to further confuse and frustrate a student of international relations. It is important for such a student not to get caught up in such differences, but to focus rather on the substantive similarities and differences between different types of TNAs, and to recognize that terminology is at some level a labelling issue, not a substantive one. With that in mind, here are some common classifications of transnational actors.

Civil Society and Civil Society Organizations (CSOs)

The term **civil society** is used in different ways in different contexts. As it relates to TNAs, it seems to have taken on both a general and a more specific connotation. In general terms, it is often used as an umbrella term to denote the sum total of nongovernmental group-based involvement in the political sphere. Such organizations represent a multitude of various groups in society, giving them a voice in public discourse and policy deliberations. International governmental organizations (IGOs) such as the World Bank and the International Monetary Fund, for example, recognize civil society as including a wide variety of business, labour, charitable, religious and other nongovernmental

> **Civil Society**, in a specific sense, refers to the sum total of transnational groups focused on helping the disadvantaged or forwarding the common good of global society. Groups in this classification, though they may also fit in other categories, can be referred to as **Civil Society Organizations**.

organizations and engage with a multitude of such groups to assist in achieving their goals. For-profit entities, such as individual businesses and privately owned mass media, are generally excluded from this definition, as are political parties and individuals. In this general connotation, some of the group types discussed below would fall under the umbrella of **civil society organizations**.

In a more specific sense, even when not expressly noted, use of the term sometimes seems to refer primarily to the constellation of organized transnational groups whose goals are oriented to the benefit of disadvantaged groups or the overall common good of global society. Such causes as defending human rights, promoting social justice, protecting the environment and facilitating peace would all fall under this category. The causes of these groups extend far beyond their membership, and much of the time those who benefit the most are those in society who cannot effectively organize on their own. Such organizations are plentiful in most open political systems, so the link between civil society and democratization is common in the literature. Some scholars (Almond and Verba 1963; Putnam 1995) contend that the health of a democratic system is at least partially dependent upon civic involvement and activity, both political and non-political. The international sphere is a different environment, to be sure, but some of the same activities (and consequences) seen within societies are also being witnessed between them at the global level. While some of these groups operate privately, others find success in partnering with various governmental organizations at the local, national, and international levels.

Nongovernmental Organizations (NGOs)

As is the case with civil society, the term nongovernmental organization (NGO) is employed in a variety of contexts by the analysts, commentators, policymakers and scholars who use it. Sometimes used generally to describe the full array of TNAs, it more commonly lends itself to discussions of formalized private organizations that use political means to achieve their goals. The term **international nongovernmental organization** (INGO) is at times employed to distinguish between those organizations that operate across national borders and those that are purely domestic in scope. A few organizations blur even this line, having an international presence while affiliate organizations or subdivisions operate exclusively within a single national setting.

> **Nongovernmental Organizations,** or **International Nongovernmental Organizations**, are more formalized transnational actors that employ political means such as lobbying and issue advocacy to achieve goals.

NGOs are often categorized on at least two dynamics: type of activity and global reach. In terms of activities, most NGOs are primarily focused either on lobbying policymakers (and others) for a particular cause, or doing the hands-on work of addressing a specific problem. The World Bank, for instance, distinguishes NGOs as being either operational or advocacy based. Operational NGOs focus on planning and implementing projects designed to address a specific problem such as poverty. Advocacy-based NGOs are organized around a larger cause, and their activities are designed influence policies that relate to that cause. A growing number of NGOs, however, now engage in some amount of both types of activities, making their classification more difficult. With regard to global reach, some NGOs are narrowly focused on one geographic region. Others have more of a regional focus, or concentrate on wider areas. Yet others are truly global in scope, with operations all over the world. Many factors contribute to this dynamic, including available resources, scope of the problem being addressed, the willingness of government bodies to allow access and other matters. Technological advancements, especially those in communication, are making it easier for some groups to extend their reach farther than they could have even a few years ago.

One particular type of NGO that has garnered substantial controversy is the government-operated nongovernmental organization (GONGO). As the name suggests, such groups are created, funded and managed by government entities, often covertly, for the purposes of furthering specific political and policy-oriented objectives. Outwardly, they are made to appear as any other NGO, privately funded and free from government control or influence. They are routinely employed by oppressive regimes worldwide to advance their objectives within rival countries or in dealings with international institutions. They are also utilized by democratic governments, however, in pursuit of both narrow and wide-ranging goals. Though some are known, many GONGOs are not, which critics contend casts suspicion and doubt upon all NGOs who are active in transnational politics.

Transnational Advocacy Networks

No transnational actor exists in isolation on the world stage. Rather, each operates as one small and integrated part of a complex and far-reaching web of individuals, groups and global dynamics that is built up around a transnational issue or idea. Drawn to this issue (and all issues) are those people and organizations with expertise in the area and a strong interest in promoting or preventing change. They have shared values and concerns, plus a level of knowledge and expertise that fosters greater communication and the deep exchange of information (Keck and Sikkink 2004). As interactions increase among these various actors, they begin to make more lasting connections with one another, leading to the development of a **transnational advocacy network**. Such networks are generally characterized as voluntary, loose, horizontal and reciprocal in nature. In recent years, this has been one of the fastest-growing types of TNAs.

> A **Transnational Advocacy Network** is a loose and horizontal association of organizations and individuals at the state and international levels who are committed to a addressing common transnational issues. This is related to **Epistemic Communities**, which are networks of professionals and other experts who share a common vision on global problems and how to best address them.

The stronger the connections between like-minded actors, the more opportunity that exists to coordinate activities, align goals or simply share information. Over time, as the network grows and strengthens, it can become a significant player in its own right in shaping the outcome of relevant political battles and policy debates. With this in mind, the creation and expansion of transnational advocacy networks has become an intentional, purposeful endeavour. More often than not, their creation is a response a sovereign entity that is either a cause of, or unresponsive to, a perceived societal problem.

Closely related to transnational advocacy networks are **epistemic communities** (Haas 1992), which are best described as networks of professionals and other experts from diverse positions and perspectives, who share a consensus about the causes, consequences and possible solutions to a societal problem. These communities can range from a few like-minded people to a network of thousands or more.

Multinational Corporations (MNCs)

Multinational corporations (MNCs) are one of the oldest TNAs on the world stage, dating as far back as the Dutch East India Company in the early 1600s. They are credited (or criticized) for their substantial role in promoting globalization and the persistence of international dynamics prominent in the Westphalian system of state sovereignty. In recent decades, some have postulated that they have become a rising challenge to the state-centred international system and, along with other TNAs, are responsible for major changes in the international system that may eventually necessitate a re-evaluation of the nature of sovereignty itself (Moksnes and

Melin 2012). The amount of global wealth held by MNCs, for example, is beyond substantial. By cross-referencing 2012 GDP figures with the 2012 Forbes Global 500 list, the enormity of these profit-driven organizations becomes evident: the combined earnings of the ten largest MNCs (eight of which are energy companies) would eclipse all but the top four national economies

> **Multinational Corporations** are said to have substantially accelerated the process of globalization, which helps them to pursue wealth through global commerce and trade. MNCs that are primarily international in nature, rather than based primarily in one country, are often labelled as being **Transnational Corporations**.

in the world. However their power and influence is measured, MNCs are – as they have been for centuries – considered prominent and important players in the development of economics, politics and culture around the world, and there are no signs that this will change any time soon.

The label of MNC most commonly refers to a for-profit corporate entity which is headquartered in one country, but with additional operations in other countries around the world. There is some disagreement on what qualifies as an MNC, based on such issues as the level of investment in foreign countries, the extent to which its business is tied to foreign markets and a diversity of nationalities among its top executives. There is no general consensus on such issues, and in practice MNCs are in most cases simply viewed as companies which operate in their home country as well as in other national and international jurisdictions. Related to this, **transnational corporations** are considered a variation of an MNC wherein the company takes on a primarily international personality, without primary allegiance to any single country. A firm's headquarters may be spread amongst different national jurisdictions, while corporate policies and strategies are oriented primarily to the global economy rather than national concerns. When the term is used, however, it is most often intended that the definitions of MNCs and TNCs be interchangeable.

As the influence of MNCs in the world continues to grow, so do the controversies that surround them. One strain of criticism centres on the profit-motivated practices of MNCs, including the exploitation of people and natural resources. Another strain focuses more on the effects that such entities have (both individually and collectively) on increased globalization, which some critics fear and others lament. In both instances, the moralistic overtones centre on a belief that MNCs have ethical responsibilities that are not always (or often) being fulfilled. Conversely, there are those who celebrate such entities as the drivers of human development and innovation, the catalyst for social and economic betterment in parts of the world and the bringing together of disparate states and societies into common dialogues that might otherwise be much more difficult to accomplish.

Grassroots Organizations and Grassroots Support Organizations (GSOs)

Grassroots organizations are those groups that rise from the ground up, driven by the needs and demands of local people who organize for common purpose. As such movements grow, local groups may connect and can then work to facilitate grassroots action in other local areas. These types of groups are generally more decentralized than other transnational organizations, allowing for flexibility and agility to deal with local problems and issues as they might arise. Central organizational structures, where they exist, tend to focus on facilitating the needs of the local and regional subsidiaries, rather than insisting upon conformity to strict and hierarchical mandates and messages.

Related to these are **grassroots support organizations**, whose purpose is to facilitate and coordinate efforts to assist the poor and disadvantaged at the local and regional levels across multiple states. Often, one prominent activity is to

> **Grassroots Organizations** typically begin at the local level, driven by the needs and demands of people with common purpose. Related to these, **Grassroots Support Organizations** often form to both facilitate and coordinate efforts to help similar grassroots groups and causes in various locations around the world.

solicit donations which are then routed to various groups and individuals at the grassroots level. There are many transnational microfinance organizations, for example, that specialize in providing small loans to groups and individuals whose activities focus on economic development, social justice and similar issues at the local and regional levels.

Overall, grassroots and grassroots support organizations are some of the most likely TNAs to take direct action to address the issues they feel need attention. While lobbying, fundraising and other functions are present, they are seen most prominently as means to an end of doing more on the ground, directly helping people on the ground where they feel their efforts are most needed.

Transnational Religious Movements

Organized religions are structured around a common belief in a deity or divine creator and adherence to a common set of ideas, stories, lessons and values that guide people to lead an ethical life. When such organizations become international in scope, they are sometimes characterized as **transnational religious movements**. Each movement is headed by a political

apparatus that governs the organization and works to pursue organizational goals on the global stage. Given the wide range of religious organizations in the world, and given the wide variance between them in terms of size, structure, resources and beliefs, it is somewhat difficult to paint with a broad brush in discussing the power and influence of such groups as a whole in international politics (Haynes 2004). Further difficulty stems from the fact that the beliefs

> **Transnational Religious Movements** cross national boundaries and are led by political organizations that pursue the religious group's goals around the world. When a state's laws, customs and political structure are based on a given religious movement, that political system is called a **Theocracy**.

espoused or the actions taken by one sect that wields influence must at times be distinguished from the beliefs of that sect's mainstream faith, whose influence may be qualitatively different. Given these and other limitations, though, it is still possible to discuss the ways in which such groups affect international discourse and transnational politics.

At the most fundamental level, religion often underpins and reinforces the moral and cultural foundations of a society, and these in turn serve to shape and influence politics and policy on an enormous range of issues. As globalization and other factors accelerate the transnational nature of religious movements, this is true to an ever-growing degree on the world stage as well. More directly, there are many ways in which these groups become involved in the political realm. At one end of the spectrum, religious organizations may serve as lobbyists for groups unable to fight for themselves, or for policies that promote their own values and objectives. This may include interaction with state leaders and institutions, IGOs other NGOs, or some combination of these. At the other end of the spectrum, governments may be structured on the basis of religious teachings or beliefs, and the leadership may preside over a political, economic and cultural system that reflects the same. In some instances, religious leaders in such **theocracies** may select the political leadership, or may assume leadership roles themselves. In turn, the state apparatus works to further the transnational interests of the governing religious group. At both ends of the spectrum and at all points in between, the significance of religious movements in shaping national and international discourse and decisions is undeniable.

Of particular concern to scholars and practitioners alike are the dangers posed by transnational religious movements that have radicalized and become militant. Such movements are much less likely to be tolerant of others' perspectives and values, allowing dogma to dictate harsh treatment for all those who oppose their own point of view. Such groups, given the right conditions, can bring about a number of different phenomena. Through the use of violent or coercive means, such actors can prod powerful groups into reclaiming lost territory from other state actors or drive religious minorities from their own territory. They can also incite minority groups toward separatist sentiment (which often turns violent), and encourage them to commit terrorist acts against national and/or international actors deemed a threat to the religion or its ideals (Kegley 2010).

Non-state Nationalist Groups

Non-state nationalist groups are connected by such things as historical legacy, cultural heritage, racial identity, common language, shared religious beliefs and other attributes, but do not enjoy the benefits of their own sovereign state. These distinctive ethnic groups are bound by a strong sense of Nationalism, an allegiance that in some cases supersedes loyalty to the sovereign state in which they reside. This nationalist self-perception becomes an integral and primary element of their identity, both individually and collectively, and can lead to a desire to obtain (or regain) territorial autonomy and political sovereignty for themselves.

> **Non-state Nationalist Groups** have in common such attributes as history, culture, racial or ethnic identity, religion and/or language. All of this is held together by a strong sense of Nationalism that can sometimes be more important to that of the nation-state in which the group resides. Nationalist groups that are spread out rather than concentrated in the place identified as their rightful homeland are often referred to as **Diasporas**.

These groups can take different forms. Many are indigenous populations that at one time may have had sovereign authority over a given territory. These groups number in the thousands, encompassing hundreds of millions of people in dozens of countries around the world. The vast majority live peacefully within the current state structure and some even have limited autonomy, such as Native Americans in North America and Aborigines in Australia. Despite this, most groups aspire to greater autonomy and utilize various conventional (and sometimes unconventional) means to achieve it. Other groups aspire to outright sovereignty, such as Palestinians in the Middle East, and engage in a wide variety of activities to achieve that goal. While these populations are geographically centralized for the most part, other nationalist groups are more accurately described as **diasporas**, where a group migrates outward to various places around the world despite retaining their nationalist identity and holding allegiance to that group. Often, these diasporas are in response to political, religious or other types of persecution by the ruling regime, and the hope of many in these groups is that through regime change they will one day be able to return home. If these population dispersions last for an extended period and become multi-generational, as is the case with Cubans in the United States, such things as group identity, allegiance and a desire to return home can be questioned.

Struggles involving ethnic minorities have been anything but peaceful in some states and regions. State attempts to assimilate, relocate or eradicate ethnic minorities have often resulted in violence on a large scale, with scores of groups deemed 'at risk' of further abuses at the hands of their resident states (Gurr 2000). The world has witnessed that such violence may arise more often in situations where the governing structure is weakened, thus giving opportunity for the minority group to take advantage. When these efforts are repressed violently by police and/or military force, larger and more sustained conflict may result. Indeed, there are times when it is the ethnic minority group that initiates the violence, often in response to perceived injustices by the ruling government and partial or complete exclusion from the legitimate political process.

The goals of nationalist groups may be categorized as integrative, revolutionary or separatist. Groups that are integrative work to gain power within the existing political system, ranging from simple inclusion into the political system to structural reform that allows for some level of power-sharing between the group and the existing government. This is most common in democratic systems, where there are institutional avenues for such groups to engage in the political process. Some groups want instead to depose the ruling regime and return to rule themselves, and so pursue revolutionary goals aimed at that purpose. This is the preferred path for many governments in exile. Still other groups wish to no longer be under the rule of their resident state, following instead a separatist path that may lead to eventual independence. Most irredentist movements follow some variation of this path, for instance. Whatever the goals, nationalist groups have largely become much more adept over the years at utilizing external actors such as NGOs, IGOs and other states to achieve success.

Transnational Criminal Organizations (TCOs)

Not all non-state actors are legitimate, positive contributors to global discourse and operations. Some groups, by their very nature, threaten the security and stability of the global arena. **Transnational criminal organizations** (sometimes referred to collectively as transnational organized crime, or TOC) are among the most pervasive and influential types of such groups, and play a major role in shaping the international landscape both politically and economically.

Differences in definitional approach among scholars and practitioners often reflect the diverse and dynamic nature of TCOs, especially since their rapid rise in profile and prominence in the 1990s.

> Distinctly negative in nature, **Transnational Criminal Organizations** are long-term formal or quasi-formal groups that conduct illegal activities across state boundaries for the purpose of private financial gain. TCOs are known to get involved in the political realm to influence or corrupt individuals or agencies, and even on occasion to overthrow an entire political system, to achieve their own illegal ends.

These differences focus on a number of factors, such as the level of formal organization and hierarchy, the nature of the members vs. the nature of activities and the distinction between organized crime and such things as terrorist organizations and insurgent groups (Wagley 2006).

Generally speaking, TCOs can be described as formal or quasi-formal organizations that persist over time, operate to some degree across (or in disregard of) state boundaries and are constituted for the purpose of financial gain through various criminal enterprises and activities. While it is true that TCOs are known to enter the political realm to influence, manipulate and at times even oust individual officials or entire governments, their ultimate purpose in doing so is to affect the system in order to maximize immediate and/or longer-term material gains, not to gain political power or to affect national or international policy for political reasons.

Internationally, TCOs are involved in a wide range of criminal activities, such as drug trafficking, human trafficking, smuggling, cybercrime, money laundering and much more. Thanks to several converging factors since the 1990s, including accelerated globalization, decentralization and destabilization in parts of the former Soviet bloc and a global trend toward deregulation, transnational crime is thriving in the twenty-first century (Williams 2001). As TCOs have evolved, many have strayed from the classic model of a formalized, hierarchical organization towards a looser, decentralized and more agile network of cells and confederate groups (Williams 2001). This newer configuration can be more reactive to the global environment and more easily hidden from government stings and investigations. Just how prominent and powerful TCOs are is difficult to measure, as much of their activity is underground and secretive. Various studies over time have estimated that organized criminal activity may account for between two and ten per cent of global GDP in recent years, though such estimates are at least partially speculative due to the hidden and secretive nature of most TCO activities. In some regions, TCO activity has served to disrupt the normal operations of society and may even threaten civil stability, thus making the normal operation of government and the economy more difficult, if not impossible. Whether it's warlords in Somalia or drug cartels in Mexico and Columbia, such groups can even threaten interstate relations and endanger international security.

Some elements of TCO activity have remained consistent over time, such as interactions with corrupt, ineffectual or unstable governments. States may utilize TCOs for such purposes as circumventing trade sanctions, and TCOs may utilize states for a safe haven and to provide opportunities for money laundering, among other activities. These enterprises prey upon government corruption and weakness so they may operate freely and without fear, and may try to influence or manipulate the political landscape to their advantage. In states where instability already exists, this could threaten sovereignty and lead to failed states, civil wars and more.

While these types of activities are still prominent, new trends are also emerging. Perhaps the most disturbing of these is the increased level of interactions with terrorist organizations and insurgent groups. For some, these are merely business transactions and temporary partnerships that occur when organizations with divergent motives come together for mutual benefit. For others, however, the evolving relationship between these actors grows deeper and more complex all the time, and the clear separations between them may be blurring (Shelley et. al. 2005). This would give distinct operational and strategic advantages to both types of groups, and make it much more difficult to manage anti-crime and counterterrorist efforts. The key question seems to be whether increased short-term interactions (sometimes labelled a *nexus*) will lead to longer-term strategic partnerships between TCOs and terrorist organizations, and so far most analysts believe this not to be likely.

Terrorist Organizations and Insurgent Groups

Among the transnational non-state actors that pose significant threats to international security and global stability, perhaps none has gotten more widespread attention in the early twenty-first century as terrorist organizations. For all of this attention, however, confusion and misperceptions persist about the nature of terrorism and about the groups that perpetrate terrorist acts. While part of this may be attributed to the 'definitional potpourri' among scholars and policymakers (Nacos 2012), much of it is the result of government officials, media outlets and others using the terrorist terminology for their own purposes to describe groups, individuals, threats and acts that may or may not be terrorism.

A working definition of **terrorism** would include several elements. First, the acts are violent in nature. This may be traditional physical violence, but in the twenty-first century must now include destructive acts in cyberspace. Second, the motives must be political in nature. This is the key distinction between terrorist organizations and TCOs for most experts. Third, the targets are civilians or otherwise seen as non-combatants. Attacks against military or other governmental targets may include nongovernment personnel, making this element more difficult to distinguish at times. Fourth, the intent of the act is to spread fear and panic to a larger audience. This is the primary reason why innocent victims are sought. Fifth, and in order to facilitate the previous goal, targets and timing are selected to maximize coverage by mass media.

> **Terrorism** involves acts of violence and destruction aimed primarily at civilians/non-combatants, in order to spread fear and panic to a larger audience through mass media and other means. For an act to be considered terrorism, the purpose in committing it and the objectives they hope to achieve must be political.

These groups form and commit such acts largely because of the convergence of their strongly held ideologies and their marginal place in the political system. Such groups typically arise in response to an unacceptable *status quo* or a profoundly unwelcomed change in the political system. Whereas most groups would work within the system to affect a desired change, those who affiliate with terror groups typically are (or feel they are) being shut out of the process, denied access and stripped of political relevance. Thus, whether for political, sociocultural or situational reasons, they are (or feel they are) powerless under the current political arrangement, and therefore must resort to violence in order to be heard. Such groups, then, tend to be more common in systems where minority voices have no legitimate, peaceful outlet of expression, such as in authoritarian regimes, or where one dominant power (regional or global) tends to dictate policy to the exclusion of all who dissent.

Much as globalization and the post-Cold War international system have affected transnational criminal organizations, so too have they had a profound impact on terrorist organizations and insurgent groups. With some variance, most terrorist organizations have little hierarchical structure and instead operate as a fluid, decentralized network of individuals and small groups (known as cells) spread out over a wide area. Changing global dynamics have made this an easier and more effective tactic to avoid detection and capture, and their successes in doing so have led other non-state actors, such as TCOs, to more frequently utilize such an approach. Also, the same economic deregulation that has made it easier for TCOs to engage in smuggling and money-laundering operations have given terrorist organizations greater freedom to move money, materials and personnel undetected across state borders.

Terrorist organizations are funded in a number of different ways. For example, some have state sponsors, who offer direct monetary support as well as indirect aid such as a safe haven, training grounds, weapons and more. This provides mutual benefits, including the opportunity for the state to utilize such groups to pursue policy goals through unconventional means. Also, some groups benefit from the donations of private organizations and wealthy individuals who share the group's ideological or strategic goals. Often, such funds are used not merely to fund operations, but also for such purposes as community development and outreach that help to win over the hearts and minds of local populations. Additionally, legitimate businesses are often used to fund terrorist operations, as well as to launder illicit funds gained elsewhere. These businesses may or may not have known connections to terrorism, and they can be found throughout the world. Finally, most terrorist organizations finance their activities at least partially through illicit and illegal activities. In this aspect of their operation, terrorist organizations behave much like transnational criminal organizations. Human trafficking, fraud, money laundering, smuggling and other criminal activities are among the most common illegal activities in which these groups engage. The drug trade in particular has gained significant attention in academic and policy circles since the 1990s. 'Narcoterrorism' refers to drug operations run by terrorist organizations, which in many cases account for most if not all of that group's external funding. A few scholars are wary of the characterization as somewhat misleading, however, preferring the term 'narco-funded terrorism' to distinguish terror groups from drug cartels (Nacos 2012), or arguing that the term is propagated by policymakers who benefit from emphasizing the linkages between the drug trade and terrorism (Miller and Damask 1996). Those who investigate the possible nexus between TCOs and terrorist organizations often focus on the drug trade as the most prominent point of convergence. And while some dismiss this cooperation as merely being lucrative business with no meeting of the minds on motives, others worry that longer-term partnerships may be blurring the lines between motives and money.

Related to, but distinct from, terrorist organizations are insurgent groups. While the two may be similar in many ways, including their utilization of violence to achieve political ends, there are significant differences between the two. The larger goal of an **insurgency** is to utilize paramilitary strategies and tactics in order to ultimately gain political power at the expense of the ruling regime. Their efforts are typically more organized, more sustained, more widespread and more intense than most terrorist organizations, and as such are best thought of as rebellions against a sovereign entity. Their targets also differ from terrorist organizations,

> As opposed to terrorism, **Insurgency** is paramilitary in nature, the primary goal being to overthrow the ruling regime and assume political power. Such groups are typically not seen as legitimate by either the ruling regime or the international community.

with a focus on military and political targets and objectives, to facilitate in the downfall of the sovereign force. Generally, such forces are not recognized as legitimate challengers to the regime by either the regime itself or the majority of the international community, thus distinguishing them from belligerents locked in a civil war. While insurgent groups sometimes employ terrorist tactics, these are typically meant as a means to a larger end, rather than political statements in their own right.

Table 7.1   Types of transnational actors

Type of Transnational Actor*	Notable Characteristic
Civil Society Organizations	Work to help disadvantaged groups or the overall common good.
Nongovernmental Organizations	Focus on either operational projects or affecting policy change.
Transnational Advocacy Networks	Groups connected by an interest in or advocacy for a shared issue.
Multinational Corporations	Priority is profit through international commerce and trade.
Grassroots Organizations	Attention is focused on addressing localized problems.
Grassroots Support Organizations	Work to facilitate local efforts or to help poor and disadvantaged people.
Transnational Religious Movements	Operate internationally to pursue their religious values and beliefs.
Non-state Nationalist Groups	Focus is on enhancing political power, gaining autonomy or statehood.
Transnational Criminal Organizations	Focus is on financial gain through a wide variety of illegal activities.
Terrorist Organizations	Engage in violent behaviour to instil fear and force political change.
Insurgent Groups	Use organized violence to affect regime change and gain political power.

* Please note that these are not mutually exclusive or discrete, as groups can fall into more than one category.

CHARACTERISTICS OF TRANSNATIONAL ACTORS

It should now be apparent that there is a vast diversity among the tens of thousands of transnational actors that currently operate. This diversity exists in several different respects, including their size of membership, geographic reach, organizational purpose, source(s) of funding and internal structure.

Size

There is certainly no shortage of large organizations on the world stage, most notably the MNCs with interests in seemingly every corner of the world. (For example, as of 2014 Coca-Cola is sold in every country on the planet except for Cuba and North Korea.) Even among non-MNCs, a few groups boast memberships of a million or more. Most groups, however, are substantially smaller, with membership rolls as large or small as are their causes and their geographic reach. Bearing in mind the state of technological advancement in the twenty-first century and given sufficient resources it is possible for just a few dedicated individuals in a very small group to make a substantial impact on an issue of importance to them. Depending on the cause, though, it may be critical to have a large number of members. Grassroots organizations, for instance, often depend on large numbers of volunteers to engage in a wide range of activities, from circulating petitions to public demonstrations. It is important to note, however, that size doesn't necessarily equal strength. Large numbers of people are sometimes difficult to manage, and many may be more likely to become passive within the organization on the belief that there are plenty of other people who will act. Conversely, groups with a smaller number of dedicated members can sometimes be much more effective than their larger counterparts.

Geography

In an increasingly globalized world, national borders are often of only limited importance to some transnational groups. Such issues as environmental protection and global health initiatives don't conform to state boundaries, and so some groups organize their reach based on the nature of the issue being addressed, regardless of these boundaries. The result of this is that while numerous groups operate on a truly global scale, an increasing number of them – perhaps 80 per cent or more – are more regional in scope as they tackle issues that are predominantly centred in one area of the world (Kegley 2010). The level and type of activity within and between states can be formal and direct, such as that of a multinational corporation, or it can be designed to exert more indirect influence on a government or its population. The proliferation of computer and telecommunications technology into more parts of the world than ever before has allowed smaller groups to have more geographic reach than they might have had only a decade or two ago.

Purpose

Different types of groups operate for a variety of purposes. The profit motive ultimately drives MNCs, while policy change or preservation marks the purpose of most issue advocacy groups on the world stage. The same is true for transnational criminal organizations and terrorist organizations, respectively, though their means of pursuing such purposes are largely illegal and unacceptable to a lawful society. Some purposes are wide ranging, while others are narrower in scope. Some are supported by a wide consensus of supporters, while others are more controversial. There are times when an actor may wish to pursue secondary purposes, which can sometimes bring accolades but can also precipitate conflict and controversy. The latter reality can sometimes be seen, for instance, when a multinational corporation takes a stand on a social or political issue within society, such as Coca-Cola's position on Apartheid in South Africa in the 1980s.

Funding and Support

There are multiple sources of funding for transnational organizations, and access to funds may depend to some extent on the type, purpose and activities of the various groups in question. MNCs get their funding primarily through profits, though some also receive additional benefits in the form of tax abatements and reductions, government incentive payments, industry-based subsidies, content-based grants and others. Other types of groups depend on various forms of private donations, some getting support from big contributors while others depend on small, grassroots giving. Yet other groups accept governmental funding in varying amounts from states and/or international governmental organizations. As was discussed earlier, there are even government-organized groups (GONGOs), which are funded substantially or wholly by the government bodies who created them in the first place. Some critics believe that these private and governmental donations, especially those from big contributors, could affect the policy stances and the activities of said groups as they are co-opted by the wealthy few. Without funding, however, nearly all group activity would soon grind to a halt, making contributions from all sources a necessary part of these groups' existence.

Internal Structure

The type of organizational structure adopted by a transnational actor is largely a function of its other characteristics. MNCs, for instance, by and large hold fast to a more traditional, hierarchical model of organization, though geographic subdivisions are sometimes given limited autonomy to act in response to the peculiarities and uniqueness of their various markets. This approach is necessary in order to maintain consistency of policy and product quality, and to hold subsidiaries and subdivisions accountable for variations from the central plan. Conversely, in order to evade detection, capture and prosecution, some transnational criminal organizations have diverged from the centralized, corporate structure. Instead, many are adopting practices most commonly seen among terrorist groups, including such things as cell-based organizational structures and more decentralized decision-making.

THE ACTIVITIES OF TRANSNATIONAL ACTORS

Fundamentally, transnational actors exist to affect change on regional or global issues of importance to them, and to influence the decisions and the decision processes of those in power at all levels concerning those same issues. This is done in a number of different ways, and often in multiple ways simultaneously. Indeed, it is important to keep in mind that virtually no transnational actor engages in any single behaviour to the exclusion of all others. Rather, groups employ multiple approaches to the task of affecting the changes that they desire. Some of these approaches are better suited to certain types of actors and certain situational parameters, and organizations are sometimes designed to capitalize on this, but no approach is the exclusive domain of any actor or group of actors.

There are several types of activities in which most TNAs take part. For example, a substantial number of groups are designed primarily to take direct action in order to address relevant problems and issues, and still others engage in direct action as a significant portion of their organizational strategy. This hands-on approach is often one of the more publicized elements of a group's efforts outside the organization. Another type of activity in which TNAs engage is lobbying. While direct action is the preferred approach toward change for some groups, others focus primarily on lobbying governments and individual decision-makers to affect change. This lobbying activity can take many forms, much of it occurring at the state level and coordinated to varying degrees at the international level. Some groups also lobby international organizations, such as the roughly 3,000 international NGOs registered to operate at the United Nations.

A third type of activity practiced by TNAs is to promote issue awareness. The goal here is to make sure all parties relevant to an issue are fully informed of the facts needed to make decisions deemed beneficial to the group. This may be done through direct dissemination of information, public ad campaigns, political activism such as demonstrations, use of social media and other internet tools and more. The proper approach depends largely on the nature of the issue, the information to be distributed, the dynamics of the political system and other similar variables. Conversely, transnational groups may focus their attention on the decision-makers themselves, serving an oversight role to ensure that their interests, no matter how wide or narrow, are promoted or protected.

Yet another activity common to most TNAs is fundraising. Whether seeking profits or soliciting donations, groups must engage in fundraising in order to facilitate the other functions of the organization. This funding may take the form of small grassroots donations, direct or indirect subsidies from governmental institutions and large donor gifts and bequests, among others. Lastly, all TNAs engage in some form of outreach. Going beyond the normal lobbying efforts, outreach encompasses efforts to create longer-term relationships with groups and individuals outside the organization but of benefit to the organization's goals and objectives. This outreach may work in both directions, as outside actors seek either to influence or to benefit from the influence of a particular transnational actor. Often, these partnerships help all parties involved to achieve their larger goals, such as when civil society organizations partner with the International Monetary Fund to pursue development initiatives for the underprivileged.

THE IMPACT OF TRANSNATIONAL ACTORS

There are seemingly countless ways, both large and small, in which transnational actors have had an impact on global affairs. Just since the turn of the twenty-first century, TNAs have been at the heart of some of the world's most significant events. It was a terrorist organization that on 11 September 2001 set events in motion that triggered a decade-long 'global war on terror' and precipitated monumental changes in how nation-states approached homeland security. It was the behaviour of multinational corporations that precipitated the global economic crisis in 2008, both in their direct actions leading to the crisis and in their efforts to lobby national governments and IGOs toward economic deregulation. And it was grassroots citizen activist groups that sparked the Arab Spring uprisings in early 2011, which saw leaders forced out of power in four countries, armed uprisings commence in two others and major demonstrations take hold in at least half a dozen more as of early 2013.

Beyond these examples of event-driven significance, there are more general ways that TNAs have impacted global affairs. These include their impact on issue advocacy and regimes, global democratization, the struggle for human rights and political liberties, the continued march of globalization and the use of soft power in the global arena.

Issue Advocacy and Regimes

For some TNAs, issue advocacy is their *raison d'être*, and global activity of this type seems to be at an all-time high. These organizations serve to empower individuals and help to spark collective action by private citizens. The stronger these efforts become, the more it is believed that power will be further diffused away from government and toward the people themselves. This could lead to a substantial transformation of global politics (Kegley 2010), if it has not already done so. It also has the effect of bringing more issues into the public eye, and pressuring states and

IGOs to address issues that even a decade or two ago would potentially be disregarded, even discarded as unimportant.

One of the more lasting impacts related to issue advocacy is the shaping of **regimes**, the sets of political, cultural, economic and moral norms and values that govern discourse and action on a given issue or set of issues. As TNAs become more involved and influential in the debates and decision processes on a given issue, the more impact they tend to have on how that issue and the actors involved in it operate into the future. For example, repeated pressure by civil society groups on the importance of protecting human rights has led governments to re-evaluate trade relations with countries that allow extensive child labour or fail to provide basic safety standards for their workers.

> A **Regime** is a set of political, cultural, economic or moral norms and values that govern discourse and action on a given set of issues. These take a multitude of forms, from informal practices to international treaties.

Global Democratization and Human Rights

Since the early 1990s, popular uprisings and increased demands for democratic reforms have stretched across the globe, including Eastern Europe, the former Soviet Union, the Middle East, East Asia and more. Spurred by the advent of advancements in communication – most notably the internet – and the seemingly unstoppable force of globalization, the last two decades have seen a massive expansion of democracy as more and more states have been forced to shed their autocratic ways in favour of granting individual liberties, civil rights and political equality to their citizens. Utilizing tools such as social media, advocacy networks and civil society organizations have been able to penetrate even the most closed societies to introduce such ideas to populations that only a few years ago might not have known of them.

These same forces of globalization and global communication have helped to spark a dramatic increase in demands for the global community to protect and defend basic human rights around the world. The UN's declaration on the 'responsibility to protect' (RtoP) is but one manifestation of this pressure, as national governments and IGOs are lobbied incessantly to intervene in regions where basic human rights are neglected, ignored or actively abused. No longer is it universally accepted in the international community that state sovereignty is inviolable, as it becomes more acceptable for states to intervene, at least in limited ways, against states who fail to protect the basic rights and security of its citizens.

Globalization and the Global Economy

The effects of globalization can be felt at all levels of human interaction and arguably in every corner of the globe. As democracy continues to spread, so do the forces of Capitalism and free market trade that contribute to this process. Multinational corporations are major drivers of this dynamic, serving to overlap and overshadow state borders and to lead global economic trends. Despite the difficulties experienced in recent years with regard to global financial crises, this economic globalization has contributed greatly to the fact that standards of living are on the rise for billions of people. This in turn has contributed to the empowerment of entire classes of people in a multitude of countries, which gives further momentum to the drive for democratization and the securing of political rights and social justice for entire societies.

Soft Power and Transnational Actors

All of this fits well with a concept out of the political science literature that has captured the attention of world leaders and leading scholars alike since the 1990s, a concept known as **soft power**. Rather than focus on traditional 'hard' power – the use of coercion and/or incentives – to influence the decisions of other actors, Joseph Nye posited that there was an alternate way that could prove much more effective. Instead of deterring or compelling others' behaviour, an actor could convince others that they want what the actor wants. In other words, the soft power approach co-opts actors into acting favourably, rather than compelling behaviour through

> Rather than relying on incentives and threats, an actor using a **Soft Power** approach convinces other actors to want what they want (democratic reform, individual liberties and so on), thus co-opting them into cooperation.

incentives and threats (Nye 2004). This attraction works when the actor puts focus on desired values and conditions, such as promoting democracy, individual liberties and human rights, among others. While it is a much longer-term and often indirect approach than are the hard power alternatives, it may lead to more lasting, peaceful solutions to potential conflicts and also contribute to greater freedom, prosperity and security for all involved. TNAs can play a central role in this approach, working in a multitude of capacities to enhance or inhibit the generation of soft power. As the perceived legitimacy of TNAs grows in the international system, their influence over the behaviour of others also grows, opening the door for these global players to have a substantial impact on global affairs.

CHALLENGES OF TRANSNATIONAL ACTORS IN INTERNATIONAL AFFAIRS

While there are indeed many issues posed by the increased importance of transnational actors, and many challenges abound by the significant shifts in the international stasis, two matters in particular may be worth greater attention and action in the short term: challenges to state sovereignty, and questions concerning legitimacy, accountability and credibility.

Challenges to State Sovereignty

The Westphalian system of sovereignty, which has shaped global affairs for over three and a half centuries, continues to be affected in meaningful and lasting ways by the increased activity and rising influence of TNAs. The extent to which boundaries have become less important and the primacy of the state has been challenged is still up for debate (Risse 2012; 2002), but there is no questioning that the impact of such groups thus far is significant. While still the primary actor in world affairs, nation-states no longer hold the only seat at the table when it comes to making important decisions, influencing the decisions of others or even setting the global agenda. At every turn, TNAs are continuously found to be present, active and influential on a wide range of issues from trade relations to international security. Power is decentralizing, thanks in no small measure to continued technological advancement, the forces of globalization and a growing sense of empowerment by an ever-increasing number of people around the world.

Challenges to the Westphalian model are arising both internationally and within states themselves, further serving to soften the grip of state sovereignty. Even small groups of people, situated in restrictive or outright oppressive systems, are finding ways of challenging the governments that repress them. As more countries around the world continue efforts toward democratization, such groups are learning the true extent of the power that they wield. In fact, in some cases it can be said that this power is the very thing driving democratization in the first place, as various autocratic governments try to reform or are pushed aside by pressure or by force. Added to this is the growing notion of **responsible sovereignty**, which has been gaining traction among scholars and the larger international community since the 1990s (Etzioni 2006). This is the idea that all states and the international community at large have a responsibility to protect all people around the world, and are obligated to violate the sovereignty of any state that fails to protect its own population. In other words, state sovereignty is conditional rather than absolute, and non-state actors may play a significant role in monitoring the bad behaviour of abusive or neglectful regimes.

> One challenge to the traditional Westphalian system is the concept of **Responsible Sovereignty**, which says that state sovereignty is conditional rather than absolute. If a state fails to protect its own people, it is the obligation of other states and the international community to intervene on their behalf. This is manifested in the UN principle of Responsibility to Protect (RtoP), and in other ways.

So, as the boundaries between system, states and citizens continue to blur and fade (Keck and Sikkink 2004), will the increasingly complex international system that is emerging serve to help or harm the prospects for peace and cooperation in the world? It seems that only time will tell for certain.

Questions of Legitimacy, Accountability and Credibility

In the Westphalian system as it has existed for centuries, the legitimate authority to govern has been held exclusively by states in the international system. As the roles and the power of TNAs continue to evolve, however, the matter of legitimacy becomes more difficult to manage. It seems that under certain circumstances and on some issues, non-state entities are accepted as legitimate actors in the decision-making process, or at least as having a legitimate role to play in issue advocacy. This raises a number of questions. What does it mean for a transnational actor to have legitimacy on issues of global import? How does this affect the process of formulating, instituting and administering laws and policies at the international level? To what extent can or should such legitimacy be codified into policy processes and procedures at the state and international levels, and with what consequences? Who benefits and who is harmed if non-state entities are given a larger or smaller voice in international affairs in this way? For the most part, the legitimacy of any transnational actor is fluid and subjective, owing as much to the perceptions of other principal players as to the social, political and situational contexts in which the issue is surrounded (Brown 2008).

Related to this is the issue of accountability. To the extent that TNAs are able to contribute to decision-making or otherwise influence matters in the global arena, how (if at all) can and should they be held accountable for their actions? To whom should they be held accountable? Does accountability mean something different for government and nongovernment actors? Many questions arise on this matter, but answers are less clear. Sanctions are clear for governmental actors partially because their clients – those that they are charged to serve – are clearly identified. But for TNAs, there are multiple clienteles with varied levels of expectation, accessibility and trust. What one audience might deem a necessary action, another audience might determine unacceptable and worthy of sanction. International law and convention seems ill-equipped to deal with such questions, as they (much like the rest of the international system) are geared to deal with states and IGOs, not TNAs. As with legitimacy, much of this depends to a large degree on the perceptions and expectations of other relevant actors, as well as the various contexts within which the issue exists.

Overall, legitimacy and accountability on their own may be sufficient to afford power and influence to a transnational actor. In the larger picture, however, it may be the case that they merely contribute to a larger sense of credibility for that actor, which is necessary and crucial if a given transnational actor is to have any substantial long-term impact on global affairs (Brown 2008).

THE FUTURE OF TRANSNATIONAL ACTORS ON THE WORLD STAGE

What does the future hold for transnational actors on the world stage? If developments over the last couple of decades are any indication, it seems their power and influence will continue to be felt in nearly every aspect of international activity. Examples of TNA successes include such international agreements as the Kyoto Protocol on global climate change, the international Landmine Convention and the creation of the International Criminal Court, to name just a few. It would be difficult to pick up a newspaper or tune into a news broadcast without seeing some manifestation of TNA efforts to affect change, and the internet is seemingly overflowing with examples and evidence of their continued efforts to bring even more political, economic, social and ethical changes at the local, national and international levels.

However, there is intense debate over the extent to which TNAs currently influence states, IGOs and the international system, and there is a wide variance of opinion concerning future prospects to do the same (Kegley 2010). At least some portion of this split in outlook can be attributed to the theoretical perspective underlying the analysis. Liberalist theories are more likely to credit TNAs for having influence and power, and it can be argued that such dynamics are consistent with the liberalist worldview and the aspirations of its adherents. Conversely, realist theories generally subscribe to the state-centric model of sovereignty, and tend to eschew any explanations that credit other international actors for having power or significant influence over states.

Overall, there are some analysts and academics who believe that TNAs have growing influence now and may be poised to challenge states for primacy in the decades to come. Meanwhile, there are some who believe that the power and influence of TNAs is overstated now and that there is no likelihood of challenging the state-centric international system anytime soon. The majority of studies in this area, though, fall somewhere in between these two extremes (Kegley 2010). For example, studies reveal that influence over policy varies significantly depending on the issue and the political landscape. It is also contended that a relatively small number of TNAs have more influence than other actors. This, however, does not happen very often, and when it does, it tends to be limited to single issues, and usually occurs when the interests of a TNA coincide with those of at least one large state power. Studies have also shown that states often use TNAs for their own purposes, influencing or outright manipulating them rather than working in tandem or being influenced by them.

In the end, it seems reasonable to contend that the influence of TNAs will continue to grow as the world continues to globalize and become more individually empowered and globally interdependent. Whether this will ever translate to a time when transnational actors become rivals for primacy in the global arena, however, seems anything but certain for now.

QUESTIONS FOR REFLECTION

1. What has accounted for the rapid growth of transnational actors on the world stage since the mid-twentieth century? Based on these factors and current dynamics, will this number decline, stabilize or continue to grow? Explain.
2. Under what conditions and on which issues do transnational actors tend to be most and least successful, and why? What factors best explain why some TNAs are more successful than others?
3. Given the greater presence and stronger influence of transnational actors in global affairs, will there be a point at which they begin to challenge the primacy of the state-centred model of international relations? Why or why not?
4. Considering the current role and future prospects for transnational actors in international relations, is it necessary for nation-states and international governmental organizations to adjust international laws and customs to accommodate them? Why or why not?
5. Overall, is the growth in prominence of transnational actors a positive or a negative trend? What are the largest positive and negative consequences of this trend continuing into the future?

REVISION QUIZ

1. Which of the following is not a characteristic of transnational actors?

   a. They are private actors
   b. They are largely non-political entities
   c. Their members are volunteers
   d. Their goals are generally policy-oriented

2. The largest era of transnational actor proliferation was/is:

   a. The mid- to late nineteenth century
   b. The period between World War I and World War II
   c. Since the 1960s
   d. Since the 2000s

3. Government-operated nongovernmental organizations garner substantial controversy because, among other reasons, they:

   a. Exist as private organizations serving the needs of the people, but are coerced into doing a government's political bidding
   b. Routinely evade, ignore or outright violate national and international laws to achieve their policy and political goals
   c. Are most commonly associated with political violence which is funded and otherwise supported by a government
   d. Are made to appear private and free from influence, but are covertly created to further a government's own objectives

4. Transnational advocacy networks and epistemic communities have members who are generally linked by:

   a. Geography and nationality
   b. Issue expertise and activism
   c. Educational background
   d. Former government service

5. Which of the following is *not* true about multinational corporations?

   a. Their influence is largely limited to the global economy
   b. They have been in existence since at least the 1600s
   c. Their wealth can sometimes rival that of whole countries
   d. They are credited or blamed for much of globalization

6. The vast majority of transnational actors operating now are:

   a. Funded through large donations and partnered with states
   b. Funded through small donations and partnered with IGOs
   c. Relatively large in membership with more of a global focus
   d. Relatively small in membership with more of a regional focus

7. The internal structures of international criminal organizations today:

   a. Are trending toward decentralized leadership and decision-making
   b. Most closely resemble the centralized, hierarchical style of MNCs

   c.   Tend to be hierarchical regionally but decentralized at the global level

   d.   Allow for decentralization of purpose with a hierarchical leadership

8. Which of the following are not activities of most transnational actors?

   a.   Direct action and lobbying

   b.   Agenda-building and feedback

   c.   Issue awareness and oversight

   d.   Fundraising and outreach

9. The influence of transnational actors on regimes:

   a.   Rises and falls primarily due to media coverage

   b.   Depends mostly on partnerships and geography

   c.   Generally increases as they become more influential

   d.   Is surprisingly negligible in all but the rarest cases

10. The UN declaration on the responsibility to protect is a manifestation of:

   a.   How powerful a small but well-organized and well-funded organization can be to compel states to act against their preferences

   b.   How important it is for states, IGOs and transnational actors to coordinate their efforts at combating illegal commerce

   c.   The pressure placed on states and IGOs to intervene into the affairs of states that fail to protect and defend their own citizens

   d.   The limitations that transnational actors face when trying to resist the will of powerful states and influential IGOs

11. The central idea behind soft power is that:

   a.   Compellence is more effective than deterrence at influencing behaviour

   b.   Deterrence is more effective than compellence at influencing behaviour

   c.   Incentives and threats are more effective than co-opting others' wants

   d.   Co-opting others' wants is more effective than incentives or threats

12. The idea of responsible sovereignty:

   a.   Is a distinct departure from the hands-off approach of state-centric sovereignty

   b.   Was the prevailing approach to sovereignty for centuries, but is now changing

   c.   Is an attractive proposition for states, but would harm transnational actors

   d.   Was once seen as the future of international relations, but has fallen from favour

13. Legitimacy, accountability and credibility can all be seen as:

    a. Obstacles faced by states and IGOs trying to limit the influence of TNAs
    b. Challenges faced by transnational actors that want more power and influence
    c. Stages that a TNA must go through to be recognized by the states and IGOs
    d. Opportunities for TNAs to challenge states and IGOs in formulating policy

14. Those holding a realist worldview most likely believe that transnational actors:

    a. Have little to no real power now, and have little prospect of it in the future
    b. Possess moderate power now, but probably won't challenge state sovereignty
    c. Are rising in power, and may one day challenge state-centric sovereignty
    d. Could be the key to overcoming the limitations of the international system

15. Looking at relevant contemporary scholarship and the historical record, it seems reasonable to contend that the influence of transnational actors:

    a. Has been overstated to this point, largely as a result of examples of successes that are not representative of the challenges that TNAs face
    b. Reached its apex in the 1990s and 2000s, as they are intrinsically unable to overcome the challenges of legitimacy, accountability and credibility
    c. Will continue to grow as the world continues to globalize, individuals become more empowered and states become more interdependent
    d. Is destined to continue expanding, due to continued globalization and increased interdependence, until they create a system of dual sovereignty

Answers: 1: b; 2: c; 3: d; 4: b; 5: a; 6: d; 7: a; 8: b; 9: c; 10: c; 11: d; 12: a; 13: b; 14: a; 15: c.

BIBLIOGRAPHY

Almond, G.A. and Verba, S. (1963) *The Civic Culture* (Princeton, NJ: Princeton University Press).
Boli, J. and Thomas, G.M., eds (1999) *Constructing World Culture: International Non-Governmental Organizations Since 1875* (Stanford, CA: Stanford University Press).
Brassett, J. and Tsingou, E., eds (2011) 'Legitimacy and Global Governance [special issue]', *Review of International Political Economy* 18(1).
Brown, L.D. (2008) *Creating Credibility: Legitimacy and Accountability for Transnational Civil Society* (Sterling, VA: Kumarian Press).
Bruszt, L. and Holzhacker, R., eds (2009) *The Transnationalization of Economies, States, and Civil Societies: New Challenges for Governance in Europe* (New York: Springer Science + Business Media).
Cohen, J. and Arato, A. (1992) *Civil Society and Political Theory* (Cambridge, MA: MIT Press).
Etzioni, A. (2006) 'Sovereignty as Responsibility', *Orbis* 50(1) (Winter), 71–85.
Gourevitch, P.A., Lake, D.A. and Stein, J.G., eds (2012) *The Credibility of Transnational NGOs: When Virtue is Not*

Enough (Cambridge: Cambridge University Press).

Gurr, T.R., ed. (2000) *People Versus States: Minorities at Risk in the New Century* (Washington, DC: United States Institute of Peace Press).

Haas, P.M. (ed.). (1992) *Knowledge, Power, and International Policy Coordination* (Edinburgh: Reaktion Books).

Haynes, J. (2004) 'Religion and International Relations', *International Politics* 41 (September), 451–62.

Haynes, J. (2001) 'Transnational Religious Actors and International Politics', *Third World Quarterly* 22(2), 143–58.

Martinez, R.A.B. (2008) 'Grassroots Support Organizations and Transformative Practices', *Journal of Community Practice* 16(3).

Heinrich, V.F. and Fioramonti, L., eds (2008) *CIVICUS: Global Survey of Civil Society, Volume 2: Comparative Perspectives* (Bloomfield, CT: Kumarian Press).

Keck, M.E. and Sikkink, K. (2004) 'Transnational Advocacy Networks in International Politics'. In K.A. Mingst and J.L. Snyder (eds), *Essential Readings in World Politics*, 2nd edition (New York: Norton).

Kegley, C.W. (2010) 'Nongovernmental Organizations and the Shape of the Global Future'. In *World Politics: Trend and Transformation*, 12th edition (Boston, MA: Wadsworth).

Kuchinsky, M. (2011) 'Nonstate Actors in International Relations'. In J.T. Ishiyama and M. Breuning, M. (eds), *21st Century Political Science: A Reference Handbook*, Vol. 1 (Los Angeles: Sage Publications).

Miller, A.H. and Damask, N.A. (1996) 'The Dual Myths of 'Narco-Terrorism': How Myths Drive Policy', *Terrorism and Political Violence* 8(1), 124.

Moksnes, H. and Melin, M., eds (2012) *Global Civil Society: Shifting Powers in a Shifting World* (Uppsala: Uppsala Centre for Sustainable Development).

Nacos, B. (2012) *Terrorism and Counterterrorism*, 4th edition (Boston, MA: Longman).

Nye, J.S. (2004) *Soft Power: The Means to Success in World Politics* (New York: Public Affairs/Perseus Books Group).

Nye, J.S. and Keohane, R.O. (1971) 'Transnational Relations and World Politics: An Introduction', *International Organization* 25(3), 329–49.

PRIF Research Department III (2012). The Relevance of Private Actors in the Transnational Sphere for Just Peace Governance. Working Paper No. 13. Frankfurt: Peace Research Institute Frankfurt.

Putnam, R.D. (1995) 'Bowling Alone: America's Declining Social Capital', *Journal of Democracy* 6(1), 65–78.

Reinalda, R., ed., (2011) *The Ashgate Research Companion to Non-State Actors* (London: Ashgate Publishing).

Risse, T., (2002) 'Transnational Actors and World Politics'. In W. Carlsnaes, T. Risse and B.A. Simmons (eds), *Handbook of International Relations* (Los Angeles: Sage Publications).

Risse, T. (2012) 'Identity Matters: Exploring the Ambivalence of EU Foreign Policy', *Global Policy* 3(s1), 87–95.

Shelley, L.I., Picarelli, J.T., Irby, A., Hart, D.M., Craig-Hart, P.A., Williams, P., Simon, S., Abdullaev, N., Stanislawski, B. and Covill, L. (2005) Methods and Motives: Exploring Links between Transnational Organized Crime & International Terrorism. Retrieved from the National Criminal Justice Research Service website: https://www.ncjrs.gov/pdffiles1/nij/grants/211207.pdf

Vakil, A. (1997) 'Confronting the Classification Problem: Toward a Taxonomy of NGOs', *World Development* 25(12), 2057–70.

Wagley, J.R. (2006) *Transnational Organized Crime: Principal Threats and U.S. Responses* (Washington, DC: Congressional Research Service, Library of Congress).

Wallace, W. and Josselin, D., eds (2001) *Non-State Actors in World Politics* (London: Palgrave).

Whitfield, L. (2003) 'Civil Society as Idea and Civil Society as Process', *Oxford Development Studies* 31(3), 379–400.

Williams, P. (2001). 'Transnational Criminal Networks'. In J. Arguilla and D. Ronfeldt (eds), *Networks and Netwars: The Future of Terror, Crime, and Militancy* (Santa Monica, CA: RAND Corporation).

Chapter 8

Nature as an Actor in International Politics

STEPHEN HOBDEN

The question of who acts in international politics has been a defining question of the subject. All discussions about the 'international' contain some notion of who the actor or actors may be, and candidates have included states, international organisation, transnational corporations and individuals. So far, however, the possibility that nature might be an actor in international politics has received little consideration. Questions related to the environment have been pondered by the main streams of thought within the discipline, though this has been as an 'add on' to their main concerns, whether this be international conflict, the possibilities for cooperation or the workings of the global economy.

This chapter, by contrast, makes the claim that not only is nature an actor in international politics, it is the actor. We can only understand human activity as embedded and constituted by the rest of nature. Such a stance is in opposition to the duality that has emerged, particularly in Western thought, which divides human beings from the rest of nature. Despite various challenges, in particular Darwin's theory of evolution, anthropocentric (or human-centred) thinking persists across the social sciences, but is particularly notable in International Politics. In making a claim about nature as the actor in international politics this chapter challenges that dichotomy.

The chapter is divided into three sections. Firstly it examines the ways in which environmental issues have been analysed in three of the central approaches to thinking about International Politics: Realism, Liberalism and Marxism. The chapter shows that while all three have engaged with environmental concerns, for all three thinking about nature has been a supplement to their main focus.

The chapter then seeks to challenge this relatively marginal focus. To do this the chapter turns to a consideration of 'big history'. Big history is literally that – a history of the universe since the big bang. The purpose of adopting such an approach is to decentre the human. Looked at in the timescale of the universe, human existence appears as an ephemeral blip, dependent on a conjunction of relatively benign cosmic and global circumstances. The implications of a decentring of the human suggests the need for considering ways of incorporating thinking about humanity within the context of the rest of nature. One way of approaching this has been the recent call for the development of a 'post-human international relations'. The third section of the chapter discusses what such an approach might comprise.

The chapter concludes that, at a time of apparent global environmental crisis, typified by climate crisis, international politics provides the best starting point for thinking about the politics of our relations with the rest of nature. However, a positive contribution to thinking about these issues will require a rethinking of much of the discipline, and a change of focus away from the purely human to the human constituted by and embedded in the rest of nature.

Key Words: Nature, Non-Human Nature, Anthropocentric, Complexity Thinking, Post-humanism.

Chapter 8

Nature as an Actor in International Politics

STEPHEN HOBDEN

INTRODUCTION

The question of who, or what, is the main actor has been a central question for theorists of international relations. All theoretical approaches hinge on the notion that a certain type of entity 'acts' in international politics. Famously and paradigmatically for realists, the state is the key actor in international politics. Liberals widen the spectrum, including states, but also individuals, transnational corporations and international organisations. Marxists see the global capitalist system as an actor. Some might claim that it is only people that act – or at least are the only significant actors. Yet theorists of international politics have been happy to populate their field of study with a variety of non-human actors, albeit that those actors are abstract human creations such as the state. One potential actor that is not considered is **nature**. International Politics is a deeply **anthropocentric** discipline, which draws a very sharp distinction between the human world and the remainder of non-human nature – which can safely be dispatched to other disciplines such as geography. A brief examination of many of the keystone texts of the discipline, such as Waltz's *Theory of International Politics*, will reveal an absence of engagement with anything outside of the human.

Nature – this is a term that is open to a multiple interpretations. In this chapter it means everything that exists in the sense that there is nothing outside or independent of nature.

Non-Human Nature – all of nature with the exception of human beings. The term is used to emphasise that human beings are not independent of nature.

Anthropocentric – literally, human-centred. The view that the human species constitutes a separate or in some way special position within nature.

This exclusionary focus on the human is deplorable for a number of reasons. First, the biosphere confronts an environmental catastrophe. The contours of this cataclysm have been widely documented elsewhere (see, especially, Speth 2008). While this is not the only crisis confronting the human race at the start of the twentieth century, and we might cite nuclear proliferation, financial crisis and global inequality as equally demanding of our attention, it is not an issue that we can overlook. Secondly, International Politics is the inevitable home for analysing the politics of global environmental questions. Certainly there are environmental problems that can be addressed at the domestic level; however in confronting the 'big' issues, such as climate chaos or species devastation, it is at the global level that action will be required. The environment does not respect national borders, and international cooperation is needed to resolve issues such as climate chaos – states cannot isolate their borders from the impact of greenhouse gas emissions. Third, human existence and human activity do not occur independently from the rest of nature. Human systems interact and depend on non-human systems such as geography, food systems, water systems and the atmosphere. Certainly some social scientists have been aware of this. Mackinder (1904) famously indicated the role of geography in determining the characteristics of geopolitics, and Braudel (1995 [1949], 231) pointed to the influence of climatic and geographic factors in the development of human societies around the Mediterranean. More recently Daniel Deudeney (1999) has revisited these geopolitical discussions as an avenue for considering 'bringing nature back in' – yet these acknowledgements mark the exception rather than the pattern.

This chapter argues not only that nature is *an* actor in international relations; it will make the argument that nature is *the* actor. To reach this point the chapter proceeds through various arguments. To begin we will look at the ways in which human–environment relations have been depicted by various theoretical positions in international relations. The point being made here is that all theoretical perspectives thus far have adopted an anthropocentric position – one that sees a sharp divide between the human and the rest of the environment. We will then take the perspective of what has become known as 'big history', both to contextualise the development of the human species, and to make the argument that human development has not occurred independently of the rest of nature. There will then follow a discussion of new developments in what has been described as a 'post-human international relations', before concluding that international relations that perceive of nature as the actor in international politics requires a rethinking of the discipline both ontologically and politically.

MAINSTREAM APPROACHES TO THE ENVIRONMENT

Since the 1990s there has been an increase in interest amongst scholars of international relations in the environment. This is to be welcomed, and this increased attention has mirrored growing disquiet about environmental questions (particularly climate chaos) in the political sphere generally. Each of the mainstream approaches, reflecting their particular focus of interest, has approached the issue in different ways. Each approach though has added the environment into its list of concerns, and viewed environmental questions through a pre-existing framework.

Realists have been, for the most part, least interested in issues related to the environment. The environment has generally been seen as an issue of low politics, and not a matter of national interest in the sense of providing an existential threat to any community – well at least amongst the great powers. This lack of interest has been ameliorated to an extent by the development of an 'environmental security' agenda. The environmental security literature is large and emerges from a variety of theoretical perspectives (Cudworth and Hobden 2011), however one issue that has been analysed is the possibility of conflict due to environmental degradation: for example, droughts leading to environmental refugees, resulting in tensions in societies receiving the refugees. Alternatively, conflict may emerge as a result of competition over scarce resources. It is with reference to this latter topic that realist writers have made the most significant contribution.

At the forefront of this thinking about security has been the work of Michael Klare (see especially 2001, 2008 and 2012). Klare has consistently argued that with the emergence of a multi-polar world and one where there is increased demand for resources to feed a

> **Michael Klare on the dangers resulting from a competition for scarce resources** – the prospects are worrying. A world of rising powers and shrinking resources is destined to produce intense competition among an expanding group of energy-consuming nations for control over the planet's remaining reserves of hydrocarbons and other key industrial materials. (Klare 2008, 7)

growing capitalist system, states will come into conflict with each other. At the forefront of his concerns has been oil, sparked by fears that the world may have reached the topping point – the maximum level of oil production after which it will become increasingly difficult to extract oil. A high level of resources is needed to sustain economic development. Countries with large populations, such as China and India, which are undergoing rapid economic development, will increasingly be competing for the dwindling resources that remain.

Oil has often been seen as the spark point for future conflict. While concerns have been raised about the 'tipping point', and in a world of finite resources, it will be reached at some point, it would appear that the world has not arrived there yet. If oil is an environmental security threat there appears to be more reason to be concerned about its continued consumption contributing to greenhouse gas emissions. If oil is a requirement to maintain what has been called 'carboniferous capitalism' (see Paterson 2009), then an even more important resource for human survival is water. Concerns over the availability of fresh water in certain regions of the world have led to concerns that 'water wars' will result (Serageldin 2009). In the World Water Development Report the UN General Secretary pointed to the possibility of water shortages leading to violent conflict. This is an area over which there is considerable debate, and although competition over access to water resources appears to be a plausible possibility, others argue that negotiations over contested water resources is more likely than actual warfare (see Barnaby 2009).

Realists then, with their emphasis on interstate conflict, incorporate discussions of environment within their pre-existing framework which emphasises the always present possibility of war between states. The environment is one more potential cause of such conflict. The arguments over water though point to a second strand in mainstream approaches to environmental issues – a liberal approach. The focus of this approach is the claim that 'the question of when, if, and how well national governments cooperate to address shared environmental problems … is central to the relationship between international relations theory and the environment' (O'Neill 2009, 1). In other words this discussion is centrally about governance.

Liberal international relations scholars have contributed considerably to discussions about environmental issues. Their perspective reflects the view that the possibility of cooperation between states is also significant in interstate relations. Liberal accounts would point to the successes that have been achieved in addressing environmental questions at the interstate level. It is comparatively unlikely that much progress could occur at the national level: the serious character of an issue such as climate chaos will encourage states to cooperate. As Elizabeth DeSombre (2007, 1) notes, 'the fact that states cannot address many environmental problems successfully impels international cooperation, and there are many situations in which all parties can benefit'. Liberal scholars also point to a variety of non-state actors that play a role in environmental issues. These would include intergovernmental organisations such as the United Nations Environment Programme, and nongovernmental organisations such as Green Peace and Friends of the Earth. While it might be acknowledged that on some issues states have been able to cooperate, such as on ozone depletion (the 1987 Montreal Protocol on Substances that Deplete the Ozone Layer is often cited as an example of successful international cooperation to confront an environmental issue), negotiations on reducing carbon dioxide emissions to counter climate chaos, which perhaps have more significant economic implications, are proving to be far less successful. Liberal writers have dominated the discussions of environmental issues, and their perspective has provided a significant account of the capacity and limits to interstate cooperation.

Both realist and liberal accounts focus on states: realists suggest that environmental issues will spark conflict between states, whilst liberal accounts suggest that states have the capacity to cooperate on environmental issues. Both remain wedded to a conception, however, that draws a sharp distinction between human and non-human nature, and remains within a framework of adding nature into the study of international relations.

Marxism might provide a more nuanced account, and at a minimum moves our attention away from the state and interstate concentration of both Realism and Liberalism. However there remains a considerable debate within the environmental movement as to the utility of Marx as a starting point for a non-anthropocentric account. Also, while there is a very lively and considerable debate and contribution from Marxists to the study of international relations, the majority of work has traced the dynamics of Capitalism as a global system rather than engaging with specifically environmental issues. Very little has changed from the observation made by Eric Laferrière and Peter Stoett (1999, 139) that there was 'a near total absence of ecological reflections within IR'. Outside of IR, and particularly within Sociology, there has been a lively debate about the significance and relevance of Marxist contributions to thinking ecologically at a global scale.

There would appear to be good reasons for an analysis of the environment within international relations as part of a Marxist project. Marx in his original formulations on Capitalism saw it as an expansionary and global phenomena, a point which has been increasingly developed by work in international political economy (see, for example Panitch and Gindin 2012). In this it breaks away from state-based formulations as depicted by both Liberalism and Realism. Marxist analyses have also developed a depiction of the historical development of industrialisation, a form of organisation which has had a negative impact on the rest of nature. More recent work, particularly in sociology, has also developed the notion of a metabolic rift.

In arguing for an approach to thinking about ecology, Jason Moore (2003, 449) argues that three insights from Marx are particularly significant: first, a co-evolutionary approach to the study of history which analyses the changing relations between human and non-human nature. Human production is dependent on nature, yet at the same time transforms nature. As Moore (2003, 450) argues, 'nature shapes and is actively shaped by society'. It is an interactive, dialectical process.

Second, that there is an ecological element to the labour theory of value. The labour theory of value points to the role of labour in the production of value, yet this is a relation which also depends on the exploitation of nature. Moore argues that Marx, significantly from an ecological perspective, does not separate these out. More specifically, 'Capital does not exploit land and labor so much as it exploits the land through labor' (Moore 2003, 250). The production of value is a specific characteristic of Capitalism, reliant on human labour and the exploitation of nature. Yet value obscures the role of labour and nature in the process of production. Furthermore, value requires that capital be constantly in motion and constantly expanding. This brings it into contradiction with nature which, as opposed to value, is not boundless. As a result, 'the production of value [which] presupposes limitless expansion ... continually finds itself in contradiction with the ecological bases of value accumulation' (Moore 1993, 451).

This mismatch between Capitalism's constant expansion compared to the ecological limits is played out in Moore's final point, Marx's analysis of metabolism and metabolic rift; a point which not only signifies the impact of capital on nature but also of its global impact. Capitalism's development created and enhanced a division between town and country, with agriculture playing a major role in the development of industrial Capitalism. But this increasingly leads to a 'metabolic rift'. Nutrients are flowing out of the rural areas into the cities but are not being recycled. Marx (cited in Moore 2003, 451) described this as the 'irreparable rift in the interdependent process of social metabolism, a metabolism prescribed by the natural laws of life itself'. Agricultural practices are part of capitalist expansion and require, in a global competitive market, the ever-greater exploitation of nature through the most efficient, industrially based Capitalism. This continually points to monoculture and the driving out of biodiversity. Because capitalist development has consistently resulted in the exhaustion of the soil in agricultural production, it has constantly required expansion of the frontiers of agriculture.

Yet while Marxist theorisations would appear to have much to offer in terms of an analysis of the development of Capitalism within nature, many within the environmental movement remain suspicious of an inherent anthropomorphism in Marx's work. For example, Mick Smith points to Marx's analysis of labour, something that Marx sees as a specifically human characteristic. Smith (2001, 87) argues that Marx's approach to labour 'limits what can and can't be said about nature and it is because of this emphasis on the dynamics of *human* labour that nature finds itself marginalised in spite of Marx's materialism'. Thus nature's role in the production process is to be consistently dominated and subordinated by human activity, as implied in Marx's (cited in Smith 2001, 88) statement that 'the labour process is an appropriation of what exists in nature for the requirements of man'. In short, while nature is the basis of all human production, Marx's account differs little from the view that nature is a resource which humans can and do draw upon. This depicts humans as some way different and special with regard to the rest of nature, a claim which ecologists would resist.

Ultimately all three of the mainstream approaches reproduce the views of humans as in some way separate from nature. For realists, nature provides yet another issue about which states may come into conflict. Geostrategic views certainly see a role for geography in influencing state behaviour, yet these fail to provide an account of humanity as embedded in nature. Likewise, liberals see the environment as an issue which can be fitted within their particular worldview – one on which states can and will cooperate to find solutions. Marxist accounts stress the historical development of Capitalism, and this provides a basis for thinking about the devastating impacts that Capitalism as a form of social organisation has had for the rest of nature. In thinking through these issues we need to consider historical developments. And in terms of thinking about the place of humans as a part of nature, and of nature as the actor in international relations, we need initially to turn to the subject of big history.

HUMANITY IN BIG HISTORY

In the Western tradition, both science and religion have developed the view of the human species as being in some ways different from other species. The religions of the book (Judaism, Christianity and Islam) all share the idea that a supernatural being created the Earth and that humans were given dominion over the rest of the creation. While much of the beliefs of religion were challenged during the period of the enlightenment, the notion that humans were significantly different remained. Other species were understood as being simply the slaves of instinct, and in effect being little more than machines. Certainly there were those who were skeptical of this view – Michel de Montaigne famously raised the question of whether he was playing with his cat, or whether his cat was playing with him, and Spinoza pointed to the common substance of which everything was made – disputing Descartes' claim that there was a mind-body duality. Despite these challenges, the prevailing, anthropocentric, view is that human beings are in some way separated or stand apart from nature.

Donna Haraway (2008, 12–13) points to four challenges that have rocked the human view of its unique position within nature. The first of these was the Copernican revolution. Instead of Planet Earth being the centre of creation, it was discovered that the Earth revolved around the Sun and, in that, was no different from the other planets in the solar system. Humanity did not occupy the central place in the universe.

Secondly the theory of evolution, propounded by Darwin in *The Origin of Species*, indicated that far from being separate from the rest of nature, human beings had developed directly from other life forms, most recently, to the horror of some of his Victorian readers, from monkeys. Darwin's evolutionary account has had a troubled history, particularly when the emphasis has been placed on the notion of the 'survival of fittest'. This led to the so-called science of eugenics and the development of views that there is a hierarchy between human ethnicities – the opposite of what Darwin intended. Additionally, while it indicated human heritage in other life forms, it could be used to argue that humanity was the most evolved and fittest species (and therefore extra special). More recent explorations have focused on Darwin's notion of adaptability rather than fitness, suggesting that evolutionary patterns are rather more tinkering than perfecting. In his book *Your Inner Fish*, Neil Shubin argues that the human body is essentially a fish with legs that has the capability to walk upright. This evolutionary heritage has left humans with all sorts of residue problems from hiccups to haemorrhoids. Someone designing a human body from scratch would come up with a more efficient or at least a more streamlined version. Likewise, Gary Marcus depicts the arbitrary character of evolution as leading to appearance of 'kluges', in other words, 'clumsy or inelegant – yet surprisingly effective – solution to a problem' (Marcus 2008, 2): the human brain being a paradigmatic example. The apparently random character of evolution has also drawn out a more significant claim. Not only is the development of the human body and mind the result of random fiddling, the existence of humanity itself might be the result of entirely contingent factors. In his discussion of the Burgess Shale formation (an area in British Colombia, Canada, famous for the large quantity of fossils), Stephen Jay Gould concluded that chance played an enormous element in evolutionary patterns. Likening these developments to the playing of a magnetic tape, he argued that were we to 'wind back the tape of life to the early days of the Burgess Shale; let it play again from an identical starting point, and the chance becomes vanishingly small that anything like human intelligence would grace the replay' (Gould 1989, 14). Ultimately, given the comparatively random character of the evolutionary process, the appearance of humanity is a complete accident.

Freudian psychology contributed another challenge to the privileged position of the human, suggesting that the subconscious plays a significant role in human activity. This challenges the priority of reason, which was taken by enlightenment thinkers as the key feature of the distinctiveness of the human. Finally, Haraway argues that the development of the cyborg – the intermelding of technology with the human – raises questions of the boundaries of what it is to be human.

To the above four challenges of the human claim to be distinct from the rest of nature we might add the perspective of 'big history'. This is history written on the largest scales, and a recent development in thinking about the place of the human species within the unfolding patterns of the universe. While humans have pondered their position within the universe, it is only in relation to recent developments in cosmology, physics, chemistry and evolutionary theory that perspectives of this magnitude have been permitted and encouraged. Big history is literally that – history within the time span of the existence of the universe (roughly 14 billion years), and within the spatial elements of the universe – possibly infinite, and possibly a multiverse. At these timescales the appearance of humans, and indeed of life on the Planet, is a very recent occurrence.

If the existence of the universe to date were compressed into one year, with the big bang occurring at the beginning of the first second of 1st January, and today being midnight on the 31st December, then the Earth was formed on 14th September; the first life on Earth appeared around about 25th September; plants began to colonise the land on 20th December; the first dinosaurs appeared on 24th December, with the first mammals making an appearance on 26th December, and the first hominids on 30th December. The 31st December has been a particularly eventful day, particularly as it proceeds thus: the first humans appear at around 10.30 pm, with stone tools being in widespread use by 11 pm; settled practices of agriculture appear at about 20 seconds after 11.59 pm, and the first cities emerge at 25 seconds to midnight; Columbus sails across the Atlantic Ocean in search of a trade route to China at 1 second to midnight; and humans develop the capacity to destroy all life on the planet immediately prior to midnight.

Yet big history doesn't restrict itself to thinking about the development of life on the Planet, it also considers the cosmological processes that led from the big bang at the origins of the universe through to the creation of stars and planets. Fred Spier points out that it was a series of fortuitous accidents which permitted life to emerge on the Planet at all. Spier applies the term 'Goldilocks principle' to these factors, in the sense that all of them had to be just right – in other words, like the bears' porridge, not too hot and not too cold. In the first instance there are physical constants that need to be at certain levels for even galaxies, stars and planets to form – slight variations in the strong nuclear force, electromagnetism and gravity would have meant that nothing would have emerged out of the plasma of elementary particles that came into existence in the very first moments of the existence of the universe. Secondly, for life to emerge on Planet Earth there was a requirement that water be available. If the orbit of the Earth had taken it closer to the Sun then any water would have boiled away, an orbit further from the Sun would have meant that water would have constantly frozen. Finally the Earth had to be of a certain size such that its gravitation pull was propitious for the appearance of life. Any smaller and the Earth would not have been able to retain its atmosphere. If it had been markedly larger then the gravitation pull would have crushed anything appearing on the Planet's surface.

From a big history perspective, a very particular set of circumstances had to exist for life at all to emerge on Planet Earth. There is some speculation that life in a very elementary sense appeared on the planet Mars, however the circumstances were not suitable for this to persist, or to develop in the multifaceted ways that it has on Earth. As noted above, according to Stephen Jay Gould the appearance of the human species is also contingent on some specific evolutionary and environmental developments. One element that climatologists have speculated on is whether there were climatic factors involved in the processes by which our ancestors made the move from living in trees to walking upright on the land. Furthermore, it is claimed that there has been a period of comparatively benign climatic conditions which have coincided with the flourishing and spreading of humanity throughout the planet (Dibley 2012, 139). Certainly it would appear that certain climatic conditions prevailed that benefited smaller mammals – and one feature of homo sapiens appears to be their phenomenal adaptability to an enormous range of climatic situations – from the heat of the deserts to the cold of the Arctic regions.

Human beings have also developed their intellectual capabilities through their interactions with the physical world. There is emerging evidence that the use of tools coincided with an increase in the size of our ancestors' brains. This suggests that it was tool use that increased intellectual ability – leading to the development of a more complex tool-making capacity. In other words there has been a symbiotic and co-evolutionary relationship between humanity and the non-animate features of the environment.

The study of big history suggests that broadly environmental features – which we might be called nature – are absolutely fundamental in understanding the appearance and development of the human species. Nature has been the central actor in terms of understanding our emergence as a species, our capacity to survive in a wide range of habitats and the development of the capacities of our brains.

Without a doubt humans are a remarkable species, who have demonstrated not only a capability to inhabit much of the land space on the Planet, but also the capability to transform the landscape – clearing the forests, and mining the layer of the planet for materials to work into tools and to provide energy sources. While all species have an impact on their environment to a certain extent (even if it's solely by eating it), there is no evidence to suggest that homo sapiens have, or have had, any competitors in terms of their capacity to transform the landscape. This extends to the impact on the climate. These impacts are so great that there is now talk of it having an impact on the geological record such that the current geological era is being called the **anthropocene**.

The extent of human transformation of the environment, particularly with regard to climate change, is to such an extent that some analysts are suggesting that the human race may not only be threatening our fellow species, but also the continued existence of human civilisation on the Planet. Various ecologists point to the very rapid rate of extinction amongst our fellow species (see, for example, Wilson 2006, 5). While species extinction has been a consistent pattern in evolutionary development, the current 'sixth great extinction' appears to be without parallel and the causes can be found in the human exploitation of the habitat and impacts of climate change. Some suggest that we are not only at the forefront of threats to our fellow species, but also to ourselves. Perhaps the most prominent of these is James Lovelock, originator of the **Gaia** hypothesis. Lovelock has argued that the Earth's biosphere can be considered as an interlocking and interdependent series of networks that have maintained a balance between the various elements of the biosphere. Human activity has disrupted this interlocking network to such an extent that the persistence of human life on the Planet is at risk. In apocalyptic terms Lovelock (2006, 147) states that 'the bell has started tolling to mark our ending … only a handful of the teeming billions alive now will survive'. While this might be an extreme view, the view of the broader threat to the human

> **Anthropocene** – a term developed by the ecologist Eugene Stoermer and chemist Paul Crutzen which is used to suggest that the current human impact on the biosphere is so great that it constitutes a geological era in its own right (see Crutzen and Stoermer 2000, Dalby 2009, 11–12).
>
> **Gaia** – a term adopted by the scientist James Lovelock to describe his notion of the biosphere as an interconnected and self-regulating system.

species is expressed by other writers (see, for example, Rees 2003, 112), or, at a minimum, the century ahead is likely to be characterised by significant levels of upheaval (Gore 2013, xv).

What these authors suggest is not that life itself on the Planet will be ended by human activity, rather that the mass extinction of species may include the human species. Life will remain on the Planet, and nature will continue without humanity – just with a different set of environmental conditions. Furthermore, it is argued by Diamond that civilisations have 'collapsed' in the past and hence the dismissal of the possibility of such events occurring in the future would be an extreme anthropocentric viewpoint – seeing the human species as some way divorced from exigencies of the rest of nature. As Diamond (2005, 498) puts it, these 'environmental problems *will* get resolved', and soon, 'the only question is whether they will become resolved in pleasant ways of our own choice, or in unpleasant ways not of our choice'.

A consideration of big history points to the de-centring of the human. Humanity has appeared at a very late stage in the life of the universe to date, on one small and insignificant Planet in one of potentially billions of planetary systems in the universe. Furthermore, it would appear that a very specific series of historical accidents contributed to the appearance of humanity as a separate species – and if Gould is correct and we replay the 'tape' of evolutionary history, the outcomes may have been remarkably different. Contrary to the approaches to the study of international relations that were considered in the first part of the chapter – which have attempted to add in nature as a supplement to existing approaches – what is required is an approach which does not separate the human from the rest of non-human nature, but rather starts with a view of humanity as 'of' nature rather than 'in' nature.

POST-HUMAN INTERNATIONAL RELATIONS

Cudworth and Hobden (2011) have argued for an approach to the study of international relations that they call post-human. Post-humanism is a potentially difficult term as it covers a variety of perspectives from transhumanism to the notion of life on the Planet following the demise of the human species. However the approach suggested here comprises a combination of a non-mechanical (or non-Newtonianism) in combination with a non-anthropocentric perspective. As already noted much of the social sciences, and international relations in particular, it has retained a human-centred viewpoint. It is perhaps not surprising that the study of the human social world, especially an undertaking such as international relations, might be preoccupied with human activity and human-created institutions, such as states and international organisations. The problem

> **Post-humanism** – a term used in a variety of ways, including transhumanism (body modification), and considerations of life on the Planet after the demise of humanity: most widely used to refer to thinking that challenges human-centredness or anthropocentrism. See for example the Post-humanities series, edited by Cary Wolfe and published by the University of Minnesota Press.
>
> **Non-Newtonianism** – the view, not that Newton was wrong, but rather that his account of physics relates to an only limited subset of reality. The Newtonian account of the world has been challenged by Einstein's theory of relativity, and by quantum mechanics. Newtonian ideas have been imported wholesale into the social sciences (for example, ideas about regularities and linearity), in the form of viewing the social world as a mechanical system. Non-Newtonian approaches (in particular certain forms of complexity thinking) challenge this view.

comes when human activity is seen as divorced from the rest of nature. International Relations in particular has confronted problems when trying to analyse environmental problems. These difficulties result from the state-focused ontology of the discipline. This fails to provide an adequate framework for thinking about human relations with the rest of nature, which do not conform to territorial borders.

International Relations has also largely adopted a mechanical approach to studying the world, attempting to understand regularities, and applying a way of thinking about the world which sees it as a machine. There has been considerable criticism of the adoption of such mechanical thinking into the social sciences (Wallerstein 2000, 30–31, Homer-Dixon 2009), yet much of the study of international relations is based on the assumptions of a mechanical view of the world, which see the persistence of regularities and a sharp divide between observer and observed.

At the core of the post-human approach is the utilisation of **complexity thinking** to counter both the mechanical and anthropocentric elements in International Relations. Complexity thinking is also a broad field within which there are competing perspectives – and in particular distinctions can be drawn between approaches which want to retain a scientific (and specifically mathematical/computer-based model) and a more philosophical approach which suggests that there is a need to rethink our ontological and epistemological assumptions. The French philosopher Edgar Morin (2007) has drawn a distinction between these two perspectives as between 'restricted' and 'general' complexity. A post-human international relations understands complexity much more as a generalised condition.

Such a way of thinking about complexity focuses on the notion of a **complex adaptive system**. A complex adaptive system can be made up of a number of elements, which interact with each other in non-linear ways and generate what complexity theorists describe as 'emergent features'. For example, the human body is made up of a number of systems – blood, respiratory,

> **Complexity Thinking** – an umbrella term for a wide variety of theoretical approaches which attempt to understand and analyse complexity, and, possibly, suggest policy options for working within a complex world. As different approaches to the study of complexity have radically different ontological and epistemological commitments, it is important to understand the basis to any claim that a complexity approach is being adopted.
>
> **Complex Adaptive Systems** – the cornerstone of may approaches to analysing complexity. Complex Adaptive Systems are seen as bounded entities, comprising heterogeneous elements which exhibit emergent features (in other words, characteristics that are not evident from a study of the individual elements). Complex adaptive systems are seen as open, and exhibit non-linear characteristics.

nervous – and when interacting together the emergent feature is an individual person. The international system could be seen as comprising a number of different types of systems – for example, states, international organisations and transnational corporations, and it is their interactions that lead to emergent features.

These systems are seen as 'open' – that is, they intersect and overlap with other systems – so, for example, the human body takes in other systems in the form of food, and can be invaded by other systems in the form of viruses. The international system could be seen as interacting with the global economic system. Complex adaptive systems also adapt to their environment, so that they can be seen as evolving in tandem with other systems. Complex adaptive systems are also viewed as operating in a network of interactions – and interactions with other systems. In the course of such interactions, systems adapt to their environment, and therefore systems are seen as co-evolving with each other – in a constant and dynamic process of change.

A further characteristic of systems is that they can be seen as 'nested'. In a nested series of systems, larger-scale systems can be seen as encompassing many smaller scale systems. Such systems interact closely with each other, while maintaining sufficient boundaries to permit their individual analysis. With reference to international relations, all human systems can be seen as nested within a global environmental system. The analysis of nested systems also allows the analysis of hierarchical relations between systems. This form of analysis has been taken furthest by the ecologists Lance Gunderson and Buzz Hollings, and their various associates. Gunderson and Hollings (2002) describe such systems as a '**panarchy**'. These are interlinked systems combining elements from both human systems with those of non-human nature. As such this approach to thinking allows us to analyse the interactions between human social systems and their overlap with the remainder of the human world (see Scheffer et al. 2002).

> **Panarchy** – a term developed by the ecologists Lance Gunderson and Buzz Holling to describe nested, overlapping and intersected collections of complex adaptive systems – particularly those that comprise both human and non-human systems.

As opposed to the state and territorial focus of much international relations theorising, the notion of a panarchy of interlinked and co-evolving systems enables the development of thinking about human–non-human relations at a variety of levels, whether global, regional or local. Hence, the biosphere can be seen as a complex adaptive system which has changed over time in parallel with the diversity of human and non-human systems. If human systems are viewed as nested within a much wider range of other systems then the duality which characterises much of the thinking within International Relations can be challenged, permitting the analysis in particular of human interactions with the rest of the environment. In this sense the environment is not 'other' and 'out there', instead human systems are one aspect of a much broader concept of nature. Human systems can thus be seen as embedded within nature – which is both constitutive of human systems, and in turn shaped by human activity. Human development has been shaped by changes in the wider environment, and now it would appear that human activity is shaping the wider environment – though it is nature that will remain whatever humans attempt to do. It is human hubris and folly to think in any other way. If human systems are perceived as nested within any number of non-human systems then it becomes possible to analyse how developments within one system can have implications for any number of other systems across the panarchy. So, for example, changes in the climate brought about by carbon dioxide emissions ripple through a range of human and non-human systems – the oceans become acidified as a result of their increased absorption of carbon dioxide, with a result on marine life. Climatic changes result in increased levels of drought in some areas, and vast increases in precipitation in others – all with potentially devastating impacts on agriculture. The life of other species is being disrupted at a phenomenal rate, making it harder for adaptation. Feedback systems can mean that processes of climate change are impacted by positive feedback loops – so, for example, as the polar ice caps melt, less of the sun's energy is reflected back into space, and hence climate warming becomes more rapid.

Ultimately human systems, from this perspective, cannot be seen as separate from the rest of nature. Contingent and random sets of events resulted in the appearance of humans on the Planet, and to an extent the contingency of those occurrences can be traced back 14 billion years. As Neil Shubin (2013) suggests, we should be aware of 'the universe within'. A post-human approach potentially provides the tools for both acknowledging the embedded character of human systems and the interactions between human and non-human nature. By breaching the distinction between human society and the rest of nature seen in much theorising of the social world, this perspective is the central character of nature as an actor. Humans certainly act, yet these actions occur within a far broader context – acknowledging this context implies a profound rethink of our politics and the analysis of international relations.

RETHINKING POLITICS: RETHINKING INTERNATIONAL POLITICS

While we have seen that various approaches to the study of international relations have attempted to incorporate an analysis of environmental issues, they have all remained decidedly anthropocentric, failing to acknowledge that humanity is within nature and not separate from it. The study of big history' points us towards thinking about the relatively insignificant existence of human beings, and of the interdependent character of their emergence and development within a range of physical and chemical processes, that lead from the big bang to the current day. From this bigger perspective, nature is the actor, and it is through the conjunction of a set of relatively benign cosmic and global circumstances that humanity in its current form has emerged. Despite the relative insignificant position within the cosmic calendar, comparatively recent developments within capacity have led to a situation where human activity is having a potentially disastrous impact on the rest of the biosphere. Certainly disastrous for many of the species with which we share the Planet, and possibly disastrous for humanity, should, on a crowded Planet, we render large sections uninhabitable.

Yet these developments do not occur outside of nature, and nature will persist regardless of the actions of one species within that greater whole. Nature is ultimately the final arbiter, and contains the limits within which human activity can persist. Humans breach these limits to their own costs. Human activity does not occur outside of nature – even when its action creates large disruptions in the rest of nature. To see humanity as outside/superior/independent of nature, or of non-human nature, as a resource to be exploited for human ends is the central characteristic of anthropocentric thinking.

International Relations is the discipline that is best placed to confront what is usually, and incorrectly termed 'the environmental crisis'. This is because issues of power dominate this area, and because the discipline seeks to understand the world as more than domestic politics. Yet so far, because of its foundations specifically in territorial space, it has found it difficult to address these issues or to consider them beyond the human. In this chapter it has been suggested that an approach to thinking about international relations from a complexity perspective offers a means of overcoming these problems.

Such an approach, a *post-human international relations*, challenges us to rethink the ontology of international relations, and the politics of international relations. Rather than starting with the territorial space – a concept which, in ecological terms, has little meaning – the ontology of the complexity inspired post-human international relations is the complex adaptive system. The world of human society comprises a series of overlapping, cross cutting and intersected systems, from the level of the individual, up to the level of international system – and these in turn are embedded and constituted by a series of systems of non-human nature – in the terms of Gunderson and Hollings, a panarchy. The notion of panarchy enables us to reconsider the framework within which we consider both human inter-relations, but also human relations with the rest of non-human nature, and how developments within one system can have implications across the panarchy.

However it is not simply a question of an ontological reorientation, as significant as that may be. What is also involved here is a political reorientation which prioritises relations with the rest of non-human nature. Three elements might be central here. Firstly, an element of humility. Compared to the great dramas of cosmic history, humanity's appearance is less than insignificant. As Simms (2013, 16) points out, dinosaurs dominated the planet for 165 million years whereas humanity's future as a species is, at a minimum, debatable, after a mere 300,000 years. The fragility and ephemeral character of existence, in terms of individual, species and biosphere, should lead us to reflect on human hubris.

Secondly, we might adopt a precautionary principle. While the notion of an impending apocalypse is one that has arisen throughout human history, for a number of writers we do appear to be approaching a crunch point in terms of relations with the rest of nature. While humanity as a species and human civilisation may not ultimately be at threat, there is ample evidence that the impact on the species with which we share the Planet is devastating. This would imply that in terms of our policy-making and action we should proceed with a degree of caution, and focus on the point that in complex systems we cannot be assured of the outcomes of our actions.

Finally, within a panarchy of interlinked human and non-human systems, priority should be given to what has been termed resilience within systems as opposed to making systems more fragile. Resilience is taken here to mean the capability of systems to adapt to changes in their environment without collapse. The impact on the resilience of human and non-human systems should be a priority in terms of all decision-making and action.

Such a combination of priorities would result in a profound reconsideration of the interconnected character of our relations with the non-human world, and of our practice. Undoubtedly humans have a capacity to impact the biosphere. However there is nothing unique to our species, whose existence, and continued existence, depends on the rest of nature. In that sense nature is the actor in international relations. The discipline that studies politics at a global scale, International Relations, has a responsibility to develop means of analysis which permit the rethinking of our relations with non-human nature, and our practice in order to, in Andrew Simms' words, 'cancel the apocalypse'.

QUESTIONS FOR REFLECTION

1. Why might traditional International Relations be considered anthropocentric?
2. What makes big history 'big'?
3. To what extent would you accept Lovelock's view that 'the bell is tolling for our ending'? Are there any actions that we can take to avoid this fate?
4. What are the main features of complexity thinking? How can these contribute to our understanding of human relations with non-human nature?
5. 'The subject of the social sciences is the actions of humans. Therefore such studies will inevitably be anthropocentric'. Discuss.

REVISION QUIZ

1. If the history of the universe were compressed into one year, the first humans appeared on:

   a. 21st June
   b. 7th January
   c. 1st January at 1 minute past midnight
   d. 31st December at 10.30 pm
   e. 1st August

2. Anthropocentrism can be defined as:

   a. The view that humans are better than the rest of nature
   b. A form of obscene behaviour
   c. The view that humans constitute a unique and separate part of existence
   d. A type of writing
   e. The view that humans should avoid nature

3. According to Neil Shubin we should embrace our inner:

   a. Ant
   b. Monkey
   c. Soul
   d. Fish
   e. Existence

4. Positive feedback:

   a. Is a style of guitar playing
   b. Is the result of writing a good essay
   c. Brings systems into equilibrium
   d. Is the opposite of climate change
   e. Results in systems becoming more unstable

5. Post-human International Relations are:

   a. International relations after humans become extinct
   b. International relations that are post-Newtonian and non-anthropocentric
   c. International relations for computers
   d. International relations for non-human animals
   e. Not international relations at all

6. Big history is:

   a. History of the most significant people
   b. History of the great powers

    c. History from the big bang to the present
    d. History encompassing all of humanity
    e. History of large buildings

7. Gaia hypothesis:

    a. Is an Italian name
    b. Is the view that the earth's biosphere acts as a self-regulating mechanism
    c. Is the view that international relations should focus on the environment
    d. Is a make of ice cream
    e. Is an account of climate change

8. We should aim to promote the resilience of systems because:

    a. This makes them stronger
    b. Resilience is a 'good thing'
    c. It increases the capability of systems to adapt to external shocks
    d. We've been told to
    e. This allows them to operate more effectively

9. The sociologist Edgar Morin has drawn a distinction between 'restricted' complexity and:

    a. 'Generalised' complexity
    b. 'All-purpose' complexity
    c. 'Mass' complexity
    d. 'Indefinite' complexity
    e. 'Finalised' complexity

10. 'Non-Newtonianism' is:

    a. The view that Isaac Newton didn't exist
    b. The claim that gravity doesn't exist
    c. The view that Newton's mechanical view of the operation of the universe isn't applicable to the study of complex systems
    d. The claim that Newton was wrong
    e. The claim that there is more to the study of complex systems than can be understood by Applying Newton's mechanical view of the operation of physical forces.

Answers: 1: d; 2: c; 3: d; 4: e; 5: b; 6: c; 7: b; 8: c; 9: a; 10: c.

BIBLIOGRAPHY

Barnaby, W. (2009) 'Do nations go to war over water?', *Nature* 458, 282–3.

Braudel, F. (1995 [1949]) *The Mediterranean and the Mediterranean World in the Age of Philip II, Volume 1* (Berkeley, CA: University of California Press).

Cudworth, E. and Hobden, S. (2011) 'Beyond environmental security: complex systems, multiple inequalities and environmental risks', *Environmental Politics* 20(1), 42–59.

Cudworth, E. and Hobden, S. (2011) *Posthuman International Relations* (London: Zed Books).

DeSombre, E. (2007) *The Global Environment and World Politics* (New York: Continuum).

Deudney, D. (1999) 'Bringing nature back in: Geopolitical theory from the Greeks to the global era'. In D. Deudney and R.A. Matthew (eds), *Contested Grounds: Security and Conflict in the New Environmental Politics* (Albany, NY: State University of New York Press), 25–57.

Dibley, B. (2012) '"The shape of things to come": Seven theses on the anthropocene and attachment', *Australian Humanities Review* 52, 139–53.

Dalby, S. (2009) *Security and Environmental Change* (Cambridge: Polity).

Diamond, J. (2005) *Collapse: How Societies Choose to Fail or Survive* (London: Allen Lane).

Crutzen, P. and Stoermer, E. (2000) 'The "anthropocene"', *Global Change Newsletter*, 41, 17–18.

Gore, A. (2013) *The Future* (London: Allen Lane).

Gould, S.J. (1989) *Wonderful Life: The Burgess Shale and the Nature of History* (New York: Norton).

Gunderson, L.H. and Holling C.S. (eds) (2002) *Panarchy: Understanding Transformations in Human and Natural Systems* (Washington, DC: Island Press).

Haraway, D. (2008) *When Species Meet* (Minneapolis, MN: University of Minnesota Press).

Homer-Dixon, T. (2009) 'The newest science: Replacing physics, ecology will be the master science of the 21st century', *Alternatives Journal* 35(4), 8–38.

Klare, M. (2001) *Resource Wars: The New Landscape of Global Conflict* (New York: Metropolitan Books).

Klare, M. (2008) *Rising Powers, Shrinking Planet: How Scarce Energy is Creating a New World Order* (Richmond: Oneworld).

Klare, M. (2012) *The Race for What's Left: The Global Scramble for the World's Last Resources* (New York: Metropolitan Books).

Laferrière, E. and Stoett, P. (1999) *International Relations Theory and Ecological Thought: Towards a Synthesis* (London: Routledge).

Lovelock, J. (2006) *The Revenge of Gaia: Why the Earth is Fighting Back – and How We Can Still Save Humanity* (London: Allen Lane).

Marcus, G. (2008) *Kluge: The Haphazard Construction of the Human Mind* (London: Faber).

Mackinder, H.J. (1904) 'The geographical pivot of history', *The Geographical Journal* 23(4), 421–37.

Moore, J. (2003) 'Capitalism as world-ecology: Braudel and Marx on environmental history', *Organization & Environment* 16(4), 431–58.

Morin, E. (2007) 'Restricted complexity, general complexity'. In C. Gershenson et al. (eds), *Worldviews, Science and Us: Philosophy and Complexity* (Singapore: World Scientific Publishing), 5–29.

O'Neill, K. (2009) *The Environment and International Relations* (Cambridge: Cambridge University Press).

Panitch, L. and Gindin, S. (2012) *The Making of Global Capitalism: The Political Economy of American Empire* (London: Verso).

Paterson, M. (2009) 'Post-hegemonic climate politics?' *British Journal of Politics & International Relations* 11(1), 140–58.

Rees, M. (2003) *Our Final Century: A Scientist's Warning* (London: William Heinemann).

Scheffer, M. et al. (2002) 'Dynamic interaction of societies and eco-systems – linking theories from ecology, economy and sociology'. in L.H. Gunderson and C.S. Holling (eds), *Panarchy: Understanding Transformations in Human and Natural Systems* (Washington, DC: Island Press), 195–240.

Serageldin, I. (2009) 'Water wars?', *World Policy Journal* 26(4), 25–31.

Simms, A. (2013) *Cancel the Apocalypse: The New Path to Prosperity* (London: Little Brown).

Shubin, N. (2009) *Your Inner Fish: The Amazing Discovery of Our 375 Million Year Old Ancestor* (London: Penguin).

Shubin, N. (2013) *The Universe Within: A Scientific Adventure* (London: Allen Lane).

Smith, M. (2001) *An Ethics of Place: Radical Ecology, Postmodernity and Social Theory* (Albany, NY: State University of New York Press).

Speth, J.G. (2008) *The Bridge at the Edge of the World* (New Haven, CT: Yale University Press).

Spier, F. (2010) *Big History and the Future of Humanity* (Oxford: Wiley-Blackwell).

Wallerstein, I, (2000) 'From sociology to historical social science', *British Journal of Sociology* 51(1), 25–35.

Wilson, E.O. (2006), *The Creation: An Appeal to Save Life on Earth* (New York: Norton).

PART III:
Topics and Issues

Chapter 9
The International Economy of World Politics

GREG ANDERSON

What is the contribution of international political economy (IPE) to the understanding and explanation of international life? At its most simplistic, IPE can be thought of as the nexus of the political relationships derived from international economic interactions. Yet, IPE is among the most eclectic of disciplines, harkening back to a more unified period of social science inquiry; a period where many contemporary disciplines such as political science, economics, history and sociology were thought of simply as political economy. As a well-defined discipline, contemporary IPE is only a few decades old. However, like our colleagues in the rest of the social sciences, we are also engaged in robust debates about what the discipline is, what questions it should be asking, of what subjects and how they should be investigated? Yet, these divisions obscure a broadly unifying purpose among IPE scholars; understanding the complex social, political and economic relationships flowing from the increasingly indistinct boundaries separating dimensions of world politics. The aim of this chapter is twofold; first, in outlining some of the principle domains of world politics of interest to scholars of IPE and, secondly, highlighting the utility of IPE as a multidisciplinary set of tools for interpreting them.

Key Words: Macroeconomics, International Relations, Interdependence, Non-state actors, Institutions, Monetary Policy, International Trade, Central Banking, Globalization.

Chapter 9

The International Economy of World Politics

GREG ANDERSON

INTRODUCTION

As US Secretary of Defense between 2000–06, Donald Rumsfeld seemed to take special pleasure in verbal jousting with journalists. In February 2002, in perhaps his most infamous engagement, Rumsfeld defended the Bush administration's interest in Iraq with an oral exploration of distinctions he saw between knowns and unknowns saying,

> *There are known knowns; there are things we know we know. We also know there are known unknowns; that is to say, we know there are some things we do not know. But there are also unknown unknowns – the ones we don't know we know.*

Rumsfeld was evidently proud enough of the exchange to name his post-office memoir after it ('Known and Unknown' [2011]). Depending on one's view of the Bush administration, and of Rumsfeld himself, the Secretary's combativeness was offensive, humorous, dissembling platitude or obvious truism. Linking Rumsfeld's knowns and unknowns to any discussion of IPE might seem a stretch of the imagination. Yet, the emergence of international political economy in the past several decades is the reflection of a whole series of knowns and unknowns arising out of the complexities of postwar global politics.

As the name of the discipline implies, International Political Economy is some mixture of the international with politics and economics. In its relatively short life as a distinct academic discipline, IPE has become the quintessential interdisciplinary field and contributed to important debates both in and, perhaps more significantly, outside the ivory tower. This chapter's contribution to this volume is intended both as a broad overview of the emergent importance of IPE in the last several decades, some of the discipline's ontological and epistemological concerns, as well as an articulation of some of the many content areas in which IPE scholars can be found. This chapter is organized into three parts.

Part I will outline the emergence of IPE as a discipline alongside changes in global politics itself that necessitated a return to an older style of integrated social science enquiry. Part II will build upon this by exploring some of the early ontological and epistemological divisions within IPE, many of which are also found throughout the social sciences, but whose manifestation in IPE results in profound contrasts of approach, purpose and outcome. Finally, Part III will attempt to outline some of the many areas in IPE where scholars are turning the field's interdisciplinary lens toward appreciating more of the world's 'known unknowns, and unknown unknowns'. Broadly, this chapter concludes that while IPE is beset with the standard disciplinary divisions and debates endemic to all social science, its interdisciplinary approach to enquiry is well-situated to appreciate the growing complexity of global politics.

PART I: OLD WINE IN NEW BOTTLES?

… more than ever, foreign policy is economic policy. (US Sen. John Kerry, 29 January 2013)

During his Senate confirmation hearings as US Secretary of State, John Kerry faced a barrage of questions about his management of foreign policy as America's top diplomat. Broadly speaking, Kerry's testimony signalled that the United States would continue playing a pivotal role in global affairs, but that the nation's diplomacy would continue to be shaped by the countless interactions among a plethora of global actors – states, sub-state, non-state, transnational, multinational, private, public and non-profit actors of all shapes and sizes – and challenges that were often beyond the capacity of the US to deal with alone – climate change, terrorism, trafficking, regional conflict, pandemic disease. While a US Secretary of State might generally be predisposed toward an emphasis on the softer side of state power – relative to the Secretary of Defense – Kerry's acknowledgement that economic policy is a fundamental, and growing, dimension of US foreign policy is revealing both for what is says about contemporary American foreign policy and the need to study dimensions of world politics, including foreign policy, through analytical lenses as sophisticated as the subject matter itself. At its most basic, the study of international political economy details the global interaction amongst factors of production and their historical, social and political ramifications.

Inter-Disciplinary Origins

The origins of international political economy arguably originate to a period when the social sciences and humanities were more unified, with fewer of the familiar divisions between disciplines and sub-disciplines. Many of us who have entered the ranks of professional academics in recent years (including myself) have been hearing about the virtues of cross-disciplinary or inter-disciplinary research and collaboration since the earliest days of our undergraduate training. As a result, a great many recent scholars have become highly inter-disciplinary in their research, breaking down many of the disciplinary silos that have segmented the social sciences and humanities into ever more narrow niches. These disciplinary silos are problematic for a variety of reasons, not the least of which is that scarce academic positions are too frequently driven by the purity of one's training wherein departments of history, economics or political science tend to seek new colleagues who have immersed themselves narrowly in those disciplines. In short, such a research program can leave one less focused on, and with less depth in, any particular disciplinary cannon or research tradition – in effect, becoming a jack of all trades, master of none.

Yet, for scholars of international political economy the outer boundaries of many social science and humanities disciplines remain unsatisfyingly rigid, ill-suited for addressing the complexities of contemporary global politics. While most scholars cite the origins of contemporary IPE somewhere in the mid- to late twentieth century, a strong case could be made that some of the earliest explorations of the relationship between the factors of production and their relationship to politics are in Plato's *Republic* from around 380BC wherein he explores elements of the division of labour (Irwin 1996, 13). However, the most prominent early political economy treatments of the nexus of economics and politics emerged from the eighteenth-century intellectual transformation from mercantilism to free trade typified by Adam Smith's 1776 classic *Wealth of Nations* (see Irwin 1996, 26–74, 75–86). Therein, Smith engaged in a detailed analysis of the relations between the state and factors of production, most famously describing the domestic efficiency gains to be had from specialization and the division of labour. However, Smith went further and argued that these same principles could augment those gains internationally by sourcing some products abroad rather than wasting resources producing them at home. While David Ricardo (1817) later built upon this in articulating the case for free trade rooted in comparative advantage, Smith's was undoubtedly one of the most famous analyses of the political and social relationships between domestic and international stakeholders in the conduct of economic policy – the principal subject matter of modern IPE scholars (see Cohen 2008, 16–19).

However, as an identifiable discipline, the origins of IPE might reasonably be traced to Susan Strange and 1970. That year, Strange published a pivotal piece in which she complained that the study of global politics had not kept up with some of the rapid changes taking place in international economic relations (Strange 1970). While there were many who both preceded and antedated Strange, and are now considered giants in the field (Polanyi 1944; Keynes 1937), it was Strange who really crystallized the problem; scholars of international politics and of macroeconomics had carved out separate intellectual worlds that were, in fact, increasingly impossible to separate:

> **Macroeconomic** – the big picture: analysing economy-wide phenomena such as growth, inflation and unemployment.

> *The economists do not even try to deal with the political aspects of international economic relations and international economic problems; and few political scientists even try to explore the economic dimension of international politics or diplomacy. (Strange 1970, 313)*

Strange's call to interdisciplinary arms was driven, in part, by the perceived weaknesses of individual disciplines within the social sciences to fully appreciate the profound changes taking place in the global postwar order. The institutionalization of large swaths of international affairs after World War II as typified by the United Nations, the Bretton Woods institutions (IMF and World Bank) or the management of trade relations through the General Agreement on Tariffs and Trade (GATT) seemed to harken a new form of international relations wherein the Westphalian state was

> **International Relations** – study of the relations of states with each other and with international organizations and certain sub-national entities (for exampe, bureaucracies and political parties).

increasingly sharing the global political stage with other actors. Moreover, many of those actors were private or transnational in character (the multinational firm), and had economic interests as their prime function, the consequences of which were often deeply political.

Then, in 1977, Robert Keohane and Joseph Nye published *Power and Interdependence*, now virtually required reading for every PhD student in political science. As Keohane and Nye wrote in the preface to the second edition, by the beginning of the 1970s,

> *The Vietnam War had become highly unpopular in the United States, and detente seemed to have reduced the importance of the U.S.-Soviet nuclear competition. At the same time,*

international trade was growing more rapidly than world product: transnational corporations were playing dramatic political roles; and from 1971 on the international monetary system was in flux. Meanwhile, the relative economic predominance of the United States was declining as the European and Japanese economies grew at more rapid rates. (Keohane and Nye 2001, xi)

The state was not about to disappear. Nor was the United States, as the dominant example about to fade away. Yet, there were clearly other actors vying for influence alongside the state (see also Keohane and Nye 1974). The oil shocks of the 1970s, the end of the Bretton Woods system and the persistent stagflation of the era with roots at home and abroad all suggested the need for a more complex analytical lens to help understand this more complex world.

Keohane and Nye gave impetus to the research programs of countless scholars, arguably spawned at least one sub-discipline of its own (globalization studies in the 1990s) and permanently inserted 'interdependence' as a core concept throughout much of the social sciences. The complex stew of global forces, and the analytical mix needed to understand them, drew scholars of all stripes – but especially international relations theorists, macroeconomists – into what has become a heavily interdisciplinary enterprise.

> **Interdependence** – mutually dependent on each other, a reciprocal relation between entities (objects or individuals or groups).

The growth of IPE since the 1970s, first as a sub-discipline of International Relations, and increasingly as a social science discipline in its own right, has been dramatic. Yet, much remains to be done in this regard as many of the disciplinary silos that wall off the social sciences from each other remain stubbornly intact. Few formal programs in IPE actually exist and, as a result, few IPE scholars were actually formally trained in this complex stew of disciplines we identify as IPE. Most have received their formal academic training in political science, economics or perhaps international affairs, later immersing themselves in the traditions of a second discipline. Regrettably, much work remains with respect to Susan Strange's call to inter-disciplinary arms. The consequences of disciplinary rigidity are felt in everything from the hiring decisions of departments to the choices of majors and minors by undergraduates. Departments, in spite of lip service to interdisciplinary research, still tend to hire those trained in traditions with which they themselves are familiar. Young scholars pursue genuinely interdisciplinary research programs at some peril to their prospects for landing a tenure-track job since they may be perceived to lack the necessary depth of training in any one discipline; jack of all trades, master of none. This in turn cascades down the pedagogical ladder all the way to majors and minors offered to undergraduates, most of which remain anchored in tradition.

For all the work that remains, IPE scholars can also be proud of the work that has been done. The discipline has important flagship journals, including *International Organization*, *World Politics*, *International Studies Quarterly*, the *Review of International Political Economy* or the *New Political Economy* (Cohen 2010). Professional associations, some of them offshoots of larger social science organizations, have emerged, some of them, like the International Political Economy Group (IPEG) in the UK or the International Political Economy Society (IPES) in the United States, becoming quite influential in just a few short years (Cohen 2008, 47–8).

For all the harmony among IPE specialists about the need to study an increasingly complex world through an interdisciplinary lens, the nexus of several disciplinary traditions in IPE brought many of the epistemological and ontological debates along with them. In fact, not only has Strange's call for more conversation between economics and political science brought many of the same debates found throughout the social sciences, it has spawned an interesting geographical divide within IPE as well. It is to that divide and the unique questions IPE brings to the study of world politics that this chapter now turns.

PART II: THE TRANSATLANTIC DIVIDE

> *We have really everything in common with America nowadays except, of course, language.*
> *(Oscar Wilde,* The Canterville Ghost, *1887)*

If one reads the key journals noted above or attends the meetings of their related associations, one could be forgiven for coming away dazed and confused. While there is broad unanimity among IPE scholars about the need for a blend of disciplinary influences in the study of world politics, there is much less when it comes to the kinds of questions that ought to be asked and the methods by which they should be explored. In the broadest of terms, IPE now occupies two very different camps, categorized by Benjamin Cohen in 2007 as the 'British' and 'American' schools of IPE (Cohen 2007).

Catherine Weaver usefully compared this split in IPE to the differing functions of the left and right sides of the brain identified by cognitive psychologists (Weaver 2009, 338–9):

Left Brain	Right Brain
Uses Logic	Uses feeling
Detail-oriented	'Big Picture'-oriented
Facts-ruled	Imagination-ruled
Words and Language	Symbols and Images
Math and Science	Philosophy and Religion
Knowing	Believes
Reality-based	Fantasy-based
Practical	Impetuous
Safe	Risk-taking

According to Weaver, the transatlantic divide within IPE is much the same, pitting causal explanation against interpretive or reflective approaches to assessing global politics. American IPE tends to be highly positivist and reductionist in its epistemological approach whereas the British school tends to reject reductionism in favour of pursuing much broader, normative questions (Weaver 2009, 339). American IPE has increasingly looked to the methodologies of economics and mathematics, the use of large-N data sets, formal modelling and a focus on quasi-experimental approaches to social science enquiry that build incrementally by focusing on narrow sets of questions. The British variant of IPE, by contrast, doubts the utility of positivist social science and is instead drawn toward post-positivist or critical approaches that focus on broad normative questions of social justice, equality, morality and ethical matters (Cohen 2007, 199–202). American IPE is oriented around solving specific problems, and purports to be value-neutral in seeking descriptions and explanations for how things work. The British variant rejects the notion that social science investigation is value-neutral and has at its core a more overtly normative political project aimed at transformation. In effect, the American school is preoccupied with what is while the British school is focused on what ought to be (Cohen 2007, 199).

The bipolar nature of IPE has spilled over into the pages of the aforementioned academic journals and professional meetings. The pages of *International Organization* and *World Politics*, for example, have become increasingly quantitative and oriented around analyses of specific policy-oriented puzzles whereas the *Review of International Political Economy* or the *New Political Economy* tend to be more pluralist in content and outlook (see Cohen 2010).

Simple classifications of the entirety of IPE into two simple categories would make appreciating the field much easier if it actually reflected reality. In fact, categorization of IPE into American and British camps offers little more than a starting point. The debate over the American and British schools has been the focus of at least one book (Cohen 2008), one special issue of *New Political Economy* (2009) and several review articles in the pages of the *Review of International Political Economy* (Keohane 2009; McNamara 2009; Maliniak and Tierney 2009). An obvious critique of the simplistic characterization of IPE as being in two camps is that many IPE scholars straddle the territory between the two. Mark Blyth of Brown University, Rhode Island, is a prime example. A British citizen trained as an undergraduate in the UK, Blyth then went to the United States for graduate training in political science where he remains. He writes:

> I have lived 'over there' for nearly two decades. Despite being both an admirer and consumer of a great deal of the work that British IPE scholars produce and being Scottish by birth, I am by training and temperament an American scholar. (Blyth 2009)

Closer to home, I began my university training as a history major (Brigham Young), only switching to international affairs for my PhD (Johns Hopkins – SAIS), and now teach at the University of Alberta in Canada. In training and temperament, coupled with my interest in foreign policy, I suppose I fall most heavily into the positivist American School. I had, for example, never heard of Robert Cox, an icon of the British School, before coming to Canada. Nor was I familiar with Antonio Gramsci or the threads of social resistance flowing through the more critical variants of IPE. Moreover, my background includes formal training in neither of the core disciplines of economics nor political science and instead is rooted in history and foreign affairs. Like many IPE scholars, the traditions of political science, and especially economics, have become my full-time hobbies. Moreover, my dabbling in a range of other disciplinary traditions, including comparative politics, security or development studies, has created in me something of a 'jack of all trades, master of none'. Yet, it is the necessity of this same disciplinary breadth that prompted Susan Strange's original call for more interaction between economics and political science.

Hence, IPE may be riven by significant differences over some of the most basic questions of epistemology and ontology (Cohen 2007, 215–6), but are in fact complementary sides of the same coin. Whereas the American school is the more dominant, some would say hegemonic, branch of IPE, the British school is more critical, with an emancipatory agenda of social change. Whereas the American school might be oriented around the resolution of narrow problems, the British school pursues grand systemic questions. Epistemologically and ontologically, the two schools (or mixtures thereof) have their strengths and weaknesses.

Stephen Walt has offered a general critique of the gap between the needs of policymakers and the kind of research generated at most universities (Walt 2005). The dominant position of American IPE has, in part, been derived from its emphasis on problem-solving research. However, for all its emphasis there, American IPE is often hostage to parsimonious model-building, econometrics and state-centrism that reduces enquiry to neat, testable hypotheses that may not have practical implications (see Underhill 2009). Moreover, the training being offered in many US schools is heavily focused on the methodologies to be applied to large-N data sets with much less emphasis on how to ask meaningful questions of the data:

> There is nevertheless a growing problem in the British school which affects the capacity of scholars to address the big questions being posed. Some of course have joined 'the other side' by demonstrating a rather slavish devotion to the US-School preference for economistic data analysis and the testing of narrow and unoriginal hypotheses. On the other hand, in Cohen's British School, the lack of analytical rigor is if anything becoming worse, deteriorating into declaratory posturing essentially devoid of empirical underpinnings and operating at a high level of systemic abstraction … which deteriorates into a sort of template oppositionalism to global capitalism, the scholarly content of which is difficult to discern. (Underhill 2009, 350)

> At the same time the US school understands that data and observation are so unproblematic we can accept them as real … the British school that data and observation are so problematic that we must dispense with them altogether. (Cameron and Palan 2009, 123)

Yet, the reader of this section might reasonably ask 'So what, who cares?' Are these not the same kinds of ivory tower debates found in other disciplines? Historians, economists, sociologists and traditional political scientists all have their epistemological, ontological and ideological differences, don't they? Moreover, some of these debates seem at odds with both Susan Strange's plea for interdisciplinary collaboration and many of the problems of the 1970s that drove the emergence of the discipline. Efforts to delineate some of the divisions within IPE are probably a natural product of the discipline's growing prominence as a stand-alone part of social science. Regrettably, some have even begun defining the split between British and American IPE as constituting two completely different disciplines (Weaver 2009; McNamara 2009). However, these same efforts are problematic for a young discipline still trying to distinguish itself as something more than a collection of international relations scholar conversant in economics. Moreover, since so many IPE scholars reside in the 'interdisciplinary middle' between several traditions, such divisions can also been seen as artificial constructions that replicate some of the inadequacies of traditional disciplinary boundaries that frustrated IPE scholars in the first place.

Nevertheless, debates over which of two or more boxes to toss IPE scholars are important for what they reveal about IPE's contribution to the study of global politics. Students of international relations are likely familiar with the basic tenets of Realism and Liberalism as two of the dominant paradigms. Although nuanced differences between them are many, a central point of contention revolved around the role of the state in international affairs. Was the state a purely sovereign entity with maximum latitude to pursue its 'interests' relative to measures of power that might constrain its behaviour? Was international cooperation merely the product of a coincidence of self-interest by two or more states? Or, were there international bodies, agreements or conventions that, by enlightened design, incentivized the subjugation of self-interest to some collective? Debates over the proper units of analysis (ontology) are seldom far from fights over how to actually measure and evaluate any of it (epistemology).

IPE has contributed to the study of world politics, perhaps regrettably, by making it more complicated. International relations scholarship has certainly expanded the range of actors deemed worthy of examination. A near-bottomless pit of non-state actors (institutions, private sector actors, social movements, interest groups, individuals) is now vying for attention alongside states as key actors in international affairs. IPE has complicated

> **Non-state Actor** – an individual or organization that has significant political influence but is not allied to any particular country or state.

this picture by explicitly adding economics to politics in the study of this complex mix of actors. British school, American school, or somewhere in between, IPE scholars of all stripes are interested in teasing apart the complex stew of problems at the heart of global politics. IPE is more than the simple addition of economics to the study of politics, or vice versa. Hence, IPE is about more than the economic incentives for actors within international politics or how politics augments or undermines economic efficiency. Instead, the totality of IPE scholarship represents an integrated whole of the economic and political relationships at all levels (state and non-state) that connect, transform and propel our global politics.

While the diversity of IPE makes the boundaries of enquiry difficult to define, there are at least six broad areas of investigation that most IPE scholars would allow are quintessentially IPE topics: International Trade, International Monetary Relations, the Multinational Corporation, Development, Globalization and, increasingly, Climate Change. The balance of this chapter is devoted to a brief examination of the merits of IPE in sorting through each of these.

> **Globalization** – the process of international integration arising from the interchange of world-views, products, ideas, and other aspects of culture. This process is most often linked to the expansion market capitalism around the world.

PART III: SOME CENTRAL PASSIONS OF IPE

Send me a one-armed economist. (President Harry S. Truman)

Harry Truman's famous quip about having his advisors send him a one-armed economist because they kept sitting on the fence by saying 'on the one hand this, on the other hand that' signals the clash between the ambiguity of social science research and the need for certainty on the part of policymakers. It was this same need for additional degrees of certainty in understanding our global politics that drove Strange to call for greater dialogue between economists and political scientists. The need to blend politics with economics in international affairs has not always been obvious. But the assumptions of the neoclassical model, such as perfect competition or information, that make the model so compelling also leave out one of the most important factors in all matters political: humans. Conversely, students of politics frequently deal with the imperatives of economic policy-making without considering the lessons and efficiency goals of economic theory. But nowhere is the need for a mix of the two (politics and economics) more obvious than in the six basic areas of focus for IPE of all ontological and epistemological stripes.

International Trade

In the spring of 2001, I was sitting on a downtown Washington, DC patio enjoying an after-work drink with a few colleagues from the Office of the United States Trade Representative. About a half an hour after we had arrived, the stretch of Massachusetts Avenue in front of the restaurant was suddenly closed by DC police, followed by hundreds of anti-globalization protesters marching against the start of the Third Summit of the Americas commencing

> **International Trade** – the exchange of capital, goods and services across international borders or territories.

that day in Quebec City. The ostensible target of their anger was the proposed Free Trade Area of the Americas that would have knit together all 34 democratically elected governments in the Western Hemisphere under a common set of liberalized trade and investment rules. The irony of watching protesters stroll past a group of government bureaucrats, many of whom had just completed official briefing books for the US delegation to the Summit of the Americas, was rich.

However, it was also indicative of why international trade is such a quintessentially IPE topic. Trade connects the factors of production and the stakeholders behind them as they cross borders, transformed, and enter increasingly global production chains. Hence, trade is also about the poisonous mix of politics and economics that is also at the heart of IPE. As Douglas Irwin's (1996) fantastic history of the evolution of free-trade thought depicts throughout, trade is among the most controversial areas of public policy. It's also evident throughout that the liberalized trading regime that has been in place for most of the postwar period, the one most of us are familiar with, and the source of some of the anxiety among Summit of the Americas protesters, has been the historical exception rather than rule.

International trade has always pitted domestic interests against their foreign counterparts, often infused with the language of economic nationalism, periodically forms of xenophobia and always complicated trade-offs for political leadership. In fact, the roots of these conflicts are inherent parts of the case in favour of trade liberalization put forward by Adam Smith (1776) and David Ricardo (1817). Smith and Ricardo reasoned that there was a heavy price (inflation) to be paid for mercantilism's emphasis on exports while limiting imports. Generally, they argued that through specialization and exchange, the market for exports could be dramatically expanded to foreign countries and domestic productive capacities enlarged to service them. By allowing other countries to do the same, and accepting some of their surplus production in exchange for domestic manufactures, there would be broad consumer benefits in the form of lower prices and product differentiation, as well as a more efficient use of domestic productive capacities that only economies of scale could bring.

At the same time, both implicitly acknowledged that there were bound to be adjustment costs with this specialization and trade. As trade between countries expanded, there would be increased specialization and the expansion of some industries at home, while others shrank and gave way to more efficient production abroad. Smith's and Ricardo's arguments were elegant, but were entirely about efficiency. Why, they reasoned, allocate more of our scarce resources into the production of those products that we can produce most efficiently, earn income from foreigners by exporting them, while ceding the production of those manufactures in which we lack natural advantage (efficiency) to foreigners and then import them to the benefit of our consumers?

For the economist in IPE scholars, the elegance of Smith's theory of absolute advantage and Ricardo's comparative advantage are compelling. Moreover, the two theories still form the basic intellectual rationale for liberalized trade. However, the politics of this liberalization are messy and, therefore, of recurring interest to scholars of IPE. As nearly every student of international trade knows, liberalization generates 'winners' and 'losers' at home and abroad. The 'winners' are those consumers who reap the benefits of lower prices and greater varieties of consumables, the employees in sectors of comparative advantage whose firms expand, hire more workers and add more shifts to supply products for export markets. In specific instances, the benefits are narrowly felt, but overall are spread broadly throughout the economy.

By contrast, the 'losers' from trade liberalization are a highly concentrated, easy to identify and frequently noisy set of stakeholders. As Ricardo argued in 1817, the process of adjustment to a more efficient form of trading relations involved a shift of workers out of sectors of comparative disadvantage and into those of comparative advantage. However, as workers are 'released' from one sector to the next, the politics of trade liberalization became complicated by the inevitable transition period. In short, agricultural workers 'released' as a result of liberalization are unlikely to find employment in high-tech computer chip design, therefore creating a problem for a nation's political leaders in advocating for liberalization in the first place. Whereas the consumer groups enjoying the benefits of liberalization are spread throughout the country and unlikely to write to their elected leadership praising their trade liberalization initiatives, unhappy factory workers that have seen their jobs move to a country that enjoys a comparative advantage are concentrated, often powerful stakeholders that only the bravest politicians are willing to take on by pointing to Smith and Ricardo.

Yet, it is these domestic stakeholders, the sectors they represent, the politics they pursue, their direct connection to their equivalents abroad, all filtered through an economic model premised on efficiency that make the study of international trade so inherently a part of IPE. However, IPE analyses of international trade also examine the implications of global and regional patterns of trade for what they say about everything from patterns of production (Soloaga and Winters 2001; Humphrey 2003; Feinberg and Keane 2006) to the relative distribution of political power in the global economy (Narlikar and Tussie 2004). A related focus of IPE scholars involves the analyses of the rules of international trade and the institutional structures that have formed around them. The distributional consequences of trade liberalization have already been noted. However, the rules that enshrine this liberalization between states involve forms of governance between them that are also the subject of intense scrutiny by IPE scholars.

For example, in 2013, the World Trade Organization (WTO) is comprised of 159 member countries, the vast majority of which are developing countries. The most recent 'round' of trade liberalization under WTO auspices, the Doha Development Round, has been in stalemate for several years because of disagreements, largely between the WTOs rich and poor members, over how to liberalize trade in agriculture (Elliot 2006). While the machinations of agricultural trade are in and of themselves interesting, the stalemate within the Doha Round is fascinating because of the

> **Institutions** – any structure or mechanism of social order-governing behaviour of a set of individuals within a given community. They consist of informal constraints (sanctions, taboos, customs, traditions and codes of conduct) and formal rules (constitutions, laws, property rights).

evident shift in power within a major international institution. The WTO, unlike the other postwar financial institutions, is a consensus-driven organization meaning that even the smallest members can veto new multilateral agreements. Hence, small and developing countries have clamoured for membership in the WTO because its rules-based structure and decision-making have reduced the importance of power within the international body (Narlikar and Tussie 2004; Lacarte-Muro and Gappah 2000; Barcelo 2005).

When one considers that the predecessor of the WTO, the General Agreement on Tariffs and Trade (GATT) began with a mere 23 members, most of which are part of the developed world, the structural change in the institutions governing global trade patterns is profound. IPE scholars have, of course, challenged the liberal notion that institutions are evidence of the reduced primacy of power in international relations and are by design and function forums for the exercise and extension of power (Krasner 1976). Moreover, scholars have also pointed to institutional structures within the WTO that incentivize the expansion of regionalism around the world. Article XXIV of the original GATT allows members to pursue regional preferences agreements so long as they are generally liberalizing (GATT 1947). Here, IPE scholars are interested in shifting patterns of regional trading relationships, many of which have devolved into significant 'trading blocks' anchored by one or more large countries; the United States in North America, Brazil in South America, Germany in Europe. How these regional preferences are distorting trading patterns, and complicating multilateral processes, is of course a focus of IPE scholars. But so too are the politics of these regional blocks as anchor countries conclude new arrangements with countries where the economic benefits are slight but the political benefits may be large. This particular set of dynamics has been popular with a variety of Marxist approaches, including world systems theorists like Immanuel Wallerstein (1974). For these scholars, large 'core' states draw smaller, 'peripheral' states into their economic and political orbit, perpetuating dependency on market access to the large state, while the large state uses the terms of preferences agreements to 'lock in' economic and political reforms favourable to the large state.

The dimensions of international trade of interest to scholars of IPE continue to proliferate and include, among other things, the effects of outsourcing (Drezner 2004; Bhagwati et al. 2004), the environment (Audley 1995; Bhagwati 2000; Droege 2012), civil society (Ayres 1999; Knudson 1998), and security (Anderson 2012; Goldfarb and Robson 2003).

International Monetary Relations

Unlike trade relations, the IPE of international monetary relations is, for some, much more abstract and less accessible to non-economists. Yet, for anyone that has followed the rapid growth of the Chinese economy and its relationship to the United States, trade relations and monetary relations between the two have become a key political lightening rod that increasingly begs for additional understanding. IPE scholars have been happy to provide it.

> **Monetary Policy** – what a central bank does to control the money supply and thereby manage demand in the economy.

An important difference between the IPE analyses of trade relative to monetary relations revolves around the issue of sovereignty. Students of the neoclassical stages of economic integration will be familiar with the fact that engaging in trade relations entails a relatively small loss of sovereign policy power on the part of the state. It is the case that the reduction of tariff barriers through multilateral or regional agreement entails some restriction of policy latitude, but really only over the imposition of tariffs and other border measures on imports.

Monetary policy, by contrast, involves the sovereign control over interest rates and the money supply. In only a select few jurisdictions has the state ceded control over its own money supply and capacity to set interest rates and thereby given up a significant degree of policy latitude. In some instances, sovereignty is pooled and delegated to a multilateral body such as, in the case of the European Union, a common central bank (The European Central Bank). Such an institution manages a common currency and interest rates for all. In other cases, such as Ecuador, the state may simply elect to adopt the currency of another country (the US Dollar), again ceding its sovereignty over monetary affairs.

These analyses are inherently about the state and its relationship to some international body. As we have seen in the debt crisis roiling the European Union in recent years, the state's relationship to the European Central Bank and the other members of the European Union has been the focus of intense scrutiny. As Ireland, Greece, Spain, Portugal and Italy have experienced varying degrees of financial turmoil, bailouts and structural adjustment imposed by other member states, the citizenry of those states have had occasion to question the merits of Euro area membership.

Analyses of monetary relations elsewhere are equally statist in orientation, but tend to focus on domestic policy institutions such as central banks whose prime function and purpose have important international spillover effects. Students of monetary economics will appreciate the trade-offs associated with the choice exchange rate regime (Caramazza and Aziz 1998). In Europe, the members of the Euro area have essentially adopted a fixed exchange rate, severely restricting their monetary policy latitude, and restricting their freedom of movement in the midst of the current debt crisis. China has nominally done the same by committing to a fixed exchange rate tied to the value of the US Dollar.

Therein reside the complicated politics of monetary relations between the two countries. Consider the complicated spillover politics of China's decision to peg the Yuan to the US Dollar (Roubini 2007; McKinnon 2007). China's export-driven development model has been built, in part, on the stability and predictability that a fixed exchange rate brings with it. As China transitions from a command, statist economy toward a more liberal, open form, it faces numerous challenges in closing inefficient state-run enterprises, and incentivizing development deeper into the Chinese mainland that authorities argue requires the stability of a fixed regime. Yet, on the other side of the Pacific, American politicians look at the fixed regime with skepticism, and at times vitriol. In their minds, Chinese authorities unfairly intervene with their pegged rate to keep the Yuan's value artificially low relative to the US Dollar, making Chinese products cheaper for Americans to purchase than domestic products, worsening the US trade deficit, and incentivizing the offshoring of American manufacturing jobs to China (Drezner 2004; Bhagwati et al. 2004). In the midst of a US economy beset by a weak recovery from a deep financial crisis, the political pressures in the United States for some kind of action have become enormous (Bergsten 2010).

The 2012 US presidential campaign was full of rhetoric about Chinese currency manipulation, Mitt Romney in particular promising to label China a currency manipulator on his first day in the White House. Romney was unsuccessful, but the pressures remain with the US Congress periodically taking legislative action to change the dynamics. Yet, currency manipulation is also one of those political allegations that resides mainly in the eye of the beholder. Central banks around the world are constantly intervening in global currency markets, even those whose currencies float and are ostensibly responsive to supply and demand signals in the marketplace. Central banks around the world, notably the US Federal Reserve and the European Central Bank, have been engaging in 'quantitative easing' by purchasing private bank

> **Central Bank** – an institution that manages a state's currency, money supply and interest rates. In some places it is called a reserve bank or the monetary authority. The US Federal Reserve, European Central Bank and Bank of England are examples.

assets, greatly expanding the potential money supply and, in theory, depreciating the value of the Dollar and the Euro relative to other currencies.

The point is that one the main functions of IPE as an interdisciplinary approach is to tease out the unique mix of politics and economics that drives so much of global politics. Trade and monetary relations are not just about trade or monetary issues, nor are they just about economics. In fact, the analysis of monetary relations between countries necessarily involves capital flows and foreign direct investment, which in turn frequently spills over into matters of international development.

The United Nations Conference on Trade and Development (UNCTAD) has since 1991 published a yearly report on global capital flows, the World Investment Report. Economic theory suggests that capital ought to flow 'downhill' in the sense that returns on capital in areas of the world in which capital is scarce (and therefore expensive) ought to attract it from areas in which capital is abundant (and therefore cheap). Until very recently, UNCTAD's reports repeatedly demonstrated that most capital flows occur between rich, capital abundant, developed economies. Very little of it flowed to the Global South where it was seemingly needed most. The potential benefits of foreign direct investment for developing countries, including direct employment, infrastructure development, technology transfer, increased local product quality and higher wages (Graham 2000), are well known to economists. However, the search for rules to govern the relationship between private multinational firms and their sovereign hosts under international law complicates FDI and spills over into the realm of politics (Salacuse 1990; 2007). The FDI flow from capital-abundant regions to those where it is scarce is significantly impeded by the ever-present threat of expropriation by the sovereign host. Over the years, thousands of bilateral investment treaties and investment provisions within trade agreements between nations have sought to govern those relations by setting terms under which Greenfield investment enters a host country (Ibid.). Prominent recent examples of expropriation, notably in the Venezuelan oil and gas sector, suggest such treaties are not sacrosanct and that host countries are not always happy with the terms of those arrangements.

Recent financial crises have also focused attention on flows of portfolio capital in and out of countries, sometimes with remarkably destabilizing velocity. Some have actively promoted the use of limited capital controls, such as the so-called Tobin Tax (Raffer 1998; McCulloch and Pacillo 2011) that would impose a transaction cost on large currency exchanges. Some have pointed to the fact that capital flight out of Asian economies during the financial crisis there in the late 1990s has strongly informed contemporary policy measures, such as the holding of large reserves, that contributed greatly to the large macro imbalances that fuelled the financial crisis in the United States (Diamond and Rajan 2009). The accumulation of large reserves in Asian central banks has, in turn, transformed patterns of FDI flows reported by UNCTAD such that developing countries such as China remain significant targets, but increasingly also sources of FDI flows (UNCTAD, World Investment Report 2011–12).

Finally, no discussion of IPE's contribution to the analysis of international monetary relations can ignore the ongoing debate about the role of the US Dollar in global finance. While the Dollar's prominence as the globe's key currency is arguably just a by-product of a postwar history that saw the United States as the world's only economy not ravaged by war, and the Dollar as the only widely accepted currency, the Dollar has had remarkable longevity as the key currency, conferring unique advantages on the United States as a global power (Eichengreen 2011, 39–68; Kunz 1995, 29–56.). With so many of the world's most important commodities priced in dollars, notably oil, the United States has been relatively immune to fluctuations in the Dollar's value relative to other currencies. The US simply buys commodities in terms of Dollars that it actually prints. However, this privilege has been most important at moments of financial crisis that would leave other nations in much more serious trouble. The United States, unlike most other nations, finances much of its overconsumption by issuing debt denominated in its own currency. Hence, while America finances its deficit spending by effectively issuing IOUs, increasingly to foreigners, it is debt that will only ever have to be repaid in Dollars the US prints in the first place. Hence, the United States doesn't have to worry about the decline in value of the US Dollar ballooning America's deficit in the midst of crisis. In fact, it is the holder of US debt abroad that might worry about declines in the value of their US Dollar holdings if the Dollar were to fall relative to other currencies (see Setser et al. 2005).

America's Dollar diplomacy would be significantly weakened were there a serious alternative to the dollar. The Japanese Yen or German Deutschmark have periodically attracted scholarly attention as possible rivals to the Dollar, but it wasn't until 1999 and the introduction of the Euro that a serious key currency rival seemed to emerge (Kunz 1995; Eichengreen 2011, 69–96). However, the ongoing European debt crisis has called into question the future of the Euro (*The Economist*, 'Holding Together' 2009) and, in effect, reaffirmed the Dollar as the globe's key currency. In spite of America's formidable economic challenges, including an anaemic recovery from a devastating financial crisis and a bleak fiscal situation, the world's investors continue to purchase US Treasury Bills in vast quantities, in effect rendering a vote of confidence in US economic prospects and the stability of the Dollar: predicting the collapse of the Dollar, or outlining its consequences as a warning to policymakers, has periodically generated a cottage industry of literature on the subject (Eichengreen 2009; 2011). However, a combination of viable alternatives and the flight from uncertainty elsewhere into Dollar assets suggest both that the Dollar will remain the globe's key currency and the Dollar as a major part of American polices at home and abroad is assured for the foreseeable future.

Whatever lies ahead for the Dollar, there's little doubt that IPE scholars will continue dissecting the complex interplay of politics and economics that undergirds monetary relations. These complexities are a never-ending source of interest for scholars because of the difficult trade-offs so often associated with the choice of exchange rate regime, the consequences of debt financing for currencies or the power that comes simply from printing the world's key currency.

The Rest

Trade and monetary relations form a sort of core subject matter common to all stripes of IPE. However, as even this brief description makes abundantly clear, IPE has extended its investigatory reach into many other areas and has the potential to do so in many more.

The multinational corporation has been the subject of intense scholarship for a very long time, dating back to the formation of the British East India Company in 1600. However, the modern multinational corporation has attracted the attention of scholars because of its role in several other areas of interest to IPE scholars. Multinationals as sources of foreign direct investment has already been noted, but the implications of private activities for international development in this regard is obvious. For developing countries, the prospect of FDI brings with it the promise of jobs, skills and technology transfer, productivity enhancing competition, greater local product quality and wage rates higher than those prevailing locally (Bhagwati 2005; Wolf 2004). However, critics of multinationals argue that many of these promised benefits fail to materialize as promised. Worse, a range of human rights activists, corporate watchdog groups and anti-corporate crusaders have periodically exposed apparent negligence on the part of firms in maintaining core labour standards throughout their entire production chain. Corporations have been major drivers of efficiency in global supply chain management that has frequently entailed extensive offshoring and outsourcing of both materials procurement and manufacturing, but also been burned by poor oversight of far-flung operations that too often resulted in embarrassing public relations fiascos for firms (Blinder 2006; Wolf 2004, 220–48).

Yet, for some analysts, the same globalization that generated the conditions in which multinationals found themselves in embarrassing situations also facilitated their exposure and resolution (Bhagwati 2005, 162–98). An interesting consequence of all of this has been the growing focus on the accountability and social responsibility of firms in a number of areas, including labour rights and environmental protection. Whereas a decade ago, corporate social responsibility was a relatively new concept to which firms largely paid lip-service, it is now a booming and vitally important component of most corporate structures. Moreover, for many firms, appealing to socially conscious consumer tastes is proving to be big business (Mohan 2009; *The Economist*, 19 January 2008). Fair trade coffee can be found in virtually all coffee shops (de Pelsmacker et al. 2005; Le Mare 2008; Arnot et al. 2005). Products manufactured in environmentally sustainable ways are a growing component of consumer purchasing behaviour.

International development has become a substantial sub-discipline of its own (Dollar and Kraay 2002; Sachs 2005, Sen 1999; Collier 2007), but is of interest to IPE scholars first and foremost because of its many implications for relations between the developed Global North and the comparatively underdeveloped Global South. But a major focus of IPE scholars in this area has been on the institutions charged with development as well as the management of elements of the global economy; namely, the Bretton Woods institutions, the World Bank, International Monetary Fund and the World Trade Organization. IPE scholars have been interested in both the internal governance of these institutions (Einhorn 2001), their effectiveness (Easterly and Pfutze 2008) and possible avenues for reform (Kenen 2001; Blinder 1999; Schott 2001). The shifting models of international development are also a growing preoccupation of IPE scholars because of their implications for GDP growth, international trade and monetary flows, as well as regional and global politics. The 2000 United Nations Millennium Development Declaration and its associated goals for significant improvements on a range of human development indicators amounted to a call to developmental arms. Renewed focus on indebtedness levels, governance reforms (Radelet 2003; Reuter and Truman 2004; Toke 2009), components of a so-called post-Washington Consensus on economic policy (Rodrik 2006; Kuczynski and Williamson 2003), appropriate levels of official development assistance (Birdsall and Williamson 2003) and even the role of private philanthropy (Werker and Ahmed 2008) have all received increased attention.

Even more recently, some of the rapidly changing dynamics of development flowing from the nation-building exercises of the 1990s (Somalia, Kosovo, Haiti), as well as the conflict zones of the early 2000s (Iraq and Afghanistan), have turned the attention of IPE scholars toward the shifting mixture of civilian and military components of development (Spearin 2008; Kinsey 2005).

Finally, one of the most interesting and complex emergent areas of IPE study is climate change. It is shaping up to be so mainly because of the intersection of so many different sub-disciplines of the social sciences and, in this case, sciences. In fact, the growing body of hard science demonstrating that climate change is caused largely by human activity (that is, productive economic activity) is beginning to bounce up against the politics and economics of IPE (Esty 1994; Audley 1995). Early work in the GATT and WTO focused on the links between productive activity and individual species protection, such as dolphins or turtles (Ibid.). Interestingly, much of that work concluded that the rules of global trade and conservation were not in competition with each other. However, global climate change and its mitigation efforts are on a different scale of importance entirely and renewed work into the compatibility of current trading rules and mitigation has only just begun (Hufbauer et al., 2009). The early evidence suggests that political clashes are on the horizon. Apart from whether developed and developing countries can decide who bears the largest burden for mitigation – rich vs. poor – and whether generations of productive activity merit paying a heavier burden, the actual mechanisms for mitigation may come into direct conflict with existing trading rules (Ibid.). For instance, as carbon life-cycle tracing for individual products becomes more finely tuned, a tax on the carbon footprint of many products as they cross borders might be away to initiate the mitigation process. However, such a tax would conflict with the process-product distinctions currently governing the non-discrimination principle within the WTO system (Esty 1994; Hufbauer et al., 2009).

CONCLUSIONS

The contribution of IPE (since its emergence as a coherent discipline in the 1970s) to the study of global politics can be read as a social science response to fundamental changes in global politics itself. As unified, sovereign states appeared to be giving way to a much more nuanced, complex and linked global politics in the 1970s, social science groped for an equally nuanced and complex set of tools with which to approach it all. Susan Strange's plea for more dialogue between economics and political science was a clarion call for just such an approach.

It was an approach that has been answered by a growing number of scholars, so many in fact, that IPE is much less a sub-discipline of international relations than a fully fledged discipline of its own, complete with internecine debates about ontology and epistemology typical of academic debate. However, at the same time IPE has become a discipline of its own, it has also spread its reach into a near-bottomless pit of areas that are merely reflective of the complexity around us. Whereas the 1970s were a period in which economics seemed to be as pivotal to understanding global political phenomenon and vice versa, relative to the high politics of military strategy, IPE has increasingly been expanding its investigatory tentacles into newish areas of contemporary global politics rooted in far more than just the mix of economics and political science. As an inherently interdisciplinary approach, IPE is well positioned to continue adapting alongside global politics itself.

QUESTIONS FOR REFLECTION

1. How can we account for the divisions within the social science on epistemological and ontological terms?
2. Are the core elements of IPE described in this chapter likely to remain the same set of core elements for the next 20 years?
3. Do the origins of IPE as a discipline suggest changes to both the discipline and its subject matter are inevitable?
4. What are the advantages of inter-disciplinarity that cannot be had within the bounds of a single discipline alone?
5. Why are British and American IPE so different?

REVISION QUIZ

1. What was the main reason for the emergence of IPE as a discipline?

   a. President Nixon issued an executive order creating it
   b. There were large shifts in global politics taking place that standard approaches to international relations didn't seem capable of explaining
   c. A subset of international relations scholars got upset at a professional meeting and walked out
   d. There were economists who didn't have enough work to do

2. Whose journal article was highly influential in starting the conversation between economics and political science?

   a. Susan Strange
   b. Milton Friedman
   c. Paul Krugman
   d. Robert Keohane

3. What are the two main disciplines that make up IPE?

   a. Botany and sociology
   b. International Relations and Macroeconomics
   c. History and English
   d. Sociology and Political Science

4. In what ways does IPE differ from traditional International Relations?

   a. IPE scholars are generally friendlier at professional meetings
   b. IPE makes the economic dimensions of politics an explicit part of their analysis
   c. International Relations scholars think economists are crazy
   d. Economists think International Relation scholars are nuts

5. Which of these titles is a famous work of modern international political economy?

   a. *Power and Interdependence*
   b. *Three Billy Goats Gruff*
   c. *Das Kapital*
   d. *Rise and Fall of the Roman Empire*

6. How are the major divisions in IPE frequently characterized?

   a. British and American
   b. Russian and Chinese
   c. Indian and Sri Lankan
   d. Australian and American

7. How are the epistemological divisions within contemporary IPE best characterized?

   a. Positivist vs. post-positivist
   b. Reflectivist vs. traditional
   c. Science model vs. interpretive models
   d. All of the above

8. What are some common subject areas IPE scholars typically focus on?

   a. International institutions
   b. Development
   c. Trade politics
   d. Monetary relations
   e. All of the above

9. One source of reflection among scholars leading to the emergence of IPE was:

   a. The geopolitics of the energy crises of the 1970s
   b. The institutionalization of many economic relationships
   c. The relative decline of the United States in the global economy
   d. The growing power of a range of non-state actors
   e. All of the above

10. IPE (complete the sentence) …

   a. Is throwback to a time when social science was more inter-disciplinary
   b. Is too complicated
   c. Is irrelevant in today's world
   d. Really stands for Inter-dependent Potato Exporters

11. Which of these key terms is most strongly associated with IPE?

    a. Interdependence
    b. Theory of the Firm
    c. Balance of Power
    d. Federalism

Answers: 1: b; 2: a; 3: b; 4: b; 5: a; 6: a; 7: d; 8: e; 9: a; 10: a; 11:**???.**

BIBLIOGRAPHY

Anderson, G. (2012) 'Securitization and Sovereignty in Post-9/11 North America', *Review of International Political Economy* 19(5), 711–41.

Arnot, C., Boxall, P.C. and Cash, S. (2005) 'Do Ethical Consumers Care About Price? A Revealed Preference Analysis of Fair Trade Coffee Purchases', *Canadian Journal of Agricultural Economics* 54(4), 555–65.

Audley, J. (1995) 'Environmental Interests in Trade Policy: Institutional Reform and the North American Free Trade Agreement', *The Social Science Journal* 32(4), 327–60.

Ayres, J. (1999) 'From the Streets to the Internet: The Cyber-Diffusion of Contention', *The Annals of The American Academy of Political and Social Science* 566(1), 132–43.

Barcelo, J. (2005) 'Developing Countries and the WTO', *Cornell Law Forum* 8(1), 8–16.

Bergsten, C.F. (2010) 'We Can Fight Fire with Fire on the Renminbi', *Financial Times*, 4 October 2010.

Bhagwati, J., Panagariya, A. and Srinivasan, T.N. (Fall 2004) 'The Muddles Over Out Sourcing', *Journal of Economic Perspectives* 18(4), 93–114.

Bhagwati, J., Panagariya, A. and Srinivasan, T.N. (2004) *In Defense of Globalization* (Oxford: Oxford University Press).

Bhagwati, J., Panagariya, A. and Srinivasan, T.N. (2000) 'On Thinking Clearly About the Linkage Between Trade and the Environment', *Environment and Development Economics* 5(4), 483–529.

Birdsall, N. and Williamson, J. (2002) *Delivering on Debt Relief: From IMF Gold to a New Aid Architecture* (Washington, DC: Institute for International Economics).

Blinder, A. (March/April 2006) 'Offshoring: The Next Industrial Revolution?' *Foreign Affairs* 85(2), 113–28.

Blinder, A. (September/October 1999) 'Eight Steps to a New Financial Order', *Foreign Affairs* 78(5), 50–63.

Blythe, M. (2009) 'Torn Between Two Lovers? Caught in the Middle of British and American IPE', *New Political Economy* 14(3), 329–36.

Caramazza, F. and Aziz, J. (1998) 'Fixed or Flexible?: Getting the Exchange Rate Right in the 1990s'. In *Economic Issues 13* (Washington, DC: International Monetary Fund).

Cameron, A. and Palan, R. (2009) 'Empiricism and Objectivity: Reflexive Theory Construction in a Complex World'. In M. Blyth (ed.), *The Routledge Handbook of IPE: IPE as a Global Conversation* (London and New York: Routledge), 112–25.

Cohen, B. (2010) 'Are IPE Journals Becoming Boring?', *International Studies Quarterly* 54(3), 887–91.

Cohen, B. (2008) *International Political Economy: An Intellectual History* (Princeton, NJ: Princeton University Press).

Cohen, B. (2007) 'The Transatlantic Divide: Why Are American and British IPE so Different?' *Review of*

International Political Economy 14(2), 197–219.

Colby, B.G. (November 2000) 'Cap-and-Trade Policy Challenges: A Tale of Three Markets', *Land Economics* 76(4), 638–58.

Collier, P. (2007) *The Bottom Billion: Why the Poorest Countries are Failing and What Can Be Done About It* (New York: Oxford University Press).

Diamond, D. and Rajan, R. (2009) 'The Credit Crisis: Conjectures about Causes and Remedies', *American Economic Review* 99(2), 606–10.

Dollar, D. and Kraay, A. (2002) 'Spreading the Wealth', *Foreign Affairs* 81(1), 120–33.

Drezner, D. (2004) 'The Outsourcing Bogeyman', *Foreign Affairs* 83(3), 22–34.

Droege, S. (2012) 'The Challenge of Reconciliation: Climate Change, Development, and International Trade', *Climate Policy* 12(4), 524–6.

Easterly, W. and Pfutze, T. (Spring 2008) 'Where Does the Money Go? Best and Worst Practices in Foreign Aid', *Journal of Economic Perspectives* 22(2), 29–52.

Easterly, W. and Pfutze, T. (2006) *White Man's Burden* (New York: Penguin).

Easterly, W. and Pfutze, T. (Summer 2003) 'Can Foreign Aid Buy Growth?', *Journal of Economic Perspectives* 17(3), 23–48.

The Economist, 'Holding Together: A Special Report on the Euro Area', 13 June 2009.

The Economist, 'Just Good Business: A Special Report on Corporate Social Responsibility', 19 January 2008.

Eichengreen, B. (September/October 2009) 'The Dollar Dilemma' *Foreign Affairs* 88(5), 53–68.

Einhorn, J. (September/October 2001) 'The World Bank's Mission Creep', *Foreign Affairs* 80(5), 22–35.

Elliott, K.A. (2006) *Delivering on Doha: Farm Trade and the Poor* (Washington DC: Institute for International Economics).

Esty, D. (1994) *Greening the GATT* (Washington, DC: Institute for International Economics).

Feinberg, S. and Keane, M. (2006) 'U.S.-Canada Trade Liberalization and MNC Production Location', *The Review of Economics and Statistics* 83(1), 118–32.

Goldfarb, D. and Robson, W. (2003) 'Risky Business: US Border Security and the Threat to Canadian Exports', In *C.D. Howe Institute Commentary* No. 177 (Toronto: C.D. Howe Institute).

Graham, E. (2000) *Fighting the Wrong Enemy: Antiglobal Activists and Multinational Enterprises* (Washington, DC: Institute for International Economics).

Hufbauer, G., Charnovitz, S. and Kim, J. (2009) *Global Warming and the World Trading System* (Washington, DC: Peterson Institute for International Economics).

Humphrey, J. (2003) 'Globalization and Supply Chain Networks: The Auto Industry in Brazil and India', *Global Networks* 3(2), 121–41.

Irwin, D. (1996) *Against the Tide: An Intellectual History of Free Trade* (Princeton, NJ: Princeton University Press).

Kenen, P. (2001) *The International Financial Architecture: What's New, What's Missing?* (Washington, DC: Institute for International Economics).

Keohane, R. (2009) 'The Old IPE and The New', *Review of International Political Economy* 16(1), 34–46.

Keohane, R. and Nye, J. Jr (2001) *Power and Interdependence*, 3rd ed. (New York: Longman Press).

Keohane, R. (1974) 'Introduction: The Complex Politics of Canadian-American Interdependence', *International Organization* 28(4), 595–607.

Keynes, J.M. (1937) 'The General Theory of Employment', *Quarterly Journal of Economics* 51(2), 209–23.

Kinsey, C. (2005) 'Challenging International Law: A Dilemma of Private Security Companies', *Conflict, Security and Development* 5(3), 269–93.

Knudson, J. (1998) 'Rebellion in Chiapas: Insurrection by Internet and Public Relations', *Media, Culture & Society* 20(3), 507–18.

Krasner, S. (1976) 'State Power and the Structure of International Trade', *World Politics* 28(3), 317–47.

Kuczynski, P. and Williamson, J. (2003) *After the Washington Consensus: Restarting Growth and Reform in Latin America* (Washington, DC: Institute for International Economics).

Kunz, D. (July/August 1995) 'The Fall of the Dollar Order: The World the United States is Losing', *Foreign Affairs* 74(4), 22–6.

Lacarte-Muro, J and Gappah, P. (2000) 'Developing Countries and the WTO Legal and Dispute Settlement System: A View from the Bench', *Journal of International Economic Law* 3(3), 395–401.

Maliniak, D. and Tierney, M. (2009) 'The American School of IPE', *Review of International Political Economy* 16(1), 6–33.

McCulloch, N. and Pacillo, G. (2011) 'The Tobin Tax: A Review of the Evidence', *IDS Research Reports* 2011(68), 1–77.

McKinnon, R. (2007) 'Why China Should Keep Its Dollar Peg', *International Finance* 10(1), 43–70.

McNamara, K. (2009) 'Of Intellectual Monocultures and the Study of IPE', *Review of International Political Economy* 16(1), 72–84.

Le Mare, A. (2008) 'The Impact of Fair Trade on Social and Economic Development: A Review of the Literature', *Geography Compass* 2(6), 1922–42.

Mohan, S. (2009) 'Fair Trade and Corporate Social Responsibility', *Economic Affairs* (December 2009), 22–8.

Narlikar, A. and Tussie, D. (2004) 'The G20 and the Cancun Ministerial: Developing Countries and Their Evolving Coalitions in the WTO', *The World Economy* 27(7), 947–66.

de Pelsmacker, P., Driesen, L. and Rayp, G. (2005) 'Do Consumers Care about Ethics? Willingness to Pay for Fair-Trade Coffee', *Journal of Consumer Affairs* 39(2), 363–85.

Polanyi, K. (1944) *The Great Transformation: The Political and Economic Origins of Our Time* (Boston: Beacon Press).

Radelet, S. (2003) *Challenging Foreign Aid: A Policy Maker's Guide to the Millennium Challenge Account* (Washington, DC: Institute for International Economics).

Raffer, K. (1998) 'The Tobin Tax: Reviving a Discussion', *World Development* 26(3), 529–38.

Reuter, P. and Truman, E. (2004) *Chasing Dirty Money: The Fight Against Money Laundering* (Washington, DC: Institute for International Economics).

Ricardo, D. (1817). *On the Principles of Political Economy and Taxation*. In *The Works and Correspondence of David Ricardo*. 11 vols. Edited by Piero Sraffa, with the collaboration of M.H. Dobb (Cambridge: Cambridge University Press), 1951–73.

Roubini, N. (2007) 'Why China Should Abandon Its Dollar Peg', *International Finance* 10(1), 71–89.

Rodrik, D. (2006) 'Goodbye Washington Consensus, Hello Washington Confusion? A Review of the World Bank's "Economic Growth in the 1990s: Learning from a Decade of Reform"', *Journal of Economic Literature* 44(4), 973–87.

Rumsfeld, D. (2011). *Known and Unknown* (New York: Penguin).

Sachs, J. (March/April 2005) 'The Development Challenge', *Foreign Affairs* 84(2), 78–90.

Salacuse, J. (2007) 'The Treatification of International Investment Law', *Law and Business Review of the Americas* 13(1), 155–66.

Salacuse, J. (1990) 'BIT by BIT: The Growth of Bilateral Investment Treaties and Their Impact on Foreign Direct Investment in Developing Countries', *International Lawyer* 24(3), 655–75.

Schott, J. (2001) *The WTO After Seattle* (Washington, DC: Institute for International Economics.)

Sen, A. (1999) *Development as Freedom* (New York: Knopf).

Setser, B., Roubini, N., Levey, D. and Brown, S. (July/August 2005) 'Our Money, Our Debt, Our Problem', *Foreign Affairs* 84(4), 194–200.

Smith, A. (1776) *An Inquiry into the Nature and Causes of the Wealth of Nations* (London: Methuen & Co.).

Soloaga, I. and Winters, A. (2001) 'Regionalism in the Nineties: What Effect on Trade?', *North American Journal of Economics and Finance* 12(1), 1–29.

Spearin, C. (2008) 'Private, Armed and Humanitarian? States, NGOs, International Private Security Companies and Shifting Humanitarianism', *Security Dialogue* 39(4), 363–82.

Strange, S. (1970) 'International Economics and International Relations: A Case of Mutual Neglect', *International Affairs* 46(2), 304–15.

Toke, A. (2009) 'Corruption, Institutions, and Economic Development', *Oxford Review of Economic Policy* 25(2), 271–91.

Underhill, G. (2009) 'Political Economy, the "US School" and the Manifest Destiny of Everyone Else', *New Political Economy* 14(3), 347–56.

Wallerstein, I. (1974) *The Modern World System, Vol. I: Capitalist Agriculture and the Origins of the European World-Economy in the Sixteenth Century* (New York/London: Academic Press).

Walt, S.M. (2005) 'The relationship between theory and policy in international relations', *Annual Review of Political Science* 8(1), 23–48.

Weaver, C. (2009) 'IPE's Split Brain', *New Political Economy* 14(3), 337–46.

Werker, E. and Ahmed, F. (Spring 2008) 'What Do Non-Governmental Organizations Do?', *Journal of Economic Perspectives* 22(2), 73–92.

Wolf, M. (2004) *Why Globalization Works* (New Haven, CT: Yale University Press).

Chapter 10
Conflict and In/Security in Global Life

SANDRA POPIDEN

This chapter introduces students to the sub-field of Security Studies. It starts by outlining the long-standing threat of great power war which tended to dominate the twentieth century. In the twenty-first century, war remains a persistent problem, but the new face war is now largely civil or internal conflict, rather than interstate wars fought between rival blocs of great powers. The chapter also highlights other trends in the security arena, such as the proliferation of nuclear and other weapons of mass destruction, increases in the number of weak states, international terrorist and cyber attacks. The chapter familiarizes students with the efforts to counter such threats, for instance through the promotion of contingency plans to safeguard WMD materials. The chapter concludes with a discussion of the evolution of the concept of security. For example, scholars who argue for a widening of the concept of security have begun to include non-military threats, such as health pandemics, environmental degradation or climate change, which challenge the traditional concept of national security advanced by Neorealist scholars. Still other scholars and policymakers advocate for a human security approach which shifts the emphasis from the security of the state to the physical security of the population.

Key Words: Great Power Peace, National Security, Hegemonic War, Nuclear Deterrence, Nuclear Proliferation, The Security Dilemma, Weapons of Mass Destruction, Loose Nukes, Asymmetric Conflicts, International Terrorism, Cyber Threats, Widening of Security, Deepening of Security.

Chapter 10

Conflict and In/Security in Global Life

SANDRA POPIDEN

World leaders 'face a moment of uncommon turbulence and high anxiety. The global economic crisis continues to shake banks, businesses, governments and families around the world. We face an extraordinary array of geopolitical and humanitarian challenges – famine in Somalia, the aftershocks of the Arab Spring, ongoing conflicts in some countries and difficult transitions in others. All this is in addition to the deeper political, economic and environmental transformations that are reshaping our world ... The terrorist threat has not gone away ... A related issue is the safety and security of nuclear installations ... In this age of anxiety, the world's people look to us for answers and action ... The U.N. remains our best hope for building a safer, more secure and just world'. (United Nations Secretary General, Ban Ki-Moon 2011)

INTRODUCTION TO SECURITY STUDIES

Perhaps no other topic in international relations has received as much attention as the causes of war and the methods for attaining security and peace. As one surveys world politics, diverse sets of security challenges continue to dominate the international agenda. Take a moment and imagine that you are the newly elected leader of your country and you choose to begin by conducting a security threat assessment. Your national security advisor begins by asking you about priorities. How do you respond? When you think about security, what images or ideas come to mind? What are the most important sources of insecurity or harm? Examine Table 10.1 and determine whether or not the most common threats are also the most dangerous ones? Next, think about the question of security for whom: states, societies, groups or individuals? Finally, what policy choices or capabilities are available that can increase the chances of achieving security and protection from harm? As you can likely imagine, there is ample room for policymakers to disagree. One's answers are likely to be influenced by differing theoretical paradigms, as well as the historical context, and the prioritization of threats across space and time.

In this chapter, we will primarily examine wars, armed conflicts and the weapons and tactics of war. Shifts in international power have historically led to major wars, which have been some of the most powerful influences that have shaped the course of international relations. Wars and conflicts remain among the most persistent security threats with the highest casualty rates. However, we will explore how

> **Great Powers** – an internationally recognized status as a military, economic, politically and culturally powerful or influential country on a global scale.
>
> **Great Power Peace** – a period without hegemonic wars fought among great powers. It is also known as the long peace between the superpowers during the Cold War and the post-Cold War transformation of the international system.
>
> **Concert of Europe** – the balance of power system that kept the peace among great powers after the Napoleonic Wars to the outbreak of World War I.

the types of conflicts, actors involved and affected and threats to security are all dynamic factors that vary over time. For example, the period since the end of World War II has been the longest period of peace among the **great powers** since the **Concert of Europe** (1815–1914). While there are far fewer wars fought between states, internal conflicts or civil wars, conflict traps and asymmetric warfare using terrorist tactics have increased.

Table 10.1   Potential security threats

Hegemonic war
Interstate war
Regional war
Civil war
International terrorism and asymmetric warfare
Cyber war, cyber terrorism, cyber crime
Weapons of mass destruction (nuclear, biological and chemical
Weak states and dysfunctional political institutions
Outlier regimes and state terrorism
Ethno-nationalist and communal conflict
Religious conflicts and militant sects
International crime and drug trafficking
Economic crises, decline and economic conflict
Climate change and environmental degradation
Food, water, and energy insecurity

The chapter begins by exploring alternative perspectives on security, beginning with a narrow conceptualization favoured by realists that became the dominant paradigm during the Cold War. **National security** was assessed by evaluating the balance of offensive and defensive military power capabilities. Security was achieved largely through **nuclear deterrence** and containment strategies. We then introduce the concept of the security dilemma, and outline the development of increasingly deadly weapons of mass destruction, as well as newer threats. These include international terrorism, organized crime, climate change and environmental degradation, migration and energy issues that now populate the crowded security agenda (COT 2007). In response to the increasing diversity and interconnectedness of threats, practitioners and scholars have argued for the widening of the scope of security studies to include economic, energy, societal and environmental dimensions.

> **National Security** – maintaining the survival of the state through use of power and tools of statecraft.
>
> **Nuclear Deterrence** – a military strategy based on the threat of nuclear armed attack to prevent actions such as an attack against one's own territory or other allied state.

Liberal scholars have also opened the black box of the state and examined how issues are elevated to state interests by governmental authorities through the actions of coalitions of groups and individuals. They also assert that there are three pillars to a liberal peace: peace among democracies, commercial liberalism and international institutions (Doyle 2005, 463). The overall system is likely to be more peaceful when these three elements are present and mutually reinforcing. When the number of democratic countries is high, greater security is likely because democracies rarely fight one another and instead use non-violent methods of conflict resolution (Russett 2005). Secondly, economic interdependence promotes peace on the **monadic**, **dyadic** and **systemic levels**, as countries that are economically interdependent have more to lose, are able to trade vs. invade for resources and thus are less likely to choose to engage in costly conflicts (Maoz 2009). Finally, international organizations, particularly those composed largely of democracies, tend to favour

> **The Kantian Tripod** – the liberal assertion that the democratic peace, commercial liberalism and international institutions, when simultaneously combined, promote peace in the international system.
>
> **Monadic Interdependence** – the share of a state's resources that is due to its relations with others.
>
> **Dyadic Interdependence** – the dimensions, or scope of dependence, and the extent of the relationship, or the opportunity cost of disrupting the relationship with the other state in the pair (dyad).
>
> **Systemic Interdependence** – the ripple effect that a change in any actor creates in the system taken as a whole.

peaceful conflict resolution by aiding in the establishment of credible commitments, dispute settlement and socialization in peaceful behaviour (Pevehouse and Russett 2006, 969).

Finally, policymakers and practitioners have also come to challenge narrow conceptions of security as insufficient to effectively deal with the problems of the twenty-first century. Since 2003 the United Nations has spearheaded a paradigm shift aimed at marshalling the effort to respond to the array of challenges in today's globalized world. The deepening of security studies means that the central focus should be on human security conceptualized as the protection of individuals' safety and welfare. Efforts to improve the human condition began with the recognition that states themselves have slaughtered some 130 million of their own citizens between 1900 and 1987, in acts of government repression and one-sided violence (Rummel 1994).

From this perspective, conflict and deprivation are interconnected and require far greater international attention. The mobilization of efforts such as the Millennium Development goals to halve the number of people living in absolute poverty by 2015 have resulted in great progress, however far too many people still live in countries stuck in under-development and conflict traps. For example, more than 800,000 people lose their lives each year to violence and 40 per cent of humanity, or 2.8 billion people 'suffer from poverty, ill health, illiteracy and other maladies' (Commission on Human Security Report 2003). One of every seven people on the planet (1.4 billion/7 billion) lives on less than $1.25 per day. According to the UN, 768 million people lack clean drinking water and 2.5 billion lack access to sanitation. They estimate that by 2050, 40 per cent of humanity will live in severely water-stressed countries and global demand for water will increase by 55 per cent.

World Bank President Jim Yong Kim stated that extreme poverty is 'the defining moral issue of our time', and from a human security approach combating deprivation is also a security imperative. Creating conditions of political and economic stability that allow for people to live without fear and to gain educational and employment opportunities are imperative. Peoples' overall level of safety is multi-dimensional and begins with physical security, or freedom from harm, but also includes political, socio-economic, cultural and environmental security. Lives and livelihoods are made less secure by poverty and conflict cycles, when health and development needs are not met. These structural factors also raise the risk of the premature death and the spread of devastating infectious diseases or pandemics. This paradigm challenges the traditional focus on states and maintains that whether or not states win or lose in war, what matters are the lives of human beings.

THE LONG-STANDING THREAT OF GREAT POWER WAR

The World Wars: Great Powers Collide to Preserve the Balance of Power

Since 1648 and the founding of the state system, threats to a state's security and survival have been viewed as arising from other states, particularly rival neighbouring ones. As the renowned Prussian military strategist Carl von Clausewitz maintained, when diplomacy (incentives) or coercive diplomacy (threats and disincentives) are not adequate to convince or compel a state to adhere to another's will, leaders can make a rational choice to engage in war to resolve the conflict. Clausewitz aptly described war as a political decision, or 'the continuation of politics by other means'. This places war in a political context as an instrument of policy or a mechanism for achieving politically desired ends. This leads realists to maintain that hard power resources are essential to ensure a state's security and survival, because 'military strength is the ultimate arbiter of conflict' (Spanier and Wendzel 1996, 147).

Interstate wars have been fought for a variety of reasons, including a perceived threat to their survival, incompatible vital or other national interests, ideological disputes or threats posed to the interests of their alliance partner. The rise of strong and revisionist states that engaged in aggressive attacks on state sovereignty or which sought to upset the balance of power through military force have historically been perceived as particularly threatening.

> **Interstate Wars** – the use of military force between two or more states, resulting in more than 1,000 battle-deaths a year.
>
> **Intra-state Wars** – a high-intensity conflict fought over issues of territory or control of the government, within a country. It is fought between organized groups and the state, resulting in more than 1,000 battle-deaths a year.

In the early twentieth century, great power states became involved in two World Wars, War I (1914–18) and World War II (1939–45), which were the largest and most devastating wars of attrition in human history. They led to a combined death toll estimated at 100 million. Chemical and biological weapons were both used in World War I, resulting in over one million casualties. Use of these dehumanizing and indiscriminate weapons led to the 1925 Geneva Protocol, which banned the use of poisonous gas as a weapon of war (Grumberger 2013). World War II was fought by Germany, Japan and Italy (the Axis) against Great Britain, the Soviet Union and the United States (the Allies). It was an even deadlier conflict and battles took place on six continents, involving all of the world's oceans. Poison gases were less frequently used on the battlefield, but were employed intermittently by Japan and by Nazi Germany to commit genocide of millions in concentration camps. Millions of soldiers also perished in conventional battles, and as the war progressed the opponents used new technologies to target each other's civilian populations.

The Axis powers used rockets to fire at civilians in England and engaged in war crimes and crimes against humanity, including large-scale massacres and genocide. Both the Axis and the Allies eventually used their airpower to fire-bomb each other's urban cities. After the unconditional surrender of Germany, the United States became the only country to use nuclear weapons.

World War II ended after Truman made the decision to drop two nuclear bombs, obliterating two Japanese cities, Hiroshima and Nagasaki. This was a decision that led to 200,000 largely civilian deaths and forced the Japanese government to submit their unconditional surrender.

Both of the World Wars were **hegemonic wars**, meaning that they were fought between conflicting alliances over supremacy and control over the entire world order. These threats to the international system itself were also fought as **total wars**, in which the objective was the unconditional military surrender of one's adversary. The objective was to defeat the opponent, occupy the rivals' capital cities and replace the opponents' political systems (Spanier and Wendzel 1996, 158). Such ambitious political and military objectives required the total mobilization of the resources of the state and society, in contrast to limited wars whose objectives stop short of unconditional surrender. Particularly after the brutality of these total wars

> **Hegemonic Wars** – system-wide or total conflicts involving great powers and minor powers for control over the international order.
>
> **Total Warfare** – state survival is in question, prompting the mobilization of the entire state and societal resources to fight. Adversaries often demand the unconditional surrender of their rival. There are also fewer constraints on the scope of conflict, as the objectives are to conquer and occupy the opponent.
>
> **Limited Warfare** – adversaries seek limited political aims, not a complete victory. There are often more restraints in fighting the war and geographical constraints.

between rival great powers' alliances, many international relations observers came to view security through the state-centric prism of realist theory.

Table 10.2   Types of war

1) Hegemonic war
2) Total war
3) Limited war
4) Civil war
5) Asymmetric war.

The Cold War: the Long Peace and the Most Dangerous Game

Security has traditionally been understood as the primary concern of states seeking to survive and flourish in the context of a self-help anarchic state system. As the Cold War progressed (1945–91), mainstream security studies focused on national security, power and achieving negative peace, defined as the absence of war. This conceptualization of security was heavily influenced by the geopolitical context of the period involving the enduring 45-year ideological struggle between the capitalist Western alliances, led by the US against their rival communist alliance, led by the Soviet Union. In 1949, despite the concerns of realists in the US, who viewed entangling alliances as dangerous, 12 states came together to form the **North Atlantic Treaty Organization**.

The centrepiece of this **collective defense** organization is Article 5 of the Treaty, which states that an attack on one member state is viewed as an attack on the alliance itself. Countries also attempted to resurrect the liberal ideas such as forming a more robust collective security organization. The UN was intended to promote international security through the development of international law and as a means for non-violent conflict resolution. Moreover, new international organizations were created to promote economic growth and monetary stability, through the Bretton Woods system, including the International Bank for Reconstruction and Development and the International Monetary Fund. The intent was to avoid the protectionism that contributed to World War II, and to help create the conditions for states to benefit from an open global economy.

> **NATO** – a collective defense organization and political/military alliance that formalized the Western transatlantic security relationship. It was created to counter the Soviet threat to Western Europe and to international security. Presently, NATO has 28 members.
>
> **Collective Defense** – the principle that an attack against one or several members is considered as an attack against all.
>
> **Collective Security** – a system, global in scope, that attempts to act together to prevent or stop state aggression. The League of Nations and United Nations were both founded on this concept.

Throughout the Cold War, both sides feared the loss of strategically important countries and came to view the world in terms of the domino theory. Rather than risk direct confrontation, due to the potential of escalation to World War III and nuclear war, the US and USSR fought proxy battles in other countries. The most notable internationalized proxy wars were in fought in Asia. Sixty years ago, the Korean War (1950–53) was a war of attrition that cost the lives of 54,246 Americans. The South Koreans lost 217,000 in military battle deaths and 1,000,000 civilian deaths. The North Koreans lost 400,000 military and 600,000 civilians, while their Chinese allies had 600,000 military fatalities (Rhem 2000). Similarly, the number of US military fatal casualties in the Vietnam War (1955–75) was 58,220. The estimates of the Vietnamese death toll are far less precise and range from 500,000 to 2,000,000, not including the casualties in Cambodia, Laos or the deaths following the end of the war when the US military withdrew and the communists took over South Vietnam (DCAS 2008).

Also during this period of bipolarity, the US and USSR also engaged in unprecedented arms racing, involving the stockpiling of conventional weapons, as well as **weapons of mass destruction** nuclear, chemical and biological weapons. For example, the United States is estimated to have produced 70,000 nuclear weapons from 1945 to the mid-1990s, while the Soviets produced 55,000 (National Resources Defense Council 1996, 2). Doctrines of containment and nuclear deterrence were developed in the context of launch-ready arsenals, which are always on alert, capable of being fired at their target within minutes and killing 100 million people within the hour.

> **Weapons of Mass Destruction** – nuclear, radiological, chemical and biological weapons with the ability to inflict mass casualties and destroy infrastructure and the environment.
>
> **Chemical Weapons** – include choking agents (phosgene), nerve agents (Sarin, soman and VX) and blister agents (mustard, lewisite and mustard-lewisite mixture).
>
> **Biological Weapons** – include anthrax, botulinum and staphylococcal enterotoxin B. Countries have conducted research on the weaponizing agents such as ricin, plague and smallpox. The effects of BW are not immediately visible, and diseases such as smallpox can be spread through person to person contact after release.

The Soviet Union also had the world's largest arsenal of **chemical weapons**, and Russia still is estimated to possess 40,000 metric tons of these chemical agents (Collina 2013). The United States had a declared arsenal of 27,771 metric tons in 1997, and since signing the **Chemical Weapons Convention (CWC)** have reduced their stockpile to 5,449 metric tons in 2010 (Ibid. 2013). According to SIPRI (2012) there are 189 signatories, and the US, Russia, Iraq and Libya have not yet met their CWC destruction deadlines for existing stockpiles.

Although the US **biological weapons** program ended under the Nixon administration in the early 1970s, great powers and other states have amassed stockpiles of bacteriological weapons. Since the 1920s, the Soviet government had an offensive weapons program that later stood in violation of the **Biological and Toxin Weapons Convention of 1972** (Leitenberg and Zilinskas 2012). The current status of Russia's programs is unclear and unverified. While the majority of states have now signed the CWC and BWC and destroyed declared stockpiles, dangers from the proliferation and use of WMD remain.

In this context of heightened tensions with enduring ideological battles fought in the shadow of potential nuclear annihilation, threats to state survival were viewed as paramount.

> **The Chemical Weapons Convention** (1997) – as a result of this legally binding arms-control treaty, outlawing the production, stockpiling or use of chemical weapons, 50,619 agent tons have been verifiably destroyed (71 percent), along with 3.95 million items and containers (46 per cent).
>
> Weaknesses in the CWC have also been exposed by the repeated use of chemical weapons in the Iran-Iraq war and by the Syrian regime in 2013.
>
> **Biological Weapons Convention** (1975) – commits signatory states to refrain from developing, stockpiling or using biological agents.
>
> According to the United Nations, implementation of the BWC treaty has been slower due to the lack of a formal verification mechanism among signatories including Iran, Pakistan, North Korea, Russia and China.
>
> The State Department in 2013 reported that while there are 170 state-parties, more than a dozen countries that have either refused to sign or ratify the convention. (Department 2013, 15).

National security was understood in strategic terms and largely evaluated in terms of the balance of military capabilities. The greatest perceived threats emanated from the opposing by rival great powers. Thus, security studies came to be understood as 'the study of the threat, use and control of military force', and the policies that states pursue in order to prepare for, prevent or fight in war against other states (Walt 1991, 212). This conceptualization privileges states and the threats that emerge from other militarily powerful states.

This was particularly appealing in the Cold War era characterized by advanced weapons technologies and the nuclear balance of terror based on the logic of **mutually assured destruction**. These factors contributed to the privileging of military dimensions of statecraft and the reliance on the logic of containment and nuclear deterrence (COT 2007, 7). The main function of military strength was to deter 'an all out attack' and preserve both the individual states and the international system (Spanier and Wendzel 1996, 148). National security and negative peace became virtually identical. Thus,

> **Mutually Assured Destruction** – the logic of that underpins the military strategy of nuclear deterrence. This means that both nuclear powers have sufficient second strike capabilities (in terms of sea, land or air platforms), that even if a state is attacked with nuclear weapons, they have the ability to strike back and reciprocate the nuclear destruction.

from a state-centric perspective, threats stem from rising great powers and the possibility of hegemonic wars of transition between the declining power and the rising powers.

Table 10.3   Chronology of major multilateral arms control treaties

Partial Test Ban Treaty (1963) – Prohibits testing of nuclear weapons in the atmosphere, underwater and in outer space (136 signatories).

Nuclear Nonproliferation Treaty (1968) – Prohibits the spread of nuclear weapons and technologies to non-nuclear weapons states (189 signatories; India, Israel and Pakistan are *de-facto* nuclear powers who are not party to the treaty).

Biological and Toxic Weapons Convention (1972) – Prohibits the production and storage of biological agents, calls for the destruction of existing stockpiles (171 signatories; 16 have not ratified; 23 have not signed).

Missile Technology Control Regime (1987) – Restricts the export of ballistic missiles and production technologies (34 signatories).

Open Skies Treaty (1992) – Allows unarmed surveillance flights over territory of signatory states (35 signatories).

Chemical Weapons Convention (1993) – Requires all stockpiles to be destroyed (181 signatories; Angola, Egypt, North Korea and South Sudan, North Korea are not parties; Israel and Myanmar signed but not yet ratified; Syria ratified the CWC in 2013).

Comprehensive Test Ban Treaty (1996) – Bans all testing of nuclear weapons (183 signatories; Pakistan, North Korea and India are not parties; China, Iran, Israel and the US have not yet ratified).

Antipersonnel Landmines Treaty (1997) – Bans the production and export of landmines, calls for removal of existing landmines (161 signatories; 36 have not signed including China, Israel, North Korea, Pakistan, Russia, Syria, US).

Convention on Cluster Munitions (2008) – Bans the use, production and transfer of cluster munitions (113 signatories; 80 states have not signed including China Israel, North Korea, Pakistan, Russia, Syria, US).

Arms Trade Treaty (2013) – Regulating the international trade in conventional arms to stop arms flows to conflict regions and to prevent human rights abusers and violators of the law of war from being supplied with arms (113 signatories; 7 ratifications; status: not yet entered into force).

Source: SIPRI Yearbook (2012); Federation of American Scientists (2013); Organization for the Prohibition of Chemical Weapons (2013); International Campaign to Ban Landmines (2013); Cluster Munition Coalition (2013).

Table 10.4   Chronology of major bilateral arms control agreements (US and Russia)

Strategic Arms Limitation Talks SALT I (1972) Agreement limited the United States to 1,054 ICBM silos and 656 SLBM launch tubes. The Soviet Union was limited to 1,607 ICBM silos and 740 SLBM launch tubes.

Anti-Ballistic Missile Treaty ABM (1972) Limited strategic missile defenses to 200 (later 100) interceptors each. In June 2002, the United States unilaterally withdrew from the ABM treaty.

Strategic Arms Limitation Talks SALT II (1979) Limited US and Soviet ICBM, SLBM and strategic bomber-based nuclear forces to 2,250 delivery vehicles and placed a variety of other restrictions on deployed strategic nuclear forces.

Strategic Arms Reduction Treaty START I (1991) Required the United States and the Soviet Union to reduce their deployed strategic arsenals to 1,600 delivery vehicles, carrying no more than 6,000 warheads, using the agreement's rules. Reductions were completed in 2001.

Strategic Arms Reduction Treaty START II (1993) Required reductions in the deployed strategic arsenals to 3,000–3,500 warheads and banned the deployment of destabilizing multiple-warhead land-based missiles. Like START I and, it required the destruction of delivery vehicles but not warheads. The agreement's deadline was December 2007, but START II was effectively shelved as a result of US withdrawal from the ABM treaty in 2002.

Strategic Offensive Reductions Treaty SORT (2003) United States and Russia pledge to reduce their strategic arsenals to 1,700–2,200 warheads each. SORT was replaced by New START on 5 February 2011.

New Strategic Arms Reduction Treaty New START (2011) Limits each side's deployed offensive strategic nuclear warheads to 1,550 and strategic delivery systems (ICBMs, SLBMs and heavy bombers) to 800. The warhead limit is 30 per cent lower than the 2,200 upper limit of SORT, and the delivery vehicle limit is 50 per cent lower than the 1,600 allowed in START I. The Treaty limits take effect seven years after entry into force, and the treaty will be in effect for 10 years, or longer if agreed by both parties.

Source: Arms Control Association, Daryl Kimball (2012) http://www.armscontrol.org/factsheets/USRussiaNuclearAgreementsMarch2010.

The Security Dilemma

The irony of the logic of the peace through strength argument, which maintains that if you want peace you must prepare for war, is that arms acquisition can actually threaten security. In an anarchic self-help world, arming oneself with deadly military forces and an arsenal of sophisticated weapons often leads to a paradoxical situation. Even states with compatible goals may still go to war because of the **security dilemma** which means that 'many of the means by which a state tries to increase its security decreases the security of others' (Jervis 1978). Actions aimed at enhancing security can actually diminish the perceptions of security of others and can lead to vicious spiralling effects with undesirable outcomes such as rising tensions, arms racing or military conflict. What one state perceives to be defensive or necessary actions to enhance their security are thought of as threatening or offensive by another state.

> **The Security Dilemma** – according to Robert Jervis (1978), many of the means by which a state tries to increase its security actually decreases the security of others, contributing to negative spiralling effects.

During the Cold War, arms racing between US and Soviet Union led to each side developing nuclear arsenals with over 10,000 active warheads. In contrast with the expectations of negative spiralling effects due to conventional arms racing between great powers, the logic of nuclear deterrence may have actually helped to mitigate the severity of security dilemma and constrain the scope of conflicts that previously escalated to total wars (Spanier and Wendzel 1996, 157). Other factors that helped to mitigate the severity of the security dilemma include the growth in democratic great powers allied with each other, states engaging in complex economic interdependence and collective action through international organizations. These trends have also contributed to the great power 'long-peace' (Ikenberry 2011).

After the fall of the Soviet Union in 1991, the US became the unrivalled global superpower, with unparalleled military, economic and soft power. As the **hegemon** in a unipolar system, the United States has capabilities and responsibilities that far outstrip any other country. The US has hundreds of military bases throughout the world, is capable of global deployment and has an arsenal of intercontinental ballistic weapons. They have advanced command, control, communication and intelligence technology and have made significant investments into the development of futuristic weapons such as the Laser-Induced Plasma Channel, unmanned vehicles and a **Ballistic Missile Defense System**.

> **Hegemony** – this refers to the preponderance of power or dominant position in the international system.
>
> **Ballistic Missile Defense System** – according to the US Missile Defense Agency, between 1985–2014, America invested $164.7 billion into the system to defend US territory from attack by ballistic missiles. This is also known as the Strategic Defense Initiative as or the Star Wars program.

In the twenty-first century, between 2000 and 2011, the world's defense spending approximately doubled, and viewed on a per capita basis, now represents approximately $260 per person. The US spent $695.7 billion on defense in 2011, and accounts for 58 per cent of the $1.9 trillion in defense spending by the world's top 10 military powers (SIPRI 2012). Only two of the top ten military powers; China and Russia are military competitors of the US, and America outspends China, the next-biggest military power, by between five- and sixfold (George

Washington University). The other top 10 military spenders are all American allies, which serves to reduce the threat perceptions that drive the security dilemma.

While the intent of increased military spending and technology are to make the US more secure, these enhanced militarily capabilities are viewed with dismay by Russia and China as undermining their security. While the Bush and Obama administrations have both attempted to reassure Russia that the SDI missile defense program is intended to counter the nuclear threat from Iran or North Korea, Russian leaders have repeatedly expressed concern that the program undermines their nuclear deterrent capabilities, promotes unchecked American offensive military capabilities and threatens to reignite arms racing.

Recent developments also confirm that Obama's 're-set' of relations with Russia has stalled – due to Russia's use of military force to destabilize another neighbouring country. However, unlike the 2008 Russian Five Day war against Georgia, in this case, Russia unlawfully annexed Ukraine's Crimean Peninsula territory and the Sevastopol naval base that the Russians had leased from Ukraine. Russia's actions and destabilization of eastern Ukraine provide significant precedents, particularly because Ukraine is Europe's second largest country by population, and largest by territory. In the strategically important Middle East, Russia also supports the Syria's Bashar al-Assad regime, which targets civilians and has repeatedly employed chemical weapons, worsening the security dilemma. This is evident in the proliferation of military aid given to adversaries on opposing sides in the Ukrainian and Syrian conflicts, in the warnings that the US and Russia are heading for a return to the Cold War, and in the potential for additional spiralling events such as interventions or armed conflicts to occur.

Tensions are also on the rise in Asia over a number of unresolved territorial disputes. The tensions of a maritime dispute over the Japanese controlled Senkaku Islands have recently risen with China engaging in military provocations in the East China Sea. In the South China Sea, China's claims have also led to escalating tensions with other neighbours, including Taiwan, and Vietnam, and the Philippines, Malaysia, and Brunei. President Obama's recent pivot to Asia and efforts to strengthen regional alliances with Japan and South Korea all illustrate the uncertainty concerning communist China's increased military spending and long-term territorial ambitions. Policymakers also face difficulties in distinguishing between offensive and defensive military capabilities, which also worsens the severity of the security dilemma (Van Evera 1998). Moreover, power transition theory holds that, in the long term, were the United State's relative military power to decline and a rising challenger's to increase, the security dilemma would likely intensify further.

Obama's Pivot to Asia – tensions are rising over rival territorial claims in the East and South China Sea between China and six neighbours, which have both hydrocarbon resources and are important shipping lanes for international trade. China has been growing increasingly militarily assertive over the Japanese controlled Diaoyu/Senkaku Islands. China's actions have led to President Obama's redeployment of military assets to Asia, strengthening diplomatic ties, and affirming that if Japanese sovereignty is attacked, the US will defend it. China also has territorial disputes with Taiwan, Vietnam, Malaysia, Brunei and the Philippines as well.

It remains to be seen if China, Russia or other rising powers or alliance partners will rise peacefully or will challenge US hegemony and lead to a military confrontation. While the logic of nuclear deterrence has mitigated the challenges involved in the security dilemma to date, the chief sources of insecurity are often the great powers themselves. 'Their greatest menace lies in their own tendency to exaggerate the dangers they face, and to respond with counterproductive belligerence' (Van Evera 1998, 93). Rather than attempts to obtain primacy, or restore a bipolar system, alternatively a multipolar system may emerge with multiple centres of power including the US, the European Union, China, Russia, India and Japan.

THE NUCLEAR THREAT AND GLOBAL SECURITY

Are More Nuclear Weapons Better?

Declassified documents show that American presidents Harry Truman and Dwight Eisenhower both considered launching preventive attacks on the Soviets to prevent them from achieving the nuclear bomb (Sagan 1996, 46). President Kennedy also rejected plans to launch preventative strikes against China to stop their nuclear weapons program (ibid., 47). Presidents Clinton and Bush also faced similar preventive war dilemmas with regard to North Korea and Iraq. This resulted in a preventive war to topple the Iraqi regime and the Koreans achieving their nuclear bomb in 2006. President Obama now faces a similar security challenge with the Iranian nuclear weapons program that he maintains poses intolerable risks. Obama has pursued policies including economic sanctions, coercive diplomacy, cyber attacks and threats of military action against Iranian nuclear sites.

Moreover, in 1981, the Israelis launched preventive military airstrikes targeting the Iraqi Osirak nuclear reactor. Operation Babylon was actually the second attack on Iraq's nuclear reactor. In the first days of the Iran-Iraq War (1980–88), Iran carried out Operation Scorch Sword airstrikes, partially damaging Iraq's nuclear reactor. In 2007, Israel launched another preventative air attack on a Syrian complex which an IAEA investigation found 'very likely' housed Syria's nuclear program (SIPRI 2012) due to the traces of uranium found at the site (Bednarz et al. 2009). At the 2012 meeting of the General Assembly, Israeli PM Netanyahu portrayed Iran as a ticking time bomb and said that they would act alone to counter the Iranian threat if Iran approaches the red line – or final stage of creating a nuclear bomb.

In addition to the dangers of preventive war arising from nuclear weapons, it is also possible, with the release of previously classified information, to determine that the security provided by the balance of terror between the superpowers was more fragile than was previously thought. Although nuclear weapons had a sobering influence on the great powers, the deterrent 'effect was neither automatic nor foolproof' (Sagan 1996, 47). Some of the most dangerous moments took place during the 13-day Cuban Missile Crisis. In 1963, the high stakes game of brinksmanship began when the Soviets sent nuclear weapons in Cuba to strengthen their ally and a U-2 spy plane was shot down over Cuba. President Kennedy threatened to invade the island and authorized a naval blockade, bringing the world to the brink of nuclear war (Allison and Zelikow 1999).

At the height of the Crisis, a US depth charge was perceived by a Soviet nuclear submarine as an attack and the military command's reaction was 'Maybe the war has already started up there … We're gonna blast them now! We will die, but we will sink them all – we will not become the shame of the fleet' (Savranskaya 2005, 246). The captain had the capacity to use their nuclear torpedoes against an American destroyer without direct orders from Moscow. They were operating under limited information and the expectation of hostilities above. A nuclear war was prevented only because of a safeguard that required three officers to authorize the launch, and one of them refused to do so. A US plane also accidentally entered Soviet airspace during the Crisis, creating another near miss. Moreover, until 1977 authorization codes and other safeguards to prevent the illicit use of nuclear weapons were rather weak. For example, without any higher authority, a member of the US Minutemen crew had the capability to fire up to 50 ICBMs due to the lack of safeguards (Blair 1977). These weak safeguards increased risks of an illicit use or act of nuclear terrorism.

Furthermore, numerous false alarms and nuclear accidents have also occurred. In 1995, Russia's early warning radar system mistook a Norwegian missile intended to explore the Northern Lights for a Trident nuclear submarine launch. Russian President Yeltsin had only minutes to decide whether to respond with a nuclear counterattack on the United States (Sastri 2004, 74). Thankfully, Yeltsin chose not to believe the intelligence and did not follow Russia's military standard operating procedures to 'launch on warning' retaliatory missiles (Burr 2001). The likelihood of miscalculations is elevated due to constraints in determining the reliability of information in minutes before the incoming missiles strike potentially their targets. Indeed, the deterioration of Russian early warning and command systems, poor maintenance, inadequate training and lowered morale are all trends that are 'almost certain to produce more false alarms in the future' (Blair 2013).

The United States had their own false warning in 1979, when a training tape to simulate nuclear war was mistakenly interpreted by the NORAD mainframe as evidence of Soviet nuclear missile attack targeting the United States (Gates 1996, 114; Burr 2001). National Security Advisor Brzezinski was called and told that the US was under nuclear attack from 250–2,200 Soviet missiles, and that the nuclear arsenal was being prepared for the President's launch command. The mistake was discovered just prior to President Carter being notified, which narrowly avoided the dilemma concerning whether or not to order retaliatory nuclear strikes. Also, 'in 1980, a 23-cent computer chip failed and generated information that looked like a large Soviet attack against the United States' (Blair 2013). Senior State Department adviser Marshal Shulman also wrote that 'false alerts of this kind are not a rare occurrence' and that there is a 'complacency about handling them that disturbs me' (Burr 2001). Similarly, in a recent book, *Dereliction of Duty*, written by Lt Col. Robert Patterson, who was responsible for carrying the nuclear 'football', wrote that President Clinton lost the codes for the nuclear football, which were needed to launch the nuclear missiles, and that they were missing for months.

Table 10.5   Chronology of Broken Arrow nuclear weapons accidents involving the US

1950: A US Air Force B-47 bomber disappeared over the Mediterranean and two nuclear capsules were not recovered.

1956: Bomber carrying two capsules of nuclear materials for nuclear bombs, en route from MacDill AFB, Florida to Europe, disappeared and no traces of the missing aircraft or crew were found.

1957–65: 100 kilograms of uranium 235 disappeared from a nuclear recycling plant in Apollo, Pennsylvania (Mazari 2009, 70).

1958: A B-47 mounting breaks, dropping an atomic bomb that falls in South Carolina, but does not explode.

1960: Bomarc air defense missile exploded melting a nuclear warhead and spreading plutonium contamination.

continued ...

Table 10.5 *concluded*

1961: Goldsboro B-52 broke up and one of the parachutes failed and two nuclear bombs fell in North Carolina. Only a single switch prevented the 4 megaton bomb, equivalent to 4 million tons of TNT, 250 times stronger than the Hiroshima bomb, from harming millions of Americans.

1965: Philippine Sea A-4E Skyhawk incident when an aircraft carrying a one megaton thermonuclear weapon fell into the sea from the aircraft carrier USS Ticonderoga 70 miles from the Ryuku Islands and was not recovered.

1966: Palomares B-52 bomber exploded during refueling and three nuclear weapons fell and contaminated Spanish territory with plutonium, one fell into the Mediterranean Sea and was recovered.

1968: Thule B-52 bomber crashed near Greenland with four nuclear weapons, radioactive plutonium contaminants were released from the destroyed weapons.

1968: USS Scorpion 400 miles south west of Azores sank with one nuclear reactor and two nuclear weapons on board that were not recovered.

1981: The US nuclear-powered ballistic missile submarine USS George Washington collided with a Japanese freighter in the East China Sea. The submarine carrying an estimated 160 nuclear warheads was damaged.

1984: The US aircraft carrier USS Kitty Hawk collided with a Soviet nuclear-powered attack submarine in the Sea of Japan. The USS Kitty Hawk was estimated to have carried several dozen nuclear weapons, and the submarine likely carried two nuclear torpedoes.

2007: B-52 bomber was loaded with nuclear weapons by mistake and flew 1,600 miles from North Dakota to Louisiana without the crew or commanders knowledge.

Source: Greenpeace International (Handler 1996) http://www.greenpeace.org/international/Global/international/planet-2/report/2006/2/handler-nuclear-accidents.pdf.

In sum, dangers emerging from preventive wars and military strikes, games of brinksmanship, false alarms and accidents have all already occurred. Although the probability of a nuclear war is low, all nuclear systems do have flaws and in many countries basic safeguards are lacking, threatening millions of lives. States have already had to face the decision to retaliate under the mistaken perception that they are under nuclear attack. These events serve to temper the degree of confidence in the logic of nuclear deterrence. Recognizing that tens of thousands of nuclear weapons no longer significantly increase their security, the US and Russia have agreed to reduce by their stockpiles by 90 per cent over their Cold War peak. Even Cold Warriors such as George Schultz, Henry Kissinger, William Perry and Sam Nunn published recommendations in 2013 calling for increased non-proliferation efforts, stating that they currently fail to match the urgency of the threat. They stress that the consequences of action are 'potentially catastrophic'.

However, some 19,000 nuclear weapons remain in the US, Russia, the UK, France, China, India, Pakistan and Israel (SIPRI 2012, 14). Moreover, a recent report by Greenpeace found that the US Navy has experienced at least 380 nuclear weapons incidents, at least 51 nuclear warheads have been lost into the sea (44 Soviet and 7 US), seven nuclear reactors (5 Soviet and 2 US) and 19 nuclear powered vessels have been deliberately dumped at sea (18 Soviet and 1 US) (Handler 1996, 2). Far less is known about the security breaches and accidents among other nuclear powers.

The Former Soviet Union and Loose Nukes

The collapse of the central Soviet government in 1991 led to a breakdown in security and sale of portions of their massive weapons arsenal. Large amounts of conventional weapons were sold

Table 10.6   Proliferation of nuclear weapons

Russia: 8,500
US 7,700
France: 300
UK: 225
China: 150
Pakistan: 125
India: 80–100
Israel: 80
North Korea: 10

Source: Global Zero Movement http://www.globalzero.org.

to actors in Sierra Leone, Rwanda, the Congo and Angola (Farah and Braun 2007). Similarly, for some unemployed nuclear scientists, members of the military and international arms dealers, Soviet weapons came to be viewed as valuable commodities to be sold for their private gain. For over 20 years, Senator Nunn has maintained that 'there is no greater threat to our nation's, or our world's, national security than the illicit spread of weapons of mass destruction' (1996). According to the IAEA, between 2005 and 2006, there were 250 reported incidents involving the unauthorized or criminal possession, theft or loss of nuclear or other radioactive materials, or the unauthorized disposal of radiological materials (UN News Center 2007). Of these incidents the UN reports that in 73 per cent of the cases the materials have not been recovered.

Moreover, between 1993 and 2006 the UN has 1,080 incidents reported by participating states, of which '275 involved unauthorized possession and related criminal activity, 332 involved theft or loss and 398 other unauthorized activities' (UN News Center 2007). These repeated examples of the lack of control over WMD sites and the presence of illicit trafficking networks expose the vulnerabilities and extent of the security threat. Even high-risk radiological materials have already been stolen, such as highly enriched uranium needed to make a nuclear bomb. The potential for materials to be stolen or sold to international terrorists intent on inflicting mass casualties is a frightening reality.

Table 10.7   Can terrorists obtain WMD? Fourteen examples of the black market in WMD materials

1. 90s: Japanese cult Aum Shinrikyo unsuccessfully attempted to purchase a nuclear weapon for $15 million from the Former Soviet Union (Lee 2003, 100). In 1995 they carried out a Sarin gas attack, killing 12 and sickening over 5,500 people in a Japanese subway.
2. 1998: Russian Federal Security Service (FSB) foiled an attempt by 'staff members' of a nuclear weapons plant in Chelyabinsk province to steal some 18.5 kilograms of highly enriched uranium (Ibid. 2003, 101).
3. 1998: US federal indictment of Osama bin Laden referred to his attempts to acquire nuclear weapons materials, going back at least to 1993. al-Qaeda member, Jamal Ahmad Al-Fadl, testified that he intended to purchase highly enriched uranium for $1.5 million from Sudan (Lee 2003, 100).
4. 2001 Bruce E. Ivins, a biologist at the US Army's Fort Detrick bio-defense lab, mailed deadly anthrax spores that killed five people.
5. 2001: Osama bin Laden met with Pakistani nuclear scientists Sultan Bashiruddin Mahmoud and Abdul Majid and discussed the potential use of WMD (Khan and Moore 2001).

continued ...

Table 10.7 *concluded*

6. 2001: Bin Laden emissary in Pakistan offered a Bulgarian businessman $200,000 to arrange for a legitimate environmental firm to buy radioactive waste from an atomic power plant in Bulgaria (Nathan and Leppard 2001).

7. 2002: US intelligence sources discovered of a laboratory in Afghanistan in which al Qaeda planned to develop biological agents such as anthrax (Gordon 2002).

8) 2002: US authorities arrested José Padilla and in 2007 convicted him on charges of supporting terrorism and conspiracy to commit murder for the plot to build and explode a radiological dirty bomb in the US (Risen and Shenon 2002).

9. 2006: Oleg Khintsagov was arrested after attempting to sell 100 grams of highly enriched uranium from the former Soviet Union for $1 million. He also offered to sell an additional two kilos to the potential terrorists, who were members of an undercover Georgian sting operation (Corso 2010).

10. 2000–10: Georgian officials say police have foiled or intercepted eight other attempts to transport weapons-grade enriched uranium via Georgia over the past 10 years, most recently in March 2010 (Ibid. 2010).

11. 1995: Chechen separatist rebels engaged in the first confirmed attempt to conduct a nuclear terrorist attack by creating a dirty bomb. A mixture of cesium-137 and dynamite was put in a Moscow park, but the bomb failed to go off (Allison 2004).

12. 2001–02: Chechen terrorists acquired radioactive materials from a Grozny nuclear waste plant and stole radioactive metals from the Volgodonskaya nuclear power station (Ibid. 2004).

13. Chechen terrorists planned to target railway systems transporting nuclear materials, hijack a Russian nuclear submarine or attack the Kurchatov Institute, housing 26 operating nuclear reactors (Ibid. 2004).

14. 2013: Ricin-laced letters mailed to President Obama, Republican Sen. Roger Wicker of Mississippi and Lee County Judge Sadie Holland.

Sources: Lee 2003; Gordon 2002; Nathan and Leppard 2001; Khan and Moore 2001; Corso 2010; Allison 2004.

Once acquired, WMD materials could easily be shipped around the globe alongside commercial goods. The UN estimates that some 500 million shipping containers cross the globe each year and that less than 2 per cent are physically inspected. The limits of modern detection methods are evident in the trafficking of drugs, fake antibiotics, weaponry and even body parts and people who are illicitly smuggled and sold on black markets. Port protection and maritime transportation, even in the US, remain one of a country's 'most serious vulnerabilities' with only about 5 per cent of the 9 million shipping containers that arrive at 361 major US ports every year being thoroughly inspected (Flynn 2006). In May 2002 there were reports that 25 Islamist extremists entered the United States by hiding in shipping containers (Ibid. 2006).

Thus, the threats in the twenty-first century are not limited to states' use of nuclear weapons by design or mistake, but also that sub-state actors have acquired them. Today there are about 1.6 million kilograms of highly enriched uranium and 500,000 kilograms of plutonium in the world, enough to make more than 125,000 nuclear bombs (Koren 2013). Particularly, in weakened states, both the knowledge from established WMD programs and the radiological materials themselves have already emerged in the illicit arms markets. The priority given to safeguarding these 'loose' nuclear materials around the world was dramatically elevated following the September the 11th terrorist attacks. However, the US $400 million dollar annual allocation for nuclear threat reduction has described as a 'shoestring' budget in relation to the size of the threat (Kaszynski 2013).

NIGHTMARE SCENARIOS: ROGUE REGIMES, WMD AND INTERNATIONAL TERRORISM

In 2002, the US National Security Strategy identified three interconnected threats posed by rogue regimes, armed with weapons of mass destruction, which could be given, sold or stolen by terrorist actors such as al-Qaeda or their affiliated networks. In Bush's 2002 State of the Union speech, he labelled Iraq, Iran and North Korea as the 'Axis of Evil' and highlighted the potential for rogue regimes armed with nuclear weapons to provide them to al-Qaeda, which would use them to reach their stated aim of inflicting millions of casualties. Intelligence found on battlefields in Afghanistan and elsewhere have provided evidence that terrorist groups are actively looking to purchase, steal or make weapons of mass destruction that would maximize casualties rather than simply raise awareness of their political demands. Presidents Bush and Obama have both publically stated that nuclear weapons pose the most catastrophic risks to humanity and that neither has confidence in the logic of containment and deterrence in the era of potential nuclear terrorism.

After 9/11, Bush initiated a **Global War on Terror**, increased human and signals intelligence collection efforts and focused US military and coalition efforts on fighting two interstate wars in Afghanistan and Iraq. These wars were initiated based on **Bush Doctrine's** assertion of the right to engage in pre-emptive (and preventive) war, extraordinary rendition and military tribunals to combat these three interconnected threats. Following the 2008 election President Obama fulfilled his pledge to end the war in Iraq in 2011 and authorized a surge of additional military troops in Afghanistan. However, he also publically committed to a significant drawdown of troops and a conclusion of American's longest war by 2014. Afghans are expected to take the lead in securing the country and the US expects to continue use a counterterrorism strike force. An estimated 8,000 to 12,000 NATO forces are also to work as military trainers and advisors.

The Obama administration has largely combated these threats through the use of technology and clandestine operations. Obama has favoured a light military presence using US Special Forces, drone strikes and precision weaponry, and has continued to enhance the powers of the presidency. Examples include operating under the Military Commissions Act (2006), which authorizes the president to classify suspected terrorist detainees as enemy combatants and deny them *habeas corpus* rights. Although Obama ended Bush's extraordinary rendition policies and enhanced interrogation techniques, he did sign the National Defense Authorization Act (2012). The NDAA authorizes the

> **Global War on Terror** – an international military campaign led by the US to eliminate the threats faced by al-Qaeda, affiliated international terrorist organizations and state sponsors of terrorism.
>
> **The Bush Doctrine** – the unifying principles of Bush's foreign policy. This includes targeting states that provide safe-haven for terrorists, launching preventive wars, promoting democracy in the Middle East and pursuing military interests unilaterally if necessary.
>
> **Pre-Emptive War** – a war launched to repel an imminent attack, such as a mobilizing army massing on your border or air force readying on the tarmac.
>
> **Preventive War** – a war launched to prevent an attack, but the target has not yet acted aggressively and is not an imminent threat at the time of the war. Preventive wars are illegal according to the UN Charter and international law.
>
> **The Obama Doctrine** – favours foreign policies that are interventionist and internationalist, not isolationist or unilateral to address non-proliferation and disarmament; the promotion of peace and security; the preservation of our planet; and a global economy that advances opportunity for all people.

president to indefinitely detain without trial a member or supporter of al-Qaeda, the Taliban or forces engaged in hostilities against coalition partners, even if detainees are US citizens. Finally, the Obama administration also continued the NSA secret bulk-data collection, including surveillance on both international and American citizens' communications. As the documents leaked by Edward Snowden have revealed, there have been radical reversals of 1970s NSA reforms, and it is now again legal for the intelligence community and NSA to secretly spy on American citizens.

President Obama has largely avoided using the term Global War on Terror and instead has targeted al-Qaeda specifically rather than initiating additional asymmetrical wars with heavy footprints. He has authorized approximately 250 drone strikes against Islamic militants, while engaging in a combination of multilateral pressure, clandestine operations and traditional as well as coercive diplomacy to counter the threats from outlier states that pursue WMD and support terrorism. However, critics of Obama's drone policy point out the civilian casualties and that the 'missile strikes that kill members of al Qaeda and its affiliates in Pakistan and Yemen do not strengthen economies, curb corruption, or improve government services' which are needed to help local leaders marginalize militants and reduce the pool of potential recruits (Rohde 2012).

Pakistan: Insecure Nuclear Weapons and Global Security

A.Q. Khan, the so-called father of Pakistan's nuclear weapons programme, is behind the most elaborate nuclear smuggling ring ever discovered. For decades until his arrest in 2004 his arms deals furthered the nuclear programs in North Korea, Iran and Libya. Despite publically admitting to selling nuclear secrets, he was pardoned, detained under house arrest for five years and released in 2009. Hailed as a hero in Pakistan, his private nuclear supplier network sold nuclear plans, centrifuges and advice to countries willing to purchase the nuclear materials. Although this network was discovered, the lack of certainty that nuclear trading rings have ceased leads to continued challenges to the NPT Treaty.

Serious risks remain as there are approximately 10,000 people in Pakistan, both military and civilians, who have access to or knowledge of nuclear weapons facilities, and could potentially circumvent the rather weak safeguards. Proliferation threats due to security gaps are most pronounced at civilian production sites rather than the storage sites more heavily guarded by the military. The procedural and mechanical safeguards for arming the weapon are also vulnerable and could be compromised. A collusion of individuals with pro-terrorist sympaties could result in the transfer 'nuclear weapons, weapons components or nuclear expertise to terrorists' such as the Pakistani Taliban or al-Qaeda (Gregory 2009).

Moreover, disturbing new revelations have emerged that during the 1999 Kargil War between nuclear armed rivals Pakistan and India, Pakistan's Inter-Service Intelligence contacted the Afghan Taliban to discuss the plan to hide nuclear weapons in western Afghanistan to 'protect them from a potential preemptive attack by India' (Sagan 1996, 49). The plan to transport and store the nuclear weapons in one of the world's most insecure states that had been involved in decades of protracted wars involving Islamic militants since 1979 underscores the potential vulnerability of the nuclear weapons. Also, recall that Afghanistan in 1999 was under the control of the Taliban and was a safe haven for al-Qaeda as they prepared for the September the 11th and other attacks.

After 9/11, Osama bin Laden also met with Pakistani nuclear scientists to discuss 'techniques for developing nuclear weapons and other weapons of mass destruction' (Sagan 1996, 52). Officially, the Pakistani government is a partner in the effort to combat militants who use terrorist tactics. Their cooperation has been key to successfully dismantling and degrading al-Qaeda's militant network. However, Pakistan faces a wide variety of crises: they are the 13th weakest state in the world, with a struggling economy and a highly factionalized government (State Failure Index 2013). The military have traditionally ruled, and elements have long-standing ties to Jihadist militants. Tribal regions of Pakistan evade government control, and the military are engaged in ongoing armed conflicts. Multiple terrorist networks are active in Pakistan and tensions with India remain high.

When Pakistan built their nuclear facilities, they feared India, and thus placed the facilities away from the border and in areas that are now central to al-Qaeda and Pakistan Taliban militancy. A number of terrorist attacks on nuclear weapons facilities have already occurred:

> These have included an attack on the nuclear missile storage facility at Sargodha on November 1, 2007, an attack on Pakistan's nuclear airbase at Kamra by a suicide bomber on December 10, 2007, and perhaps most significantly the August 21, 2008 attack when Pakistani Taliban suicide bombers blew up several entry points to one of the armament complexes at the Wah cantonment, considered one of Pakistan's main nuclear weapons assembly sites. (Gregory 2009)

In addition, there are also fears that Pakistan's military is playing a 'double game' by cooperating with the United States while also supporting militants who launch terrorist attacks and target NATO forces (Riedel 2012). This concern apparently contributed to Obama's decision not to inform Pakistan of the Seal Team 6 operation to capture or kill Osama Bin Laden on their soil. OBL's safe house compound was located only one mile from Abbottabad, Pakistan's equivalent of West Point. For decades, the ISI have supported the rise of the Taliban and other radical Islamist groups, including the Haqqani network and Laskar-e-Taiba. They engage in armed conflict and terrorist attacks in Afghanistan, Kashmir and elsewhere. Former chairman of the Joint Chiefs of Staff, Admiral Michael Mullen, stated that the Haqqani network 'has long enjoyed the support and protection of the Pakistani government and is, in many ways, a strategic arm of Pakistan's Inter-Services Intelligence agency' (Jones 2011).

Elements within the ISI allegedly continue to provide protection for some of the most active Islamist terrorist organizations, such as L-e-T who attacked the Indian Parliament (2001), and Mumbai (2008), killing 164 and injured 300. L-e-T also has a history of 'documented links to Al Qaeda and has trained many of the militants who landed in US and British jails since 9/11' (Schmidt and Gorman 2008). For example, Abu Zubaydah, a senior al-Qaeda leader was arrested in 2002 from an L-e-T safe house in Pakistan proving the extent of their close connections (Crenshaw 2013). L-e-T serves as a gateway for Western converts, such as the Shoe Bomber, who have already demonstrated the operational capabilities needed to mount attacks, even on the American homeland (Tankel 2013).

Concerns about the military and ISI are amplified by the fact that they have nuclear command and control capabilities. Security experts worry that nuclear weapons might fall into the hands of terrorists willing to use them, due to 'untested security systems … and no shortage of Islamist militants' (Council on Foreign Relations 2006). While the regime headed by General Musharraf was ousted from power in 2008, and Pakistan is now ruled by an elected leader, the relationship with the US has deteriorated. A former Pakistani ambassador to Washington referred to the relationship as almost adversarial, particularly when US drone strikes kill civilians or Pakistani soldiers. The potential dangers of Pakistan's WMD programs are multifaceted and many 'more steps must be taken before the threat is neutralized and Pakistan's nuclear weapons no longer pose an existential danger to the rest of the world' (Gregory 2009).

Iraq: Brinksmanship between Enduring Rivals and Preventative War

Since the First Gulf War in 1990, Iraq has been perceived as a growing threat to the American and regional allies Saudi Arabia and Egypt due to his actions in attempts to dominate the Middle East and influence oil prices. Actions including Hussein's invasion of Iran (1980–88) and Kuwait (1990–91), and actively pursuing nuclear weapons until at least 1998 illustrate the ambition to become the dominant regional power. Finally, the dictator exhibited a pattern of using chemical weapons both against the Iranians and Iraqi Kurds. Following the 9/11 terrorist attacks, the Bush administration viewed the history of Iraqi aggression and the pursuit of WMD as unacceptable risks that prompted a US-led coalition to invade and topple the Hussein dictatorship in 2003. The George W. Bush administration repeatedly maintained that they 'don't want the smoking gun to be a mushroom cloud' and that the Iraqi regime posed an imminent threat to US national security and international security (Rice 2003).

In a speech before the United Nations, Secretary of State Colin Powell stated that Western intelligence had evidence that Hussein was pursuing WMD programs in violation of the treaty that ended the First Gulf War (1990–91), and more than a decade of UN resolutions requiring disarmament. The combination of their alleged failure to comply with UN Security Council resolutions by continuing to pursue weapons of mass destruction programs and patterns supporting terrorism (although the asserted links to al-Qaeda were found not to be based on sound intelligence) provided the rationale for the initiation of the Second Gulf War (2003–11). Although the war deposed Hussein, much of the cited intelligence was later found not to be based on credible sources, and an ongoing nuclear weapons program was never found.

The human and financial costs of the Iraq War are staggering, with an insurgency developing, terrorist acts triggering sectarian violence and a full-scale civil war. The nearly decade-long occupation was estimated to cost a trillion dollars, and the deaths are estimated at 150,000–250,000 Iraqis, largely civilians, while 4,486 American died out of the total coalition losses of 4,804 lives. Although Iraq was successfully disarmed by the UNSCOM inspectors following the First Gulf War, Hussein refused to expose this perceived weakness to the Iranians and Americans. Thus, policy choices, informational asymmetries and miscalculations culminated in a protracted and costly war over a non-existent nuclear program, with dire consequences. Following the withdrawal of US forces, Iraq is now ruled by democratically elected leaders, but ranks ninth worst on the State Failure Index (2012) and is the fifth least peaceful country (Global Peace Index 2012). Iraq remains one of the most violent places on earth as terrorist attacks occur more frequently there than almost anywhere else in the world.

North Korea: the Newest Member of the Nuclear Club

The Korean Peninsula remains one of the most fortified and militarized regions in the world. The Korean War (1950–1953) ended without a formal peace agreement and tensions and hostilities persist. The North is one of the most isolated and repressive dictatorships on the planet. The regime's rejection of the NPT non-proliferation regime and pursuit of nuclear weapons has cost dearly. During the 1990s, approximately one-tenth of the population starved to death. With few exports, the North sells their ballistic missile and military technologies to other authoritarian regimes, which undermines the Nuclear Non-Proliferation Treaty, increases perceptions of insecurity and contributes to increased military spending.

The North Korean regime currently has a million-man army opposing 650,000 South Korean and 28,500 US soldiers with only a narrow demilitarized zone dividing them. Recent incidents such as torpedoing a Southern warship (2010), using artillery to shell Southern territory (2011 and 2014), Kim Jon-un's threatens to nuke the South and America, ballistic missile launches over Japanese territory, three nuclear tests and threats of a looming fourth have heightened fears of renewed armed conflict. Were a war to break out, estimates put the loss of lives at more than 500,000 in South Korean alone (Bennett and Shambaugh 2010, 181).

The Clinton administration responded to this threat by pursing a diplomatic track that culminated the 1994 Agreed Framework. The North agreed to give up their nuclear weapon program in exchange for the normalization of relations, fuel and the building of two nuclear power reactors. However, both sides maintained that the other was not living up to the agreement, and the Yongbyon nuclear facilities were reactivated. They also withdrew from the NPT and successfully tested their atomic bomb in 2006. Now a member of the nuclear club, they are unwilling to dismantle their nuclear reactors. Agreements were signed in 2007 and 2012, in which the North agreed to halt their long-range missile launches, enrichment activities and nuclear tests in exchange for food aid. However, the regime continues to engage in provocations. A dangerous game of nuclear brinksmanship with the United States and South Korea continues.

Following the testing of the nuclear bomb, the US has largely been deterred from initiating a military conflict and has favoured multilateral sanctions and multi-party talks. The grudging acceptance of North Korea's nuclear weapons without Western military retaliation has provided a potential lesson for the Iranians. While in 2007 the Bush administration hailed the agreement as an exemplary model for Iranian negotiations, the North has provided a precedent of a different sort. For years they have employed deceptive tactics to continue their nuclear program despite the 6+1 party negotiations and agreements, international isolation and threat of war.

Iran: The 10th Member of the Nuclear Club?

The question of what actions are justified when facing hostile states with a history of supporting acts of terrorism, pursuing weapons of mass destruction and the potential that they may fall into the hands of terrorist organizations has not receded. Western powers fear that a nuclear-armed Iran will be emboldened to increase their support for terrorism and lead to further proliferation in the politically unstable Middle East. Even if Iranian government is deterred and refrains from giving or selling WMD plans, components or materials to other rogue regimes or international terrorists, their presence increases the threats of 'loose' WMD materials being illicitly acquired by non-state actors.

President Obama has repeatedly stated that the threat from a nuclear Iran cannot be contained and that the US will 'do what is necessary' and 'will do anything to make sure that Iran doesn't get nuclear weapons'. He has also made clear that 'all options are on the table' including diplomacy, economic sanctions and the use of military force (Associated Press 2013).

In 2013, Iran had a presidential election which replaced the fire-brand Mahmoud Ahmadinejad with a more moderate President Hasan Rouhani. He was authorized by the Iranian Supreme Leader Ayatollah Ali Khamenei to agree to an interim agreement to freeze parts of the nuclear program in return for between $7 billion and $20 billion in sanction relief. As of this writing, four rounds of negotiations have taken place, with the latest making no progress toward achieving a final deal by the July 2014 deadline. Thus, it remains to be seen whether a diplomatic deal can be reached that can avert war. For now, the prospect of (P5+1) negotiation opens up the possibility that Iran could give up its nuclear weapons program in exchange for the removal of the crippling economic sanctions, a normalization of relations or security guarantees.

CONTINGENCY PLANS FOR SAFEGUARDING WMD WHEN REGIME COLLAPSE AND STATES FAIL

A central problem of time is how to strengthen weak states, particularly those that are in critical danger of state failure. As the case of the former Soviet Union illustrates, as regimes lose their grip on power, windows of opportunity emerge when countries' weapons stockpiles become vulnerable targets. The lowering of the barriers to arms proliferation are particularly likely when states are unable to safeguard stockpiles, such as in cases of regime transition, civil war or state failure. As the Iraq and Libyan wars underscore, regime collapse can lead to large caches of conventional weapons being seized by sub-state actors. Although they used their oil wealth to purchase vast arsenals, the likelihood of WMD getting into the hands of sub-state actors was substantially reduced by preventative action taken by the international community.

Iraq and Libya: Disarmament Prior to War and Regime Change

Bowing to international pressure, Iraqi WMD programs and stockpiles were largely destroyed after years of international isolation and sanctions. UNSCOM in Iraq (1991–1998), faced years of Iraqi deception, minimal or noncompliance. Without such an effort, the fall of the regime would have posed a far greater threat to international security. In both Iraq and Libya the countries degenerated into protracted wars as entrenched authoritarian regimes refused to give up power. According the UN, the Libyan Civil War resulted in between 10,000–25,000 deaths, many of them civilians. Both Qaddafi and Hussein demonstrated a willingness to engage in large-scale massacres to preserve their rule and in the Libyan case this prompted a NATO no-fly zone and airstrikes. Using counterfactual logic, had the international community not disarmed their large WMD stockpiles prior to the collapse of the regimes, they may have been looted alongside the conventional weapons, oil and priceless national treasures.

In Libya, Qaddafi only renounced his WMD program after a shipment of uranium enrichment materials he illicitly purchased from the A.Q. Khan nuclear smuggling network was intercepted in 2003 as part of the enhanced Proliferation Security Initiative port security measures. Fearing regime change, he quickly signed the relevant international treaties, built destruction facilities and allowed international IAEA inspectors in. Although most of the Qaddafi's tons of mustard gas were destroyed, shortly after the overthrow and death of Qaddafi at the hands of regime's opponents in 2011, opposition forces discovered chemical weapons caches with hundreds of battle-ready warheads loaded with mustard gas (Warrick 2013).

In 2012, the new transition government confirmed that the former Qaddafi regime failed to report elements of an ongoing chemical weapons program in violation of international law. Qaddafi had undeclared chemical weapons storage sites with at least nine metric tons of mustard gas that have not yet been destroyed (Nuclear Threat Initiative NTIa). The new government also found 6,400 barrels of the 'yellowcake' uranium at a warehouse in Sabha and is deciding whether or not to use them for nuclear power (NTIb). The IAEA confirms that Libya is now compliant in nuclear disarmament. However, the destruction of existing WMD stockpiles is an expensive and lengthy process, and the presence of al-Qaeda militants and the rise of well-armed sub-state actors means that the challenges of properly safeguarding these facilities remain. Lastly, the true extent of the looting of unguarded Libyan armories and weapons depots is unknown, but the weapons are already contributing to the violence in Egypt and Syria.

Syria: Civil War and the First Use of Chemical Weapons in the Twenty-first Century

Over the last three years, Syria has dramatically imploded with the nation breaking down into a bloody internationalized civil war that has cost 160,000 lives. The war has contributed to regional insecurity through mechanisms of diffusion (including foreign involvement) and contagion (spreading across borders). American intelligence also point to the presence of al-Qaeda extremists in Syria's civil war and deputy director of the CIA, Michael Morrell (2013), asserted that the existence of one of the world's largest stockpiles of chemical weapons posed the greatest threat to US national security. If the Syrian regime collapses, power vacuums may allow Syria to become al-Qaeda's new safe haven, rivalling Yemen and Pakistan. Before Syria agreed to turn over their chemical weapons, the Pentagon estimated that it would require 75,000 troops to seize Syria's chemical stockpiles.

On 21 August 2013, French and US intelligence indicated that Branch 450 of the Syrian military – supporting of the Alawite minority led regime – used rockets capable of delivering up to 60 litres of nerve agents in urban areas. Agencies estimate that there are 1,000 tons of chemical weapons located in 50 sites across the country and thousands of delivery munitions including ballistic missiles, artillery rockets and bombs (BBC 2013). Syrian rebels are allegedly receiving training from military contractors to secure the chemical weapons and warnings and assistance have been sent to neighbouring countries. Iraq and Jordan are on the frontlines of efforts to seize illicit materials that may be smuggled out of Syria. Detection is complicated by the sheer scale of the displacement – some two million refugees have fled the conflict.

These events have led to President Obama's foreign policy reversal, from not providing lethal military aid to the rebel factions to now doing so, and also sending a costly signal that he was ready to authorize a military air strike against the Assad regime for gassing over 1,000 people. He threatened a set of precision strikes to punish the regime for using chemical weapons and to deter its future use. He stated that 'when, with modest effort and risk we can stop children from being gassed to death and thereby make our own children safer in the long run, I believe we should act' (Obama 2013). The threat prompted Russian President Putin to pressure Syria to sign to the Chemical Weapons Ban and agree to dismantle their chemical weapons program by 2014.

However, the UN's efforts to disarm Iraq and Libya illustrate the difficulties in verifying and enforcing international law. States may lack commitment to compliance and may seek to evade transparency and deceive IAEA inspectors by not providing a full account of their stockpiles. The challenges in Syria are compounded by the dangers involved in locating and destroying 1,000 metric tons of WMD during a raging civil war. The disposal of WMD is a long, expensive and dangerous process and even under the best case conditions the threats from their massive weapons stockpiles will likely persist. The likelihood of the regime losing control over their remaining WMD arsenal is a concern, as groups branded terrorists by the Obama administration are targeting military bases that serve as major production centres (Whitlock and Morello 2012).

North Korea: An Imminent Collapse?

As these cases illustrate, dangers to global security can emerge not only from aggressive states but also from state failure and regime change. With the death of Kim Jong-il in 2011 and the succession of his son Kim Jong-un, North Korea is in the midst of a leadership transition and is plagued by persistent economic failure that increases the likelihood of regime collapse. North Korea is the 22nd weakest state in the world and a recent RAND Corporation report claims that the regime is facing impending collapse (Bennett 2013). The potential for a lengthy period of instability and variety of simultaneous crises have prompted the US and ROK to strengthen their alliance and consider the development of contingency plans.

Issues of concern include how to respond to a potential civil war, natural disasters, massive refugee flows, kidnapping of ROK citizens or loss of control over weapons of mass destruction (Center for US-Korea Policy 2009, 3). The RAND Corporation has also estimated that 'based on optimistic assumptions about how the collapse might occur' between 260,000 and 400,000 ground force personnel would be required to stabilize North Korea (Bennett and Lind 2011, 86). As North Korea lies on China's border, any American intervention to secure the North's chemical, biological and nuclear weapon is laden with dangers. As the US learned in the Korean War when it shifted from containment to rollback, American presence near China's borders can lead to conflict with China. The consequences of the collapse of the northern militarized regime are sufficiently dire that analysts estimate it could require a military operation with US troop commitments in excess of that for both Iraq and Afghanistan.

Pakistan: At Greatest Risk of Nuclear Terrorism?

Similarly, Pakistan is a large country of 170 million, and nearly two-thirds of the population lives on less than two dollars a day with rising inequality and scarcity. Further, 40 per cent of Pakistani children are not in primary school, leading to high youth unemployment and lowering the country's development potential (World Economic Forum 2013). Moreover, Pakistan faces the difficult task of establishing civilian rule, as elected leaders face threats from within their own military, from insurgents or from an Islamic coup. According to the Nuclear Threat Initiative, a number of serious security threats have already occurred:

In 2007, a suicide bomber attacked a bus carrying workers to the Sargodha air base, which is believed to house nuclear weapons. The following month, a school bus was attacked outside Kamra air base, which may also serve as a nuclear storage site. In August 2008, Pakistani Taliban suicide bombers attacked what experts believe is the country's main nuclear-weapons assembly depot in Wah cantonment. Recently, militants invaded a major Pakistani naval base near Karachi, blowing up two P-3C Orion surveillance planes and killing at least 10 people ... In a series of interviews, several Pakistani officials told National Journal that investigators suspect the militants had help inside the complex. Experts believe that nuclear-weapon components were stored nearby. (Goldberg and Ambinder 2011)

The US has developed contingency plans to use using military force to secure Pakistan's 125 nuclear weapons located at 15 different facilities. This is a policy option to deal with worst-case scenarios occurred involving unacceptable risks to American or international security, such as international terrorists gaining control of radiological materials (Richelson 2009, 207–15). According to the former deputy counterterrorism director, Pakistani nukes remain 'one of the highest priorities of the U.S. intelligence community' (*Times of India* 2011). In 2010, military assistance to Pakistan totalled $2.5 billion, and there is considerable debate as to whether or not to cut aid aimed at enhancing the US partnership with Pakistan.

In sum, the dangers posed by WMD remain pressing concerns more than 20 years after the end of the Cold War. While the threat of deliberate use of nuclear weapons against another state has been reduced due to the decline in ideological conflicts and rise of international conventions, numerous dangers remain. A number of states have undeclared stockpiles and have not signed or complied with WMD conventions. President Obama has made nuclear weapons a centrepiece of his foreign policy agenda, including the permanent institutionalization of the Global Initiative to Combat Nuclear Terrorism partnership of 83 states.

Moreover, in 2010, Obama initiated the Nuclear Security Summit to develop norms to safeguard and reprocess nuclear materials and to address states who fail to comply with international law. A second Nuclear Summit in 2012 resulted in a communiqué focused on increasing cooperation to prevent nuclear terrorism and to prevent illegal trafficking. The bilateral New Start Treaty with Russia also limits both countries to 1,550 deployed strategic nuclear warheads, and Obama pledged to reduce the number unilaterally to 1,000. These efforts demonstrate the degree of concern placed on deadly technologies capable of killing millions in minutes, as well as the size of the existing security gaps in the existing WMD regimes.

Africa's Deadliest War – also known as Africa's world war, fought between the DRC government and its supporters, Angola, Namibia and Zimbabwe vs. rebel groups backed by Uganda and Rwanda. The war has led to horrifying human tragedies and the looting of the DRC's vast energy and mineral resources. For example, the DRC has at least two-thirds of the world's coltan resources, which are illegally extracted and sold to companies to become part of computers, tablets and mobile phone technologies. This has prompted Congolese activists to continue to ask: how many children may have died for you to have your mobile phone? For more on this issue, watch the documentary film *Blood in the Mobile* by Frank Piasecki.

THE NEW FACE OF WAR IN THE TWENTY-FIRST CENTURY: ASYMMETRIC CONFLICTS

The Changing Trends in War

Contrary to Samuel Huntington's expectations that the dominant form of violence would be between civilizations, the most immediate threat to global peace emerges from within states. More than one-third of UN members have been affected by armed conflicts and civil war. Internal wars are the most common and persistent form of violence in the international system. Thus, they remain the most frequent security challenges that the international community faces. For example, the deadliest conflict since World War II was actually an internationalized civil war in the Democratic Republic of the Congo (1998–2008), which killed 5 million people, led to massive refugees and internal displacement and over 300,000 rapes. The war involved substantial looting of the DRC's natural resources by three different national rebel movements and some 14 foreign armed groups. It also led to the largest and most expensive UN peace-building operation that continues to face significant challenges in reducing violence in the Eastern Congo.

Between 1946 and 1999, there were 25 interstate wars resulting in 3.3 million battle-deaths, averaging three months. There were also 127 civil wars with 16.2 million battle-deaths, lasting on average six years (Fearon and Laitin 2003). Similarly, the vast majority of the 248 lower-level armed conflicts are also within states. In 2011, there were six wars and 37 ongoing armed conflicts, up from 31 the year before (Themnér and Wallensteen 2013, 565). Despite the recent declines in internal conflicts since the late 1990s, violence has increased over the last five years. The increase is largely driven by conflicts in the South Asia and MENA regions.

Table 10.8   Armed conflicts active in 2011

Location	Incompatibility	Year	Intensity
Europe			
Russia	Territory (Caucases Emirate)	2007–11	Minor
Middle East			
Iran	Government	2005–11	Minor
Iraq	Government	2004–11	Minor
Israel	Territory (Palestine)	2000–11	Minor
Syria	Government	2011	Minor
Turkey	Territory (Kurdistan)	1984–2011	Minor
Yemen	Government	2009–11	War
Asia			
Afghanistan	Government	2003–11	War
Cambodia, Thailand	Territory (common border)	2011	Minor
India	Territory (Kashmir)	1989–2011	Minor
	Government	1996–2011	Minor
Myanmar	Territory (Kachin)	2011	Minor
	Territory (Karen)	2005–11	Minor

Location	Incompatibility	Year	Intensity
Pakistan	Territory (Baluchistan)	2011	Minor
	Government	2007–11	War
Philippines	Territory (Mindanao)	1993–2011	Minor
	Government	1999–2011	Minor
Thailand	Territory (Patani)	2003–11	Minor
Tajikistan	Government	2010–11	Minor
Africa			
Algeria	Government	1991–2011	Minor
Central African Republic	Government	2009–11	Minor
Ethiopia	Territory (Ogaden)	1998–2011	Minor
Ethiopia	Territory (Oromiya)	1998–2011	Minor
Ivory Coast	Government	2011	Minor
Libya	Government	2011	War
Mauritania	Government	2010–11	Minor
Nigeria	Government	2011	Minor
Rwanda	Government	2009–11	Minor
Senegal	Territory (Casamance)	2011	Minor
Somalia	Government	2006–11	War
South Sudan	Government	2011	Minor
Sudan	Territory (Abyei)	2011	Minor
	Government	1983–2011	War

Source: Themner and Wallensteen (2012).

Civil wars are also longer, more likely to reoccur and less likely to end through a negotiated settlement than interstate wars. Combatants in almost half of all civil wars never attempt to negotiate, and even in the minority of cases in which a peace treaty is signed to end the war, the dominant trend is that they are 'likely to experience renewed violence in the future' (Walter and Snyder 1999, 1). Moreover, separatist conflicts fought over territory are often more intractable than other civil wars (Walter 2003). The number of conflicts involving issues of self-determination and autonomy has almost doubled since 1984 and they last more than twice as long as other civil wars, with even higher recidivism rates (Walter 2006).

Mary Kaldor (1999) termed these conflicts 'new wars' which are often less concerned with the conventional ideological battles, and increasingly involves ethno-nationalist and religious dimensions. Studies find as many as 23 to 25 million total war-related deaths in under-developed nations in the last half century can be 'attributed to violent conflict underlined by significant overtones of identity or ethnonationalism' (Conteh-Morgan 2004, 193):

> The critical cause of ethnonationalist conflict is the interaction of three factors: interethnic hostility, elite outbidding within groups, and a security dilemma confronting them … all three necessary conditions are dependent on the existence of economic deprivation, opportunity, and a situation of de facto anarchy (Conteh-Morgan 2004, 200).

Particularly when a state weakens and is unable to provide security and other public goods to the population, fears rise and conflicts arise out of the emerging **strategic dilemmas** (Lake and Rothchild 2001). Moreover, since 2000, 43 per cent of civil wars have been religious and religious ideology is one of the 'leading motivations for most transnational terrorist attacks' (Shah and Toft 2006).

> **Strategic Dilemmas** – according to James Fearon (2005), strategic dilemmas include the security dilemma, asymmetric information, problems of credible commitment and issue indivisibilities.

Table 10.9   The 16 ongoing United Nations peacekeeping operations

- 69 Peacekeeping operations since 1948
- Approved resources of $7.83 billion (2014), .5% of world annual military expenditures
- 122 countries contribute to the 118,111 field personnel and support of peace-building missions
- Peacekeepers monitor cease-fire and armistice agreements, work to prevent the escalation of incidents, and in some cases to protect civilians and support transition processes.

1. *United Nations Organization Stabilization Mission in the Democratic Republic of the Congo* (MONUSCO), since 2010: 25,698 total personnel strength, budget (2013–2014) $1,456,378,300
2. *African Union-United Nations Hybrid Operation in Darfur* (UNAMID), since 2007: 22,623 total personnel strength, budget (2013–14) $1,335,248,000
3. *United Nations Mission in the Republic of South Sudan* (UNMISS), since 2011: 11,351 total personnel strength, budget (2013–14) $924,426,000
4. *United Nations Multidimensional Integrated Stabilization Mission in Mali* (MINUSMA), since 2013: 8,035 total personnel strength, budget (2013–14) $602,000,000
5. *United Nations Operation in Côte d'Ivoire* (UNOCI), since 2004: 10,736 total personnel strength, budget (2013–14) $584,487,000
6. *United Nations Stabilization Mission in Haiti* (MINUSTAH), since 2010: 9,755 total personnel strength, budget (2013–14) $576,619,000
7. *United Nations Interim Force in Lebanon* (UNIFIL), since 1978: 11,162 total personnel strength, budget (2013–14) $492,622,000
8. *United Nations Mission in Liberia* (UNMIL), since 2003: 8,931 total personnel strength, budget (2013–14) $476,329,800
9. *United Nations Interim Security Force for Abyei, Sudan* (UNISFA), since 2011: 4,311 total personnel strength, budget (2013–14) $329,108,600
10. *United Nations Truce Supervision Organization* (UNTSO), the UN's first peacekeeping mission in the Middle East, since 1948: 382 total personnel strength, budget (2013–14) $70,280,900
11. *United Nations Mission for the Referendum in Western Sahara* (MINURSO), since 1991: 508 total personnel strength, budget (2013–14) $60,475,700
12. *United Nations Peacekeeping Force in Cyprus* (UNFICYP), since 1964: 1,145 total personnel strength, budget (2013–14) $56,604,300
13. *United Nations Disengagement Observer Force in Syria* (UNDOF), since 1974: 1,406 total personnel strength, budget (2013–14) $60,654,500
14. *United Nations Interim Administration Mission in Kosovo* (UNMIK), since 1999: 368 total personnel strength, budget (2013–14) $44,953,000
15. *United Nations Military Observer Group in India and Pakistan* (UNMOGIP), since 1949: 113 total personnel strength, budget (2013–14) $21,084,400
16. *United Nations Multidimensional Integrated Stabilization Mission in the Central African Republic* (MINUSCA), Security Council authorized deployment of 11,820 total personnel, to begin their mission in September 2014 to protect civilians and support the transition process.

Source: United Nations Peacekeeping Factsheet (10 April 2014) http://www.un.org/en/peacekeeping/resources/statistics/factsheet.shtml.

Civil wars often cause a considerable loss of life, refugee crises, economic devastation and the destruction of political, economic, legal and civil society (Collier et al. 2004). They also undermine regional stability and strain the UN, AU and NATO's ability to respond. Furthermore, in contrast to World War I, when 90 per cent of casualties were soldiers and ten per cent civilians, in the late twentieth century civil wars, 'more than 80 per cent of the casualties were civilians' (Conteh-Morgan 2004, 278). Internationalized civil wars, such as in Syria, tend to have the highest death tolls (Lacina 2006), with negative legacies that persist for decades after the shooting stops (Collier et al. 2004). The total economic impact of containing violence was an estimated $9.46 trillion in 2012, or equivalent to 11 per cent of global GDP (Global Peace Index 2013). If the cost of violence could be reduced by 50 per cent, this would generate enough money to repay the debt of the developing world, provide enough money for the European stability mechanism and fund the additional amount required to fund the Millennium Development Goals (Ibid. 2013).

In addition, there is also evidence that civil wars, international criminal networks and the drug trade are interconnected. For example, Mexican drug cartels use the $25 billion dollars annual income from the US market to increase their capabilities to fight the government in the Mexican drug war (2006–present) that has lead to over 60,000 deaths. Similarly, the Taliban fund their insurgency through opium, which is the country's most lucrative industry and accounts for 92 per cent of the global output. Valued at $4 billion, or half the value of Afghanistan's GDP in 2008, opium allows the Taliban to threaten the government and fund their armed campaign (UNODC).

In 2009, the value of illicit trade around the globe was $1.3 trillion and the profits from the drug trade were $322 billion dollars (UN Report 2012). The drug trade is equivalent to 1 per cent of the world's GDP, higher than the GDP of 88 per cent of all countries (UNODC). The networks and linkages between conflict zones, international terrorism and international crime have grown, often due to the need to raise revenues through the international drug trade. Numerous transnational criminal networks are also involved in the illicit trafficking of people, natural resources and arms.

International Terrorism

Terrorism is commonly defined as 'premeditated, politically motivated violence perpetrated against noncombatant targets by sub-national groups or clandestine agents' (NCTC 2011). In 2011, international terrorist networks killed over 12,000 and injured 45,000 people in attacks in 70 countries around the world, with Muslims suffering between 82 and 97 per cent of fatalities in recent years. Approximately two-thirds of all terrorist attacks that occurred across the world took place in just three countries, Afghanistan (3,353), Iraq (3,063) and Pakistan (2,033), followed by Somalia (1,001) and Nigeria (593) (NCTC 2011, 9). The fact that al-Qaeda and their affiliates have primarily killed Muslim civilians has decreased public support for their groups and they have consistently failed to gain a basis of support among the Muslim masses.

While the majority of core al-Qaeda members have been killed or captured significantly degrading their capabilities to carry out large-scale attacks, terrorist threats remain among some 60 different countries. Terrorist threats continually evolve and attacks by al-Qaeda affiliates in Afghanistan, Pakistan and Yemen are steadily increasing. Terrorist attacks are at a five-year high in Africa and the Western Hemisphere largely due to Nigeria's Boko Haram and Colombia's FARC rebels (NCTC 2011, 9). Moreover, as the 2013 attack by Al-Shabaab on a Nairobi Kenya

Table 10.10   Sample of recent terrorist attacks

Nigeria, January 2012: Islamist Boko Haram launch gun and bomb attacks in northern Nigeria on five police buildings, two immigration offices and the local headquarters of the State Security Service, killing at least 178.

Afghanistan, April 2012: Dozens of Taliban launch coordinated attacks on embassies, NATO bases, parliament and government buildings in Kabul and three eastern provinces.

Pakistan, January 2013: Bombing of a snooker hall kills 115 people and wounds over 270 in Quetta, a city of Hazara Shiites. Attack is carried out by Lashkar-e-Jhangvi, a Sunni militant group with strong ties to the Pakistani Taliban.

Syria, January 2013: Explosions at the University of Aleppo kill 83 and wound 160 people. No group claimed responsibility and activists claim that the Syrian government was responsible.

Algeria, January 2013: al-Qaeda linked militants took 800 people hostage at the Tigantourine gas facility and the siege resulted in 37 hostage deaths and 29 militant deaths.

United States, April 2013: Two self-radicalized brothers detonated bombs at the Boston Marathon, killing 3 and injuring at least 264.

Afghanistan, June 2013: Afghan Taliban suspected in poison gas attacks that sent hundreds of girls to hospitals from multiple schools.

Yemen, September 2013: al-Qaeda in the Arabian Peninsula, are responsible for a series of failed bomb plots against the US launched a coordinated attack on Yemeni military installations, killing 38 troops and wounded dozens.

Kenya, September 2013: Al-Shabaab militants linked with al-Qaeda attacked the Westgate mall in Nairobi, holding hostages, injuring 175 and torturing and killing some 38 people. The mall attack was the deadliest in Kenya since al-Qaeda bombed the US Embassy in 1998, killing 213 people.

Nigeria, April–May 2014: The terrorist group Boko Haram kidnaps over 200 school girls and expresses the intent to sell them into slavery, while engaging in a bomb campaign, including targets such as a market and hospital, which killed 46 and injuring dozens.

---

shopping mall, killing 68 people illustrates, Al-Shabaab is of particular concern because this Somali Islamist group recently pledged their alliance to al-Qaeda. Of all of al-Qaeda's affiliated groups, they have the deepest linkages with the US, with supporters in Seattle, St Louis, San Diego, Minnesota, Maryland, Ohio and Alabama. Fifteen Americans have died fighting for Al-Shabaab and four Americans have become suicide bombers (Bergen and Sterman 2013).

As Obama acknowledged during a speech at the National Defense University, military solutions to the terrorist problems are insufficient. He maintains that in order to effectively address the threats from terrorism, the US must refrain from initiating costly, large-scale interventions, and instead seek to mobilize allies and develop partnerships with states facing terrorist threats. The international community must address the underlying causes and conflicts that feed extremism and recruitment. Conflict prevention efforts such as confidence-building, power-sharing arrangements, good government, pro-poor economic growth and education for employment opportunities are key to shrinking the pool of unemployed youth recruits and can build resilience against future terrorist attacks. In a commencement speech for the US Military Academy in West Point in May 2014, President Obama again called for the promotion of greater freedom and tolerance to combat extremism. He also called upon Congress to allocate an additional $5 billion for a new counterterrorism partnership to continue to train and build capacities and relationships with countries on the frontlines: such as Yemen, Somalia, Libya, Mali, Jordan, Lebanon, Turkey, Iraq and Pakistan.

Table 10.11   US State Department's designated foreign terrorist organizations

Date Designated	Name
10/8/1997	Abu Nidal Organization (ANO)
10/8/1997	Abu Sayyaf Group (ASG)
10/8/1997	Aum Shinrikyo (AUM)
10/8/1997	Basque Fatherland and Liberty (ETA)
10/8/1997	Gama'a al-Islamiyya (Islamic Group) (IG)
10/8/1997	HAMAS
10/8/1997	Harakat ul-Mujahidin (HUM)
10/8/1997	Hizballah
10/8/1997	Kahane Chai (Kach)
10/8/1997	Kurdistan Workers Party (PKK) (Kongra-Gel)
10/8/1997	Liberation Tigers of Tamil Eelam (LTTE)
10/8/1997	National Liberation Army (ELN)
10/8/1997	Palestine Liberation Front (PLF)
10/8/1997	Palestinian Islamic Jihad (PIJ)
10/8/1997	Popular Front for the Liberation of Palestine (PFLF)
10/8/1997	PFLP-General Command (PFLP-GC)
10/8/1997	Revolutionary Armed Forces of Colombia (FARC)
10/8/1997	Revolutionary Organization 17 November (17N)
10/8/1997	Revolutionary People's Liberation Party/Front (DHKP/C)
10/8/1997	Shining Path (SL)
10/8/1999	al-Qa'ida (AQ)
9/25/2000	Islamic Movement of Uzbekistan (IMU)
5/16/2001	Real Irish Republican Army (RIRA)
9/10/2001	United Self Defense Forces of Colombia (AUC)
12/26/2001	Jaish-e-Mohammed (JEM)
12/26/2001	Lashkar-e Tayyiba (LeT)
3/27/2002	Al-Aqsa Martyrs Brigade (AAMB)
3/27/2002	Asbat al-Ansar (AAA)
3/27/2002	al-Qaida in the Islamic Maghreb (AQIM)
8/9/2002	Communist Party of the Philippines/New People's Army (CPP/NPA)
10/23/2002	Jemaah Islamiya (JI)
1/30/2003	Lashkar i Jhangvi (LJ)
3/22/2004	Ansar al-Islam (AAI)
7/13/2004	Continuity Irish Republican Army (CIRA)
12/17/2004	Libyan Islamic Fighting Group (LIFG)
12/17/2004	al-Qaida in Iraq (AQI)
6/17/2005	Islamic Jihad Union (IJU)
3/5/2008	Harakat ul-Jihad-i-Islami/Bangladesh (HUJI-B)
3/18/2008	al-Shabaab
5/18/2009	Revolutionary Struggle (RS)
7/2/2009	Kata'ib Hizballah (KH)
1/19/2010	al-Qa'ida in the Arabian Peninsula (AQAP)
8/6/2010	Harakat ul-Jihad-i-Islami (HUJI)
9/1/2010	Tehrik-e Taliban Pakistan (TTP)
11/4/2010	Jundallah
5/23/2011	Army of Islam (AOI)
9/19/2011	Indian Mujahedeen (IM)
3/13/2012	Jemaah Anshorut Tauhid (JAT)
5/30/2012	Abdallah Azzam Brigades (AAB)
9/19/2012	Haqqani Network (HQN)
3/22/2013	Ansar al-Dine (AAD)

Source: US Department of State (2013) http://www.state.gov/j/ct/rls/other/des/123085.htm.

Cyber Threats: Multifaceted and Rapidly Evolving Challenges

Intelligence communities are increasingly concerned that states or terrorist networks will evolve the technological capabilities needed to launch cyber attacks and harm **critical infrastructure**, economic, governmental or military targets. For example, in 2013, former National Coordinator for Counter Terrorism Richard Clark revealed the vulnerability of the private sector soft targets and cited repeated attacks on the US electrical grid by hackers. He has been particularly vocal about the potential for information cyber wars with China, Russia, Iran or North Korea. Recently heads of the intelligence officials testified that we are not prepared for the equivalent of a cyber Pearl Harbor. The Director of National Intelligence James Clapper (2013) remarked,

> **Critical Infrastructure** – refers to the assets that are crucial for the functioning of society, including a country's water, food, energy, communication and transportation, banking, governmental and military systems.

> In my almost 50 years of intelligence, I do not recall a period in which we confronted a more diverse array of threats, crises, and challenges around the world … the world and our threat environment is changing.

Thus, security threats arise from rival states and weak states, as well as from an array of non-state actors that include terrorists and criminal cyber hackers. The number of cyber attacks on critical infrastructure in the US alone in 2012 increased 68 per cent to 200,000 in one year (Homeland Security 2013). The increased surveillance powers given to intelligence agencies since 9/11 and the creation of the US Defense Department's Cyber Command both illustrate the growing recognition of cyber threats. Actors are repeatedly launching attacks on targets with malware, Trojans, worms, viruses and logic bombs.

EVOLVING CONCEPTIONS OF SECURITY

The Widening of Security: Expanding the Dimensions of Security

Events such as the unexpected fall of the Soviet Union, the 9/11 attacks and the 2008 global recession all illustrate the deficiencies of relying exclusively on narrow conceptions of national security, based on interstate threats and military dimensions of statecraft. The concept of national security has been broadened to encompass dimensions such as economic, energy, food, border, health, cyber and environmental security. Intelligence agencies and policymakers have increasingly come to realize the need for a wider perspective because of the requirement of developing a multi-dimensional strategy to combat terrorism effectively. For example, the CIA now collects and analyses information about international terrorism, WMD proliferation, international organized crime, drug trafficking and the shadow economies that fund them. They also gather intelligence on cyber attacks, regional conflicts, counterintelligence threats and the effects of environmental and natural disasters.

   A growing number of scholars have also asserted that the concept of security must be broadened to include additional threats to state and societal security (Buzan 1991; Buzan et al. 1997). The Copenhagen School examines five main dimensions of security: military, political, economic, societal and environmental. *Military security* involves the relative capabilities and perceptions of the intentions of states. *Political security* involves state stability, while *economic security* involves states' ability to acquire resources and opportunities needed to support state power and contribute to general welfare. *Social security* concerns the status of traditional patterns of identity and *environmental security* involves life support systems. They also focus on explaining why and how issues become integrated as part of the national security policy agenda.

As the Obama administration's 2010 National Security Strategy recognizes, American national security is 'inexorably intertwined' with the pursuit of three other national interests, including prosperity in an open global economic system, respect for universal values and an international order strengthened by US leadership and cooperation to promote peace, security and opportunity (Obama NSS 2010).

Moreover, recent advances in our understanding of the causes and consequences of climate change have led to a greater awareness of the concept of environmental and global security. The IPCC climate change research group has documented that carbon dioxide increased 40 per cent since pre-industrial times, the mean sea level has risen more than 7 inches in the last 100 years and is expected to rise another 10 to 30+ inches in the twenty-first century. The shrinking of glaciers and ice sheets are attributed to the rise of global surface temperatures, which are expected to continue to rise, in conservative estimates, between 2 to 3 degrees (Hjelmgaard and Rice 2013). Many of the planet's life support systems are in decline or showing signs of difficulties coping with the changes brought on by industrialization. New security paradigms explore the interconnections between a diverse set of security concerns – environmental, food, water and energy security. While the balance of evidence that environmental insecurity directly impacts a country's likelihood of war is rather mixed, it does contribute the long-term fragility in weaker states. As extreme climate conditions and natural disaster shocks lower socio-economic development, they can contribute to the destabilizing conditions favourable for insurgencies in weak states.

The Deepening of Security: Prioritizing Human Survival and Welfare

The United Nations has been at the forefront of promoting a paradigm shift to **human security**. A human security approach focuses on the interdependent dimensions of protecting individuals and places a premium on prevention efforts (Commission on Human Security 2003). One example of immense suffering and a human rights crisis was the first genocide of the twenty-first century, in Darfur, Sudan. The government of Sudan unleashed Arab militias, or Janjaweed (devil's on horseback), to engage in the mass killing and rape of civilians, burning villages and destroying livelihoods. According to the United Human Rights Council, the genocide in Darfur has cost nearly half a million lives, displaced 2.5 million Sudanese and led nearly 5 million Darfuris to rely on international aid to survive.

> **Human Security** – is narrowly defined by the UN Development Programs as safety from such chronic threats as hunger, disease and repression. It is also more widely defined as a means of protection from hurtful disruptions in the patterns of daily life – whether in homes, in jobs or in communities. Such threats can exist at all levels of national income and development.

The human security perspective has also been appealing to critical theorists because it raises awareness about structural violence and the status of vulnerable populations. For example, neglect in terms of infanticide, disparities in nutrition and health care have led to the deaths of 100 million 'missing' women in China and South Asia, West Asia and North Africa. Women and children also make up more than 60 per cent of the hungry, and are disproportionally at risk of becoming refugees, victims of sexual violence, human trafficking or modern-day slavery. Millions of children have been victims of armed conflict and it is estimated that 300,000 kids have been turned into child soldiers (Kegley and Blanton 2013, 445). A human security perspective highlights the condition of the most vulnerable populations of the world and the threat to human lives and wellbeing stems from sources including structural conditions, government policies and non-state actors.

Threats include 'chronic and persistent poverty, climate related disasters, organized crime, human trafficking, health pandemics, and sudden economic and financial downturns' (UNOCHA 2013).

Indeed,

> the world is interdependent in areas as diverse as financial markets, infectious diseases, climate change, terrorism, nuclear peace and safety, product safety, food supply and water tables, fish stocks and ecosystem resources. In addition to their potential for provoking interstate military conflicts, these are all drivers of human insecurity because of the threat they pose to individual lives and welfare. (Thakur 2011, 3)

From this perspective, the fact that every 3.6 seconds someone dies from starvation, someone dies every 13 seconds from HIV/AIDs and a child dies every 30 seconds from Malaria require additional concerted action. Armed conflicts are also of particular significance to human security, as they aggravate poverty and lower the quality of life, potentially undermining national, regional and global security. Armed conflicts are also primary drivers of food insecurity, human rights violations and human displacement. They also impede investment, harm economic growth and divert resources away from human development (UNODA 2013). Wars are development in reverse and fighting often destroys the educational, health, employment, legal, governmental and critical infrastructure that people depend on. They also provide an attractive location for international terrorists and criminal networks that disproportionately harm civilians.

Around the globe, people are facing food, fuel and financial crises. Environmental degradation and climate change are other important sources of insecurity as humans are affected by extreme weather patterns, the rising of the global surface, atmospheric and ocean temperatures and rising oceans. The loss of snow cover contributes to water and food scarcity and the unprecedented use of finite underground aquifer resources. The potential for future dangers are highlighted by the UN estimates that the global population will to soar to 11 billion by 2100. Already by 2025, the global population will reach to 7.9 billion and 9 out of every 10 people on the planet will live in a developing country. Population growth and climate change are expected to continue to disproportionately affect people living in developing countries, particularly in Africa and Asia. The corresponding dangers of malnutrition and famine are likely to be exacerbated in countries with the weakest capacity to protect vulnerable populations. Thus, the spectrum of threats in this century is far more expansive than in the past. In order to address such trans-sovereign threats, increased cooperation on prevention and mitigation efforts involving both state and non-state actors are required.

CONCLUSION

In this chapter we examined a variety of ways academics and policymakers define security and insecurity. We have also explored how the changing trends in war and the evolution of technology continue to affect threat perceptions. The security agenda has been widened from the narrow focus on interstate wars and conventional munitions to include threats from WMD, asymmetric conflicts, terrorism, cyber attacks and climate change. The security agenda has also been deepened to include non-traditional threats such as disease, environmental degradation and climate change that negatively impact human security and welfare. A human security approach of prioritizing people provides a stark contrast with traditional neorealist structural theories that focus on great power politics. Proponents of a human security approach assert that the path to enduring security is through the building of positive peace. This involves promoting mutually beneficial relationships, human capital and good governance, human rights, battling corruption and ensuring an equitable economy that promotes opportunities for all.

QUESTIONS FOR REFLECTION

1. What are the primary threats to security from the realist, liberal, and human security perspective?
2. How are realist, liberal, and the human security approaches to managing insecurity different?
3. What are the most common forms of war?
4. How do wars happen? What can be done about them?
5. Is a hegemonic war of transition likely? If so, what states are likely to be involved in the balancing coalition?
6. What are the implications of the rise in asymmetric warfare?
7. What is the difference between the non-proliferation regime and counter proliferation efforts such as the Proliferation Security Initiative?
8. Where are terrorist attacks most common and who do they primarily effect?
9. Where are civil wars most common and who do they primarily effect?
10. Who do separatist and civil wars last so much longer than interstate wars?
11. How has the terrorist threat evolved over time? What should be done about the cyber threats?
12. What are the contending explanations of the 'long peace'?
13. Is disarmament possible, likely or necessary?
14. Should we negotiate with rogue regimes?
15. What are the strengths and weaknesses of the realist, liberal and human security paradigms?

REVISION QUIZ

1. A failed state is:

   a. A political unit in which citizens identify with the state and see the state as legitimate, it has a monopoly over the use of force and is able to provide citizens with services
   b. A political unit in which citizens are cosmopolitan and less nationalistic
   c. A state that does not command the loyalty of its citizens because it does not meet basic responsibilities, control its territory or monopolize the use of force
   d. A state that favours multilateral intervention

2. A state that has the political, economic and military resources to shape the world beyond its borders and has the capacity and potentially the will to define the rules of the international system is most likely a:

   a. Small state
   b. Middle power
   c. Great power
   d. Premodern state

3. What type of balance of power did the world system have during the Cold War?

   a. Multilateral
   b. Biploar
   c. Multipolar
   d. Unipolar

4. What type of system have we had since the collapse of the Soviet Union in the early 1990s?

   a. Unilateral
   b. Multilateral
   c. Multipolar
   d. Unipolar

5. Which of the following is not a potential flashpoint in US–Chinese?

   a. Taiwan
   b. Senkaku Islands and Japan
   c. Hawaii
   d. North Korea

6. How many people on the planet are living on less than $1.25 per day (absolute poverty)?

   a. 1.4 billion people
   b. 2.5 billion people
   c. 4 billion people
   d. 80 per cent of humanity

7. Terrorism is:

    a. A tactic of the weak
    b. A strategy of the weak
    c. Any violence used for political change
    d. A guerilla war

8. The concept of human security refers to:

    a. Civil liberties guaranteed in a written document, including inalienable rights such as life, liberty and pursuit of happiness
    b. Maintaining the survival of the state through use of power and tools of statecraft
    c. The measures taken by states and international organizations to ensure their survival and preservation of their societies
    d. The security of individuals, including their physical safety, their economic and social wellbeing, respect for their dignity and the protection of their human rights

9. The concept of national security refers to:

    a. Civil liberties guaranteed in a written document, including inalienable rights such as life, liberty and pursuit of happiness
    b. Maintaining the survival of the state through use of power and tools of statecraft, including military actions, diplomacy, economic resources, international agreements and alliances
    c. The measures taken by states and international organizations to ensure their survival and preservation of their societies
    d. The security of individuals, including their physical safety, their economic and social wellbeing, respect for their dignity and the protection of their human rights

10. The concept of global or international security refers to:

    a. Civil liberties guaranteed in a written document, including inalienable rights such as life, liberty and pursuit of happiness
    b. Maintaining the survival of the state through use of power and tools of statecraft
    c. The measures taken by states and international organizations to ensure their safety, survival and the preservation of their societies
    d. The security of individuals, including their physical safety, their economic and social wellbeing, respect for their dignity and the protection of their human rights

11. The call for a 'widening' of the concept of security means:

    a. Expanding the dimensions of security to include non-military threats to nations and the international system, including economic, political, social and environmental policy areas
    b. Focusing on military threats to the state
    c. Focusing on threats to humanity
    d. Prioritizing threats the threats that individual humans face

12. The call for a 'deepening' of the concept of security means:

    a. Expanding the dimensions of security to include non-military threats to nations and the international system
    b. Focusing on military threats to the state
    c. Focusing on threats to humanity
    d. Prioritizing the threats that individual humans face

13. Child soldiers fight in approximately 75 per cent of all armed conflicts fought today. Approximately how many child soldiers are fighting?

    a. 100,000
    b. 25,000
    c. 40,000
    d. 300,000

14. If effective action is not taken to mitigate the effects of climate change, scientists predict that how much of humanity will be living under severe water stress by 2050?

    a. 10 per cent
    b. 20 per cent
    c. 40 per cent
    d. 60 per cent

15. If nothing is done to curb fossil fuel emissions, which of the following is not a scientific prediction about the effects of climate change on average weather and events by 2100?

    a. Glaciers and ice sheets will contribute to rising seas and coastal flooding
    b. Melting glaciers and ice sheets, and when paired with rising populations will lead to an over 50 per cent increase in the demand for fresh water
    c. The global surface temperature will rise by at least 2 to 3 degrees
    d. The global surface temperature will rise by less than 1 degree

16. The Strategic Defense Initiative:

    a. Is a US Defense Department DARPA-created exo-skeleton military project
    b. Is an unmanned aerial vehicle
    c. Is a controversial defensive missile shield that would destroy offensive missiles in flight
    d. Is a program aimed at increasing counterterrorism cooperation

17. The Security Dilemma refers to:

    a. A period of détente between the East and West in the 1970s
    b. The rise of NATO and the EU
    c. The idea that states have a legal right to enforce international law against aggression
    d. The spiralling effect that can occur when one state arms, and others then react by arming, resulting in declines in national security as their arms increase.

18. Which of the following does the UN not include in its references to weapons of mass destruction?

    a. Chemical weapons
    b. Biological weapons
    c. Nuclear weapons
    d. Small arms

19. Which of the following is *not* referring to characteristics of asymmetric conflicts?

    a. It refers to a conflict between actors who are equal in weapons and technology
    b. It refers to a conflict between actors who are unequal in weapons and technology
    c. Guerrilla warfare
    d. Terrorist attacks

20. Approximately how much did the United States spend on national defense in 2011?

    a. $200 billion
    b. $400 billion
    c. $500 billion
    d. $700 billion

21. Which of these terms best describes the type of global foreign policy strategy asserted by President Barack Obama and the US government?

    a. Internationalist and interventionist
    b. Detachment
    c. Isolationist
    d. Unilateral

22. During President Barack Obama's first two years in office (2009–10), which of the pillars of his foreign policy consumed his efforts?

    a. The global economic crisis
    b. The war on terrorism
    c. Global warming
    d. Universal health care

23. Which of the following refers to dyadic interdependence, which is used to test the validity of commercial liberal theory about the pacific effects of international trade?

    a. International interdependence or trade levels of all countries in the system;
    h International interdependence or trade levels of all sub-groups in the system;
    c. International interdependence or trade levels between all possible trading pairs in the system;
    d. The number of states who engage in international trade in the system.

24. Which of the following does not refer to the Bush Doctrine?

    a. It aimed to counter the threat stemming from rogue regimes, armed with WMD, and
       their potential use by terrorist organizations
    b. It included launching preventative wars and promoting democratic principles to topple
       threatening regimes
    c. It relied primarily on containment and nuclear deterrence strategies
    d. It included targeting states that provide safe havens to terrorism, and pursuing other
       military interests unilaterally if necessary

25. How many nuclear weapons do Russia and the US possess?

    a. 1,000 (Russia) and 5,000 (US)
    b. 8,500 (Russia) and 7,700 (US)
    c. 10,000 (Russia) and 50,000 (US)
    d. 700 (Russia) and 700 (US)

Answers: 1: c; 2: c; 3: b; 4: d; 5: c; 6: a; 7: a; 8: d; 9: b; 10: c; 11: a; 12: d; 13: d; 14: c;
15: d; 16: c; 17: d; 18: d; 19: a; 20: d; 21: a; 22: a; 23: c; 24: c; 25: c.

BIBLIOGRAPHY

Allison, G. and Zelikow, P. (1999) *Essence of Decision: Explaining the Cuban Missile Crisis* (New York: Pearson Press).

Allison, G. (2004) 'Nuclear Terrorism: How Serious a Threat to Russia? Russia in Global Affairs', September/October 2004. Available at: <http://belfercenter.hks.harvard.edu/publication/660/nuclear_terrorism.html> [Accessed 7 December 2012].

Autesserre, S. (2010) *The Trouble with the Congo: Local Violence and the Failure of International Peacebuilding* (Cambridge: Cambridge University Press).

Bednarz et al. (2009) 'Peace Without Syria Is Unthinkable. SPIEGEL Interview with Syrian President Bashar Assad', 19 January 2009. Available at: <http://www.spiegel.de/international/world/spiegel-interview-with-syrian-president-bashar-assad-peace-without-syria-is-unthinkable-a-602110–2.html>.

Bennett, B. (2013) 'Preparing for the Possibility of a North Korean Collapse. The RAND Corporation. National Security Research Division'. Available at: <http://www.rand.org/content/dam/rand/pubs/research_reports/RR300/RR331/RAND_RR331.pdf>.

Bennett, B. and Lind, J. (Fall 2011) 'The Collapse of North Korea: Military Missions and Requirements', *International Security* 2(36), 84–119. Available at: <http://belfercenter.ksg.harvard.edu/publication/21393/collapse_of_north_korea.html>.

Bennett, A. and Shambaugh, G. (2009) *Taking Sides: Clashing Views in America's Foreign Policy* (Columbus, OH: McGraw-Hill/Dushkin).

Bergen, P. and Sterman, D. (2013) 'Al-Shabaab's American Allies', CNN, 23 November 2013. Available at: <http://www.cnn.com/2013/09/23/opinion/bergen-al-shabaab-american-ties/index.html>.

Blair, B. (2013) 'Russian Roulette', Frontline Interview of Senior Fellow at the Brookings Institute. Available at: <http://www.pbs.org/wgbh/pages/frontline/shows/russia/interviews/blair.html>.

Blair, B. (September 1977) 'The Terrorist Threat to World Nuclear Programs', *The Journal of Conflict Resolution* 31(3), 379–403. Available at: <http://web.archive.org/web/20120419032140/http://www.cdi.org/blair/terrorist-threat.cfm>.

Burr, W. (ed.) (2001) 'Launch on Warning: The Development of U.S. Capabilities, 1959–1979', National Security Archive Electronic Briefing Book No. 43. Published – April 2001. Available at: <http://www2.gwu.edu/~nsarchiv/NSAEBB/NSAEBB43/>.

Burr, W. (ed.) (2001) 'The 3 A.M. Phone Call', The National Security Archive Briefing 371, George Washington University. Available at: <http://www2.gwu.edu/~nsarchiv/nukevault/ebb371/>.

Buzan, B. (1991) *People, States & Fear: The National Security Problem in International Relations* (North Carolina, NC: University of North Carolina Press).

Buzan, B. et al. (1997) *Security: A New Framework for Analysis* (Colorado, CO: Lynne Rienner Publishing).

Center for U.S.-Korea Policy (2009) 'North Korea Contingency Planning and U.S.-ROK Cooperation', The Asia Foundation. Available at: <http://asiafoundation.org/resources/pdfs/DPRKContingencyCUSKP0908.pdf>

Cha, V. and Kang, D. (2003) *Nuclear North Korea: A Debate on Engagement Strategies* (New York: Columbia University Press).

Clapper, J. (2013) Director of National Intelligence. United Press International. 'Official: US Faces Diverse Threats', 13 March 2013. Available at: <http://www.upi.com/Top_News/US/2013/03/13/Official-US-faces-diverse-threats/UPI-15151363156505/#ixzz2etu394BS>.

Clausewitz, C. (1989) *On War* (Princeton, NJ: Princeton University Press).

Collier, P. and Hoeffler, A. (2004) 'Greed and Grievance in Civil War', *Oxford Economic Papers* 56(4),563–96.

Collina, T. (2013) Research Director, Arms Control Association. Available at: <http://www.armscontrol.org/factsheets/cbwprolif>.

Conteh-Morgan, E. (2004) *Collective Political Violence: An Introduction to the Theories and Cases of Violent Conflicts* (New York: Routledge Press).

Corso, M. (2010) 'Tbilisi Grants Early Release to Weapons-Grade Uranium Smuggler', 22 June 2010, *Eurasianet*. Available at: <http://www.eurasianet.org/node/61374>.

COT Institute for Safety, Security and Crisis Management (2007) 'Notions of Security: Shifting Concepts and Perspectives', *Policy Paper*, 15 February 2007.

Council on Foreign Relations (2006) 'Loose Nukes', *Backgrounder*, January 2006. Available at: <http://www.cfr.org/weapons-of-mass-destruction/loose-nukes/p9549>.

Defense Casualty Analysis System (DCAS) (2008) 'Vietnam Conflict Extract Data Files', Electronic Records Reference Report, 29 April 2008. Available at: <http://www.archives.gov/research/military/vietnam-war/casualty-statistics.html#category>.

Doyle, M. (2005) 'Three Pillars of the Liberal Peace', *American Political Science Review* 99(3), 463–6.

Failed State Index (2012) 'The Fund for Peace'. Available at: <http://ffp.statesindex.org/>.

Farah, D. and Braun, S. (2007) *Merchant of Death: Money, Guns, Planes, and the Man Who Makes War Possible* (New Jersey: John Wiley & Sons).

Fearon, J. and Laitin, D. (2003) 'Ethnicity, Insurgency, and Civil War', *American Political Science Review* 97(1), 75–90.

Fearon, J. (Summer 2004) 'Separatist Wars, Partition, and World Order', *Security Studies* 13(4), 394–415.

Fearon, J. (1995) 'Rationalist Explanations for War', *International Organization* 49(3), 379–414.

Flynn, S. (2006) 'Targets for Terrorism: Ports', Council on Foreign Relations, January 2006. Available at: <http://www.cfr.org/border-and-port-security/targets-terrorism-ports/p10215>.

Gates, R. (1996) *From the Shadows: The Ultimate Insider's Story of Five Presidents and How they Won the Cold War* (New York: Simon & Schuster), 114.

George Washington University (2012) 'Face the Facts, A Project by the George Washington University', 6 August 2012. Available at: <http://www.facethefactsusa.org/facts/in-dollars-for-defense-were-still-1-with-a-bullet-infographic/>.

Georgy, M. (2012) 'Pakistan and U.S.: Allies Without Trust', Reuters, 4 June 2012. Available at: <http://www.reuters.com/article/2012/06/04/us-pakistan-usa-idUSBRE85303J20120604>.

Globalsecurity.org (2013) 'Ukraine Special Weapons'. Available at: <http://www.globalsecurity.org/wmd/world/ukraine/index.html>.

Goldberg, J. and Ambinder, M. (2011) 'The Pentagon's Secret Plans to Secure Pakistan's Nuclear Arsenal', National Journal, *Nuclear Threat Initiative*, 9 November 2011. Available at: <http://www.nti.org/gsn/article/the-pentagons-secret-plans-to-secure-pakistans-nuclear-arsenal/>.

Gordon, M. (2002) 'U.S. Says It Found Qaeda Lab Being Built to Produce Anthrax', *The New York Times*, 23 March 2002, A1.

Gregory, S. (2009) 'The Terrorist Threat to Pakistan's Nuclear Weapons', Combating Terrorism Center Sentinel, West Point. 2:7. Available at: <http://www.ctc.usma.edu/posts/the-terrorist-threat-to-pakistan%E2%80%99s-nuclear-weapons>.

Grumberger, J. (2013) 'Briefing: Chemical Weapons. Fund for Peace', 19 September 2013. Available at: <http://library.fundforpeace.org/ttcvr1313>.

Handler, J. (1996) 'Nuclear Accidents. Greenpeace International'. Available at: <http://www.greenpeace.org/international/Global/international/planet-2/report/2006/2/handler-nuclear-accidents.pdf>.

Hjelmgaard, K. and Rice, D. (2013) 'U.N. Global Warming Report Puts Humans on the Hot Seat', *USA TODAY*, 27 September 2013. Available at: <http://www.usatoday.com/story/weather/2013/09/27/global-warming-report-intergovernmental-panel-on-climate-change/2878853/>.

Hersh, S. (1992) 'U.S. Secretly Gave Aid to Iraq Early in Its War Against Iran', New York Times. Published: 26 January 1992. Available at: <http://www.nytimes.com/1992/01/26/world/us-secretly-gave-aid-to-iraq-early-in-its-war-against-iran.html?pagewanted=all&src=pm>.

Ikenberry, J. (2011) 'Review of: Dangerous Times? The International Politics of Great Power Peace', Fettweis, C. *Foreign Affairs*. May–June 2011. Available at: <http://www.foreignaffairs.com/articles/67755/christopher-j-fettweis/dangerous-times-the-international-politics-of-great-power-peace>.

Jervis, R. (1978) 'Cooperation under the security dilemma', *World Politics* 30(2), 167–214.

Jones, S. (2011) 'Why the Haqqani Network is The Wrong Target To Save Afghanistan, Deal With the Taliban', *Foreign Affairs*, 6 November 2011. Available at: <http://www.foreignaffairs.com/articles/136646/seth-g-jones/why-the-haqqani-network-is-the-wrong-target>.

Kaldor, M. (1999) *New and Old Wars: Organized Violence in a Global Era* (Stanford CA, Stanford University Press).

Kaplan, R. (2006) 'When North Korea Falls', *Atlantic Monthly*, 1 October 2006. Available at: <http://www.theatlantic.com/magazine/archive/2006/10/when-north-korea-falls/305228/> [Accessed 1 September 2013].

Kegley, C. and Blanton, S. (2013) *World Politics: Trend and Transformation* (Boston, MA: Cenage Learning).

Kaszynski, M. (2013) 'Nunn-Lugar Cooperative Threat Reduction Program', *American Security Project*. Available at: <http://americansecurityproject.org/ASP%20Reports/Ref%200068%20-%20The%20Nunn-Lugar%20Cooperative%20Threat%20Reduction%20Program.pdf>.

Kimball, D. et al. (2012) 'Media Backgrounder: Nuclear Weapons and the Foreign Policy Debate', Arms Control Association, 22 October 2012. Available at: <http://www.armscontrol.org/pressroom/Media-Backgrounder-Nuclear-Weapons-and-the-Foreign-Policy-Debate>.

Ki-Moon, B. (2011) UN Secretary-General Ban Ki-Moon's Press Conference, UN Department of Public Information, New York, 15 September 2011. Available at: <http://www.un.org/News/Press/docs//2011/sgsm13803.doc.htm>.

Ki-Moon, B. (2013) 'Humanitarian Situation in Syria Outpacing Aid Efforts, Secretary General Warns at G-20 Summit, Citing "Terrible and Tragic" Statistics', 5 September 2013. Available at: <http://www.un.org/News/Press/docs/2013/sgsm15257.doc.htm>.

Khan, K. and Moore, M. (2001) '2 Nuclear Experts Briefed Bin Laden', *Washington Post*, 12 December 2001, A1, A23.

Koren, M. (2013) 'Top Ten Cases of Nuclear Thefts Gone Wrong', *Smithsonian Magazine*, 4 February 2013. Available at: <http://www.smithsonianmag.com/science-nature/Top-Ten-Cases-of-Nuclear-Thefts-Gone-Wrong-189690171.html>.

Lacina, B. and Gleditsch, N.P. (2005) 'Monitoring Trends in Global Combat: A New Dataset of Battle Deaths', *European Journal of Population* 2(3), 145–66. Available at: <http://www.prio.no/CSCW/Datasets/Armed-Conflict/Battle-Deaths/The-Battle-Deaths-Dataset-version-20/>.

Lacina, B. (2006) 'Explaining the Severity of Civil Wars', *Journal of Conflict Resolution* 50(2),276–89.

Lake, D. and Rothchild, D. (2001) 'Containing Fear: The Origins and Management of Ethnic Conflict'. In: M.E. Brown (ed.), *Nationalism and Ethnic Conflict* (Cambridge, MA, and London: MIT Press), 126–60.

Lee, R. (2003) 'Nuclear Smuggling: Patterns and Responses'. Available at: <http://strategicstudiesinstitute.army.mil/pubs/parameters/articles/03spring/lee.pdf>.

Leitenberg, M. and Zilinskas, R. (2012) *The Soviet Biological Weapons Program. A History* (Cambridge, MA: Harvard University Press).

Love, M. (2007) *Beyond Sovereignty: Issues for a Global Agenda* (Belmont, CA: Thomson Wadsworth).

Maoz, Z. (2009) 'The effects of strategic and economic interdependence on international conflict across levels of analysis', *American Journal of Political Science* 53(1), 223–40.

Mazari, S. (2009) 'The Threat of Nuclear Proliferation amongst Non-State Actors in South Asia'. In: Sisodia, N. et al. (eds), *Proliferation and Emerging Nuclear Order* (New Delhi, India: Academic Foundation).

Mowatt-Larssen, R. (2010) 'Al Qaeda Weapons of Mass Destruction Threat: Hype or Reality?' Paper, Belfer Center for Science and International Affairs, January 2010. Available at: <http://belfercenter.ksg.harvard.edu/files/al-qaeda-wmd-threat.pdf>.

Nathan, A. and Leppard, D. (2001) 'Al-Qaeda's Men Held Secret Meetings to Build Dirty Bomb – Bin Laden's Nuclear Plot – War on Terrorism', *The Sunday Times* (London), 14 October 2001. Available at: <http://global.factiva.com/en/arch/display.asp>.

Nuclear Threat Initiative (2013a) 'Libya: Country Profile'. Available at: <http://www.nti.org/country-profiles/libya/>.

Nuclear Threat Initiative (2013b) 'Fate of Libya's "Yellowcake" Uranium Still in the Air', 23 September 2013. Available at: <http://www.nti.org/gsn/article/fate-libyas-uranium-still-air/>.

Nunn, S. (1996) 'Cooperative Threat Reduction', Statement before the Senate Permanent Subcommittee on Investigations, 13 March 1996. Available at: <http://www.fas.org/spp/starwars/congress/1996_h/s960313a.htm>.

Nunn-Lugar Scorecard (2012) Senator Richard Lugar's webpage, May 2012. Available at: <http://lugar.senate.gov/nunnlugar/scorecard.htm>.

Obama, B. (2010) US National Security Strategy, Office of the President of the United States, White House, p. 17. Available at: <http://www.whitehouse.gov/sites/default/files/rss_viewer/national_security_strategy.pdf>.

Obama, B. (2013) 'All Options Are On The Table With Iran', CBSDC/AP, 20 March 2013. Available at: <http://washington.cbslocal.com/2013/03/20/obama-all-options-are-on-the-table-with-iran/>.

Ogata, S. et al. (2003) United Nations Commission on Human Security Report Outline, 'Human Security Now', New York. Available at: <http://www.unocha.org/humansecurity/chs/finalreport/index.html>.

Paine, C., Cochran, T. and Norris, R. (1996) 'The Arsenal of the Nuclear Weapons Powers: An Overview', Canberra Commission Issue Paper, National Resource Defense Council, Inc. Washington DC. Available at: <http://docs.nrdc.org/nuclear/files/nuc_01049601a_160.pdf>.

Patterson, R. (2004) *Dereliction of Duty: Eyewitness Account of How Bill Clinton Compromised American National Security* (Washington, DC: Regnery Publishing).

Pevehouse, J. and Russett, B. (Autumn 2006) *International Organization*, 60(4), 969–1000.

Rhem, K. (2000). 'Korean War Death Stats Highlight Modern DoD Safety Record', American Forces Press Service, US Department of Defense, Washington, DC, June 8, 2000. Available at: <http://www.defense.gov/News/NewsArticle.aspx?ID=45275>.

Rice, C. (2003) Transcript of Interview of the US National Security Advisor, Condoleezza Rice by Wolf Blitzer. *CNN*, 7 September 2003. Available at: <http://transcripts.cnn.com/TRANSCRIPTS/0309/07/le.00.html>.

Riedel, B. (2012) 'Double Game Deepens', The Brookings Institute, 6 April 2012. Available at: <http://www.brookings.edu/research/opinions/2012/04/06-double-game-pakistan-riedel>.

Reuters (2011) 'Up to 15,000 Killed in Libya War: U.N. Rights Expert', Reuters, 9 June 2011. Available at: <http://www.reuters.com/article/2011/06/09/us-libya-un-deaths-idUSTRE7584UY20110609>

Richelson, J. (2009) *Defusing Nuclear Armageddon: Inside NEST, America's Secret Nuclear Bomb Squad* (New York: W.W. Norton and Company).

Risen, J. and Shenon, P. (2002) 'Traces of Terror: The Investigation. U.S. Says It Halted Qaeda Plot to Use Radioactive Bomb', *The New York Times*, 10 June 2002, A1.

Rohde, D. (March/April 2012) 'The Obama Doctrine: How the President's Drone War is Backfiring', *Foreign Affairs*. Available at: <http://www.foreignpolicy.com/articles/2012/02/27/the_obama_doctrine?page=0,4&wpisrc=obinsite>.

Rummel, R.J. (1994) 'Power, Genocide, and Mass Murder', *Journal of Peace Research* 31(1), 1–10.

Russett, B. (2005) 'Bushwhacking the democratic peace', *International Studies Perspectives* 6(4), 395–408.

Sagan, S. (September/October 1996) 'How to Keep the Bomb From Iran', *Foreign Affairs* 85(5), 45–59.

Saito, M. (2013) 'Tritium Levels Reach New High at Wrecked Fukushima Nuclear Plant', Reuters, 12 September 2010. Available at: <http://www.reuters.com/article/2013/09/12/us-japan-fukushima-radiation-idUSBRE98B0SH20130912>.

Sanger, D. and Schmitt, E. (2012) 'Pentagon Says 75,000 Troops Might Be Needed to Seize Syria Chemical Arms', *New York Times*, 15 November 2012. Available at: <http://www.nytimes.com/2012/11/16/world/middleeast/pentagon-sees-seizing-syria-chemical-arms-as-vast-task.html?pagewanted=all&_r=0>.

Savranskaya, S. (2005) 'New Sources on the Role of Soviet Submarines in the Cuban Missile Crisis', *Journal of Strategic Studies*, 28(2), 233–59. Available at: <http://belfercenter.ksg.harvard.edu/files/CMC50/SavranskayaJSSNewsourcesonroleofSovietsubmarinesinCMC.pdf>.

Sastri, M. (2004) *Weapons of Mass Destruction* (New Delhi: S.B. Nangia, A.P.H Publishing Corporation), 74.

Schmidt, S. and Gorman, S. (2008) 'Lashkar-e-Taiba Served as Gateway for Western Converts Turning to Jihad', *Wall Street Journal*, 4 December 2008. Available at: <http://online.wsj.com/article/SB122834970727777709.html?mod=googlenews_wsj>.

Schultz, G., Perry, W., Kissinger, H. and Nunn, S. (2013) 'Next Steps in Reducing Nuclear Risks', *Wall Street Journal*, 5 March 2013. Available at: <http://online.wsj.com/news/articles/SB10001424127887324338604578325912939001772>.

Sen, A. (2009) 'More Than 100 Million Women Are Missing', *The New York Review of Books*, 20 December 1990 Issue. Available at: <http://www.nybooks.com/articles/archives/1990/dec/20/more-than-100-million-women-are-missing/?pagination=false>.

Seward, A. (2005) 'Combating Proliferation: Assessing the Russian Nuclear Threat', *Journal of Public and International Affairs*, Princeton University. Available at: <ttp://www.princeton.edu/jpia/past-issues-1/2005/9.pdf>.

Shah, T and Toft M. (July/August 2006) 'Why God is Winning', *Foreign Policy*, 42–3.

Shelton, H. (2010) *Without Hesitation: The Odyssey of an American Warrior* (New York: St Martin's Press).

SIPRI Yearbook (2012) *Armaments, Disarmament and International Security* (Solna, Sweden: Stockholm International Peace Research Institute).

Spanier, J. and Wendzel, R. (1996) *Games Nations Play* (Washington, DC: CQ Press).

Stanford University (2013) Lashkar-e-Taiba. Mapping Militant Organizations Project. Project Director, Martha Crenshaw. Available at: <http://www.stanford.edu/group/mappingmilitants/cgi-bin/groups/view/79>.

Tankel, S. (2011) 'Lashkar-eTaiba: Past Operations and Future Prospects', New America Foundation, 27 April 2011. Available at: <http://newamerica.net/publications/policy/lashkar_e_taiba>.

Tankel, S. (2013) 'Lashkar-e-Taiba Capable of Threatening U.S. Homeland', Testimony 12 June 2013, House Homeland Security Committee. Available at: <http://carnegieendowment.org/2013/06/12/lashkar-e-taiba-capable-of-threatening-u.s.-homeland/g9z7#>.

Tap, C. et al. (2008) 'Iraq War mortality estimates: A systematic review', *Conflict and Health* 2(1). Available at: <http://www.conflictandhealth.com/content/2/1/1>.

Times of India (2011) 'US has "Snatch-and-Grab" Plan for Pak's Nuclear Weapons', 6 August 2011. Available at: <http://articles.timesofindia.indiatimes.com/2011-08-06/pakistan/29858131_1_nuclear-arsenal-pakistan-army-abbottabad>.

Thakur, R. (June 2011)The United Nations in Global Governance: Rebalancing Organized Multilateralism for Current and Future Challenges, United Nations General Assembly 65th Session Thematic Debate on the United Nations in Global Governance. UN Headquarters. Available at: <http://www.un.org/en/ga/president/65/initiatives/GGStatements.html>.

Themnér, L. and Wallensteen, P. (2013) 'Armed Conflict, 1946–2012', *Journal of Peace Research* 50(4).

United Nations Office for Disarmament Affairs (2013) 'Small Arms'. Available at: <http://www.un.org/disarmament/convarms/SALW/>.

United Nations News Centre (2007) 'Illicit Trafficking, Theft of Nuclear Materials "A Persistent Problem" UN Agency Reports', 12 September 2007. Available at: <http://www.un.org/apps/news/story.asp?NewsID=23774#.UkMVNX-DnDB>.

United Nations Report (2012) Thematic Debate of the 66th session of the United Nations General Assembly on Drugs and Crime as a Threat to Development, On the occasion of the UN International Day against Drug Abuse and Illicit Trafficking, 26 June 2012 – New York Available at: <http://www.un.org/en/ga/president/66/Issues/drugs/drugs-crime.shtml>.

United Nations Office on Drugs and Crime (UNODC) (2012) 'World Drug Report'. Available at: <http://www.unodc.org/unodc/en/data-and-analysis/WDR-2012.html>.

US National Counter Terrorism Center (NCTC) (2011) 'Report on Terrorism'. Available at: <http://www.nctc.gov/docs/2011_NCTC_Annual_Report_Final.pdf>.

US Department of State (2013) 'Adherence to and Compliance with Arms Control, Nonproliferation and Disarmament Agreements and Commitments', July 2013. Available at: <http://www.state.gov/t/avc/rls/rpt/2013/>.

Van Evera, S. (1998) 'Offense, Defense, and the Causes of War'. In M.E. Brown, O.R. Coté, S.M. Lynn-Jones and S.E. Miller (eds), *Theories of War and Peace* (Cambridge, MA: MIT Press), 92–135.

Walt, S.M. (1991) 'The renaissance of security studies', *International Studies Quarterly* 35(2), 211–39.

Walter, B. (2003) 'Explaining the Intractability of Territorial Conflict', *International Studies Review* 5(4), 137–53.

Walter, B. (2006) 'Information, Uncertainty and the Decision to Secede', *International Organization* 60(1), 105–35.

Walter, B.F. and Snyder, J.L. (eds) (1999) *Civil Wars, Insecurity, and Intervention* (New York: Columbia University Press).

Warrick, J. (2013) 'Lessons from Iraq, Libya Loom Large as Diplomats Ponder Syrian Weapons Probe', *Washington Post*, 4 September 2013. Available at: <http://www.washingtonpost.com/world/national-security/lessons-from-iraq-libya-loom-large-as-diplomats-ponder-syrian-weapons-probe/2013/09/14/5440f544-1d70-11e3-a628-7e6dde8f889d_print.html>.

Whitlock, C. and Morello, C. (2012) 'U.S. Plans for Possibility that Assad Could Lose Control of Chemical Arms Cache', *Washington Post*, 16 December 2012. Available at: <http://articles.washingtonpost.com/2012-12-16/world/35864232_1_chemical-weapons-chemical-arms-free-syrian-army>.

World Bank (1999) *World Development Indicators* Washington, DC: World Economic Forum. 2013. Global Agenda Council on Pakistan 2013. Available at: <http://www.weforum.org/content/global-agenda-council-pakistan-2013>.

Zenko, M. (November 2010) 'Toward Deeper Reductions in US and Russian Nuclear Weapons, Council on Foreign Relations Special Report'. Available at: <http://www.cfr.org/united-states/toward-deeper-reductions-us-russian-nuclear-weapons/p23212>

Chapter 11
Global Inequality

EUNYOUNG HA AND JULIA HYEYONG KIM

Global inequality – that is, income gap between the high-income and the low-income countries – has generally increased at the same time as globalization has enlarged in recent decades. Proponents of globalization argue that globalization, such as freer trade and more mobile capital flows, helps both advanced economies and developing economies grow faster by providing low-cost goods at home and access to new markets abroad. On the other hand, opponents of globalization insist that globalization exacerbates the existing bias against developing countries in the global economic system, which is inherently structured to favour the advanced economies. Has globalization caused the global inequality? Is the market integration unfair to less developed countries, as anti-globalization protesters insist? Or, has globalization helped developing countries to achieve higher economic growth and reduce poverty as globalization proponents argue?

   To answer these questions, this chapter reviews key theories on globalization and economic growth: liberalism, neoliberalism, Marxism, structuralism and dependency theory. This chapter also examines two development strategies adopted by developing countries: Import Substitution Industrialization (ISI) strategy and Export-Oriented Industrialization (EOI) strategy. Based on structuralism and dependency theory, Latin American countries adopted Import Substitution Industrialization (ISI) strategy, while East Asian countries chose Export-Oriented Industrialization (EOI) strategy. This chapter reviews how these two strategies led the two regions to different economic development. Finally, this chapter will discuss international and domestic efforts to alleviate global inequality.

Key Words: Global Inequality, North-South System, Liberalism, Comparative Advantage, Absolute Advantage, Opportunity Cost, Modernization Theory, Neoliberalism, Marxism, Structuralism, Dependency Theory, Falling Terms of Trade, Low Price Elasticity of Demand, Modern World System, Import Substitution Industrialization (ISI) Development, Export-Oriented Industrialization (EOI), Community Economy, Race to the Bottom.

Chapter 11

Global Inequality

EUNYOUNG HA AND JULIA HYEYONG KIM

INTRODUCTION

Over the last few decades, the impacts of globalization have become a major source of concern among researchers, policymakers, activists and politicians. Has the integration of nations into a global system of trade and investment helped developing countries grow their economies? Or has it led to outsized gains by richer nations and increasing inequality? The proponents of globalization argue that globalization helps advanced economies by providing low-cost goods at home and access to new markets abroad. Proponents also argue that globalization benefits developing countries by creating opportunities for export-based growth and opening the way for foreign investments, which modernize the economies of low-income nations. Research shows that the poverty level in low-income countries has declined with their integration into the world market. In 1980, over 83 per cent of people living in low-income nations lived on under $2 per day. In 2010, after successive waves of globalization, that had fallen to just over 74 per cent (World Bank 2013).

On the other hand, those opposed to globalization argue that the increasing trade and investment of the past decades has exacerbated the existing economic inequality between advanced economies and less developed countries. According to them, free trade and capital mobility perpetuates an unfair world economic system where highly industrialized nations exploit those who are less developed. In their view, because international trade takes place within a world system that is structurally biased, globalization favours the already advanced economies and deepens the economic gap between the advanced economies (clustered in the Northern hemisphere) and developing nations (who are more commonly found in the Global South).

Opponents of globalization point to **global inequality**, the growing gap between high- and low-income nations, which has increased as globalization has grown. Figure 11.1 shows per capita gross domestic product (GDP) in constant US dollars (2005) from 1960 to 2010 for

Global Inequality – income gap between developed and developing countries.

Liberalism –the classical economists such as Adam Smith argue that the market should be left alone (free market) and wealth should be created through the division of labour.

Neoliberalism – Neoliberal economists argue that state intervention should be minimal and a country can grow best through free trade and capital markets. According to them, state intervention in developing countries distorts the market and prevents economic growth. After the 1980s, liberalism once again became the main school of economics.

Marxism – Karl Marx argued that capitalism creates an unfair system where capital owners exploit the labour. Neo-Marxism argues that developed countries in the capitalist global economy exploit developing countries.

Structuralism – Structuralists emphasize the unfairness inherent in the structure of the international economic system. They argue that the existing structure of the economic system allows developed countries to extract wealth from developing countries and maintain their dominance in the international market.

four different income groups: high-income countries, upper-income countries, lower-middle-income countries and low-income countries. Because GDP growth in developing countries is often offset by higher population growth, GDP per capita (GDP divided by population) allows the comparison of economies across different kinds of nations. Looking at Figure 11.1, we can see that GDP per capita for high-income countries has increased at a much faster rate than GDP per capita for other nations in recent decades. In other words, while wealthy nations have benefited greatly, middle- and lower-income countries have only seen modest growth.

Has globalization caused this global inequality? Is the market integration unfair to less developed countries, as anti-globalization protesters insist? Or, has globalization helped developing countries to achieve higher economic growth and reduce poverty despite growing populations, as globalization proponents argue? To answer these questions, this chapter reviews key theory on globalization and economic growth, examines the development strategies adopted by developing countries and discusses possible solutions to rising global inequality. This chapter is organized as follows. First, we will review **Liberalism** and **Neoliberalism**, which are often cited by globalization proponents. Second, we will review **Marxism**, **Structuralism** and **dependency theory**, which are often highlighted by anti-globalization commentators. Third, we will examine two development strategies adopted by developing countries: **import substitution industrialization (ISI)**, which has been adopted by many Latin American countries and **export-oriented industrialization (EOI)**, which has been frequently used by East Asian countries. Finally, we will discuss several international and domestic efforts to alleviate global inequality.

The Dependency Theory – the dependency theorists argue that countries in the Global North (developed countries) make the South (developing countries) dependent on them. According to them, because the North does not help the South industrialize but extracts raw materials, the South can never catch up with the North in the existing world economic system.

Import Substitution Industrialization (ISI) Development – Import Substitution Industrialization (ISI) Development strategy is a development strategy adopted by Latin American countries in the 1960s and the 1970s. Based on the dependency theory and structuralism, ISI strategy stressed national economic independence and promoted inward-oriented economic policies. Based on this strategy, Latin American countries limited the imports of consumer goods and subsidized infant industries to produce them domestically.

Export-Oriented Industrialization (EOI) Development Strategy – Export-Oriented Industrialization (EOI) Development strategy is a development strategy adopted by East Asian countries throughout the 1960s, the 1970s and the 1980s. EOI strategy promoted outward-oriented economic policies. Based on this strategy, East Asian Tigers such as South Korea, Taiwan, Hong Kong and Singapore promoted free trade and subsidized manufacturing industries that produced export goods.

GLOBALIZATION AND ECONOMIC DEVELOPMENT I: CLASSICAL ECONOMICS AND NEOLIBERAL ECONOMICS

The classical liberal economists of the eighteenth and nineteenth centuries argued that nations would grow through free trade and a reduction in government control of prices. According to Adam Smith (1723–90), the market is best operating with its 'invisible hand', and more wealth is created through the division of labour in the market. Therefore, market provides the best regulatory institution when domestic government does not interfere with it. In a capitalist

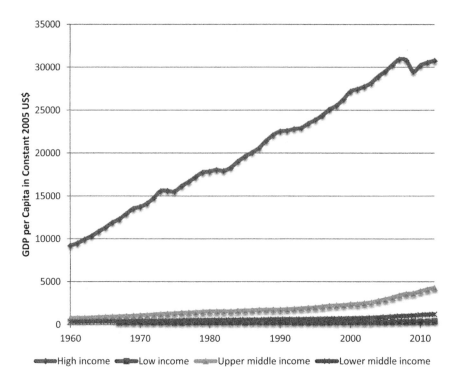

Figure 11.1   GDP per capita in constant 2005 US Dollars (1960–2012)
Data source: World Development Indicators 2013.

economy, individuals' self-interests guide them to make rational choices in the market. The self-interested people are yet regulated by competition under free market. For instance, producers cannot set high prices on goods because they have to compete with each other under a free market. The producers can win the competition when they provide better quality at a cheaper price. Consumers are also constrained by the market competition because they also compete with each other. Consumers can win the competition and buy the goods when they are willing to pay more for the goods. Under the perfect market competition, government intervention only distorts allocation of resources because it fixes the market price at an inefficient level.

David Ricardo (1772–1823) developed the theory of free trade and economic growth based on **comparative advantage** (see textbox below for further explanation). When a country can produce a good at lower cost than any other countries, the country has an **absolute advantage**. When the country specializes in the product with an absolute advantage it can gain benefits out of trade. However, according to Ricardo, countries do not need to have this absolute advantage to gain benefits from trade. If a country specializes in a product with comparative advantage it still benefits from international trade. After all, if all of the countries in the world specialize in goods and services with a comparative advantage and trade them with each other, all of them should get benefits out of the free trade and total welfare in the world increases (Balaam and Dillman 2011).

David Ricardo and Comparative Advantage:

Ricardo was a successful businessman, politician and economist, who ardently supported abolition of the British Corn Laws of the early 1800s. The Corn Laws, which limited international trade in grains, imposed heavy costs on the emerging industrialists of the era by driving up food prices. When the Corn Laws were finally abolished in 1846, the British economy grew rapidly because cheaper foods allowed industrialists to pay lower wages and devote capital to expand industrialization. Free trade also allowed access to overseas export markets. As the United Kingdom grew into the 'workshop of the world', the 'liberal' theories of classical economists — that free trade was the most effective way to promote economic growth — were vindicated.

Ricardo argues that even if a country does not have an **absolute advantage** in producing commodities, it can still benefit from trade because of **comparative advantage**. This is due to the **opportunity costs** of producing different commodities. Consider a hypothetical economy where two nations, A and B, produce two goods, shirts and radio as shown in Table A below. Country A can produce 1 unit of shirts with 4 hours of labour while B produces 1 unit of shirts with 6 hours of labour. Likewise, A produces 1 unit of radio with 6 hours of labour while Country B produces 1 unit of radio with 12 hours of labour. In other words, A can produce both shirts and radio more efficiently; thus, A has an absolute advantage in producing both products.

Opportunity Cost – the amount of good that has been surrendered to produce another good.

Absolute Advantage – when a country can produce a unit of a good with less cost (for example, labour) than another country, this country has an absolute advantage over the other country in producing that good.

Table A. Comparative costs of production (cost per unit in hours of labour)

	Shirts	**Radio**
Country A	3 hours	6 hours
Country B	4 hours	10 hours

Despite this, there is a comparative advantage that trade can unlock. For Country A, the hours of labour required to produce 1 unit of radio (6 hours per radio) would produce 2 units of shirts (because 1 unit of shirts requires only 3 hours). For A, the opportunity cost of producing radio is 2 units of shirts. That is, in order to produce 1 unit of radio, 2 units of shirts were given up.

For Country B, the hours of labour required to produce 1 unit of radio (10 hours per unit) will produce 2.5 units of shirts. For B, the opportunity cost of producing radio is 2.5 units of shirts. Comparing Country A and Country B, the opportunity cost of producing radio is cheaper in Country A (1 unit of radio = 2 units of shirts) than in Country B (1 unit of radio = 2.5 units of shirts). Country A has a comparative advantage in producing radio.

Comparative Advantage – when a country is relatively more efficient at producing a good or service (producing at a cheaper opportunity cost over another good or service), the country can specialize in that production, even if it does not have an absolute advantage in production of that good or service, and trade for other goods. Both trading countries will benefit as long as they have relatively different production efficiencies. For Country B, the hours of labour required to produce 1 unit of shirts (4 hours per unit) will produce 0.4 unit of radio (4 hours of labour to make a unit of shirt can produced 0.4 unit of radio). For Country B, the opportunity cost of producing shirts is 0.4 unit of radio given up. For Country A, the opportunity cost of producing shirts is 0.5 unit of radio given up (3 hours of labour to make a unit of shirt can produce 0.5 unit of radio). Therefore, Country A's opportunity cost of producing shirts (0.5 unit of radio given up) is bigger than the opportunity cost of producing shirts for Country B (0.4 unit of radio given up), meaning that Country B has a comparative advantage in producing shirts.

In summary, Country A is *relatively better* at producing radio than is Country B, and Country B is *relatively better* at producing shirts than Country A. Therefore, it is mutually beneficial for each country to concentrate on producing one product and to trade with the other in order to increase their overall welfare.

Table B below shows how both countries can mutually benefit from trading with each other. Suppose that Country B has 150 labour hours available for total production. Before trade, let's say that Country B produces and consumes 15 units of shirts (which requires 60 hours of labour input) and 9 units of radio (which requires

continued ...

Comparative Advantage (*continued*)

90 hours of labour input). Let's assume that Country A has fewer resources with 120 hours of labour input available. Before trade, Country A produces and consumes 20 units of shirts (60 hours of labour input) and 10 units of radio (60 hours of labour input).

Now, let's say both countries devote their labour to specialize in the production of the good that they have a comparative advantage in. Country A only produces radio with 120 hours of labour input, and Country B only produces shirts with 150 hours of labour input. Country A now produces 20 units of radio (120 hours divided by 6 hours) while Country B produces 37.5 units of shirts (150 hours divided by 4 hours). In this fashion, specialization and trade have enabled total world production to increase (from 35 units of shirts to 37.5 units of shirts and 19 units of radio to 20 units of radio), so overall welfare of the world has increased.

Table B. Change in production of shirts and radio after trade

	Before Trade		After Trade	
	Shirts (hours of labour)	Radio (hours of labour)	Shirts (hours of labour)	Radio (hours of labour)
Country A	20 units (60 hours)	10 units (60 hours)	0	20 units (120 hours)
Country B	15 units (60 hours)	9 units (90 hours)	37.5 units (150 hours)	0
Total	35 units	19 units	37.5 units	20 units

Sources: Balaam and Dillman 2011; Oatley 2012; Ravenhill 2011.

In this fashion, the division of labour and specialization in the production also increases the welfare of both the North (developed economies) and the South (developing economies). The cost of production is determined by three factors of production: capital, labour and land. The production becomes cheaper when a good is produced with the most abundant factor. For example, if a country has lots of labour (for example, a large population) compared to capital and land, it is cheaper for the country to produce a good for which it needs lots of labour (for example labour-intensive industry). Because advanced economies (or the North) are relatively abundant in capital and skilled labour, they should specialize in capital-intensive industries or high-tech industries. On the other hand, less developed countries, which are relatively abundant in unskilled labour, should produce labour-intensive manufacturing industries (or agricultural products). As long as developed and less developed countries produce goods and services based on their comparative advantage, free trade should benefit both of them, increasing the total welfare of the world. Surpluses from specialization can be reinvested or exchanged for more goods, increasing production, thereby stimulating growth in the South as well as in the North.

Neoliberalism, named as a renewal of orthodox economic Liberalism in the early 1980s, emphasizes a limited role of state in economy because state intervention distorts the operation of the market, leading to mismanagement of economy and even economic crisis. According to Neoliberalism, government should lower tax rates so business and investors can reinvest their income, and government should deregulate the banking system so that private capital can have free access to foreign countries. Developing countries should privatize state-owned enterprises to reduce inefficiency and cut back the size of the public sector, which was considered a deadweight on the economy. This policy direction, widely known as the Washington Consensus, emerged during the 1960s and the 1970s, and became the core policy direction of the international financial institutions such as the IMF and the World Bank throughout the 1990s and the early 2000s. When the communist bloc collapsed, Neoliberalism gained even more sway as the post-communist countries promoted neoliberal *laissez-faire* economic policies. Based on Neoliberalism, the IMF and the World Bank have encouraged free trade and capital movements.

According to liberal and neoliberal economist views, the capital market liberalization can bring benefits to less developed countries, which are less endowed with capital. Instead of borrowing money from outside, developing countries can attract foreign investments, generate employment and achieve domestic economic growth. The capital development in developing countries help the labour-intensive industries in less developed countries to increase productivity by enhancing technology and/or buying better equipment. As the labour productivity increases, workers' income shares increase, which ultimately expedites economic growth. The capital development also gives developing countries a chance to develop capital-intensive industries, which have higher returns to investment than labour-intensive or low-skilled industries.

In particular, multinational corporations (MNCs), which are the major source of foreign direct investment (FDI), create employment opportunities in developing countries and usually pay higher wages as well (Feenstra and Hanson 1997). The multinational corporations (MNCs) also transfer technology to developing countries, provide new personnel and ideas and build new production facilities, thus furthering industrialization. Even if the transferred technology is not the most advanced one (since MNCs are unlikely to transfer the newest technologies), the economies of less developed countries still benefit greatly from improved technology and business practices (Hermes and Lensink 2003). Thus, in the liberal and neoliberal perspective, the best way to reduce global inequality is to promote free trade, reduce government intervention and actively seek foreign investment.

In the same vein, modernization theory argues that developing countries can achieve economic growth by following the same path as advanced economies. The **Modernization Theory** views the development process as linear (see textbox for Rostow's argument on the Stages of Growth). As traditional, agricultural society 'modernizes' its economic, social and political values, it can become a modern and industrial society. Therefore, the obstacles against the economic development of developing countries are not the unfair world economic system being against them, as anti-globalization scholars contest, but in fact their social and political limitations, such as inefficient and corrupt political administration, weak property rights and weak rule of law (that is, lack of legal system) and inadequate mobilization of domestic resources. To catch up with advanced economies, developing countries should reform these internal deficiencies by embracing the Western economic, cultural, political and social values. The inefficient and corrupt political administration should be modernized by making the population become more involved in mass politics. The property rights should be improved by setting up the legal system, which protects investors from confiscation. The resources should be mobilized by attracting more foreign investments (Thomas 2005). The modernization theory as well as liberal and neoliberal economic theory has affected the development strategies of East Asian countries, which adopted 'export-orientation industrialization' (see the next section on Theories in Practice for further discussion).

The Modernization Theory, Walt Whitman Rostow and the Stages of Growth:

The Modernization theory – one of the major schools of thought that has grown out of liberal economic thinking. Modernization theory explains the modernization process as a multi-step, linear evolution that involves social mobilization, and socio-economic transformation. For example, the modernization process for mediaeval England began when peasants moved from rural to urban areas and from agriculture to industrial and commercial work. As English peasants moved away from the feudal order, they accepted new social, political and cultural systems. They became consumers who needed to buy food and subsistence and eventually assimilated into urban culture. They formed labour unions and began to participate in mass politics.

  According to Rostow, development is a linear process that begins in traditional society, where primary goods are produced in agriculturally based societies and trades are usually limited and based on the barter system. Next, the society moves into the stage of 'preconditions for takeoff into self-sustaining growth'. Then, society moves to 'take off' conditions and then onto the 'road to maturity'. Finally, society reaches 'the age of high mass consumption'. Rostow argues that this 'take off' would come from an increase in investment, manufacturing sectors and institutions that can support this expansion of economy and industrialization.

Sources: Deutsch, K.W. (1961) 'Social Mobilization and Political Development', *American Political Science Review* 55(3), 493–514; Rostow, W.W. (1960) *The Stages of Economic Growth: A Non-communist Manifesto* (New York: Cambridge University Press).

GLOBALIZATION AND ECONOMIC DEVELOPMENT II: MARXISM, STRUCTURALISM AND DEPENDENCY THEORY

Criticism of globalization is often based on three theories of political economy: Marxism, Structuralism and dependency theory. Karl Marx (1818–83) famously questioned the capitalist system and its unfairness and suggested Communism as an alternative to Capitalism. Similarly, contemporary Marxists argue that the international economic system is inherently unfair to the developing countries, and advanced economies are exploiting under-developed economies. Developing countries are manipulated by advanced countries, not because they are deficient but because the existing international economic system is biased against the developing countries. The structure of global economy is set up in a way that allows the advanced economies to grow faster at the expense of the developing countries. In the existing trade system, the advanced economies do not help developing countries to grow and reduce the global inequality, but they just extract wealth from under-developed economies and impoverish them further. Unless the unjust world economic system is reformed, under-developed countries will continue to be exploited by developed ones.

  Based on Marxism, Structuralism has broadened the argument that the existing international economic system is *structurally* biased and it cannot be corrected without the structural reform of the international system or government interventions. Following Structuralism, the dependency theory argues that advanced economies (**the North**) extract resources and exploit cheap labour in developing countries (**the South**) – thus making the South dependent on the North's capital for short-term profits. According to the dependency theory, markets alone would not automatically bring growth to the developing world as Liberalism or the modernization theory suggests. Because the existing international market system is incompetent to promote growth for developing countries, governments in developing countries have to intervene to achieve economic growth.

According to Structuralism and the dependency theory, free trade in the current international market enhances economic welfare only for developed countries: it is because the primary goods (for example, natural resources, food, and beverages), which are mainly produced and exported by developing countries, have (**falling terms of trade.**) According to the liberal and neoliberal economists, developing countries have comparative advantages in primary goods and they should profit most by specializing in the

> **The North and South System** – the system that describes the relationship between the developed (core) countries and the less developed countries (periphery).
>
> **Falling Terms of Trade** – falling terms of trade of primary goods means that one needs to pay more units of primary goods (for example agricultural products) to get the same units of industrial goods (for example manufactured products) at later time.
>
> **Low Price Elasticity of Demand** – price elasticity indicates the per cent change in quantity of demand relative to 1 per cent change in price. Low elasticity of price over demand means that as price goes down, demand will not go up as fast as it should.

production of the primary goods and exporting them. However, according to Raúl Prebisch (1901–86), an Argentine economist who advanced the study of development economics, a developing country cannot achieve economic growth through a developing agricultural sector because the primary (exported) goods create falling terms of trade compared to industrial (imported) goods. This is because primary goods from developing nations have **low price elasticity of demand**.

When a product has low price elasticity of demand, as the price goes up (or down) demand does not move equally: for example, when you lower the price of coffee (a common primary good), would the world demand for coffee go up accordingly? Not likely. People will not drink far more coffee just because the price goes down. Similarly, people would not go and buy lots of rice although it is on sale at a supermarket. When the demand for primary goods goes up, the price of primary goods does not go up as much, either. This is because consumers can easily substitute other primary goods. For example, if the price of coffee goes up, a consumer can substitute coffee with tea. Moreover, competitors can easily enter the agricultural trading market because they do not need much technology or capital to produce primary goods (ease of entry). Therefore, the price of primary goods has not changed much over time in the international market. On the contrary, industrial (manufactured) goods have higher price elasticity over demand. For example, if the price of an iPad goes down by half, the demand for the product will increase accordingly. Consumers purchase more industrial goods as their countries become more modernized and new technological products are introduced. Therefore, the demand and price of industrial goods also tend to grow over time in the international market.

Why does the low price elasticity of primary goods matter? It is because the low price elasticity leads to falling terms of trade of primary goods in the world market. Falling terms of trade of primary goods means that one needs to pay more units of primary goods (for example agricultural products) to get the same units of industrial goods (for example manufactured goods) at later time. Going back to our previous examples, you need more pounds of coffee or sales of coffee to buy the same iPad. You export coffee to earn dollars, while you import iPad and pay for it with the earned dollars (foreign earnings). If your 1 lb of coffee brought $1 in the past, you had to export 100 lbs of coffee to import a $100 iPad. Let's say that your coffee price did not change over the years, so you still export 100 lbs of coffee to get $100, but now the iPad is $150 per piece. In order to buy the iPad, you now have to export 150 lbs of coffee. Likewise, the purchasing power of primary goods falls over time relative to the purchasing power of industrial goods, resulting in falling terms of trade of primary goods. The South will have to export more and more primary goods in order to import industrial goods. The winners of free trade will always be developed countries as long as developing countries export primary goods following their comparative advantages.

According to the dependency theory, capitals do not automatically flow into developing countries, either. Because developing countries have low productivity, returns on investment are neither profitable nor promising. Investment risk is also higher in developing countries because of unstable political situations and the lack of rule of law. Therefore, dependency theorists argue that foreign capitals flow into developing countries only to extract raw materials and natural resources and to exploit cheap labour. Multinational corporations (MNCs) invest into developing countries to obtain cheap labour and maximize their profits. Developing countries have to compete to lower the labour standards (for example minimum wages) to attract more foreign capital investments. This leads to the **race to the bottom** of labour standards and helps multinational corporations to exploit the unskilled labour in developing countries (see the textbox for Race to the Bottom below).

Race to the Bottom and Manhole Covers Made in India

Opponents of globalization often argue that globalization results in a race to the bottom. This argument holds that in order to attract more foreign capital and to become more competitive in the world economy, developing countries will compete to lower labour and environmental standards and reduce minimum wages. Highly mobile multinational corporations will go to the area where wages are cheapest and labour and environmental regulations are minimal.

For example, an investigation of Indian companies making manhole covers for US cities found that the workers were forced to make products barehanded, barefooted and with almost no personal protection. New York City officials responded that they were required to buy the lowest priced manhole covers and Indian versions of this product were from 20 to 60 per cent cheaper than ones made in the US. The workers in India earn a few dollars a day and the trade unions in India did not concern themselves with the low-wage workers like manhole cover makers. Anti-globalization protestors argue that this is a clear case of the race to the bottom and a case of exploitation of the South by the North.

Another example is that ship-breaking industry, which is considered the most dangerous and environmentally hazardous work, has flourished in developing countries with cheapest labour such as Bangladesh, India, Pakistan, China and Turkey.

Source: Timmons, H. and Huggins, J.A. (2007) 'New York Manhole Covers, Forged Barefoot in India', *The New York Times*. Available at: http://www.nytimes.com/2007/11/26/nyregion/26manhole.html..

As one of the variants of Structuralism and the dependency theory, the **modern world system theory** argues that the *core*, the North, is the centre of the existing international market which benefits from the existing world trade system, while the *periphery*, the South, is the provider of resources for the North. Industrialization in under-developed countries is a mere means to extract natural resources or primary goods that are scarce in industrialized economies (see the text box, **The Banana Trade War** below). Immanuel Wallerstein formulated the modern world system theory by dividing the world system into three 'socioeconomic units': core, semi-periphery and periphery (Balaam and Dillman 2011). The 'core', Northwest Europe, moved away from the

---

The Banana Trade War

The so-called Banana Trade War began when the European Union (EU) put into place protectionist measures to restrict the imports of banana from the United States-based multinational corporations, Chiquita and Dole, operating mainly in the Dominican Republic and other Central American countries. The EU favoured banana imports from Jamaica, which, as a former colony, was allowed tariff-free access to the EU. After an intensive lobbying campaign by Chiquita, the US government filed a complaint via the World Trade Organization (WTO). After long trade wars that involved many punitive trade restrictions on products other than bananas, the US and the EU reached an agreement, which basically ended the EU's protectionist measures against the US bananas.

Although the Banana Trade War was a dispute between two advanced economies – the US and the EU – the ruling by the WTO greatly affected small countries in the Caribbean region like Jamaica. Once the ruling went into effect, small farmers were no longer able to compete against Chiquita and Dole in price, and exports of bananas from the Caribbean region fell dramatically. In the perspective of the US and Chiquita, the EU protectionist measures violated fair trade agreements. However, from the perspectives of small banana suppliers, the dispute shows another bias in the North-South trading system.

Sources: 'The Bad Blood Behind Bananas', *Financial Times*, London Edition. 5 March 1999.

---

agricultural sector into the high-skilled and capital-intensive industrial sector. The 'periphery', Eastern Europe, provides the basic necessities and primary goods such as raw materials and agricultural goods to the core and serves as the agricultural sector of the core countries. The 'semi-periphery', Mediterranean Europe, provides low-cost light-industry manufactured consumer goods with their cheap labour to the core. The international trade system is merely set up so that the North (the core) can create more surpluses and sell goods and services with higher profits. The North is not interested in the economic growth of the periphery. It always extracts cheap raw materials from the periphery through unequal exchange (trade) to enhance its self-interests – to accumulate more wealth. This division of units of region (Northwest Europe, Eastern Europe and Mediterranean Europe) can be easily applied to North America (the US) as the core, Latin America or Africa as the periphery and East Asia (South Korea and later China) as the semi-periphery.

Structuralism and the dependency theory were popular among scholars in developing countries during the 1960s and the 1970s and influenced the development strategies of the majority of developing countries. The main strategy is that if private initiative fails, then state needs to be the provider of the capital in order to produce goods and services and to ensure economic growth. Therefore, government needs to provide the basic infrastructure such as road or railways and public services such as education and health to the poor. Throughout the 1960s and the 1970s, the dependency theory had dominated the research of economic development and dictated the development strategy of the South. In particular, Latin American countries have adopted import substitution industrialization (ISI) strategies, which were suggested by the dependency theory (see the next section for further discussion).

The Modern World System Theory – according to Immanuel Wallerstein, the world economic system can be divided into three units: core, semi-periphery and periphery. The core extracts wealth and resources from the periphery. The periphery provides primary goods such as raw materials and agricultural goods to the core. The semi-periphery provides low-cost light-industry manufactured consumer goods to the core. The world trade system is set up for the core to create more surpluses and higher profits.

THEORIES IN PRACTICE: IMPORT SUBSTITUTION INDUSTRIALIZATION (ISI) VS. EXPORT-ORIENTED INDUSTRIALIZATION (EOI)

In 1944, right after World War II, 44 countries gathered together in a small town, Bretton Woods, to set up a new international political and economic order. To achieve harmony and peace in the international system, they made various efforts to remove barriers to international trade. However, they agreed that just promoting free trade was not enough to achieve world economic integration. Before World War II, most countries competitively devalued their currencies (for example setting their currencies, and thus products, below the real value) in order to make their goods cheaper and more competitive in the international market. This competitive devaluation resulted in isolationist economic policies and protectionist measures, which eventually led to trade wars. Learning from the experience, the countries gathered at Bretton Woods and established the *Dollar-Gold Standard*, setting their currencies to the US dollar, which was then fixed to gold. The Bretton Woods system also created the International Monetary Fund (IMF) to stabilize the global financial system and provide loans to countries experiencing the currency crisis and the World Bank (formerly known as International Bank for Reconstruction and Development) to help war-torn and poor countries by providing long-term loans.

However, from the start, the Bretton Woods system set aside the price control of primary goods and commodity trade agreements as less important issues, even though these were the most important issues for developing countries. Because Latin American countries exported mostly commodities (for example raw materials, cash crops and staples), they were concerned about commodity trade agreements. Still, they welcomed the creation of the IMF and the World Bank, hoping that they would get secure and cheap loans and technological assistance. As the US focused on containing the Soviet Union during the Cold War, more attention was given to European countries and East Asian nations who bordered the communist countries of the Soviet bloc. During this period, most US capital was invested into Western Europe, Japan and South Korea (and later Vietnam after the Vietnam War).

The General Agreement on Tariffs and Trade (GATT) was established in 1947 to further expand free trade. However, GATT focused on eliminating trade barriers on manufactured consumer goods, again avoiding the problems of primary commodity trade and agricultural products – and again reflecting the interests of the North as opposed to the South. Thus, as Structuralism and dependency theory argue, post-World War II institutions and trade agreements seemed to reinforce the existing North-South dynamic, which was biased against the South. As a result, and as suggested by Structuralism and the dependency theory, Latin American countries turned to nationalistic, inward-looking economic policies during this period.

Import Substitution Industrialization (ISI)

As an alternative to liberal economic development, the dependency theory suggests nations to use the import substitution industrialization (ISI) strategy. This approach calls for nations to substitute domestically produced goods for imported products. In the 1960s and the 1970s most of the developing countries in Africa, East Asia and Latin America adopted this development strategy (East Asian Tigers were exceptions: Singapore and Hong Kong have always pursued free market policy. Taiwan and South Korea adopted the ISI strategy in the early 1960s, but they quickly moved to export-oriented industrialization (EOI) strategies). Governments in developing countries chose 'infant industries', which could produce consumer products domestically, and protected them until they developed sufficiently to compete against more sophisticated and cost-effective imported products. To do this, governments set tariff and non-tariff barriers (for example quotas or standards that favoured domestic producers) to make imported goods less competitive compared to the domestically produced equivalents. Governments also helped infant industries borrow money easily with lower interest rates and government guaranteed loans. They also issued 'mandatory sectoral allocations', which mandated a portion of bank funds to be allocated to certain industrial sectors. Another strategy countries taking the ISI route followed was to set the local currency higher than its real value so the currency became highly overvalued. Overvaluation means that the currency is sold at a higher price than its real value. When a currency is overvalued (against the hard currency, usually the US dollar), one has to pay more in US dollars to buy one unit of that currency. This makes borrowing money outside (that is, US dollars) cheaper.

The dependency theory also suggested that developing countries should emphasize trade and investment with other developing countries. Thus, instead of the North-South trade, which was deemed unfair to developing countries, developing countries were advised to trade with countries in a similar stage of development. This would permit developing countries to enjoy similar economies of scale, to develop their own technologies and to become competitive in the international market. In fact, developing countries have made several bilateral or regional free-trade agreements such as ASEAN (Association of Southeast Asian Nations), Mercosur (Southern Common Market) and Comunidad Andina (Andean Community of Nations).

However, ISI strategies have brought several problems to Latin American countries. First, the ISI approach led to declines in agricultural production, which resulted in food shortages and a reduction in foreign earnings to pay for imports. Because governments in Latin American countries considered the agricultural sector as less effective in promoting economic development, they discouraged the expansion of the agricultural sector. Governments levied higher taxes on agricultural exports to increase revenues to support the industrial sector and put price controls on food and staples to make these products cheaply available to the industrial and urban sectors. Instead of providing foods and basic goods at cheaper prices, the government let the industrial sector set labour wages at a lower level to make more profits. However, as a result, food production declined, causing food shortages and high inflation. Because agricultural products had comparative advantages in the international market, export sales of agricultural goods were a major source of export income to Latin American countries. As the agricultural sector declined, export sales of agricultural goods declined and Latin American countries faced serious balance of payment problems.

Second, the infant industries developed under the ISI strategy never became globally competitive. Governments in Latin America put price controls on consumer goods to protect the infant industries and to guarantee their profitability. Under price controls, infant industries could sell their products at higher prices in the domestic market. They did not have an incentive to innovate and make their industries competitive in the international market. Even if they had tried, they could never compete against the highly advanced technological products of developed economies.

Third, the ISI strategy paradoxically made the Latin American countries rely more on imported consumer goods. The overvalued local currency (which also made domestic products overvalued) made imported goods cheaper than domestically produced goods. Thus, governments were compelled to place significant tariff and non-tariff barriers on imported goods. These barriers created their own problems such as black markets for imported goods and government corruption with increased bureaucratic red tapes.

Finally, Latin American countries relied on external debts to make up for the decline of the exports of primary goods and the increase of imported goods. Borrowing money was very easy in the late 1970s because of readily available petrodollars and low world interest rates. As oil prices rose sharply in the 1970s, oil-exporting countries had a sudden surge of revenue and put their money in the international banks. The banks, in turn, lent these petrodollars to developing countries. Because Latin American governments guaranteed the loans, international banks were more than happy to lend them money. The real interest rate was low, and the real international interest rate became negative from 1974 to 1979 (which implied that lenders could pay back less than what they owed). Of course, banks lent loans in dollars to Latin American countries because dollars were more stable than their local currencies. Latin American countries were fine with the loans in dollars because dollars were cheaper to them with the overvalued local currencies.

However, as exports of primary goods declined and imports increased, Latin American countries did not have enough currency to pay the interests on their debt. Some Latin American nations borrowed more money (in dollars) to service (pay for) the existing debts, which resulted in a vicious cycle of growing debt. Making the situation worse, the US Federal Reserve increased the interest rate in 1979 in order to slow down the overheated US economy, which decreased consumer demand in the US market and in turn suppressed global demand. Under the decline of global consumer demand, Latin American countries could not export their products enough to generate the hard currency and service their dollar-denominated debts. At the end of 1982 the total debt service in Latin America was 47.6 per cent as a share of the exports of goods and services. Latin American countries were no longer able to service the debt from export earnings, and external debts were ballooning out of control. In August 1982, Mexico finally announced that it would not be able to pay back foreign debts, which had a domino effect on other developing countries in the region (Franko 2007). As ISI policies failed to help developing countries to grow economically and reduce the global economic inequality, the dependency theory fell out of favour.

Export-Oriented Industrialization (EOI)

In contrast to Latin America nations, East Asian countries (that is, Hong Kong, Taiwan, Singapore and South Korea) have chosen an export-oriented industrialization (EOI) strategy and enjoyed a remarkable economic growth. Despite the popularity of dependency theory in developing nations, the four Asian Tigers followed more or less liberal economic policies: Hong Kong and Singapore pursued laissez-faire economic policies with little intervention from government; South Korea and Taiwan adopted export-oriented development policies (although their governments also intervened into the market to promote exports). According to the *World Bank Report on East Asian Miracle, Economic Growth and Public Policy* (World Bank 1993), average rates of trade protection (per cent calculated as tariffs plus the tariff equivalent of import quotas) for the Asian Tigers were roughly half the level of nations in other regions. For example, the average rate of trade protection (per cent) in 1985 was only 24 per cent in the high performance Asian economies such as Hong Kong, Taiwan, Singapore and South Korea, while it was 46 per cent in South America, 34 per cent in Sub-Saharan Africa and 42 per cent in other Asia (Bangladesh, Cambodia, Lao P.D.R., Myanmar, Pakistan, Sri Lanka and Vietnam).

The export-oriented industrialization (EOI) is inherently less protectionist than import substitution industrialization. Under the EOI strategy, governments still intervene in the market – but do so to provide export credits and subsidize export-competitive sectors of the domestic economy (which make exported products more competitive in the international market). East Asian countries also protected infant industries with import restrictions in the early stages. However, infant industries were protected not to substitute the imported goods domestically, but to create export-competitive products for the international market. Exporters demand more liberalization of the market so that they can also have freer access to trading partners' markets. They also prefer low tariff and non-tariff barriers because they have to import raw materials and intermediate goods to produce their goods. For example, the South Korean government in the 1970s and the 1980s put lower restrictions on intermediate inputs (for example raw materials for consumer goods) so that exporters can use them for their production. Also, trading partners tend to be more lenient and less retaliatory towards EOI policies (for example export credits) as compared to ISI policies (for example import tariffs against their own goods) (Krueger 1990).

Export-oriented industrialization is also better for economic growth for several reasons. First, export-promoting countries can earn foreign exchange earnings through exports and can build up large foreign currency reserves. Large foreign currency reserves encourage financial market stability and thus make EOI nations more attractive to foreign investors (since there is less risk of sudden devaluation and less risk of default on external debts). Second, the EOI approach helps markets become diversified more quickly and thus the domestic economy becomes increasingly flexible. On the other hand, industries under ISI policies expand only up to the size of the domestic market. Because the products created by infant industries are usually of lower quality and higher prices, they are less competitive in the international market. Because the domestic market is usually small, ISI policies encourage short production runs, which prevent companies from realizing increasing returns to scale. For example, the steel industry under the ISI strategy will produce only a small number of molds and shapes for metal production, which further reduces competitiveness. However, the steel industry under the EOI strategy has to produce all sorts of shapes flexibly because it is playing to the wider world market. Because it has larger consumer base, it can create more efficient factories and make longer production runs, both of which tend to make products more cost-effective. Lastly, East Asian countries devalued their local currencies to promote exports. The devaluation of the local currency means that it loses its value against the hard currency (usually US dollars), which makes exports cheaper in dollars as well. The devalued local currencies of East Asian countries made their exported products more competitive in the international market, while making imported products less attractive to the domestic consumers.

Following the EOI approach, East Asian countries enjoyed a remarkable run of economic growth throughout the 1970s, 1980s and the 1990s. Figure 11.2 shows the change of GDP per capita for East Asian countries and Latin American countries. As the figure shows, the four East Asian countries outperformed Latin American countries more than three times over the 30 years.

Furthermore, the East Asia Tigers survived the debt crisis in the 1980s, which significantly harmed Latin American and other developing countries. East Asian countries also had high foreign debts because they borrowed heavily from outside to develop their industries in

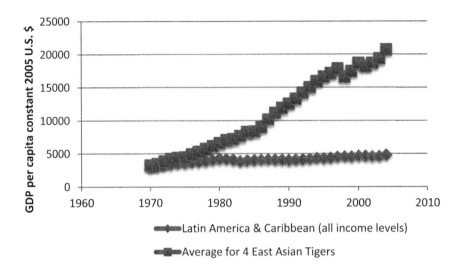

Figure 11.2   The change of GDP per capita (constant 2005 US $) for the East Asian countries and Latin American countries (1970–2004)

Data source: World Development Indicators 2013, and Statistical Yearbook of the Republic of China, various years.

the 1970s. However, they had large foreign reserve to survive the debt crisis because of large exports and high economic performance. Their external debts were also in their own currencies, not in dollars. International banks allowed East Asian countries to borrow in their currencies because they had high economic growth with low inflation (for example, abstaining from printing money recklessly to expand revenues). For example, South Korea's foreign debt by 1984 was the fourth largest in the world and equalled more than half of its GNP (Gross National Product) in 1985. However, South Korea never lost its credit from foreign creditors and lenders because of its high export to GNP ratio and rapid economic growth. In 1985, the South Korean government started to service its external debts ahead of schedule.

However, the validity of neoliberal perspective was challenged when East Asian countries were hit by the financial crisis of 1997–98. Along with pursuing EOI strategies, East Asian countries rapidly liberalized their financial markets in the early 1990s. Because East Asian countries were growing steadily, pursuing sound macroeconomic policies, and offering higher interest rates than other regions, international capital was attracted to the Tigers. Private capital invested in East Asia grew from $20 billion in 1986, to some $250 billion by 1996. However, as the Japanese yen and the Chinese Yuan became devalued (against US dollars), and Asian countries did not devalue their currencies accordingly, local currencies in Asia became relatively overvalued in the early 1990s. The overvaluation of local currencies and low inflation rates made dollars artificially cheaper and encouraged excessive international borrowing (in dollars), resulting in balance of payment problems. In early 1997, international investors started to suspect that the Thai government would not be able to defend their fixed exchange rate and began to sell the Thai currency (the baht). Once investors began to pull their money out, the Thai government quickly exhausted its foreign reserves and had to give up its fixed exchange rate, resulting in sharp fall in value for the baht and a financial crisis. The crisis spread to the other Asian countries such as South Korea, Indonesia and Malaysia, with serious impacts to all of the affected economies.

Still, most developing countries nowadays abandoned the ISI strategy and embraced the neoliberal economic policies. Developing countries tried to integrate into the international global market by liberalizing their domestic market, reducing restrictions on foreign capital, providing greater investment security, reducing government spending and public debt and restructuring the public sector. However, most developing countries did not experience the dramatic growth of the four East Asian Tigers. The social and political conditions in developing countries often prevented them from fully achieving the benefits promised by neoliberal reforms. In order for neoliberal policies to work, privatization must proceed simultaneously with the liberalization of trade, capital market and labour market. However, in many developing nations outside of Asia, public perception of Neoliberalism was tainted by the legacy of colonialism – and thus the public usually did not support neoliberal policies. Therefore, politicians were not able to implement comprehensive neoliberal policy portfolios, but adopted only some pieces. For instance, many post-communist countries could not privatize the public sector because of the strong opposition from labour unions, while they made the drastic reform on basic subsidy programs that hurt the poorest of the poor. In 1989 President Pérez of Venezuela launched his neoliberal reform package, called 'the Great Turnaround'. As a part of the reform, he raised bus fares, and low-wage workers could not go to work because of the high bus fares, which caused a popular uprising against the government. Pérez was finally impeached, and his successor ended the reforms.

Often, the neoliberal policies caused many problems when they were passed and implemented without regard to social and political conditions. For example, the IMF provided development loans to Jamaica and put a condition to cut government spending. To meet the condition the government closed most of public schools and health clinics, which harmed mostly the poor. In short, for developing nations, the path to neoliberal reform is strewn with obstacles. Governments are required to enact a comprehensive plan of reform across every sector of the economy. The scope and complexity of the required changes can often vex developing governments, and errors can redound harshly across societies without sufficient safety nets.

CONCLUSION

After the tumultuous history of the past decades, a new consensus in favour of free trade has begun to emerge. Instead of blaming the North for exploiting the South and protecting domestic markets, developing countries have successfully argued that to ensure a level playing field, industrialized nations must remove barriers to their products. To promote free and fairer trade, developing nations have been active participants in the reform of international organizations such as the GATT and the WTO. Developing countries have also tried not to follow the neoliberal reform blindly but to employ prudent fiscal and monetary policies to avoid the pitfalls of globalization.

As developing nations have grown more savvy about trade, the international community also now better understands that globalization is a double-edged sword. With this knowledge, leaders of international institutions have helped push forward reforms to reduce global inequality.

In 2001, for instance, the WTO launched the Doha Development Round to promote fairer trade between developed and developing countries, particularly on agricultural commodities.

Historically, the increasing economic gap between the rich and poor countries enlarged the economic and political tensions between the countries and made international economic and political system unstable. To promote free trade and keep the favourable international economic environment, developed and developing countries should cooperate with each other and make conscious efforts to reduce global inequality.

Grassroots Movement and 'Community Economies'

Globalization has been blamed for eliminating local and cultural diversity and making the economy more impersonal. Recently, J.K. Gibson-Graham and other scholars propose that developing countries can empower communities and develop local markets through democratic grassroots (bottom-up) movements. They argue that community-based economies, which are based on cooperation, could create an alternative to the neoliberal Capitalist economies, which are based on competition. Community-based economies value cooperation and ethics over competitiveness and efficiency, and thus promote personal, social and ecological survival of small producers. For example, in northern Mindanao, the Philippines, a rice mill was built as a part of the community economy projects to serve the whole local community of farmers.

More information is available at http://www.communityeconomies.org/Home.

QUESTIONS FOR REFLECTION

1. Does globalization increase global inequality? How would neoliberalists or structuralists answer this question? What supporting data or evidence can be used to support either position?
2. How convincing is Immanuel Wallerstein's categorization of the world economic system into core, semi-periphery and periphery? Do these divisions seem defensible in the contemporary economic setting?
3. The import substitution industrialization (ISI) strategy ultimately failed to stimulate economic growth in the developing world and to close the income gap between the North and the South. If someone claims that therefore the dependency theory is no longer valid because the empirical experiment failed, what would be your response? On the other hand, do recent financial crises (such as the 1997 Asian Financial crisis or the 2007 global financial crisis) support the dependency theory?
4. Does free trade stimulate economic growth in developing countries? Why or why not?
5. After studying the chapter, what do you think is the best solution for global inequality? Do you think a general solution is possible? Or do you think individual cases require different approaches?

REVISION QUIZ

1. Which of the following is an incorrect statement about Liberalism?

   a. David Ricardo supported free trade and abolishment of the British Corn Laws.
   b. One of the arguments for free trade of 'corns' was that the British products would become more competitive in the world market once food price declined.
   c. According to Adam Smith, a free market regulates itself because self-interest regulates individuals.
   d. Free trade promotes economic growth when countries develop industries based on comparative advantage.

2. Which of the following policies is not supported by Neoliberalism (Washington Consensus).

   a. Less government intervention in the economy.
   b. Deregulation of the banking system.
   c. Privatization of state-owned enterprises.
   d. Higher taxes and increased government spending.

3. Which of the following statements correctly describes Structuralism?

   a. Structuralism has roots in writing by John Stuart Mill.
   b. The biggest question for Structuralism is whether the capitalist market system is fair.
   c. Structuralism argues that the economic relation between the North and the South is unfair because the South (core) exploits the North (periphery).
   d. Agricultural pessimism argues that agriculture succeeds to produce economic growth because of falling terms of trade of primary goods against industrial goods.

4. Which of the following statements does not correctly describe Structuralism?

   a. Dependency theory argues that if capital moves, it moves only to extract profits from backward countries.
   b. Prebisch argues that primary export goods have falling terms of trade against industrial imported goods.
   c. Countries in the semi-periphery provide labour-intensive manufactured goods to the core.
   d. Dependency theory argues that the periphery cannot grow because the international trading system is inherently unfair to developing countries.

5. Which of the following concepts is incorrect regarding Economic Liberalism?

   a. Political Liberal
   b. Adam Smith's 'invisible hand'
   c. David Ricardo's comparative advantage
   d. Corn Laws abolished in Britain

6. Fill in the blank: A _____ is a phenomenon of developing countries competing to lower wages so that they can attract more foreign capital and become more competitive in the world market.

   a. Race to the high growth rate
   b. Race to the finish line
   c. Race to the bottom

7. For most of developing countries, capital is a scarce factor of production. How did developing nations make up for the scarcity of capital, which is crucial for economic development and industrialization? Which of the following statement(s) is/are incorrect (there could be more than one answer)?

   a. They nationalized the banks so that banks could provide long-term loans to industrial sector with low interests.
   b. Governments required banks to allocate some funds to newly industrialized sectors (that is, infant industries).
   c. They overvalued their currency by fixing the exchange rate and imported capital goods more cheaply.
   d. Government issued guarantees of loans to agricultural sector.

8. Applying Wallerstein's argument, which of the following is a correct match between the category and the country or region?

   a. The core – the Mediterranean
   b. The semi-periphery – Northwest Europe
   c. The core – East Asia
   d. The periphery – South America

9. Which of the following is a correct statement explaining falling terms of trade?

   a. Falling terms of trade is the base of the modernization theory.
   b. Falling terms of trade explains how one needs more units of agricultural goods to exchange for the same number units of manufactured consumer goods.
   c. Falling terms of trade idea was first introduced by David Ricardo.
   d. Falling terms of trade means that the price always goes down for manufactured goods.

10. Which of the following is not a part of the anti-globalization movement?

   a. North-South system
   b. Modern World System
   c. Falling terms of trade
   d. Comparative advantage

Answers: 1: c; 2: d; 3: b; 4: c; 5: a; 6: c; 7: d; 8: d; 9: b; 10: d.

BIBLIOGRAPHY

'The Bad Blood Behind Bananas'. *Financial Times*, London Edition, 5 March 1999.

Balaam, D.N. and Dillman, B. (2011) *Introduction to International Political Economy*, 5th edition (Boston, MA: Pearson Education).

Baylis, J., Smith, S. and Owens, P. (2011) *Globalization of World Politics: An Introduction to International Relations*, 5th edition (New York: Oxford University Press).

Bulmer-Thomas, V. (2013) *The Economic History of Latin America Since Independence*, 3rd edition (New York: Cambridge University).

Deutsch, K.W. (1961) 'Social Mobilization and Political Development', *American Political Science Review* 55(3), 493–514.

'Fashion chains sign accord to help finance safety in Bangladesh factories', *The Guardian*, 13 May 2013.

Feenstra, R.C. and Hanson, G. (1997) 'Foreign Direct Investment and Relative Wages: Evidence from Mexico's Maquiladoras', *Journal of International Economics* 42(3–4), 371–93.

Franko, P. (2007) *The Puzzle of Latin American Economic Development*, 3rd edition (Lanham, MD: Rowman & Littlefield).

Gerschenkron, A. (1962) *Economic Backwardness in Historical Perspective* (Boston, MA: Harvard University).

Grieco, J.M. and Ikenberry, G.J. (2003) *State Power and World Markets: The International Political Economy* (New York: W.W. Norton & Company).

Ha, E. (2012) 'Globalization, Government Ideology, and Income Inequality in Developing Countries', *Journal of Politics* 74(2), 541–57.

Hermes, N. and Lensink. R. (2003) 'Foreign Direct Investment, Financial Development and Economic Growth', *The Journal of Development Studies* 40(1), 142–63.

Kingstone, P. (2011) *The Political Economy of Latin America: Reflection on Neoliberalism and Development* (New York: Routledge).

Krueger, A.O. (1990) 'Comparative Advantage and Development Policy Twenty Years Later'. In: A.O. Krueger (ed.), *Perspectives on Trade and Development* (Chicago, IL: University of Chicago).

Oatley, T. (2012) *International Political Economy*, 5th edition (New York: Pearson Education, Inc.).

Peréz-Liñán, A.S. (2006) *Crises Without Breakdown: Presidential Impeachment and the New Political Instability in Latin America* (ms. Department of Political Science, University of Pittsburgh).

Ravenhill, J. (ed.) (2005) *Global Political Economy* (Oxford: Oxford Press).

Rostow, W.W. (1960) *The Stages of Economic Growth: A Non-Communist Manifesto* (Cambridge: Cambridge University Press).

Spero, J.E. and Hart, J.A. (2003) *The Politics of International Economic Relations*, 6th edition (Belmont: Wadsworth/Thomson Learning).

Timmons, H. and Huggins, J.A. (2007) 'New York Manhole Covers, Forged Barefoot in India', *The New York Times*. Available at: <http://www.nytimes.com/2007/11/26/nyregion/26manhole.html>.

Thomas, C. (2005) 'Globalization and Development in the South'. In: J. Ravenhill (ed.), *Global Political Economy* (Oxford: Oxford University Press).

Wallerstein, I. (1974) *The Modern World-System* (Berkeley, CA: University of California).

World Bank (1993) *The World Bank Report on East Asian Miracle, Economic Growth and Public Policy*.

World Bank (2013) *World Development Indicators*. Available at: <www.worldbank.org>

Chapter 12
Shifts in World Power

LUI HEBRON

One of the central areas of interest and topic of discussion among students of international political economy is the perceived multifaceted shift away from the economic, political and cultural predominance of the developed G7 countries of Britain, Canada, France, Germany, Japan, Italy and the United States and towards the interests, values, goals and objectives of the emerging market economies of the developing world in global affairs. Within this context, special attention has been given to the accession of the so-called BRICs states – Brazil, Russia, India, China and South Africa – on the geo-economic consciousness of international relations scholars, economic policymakers and investors alike. The significance of this shift is striking because of the potential impact these 'rising economic stars' acting in unison will have as a powerful economic bloc in at once challenging and reshaping the global balance of power. With the BRICs projected to assume a more prominent profile on the global economic stage over the coming decades, are we witnessing a transformational shift in history when the international economy's centre of power and its oversight decisively pivots away from the exclusive trilateral club dominated by the United States, Western Europe and Japan towards a more inclusive, multipolar and equitable world order? This chapter is segmented into four sections to assess the functional accuracy of the BRICs designation as potential player and centre of power in the structure and relations of the international economic order: the first section presents a brief overview of the historical and theoretical orientation of the BRICs as a classification as well as the geo-economic paradigm. The second section provides a SWOT analysis of the BRICs states by highlighting the key Strengths, exposing the main Weaknesses, exploring the most promising Opportunities and discussing the most pertinent Threats of the organization. The third section scrutinizes the functionality of the term as a viable analytical category. The concluding section reflects on the future of the BRICs in the global economy. This study suggest that the BRICs states concept does to a certain extent capture the reality of the global shift in economic power. The centre of geo-economic power is clearly expanding beyond the advanced industrialized world of the Global North. At the same time, their increased economic capabilities and dynamism should not be viewed as a threat to the order and stability of the international system. For while the BRICs states clearly want a bigger role in the global economy so as to be able to rewrite the rules of governance for the international economic system, they are also cognizant of the fact that they have greatly benefited from the present global economic system as currently constituted. Hence, for all their statements complaining about the imbalanced structure of the world economy and despite their publicized positions to have a greater voice in global economic affairs, the BRICs appear to want to bring about these changes as an insider power broker and not as an outside challenger – based on their behaviour and actions over the past ten years.

Key Words: International Political-Economy, G7, Geo-economic, BRICs, Geopolitical, SWOT Analysis, GDP, Power Transitions, World Bank, International Monetary Fund, World Trade Organization, Next 11, E-7: Emerging 7, CIVETS, 3G: Global Growth Generators.

Chapter 12

Shifts in World Power

LUI HEBRON

INTRODUCTION: THE RISE OF THE BRICS AND ITS POTENTIAL GEO-ECONOMIC IMPLICATIONS

One of the central areas of interest and topic of discussion among students of **international political economy** is the perceived multifaceted shift away from the economic, political and cultural predominance of the developed **G7** countries of Britain, Canada, France, Germany, Japan, Italy and the United States and towards the interests, values, goals and objectives of the emerging market economies of the developing world in global affairs. Within this context, special attention has been given to the accession of the so-called **BRICs** states – Brazil, Russia, India, China and South Africa – on the **geo-economic** consciousness of international relations scholars, economic policymakers and investors alike. In a little more than a decade, these five newly emerging market economies collectively have

> **International Political Economy** – explores the relationship between states and markets.
>
> **G7** – international organization composed of the seven largest economies of the globe.
>
> **BRICs** – the largest and fastest growing economies among the emerging market states.
>
> **Geo-economic** – the international economic relations among states that takes into account security considerations.

become a leading force in pushing forward their agenda calling for the peaceful and orderly transformation of both the structure of the global economy and the international economic relations between states. The significance of this shift is striking because of the potential impact these 'rising economic stars' acting in unison will have as a powerful economic bloc in at once challenging and reshaping the global balance of power. Indeed, due to the member states' belief and aspiration that they should play a more prominent role and exert greater influence in global economic affairs, they are already wielding increasingly wider relevance and more important impact on both the evolution and formation of a more multipolar world structure as well as the rules governing international commerce and economic policy.

With their improving economic standings, as measured by their strong currencies, rising market capitalization, infrastructure building boom, rapid growth and increasing volume of their national economy, high levels of education, expanding middle classes and larger roles as super regional powers, the BRICs collectively account for a hefty share of international economic activities and have become important participants in the global economic order. By 2050, the BRIC states are projected to rank in the top six (China 1st, India 2nd, Brazil 5th and Russia 6th) of the world's largest economies, and their combined economies could eclipse all the economies of the richest countries in the world (Goldman Sachs 2003). It has been further observed that as the group's economic power, status and the like have increased, they have become more assertive in projecting their geo-economic interests and policy agendas on the world stage (please refer to Figure 12.1).

With the BRICs projected to assume a more prominent profile on the global economic stage over the coming decades, are we witnessing a transformational shift in history when the international economy's centre of power and its oversight decisively pivots away from the exclusive trilateral club dominated by the United States, Western Europe and Japan towards a more inclusive, multipolar and equitable world order? Will they be able to leverage their economic cooperation into a greater role on the world stag? If so, what are the geo-economic implications of the BRICs' increased status and profile in the worldwide economy? In particular, will these states be defenders or challengers to the *status quo*? Will they contribute more or less to the world's peace and stability?

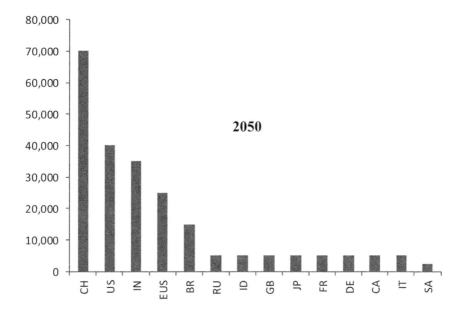

Figure 12.1   Projected World Rankings
Source: Global Sherpa.

This chapter is segmented into four sections to assess the functional accuracy of the BRICs designation as potential player and centre of power in the structure and relations of the international economic order: the first section presents a brief overview of the historical and theoretical orientation of the BRICs as a classification as well as the geo-economic paradigm. The second section provides a SWOT analysis of the BRICs states by highlighting the key Strengths, exposing the main Weaknesses, exploring the most promising Opportunities and discussing the most pertinent Threats of the organization. The third section scrutinizes the functionality of the term as a viable analytical category. The concluding section reflects on the future of the BRICs in the global economy.

CONCEPTUAL AND THEORETICAL ORIENTATION: BRICS AND SHIFTING ECONOMIC REALITY

Jim O'Neill, an economic analyst at the investment banking firm of Goldman Sachs, is universally credited with coining the catchy BRIC acronym to spotlight and symbolize the rise of these once-poor countries into major emerging powerhouses in the global economy (Goldman Sachs 2001). This select group is distinguished from other developing states by their potential capabilities to become among the world's largest and most significant economies in the twenty-first century due to their impressive demographic, geographic and market size. The four original BRIC countries collectively represented 40 per cent of the planet's total population, comprised over a quarter of the earth's landmass encompassing three continents and accounted for more than 25 per cent of global **GDP**. The BRICs became BRICsso in 2011 when South Africa was officially granted membership to the group. With the addition of South Africa, the BRICs' footprint increased to encompass 43 per cent of the planet's total population and 30 per cent of the earth's landmass spread over four continents, though its share of global GDP was unchanged at more than 25 per cent.

> **GDP** – Gross Domestic Product – refers to the total monetary value of all the goods and services produced by a country in a year.

In terms of size, growth and power projection, Brazil, Russia, India and China stand head-and-shoulders above other emerging markets and developing countries. Though South Africa possesses the continent's largest economy, it clearly does not measure up to its BRIC partners as it is neither an economic powerhouse nor has the profit potential and/or productivity of the other member states of the organization. For these reasons, many economists and analysts (including O'Neill) have questioned the country's inclusion in the consortium. What South Africa lacks in geographic, population and market size, however, is compensated by its ability to serve as a valuable agent for the bloc's member states to establish greater trade opportunities and deeper cooperation with the other countries on the continent. Framed in this larger context, South Africa's membership is a vital component of the BRICs leadership's plan to expand the organization's footprint into the strategically critical and potentially profitable African continent. In so doing, the BRICs as a whole have come to epitomize the upward mobility of the globe's largest and most dynamic emerging economies and their potential impact on the global economic, and increasingly, political order.

Power transitions are a recurring phenomenon and issue area in global politics. According to Doran (2003), Organski and Kugler (1985), Kennedy (1987) and Gilpin (1981), world history and international politics is littered by the periodic clash between great and emerging powers due to a rising state's desire to reorganize the international system to better serve its interests. Specifically, structural changes in the distribution of power has often led to the struggle between the ascending state's efforts to renegotiate the rules and institutions commensurate with its growing economic, military and geopolitical clout in the global system and the declining states' goal

> **Power Transitions** – refers to the transfer of power or the reshuffling of positions in the hierarchy of states.
>
> **World Bank** – an international financial institution that provides loans to developing countries for capital programs.
>
> **International Monetary Fund** – an organization working to foster global monetary cooperation and to secure financial stability around the world.
>
> **World Trade Organization** – an international financial institution that provides loans to developing countries for capital programs.

of minimizing their own weakened position and maintaining the *status quo*. Invariably, these points in time are rife with the potential for worldwide conflict, if not war.

The current international order was established in the aftermath of World War II. What distinguishes this system from the failed structural arrangement it replaced as well as the previous orders that have littered the landscape is the creation of rule-based, multilateral institutions and regimes (**World Bank**, **International Monetary Fund**, **World Trade Organization**) that are inclusive and expansive, and thereby facilitate and encourage the increased engagement and integration of emerging powers within the established structure.

The two distinctive features of the current global order make the possibility of a less traumatic power transition more likely. First, since this Western-based order is founded on the coordinated participation of states across all geographic, developmental and demographic strata, it provides the notable capacity to accommodate the aspirations of rising powers. Specifically, the inclusive character of this system has created a favourable international environment which grants rising states the opportunity to advance their economic and geopolitical goals and thereby enhance their status and authority within it. The significance of this arrangement is the recognition and acquiescence by the leading powers for the ascension of other states to major power status.

Second, whatever its deficiencies, the current order has an extraordinarily comprehensive, durable and widely sanctioned arrangement of global and regional multilateral rules and institutions. The significance of the ruled-based character of this system means that state sovereignty, the rule of law and shared authority (that is, the continuous process of give-and-take regarding economic, politic and security issues) over the global system are part of the operating logic of the order. And in so doing, protects the interests of all states, for the system ensures that power is exercised within the rules and institutions. That the order has evolved so as to make it so expansive and so institutionalized that a rising state has no choice but to become a full-fledged member of it has laid the basis for unprecedented levels of cooperation.

GEO-ECONOMICS AND SWOT ANALYSIS: REALITY AND POTENTIAL

Given that economic performance and power rise are the key criteria and dimensions upon which the BRICs states are classified, a geo-economic focused **SWOT analysis** would be the most appropriate analytical strategy by which to examine the evolving position and role of the BRICs' grouping in the international area. Geo-economics refers to the complex intersection between markets and states on a global scale that takes into account the market-centric/borderless focal point of economic flows when analysing economic relations between countries. The geo-economic paradigm more accurately corresponds to the realities of the contemporary global economic order in which the free flow of goods, services, information and so on, with or without the consent of states, is the hallmark of the globalizing process. SWOT analysis combines the internal strengths and weaknesses of a country with the external opportunities and threats inherent in international relations to examine a state's assets and liabilities when conducting its global economic affairs. To that end, the Strengths and Weaknesses of the BRICs states, as well as the Opportunities and

> **SWOT Analysis** – focuses on the Strengths, Weaknesses, Opportunities, Threats to determine the economic power and influence of a state.

Threats with which they must navigate in pursuit of greater economic power and larger role in the global economy, is explored.

STRENGTHS

Several factors are conducive to the long-term, stable growth of the BRICs. First, their 'late-comers' status has allowed them to take advantage of implementing advanced technologies and management practices developed and refined elsewhere. Their concerted efforts to increase investments in STEM (science, technology, engineering, and math) research has moved them to the head of the class as centres where high-value-added products are developed and manufactured. No longer content to simply be known as second-rate producers of cheap goods, each state's leading corporations have transformed themselves into world-class manufacturers of smartphones, software, rocket engines and planes. For example, Brazil's Embraer dominates the world market for small and mid-size civilian aircrafts, Russia is a global leader in rocket launchers, India's software companies are globally respected, Chinese telecommunications equipment-makers were selected by Apple to manufacture their best-selling iPhone and South Africa has become a centre for automotive industry assembly and components.

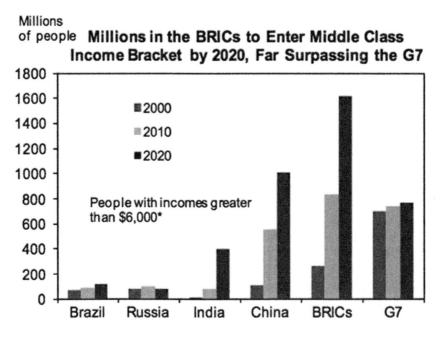

Figure 12.2   BRICs middle class

Second, the group's huge population, territorial footprint and market size combined with their breathtaking industrialization, breakneck urbanization and improving living standards all have strong potential to stimulate robust economic growth and domestic demands. Their rapid economic growth has not only lifted hundreds of millions of people out of poverty, but is also projected to bring about a large consumer-oriented middle class that would power the BRICs' economic development. And with the expansion of the BRICs' middle-class population forecasted to more than double that of the G7 economies, this bloc of states is projected to be the main engine driving the expansion of the global economy in the coming decades (please refer to Figure 12.2).

Third, their increased integration to and greater openness to the globalizing world order has elevated the global economic significance of the BRICs. Between 2000 and 2008, the BRICs contributed around 30 per cent of global growth, their combined share of total world economic output rose to 22 per cent and their average annual economic growth of 8 per cent was nearly double that of the global average of 4.1 per cent. Additionally, their 43 per cent control of global foreign exchange reserves continues to rise. It has already been projected by numerous economists and policymakers that if current trends hold, the BRICs collective economies will not only become the main engine of demand growth and spending power in the next 20 to 30 years as they surpass the combined economies of the G7 states by 2050, but as a bloc will dominate the global economy for most of this century. Given the high rate of return on their past performance, many analysts not surprisingly consider the BRICs to be a good place for future investments.

WEAKNESSES

Each of the BRICs states are vulnerable to various issues and challenges that if left unresolved could negatively impact their ability to sustain the robust growth of their economy. First, all five of the BRICs suffer from a reputation for having a corrupt business environment due to their 'arcane tax and legal systems, changeable customs regimes, unscrupulous self-dealing, and self-serving joint venture partnerships' (Altman 2012). By hindering their ability to attract foreign investors, all five states are painfully discovering that corruption is imposing a 'tax' on their economies that could stifle their economic growth. Specifically, their reputation for a non-existent or rudimentary corporate governance and accounting standards has marked the BRICs as having an unreliable business climate. According to the 2013 Corruption Perception Index compiled by Transparency International, Brazil and South Africa are ranked 72nd, China 80th, India 94th and Russia 127th out of 175 countries (2013 Corruption Perception Index, Transparency International http://cpi.transparency.org/cpi2013/results/). Corroborating these findings is the World Bank's 2013 Ease of Doing Business Rankings in which Russia is ranked 92nd, China 96th, Brazil 116th, India 134th (2013 Ease of Doing Business Rankings, World Bank http://data.worldbank.org/indicator/IC.BUS.EASE.XQ). South Africa to its credit is within the top 50 with a ranking of 41st. The need to more vigorously reform their business practices such as strengthening their legal system and instituting better oversight of businesses becomes all the more urgent given the potential slowdown in economic progress that can result from being red-flagged by both the Transparency International and World Bank rankings.

The second challenge they all face revolves around the ability to maintain the high growth rate of their economy. For as with most developing countries and emerging economies, the political legitimacy and authority of the government are ultimately and intimately linked to the leadership's ability to meet the sky-high expectations for economic success of the populace. Moreover, as World Bank President, Jim Yong Kim, noted in June 2013: 'If you lift your people out of extreme poverty, it's not like they're going to say, "Great, now we're all set, we don't want anything else"' (Bloomberg 2013). Indeed, rising pressures from recently empowered middle classes for more spending and better services has actually resulted in the outbreak of protests during the spring and summer of 2013 in Brazil, Russia, India and China. Unless or until governments are able to satisfactorily respond to denizens' questions of 'where their taxes are being spent' and 'if it is the best way to allocated limited resources', instances of civil unrest by a middle class whose numbers have swelled during the past decade and frustrated with corruption will likely be a part of the political landscape in the short to medium term. Unfortunately for the BRICs, failure to sustain growth has been the historical norm. History is littered with scores of emerging markets who were not able to maintain their initial momentum and consequently did not reach the promise land of developed state status. The fear that the five countries will not be able to live up to their economic potential is an ever present concern. Hence, with no guarantee that the BRICs can sustain their blistering growth rates, combined with the vulnerability that accompanies an under-developed political milieu, a sudden downturn in economic growth paired with serious political unrest that usually follows could easily derail the BRICs' quest to join the ranks of the political-economic elites.

Third, and ironically, even if each of the BRICs are able maintain their breakneck growth rate, that success could ultimately have a detrimental effect by creating and/or increasing the call for political change, and thereby undermining the nation's stability. History has repeatedly shown that once a country's population reaches a certain level of income and education, its citizens begin to expect, if not demand, a greater voice in governance. As functioning democracies, the transition to greater political liberalization and participation should not be a problem for Brazil, India or South Africa. For China and Russia, however, this next phase of their political evolution may be problematic. China is an authoritarian state and the communist leadership shows no sign that it is willing to cede any of its powers to its denizens. Russia, in contrast, is a democracy, but increasingly in name only.

OPPORTUNITIES

Globalization offers the BRICs new opportunities for greater engagement in the international economic community. First, the group's ever deepening links to the global capitalist economy allows for increased opportunities for geo-economic as well as geopolitical cooperation. This increased integration between the BRICs and other nations, in turn, could very well bring about the expansion of worldwide views regarding how to construct a more balanced global economy, how to improve international economic governance and how to promote democracy in world affairs.

Second, their sustained growth indicates a sea change of economic power away from the developed world and towards the emerging market states as the BRICs have steadily increased their share of the global economy. The accelerated growth and development of the consumer market as stimulated by the industrialization process in the emerging economies, for example, will provide new opportunities for dynamic, export-oriented companies. For this reason, they are poised to become the globe's main engine of demand and spending power. That it was the BRICs who came to the rescue during the 2008–09 financial crisis provides a harbinger of the worldwide importance of the BRICs' economic engine in driving the global recovery and stimulating future development in the twenty-first century.

Third, they share the common goal of achieving greater economic independence and a truly inclusive, multipolar world order. To that end, a study was commissioned in late 2012 to examine the feasibility of establishing a BRICs Development Bank. Envisioned as an alternative to the World Bank and International Monetary Fund, the self-financed bank is intended to stimulate and intensify economic cooperation in commerce, finance and infrastructure construction among the member states. The proposed bank was approved during the 2013 Summit meeting and is scheduled to open for business in early 2014.

THREATS

Like all states, the BRICs must deal with geo-economic and geopolitical obstacles and challenges in their quest for rapid economic growth and greater global role on the world stage. First, one big drawback with being export-oriented economies highly dependent on the consumers of the developed economies is that the BRICs have all been negatively impacted by the weak economies of its Western trading partners. With the onset of the international financial downturn triggered by the housing bubble and banking crisis in developed nations, the BRICs' economies were badly hurt from the sharp contraction in world trade. The diminished demand for its exports resulted in the dramatic three-year decline in GDP growth. This disturbing trend prompted policymakers and students alike to question whether or not the BRICs countries have the capability to become the engines of global growth. Bloomberg reported that 'despite a decade of prosperity', their economies 'have been slowing since 2010' with their 'stocks, bonds and currencies' all 'falling out of favor' (Bloomberg 2013).

Second, the BRICs are also increasingly facing greater competition from other emerging market economies in the developing world. Colombia, Mexico, Turkey, Nigeria, Indonesia, Pakistan, South Korea, Iraq, Philippines, Nigeria, Mongolia, Bangladesh, Egypt, Vietnam and Sri Lanka have variously been identified by Goldman Sachs (**Next 11**), Pricewaterhouse Coopers (**E-7: emerging 7**), *The Economist* ('**CIVETS**') and Citigroup (**3G: Global Growth Generators**) as the next group of economic superstars. Though not in the same league in terms of market size and territorial footprint as that of the BRICs, these once and future rising economic stars nevertheless have in common a large, young, consumer-oriented population, and are export-driven businesses seeking to expand their international market share

Next 11 – Bangladesh, Egypt, Indonesia, Iran, Mexico, Nigeria, Pakistan, the Philippines, Turkey, South Korea, Vietnam.

E-7: emerging 7 – Brazil, China, India, Indonesia, Mexico, Russia, and Turkey.

CIVETS – Colombia, Egypt, Indonesia, Turkey, South Africa, Vietnam.

3G: Global Growth Generators – Bangladesh, Egypt, India, Indonesia, Iraq, Mongolia, Nigeria, the Philippines, Sri Lanka, and Vietnam.

by take full advantage of the diverse opportunities in the global market-place. So confident are economic analysts of the growth potential of this next group of emerging market states that Professor Jerry Haar, Director of the Pino Global Entrepreneurship Center at Florida International University in Miami, declared: 'The BRICs are yesterday's news' (Stokes 2012).

Third, aside from the long-running objective of a greater voice and influence in international relations, the individual members of the alliance do not necessarily share common geo-economic and/or geopolitical interests or goals. As a result, what the BRICs stand for as well as the group's mandate remains unclear. This situation is perhaps a function of the fact that they are not very economically cohesive as their growth and development is often generated through different and sometimes competing means. For example, as major energy producers, it is in Brazil's and Russia's best interests for energy prices to remain high. High energy prices, however, are not welcome news for the two major energy consumers of India and China. As they continue to secure the raw materials they need to power their growth, China and India are destined to become economic rivals. Though Beijing looks to Brazil to be its major supplier of commodities and Brasilia, in turn, owes part of its economic success to its trading relationship with China, the two rising powers are also competitors for Africa's untapped resources. All five BRICs states also compete with one another on exports to developed markets. Then there are the simmering geopolitical rivalries between the neighbouring nuclear powers of Russia, India and China. India and China are both in the midst of upgrading and expanding their naval and air forces so as to be better able to at once protect their vast coastlines and project their maritime power on a wider area of the Indian Ocean and South China Sea. Back on land, the disputed border between China and India remains highly militarized. In like manner, Russia and China continue their tussle over territory along their shared border, and watch each other jealously as both vie for greater influence in central Asia. In this highly competitive milieu, one in which the coalition's member states' individual interests and goals are very diverse, each BRICs' priorities and agenda tends to trump any public declaration of collaboration on world political-economic issues. A summary of the SWOT analysis is presented in Table 12.1.

Table 12.1   SWOT analysis

Strengths	Weaknesses
Increased STEM research	Corrupt business environment
Expanding middle class	Rising economic expectations
Greater power in global economy	Potential for political instability

Opportunities	Threats
Greater geo-economic cooperation	High dependency on developed economies
Engine of demand and spending power	Competition from other emerging economies
Inclusive, multipolar world order	Conflicting goals and interests

FINDINGS: CLEVER ACRONYM BUT NOT READY FOR PRIME-TIME

Two conclusions can be deduced from the foregoing SWOT analysis. On the one hand, it would appear to be highly debatable to view the BRICs regime as a coherent, unified, distinguishable actor in the international political-economic system. For other than their size and economic potential, the general consensus by many observers (that is, scholars, policymakers and investors) is that due to the dissimilarity and absence of internal coherence between and among the five emerging markets as well as the undeveloped/under-developed institutional structure of the organization, the BRICs do not represent a true geo-economic bloc or geopolitical force.

As Harsh V. Pant of King's College pointedly observed: '[Y]et another summit and ritual show of unity won't hide the emptiness at the core of the BRICs' (Pant 2013).

Furthermore, the economic and political difference between members of the coalition, in terms of geo-economic goals and geopolitical interests, are such that not only do three of the five countries have a number of unsolved territorial issues with each other, but trade disputes have increasingly become the norm between the member states. When issues of vital national interests are at stake, autonomous decision-making frequently triumphs over mutual cooperation to achieve global common goals and objectives. Unless or until the five member countries are able to overcome their individual differences and begin to operate as a coherent body required for more effective action, the BRICs at best will remain a passive participant in global economic affairs. The disparate and unnatural grouping of these states prompted *The Economist* to describe the BRICs as a clever 'acronym in search of a role'. (*The Economist* 2012). Yevgeny Yasin, the head of research at the Russian Higher School of Economics, was even more critical in his assessment of the BRICs when he stated: 'Bric has no future ... I believe it will remain an informal club in form and essence' (FT Reporters 2009). Given the fact that the 'bloc' is merely a loosely woven *ad hoc* group, these negative, if not dismissive, perceptions of the BRICs are understandable.

The larger implication is that the BRICs group as presently constituted is not yet currently capable of playing a leading, power broker role on the global stage. Indeed, the absence of shared values among the BRICs has greatly limited the group's cooperative ability to present a united, cohesive front on international economic issues. Despite a decade of rapid growth of their economies, it is not clear if this economic might can be translated into political power at the global level. The BRICs' ascension as a major actor in international economic relations remains in the distant future for while the member states may already be economic powerhouses, the alliance remains a political and diplomatic lightweight. Hence, for the time being, the rise of the BRICs states will not bring about a reconfigured global economic order to the world.

On the other hand, there is no question that the BRICs have distinguished themselves from the other emerging market economies and developing countries, and by the grouping's very existence is significantly influencing, if not yet changing, geo-economic relations in the world towards one in which a more multipolar system whereby several countries and/or blocs will share global leadership is slowly being established. The findings from SWOT analysis clearly indicates that during the time frame in which the five states have been grouped, Brazil, Russia, India, China and South Africa have become economically and politically more powerful. So, though the notion of the BRICs as a coherent, unified bloc in the world system appears to be forced, the five countries nevertheless merit special attention for each has provided a distinct contribution and another dimension to the study of the globalizing world order within which it is embedded.

The key is to look at the BRICs as individual countries with unique sets of strengths, weaknesses, opportunities and threats with the potential to greatly influence and impact the international political economy.

With Brazil specializing in agriculture, Russia in commodities, India in services, China in manufacturing and South Africa in precious metals, each individual BRICs state has been able to specialize in a specific niche area based on its comparative advantage. By focusing on their strengths, they can fully exploit and expand the opportunities for greater economic interaction which in the future has the possibility to deliver them increased influence in geo-economic and geopolitical affairs and a larger and louder voice in international relations and global governance issues. The BRICs' aspiration to rewrite the governing rules of global commerce could still come to fruition in the long term.

CONCLUSION: BRIC STATES AND A NEW GLOBAL ECONOMIC ORDER

This study suggests that the BRICs states' concept does to a certain extent capture the reality of the global shift in economic power, however unnatural and forced the grouping. The centre of geo-economic power is clearly expanding beyond the advanced industrialized world of the Global North. And leading this sea change are the BRICs. At the same time, their increased economic capabilities and dynamism should not be viewed as a threat to the order and stability of the international system. For while the BRICs states clearly want a bigger role in the global economy so as to be able to rewrite the rules of governance for the international economic system, they are also cognizant of the fact that they have greatly benefited from the present global economic system as currently constituted. Hence, for all their statements complaining about the imbalanced structure of the world economy and despite their publicized positions to have a greater voice in global economic affairs, the BRICs appear to want to bring about these changes as an insider power broker and not as an outside challenger – based on their behaviour and actions the past ten years.

QUESTIONS FOR REFLECTION

1. What are the major characteristics of the BRIC states?
2. What challenges do the BRICs pose to the current state system?
3. Explain the concept/meaning of 'emerging market'.
4. Is free trade beneficial or detrimental to the world system?
5. What have been the main limitations to the effectiveness of the BRICs?
6. How has the rise of the BRICs changed international relations?
7. Discuss the criticisms of the BRICs as a group. Are such criticisms valid?
8. Assess the impact of the BRICs to expand distribution of power around the world.

REVISION QUIZ

1. Who first developed the idea of BRICs?

   a. Antoine W. van Agtmael
   b. Edward Luttwak
   c. Price Waterhouse Coopers
   d. Jerry Haar
   e. Jim O'Neill

2. The year in which the addition of the BRICs as an actor in International Relations was:

   a. 2000
   b. 2001
   c. 2002
   d. 2003
   e. 2004

3. Who were the original BRIC states?

   a. Belize, Romania, Italy, Costa Rica
   b. Bolivia, Rwanda, Indonesia, Chad
   c. Brazil, Russia, India, China
   d. Bhutan. Russia, Ivory Coast, Columbia
   e. Bulgaria, Romania, Israel, Cambodia

4. Which country was invited to become the fifth member of the BRICs?

   a. Sweden
   b. South Africa
   c. Sri Lanka
   d. South Korea
   e. Sudan

5. Which of the BRIC states are democracies?

   a. India and Brazil
   b. Russia and India
   c. Brazil and Russia
   d. China and Brazil
   e. India and China

6. Which of the BRIC countries have an authoritarian political system?

    a. China and Brazil
    b. India and Russia
    c. Brazil and Russia
    d. Russia and China
    e. India and China

7. Which BRIC states are the most integrated (trade dependent) on the global economy?

    a. Russia, India, China
    b. Brazil, Russia, India
    c. Brazil, Russia, China
    d. India, China
    e. Brazil, India, China

8. Which BRIC state(s) is/are net exporters of oil and gas?

    a. Brazil, Russia, India, China
    b. Brazil, Russia, India
    c. Brazil, Russia
    d. Brazil, China
    e. None of the above

9. Which of the following is not considered a strength of the BRICs?

    a. 'Late-comer' status
    b. Huge population
    c. Integration and openness to the world
    d. Improving living standards
    e. None of the above

10. Which of the following are weaknesses of the BRICs?

    a. Corrupt business environment
    b. Weakening growth rate
    c. Lack of democracy
    d. None of the above
    e. Both 'b' and 'c' only

11. Which of the following does NOT pose as an opportunity of the BRICs?

    a. Inclusive, multipolar world order
    b. Greater economic interdependence
    c. Opportunities for geo-economic cooperation
    d. Main engine of growth
    e. None of the above

12. Which of the following does NOT pose as a threat to the BRICs?

    a. Weak economies of the West
    b. Competition from other emerging economies
    c. Divorced from reality
    d. Lack of common geo-economic and geopolitical goals
    e. None of the above

13. One potential positive outcome(s) of the rise of BRICs on the world stage is:

    a. Support for the existing world order
    b. A movement towards a multipolar world order
    c. The movement back to a bipolar world order
    d. 'a' and 'b' only
    e. 'a' and 'c' only

14. What is the term used to depict countries whose standards of living has risen sharply over the years owing to substantial industrialization?

    a. Newly industrializing countries
    b. Emerging markets
    c. Asian Tigers
    d. Dragon Economies
    e. Global North

15. What year are the BRICs GDP projected to surpass that of the G7 states?

    a. 2015
    b. 2020
    c. 2025
    d. 2030
    e. 2040

Answers: 1: e; 2: b; 3: c; 4: b; 5: a; 6: d; 7: c; 8: c; 9: e; 10: d; 11: e; 12: c; 13: d; 14: b; 15: d.

BIBLIOGRAPHY

Altman, D. (2012) 'Reaching Tomorrow's Consumers', *Foreign Policy Magazine*, 8 October 2012.
Bloomberg (2013) 'Discontent Hits BRIC Nations as Economic Growth Slows', *South China Morning Post*, 24 July 2013.
Doran, C.F. (2003) 'Power Cycles Theory and Global Politics', *International Political Science Review* 24(1).
The Economist (2012) 'Trillion Dollar Club', 15 April 2012.

FT Reporters (2009) 'Bric quartet defined by differences', *Financial Times*, 15 June 2009.

Kennedy, P. (1987) *The Rise and Fall of Great Powers* (New York: Vintage Books).

Gilpin, R. (1981) *War and Change in World Politics* (Cambridge: Cambridge University Press).

Goldman Sachs Global Economics Paper No. 66 (30 November 2001) Building Better Global Economic BRICs. Available at: <http://www.gs.com>.

Goldman Sachs Global Economics Paper No. 99 (1 October 2003) Dreaming with BRICs: The Path to 2050. Available at: <http://www.gs.com>.

Organski, A.F.K. and Kugler, J. (1980) *The War Ledger* (Chicago, IL: University of Chicago Press).

Pant, H.V. (2013) 'BRICs Not That Sturdy', *YaleGlobal Online Magazine*, 22 March 2013.

Stokes, D. (2012) 'The decade of the CIVETS', *Business Without Borders*, 7 May 2012.

2013 Corruption Perception Index, Transparency International Available at: <http://cpi.transparency.org/cpi2013/results/>.

2013 Ease of Doing Business Rankings, World Bank Available at: <http://data.worldbank.org/indicator/IC.BUS.EASE.XQ>.

Chapter 13
Identity Politics on the World Stage

DAVID MUCHLINSKI AND DAVID SIROKY

In the late 1980s and early 1990s the scholarly study of world politics was dramatically altered as the Soviet Union finally collapsed. In its wake, the Soviet Union left behind something that it was supposed to have done away with – nationalism and expressions of national identity. As the Soviet Union crumbled, conflict erupted between various ethnic groups remaining in the former Soviet republics. Russians, Armenians, Chechens, Georgians and Tajiks all engaged in open and violent conflict in the name of national and ethnic identity. Why was nationalism such a force for violent conflict in the early 1990s when it had remained dormant for much of the Soviet era? And why did these various ethnic groups still identify with their ethnic kin when the Soviet Union was supposed to have replaced their loyalty to their kin with loyalty to the cause of revolutionary Communism?

The devastating effects of ethnic conflict re-emerged elsewhere in Europe during the same period as the former nation of Yugoslavia collapsed into several distinct states. Serbia, led by a nationalist leader in Slobodan Milosevic, engaged in a brutal and protracted war against Kosovars, Croats, Bosnians and Albanians. At the end of the twentieth century, Europeans were shocked to learn that concentration camps had once again been constructed under their noses. The wars of the former Yugoslavia claimed over 100,000 lives, and displaced over four million people.

This chapter explores the powerful effects identity – especially ethnic identity – has on international politics. Though at one time understudied, scholars of world politics have become interested in issues of identity as it has become clear that the field's main theory, neorealism, has failed to account for a variety of events such as the violent dissolution of the former Yugoslavia, increases in religious extremism and the effects these events have on world politics. This chapter introduces the study of identity and ethnicity in the context of a heated debate between two prominent scholars of world politics: Francis Fukuyama and Samuel Huntington. The chapter discusses in depth how students of world politics should understand issues of identity, and explores how identity and ethnicity affect important issues – like domestic and international conflict – in the study of world politics.

Identity is a difficult concept to grasp in the study of world politics. Are identities fixed from birth, or are individuals able to alter their identity throughout their lifetime? What makes ethnicity and identity a powerful force for mobilization in some instances and not others? How should scholars of world politics conceive of ethnicity and identity? This chapter addresses many of these questions. The chapter introduces concepts such as Primordialism and constructivism with regard to identity while exploring how the study of ethnicity itself often shapes how identity is defined. No longer a marginal field of study in world politics, the study of identity is not firmly established in the mainstream of the discipline.

Key Words: Activated Identity, Civilization, Constructivism, Ethnicity, Identity, Nominal Identity, Primordialism, Socially Constructed.

Chapter 13

Identity Politics on the World Stage

DAVID MUCHLINSKI AND DAVID SIROKY

INTRODUCTION

Theories of world politics have historically kept questions of identity hidden in the antechamber of the sub-field. Recent studies on identity and international relations by prominent scholars suggest that this may be changing (Mearshimer 2011; Snyder 2011; Toft, Philpott and Shah 2011; Toft 2010; Hale 2008: Cederman, Min and Wimmer 2010; Cederman, Weidmann and Gleditsch 2010; Cederman, Girardin and Gleditsch 2009; Posen 1993). Moreover, contemporary events in world politics, such as the onset of new civil wars, armed insurgencies and sectarian violence in Iraq, Syria and Afghanistan, the overthrow of despotic Middle Eastern regimes by popular protest, terrorist attacks carried out by Islamist organizations such as Al-Qaida, and many other examples, point to the powerful influence of identity on the world stage.

During the Cold War, policymakers and scholars of world politics were preoccupied with the superpower rivalry between the United States and the Soviet Union. World politics was viewed as a struggle for domination between great powers. The United States and the Soviet Union – and the grand ideologies that they represented – were thought to be the only political entities that influenced high politics. To the extent that identitarian groups (such as ethnic groups or religious sects) influenced world politics, it was assumed that they were assisted either by Washington or Moscow. When the Cold War ended, the scholarly community was caught unawares by identity issues. Just as ethnic cleansing during World War II was fading from memory, the population of Europe was shocked to learn that, from 1991–99, concentration camps had been set up by Serbian forces with the explicit goal of ethnically cleansing Bosnians, Croats and other non-Serb ethnic groups (Toal and Dahlman 2011; Guss and Siroky 2012). Similar dynamics among Hutu and Tutsi ethnic groups in Rwanda left half a million people dead in the course of just over 100 days (des Forges 1999). In both of these conflicts, identity played a large role.

The collapse of the Soviet Union also had an ethnic hue. Ethnic elites in the various Soviet republics framed their economic problems in ethnic terms (Giuilano 2010). Ethnicity provided individuals with a means to interpret events happening around them in the world and to reduce cognitive uncertainty regarding these events (Hale 2008). Ethnic groups in the Soviet Union feared mistreatment by Moscow, and to the extent that they were ethnically different from the majority Russian populations in many areas of the Soviet Union, sought to redress this fear of discrimination through secession. Strong emotions – including fear, hatred and resentment – may spur such groups to engage in conflict in order to redress these grievances (Petersen 2002). In the wake of the collapse of the Soviet Union and the fragmentation of that once homogenous state into various ethnically homogenous states, scholars of world politics began to take identity issues more seriously in world politics.

This chapter will address many of these theories and take stock of what we currently know about the role of ethnicity in world politics. In the course of reviewing the major theories of identity, it will situate them in the context of a 'great debate' involving two scholars of world politics, and show how their arguments bear on identity issues in world politics today. Because the scholarly literature on identity is too vast to condense into one chapter, we will focus our attention on an especially important form of identity politics on the world stage – **ethnic** politics. Other aspects of identity influence world politics, including class, gender and sexual orientation, but we limit our attention here to ethnicity, with brief mention of religious identity, and forego some coverage in the hopes of increasing precision.

IDENTITY: WHAT IS IT?

Scholars of world politics define **identity** as a social category – such as Latino, African-American, Frenchman, Japanese, Muslim, Christian, Jew and so on. Typically, individuals belonging to such groups take some pride in their membership, and view it as a more or less unchangeable and socially consequential attribute (Fearon and Laitin 2000). The two key features that tend to be crucial are clear rules of membership that determine who is (and who is not) a member, and characteristics (like beliefs, desires

> **Identity** – a social categorization by which social and political actors are defined. Those adhering to a certain identity view it as consequential.

and physical attributes like skin colour) thought to be typical of the category, or behaviours expected of members in certain situations. To give a concrete example, male Orthodox Jews in Jerusalem's Mea Shearim neighbourhood wear distinctive long black coats and top hats, while women wear dresses that cover their ankles and have long sleeves. Married women wear head coverings and men grow long beards. An outsider can easily identify a member of that community by their distinctive dress. Strict observance to the laws of Judaism is used to define membership in the community, and exclude all others.

In sum, identity serves at least three critical functions. First, an identity is a social marker, it designates to which group of things an actor or object belongs. Second, since identity acts as a social marker, it also provides individuals with appropriate social roles to follow. That is, it can act like a script that individuals follow in order to provide meaning to how they act in different social settings. For example, Mormons abstain from drinking coffee and alcoholic drinks. Immigrants from France may like to congregate in certain cafes to discuss French politics or cinema while drinking wine. French Mormons may congregate in the same cafes, but will abstain from drinking coffee or wine. Third, an identity provides a way for individuals to interpret and make sense of the world around them. For example, a religious identity can provide a way for individuals to make sense of world events. Religious individuals may think they have been blessed with divine fortune, or cursed by evil forces, depending on how events unfold. Religious identity thus offers individuals a way to interpret the world and to make sense of why certain events happen the way they do.

In political science, identity had four broad meanings (Brubaker and Cooper 2000). One involves understanding identity as the grounds for a particular social or political action. Here, identity is invoked, as opposed to interest, so as to highlight non-instrumental modes of political action. It is used to underscore how collective action is governed by particular self-understandings rather than by pure self-interest. Second, identity can be understood as a collective institution describing how a group of individuals are related and share similar characteristics. The similarities among members of a particular identity group may be objective – for example, skin colour – but are also frequently mixed with a strong subjective and socially constructed component – dark is lower in the social hierarchy than light skin in many places, but this ordering is not objective. It is simply pervasive. Third, identity may refer to some fundamental condition of a social actor – something foundational for that individual or group. We will refer back to this concept of identity later on when we discuss theories of identity broadly known as Primordialism. Finally, identity is understood as the ephemeral product of multiple and competing discourses. Here, identity is invoked to highlight the multiple, ever changing and fragmented nature of an individual's concept of 'the self'. This strand of thinking is particularly characteristic of post-structuralist and post-modern theories of social science that view identity as fundamentally socially constructed.

Identity is a category of practice, but identity is also used in other more political ways. Politicians and political entrepreneurs make appeals to identity in order to persuade people to understand themselves and their interests in particular ways, or to vote for certain candidates. Segregationist politicians in the American South during the civil rights era bridged the class divide between white voters and appealed directly to their concept of race. In doing so, many of these politicians were able to garner large amounts of support for segregationist policies, including Jim Crow laws. Similarly, Martin Luther King Jr and other African-American civil rights leaders were able to unite other African-Americans against this agenda.

In order to understand the effects of identity on *world* politics, as opposed to individual and group behaviour in domestic politics, we turn to a debate between two important scholars – Francis Fukuyama and Samuel Huntington.

THE END OF HISTORY OR THE CLASH OF CIVILIZATIONS?

Scholarly interest in identity politics, including the study of ethnic politics, blossomed with the collapse of the Soviet Union, and overtook the all-consuming superpower rivalry between the Soviet Union and the United States. During the Cold War, states were the primary actors in world politics. The international arena was viewed as an anarchic battleground where great powers strove to dominate other great powers. The main focus of international security was to prevent a nuclear confrontation between the United States and the Soviet Union. This thinking left little room within existing theories of international politics for identity. If identity mattered at all, it was a concern for domestic politics, and systemic Realism was unconcerned with domestic politics. As a result, identity issues were relegated to a dim corner of the study of world politics.

When the Soviet Union came to an end, after over half a century of Soviet rule that was supposed to replace loyalty to one's ethnic kin with loyalty to the Soviet state, Kazaks, Uzbeks, Chechens, Ukrainians, Georgians and other ethnic groups still remained, and still identified themselves according to their ethnic identities. Marxist ideology proposed that modern nations were simply the results of the capitalist mode of production. It predicted that, with the end of Capitalism, the nation as an ordering principle for social and political relations would simply disappear. Yet 60 years of Soviet rule could not wipe Nationalism away. As the Soviet Union fell, nationalist movements rose up to challenge Moscow's rule.

Realism could not explain why various domestic groups would choose to organize themselves along ethnic lines. The dominant theory of world politics had misfired on two fronts. First, it failed to predict the break-up of the Soviet Union (Kuran 1991). Second, it had failed to predict the rise and power of nationalist movements across the former Soviet Union. State death was supposed to occur only as a product of war when one state militarily defeated another, not as a result of ethnic mobilization. Yet the fall of the Soviet Union and rise of the Russian Federation was mostly peaceful (Bunce 1999; Giuilano 2010). Scholars wondered if the fall of the Soviet Union heralded a new era of peace, or if the return to a multipolar world would bring with it the potential for new conflicts (Mearsheimer 1990). The future of world politics became the subject of an important debate between two scholars – one envisioned the end of history and thus an era of peace, whereas the other forecasted a future filled with conflict along civilizational – that is, ethic – lines. Rather than basing their analyses on realist theories of international politics, they took a new direction, and focused on the concept of identity.

Francis Fukuyama: the End of History and the Last Man

Francis Fukuyama fired the opening salvo in this debate. His theory contended that the collapse of the Soviet Union presented a unique opportunity for the United States and for the entire Western world. Relying on history and philosophy to construct his argument, Fukuyama argued over time the world had come to be governed less by 'traditional' ideologies such as religion, Feudalism and the divine right of kings, to modern democracy and private Capitalism, which offers the world the twin benefits of individual freedom and the creation of vast amounts of private wealth. The power of these two forces, Fukuyama claimed, would culminate in what he called 'the end of History' (capital H). Fukuyama claims that the end result of history is the inevitable triumph of democracy over more antiquated systems of government and the victory of individual freedom over the forces of both ancient tradition and modern Communism.

Two factors played a key role in this story. First, capitalist economics has placed the individual at the centre of an important and influential intellectual tradition. The individual is the master of his or her own destiny, and the right of the individual to pursue that destiny is seen as the ultimate moral and political good. Economics shows us the way societies must mature to compete successfully in the world. The nature of economic competition is such that nations reject free markets at their own peril, for those that cannot compete will disappear from the world stage. Their social customs, intellectual contributions and even their military victories are doomed to fade into historical obscurity. The second dynamic that Fukuyama points to is the worldwide impact of this ideology. Fukuyama highlights the movements for greater personal freedom that spread across the former Soviet Union as dispositive evidence that the natural desire for humanity is to live in a free and open society where individuals are unencumbered and allowed to reach political, economic and intellectual maturity. The collapse of the Soviet Union, in this view, was thus completely natural, since totalitarianism was antithetical to human nature.

Fukuyama makes a distinction between history, with a small h, and History, capitalized. When referring to history, Fukuyama simply refers to events that occur over time, while History is understood to be 'a single evolutionary process' (Fukuyama 1992, xii). History as a single evolutionary process is linear, moving from traditional societies governed by autocratic monarchs and absolutist rulers to modern, liberal, democratic and capitalist governments. Fukuyama argues that the formulation of the scientific method and the resulting scientific discoveries during the Renaissance and European Enlightenment allowed societies, especially European societies, to improve technologically, to industrialize and to compete against other societies that failed to instil a spirit for scientific discovery, did not develop economically and were thus relegated to the dustbin of history. Liberal democracy, Fukuyama claims, is the superior form of government, for it fosters an open ethos of inquiry, freedom of ideas and the development of science. As a result, democracies develop strong economies and armies, allowing them to compete against other forms of government and to triumph. Liberal democracy recognizes freedom from governmental control of individuals, protects private property and separates religion from governance, so that all people are seen as equals, and provides for the free and fair election of representative politicians who are held accountable by the public.

Those societies that have become liberal democracies have built up the capacity over time to exploit science, technology, economics and superior governance, and will hence become stronger than those that have not. Eventually, in order to compete with the most powerful states in the world, all societies will seek to take advantage of this source of strength. As realist theories of international relations suggest, all societies struggle for power internationally and, since democratic states are the most powerful and most competitive, all states will seek to converge on the path towards becoming democratic and capitalist in order to successfully compete with other states. It is in each state's interest to do so in order that it does not fall behind and become a state that can no longer compete in the international battle for power and supremacy, which all nations constantly wage. Many but not all countries are already democratic. Fukuyama claims those nations that are not democratic are still mired in History. It is these nations, with their systems of government that are still ruled by 'backwards' systems, including ethnic kinships, totalitarian dictators or religious absolutists, that pose the major problem for world politics in the future. Of course, these nations struggle for power against liberal democracies in the international system, and Fukuyama is quick to point out that they will not survive without democratic reforms. In the interim, they will pose problems on the world stage.

Here, Fukuyama comes to his central problem: identity. For Fukuyama, any identity that is not crafted to be liberal, democratic and capitalist is problematic. Identities based on traditional institutions, for example, ethnicity or religious creed, must be replaced. That an individual refers to himself first as a Muslim and second as a citizen of Iran, for example, is problematic for Fukuyama, for it shows that History still has a powerful hold in such a society. Religion represents an ethos of anti-Enlightenment, a rejection of science in favour of supernatural explanations, and a preference for absolutist government steeped in religious law rather than tolerant, secular and democratic rule. For the people who still suffer under such regimes, Fukuyama claims that the only route to political empowerment must come through democratic change and the creation of a more democratic identity to replace that of the old and more traditional society.

For Fukuyama, identity can be good or bad. Identities based on liberal democratic notions, such as Frenchman, citizen, American, capitalist or cosmopolitan, are acceptable in Fukuyama's worldview, for these kinds of identities are modern and not mired in History. Identities based on ethnicity, such as Kurd, Muslim, Catholic or Ibo, are problematic for Fukuyama, for societies where more individuals identify themselves according to their ethnic identity are still mired in History and it is precisely in those societies where social ills develop. These societies have not developed strong political and economic institutions. People in these societies are more likely to be poor, and these societies are more likely to be riven by conflict. Fukuyama's vision, however, is optimistic, for he sees all societies inevitably transitioning towards modern Western liberal regimes in which parochial identities will be replaced by more modern ones.

Samuel Huntington: The Clash of Civilizations

In 1993, Samuel Huntington published an article in the journal *Foreign Affairs*, 'The Clash of Civilizations?', which presented a more pessimistic prediction for the future of world politics. Rather than seeing the development of a global liberal democratic identity, Huntington predicted that, with the end of the Cold War, identities would become increasingly fractured and conflictual along **civilizational** lines. Instead of economic prosperity

> **Civilization** – the penultimate cultural ordering of social groups and the broadest category of cultural identity.

and democracy leading the world to greater peace and prosperity, the great divisions among individuals and the resulting sources of conflict will be primarily cultural and civilizational.

Like Fukuyama, Huntington also relies on the concept of social evolution to make his argument but, unlike Fukuyama, Huntington claims that the natural process of social evolution differs between civilizations. For Huntington, civilizations are 'cultural entities' that include villages, regions, ethnic groups, nationalities and religious groups. The culture of a village in southern Italy may be different from a village in the north, but these Italian villages will share a common culture that distinguishes them from German villages. European communities, in turn, share cultural identities that differentiate them from Arab or Chinese communities. Arabs, Chinese and Europeans share no common cultural traits, according to Huntington's typology, and thus a civilization is the highest cultural grouping of people and the broadest level of cultural identity. Huntington claims that conflicts between civilizations are natural and inevitable as different cultures provide civilizations with different ways of viewing the world.

Civilizational identity provides an individual with membership in a social group, rules for individual behaviour and a unique way of making sense of the world around them. Civilizations are differentiated from each other by history, language, culture, tradition and religion (Huntington 1993, 25). Huntington says these differences are the product of centuries of social evolution and are thus more fundamental than political ideologies. Over the centuries, Huntington claims, civilizational conflicts have been the most prolonged and the most violent.

Scholars of world politics have been quick to realize the value of both Fukuyama's and Huntington's arguments about the role of identity in world politics. Whether scholars believe that identity is something primordial and unchanging, or more instrumental and socially constructed, informs theories of identity in world politics. We now turn to an in-depth discussion of these theories.

THE NATURE OF IDENTITY

Identity most often refers to an umbrella concept that encompasses groups differentiated by race, ethnicity, language and religion. It also covers smaller groups including tribes, castes and regional identities (Horowitz 1985). **Ethnic groups**, which are our focus in this chapter, are defined as social groups for which eligibility for membership is determined by attributes associated with – or believed to be associated with – ancestral descent. Scholars who study ethnicity often treat ethnicity as arising from a familial resemblance (Fearon 2006; Chandra 2006; Horowitz 1985). Such attributes can include traits inherited genetically (for

> **Ethnic group** – a social group for which membership is determined by descent from one's ancestral kin.

example, skin colour, gender, eye colour, height and hair colour), through cultural inheritance (for example, language), or through the course of one's life (for example, ritual scarification, or specific patterns of speech) (Chandra 2006, 400). Two primary lenses for understanding identity – and specifically ethnicity – can be found in Huntington, Fukuyama and many of the other scholars cited in this chapter. They are **Primordialism** and **Constructivism**, and these theories are based on fundamentally different assumptions and make distinct predictions, yet more often than not the hard line between these two schools of thought is overemphasized. It is more accurate to characterize them as two poles along a latent dimension in which identity is hard and fixed at one hand, and soft and fungible at the other (Horowitz 1998).

> **Primordialism** – the belief that an individual's identity is fixed and unchanging. Often primordialists refer to identity through certain immutable characteristics like biology or ethnic ancestry.
>
> **Constructivism** – the theory that certain aspects of one's identity are not fixed and unchanging, but instead malleable and fluid.

Primordialist Theories of Ethnicity

There are several ways in which primodial and constructivist theories of ethnicity differ, but the main differences can be reduced to hard views versus soft views of ethnicity, with 'hard' and 'soft' referring to the malleability of ethnic identity (Horowitz 1998). Hard views of ethnicity are often referred to as primodialist, because scholars working in this tradition view ethnic identities as primordial identities that are fixed at birth, ascriptive, firmly bounded and engendering strong bonds of group loyalty and solidarity which persist over time and incline communities towards a strong sense of ethnocentrism which make ethnic groups hostile to non-co-ethnic groups and likely to pursue conflict. Scholars who view ethnic identities in this way view them as fixed in stone, and emphasize the affective properties of ethnicity (Brown and Langer 2010). Ethnicity is the natural end result of biological differences or long historical processes that have shaped distinct cultures (van den Berghe 1978). Because ethnicity is derived from biology and history, primordialists generally view ethnic identities as slow changing and in effect largely fixed.

'If you were born poor, you may die rich. But your ethnic group is fixed' (*The Economist*, 14–21 May 2005, 80, quoted in Chandra 2012). Each person belongs only to one ethnic group whose boundaries remain fixed and unchanging over generations. Mountains erode over time, glaciers recede, cities are created and disappear, but through all those events, ethnic identities remain more or less the same (Chandra 2012).

Primordialists thus understand ethnicity as 'a primordial attachment that stems from the "givens" of social existence … congruities of blood, speech, custom and so on, are seen to have an ineffable, and at times, overpowering, coerciveness in and of themselves. One is bound to one's kinsman … as the result not merely of personal affection, practical necessity, common interest, or incurred obligation, but at least in great part by virtue of some unaccountable absolute import attributed to the very tie itself' (Geertz 1973). These ties generate a sense of community, and because an ethnic group consciously defines itself as a community in this way, this awareness necessitates an awareness of other communities. Ethnic identities and senses of affiliation are highly charged and central to an individual's sense of self. The awareness of others spills over through psychological mechanisms into conflict and violence. In particular, emotions including fear, resentment and hatred can motivate individuals to engage in conflict against other groups (Petersen 2002).

A prominent example of primodialist theorizing is contained in an op.-ed written by two prominent political scientists for the New York Times (Mearsheimer and Van Evera 1999) during the aftermath of the Bosnian Wars that shook the former Yugoslavia throughout the 1990s. The federation of Yugoslavia broke into constituent states beginning in the 1990s, and conflict within the Balkans coalesced along ethnic lines. Ethnic Serbs, led by a nationalist government, began a brutal campaign of ethnic cleansing against other ethnic groups in the region including Croats, Bosnian Muslims and Kosavars. Mearsheimer and Van Evera attribute this destructive conflict (in which 140,000 people were killed and more than four million were displaced) to deep-seated and historical hatreds that these groups have harboured against one another for centuries. Mearsheimer and Van Evera conclude that ethnic cohabitation will fail because these groups are fundamentally different from one another and long-running grievances and ancient hatreds make conflict the only outcome as long as these groups are integrated. They claim that ethnic separation is the only way to promote peace. They write, 'the history of Yugoslavia since 1991 shows that ethnic separation breeds peace, while failure to separate breeds war. Slovenia seceded from Yugoslavia with little violence in 1991 and has sense been at peace with itself and its neighbors. The key is its homogeneity: 91 per cent of the people are Slovenes: less than three per cent are Serbs'.

While the extreme primordialist viewpoint is still prominent in journalistic media like newspapers and magazines, among academics the strict version of the theory has fallen out of favour. Consequently, it is now very rare to find a political scientist who openly advocates a primordialist position (Chandra 2001). Further, the primordialist view runs into a great deal of trouble when attempting to explain ethnic conflict. Whereas it is entirely possible that ethnic affiliations produce strong emotions and these emotions can drive individual behaviour, primordialists have generally failed to provide a convincing explanation as to why ethnic affiliation rather than other aspects of identity are so emotive, or why violence occurs at some times, and in some places, but not others.

While Ukrainians and the Baltic Republics choose to break away from the Soviet Union in 1991, the Central Asian Republics remained within the structure of the USSR (Hale 2008). Additionally, when some states in India were swept by riots between Hindus and Muslims in 2002, others were not. Some states remained peaceful even though they bordered other states where widespread violence occurred (Varshney 2003). Even within states where ethnic conflict has raged, there is regional variation in violence that remains to be explained. Despite the reports of massive violence across Iraq after the fall of Saddam Hussein, only five of Iraq's 104 districts averaged more than three incidents of significant violence per 1,000 residents from 2004 to 2008, and within these violent districts, some were more violent than others (Berman, Shapiro, and Felter 2011). The question for primordialist theories is why is ethnic conflict so variable? Even the Yugoslav case referred to by Van Evera and Mearsheimer fails a strict primordialist test, for even the supposed 'age-old enemies' of Serbia, Bosnia and Croatia have been at peace for far longer than they have been at war (Hale 2008). Another question is why conflicts *within* civilizations appear more common than conflicts *among* civilizations. If ancient hatreds do not explain the prevalence of ethnic conflict and the salience of ethnic identity, but ethnic conflict remains common where individuals still show strong affiliation with their ethnic identity, how do we explain ethnic conflict? In answering this question, scholars have turned towards a different conception of ethnicity. They have moved away from viewing ethnicity as something primordial and fixed to conceptualizing ethnicity as something that can be molded and constructed. If primordialists view ethnicity as set in stone, these scholars view it as made of putty (Horowtiz 1998, 2).

Constructivist Theories of Ethnicity

Constructivism is less a theory of ethnic identification than a family of theories regarding ethnicity and ethnic identity. Whereas primodialist theories regard ethnicity as a given, constructivist theories contend that the meaning individuals attach to their ethnic identities is **socially constructed**. By emphasizing that it is socially constructed, scholars imply that an ethnic identity is not fixed and unchanging, but rather fluid and malleable. If primordialists view ethnic identity as always salient, constructivists stress that ethnicity is only relevant in certain social cases. Ethnicity is socially relevant when people notice and condition their actions on ethnic distinctions (Fearon 2000). Social relevancy, however, does not

> **Socially constructed** – the meaning or interpretation of an identity is not fixed by immutable characteristics like biology, but is determined by the relevance of certain political attributes of that identity.

make ethnicity politically relevant. Ethnicity is politicized when political coalitions are organized along ethnic lines, or when access to political and economic resources is dependent upon ethnicity (Fearon 2000; Wimmer, Cederman, and Min 2009). By themselves, social relevance and politicization are insufficient to explain conflict between ethnic groups. Ethnicity can be socially relevant without being politicized, and politicization matters little if people do not notice or act on the basis of recognized ethnic differences. Only when both factors are present, constructivists claim, are the conditions for ethnic conflict primed.

Constructivist theories of ethnicity do not depart wholly from primordialist theories. Despite recognizing that ethnic identities change over time according to varied circumstances, constructivists still define ethnic identity as a subset of identities for which descent based attributes are necessary (Chandra 2012; Fearon 2000). These theories differ from primordialist theories by splitting ethnic identity into two different categories. Ethnic identities can be either **nominal** or **activated**. Nominal ethnic identities are ethnic categories for which an individual's descent-based attributes make her eligible for membership of that particular group. Activated identities are a subset of nominal identities for which an individual attaches importance to or

> **Nominal Identity** – ethnic categories based on attributes related to ancestral descent.
>
> **Activated Identity** – a subset of nominal identities that are considered to be especially important to individuals identifying themselves according to a certain categorization.

professes to be an especially salient aspect of their identity. Ethnic identities may be activated by the individual, or may be activated by one's co-ethnics. For example, the number of Muslims in Bosnia increased by more than 75 per cent between 1961 and 1971. During the same period, the number of individuals who identify themselves as Yugoslavs in Bosnia decreased by 84 per cent (Bringa 1995, 28, cited in Chandra 2012). During this ten-year period in Yugoslavia, something happened that caused Bosnian Muslims to cease thinking of themselves as Yugoslavs and instead caused them to identify with their religious identity. Constructivist theories of ethnic identity seek to understand why and how such dramatic changes in the relevance of ethnicity occur and what impacts, if any, these changes might have on the likelihood of ethnic conflict.

Constructivists stress the fluidity of ethnic identities. But why are ethnic identities fluid, and when might they change? Constructivist scholars stress the importance political factors have in influencing individuals to activate one aspect of their nominal ethnic identities rather than other aspects. Access to political power and economic resources takes pride of place in these accounts of ethnicity. Horowitz (1985) remarks that during the 1953 reorganization of Madras state in India, the separation of Tamil Nadu from Andra Pradesh took place. Horowitz writes that in Madras state, 'with large Tamil and Telugu populations, cleavages within the Telugu group were not very important. As soon as a separate Telugu-speaking state was carved out of Madras, however, Telugu subgroups quickly formed the basis of political action' (Horowtiz 1985, 66). Ethnic differences among the Telugu and Tamil groups were unimportant until a separate Indian political unit was created for the Telugu ethnic group. From that point on, the Telugu ethnic identity became important and activated because it could guarantee access to political power and economic resources from the Indian state. In Africa, studies have shown that people tend to identify themselves more along ethnic lines as presidential elections draw closer. In Zambia, for example, ethnic coalitions formed along the lines of language or tribe, depending on whether the elections were at the national or local level respectively (Posner 2002). Further, for every month closer a country in Africa is to a presidential election, ethnic identity for Africans increases in salience by 1.8 per cent (Eifert, Miguel and Posner 2010). The governing institutions of a state can also affect how groups mobilize to seek political power. In Zambia and Kenya, ethnic groups organize along narrow aspects of their activated identities, such as tribe or clan, when states are governed by single parties. When these countries are governed by multiparty systems, ethnic groups emphasize broader aspects of their identity including region, language and religion (Posner 2007). One party systems provide incentives for individuals to identify themselves as members of small and localized groups like clans. One-party systems shrink the locus of political competition to smaller and more local parliamentary districts, thus giving incentives for individuals to vote for candidates who share similar ethnic identities. Voters vote for candidates who can redistribute needed resources towards their own ethnic group. Voters assume that co-ethnics are most likely to do this. In multiparty systems, electoral competition moves from the local to the national level, forcing individuals to identify with broader coalitions of voters. Individuals will thus have incentives to activate broader aspects of their ethnicities including language, religion and region of origin.

Constructivists stress that individuals activate aspects of their latent, nominal ethnic identities at different times, often for strategic reasons. Contrasting the primordialist argument where ethnic groups are locked perpetually in conflict because of ancient hatreds and animosities, constructivists contend that individuals are primarily rational actors. They choose which aspects of their ethnic identities to activate at different times depending on what the benefit of activating a certain aspect of one's identity might have. Individuals are not unthinking automatons who engage in conflict with others simply because of differences in how they choose to define each other. Nowhere is this clearer perhaps than in Malawi and Zambia where two ethnic groups, the Chewe and Tumbuka, reside (Posner 2004). In Malawi, relations between the two groups are often antagonistic, while in Zambia, relations between the same groups are peaceful. In Malawi, the Chewe and Tumbuka see each other as political adversaries and the two groups have generally voted for opposing political parties. In Zambia, these groups see each other as electoral allies and vote for the same political parties. Why, when all aspects about these two groups remain the same across the border between Malawi and Zambia, does their behaviour differ? In Zambia, neither the Chewe nor Tumbuka are large enough compared to the rest of the national population to significantly impact the results of national elections. Hence, there is little reason for these groups to differentiate themselves. They join the same political coalition to gain access to political and economic resources that are then distributed between the two groups. In Malawi, however, these two groups represent large segments of the population and hence serve as powerful political coalitions. Electoral competition between the two groups translates into competition over resources. Each group wants to maximize its slice of the political and economic pie. Hence, political competition has spilled over into competition between the two ethnic groups. The relative sizes of these ethnic groups in either country constitute a basis for political power, and thus the likelihood of electoral conflict between the two groups.

PRIMORDIALISM, CONSTRUCTIVISM AND THE GREAT DEBATE

Constructivism represents a major departure from primordialist theorizing about ethnicity. Yet Primordialism's influence on the study of identity in international politics remains. Further, whereas Constructivism offers a more theoretically nuanced way to study ethnicity, many of its arguments remain difficult to incorporate into our theories of ethnicity and international relations (Chandra 2012). Although it makes sense to speak of the fluidity of ethnicity on the one hand, many studies of ethnicity in international politics implicitly assume the stability and permanence of ethnic identity when crafting ethnicity as an object of study. It is difficult to capture the fluidity of ethnic identities. Have the categories of Chewe or Tumbuka persisted in Zambia and Malawi since Posner's study in 2004? Where did these ethnic identities even come from? Have these groups always identified themselves according to these descriptive labels, or were they once known by other designations? In the former Yugoslavia, a similar problem remains. The splintering of Yugoslavia occurred along ethnic lines, but where did these ethnic identities come from? Primordialist theories still pervade our thinking about ethnicity. Our use of ethnic categories like Serb, Chewe, Hutu, Russian, Native American, Latino and so on implicitly set these groups apart from others by defining what these groups share in common, and how they differ from other groups that are unlike them.

Although scholars recognize that ethnic identities do change, they often attempt to place these changes into recognizable categories based primarily on primordialist thinking. An identity based on an African clan or tribe may give way to one based on language, depending on the electoral context, but we still consider both these identities as arising from some primordial aspect of identity which is unlikely to change much over time. Often the categories into which we fit an identity are already given beforehand so that we can easily categorize them into neat compartments that are easy to study because they have characteristics which are already known, like skin colour, language, religion, caste and so on. Whereas the theoretical problems with Primordialism are widely acknowledged, our empirical analyses remain embedded in the primordial framework. Ultimately, to make sense of identity, some limits must be put on how individuals can define themselves. This generally means fixing the borders of identity at some point, and this point is often subjective. While Constructivism has rightly pointed out the arbitrariness of these borders, they are still widely employed to analyse identity. Despite its limitations, Primordialism offers justifications for the borders that must inevitably be placed around identities. Scholars must keep in mind the arbitrariness of these borders, however, lest we slip back into the depths of essentialism.

QUESTIONS FOR REFLECTION

1. How do scholars of political science conceptualize identity? What are the three main functions identity provides to individuals?
2. Why have scholars of international politics only recently begun to study issues related to identity?
3. What is Primordialism? How do primordialists understand ethnicity and what predictions do they make regarding the likelihood of conflict between ethnic groups?
4. How do constructivist theories of identity and ethnicity differ from primordialist theories? What is the difference between a nominal and activated identity?
5. What predictions did Huntington and Fukuyama make regarding identity, ethnicity and conflict? Where did they go wrong, and in what ways have their theories been empirically verified?
6. What common ground do primordialist and constructivist theories of identity share? What roles do primordialist conceptions of ethnicity play in constructivist theories?

REVISION QUIZ

1. When social scientists refer to identity, they mean:

    a. An ordering principle an individual uses to make sense of the world
    b. A fluid and amorphous discourse which defines an individual
    c. A social category defined by membership requirements and physical characteristics
    d. A political ideology

2. During the Cold War, scholars of international relations:

    a. Studied issues of identity in great detail
    b. Were not concerned with the political ramifications of identity politics

   c. Were concerned with explaining the rise of transnational terrorism

   d. Were primarily interested in explaining variation in the severity of civil wars

3. Francis Fukuyama's concept of History is best understood as:

   a. A single evolutionary process

   b. The occurrence of random and haphazard events

   c. The study of past events

   d. The superpower rivalry between the United States and the Soviet Union

4. Huntington predicted that the major outbreaks of violence would occur between:

   a. States

   b. Civilizations

   c. Religious groups

   d. The United States and the Soviet Union

5. Primordialists consider ethnic identity to be:

   a. Socially constructed

   b. Fluid and changing

   c. Devoid of meaning

   d. Derived from biology and history

6. Constructivists emphasize two features of ethnic identity. They are:

   a. Nominal and activated

   b. Activated and purposive

   c. Nominal and primordial

   d. Constructed and primordial

7. Ethnic identity is determined by:

   a. A familial resemblance

   b. Ancestral descent

   c. Religion

   d. Both 'a' and 'c'

8. Constructivism and Primordialism:

   a. Are two completely contrasting theories of identity with nothing in common

   b. Are rooted in biological theories of ethnicity

   c. Two poles along a latent dimension in which identity is hard and fixed at one hand, and soft and fungible at the other

   d. Are different ways of expressing membership in an ethnic group

9. An individual's nominal ethnic identity is defined as:

   a. Any characteristic which is typical of the group and required for membership
   b. Any characteristic which an individual feels is especially salient
   c. Skin colour
   d. Any politicized aspect of a person's identity

10. Despite its lack of favour within the scholarly community, Primordialism is still utilized in studies of identity and international relations because:

   a. Ethnic differences actually do derive only from biology
   b. It emphasizes the fluid nature of ethnic identification
   c. It helps set boundaries between ethnic groups, making scientific study of ethnicity and identity possible
   d. It explains why ethnic groups engage in conflict

Answers: 1: c; 2: b; 3: a; 4: b; 5: d; 6: a; 7: d; 8: c; 9: a; 10: c.

BIBLIOGRAPHY

Berman, E., Shapiro, J and Felter, J. (2011) 'Can Hearts and Minds be Bought?: The Economics of Counterinsurgency in Iraq', *Journal of Political Economy* 119(4), 795.

Bringa, T. (1995) *Being Muslim the Bosnian Way: Identity and Community in a Central Bosnian Village* (Princeton, NJ: Princeton University Press).

Brown, G. and Langer, K. (2010) 'Conceptualizing and Measuring Ethnicity', JICA-RI Working Paper No. 9.

Bunce, V. (1999) *Subversive Institutions: The Design and Destruction of Socialism and the State* (New York: Cambridge University Press).

Brubaker, R. and Cooper, F. (2000) 'Beyond "Identity"', *Theory and Society* 29, 1–47.

Cederman, L.E., Min, B. and Wimmer, A. (2010) 'Why do Ethnic Groups Rebel?: New Data and Analysis', *World Politics* 62(1), 87–119.

Cedeman, L.E., Girardin, L. and Gleditsch, K.S. (2009) 'Ethnonationalist Triads: Assessing the Influence of Kin Groups on Civil Wars', *World Politics* 61(3), 403–37.

Cederman, L.E., Weidmann, B. and Gleditsch, K.S. (2010) 'Horizontal Inequalities and Ethno-Nationalist Civil War: A Global Comparison'. Paper prepared for the annual meeting of the American Political Science Association, 20–25 September 2010.

Chandra, K. (2001) 'Cumulative Findings in the Study of Ethnic Politics', *APSA-CP* (Winter) 12, 7–11.

Chandra, K. (2006) 'What is Ethnic Identity and Does it Matter?' *Annual Review of Political Science* 9, 397–424.

Chandra, K. (2012) *Constructivist Theories of Ethnic Politics* (Oxford: Oxford University Press).

des Forges, A. (1999). 'Leave No One to Tell the Story. Genocide in Rwanda'. Human Rights Watch, Available at: <http://www.hrw.org/legacy/reports/1999/rwanda/>.

Eifert, B., Miguel, E. and Posner, D. (2010) 'Political Competition and Ethnic Identification in Africa', *American Journal of Political Science* 54(2), 494–510.

Fearon, J. (1994) 'Ethnic War as a Commitment Problem'. Unpublished Manuscript.

Fearon, J. (2006) 'Ethnic Mobilization and Ethnic Violence'. In B. Winegast and D. Wittman D. (eds), *The Oxford Handbook of Political Economy* (New York: Oxford University Press).

Fearon, J. and Laitin, D. (2000) 'Violence and the Social Construction of Ethnic Identity', *International Organization* 54(4), 845–77.

Fukuyama, F. (1992) *The End of History and the Last Man* (New York: Free Press).

Geertz, C. (1973) *The Interpretation of Cultures* (New York: Basic Books).

Giuilano, E. (2010) *Constructing Grievance: Ethnic Nationalism in Russia's Republics* (Ithaca, NT: Cornell University Press).

Guss, J. and Siroky, D. (2012) 'Living with Heterogeneity: Bridging the Ethnic Divide in Bosnia', *Comparative Sociology* 11, 304–24.

Hale, H. (2008) *Foundations of Ethnic Politics: Separatism of States and Nations in Eurasia and the World* (Cambridge: Cambridge University Press).

Horowitz, D. (1985) *Ethnic Groups in Conflict* (Berkeley, CA and London: University of California Press).

Horowitz, D. (1998) 'Structure and Strategy in Ethnic Conflict'. Paper presented for the Annual World Bank Conference on Development Economics, Washington, DC, 20–21 April 1998.

Huntington, S. (Summer 1993) 'The Clash of Civilizations?' *Foreign Affairs* 72(3), 22–49.

Kuran, T. (1991) 'Now Out of Never: The Element of Surprise in the East European Revolution of 1989', *World Politics* 44(1), 7–48.

Mearsheimer, J. (1990) 'Back to the Future: Instability in Europe after the Cold War', *International Security* 15(1), 5–56.

Mearsheimer, J. (2011). 'Kissing Cousins: Nationalism and Realism'. In Progress.

Snyder, J. (ed.) (2011) *Religion and International Relations Theory* (New York: Columbia University Press).

Mearshimer, J. and Van Evera, S. (1999) 'Redraw the Map, Stop the Killing', *New York Times*, 19 April.

Posner, D.N. (2002) 'The Colonial Origins of Ethnic Cleavages', *Comparative Politics* 35(2), 127–46.

Posner, D. (2007) 'Regime Change and Ethnic Cleavages in Africa', *Comparative Political Studies* 40(11), 1302–27.

Posner, D. (2004) 'The Political Salience of Cultural Difference: Why Chewas and Tumbukas Are Allies in Zambia and Advesaries in Malawi', *The American Political Science Review* 98(4), 529–45.

Petersen, R. (2002) *Understanding Ethnic Violence: Fear, Hatred, and Resentment in Twentieth-Century Eastern Europe* (Cambridge: Cambridge University Press).

Posen, B. (1993) 'The Security Dilemma and Ethnic Conflict', *Survival* 35(1), 27–47.

Toal, G. and Dahlman, C. (2011) *Bosnia Remade: Ethnic Cleanings and its Reversal* (Oxford: Oxford University Press).

Toft, M. (2010) *The Geography of Ethnic Violence: Identity, Interests, and the Indivisibility of Territory* (Princeton, NJ: Princeton University Press).

Toft, M.D., Philpott D. and Shah, T.S. (2011) *God's Century: Resurgent Religion and Global Politics* (New York: W.W. Norton).

van den Berghe, P. (1978) 'Race and Ethnicity: A Sociological Perspective', *Ethnic and Racial Studies* 1(4), 401–11.

Varshney, A. (2000) *Ethnic Conflict and Civic Life: Hindus and Muslims in India* (New Haven, CT: Yale University Press).

Chapter 14
Imposing Internal Order on States

CHRIS WILSON

The principle of non-interference in the sovereign affairs of other states has long been the foundation of order in the international system. The rule protects small states from the predations of the strong and precludes military adventurism except in self-defence. Yet in reality, intervention has a long history in international politics. States have frequently intervened in the domestic affairs of other states. Often this is to protect their political or economic interests. On other occasions, states have been motivated by a desire to protect vulnerable populations from mass killings by their governments or in the context of a failed state. In some cases, threats to regional security or to human rights have motivated some states to effect regime change through invasion or other military means.

This chapter examines the practice of military intervention in sovereign states. Concepts covered in the chapter include humanitarian intervention, the Responsibility to Protect (R2P) and forced Regime Change. While humanitarian intervention was based on the principle that the international community had a right to intervene in cases of serious crimes against humanity, R2P rested more on the notion that it had an obligation to do so. Regime Change involves the forceful removal of a government from power for humanitarian or strategic reasons.

The chapter discusses when and why states might seek to militarily intervene in other nations and the legal, moral and practical obstacles to such action. It considers the relative strength of humanitarian versus strategic motivations and asks when the international community will act to halt mass killings, crimes against humanity and genocide. It finds that a complex combination of altruism, interest and a favourable regional environment is necessary for intervention on humanitarian grounds. Despite claims of an emerging norm of R2P, intervention for strategic rather than humanitarian purposes remains the most common practice in international politics.

Key Words: State Sovereignty, Humanitarian Intervention, Responsibility to Protect, Regime Change, Rogue States.

Chapter 14

Imposing Internal Order on States

CHRIS WILSON

INTRODUCTION

State sovereignty is not what it was. Whereas once the principle of non-interference in the domestic affairs of nation-states was near sacrosanct (if not always recognized in practice), today the legitimacy of state authority is seen as 'contingent' upon developments within the country. Calls for intervention in the domestic affairs of states have become increasingly common since the end of the Cold War. Interventions range from the direct use of military force to peaceful measures to alter the domestic arrangements of states. This chapter will focus on military intervention, particularly on those with the goal of bringing to a halt severe humanitarian crises or human rights abuses or to oust an existing regime.

Within the notion of contingent sovereignty there remains debate over what sovereignty should be contingent *upon*. Throughout the first post-Cold War decade, extreme violation of human rights was seen as a legitimate reason for the violation of the principle of non-interference. If a state government proved unable to protect its population against extreme human rights violations, or was committing them itself, the international community claimed it had a right to intervene. By the end of that decade however, and particularly following the attacks on the United States in September 2001, the main rationale for intervention in other states was the removal of threats to international security seen as developing within a state. An emerging norm of **humanitarian intervention** and a **Responsibility to Protect** animates a great deal of debate in international fora, and has influenced multilateral action such as the recent intervention in Libya. However geostrategic interests, in particular the security concerns of the great powers, continue to determine when and where the international community will impose order on sovereign states.

Debates concerning intervention in the domestic affairs of states often revolve around the actions of the United States. The United States has a history of intervention in other states which few other countries can match, has led most notable international interventions, often faced the largest proportion of the cost and is often seen as the 'world's policeman', the only power capable of acting to halt grievous human rights abuses. There are far fewer restrictions on the use of force by the United States than for other states. Perhaps unfairly, the United States is often criticized for military interventions which many other countries support but do not have the military power to conduct themselves. Accordingly, this chapter will devote considerable attention to the approach of the United States towards intervention.

PRINCIPLES OF STATE SOVEREIGNTY

Since the Peace of Westphalia which ended the Thirty Years' War, the principle of state sovereignty has been considered the bedrock of international society and order. State sovereignty places the state as the ultimate holder of authority over its own affairs. States are recognized as sovereign by their peers (other states) with sole authority to exercise power over their citizens. The principle of non-interference was seen as both a means

> **State Sovereignty** – a single government has independent authority over a geographical territory.

of maintaining international stability in an anarchical international system with no overarching authority and of protecting smaller states from the predations of larger powers. The principle made all states equal, and equally free from foreign interference.

The principles of state sovereignty and non-interference were reaffirmed in the United Nations Charter in 1945: Article 2 (4) states that 'all members shall refrain in their international relations from the threat or use of force against the territorial integrity or political independence of any state'. Chapter VII states two exceptions to this proscription; when force is necessary in self-defence or when such action is authorized by the United Nations Security Council, generally when the target state poses a threat to 'international peace and security'.

Yet the principle of state sovereignty has been far more contested and less an iron-clad principle of international affairs than is sometimes presumed. As with all laws, proscription on the intervention in the domestic affairs of other states has restricted but not totally prevented the behaviour it seeks to control. Indeed, there have been forceful interventions in the domestic affairs of numerous states since the signing of the UN Charter. In many of these cases this military intervention has been in the absence of threats to international security or the necessity of self-defence and has not been authorized by the Security Council. External powers have overthrown ruling regimes, both through direct military action by a foreign power, such as the United States' overthrow of Manuel Noriega in Panama, and more indirect support for domestic coups such as assistance by the United Kingdom and United States in the overthrow of the democratically elected Iranian Prime Minister Mohammed Mossaddegh in 1953. Intervention for primarily humanitarian reasons has also occurred frequently, both with United Nations Security Council authorization and without. The following sections outline the background, motivations and practice of humanitarian intervention and **regime change**. A subsequent section discusses a range of criticisms of these military interventions.

THE NORMS AND PRACTICE OF HUMANITARIAN INTERVENTION AND R2P

The norm of humanitarian intervention is said to have its foundation in Kantian ethics, the notion that all humans are equal and form a community of obligation stretching across state borders. Since the first Geneva Convention in 1864, and particularly since World War II and the Holocaust, legal limits on intervention in the domestic affairs of states have been loosened by a range of other legal instruments which require states to refrain from

> **Humanitarian Intervention** – forceful intervention with the stated goal of halting human rights violations or suffering.

persecuting or killing their own citizens. After the horrors of the Holocaust, the international community stated its determination to prevent such atrocities occurring again. The resulting legal agreements include the Genocide Convention and the Universal Declaration of Human Rights. Despite this legal framework, however, several large genocides and mass killings did take place during the Cold War as great power rivalry and other geopolitical considerations prevented intervention. These included the killing of 500,000 people identified with the Left in Indonesia between 1965 and 1966 and approximately 2 million class enemies of the Khmer Rouge in Cambodia in the 1970s.

Calls for humanitarian intervention became far more common from 1990 with the end of the Cold War. Several international developments coincided to cause this increased number of potential and actual interventions: the end of great power rivalry made the use of force more feasible; policymakers in the West enjoyed a sense of hubris with the defeat of liberal democracy's main ideological rival in the Soviet Union; and there was an increase in intra-state mass killings as the Soviet Union disintegrated. Proponents of humanitarian intervention have commonly called for action in two situations: extensive and systematic human rights abuses by regimes against a section of the population, and during 'state failure' where political order has completely broken down and conflict and lawlessness is leading to turmoil and suffering.

There were several successful interventions with humanitarian goals and impacts in the decade following the end of the Cold War. The Australia-led intervention into East Timor (now Timor Leste) is one such example. After over 20 years of Indonesian occupation, in 1999 the Timorese people voted overwhelmingly for independence, rather than autonomy within the Indonesian state. Immediately, pro-Indonesia Timorese militias, by some accounts organized and directed by the Indonesian military, began a rampage of killings and destruction. After pressure from the President of the United States and Australia, and reliant on foreign assistance during the height of the Asian Financial Crisis, the Indonesian government agreed to an international intervention (INTERFET – International Force for East Timor) authorized by UN Security Council Resolution 1296/1999. This intervention successfully halted the violence and allowed the transition to UNTAET (United Nations Transitional Administration in East Timor).

Yet, in general, the determination and momentum to stop humanitarian abuses which appeared to be building following the end of the Cold War quickly began to dissipate and several extensive killings were allowed to continue unchecked. In Rwanda, over 500,000 Tutsis and moderate Hutus were killed in 1994 by Hutu extremists connected to the ruling regime. In Bosnia over 100,000 are thought to have been killed between 1992 and 1995 and thousands more were killed in nearby Kosovo in 1999. Single incidents of mass killings were not prevented despite widespread knowledge of their impending occurrence such as the massacre of 8,000 Bosnian Muslims at Srebrenica. When perpetrators were halted it was often local opponents which did so, such as the Tutsi RPF ending the Rwandan Genocide for example.

Recognizing the ongoing failure to effectively halt and prevent mass killings, the United Nations Secretary General, Kofi Annan, stated that the international community needed to find a way to overcome the contradiction between state sovereignty and restrictions on the use of force and the obligation to protect human rights. In turn, the Canadian government formed the International Commission on Intervention and State Sovereignty (ICISS). The result was the ICISS Report which laid out several principles for a more effective response to humanitarian crises, principles now known as the 'Responsibility to Protect' or R2P.

R2P lays out a three step series of obligations. First, each state has the responsibility to protect its own citizens from four forms of mass killings: genocide; war crimes; ethnic cleansing; and crimes against humanity. Second, the international community has a responsibility to help states protect their own citizens from these crimes. Thirdly, the international community has a responsibility to take action when the state has failed to do so. Non-violent measures such as economic sanctions on a regime should be attempted first with military intervention to only be used as a last resort. The report prescribed that interventions must be authorized by the Security Council but asked permanent members not to use their veto powers when their vital interests are not at stake and when the majority of the council supports intervention. Interventions must have the 'right intention' to halt suffering, be proportional and have reasonable prospects of success.

> **Responsibility to Protect** – states and the international community have an obligation to prevent and halt mass atrocities.

R2P faced criticism and opposition, particularly from many in the developing world who claimed that the norm was another means of powerful states imposing their will on the less powerful. In effect, however, the ICISS principle of R2P was far from radical. The Professor of Political Science, Thomas Weiss, argued that by requiring large-scale killing or ethnic cleansing for an intervention to occur, R2P actually set a higher threshold than that already used by the Security Council. Attempted restrictions on the use of the Security Council veto had also been rejected as was a statement regarding an 'obligation to rebuild' (Bellamy 2010, 9). Alex Bellamy argues that the conservative nature of R2P vis-à-vis existing practise was due to the need to achieve consensus within the United Nations.

Despite the objections to R2P, 150 states accepted the principle at the United Nations World Summit in 2005. But the language of the statement suggested its future application was unlikely to proceed without considerable debate: 'we are prepared to take collective action, in a timely and decisive manner, through the Security Council, in accordance with the Charter, including Chapter VII, on a case-by case basis and in cooperation with relevant regional organizations as appropriate, should peaceful means be inadequate ...'.

After vociferous debate the Security Council went on to adopt Resolution 1674 reaffirming the General Assembly's support for R2P. The Secretary General subsequently released a report entitled *Implementing the Responsibility to Protect*, which listed three pillars which aligned to the three phases of responsibility on the ICISS Report. Pillar Three, 'the international community's responsibility to take timely and decisive action', reiterated that all peaceful means be exhausted and, if these fail, to use more forceful means in accordance with the United Nations Charter.

This report was also criticized, primarily for its focus on prevention. Critics claimed that preventative measures were already part of the normal approach to dealing with human rights abuses and so the report altered little. In addition, it is difficult enough to mobilize states to respond when mass killings are already occurring, so the critics opined, asking them to act before such events is almost impossible. Critics have also pointed out that the report does not specify the threshold of intervention. What level of atrocities triggers the responsibility to intervene? The report refers to 'large-scale loss of life' and ethnic cleansing without quantifying 'large-scale'. It also does not specify when responsibility passes from the state to the international community, a crucial issue in any potential implementation of R2P.

R2P was first successfully applied by the international community during the post-election violence in Kenya in 2007 and 2008. As the violence erupted, the UN Secretary General Ban Ki

Moon referred to R2P and reminded the Kenyan leaders of their responsibilities. Former United Nations Secretary general Kofi Annan led a diplomatic mission to persuade the two presidential candidates Odinga and Kibaki to share power and urge their followers to halt the violence. The fact that the crisis was stopped through peaceful means, that is, diplomatic intervention by the international community, is seen as a major success of R2P, although it is unclear whether any international intervention would have been forthcoming had these diplomatic measures not been successful.

However, some observers have questioned why an intervention often seen as representing the successful implementation of R2P involved neither ethnic cleansing nor genocide while other cases which have exhibited much higher levels of mass killings have not seen intervention (Bellamy 2010, 55). The issue of selectivity in military intervention is discussed below. Given the many cases of regime violence which have not faced calls for the application of R2P, the Kenyan case suggests that the principles may be most appropriate to bringing an end to horizontal, communal violence.

INTERVENTIONS FOR REGIME CHANGE

While norms of humanitarian intervention and R2P have struggled to determine state action since their inception, the United States and several other states have been increasingly motivated by a desire to intervene in states so as to eradicate what they see as brewing threats to their own security or interests. Often the goal of such interventions is nothing less than the overthrow of the governing regime and its replacement with another which, it is hoped, will be less recalcitrant, a strategy now commonly known as Regime Change. Regime Change has most commonly been pursued in three contexts: firstly, in cases where a regime is committing grave humanitarian abuses against its people; secondly, when the regime is considered to pose a security risk to the region or internationally; and thirdly, when a regime is considered to threaten the economic interests of powerful states.

> **Regime Change** – the forced replacement of one government by another.

While policies associated with the goal of Regime Change gained increased attention and notoriety during the George W. Bush presidency following the tragic events of September 11 2001, in fact they have a long history in international politics. In 1953 the United States and United Kingdom assisted groups within Iran to bring down the Mossadegh Government and install Shah Reza Pallavi in power. In 1965 and 1966 the United States, United Kingdom and Australia provided some support to the Western-oriented General Suharto as he overthrew the left-leaning President Sukarno and eradicated the Indonesian Left, with perhaps 500,000 people killed. However, like the question of humanitarian intervention, the concept and practice of regime change has assumed increased prominence since the end of the Cold War.

Regime change has often, at least in rhetoric, been linked to the goal of democracy promotion, a goal that gained added impetus with the dissolution of the Soviet Union, the main competitor to liberal democracy. Supporters of the overthrow of Saddam Hussein in Iraq hoped that regime change would flow on to many other despotic regimes in the Middle East. Spreading democracy was seen as more than just a moral goal however. In the post-Cold War world, democracy became seen as a crucial link between domestic and international order. The theory of the Democratic Peace argued that democracies rarely fought wars with each other because of the influence of popular opinion, economic integration and their support for multilateral processes (see Russett 1994).

Regime Change surged to the forefront of US foreign policy following the terrorist attacks on New York and Washington DC in September 2001.

The Bush administration stated that it would no longer 'stand idly by' while **rogue states** gathered the means to attack the United States and its allies. The United States would take pre-emptive action to remove these threats, replacing recalcitrant regimes with others more willing to follow the rules of international society. Central to this rationale were concerns over nuclear weapons, whether used by regimes themselves to attack US interests and allies or through falling into the hands of terrorists through proliferation or state weakness.

> **Rogue States** – governments seen as violating international law or posing a threat to international security.

President Bush stated in his State of the Union address in early 2002: 'We must prevent the terrorists and regimes who seek chemical, biological, or nuclear weapons from threatening the United States and the world … I will not wait on events while dangers gather'. The focus on nuclear threat was emphasized through the president's naming of an 'Axis of Evil' of Iraq, Iran and North Korea, all of which the administration claimed already possessed nuclear weapons capability or were seeking to develop one. Regimes also became a target if they were seen as providing a sanctuary to terrorists.

There are several main methods of achieving regime change through the use of force. Most visible is the direct military targeting of a regime to force its collapse, either through invasion or air strikes. The ousting of the Saddam Hussein regime in Iraq in 2003 and the Taliban in Afghanistan in 2001 were the most contentious and dramatic cases of such an approach of forceful regime change. While both military operations sought the overthrow of the ruling regimes in each country, only that against Afghanistan enjoyed broad international support and authorization by the United Nations Security Council. More recently, several states including the United States and United Kingdom, with broad international support, used air strikes to facilitate the overthrow of Libyan leader Muammar Gaddafi, as discussed further below.

Another avenue for effecting regime change is providing support to either dissidents or to rebels in civil wars. In some cases, different foreign actors provide support to opposing sides, making the conflict more deadly and resistant to resolution. As discussed further below, a number of states currently provide military and non-military support to the Syrian opposition as it wages a civil war against the regime of President Bashar al-Assad. The Obama administration has stated that it is providing $25 million of non-lethal assistance to the rebels. At the same time, Iran is currently providing support to the Assad regime with which it has close political and cultural ties. Similarly, some observers of the 2004 overthrow of Jean Bertrand Aristide in Haiti claim the coup was supported, perhaps triggered by the United States and France.

In other cases, foreign powers have assisted states to overthrow the regime in a neighbouring country. Washington provided training and support to the Ethiopian regime, despite its growingly repressive character, prior to and during its 2006 invasion of Somalia (*USA Today*, 1/8/2007). The United States sought the removal of the Islamic Courts Union in Somalia, a coalition of militias which had recently assumed power and which the US suspected of forming links with al-Qaeda. The United States remains involved in the fight against Islamist factions within

Somalia, particularly Al-Shabab, providing military aid and training to troops from neighbouring states. This involvement is in stark contrast to the lack of intervention to halt the killing of an estimated 15,000 civilians in Somalia since the invasion, caused in part by Ethiopia's invasion and attempted regime change.

OPPOSITION TO INTERNATIONAL INTERVENTION

International intervention remains one of the most contentious issues in world politics. State and non-state actors have opposed military intervention for both humanitarian or strategic purposes. Most important in this regard has been the opposition presented by permanent United Nations Security Council members Russia and China but forceful intervention has polarized the community of states. Many states, often those with a history of colonial occupation, strongly resist international interference in their domestic affairs (Evans 2008, 285). The interventions in Kosovo, Afghanistan, Iraq and Libya have all faced opposition to varying degrees. In the following discussion, criticisms of international intervention are divided into four interrelated categories: the *moral issues* involved; the *selectivity* of intervention; the likely *efficacy* of interventions; and the *political will* necessary for intervention.

Moral Issues

In addition to the legal transgressions associated with violating the principle of state sovereignty, there are a number of criticisms of humanitarian intervention based on moral concerns. Differing opinions on humanitarian interventions are often formed along the cleavage between Western and Non-Western states. Many in the West continue to see intervention as inherently altruistic, while many in the Global South see claims of a right to intervene as a means of maintaining Western dominance. Critics of humanitarian intervention have pointed out an inherent injustice in that those states which seek to intervene are also those which determine what forms of human rights abuses require intervention (Ayoob 2002, 81). The R2P process, and the requirement of United Nations Security Council authorization, may be as far as the international community can go in reducing these concerns.

An important criticism of humanitarian intervention revolves around the irony of using violent force to save lives. Similarly, the use of military force, strategies of 'Shock and Awe' for example, to bring democracy and freedom has been highly contentious. The air strikes and other military operations involved in interventions often lead to civilian casualties. The arming or aiding of militias opposing a regime and its forces, such as the Rwandan Patriotic Front or the Kosovo Liberation Army, is also morally ambiguous, as many are themselves involved in atrocities against civilians (Valentino 2011, 63). Many third-party interventions into conflicts between regimes and minorities only serve to worsen the violence.

A related argument against humanitarian intervention is known as moral hazard. Having seen intervention to halt human rights abuse elsewhere, minorities may rise up and provoke a violent response from the regime so as to stimulate international sympathy and rescue (Kuperman 2005). For example, some observers claimed the Kosovo Liberation Army deliberately provoked violence from the Serbian authorities so as to trigger intervention. If the hoped-for intervention is later than expected, or fails to arrive, the cost to the insurgents and their community can be severe (Valentino 2011, 65).

As with opposition to humanitarian intervention, a leading criticism of attempts at regime change is that it undermines the principles of state sovereignty and freedom from interference in internal affairs by foreign actors. As such, opponents fear it will undermine the main legal avenue for maintaining international order and avoiding war and believe it must only be used in cases of self-defence as specified in Article 51 of the United Nations Charter. While attack from another state clearly meets this requirement, some jurists and governments have argued that self-defence also applies to an 'imminent threat'. Therefore, military intervention with the goal of regime change may be considered legal if that regime poses an immediate threat to the state carrying out the pre-emption.

This claim was central to the justifications offered by the Bush administration for the invasion of Iraq. Firstly, officials argued, how do we know if a threat is imminent? Contemporary security threats do not come in the form of armies massing on the border but involve plots which are not easily detected. And containment, the chosen strategy during the Cold War, will clearly not work against stateless or transnational militant groups such as al-Qaeda. Given their clandestine nature, mobility or locations within civilian populations, such groups will simply not have the same concerns over retaliation that mutually assured destruction holds for state regimes. Therefore states such as the United States cannot wait for an attack but must act before it is too late. The failure to find weapons of mass destruction in Iraq, or evidence of links with al-Qaeda or any evidence of planning for an attack against the United States or its allies has greatly undermined such claims however.

The issue of unilateralism became highly contentious during the George W. Bush presidency when the US administration demonstrated its willingness to use military force to overthrow regimes which threatened the US and its allies with or without authorization by the United Nations. Disagreement emerged between the United States and many of its normal allies in Europe, most of which preferred a multilateral approach to problems such as Iraq. Many were concerned that unilateral action without authorization by the Security Council would not only destabilize the region but undermine the authority of the United Nations.

Other opponents criticize intervention for humanitarian purposes from a realpolitik perspective. These critics claim that it is both morally unacceptable and foolish for the United States or other intervening power to risk the lives of its own soldiers when its own interests are not at stake in the crisis and may in fact be undermined by any intervention. These concerns are discussed further below.

Selectivity

A frequent criticism of international intervention concerns the issue of selectivity. Intervention is after all discretionary, there is no greater authority forcing those with the power to intervene to halt human rights abuses to do so. Global or regional powers therefore decide when they intervene in individual cases.

Many human rights abusing states are therefore not the subject of intervention. Indeed, the list of countries with conflicts and mass killings by regimes which have not seen intervention is far longer, and the numbers killed in them far larger, than those which have seen intervention (Brown 2003, 32). Many more cases of mass killings of civilians have not triggered calls for an R2P intervention than have seen coordinated international action. The 2008–09 invasion of Gaza by Israel led to approximately 1,200 mostly civilian casualties but saw little international response. As discussed, the death of over 15,000 civilians since the 2006 invasion of Somalia by Ethiopia has not triggered an R2P intervention. The ongoing killings of civilians in Iraq and Afghanistan have also not been discussed in terms of R2P.

Proponents of R2P and intervention offer several responses to this criticism. The first is that it is not possible to save everyone or to right every wrong. This was the position argued by the United Kingdom's Prime Minister Tony Blair in 1999 as part of his justification for NATO intervention in Kosovo. Just as in the domestic affairs of states, there are many more problems than there are solutions. States may act to halt mass killings in one location but not another; it is simply not possible to mobilize the necessary will and resources to intervene in every case. In addition, the process of gathering multilateral participation and agreement, obtaining United Nations Security Council authorization and then organizing the logistics of an intervention, is lengthy and time-consuming. Mass killings do not wait while this process is pursued; some of the worst killings escalate rapidly with many deaths over a brief time period, such as Rwanda's 100 days in which over 500,000 were killed.

These responses have not deterred critics from contending that this selectivity demonstrates that states will only intervene if it is in their vital national interests to do so. They believe that many supposedly humanitarian interventions are instead military adventurism designed to further strategic or economic goals. Humanitarian intervention is merely another tool by which the strong circumvent the barriers of state sovereignty to dominate the weak. One response to this claim is that interventions may still be considered humanitarian so long as the outcome involves the saving of lives. Whether or not this humanitarianism was the primary motive of the intervening states should not stop us celebrating this positive result (Wheeler 1996, 40).

Opponents of regime change claim that this foreign policy goal is also carried out selectively, targeting only those states which threaten American and Western interests while ignoring other states which are undemocratic, human rights abusers or possess or seek nuclear weapons but which are allies of those powers (Pakistan for example) or important economic partners (Saudi Arabia). Forceful democracy promotion also faces criticisms in terms of selectivity. Why, many opponents ask, if democracy promotion is one goal of military intervention in Iraq and elsewhere, do other authoritarian regimes not only escape such pressure but are actively sustained in power through military and other assistance and security guarantees? And who decides which undemocratic regimes most require regime change? Does not the decision to impose democracy on another state without consensus from the community of states through the United Nations create a contradictory and hypocritical situation?

The issue of security threat again inevitably comes to the fore. Military intervention, whether to spread democracy or to protect human rights, is far more likely if the state in question presents a strategic threat to the region or globally. Even more importantly, however, likely targets for intervention and regime change are invariably those which do not possess a powerful ally, particularly a permanent member of the Security Council. As one example, Saudi Arabia faces no such threat despite a terrible human rights record and being the major disseminator of Wahabbist ideology seen as central to a great deal of terrorism.

Efficacy

Another group of arguments in opposition to international intervention revolves around questions of efficacy. How can military interventions be both the policy of last resort but also timely enough to save lives? (Wheeler 1996, 34). As already discussed, mass killings have often caused numerous deaths by the time potential interveners have become aware of the events and agreed on the necessity of action. By the time such action is organized and implemented, it is often already too late. Many opponents are also doubtful that invading states will be willing to provide the necessary resources and 'boots on the ground' to maintain order and prevent conflict after the intervention, and to establish a functioning political system and infrastructure. Critics have also questioned whether regime change will ultimately bring greater freedom. By 2011, Iraq and Afghanistan, the two countries militarily freed from repressive regimes by the United States and its allies, were still listed as 'Not Free' by Freedom House.

Indeed, the use of force almost always leads to unintended consequences. Those advocating the use of military intervention in a country are often not familiar with local social and political dynamics nor the ethnic tensions that may erupt with the introduction of outside force. Any military intervention therefore carries the risk of worsening rather than improving the situation. Using military power against a regime or party to a conflict can escalate the violence, or draw in neighbouring states. NATO's bombing of Serbia is often considered to have stimulated far worse violence and the displacement of many thousands of Albanians by Serb forces. Yet such arguments hold less weight in those cases where mass killings or genocide are already occurring, in such cases the risks of exacerbating the situation appear slight.

Some scholars have taken these doubts over the effectiveness of intervention to its logical conclusion and argued that allowing the belligerents in a civil war or other conflict the opportunity to militarily defeat the other is a more effective means of ensuring sustainable peace. Enforced peace settlements, often by third-party intervention, only serve to give the belligerents time to regroup for a further phase of fighting. As Luttwak puts it, 'the key is that the fighting must continue until a resolution is reached. War brings peace only after passing a culminating phase of violence' (Luttwak 1999, 36). There are several important responses to such a policy, however, including the human rights abuses which often accompany military defeat (such as occurred in Sri Lanka in 2009) and the long-term damage such a victory would do to the legitimacy of the state.

Regime change also faces a great deal of opposition on account of its potential consequences. The overthrow of Saddam Hussein was clearly a worthwhile goal in terms of removing a repressive dictator who posed a threat to regional and other states. Yet those with knowledge of Iraq and the region criticized the impending forceful regime change for the impact it would likely have on domestic and regional stability and the relations between Western and Islamic societies. These criticisms proved accurate, with the onset of terrible sectarian violence between Sunni and Shia and the destabilization of a regional balance of power between Sunni and Shia-dominated states (Litwak 2012, 110–11). Similarly, the recent overthrow of Muammar Gaddafi in Libya is seen as a major cause of the subsequent coup in neighbouring Mali. Tuareg soldiers from the north of Mali who had been fighting for the Libyan president returned home after his downfall and took control of the north of the country, in turn triggering a coup in the capital, Bamako, overthrowing President Amadou Toumani Toure. There are therefore strong arguments that regime change increases rather than decreases regional insecurity.

There is also some concern that forceful attempts at regime change of states with nuclear weapons programs (such as was the stated rationale for the invasion of Iraq) may encourage other states (such as Iran) to expedite their nuclear programs so as to preclude similar military intervention against them (Heisbourg 2000, 15). Military regime change against states without WMD capability may illustrate to some nervous states that it is safer to have that capability.

Will

Given the large number of powerful legal instruments which provide outside powers the right to intervene to halt grievous human rights abuses, most notably the Genocide Convention, the failure to arrest mass killings was never a question of legal constraints but rather a lack of political will. While perhaps concerned about the massive loss of life, states capable of intervening face not only a lack of strategic interest in stability in the country but also the great financial cost of military intervention and the risk of losing the lives of its own troops to protect people in a remote region. Critics decry the opportunity costs of humanitarian interventions – the amount of money spent which could have been used more profitably elsewhere. Valentino states this in blunt terms: 'Washington spent between $280,000 and $700,000 for each Somali it spared (through its intervention)' (Valentino 2011, 67).

Politicians in those countries most willing or able to intervene for humanitarian purposes face domestic political considerations. While a successful humanitarian intervention can win a politician support from his or her constituents, a failed mission can be politically disastrous, making the risk involved often too great. Part of the reason for a lack of United States support for a greater troop commitment to UNAMIR before and after the genocide was the recent deaths of its own troops in the humanitarian mission in Somalia.

Concerns over institutional reputation may also influence a failure to intervene on the part of the United Nations and other international organizations. Barnett makes a strong case that a lack of support for intervention in Rwanda within the United Nations was to some extent motivated by a concern to protect the interests and reputation of the organization (Barnett 2010). A failed intervention so soon after Somalia could have been fatal to the institution's reputation and credibility.

CONCLUSIONS: THE ONGOING STRUGGLE OF HUMANITARIANISM

State sovereignty, now, as in the past, provides little obstacle to the imposition of order by foreign states. Different actors, both state and non-state, still appeal to humanitarian and strategic concerns to advocate for intervention into the domestic affairs of states. But despite a golden era of humanitarianism in the 1990s and the 'emerging norm' of R2P, the most common motivation for intervening powers remains their own strategic and material interests. Norms of humanitarian intervention continue to struggle for influence over state behaviour. If R2P was emerging from its inception with the ICISS Report, the terrorist attacks on New York and Washington DC of September 2001 quickly returned it to a subordinate position behind security and other concerns. While a desire to protect human life and end repression and tyranny most certainly play a role in motivating governments and the officials within them to undertake military operations, such concerns remain neither sufficient nor even necessary considerations for intervention. The great many other cases of mass killing in which intervention does not occur, the Sudan, Rwanda, Syria and Gaza for example, demonstrate that a concern to halt serious human suffering does not alone automatically trigger intervention.

A combination of altruism, interest and a conducive regional or international system are necessary to motivate states to lead or join military action. Norms, interests and structure therefore interact to influence the occurrence of intervention. The rareness of all three being conducive to intervention simultaneously explains the relative lack of international action compared to cases of mass atrocity and killing occurring across the globe.

Intervention to halt abusive regimes is far more likely if it involves a strategic or economic interest for the intervener(s). These interests may be caused by the human rights abuse itself, such as concerns over refugee flows or regional instability, or can be pre-existing and pre-date the violence, such as gaining or maintaining access to natural resources. Secondly, the regional and international situation influences the decision-making process of potential interveners. Two main structural conditions appear important in this regard – the degree of diplomatic isolation and military strength of the target state. The lack of a friend in high places, most notably an ally on the United Nations Security Council, appears to make states more vulnerable to outside intervention. And secondly, those states with substantial military capability are clearly far less likely to be the target of military intervention than those with small, or decaying and disorganized militaries. Two recent cases of intervention and non-intervention, Libya and Syria, illustrate this combination of and interplay between norms, interests and structure. The two cases are discussed in the boxes below.

The proscription on intervention in the domestic affairs of states has always been a principle rather than an inviolable law of international affairs. Interventions in the domestic affairs of states have occurred frequently since the principle was enshrined in the United Nations Charter. These interventions have more frequently been motivated by strategic, energy and other interests rather than pure humanitarianism. Humanitarian concerns continue to drive a great deal of debate in the United Nations and other international and national fora and the recent development of the Responsibility to Protect doctrine has given new life to this debate. Despite some practical and conceptual weaknesses involved in the R2P doctrine, the concept is a necessary step towards gaining agreement on the use of force to halt violence against innocent civilians. Yet when and where the international community will intervene remains determined above all by geopolitical considerations as shown by the contemporary cases of Libya and Syria. The fact that powerful states almost always need a strategic or other interest to intervene militarily in another state should not detract from the often humanitarian effect of these interventions. Yet the geopolitical obstacles to humanitarian intervention mean that the majority of violent regimes creating humanitarian crises are likely to face little intervention.

Libya

When protests and calls for democracy began in Libya in January and February 2011, just as they did in Egypt, Tunisia and elsewhere, the regime of Muammar Gadhafi used substantial military force to suppress the rebellion. Gadhafi's history of terrorism abroad, weapons proliferation and nationalization of oil production had long given the United States and other states an interest in ousting him and his regime. Yet his decision to disarm, taken in the wake of the 2003 invasion of Iraq, had greatly thawed relations between he and the United States and United Kingdom. With his attacks against protesters and civilians, however, the United States and other powers abandoned these closer relations. Popular opinion also supported action to stop the violence, with polls suggesting that the American public supported air strikes against Libyan forces. Subsequent airstrikes carried out by NATO along with other assistance to rebels in Libya has been seen as the most prominent case of R2P principles in action.

During deliberations over action against the Gadhafi regime, the Security Council avoided any mention of regime change, focusing instead on protecting civilians. Russia and China both abstained from the vote on a no-fly zone and air strikes, as did non-permanent sitting members Brazil, Germany and India. The United Nations Security Council authorized a no-fly zone over Libya and for member states to take measures to protect civilians. With Resolution 1973, the Responsibility to Protect doctrine had come into effect. This was the first time the United Nations Security Council had authorized the use of force against a sovereign government on the basis of R2P. Soon after, the United States, United Kingdom and France began to carry out strikes against the regime's military forces and the Libyan insurgents overran Tripoli. One of the doctrine's architects, the former Australian Foreign Minister, Gareth Evans, called the intervention 'a textbook case of the R2P norm acting exactly as it was supposed to'. The Libyan intervention also demonstrated that the Obama administration had returned the United States to a multilateral approach to dealing with human rights abusers and problematic states, abandoning the George W. Bush administration's unilateralism.

While the Libyan intervention can rightly be seen as a successful case of the international community acting to halt human rights abuse, the case was rather unique. Gadhafi lacked what many other dictators possess, a powerful state friend willing to oppose intervention both in international fora and through providing security guarantees. Indeed, Gadhafi was considered an enemy by many in the region and globally. In an unprecedented step, the Arab League voted to support the use of force to protect civilians in Libya. With this, the Obama administration began to support and advocate military intervention in cooperation with other governments.

Syria

The far worse civil war in Syria, which began shortly after the intervention in Libya, has provided a far harder case for proponents of international intervention. With perhaps 120,000 lives lost and one million refugees to have fled the country at the time of writing this chapter, Syria is among the worst humanitarian catastrophes to occur in the twenty-first century. Yet, unlike the case of Libya, little has been done to halt the violence. This is primarily due to the nature of the international relationships involved. Syria is itself militarily strong but more importantly possesses both strong allies on the Security Council and powerful regional allies willing to engage militarily to support the regime. Russia and China have taken a united position preventing the foreign ousting of the Assad regime and vetoing three United Nations Security Council Resolutions imposing sanctions on the regime. While Russia has long had close relations with the ruling Assad family, analysts state that the administration is also concerned over the emergence of an Islamist regime in Syria if the opposition was to gain power and with the potential for instability in the Middle East.

The United States and NATO have some strategic interest in intervening in the conflict and in the fall of Assad. Most notably, many Western states would welcome the removal of the sanctuary given to the regional terrorist organization Hezbollah. But these concerns are not sufficient to overcome the *realpolitik* constraining all parties involved in the conflict. Other factors appear to be influencing the lack of momentum for international action. The United States is also concerned about the ascension of an Islamist regime with links to organizations such as Hezbollah or Al Qaeda. The presence of chemical weapons in Syria increases these concerns, as this capability would be transferred to the incoming regime.

Although direct military action has not been forthcoming because of the diplomatic impasse in the United Nations Security Council, regional and international states have provided aid and support to both sides in the conflict. In December 2012 the United States recognized the Syrian rebels as a formal opposition to the regime and began to increase training and other non-military assistance to the coalition. Analysts claim this was in response to the growing influence of Al Qaeda-linked organizations within the opposition coalition. At the same time as providing assistance to non-Islamist groups, the US administration listed one militia involved in the coalition on its list of terrorist organizations, further supporting this analysis. In addition, there is evidence that Sunni states in the Middle East have been supplying the rebels with weapons. Similarly, the regime itself is also receiving military and non-military aid. Syria's neighbour and ally, Iran, with both close diplomatic, strategic and ethno-religious ties to the Syrian regime, has provided military support to the regime. As such, the volatile regional environment and existence of powerful friends to the Assad regime have thus far precluded any meaningful armed intervention despite the devastating humanitarian toll of the conflict.

QUESTIONS FOR REFLECTION

1. What are the three stages of responsibility in R2P?
2. Is humanitarian intervention now more likely since the emergence of the norm of a Responsibility to Protect?
3. Under what conditions is regime change through military means justified?
4. Why did the international community intervene in Libya but has thus far failed to do so in Syria despite a far greater humanitarian crisis in the latter case?
5. What are the main arguments against military intervention in the domestic affairs of states?

REVISION QUIZ

1. The principle of state sovereignty is most associated with which Treaties?

    a. West Sussex
    b. East Lothian
    c. Brussels
    d. Westphalia

2. Which chapter of the UN Charter proscribes states from using or threatening force against another except in self-defence or to prevent a threat to international security?

    a. Chapter V
    b. Chapter VII
    c. Chapter II
    d. Chapter III

3. R2P stands for which phrase?

    a. Responsibility to Provide
    b. Right to Protect
    c. Responsibility to Protect
    d. Requirement to Partition

4. Which intervention is considered the main success stories of R2P?

    a. Syria
    b. Rwanda
    c. Libya
    d. Kosovo

5. When did the United Nations World Summit accept the principles of R2P?

    a. 1996
    b. 2001
    c. 2003
    d. 2005

6. What year was the intervention in East Timor?

    a. 1999
    b. 1996
    c. 2001
    d. 2000

7. Sanctions against the Assad regime in Syria were vetoed by which P5 members of the UN Security Council?

    a. US and UK
    b. France and Russia
    c. Russia and China
    d. US and China

8. Which theory states that democracies do not fight wars against each other?

    a. Democratic Prevention
    b. Democratic Peace
    c. R2P
    d. The People's Peace

9. Which concept states that a likelihood of intervention may actually cause crises by encouraging minorities to rebel against the government?

    a. Information Asymmetries
    b. Moral Hazard
    c. Domino Theory
    d. Dukes of Hazzard

10. Which country invaded Somalia in 2006?

    a. France
    b. Mali
    c. United States
    d. Ethiopia

Answers: 1: d; 2: b; 3: c; 4: c; 5: d; 6: a; 7: c; 8: b; 9: b; 10: d.

BIBLIOGRAPHY

Ayoob, M. (2002) 'Humanitarian Intervention and State Sovereignty', *The International Journal of Human Rights* 6, 1, 81–102.

Barnett, M.N. (2010) *The International Humanitarian Order* (London and New York: Routledge).

Bellamy, A.J. (2010) *Global Politics and the Responsibility to Protect: From Words to Deeds* (London and New York: Routledge).

Brown, C. (2203) 'Selective humanitarianism: in defense of inconsistency'. In D.K. Chatterjee and D.E. Scheid (eds), *Ethics and Foreign Intervention* (Cambridge: Cambridge University Press).

Evans, G. (2008) 'The Responsibility to Protect: An Idea Whose Time Has Come … and Gone?', *International Relations* 22.

Fukuyama, F. and McFaul, M. (Winter 2007–08) 'Should Democracy Be Promoted or Demoted?', *Washington Quarterly* 31(1), 23–35.

Heisbourg, F. (2000) 'Europe's Strategic Ambitions: The Limits of Ambiguity', *Survival* 42(2), 5–15.

Jones, B.D. (2011) 'Libya and the Responsibilities of Power', *Survival: Global Politics and Strategy* 53(3), 51–60.

Kuperman, A.J. (2005) 'Suicidal rebellions and the moral hazard of humanitarian intervention', *Ethnopolitics* 4(2), 149–73.

Litwak, R.S. (2012) *Outlier States: American Strategies to Change, Contain, or Engage Regimes* (Washington DC: Woodrow Wilson Center Press).

Luttwak, E.N. (1999) 'Give war a chance', *Foreign Affairs* 78(4), 36–44.

Russett, B. (1994) *Grasping the Democratic Peace: Principles for a Post-Cold War World* (Princeton, NJ: Princeton University Press).

Valentino, B.A. (November/December 2011) 'The True Costs of Humanitarian Intervention: The Hard Truth About A Noble Notion', *Foreign Affairs* 90(6).

Wheeler, N.J. (1996) 'Making Sense of Humanitarian Outrage', *Irish Studies in International Affairs* 7(1), 31–40.

Chapter 15
Borders, Immigration and State Transformation

ALEX BALCH

The international movement of persons makes visible the contours of the state – and state power – in the context of the international system. This is why questions around migration, borders, refugees and citizenship can be central for the study of international relations. As a subject which is always close to questions of identity and power, migration has the capacity to break open debates over the role of the state, and its future local, regional and global transformations. This chapter will clarify key terms and explore contemporary migration controls as internal security practice by examining some of the key material and ideational impacts of changing patterns of human mobility in the twenty-first century. It is organized into four main sections.

The chapter begins by asking why we as IR scholars should be interested in these topics, and exploring the ways in which migration and citizenship is relevant to studying the changing power of the state in the international system. The second section offers some context by providing a brief history of the development of migration controls, finding that with some exceptions most states only developed migration controls at the beginning of the twentieth century. Historiographical issues and dominant narratives around migration are examined, and these are linked to the development of the discipline of International Relations. The third section then goes on to analyse contemporary international relations in this area through an examination of three case studies.

The first of these, on border controls, explores changing patterns of border governance and how migration is a topic that is often central to critical security studies. The second looks at the refugee system and how it provides some hope of a liberal regime, although the difficulties in protecting human rights for migrants symbolizes the inherent problems of IR. The third case is that of international labour migration where, despite obvious economic benefits for states, there has been little progress in developing international systems of governance. However, there are signs of convergence in the ways in which states deal with economic migration. The final section then moves on to consider the next steps in terms of the future options for border and migration controls, including discussion of global governance, the possibilities for a border-free world and resurgent national sovereignty. It concludes, even in the context of radical transformations of the state – some of them attributable to migration and its effects – resurgent nationalism will always tend to trump regional and international efforts that aim to remove control of borders and migration from the hands of states.

Key Words: Migrant/Migration, Sovereignty, Refugee, Asylum-Seeker, Citizenship, (Non)-Refoulement, UNHCR, IOM, ILO.

Chapter 15

Borders, Immigration and State Transformation

ALEX BALCH

INTRODUCTION

Why, as IR scholars, should we be interested in borders and **migration**? One reason is that the act of crossing borders by groups and individuals brings to light many important human aspects of the subject of IR. Focusing on these issues allows us to think about how states are defined, how they connect with their populations and how the international flow of people is managed. These subjects should not be seen as merely a minor or marginal aspect of IR – they deserve to be fully incorporated as part of the mainstream research agenda – they are central to many questions touching upon both theory and practice. In the conceptual sense they serve to highlight the importance of understanding different levels of analysis (for example, **citizenship**: individual-state-system), the relevance of shared normative principles in the international space (for example, borders: order-**sovereignty**-territoriality) and the difficulties of international cooperation over pressing contemporary political issues (for example, migration: governance-rights-security). Moreover, if states are no longer the only actors in international politics we also need to pay attention to the growing power of other actors – IGOs (intergovernmental organizations) and NGOs (non-governmental organizations) – operating in the field of migration. There may be little in terms of formal international agreements outside regional systems such as the European Union (EU), but the role of the United Nations High Commissioner for Refugees (UNHCR) and others such as the International Organization for Migration (IOM), for example, shows how other actors can assume important functions in the international management of migration.

Migrant/migration – defining a 'migrant' is not as simple as it sounds. Many, but not all, countries accept the United Nations definition of 'long-term international migrant' as 'a person who moves to a country other than that of his or her usual residence for a period of at least a year ... so that the country of destination effectively becomes his or her new country of usual residence'. As John Salt explains: 'The answer to the question "what is migration" is by no means straightforward. International migration is a sub-category of a wider concept of "movement", embracing various types and forms of human mobility (from commuting to emigration) ... What we define as immigration becomes an arbitrary choice and may be time specific. Migration streams are dynamic, involve different types of people and motivations, have different roles and different implications for host societies, and are influenced and managed by different agencies and institutions'. (Salt 2005)

Citizenship – the idea of citizenship can be traced back to classical times, but the contemporary concept is based on enlightenment ideas about the modern state as based on a contract between state and citizen (Joppke 1998). T.H. Marshall (1950) famously demonstrated how citizenship has operated as a unifying and homogenizing force since the eighteenth century, gradually extending to most of the population and including in stages civil, political and finally social rights. For Brubaker (1992), citizenship is 'an international filing system, a mechanism for allocating persons to states'.

Sovereignty – although most people understand sovereignty as the 'power of the state', there are at least three different types (de facto, de jure and coercive), and many different conceptions, for example the Hobbesian view of sovereignty as absolute and indivisible versus Rousseau's idea of sovereignty as the general will of the people. Immigration has been used by many authors as a useful 'lens' with which to consider state sovereignty. According to Agamben (2005), the immigration detention centre is where sovereignty is 'produced' – where the government can decide on the 'state of exception'. For Sassen (1996), immigration is central to the transformation of state sovereignty – 'denationalizing' key economic institutions/spaces and 'renationalizing' politics.

UNHCR – the United Nations High Commissioner for Refugees. This UN agency was set up six months before 1951 Geneva Convention. Initially a temporary structure it has gradually been extended/expanded. Responsibilities include returnees, stateless persons and some internally displaced. In 2013 the UNHCR employed over 6,000 staff.

IOM – the International Organization for Migration functions as a service organization for states in helping facilitate 'orderly flows' and carrying out deportations. In 1998 the IOM had 67 state members but by 2009 this had risen to 127. The organization has over 7,000 staff, and an annual budget of over $1bn. The IOM tends to use language of human rights, but it has no formal mandate to monitor human rights abuses or to protect the rights of migrants and other persons. According to Ashutosh and Mountz (2011, 21) the IOM 'enforces the exclusions of asylum seekers and maintains the central role of nation-states in ordering global flows of migration'.

In terms of the praxis of international relations, the ability to draw or redraw your own, or another state's borders has always been a marker of power in the international system. Likewise, the development of policies over citizenship and migration can provide invaluable information about differences between states, and the way in which they connect to one another. Indeed it is often noted that it is through the attempt to physically move across national boundaries that we render meaningful concepts like sovereignty, citizenship and human rights. More than this, borders often become monuments that serve as powerful reminders of the contemporary reality (and past failures) of International Relations. Nowhere could this be more obvious than at the symbolic barriers to movement erected in Berlin, the West Bank or Tijuana (see pictures). The events of 1989 inspired much optimism about the end of division in Europe, and begged the question of whether we could dare hope of a (some would say utopian) future with fewer borders, where everyone could enjoy freedom of movement – not just those in the rich, privileged states? We are certainly living in an era of unprecedented levels of global mobility.

In quantitative terms the total amount of human movement across borders is enormous and increasing. According to the UNWTO World Tourism Barometer International, tourist arrivals went above one billion for the first time in 2012 (1.035 billion), with more growth coming from emerging economies in Asia and the Pacific. Yet we are also living in a time where individuals who travel across borders are increasingly subject to intrusive checks and searches – of their belongings, their documents and even their bodies. Despite this, international migration remains a growing phenomenon in the twenty-first century. Since 2000 the total number of international migrants has increased every year to reach over 215 million today. However, that amounts to only around 3 per cent of the world's population, meaning that the vast majority of people do not tend to migrate.

Power over who can – and who cannot move in and out of a state is considered one of the basic foundations of sovereignty. The granting of citizenship, visas and work permits represents one of the goods over which every state jealously guards control. Yet this control is by its very nature transactional and reciprocal, a prism through which we observe international relations in action. The sheer complexity of visa arrangements between states and free movement rules within regional entities such as the EU tell us a great deal about the challenges of international cooperation. However, it should not be overlooked that human mobility provides the oil in the wheels of international negotiations. The practice of international relations has always been dependent upon the capacity for states to tolerate certain forms of free movement for privileged groups (for example for diplomats). In short, border and migration controls provide an invaluable lens with which to observe the contours of the state, and the international system in which states are embedded. Or as Aristide Zolberg said, the history of migration controls is about understanding 'the walls that states build, and the doors that they open in them' (Zolberg 1989).

Borders are therefore very important for our understanding of IR. Depending on which side you are on, they can often mean life or death. They are not just the physical expression of state power (Pickering and Weber 2006); they also indicate the depth of political division in the international sphere. As Roger Dion (1947) wrote, in the immediate aftermath of World War II: 'the line separating a democratic country from a totalitarian one can be in 1940 more difficult to cross than a formidable mountain barrier'. There are numerous examples where borders have assumed enormous significance in political terms. In the twentieth century the borders around what became the Warsaw Pact were synonymous with the great ideological division of the Cold War where the world was cleaved in two by an 'iron curtain'. In the nineteenth century the China/Korea border was almost completely sealed by a desert barrier (as described by Freiherr von Richthofen (1984)), but in the twentieth century this division would be overshadowed by another 'border' between the Global North and Global South.

Migratory phenomena do not only have impacts on states – increasing restriction on cross-border movement can also lead to growth in irregular movement and trafficking and smuggling of migrants, which can pose serious threats to human rights (ILO 2010, v). Borders are more than symbolic, they have real and sometimes terrible human consequences, dividing families and causing people to lose their lives in efforts to cross them. The division between Southern Europe and Northern Africa is at certain points just a few miles wide, but increasing numbers are dying trying to cross. In 2011 at least 1,500 people were known to have lost their lives attempting to cross the Mediterranean (Strik 2012). The state response is to fortify and strengthen border defenses: fears of unwanted flows of migrants can function as a powerful rationale for the increase of state power. As Koulish (2012) describes in his entertaining (if disconcerting) description of the use of extra-constitutional 'plenary' powers in the US:

> In a manner similar to superhero cartoons, the government is on a mission to repel or least subdue unwanted evil (foreign) advances across territorial borders, and relies on plenary powers in achieving its ends. A Manichaean narrative of good against evil creates the moral authority for such power. With each storyline, or immigrant flow, a risk is constructed, exacerbated and then overcome.

STATES, BORDERS AND CITIZENS: A BRIEF HISTORY OF MIGRATION AND THE STATE

How can we explain the way in which states organize their border and migration controls, and the reasons why they are more (or less) reluctant to cede control to regional or international systems of governance? The next two sections begin to answer this question by first providing an historical context, and second by analysing actual international relations as they currently exist in this area.

The historical approach provides a good starting point because it helps us to explore how ideas have developed over time around the international movement of persons. By situating our contemporary concerns within a more thorough understanding of the historical trajectory of ideas around movement and migration we can try and avoid the problem of presentism. As Schmidt (2002, 8) points out: 'the problem with presentism is not that historical analysis is utilized to make a point about the present, but that history is distorted as it is reconstructed to legitimate or criticize a position that the writer has set out in advance to support or to undermine'.

When talking with students about the history of migration as a political and policy issue, they often seem amazed by how recently states became concerned about these issues. The assumption made by many is that we must have always been obsessed by the problems of migration. However this political preoccupation is a relatively recent phenomenon, at least for a large part of the world. Whilst it is true that the first laws on migration in the US are now more than 200 years old (late eighteenth-century legislation concerning the incorporation of 'white' newcomers), in Northern and Western Europe most migration rules were not set out until the beginning of the twentieth century. In Southern Europe it was as late as the 1970s and 1980s before any substantive migration laws were written. In many cases this was for the simple reason that these countries did not expect high levels of inward migration. Indeed most European countries were sending, rather than receiving, migrants until the second half of the twentieth century. Generally speaking, it is only when the balance between those leaving, and those arriving, shifts in favour of the latter that states make any real effort to construct systems to control migration.

Migration in the Nineteenth and Twentieth Centuries

The purpose here is not to present a detailed description of patterns and flows of people over time. Rather it is to highlight some of the historiographical issues around thinking on migration. Historians are understandably frustrated by the lack of any long-term perspective when it comes to contemporary discussions of global migration. This, they argue, contributes to an unfortunate tendency for moral panics to frequently reoccur when it comes to these topics (Lucassen, Lucassen and Manning 2010, 4–5). But this is not the only problem when it comes to debates over the topic. There are many examples of where migration has been misrepresented by historians in order to serve other contemporary political demands. An obvious example is the teleological practice of weaving migratory flows into the story of nation building to fit conveniently within a nationalist agenda. Then there is the even broader 'atlanticist' narrative which paints the inaccurate picture of migration as a largely trans-Atlantic story tied to a deterministic vision of globalization as the triumph of 'Western civilization' (McKeown 2004).

This bias of course hides a number of facts about migration that are often ignored, namely that all human population is a result of some kind of migration; that large flows of people occurred long before we began to count international movement of people as 'migration'; and that the supposed 'age of migration' to the Americas in the nineteenth century was matched by similar flows before, during and after in Asia and Africa (McKeown 2004).

It is important to remember that it was during the late nineteenth-/early twentieth-century era that the discipline of IR was born in formal terms. It is instructive to read some of the early academic writing published in this period to see how it was skewed by the thinking of the time. Ideas we would now dismiss as racist flowed freely through the pages of the *Journal of Race Development* (now *Foreign Affairs*) (Blatt 2004). The concerns of many on the Left in the first decades of the twentieth century for the cause of 'dependent' peoples barely concealed virulent white supremacism (Vitalis 2000). In the course of the twentieth century, ideas about migration would be transformed time and again by events: the horrors committed by Hitler's Germany and its allies; the huge numbers of **refugees** created by two world wars; massive waves of postwar migration to Europe fuelled by postwar reconstruction; and resurgent globalization creating demands for all kinds of workers in a new 'global marketplace' for skills.

The influence of fascist regimes and their radical plans in the early part of the twentieth century meant not only the eventual discrediting of eugenicist ideas – they also contributed to what would happen in the second half of the century. This included the creation of the refugee system, based on principles of human rights and **non-refoulement** (see subsequent section on the refugee system). Extended economic growth and changing patterns of migration in the postwar period also meant that a succession of countries, particularly in Europe, shifted from 'sending' to 'receiving' states. These developments, alongside the acceleration of processes of globalization in the later part of the twentieth century meant that migration became a key issue for a larger and larger number of states. For some, migrants 'posed a fundamental challenge to the nation-states of Europe and America. They have compelled these countries to reinterpret their traditions, to reshape their institutions, to rethink the meaning of citizenship – to reinvent themselves, in short, as nation-states' (Brubaker 1992, 215). Indeed, according to James Hollifield, the emergence of an international labour market by the end of the twentieth century helped create what he has described as the rise of the 'the migration state' (2007, 77–82).

States, Borders and Citizens in the Contemporary International System

What do these developments mean for our understandings of IR? What would the established theories of IR expect to see unfolding at the international level? Although this is a relatively under-studied area, some authors have successfully applied IR theories to the politics of international migration (Hollifield 2012; Meyers 2000). The IR theories approach can help understand how states behave in the international system, and explain why they adopt certain approaches towards migration. As we know, realist interpretations see the state as acting selfishly in its own material or ideological interests, while liberal interpretations emphasize the importance of shared values and the mutual gains available to states through international cooperation.

If we apply this to borders and migration, we see a dilemma between the principles of sovereignty and territoriality on the one hand, and the benefits of international regimes and significance of universal values such as human rights on the other. For neo-Marxists the analysis is different, but equally clear: migrants in effect become the global proletariat – an 'industrial reserve army' – or a structural part of economies where the exploitation of labour is necessary for capitalist development (Castles and Kossack 1972).

Analysis of migration policies at the end of the twentieth century generally supported the realist notion of a challenge to the sovereignty of nation-states (Joppke 1998), and the organization and boundaries of their welfare-states (Bommes and Geddes 2000). Since then, however, there have been significant developments at the international level. We now explore these through three cases of international relations in areas relating to the topic of this chapter: border controls, labour migration and the refugee system. Each case will look at evidence of convergence/divergence in state practices or of international cooperation, and how these reflect on realist/liberal understandings of IR.

BORDER CONTROLS

Territorial borders have always been synonymous with security of the state, but the emergence of migration as a security issue has transformed what we mean by borders. It has led to a simultaneous movement of borders inwards – that is, limiting access to rights/benefits to non-citizens – and outwards – that is, stopping potential visitors through visa controls. Needless to say these developments have not escaped the attentions of critical security studies scholars. The securitization of migration as a policy issue was first seriously studied in the 1990s (Weiner 1993; Buzan, Wæver, and de Wilde 1998). Scholars noted how politicians presented migration as an existential threat to society and how this allowed for a stepping up of activities at the border. As Buzan (1993, 45) explains, the presentation of migration as a security problem is based on a specific notion of a (static) identity:

> … the threat of migration is fundamentally a question of how relative numbers interact with the absorptive and adaptive capacities of society … This threat works on the societal level when the incoming population is of a different cultural or ethnic stock from those already resident. It is amplified when migrants seek to maintain their identity rather than adapting to that prevailing in their adopted country.

Critical security scholars argue that when politicians (and academics) raise security fears over migration, the government enjoy *carte blanche* to expand state powers. These can be over physical, external borders, but also through the internal borders of the state, for example with policies over access to citizenship or access to territory – where **asylum** can be claimed. On the other side of the debate, the main challenge to this securitization of borders and migration controls has been through the rhetoric of human rights.

Changing patterns of border governance in the twenty-first century have led to questions over whether we are witnessing a global or regional reordering of borders. For some 'the border is everywhere' (Lyon 2005) and the state has completely colonized and monopolized control over legitimate forms of human mobility (Torpey 1998). Organizations such as the IOM are important here because their growing role demonstrates a shift from an emphasis of unified control over national territory to a networked command over global space (Ashutosh and Mountz 2011).

The implications of the terrorist attacks of 11th September 2001 are of course highly significant. The initial reaction of the US was to turn to border controls – instantly close the borders with Mexico and Canada and focus on greater migration enforcement, despite the fact that most of the hijackers arrived on tourist visas (Alden 2009). We are certainly seeing increasing 'remote-control' by receiving states where the border is extended beyond the physical territorial limits to prevent potential migrants getting on planes in the first place (Guiraudon 2003). It is frequently held that a legacy of the 'war on terror' is the new US 'homeland security' paradigm. This paradigm is characterized by a professionalization and federalization of border security and enforcement, drawing heavily on new technologies and the private sector. Some have raised concerns that this paradigm is spreading to the EU and beyond (Koslowski 2008; Hobbing and Koslowski 2009).

In some ways these developments present a puzzle because they often have little impact on their supposed target, that is, migration flows (Cornelius 2005). Instead they tend to create a series of unintended – and unwanted – consequences (Grewcock 2007). Furthermore, these are interesting cases of expanding state power in an era of cut-backs and deregulation. As Karyotis (2012) shows in Greece, and Alden (2012, 107) demonstrates in the US, commitments to limit or reduce the role of the state can be disregarded when it comes to security and the fight against illegal migration.

There is evidence of a massive expansion of state power and capacity in the area of border governance. In the case of the US this can be observed quite clearly with the amount of resources made available for these activities. Spending on migration enforcement and border control in the US has spiralled – by 2012 it was nearly 15 times higher than it was in 1986. Between these two dates the country spent an (estimated) $186.8 billion but could not stop the population of irregular migrants increasing to an (estimated) 11 million (Meisner et al. 2013).

Perhaps even more important at the regional and global levels has been the trend towards the application of new technologies to border control and migration enforcement (Dijstelbloem and Meijer 2011). Individual states – and regional organizations such as the EU – are building sophisticated systems that range from complex surveillance systems at the border to increasing use of databases to track and record movement.

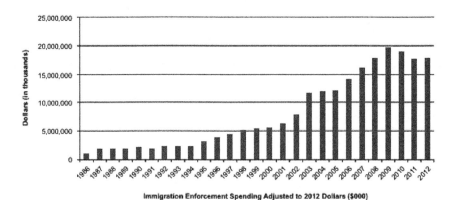

Immigration Enforcement Spending Adjusted to 2012 Dollars ($000)

Figure 15.1   Migration enforcement and border control in the US
Source: Meisner et al. (MPI) (2013, 4).

Returning to the significance for IR theories, the implication is that an international regime of sorts is emerging with the US as highly influential. In other words, a new imposed global order of security and mobility, with border systems aligned with US policies. This formal cooperation based on shared values and concerns over security would support liberal understandings of IR. However, there is also an underlying system of covert activity relating to international movement that would point to realist interpretation. These include the construction of foreign US detention facilities on sovereign territory – described by Dick Marty (the EU's rapporteur on secret rendition), as the 'global spider's web' (Council of Europe 2006, 10). In addition, the prospect of a truly global international regime of border security has other problems. It is not clear that many other states or regional organizations have the political or financial capacity to emulate the enormous operations put together by the US state, for example with the US-VISIT programme.

THE REFUGEE SYSTEM

A human rights approach to borders, citizenship and refugees offers a useful counterpoint to the usual security based focus of states. It is also synonymous with liberal understandings of IR. Realists would counter that while the human rights system exists, states often break the rules and the whole system will collapse unless there are clear benefits to those involved. As the well-known realist scholars Carr and Morgenthau would argue, while states might say they are willing to abide by universal moral values, this is only as long as they align with narrow national self-interest.

Despite the cynicism of the realist approach, there are certain areas where we can see developed, and less developed, international regimes that govern migration based on human rights. The most notable is that which was initiated by the 1951 Geneva Convention, and the accompanying UN agency – the UNHCR. Agreed by the international community, the Geneva Convention addressed some of the issues highlighted by the horrors of World War II, particularly the vulnerability of refuges and stateless persons. Other attempts to develop protections at the international level, such as the International Convention on the Protection of the Rights of All Migrant Workers and Members of Their Families (ICRMW), have had more disappointing results (see ICJ 2011).

The facts and figures on international refugees collected annually by the UNHCR demonstrate the enormous numbers of people who find themselves effectively homeless and often in desperate circumstances. No less than 42.5 million people ended 2011 either as refugees (15.2 million), internally displaced (26.4 million) or in the process of seeking asylum (895,000). Most of these refugees emanate from some of the poorest parts of the world, and the figures show where the greatest burden tends to fall: on neighbouring states that are often equally poor. In 2011 Pakistan was host to the largest number of refugees worldwide (1.7 million), followed by the Islamic Republic of Iran (887,000).

The data on asylum claims is also instructive – and demonstrates that it is not just European states that process large numbers of claims. In contrast to the geography for total numbers of refugees – here the states involved are often (but not always) in the rich north. They are also often receiving states for other forms of migration. In 2011 more than 876,100 people submitted individual applications for asylum or refugee status. Although the United States of America (76,000) and France (52,100) were among those with the highest numbers of claims, the top destination was actually South Africa, with close to 107,000 asylum claims (one tenth of applications globally) (UNHCR Global Trends 2011).

States' obligations under the 1951 Geneva Convention include cooperation with UNHCR and the principles of non-refoulement and non-reciprocity (see glossary of terms). However, it is important to note that the Convention is silent on procedures for determining status. Some might question whether the system is now out of date – the original convention was designed to deal with aftermath of World War II and the world is now a much changed place. However, according to the UNHCR on its fiftieth anniversary, the Convention is more relevant than ever, because 'recurring cycles of violence and systematic human rights violations in many parts of the world are generating more and more intractable displacement situations' (UNHCR 2001).

There have, however, been a number of unanticipated problems, including serious imbalances in burden and responsibility sharing, and the system has come under additional pressure due to concerns about certain forms of unwanted migration: 'countries that once generously opened their doors to refugees have been tempted to shut those doors for fear of assuming open-ended responsibilities, of abetting uncontrolled migration and people-smuggling, or of jeopardizing national security' (UNHCR 2001, 6).

Overall, and in contradiction to the standard realist interpretation of IR, the resilience of the refugee system has been impressive – and this is mainly due to the moral/ethical power of the Convention. However, the tension between this power and the instinctive tendency for states to pursue their own interests is self-evident. This can be seen in the way states have been able to gradually erode the basic principles upon which the Convention was based. As Gibney (2008) claims, in the case of Britain, 'the institution of asylum, while established to serve humanitarian goals, has become, in early twenty-first century Britain, a justification for boosting the coercive powers of the state'.

For many, the refugee system and the difficulties in protecting human rights for migrants symbolizes the inherent problems of IR. The double standards of states that are signed up to the Convention, yet use complex methods to deny asylum to all but the bare minimum of refugees, add weight to cynical realist arguments about universal moral values. Those critical of the ways in which states deal with borders and migrants typically employ the language of human rights: this is because human rights has become the common language of social criticism in global politics (Beitz 2009). A key complaint is the narrow nature of international cooperation on human rights: 'in this world, migrants have rights, but no or little way to make use of them or ask for their respect. They are legally voiceless' (ICJ 2011). For its liberal supporters, the concept of fundamental human rights is universal and therefore should in theory apply to all persons regardless of their migration status. Indeed the Universal Declaration of Human Rights (UDHR) affirmed (1948) that: 'all human beings are born free and equal in dignity and rights'. However, international law generally applies to states, not individuals, and so it is up to states to implement and protect human rights.

Although outside the scope of this chapter, since 2000 there has also been a coordination of activities to deal with criminal aspects of international movement of persons. This has been through efforts to combat transnational organized crime (TOC), specifically human trafficking and human smuggling. Coordinated international efforts were formally launched by the UN Palermo agreements in 2000. These have often claimed to employ a 'human rights approach' but there are questions over the actual motivations of states to cooperate over these areas. Despite this problem, in some areas we are seeing an increasing use of international law to open up national legal systems to respect human rights for all those citizens and non-citizens in their territories. The obvious example is in Europe where individuals can take cases before the European Court of Human Rights (ECHR).

INTERNATIONAL LABOUR MIGRATION

The twenty-first century has been notable for the increasing interest in states in the economic benefits of migration. As our knowledge of the impacts of migration gradually expands, states have become increasingly aware of the multiple ways in which the international movement of labour can have important economic implications (Balch 2010). This is both in the sense of global development and in terms of the economic interests of receiving and sending states. The former compete not just for the most skilled and talented migrants, but also the cheapest and hardest working. Arguments for increased migration for these states are dominated by supply-side arguments over labour flexibility, demographic issues and the potentially positive net benefit of migration to the national economies. Sending states seek maximum benefit from their diasporas through remittances and the prospects of valuable skills through return migration. Estimates are that remittances in 2015 will amount to over $530 billion (World Bank 2012).

ILO – the International Labour Organization is one of the oldest international organizations (established in 1919 by the Treaty of Versailles) and is now the UN agency that produces and monitors international standards regarding labour. It has 183 (state) members, around 1,700 staff. Agreements regarding migrant workers were first proposed by the ILO in 1949 (Migration for Employment Convention C97) and there have since been a number of other Conventions (see ILO 2010).

However, despite these apparently common interests, when it comes to international labour migration there has been little in the way of significant international agreement. Attempts to incorporate labour migration within the General Agreement on Tariffs and Trade (GATT) were not considered successful – only applying to a small number of intra-company transferees. A good example of the problem is the difficulties in securing equal rights for migrant workers, as explained in the previous section. There have been many international conventions put forward by the **International Labour Organization (ILO)** that have either not been signed or ratified by enough states. Indeed with the International Convention on the Protection of the Rights of All Migrant Workers and Members of Their Families (ICRMW), all of those that signed were sending states. The ILO attempted to kick-start an international discussion on global governance with the launch of the Global Commission on International Migration (GCIM). A key finding of the commission was that 'the international community has failed to capitalize on the opportunities and to meet the challenges associated with international migration' (GCIM 2005).

What we do see is significant tendency towards convergence among receiving states with regard to their approach towards international labour migration. As observed by Cornelius and Tsuda (2004, 15), labour-importing countries 'are coming to resemble each other in important ways'. A wide range of explanations have been put forward for policy convergence (for a review, see Meyers 2002), but the OECD has noted that since 2000 many countries have instigated major institutional and structural reforms in the way that countries deliver policy on labour migration

(OECD 2009). The shift among receiving states has seen straightforward migration restriction incrementally replaced by a language of migration 'management' (Balch 2010).

There are several problems for both sending and receiving states in establishing an international regime, and these point to realist arguments about the importance of national self-interest. There is the obvious issue that the limits of sovereignty beyond national territory make it difficult to control and manage migration flows that begin or end outside their borders. This might theoretically point to demand for an international regime, but no such regime exists. A key explanation is that while states they have a common interest in extracting value from migration, large (and powerful) receiving states can 'free-ride' the system because they do not need to join an international regime. As Koslowski concludes, they can unilaterally recruit all the migrant labour they need (2008, 103). Perhaps the best opportunity for a 'post-national' arrangement for labour migration is provided by the EU. However, despite significant integration, labour migration policy remains an area where national sovereignty is jealously guarded. While the Schengen arrangements remove some border controls, complaints by the larger migrant-receiving states still hold sway and demonstrate the continued dominance of national interests, even here (Carrera 2011).

CONCLUSIONS

The choice of cases highlights that the topic of borders/migration stands at the intersection of economics, security and human rights. These are of course overarching themes that connect to ways of thinking about almost all debates in contemporary politics and IR. The issues raised by migration touch upon all three of these themes in different ways. Most would agree that we are living in an era defined by the complex forces of globalization. Large parts of the globe are experiencing change at breathtaking pace, and living through dynamic and critical transformations – and these changes are not only economic, they are also political, social and cultural. They create various challenges for states and the international community and can thus present a tension between issues of economics, security and human rights.

A further theme is that of identity. Questions of identity have dominated the study of borders, citizenship and migration, meaning the subjects are traditionally more within the domain of political studies than IR. This is not least because the subject lends itself to a sustained focus on the nature of the liberal state for political theorists. As the French sociologist Sayad said, thinking about migration means thinking about the state and that it is 'the state that is thinking about itself when it is thinking about immigration' (Sayad 2010, 166). The argument of this chapter is that the strong emergence of migration and borders as issues of international concern in the twenty-first century means that we are now in an era where thinking about these issues helps us to think about the international system itself.

What does the evidence presented in this chapter suggest are the most feasible options for the international system when it comes to borders and migration? To conclude this chapter it is interesting to consider different scenarios and to ask which is the most likely to dominate international relations.

Will we ever see a formal system of global governance on migration? The previous analysis of different international regimes around borders and migration found some evidence of international cooperation – mainly with reference to aspects of security and human rights. The perhaps more surprising finding was that, despite the opening up of national markets through globalization of trade, when it comes to the international flow of people, states still act in a very self-interested way, with a 'zero-sum' approach.

The UN system offers the only real prospect of any formal system of global governance with regards to borders and migration, but outside the tightly circumscribed refugee regime there has been little in the way of concrete agreements. While the ILO has made some efforts to move towards a more 'soft' and cooperative regulatory approach (Baccaro and Mele 2012), its top-down model of setting standards and encouraging states to sign up has been only partially successful. Dealing with labour migration is a good example of this and has proven to be a particularly troublesome area for the ILO. As with all human rights issues, there are serious challenges around implementation and enforcement that all rely on the willingness of state signatories: the result is that in the absence of global governance we have less formalized types of cooperation flourishing – as demonstrated in the discussion of border security.

Perhaps the most radical scenario for the future is that of open borders – or 'no borders' at all. There has been a small, but growing, group of people who call for the removal of all national borders and allow for the free flow of people globally. This campaign is at times incoherent and mixes a range of issues around political, social and economic arguments (Anderson et al. 2009). However, a key point of principle for many within this campaign is that it is morally indefensible to deny freedoms to people on the basis of their nationality (Bagaric and Morss 2005, 27). For Joseph Carens there is a liberal logic to the incremental dismantling of inequalities between groups. For him this logic springs from the embedded liberal values that exist within most industrialized economies. These values have within them a desire for a continual expansion of the franchise, thus incorporating outsiders or newcomers 'to commit ourselves to open borders would not be to abandon the idea of communal character but to reaffirm it. It would be an affirmation of the liberal character of the community and of its commitment to principles of justice' (Carens 1987).

While for many this seems a utopian dream, for others, 'open borders are an inevitable long-term consequence of globalization, as well as a policy option for addressing North-South inequalities and a moral touchstone for the global extension of human rights' (Casey 2010). There is certainly historical precedent for such an arrangement. As supporters of 'no borders' point out, if one looks beyond the past 100 years or so of migration policies, there was a time when borders and controls as we now know them did not exist (Hayter 2003).

Nevertheless, perhaps the most obvious and likely future scenario is that of national sovereignty trumping any regional or international efforts to remove control of borders and migration from the hands of states. The evidence gathered here offers a mixed picture, and with the possible exception of the EU does not point to a future with fewer borders. Indeed the case study on border controls demonstrated the enduring power of sovereignty and how it can be resurgent in an era of globalization. The example of the international refugee system showed how IR can move beyond narrow self-interest, albeit in a limited way that remains at the mercy of state-based manipulation. Finally, the case of international labour migration showed the relevance of inequality in the international system. The division between different kinds of states – rich and poor, receiving and sending – means different, and sometimes conflicting, interests. This is likely to continue to act as a powerful obstacle to radical solutions or meaningful developments in global governance over migration and border controls.

QUESTIONS FOR REFLECTION

1. Why is migration such a difficult subject for states when it comes to international cooperation?
2. Is it inevitable that states will always restrict migration or is it possible that we will one day live in a world without borders?
3. What is the best way to protect everyone's human rights – including those of migrants and refugees?
4. Which is the most appropriate way of thinking about the implications of migration – a problem of economics, security or human rights?
5. Why has the 'Homeland Security' paradigm had such an influence beyond the borders of the United States?

REVISION QUIZ

1. Which country was the largest recipient of asylum claims among industrialized countries in 2013?

    a. France
    b. Germany
    c. UK
    d. US

2. Which out of the following countries hosted most refugees in 2012?

    a. France
    b. Germany
    c. Iran
    d. Pakistan

3. How many people in the world were classed as 'forcibly displaced' in 2012?

    a. 11.8 million
    b. 34.1 million
    c. 42.5 million
    d. 45.2 million

4. How much did the US spend on border enforcement between 1986 and 2012?

    a. $67.4 billion
    b. $93.1 billion
    c. $186.8 billion
    d. $265.9 billion

5. According to the US Department of Homeland Security (DHS) how many irregular migrants were estimated to be resident in the US in 2012?

   a. 1 million
   b. 11 million
   c. 111 million
   d. 150 million

6. Worldwide, what were the number of international tourist arrivals in 2013 according to the United National World Tourism Organization?

   a. below 100 million
   b. between 100 million and 500 million
   c. between 500 million and 1 billion
   d. over 1 billion

7. According to the UN definition, how long does a person need to stay in a foreign country to be counted as an international migrant?

   a. 1 month
   b. 6 months
   c. 12 months
   d. 24 months

8. What percentage of the world's population are migrants?

   a. Around 1 per cent
   b. Around 3 per cent
   c. Around 10 per cent
   d. Around 25 per cent

9. What sort of organization is the IOM – International Organization for Migration?

   a. Think-tank
   b. Non-governmental organization
   c. Intergovernmental organization
   d. None of the above

10. What is/was the GCIM?

   a. General Council on International Migration
   b. Great Country of International Migration
   c. Greek Committee on International Migration
   d. Global Commission on International Migration

11. What was the original name of the IR publication now known as 'Foreign Affairs'?

a. Journal of International affairs
b. Journal of Race Development
c. Review of International Affairs
d. International Development

Answers: 1: b; 2: d; 3: d; 4: c; 5: b; 6: d; 7: c; 8: b; 9: c; 10: d; 11: b.

BIBLIOGRAPHY

Agamben, G. (2005) *State of Exception* (Chicago, IL: Chicago University Press).

Alden, E. (2009) *The Closing of the American Border: Terrorism, Immigration, and Security Since 9/11* (New York, NY: Harper Perennial).

Anderson, B. et al. (2009). 'Editorial: Why No Borders?'. *Refuge* 26(2), 5–18.

Ashutosh, I. and Mountz, A. (2011) 'Migration management for the benefit of whom? Interrogating the work of the International Organization for Migration', *Citizenship Studies* 15(1), 21–38.

Baccaro, L. and Mele, V. (2012) 'Pathology of Path Dependency? The ILO And The Challenge Of New Governance', *Industrial and Labor Relations Review* 65(2), 195–224.

Bagaric, M. and Morss, J. (2005) 'State Sovereignty and Migration Control: The Ultimate Form of Discrimination?'. *Journal of Migration & Refugee Issues* 25.

Baker, G. (2011) 'Right of entry or right of refusal? Hospitality in the law of nature and nations', *Review of International Studies* 37(3), 1423–45.

Balch, A. (2010) *Managing Labour Migration in Europe: Ideas, Knowledge and Policy Change* (Manchester: Manchester University Press).

Beitz, C.R. (2001) 'Human rights as a common concern', *American Political Science Review* 95(2), 269–82.

Blatt, J. (2004) '"To bring out the best that is in their blood": Race, reform, and civilization in the journal of race development (1910–1919)', *Ethnic and Racial Studies* 27(5), 691–709.

Bommes, M. and Geddes, A. (2000) *Immigration and Welfare: Challenging the Borders of the Welfare State* (London, Routledge).

Brubaker, R. (1992) *Citizenship and Nationhood in France and Germany* (Harvard, MA: Harvard University Press).

Buzan, B., Wæver, O. and de Wilde, J. (1998) *Security: a New Framework for Analysis* (Boulder, CO: Lynne Rienner).

Carens, J.H. (1987) 'Aliens and citizens: the case for open borders', *The Review of Politics* 49(2), 251–73.

Carrera, S. (2011) 'The EU's Dialogue on Migration, Mobility and Security with the Southern Mediterranean Filling the Gaps in the Global Approach to Migration', CEPS (Centre for European Policy Studies): Brussels.

Casey, J.P. (2010) 'Open borders: absurd chimera or inevitable future policy?', *International Migration* 48(5), 14–62.

Castles, S. and Cossack, G. (1972) *Immigrant Workers and Class Struggle in Western Europe* (Oxford: Oxford University Press).

Castles, S. and Miller, M. (2009) *The Age of Migration: International Population Movement in the Modern World* (Basingstoke: Palgrave Macmillan).

Cornelius, W. and Tsuda, T. (2004) 'Controlling Immigration: The Limits of Government Intervention'. In W. Cornelius, T. Tsuda, P. Martin and J. Hollifield (eds), *Controlling Immigration: A Global perspective* (Stanford, CA: Stanford University Press).

Cornelius, W. (July 2005) 'Controlling "Unwanted" Immigration: Lessons from the United States', *Journal of Ethnic and Migration Studies* 31(4), 775–94.

Dijstelbloem, H. and Meijer, A. (eds) (2011) *Migration and the New Technological Borders of Europe* (Basingstoke: Palgrave Macmillan).

Dion, R. (1947) *Les frontières de la France* (Paris: G. Monfort).

Freeman, G. (1995) 'Modes of Immigration Politics in Liberal Democratic States', *International Migration Review* 29(4), 881–902.

Freiherr von Richthofen, F. (1984). *China, Ergebnisse eigner Reisen und darauf gegründeter Studien* (Berlin: D. Reimer).

GCIM (Global Commission on International Migration) (2005) 'Migration in an Interconnected World: New Directions for Action'. Report of the Global Commission on International Migration, 5 October 2005. Available at: <http://www.unhcr.org/refworld/docid/435f81814.html> [accessed 7 March 2013].

Gibney, M.J. (2008) 'Asylum and the Expansion of Deportation in the United Kingdom', *Government and Opposition*, 43(2), 146–67.

Grewcock, M. (2007) 'Shooting the passenger: Australia's war on illicit migrants'. In M. Lee (ed.) *Human Trafficking* (Cullompton, UK: Willan Publishing).

Guiraudon, V. (2003) 'Before the EU Border: Remote Control of the "Huddled Masses"'. In K. Groenendijk, E. Guild and P. Minderhoud (eds), *In Search of Europe's Borders* (The Hague: Kluwer).

Hayter, T. (2003). 'No Borders: The Case against Immigration Controls', *Feminist Review* 73, 6–18.

Hobbing, P. and Koslowski, R. (2009) 'The Tools Called to Support the "Delivery" of Freedom, Security and Justice: A Comparison of Border Security Systems in the EU and in the US', Briefing Paper, European Parliament, DG Internal Policies, Citizens Rights and Constitutional Affairs, Committee on Civil Liberties, Justice and Home Affairs, PE 410.681.

Hollifield, J. (2007) 'The Emerging Migration State'. In A. Portes, J. DeWind (eds), *Rethinking Migration: New Theoretical and Empirical Perspectives* (Oxford, NY: Berghahn Books).

Hollifield, J. (2012) 'Migration and international relations'. In M. Rosenblum and D. Tichenor (eds), *The Oxford Handbook of the Politics of International Migration* (New York: Oxford University Press).

ICJ – International Commission of Jurists (2011) 'Migration and International Human Rights Law'. Available at: <www.icj.org/dwn/img_prd/PGNo6-ElectronicDistribution1.pdf>.

ILO (2010) 'International labour migration: a rights-based approach'. International Labour Organization: Geneva.

Joppke, C. (1998). *Challenge to the Nation-State: Immigration in Western Europe and the United States* (Oxford, NY: Oxford University Press).

Karyotis, G. (2012) 'Securitization of Migration in Greece: Process, Motives, and Implications', *International Political Sociology* 6(4), 390–408.

Keynes, J.M. (1935) *The General Theory of Employment, Interest and Money* (Cambridge: Cambridge University Press).

Koslowski, R. (2008) 'Global Mobility and the Quest for an International Migration Regime', Center for Migration Studies (special issue): International Migration and Development: Continuing the Dialogue: Legal and Policy Perspectives, 21(1), 103–43.

Koulish, R. (2012) 'Spiderman's Web and the Governmentality of Electronic Immigrant Detention', *Law, Culture and the Humanities*, 1–26.

Lucassen, J., Lucassen, L. and Manning, P. (2010) *Migration History in World History: Multidisciplinary Approaches* (Boston, MA: Brill Academic Publishers).

Lyon, D. (2005) 'The border is everywhere: ID cards, surveillance and the other'. In E. Zureik and M. Salter (eds), *Global Surveillance and Policing: Borders, Security, Identity* (Cullompton: Willan).

Marshall, T.H. (1950) *Citizenship and Social Class* (Cambridge: Cambridge University Press).

McKeown, A.M. (2004) *Melancholy Order: Asian Migration and the Globalization of Borders* (New York: Columbia University Press).

Meisner, D., Kerwin, D.M., Chishti, M. and Bergeron, C. (2013) *Migration Enforcement in the United States: The Rise of a Formidable Machinery* (Washington, DC: Migration Policy Institute).

Meyers, E. (2000) 'Theories of International Immigration Policy – A Comparative Analysis', *International Migration Review* 34(4), 1245–82

Meyers, E. (2002) 'The Causes of Convergence in Western Immigration Control', *Review of International Studies* 28, 123–41.

OECD (2009) Sopemi Report 2008, Organisation for Economic Co-operation and Development (OECD).

Pickering, S. and Weber, L. (eds) (2006) *Borders, Mobility and Technologies of Control* (Dordrecht: Springer).

Salt, J. (2005) 'Types of migration in Europe: implications and policy concerns', Council of Europe: Strasbourg.

Sassen, S. (1996) *Losing Control? Sovereignty in an Age of Globalization* (New York: Columbia University Press).

Sayad, A (2010) 'Immigration and "state thought"'. In M. Martiniello and J. Rath (eds), *Selected Studies in International Migration and Immigration Incorporation* (Amsterdam: Amsterdam University Press).

Schmidt, B.C. (2002) 'On the History and Historiography of International Relations'. In W. Carlsnaes, T. Risse and B.A. Simmons (eds), *Handbook of International Relations* (London: Sage Publications).

Strik, T. (2012) 'Lives lost in the Mediterranean Sea: who is responsible?' 2012 Report for the Committee on Migration, Refugees and Displaced Persons Council of Europe Parliamentary Assembly (Rapporteur: Ms Tineke Strik, Netherlands, Socialist Group).

Torpey, J. (1998) 'Coming and Going: On the State Monopolization of the Legitimate "Means of Movement"', *Sociological Theory* 16(3), 239–59.

Vitalis, R. (2000) 'The Graceful and Generous Liberal Gesture: Making Racism Invisible in American International Relations', *Millennium: Journal of International Studies* 29(2), 331–56.

Weiner, M. (1993) *The Global Migration Crisis: Challenge to States and to Human Rights* (New York: HarperCollins).

World Bank (2012) 'Migration and Development Brief' No. 19, November 2012. Available at: <http://siteresources.worldbank.org/INTPROSPECTS/Resources/334934-1288990760745/MigrationDevelopmentBrief19.pdf>.

Zolberg, A. (1989) 'The Next Waves: Migration Theory for a Changing World', *International Migration Review* 23(3), 403–30.

Chapter 16
The Media and International Relations

ANNE ALY

This chapter explores the complex and often debated relationship between the media and international relations. It examines arguments that the media has a deep and significant impact on how governments shape their foreign policy and how individuals and groups of people are also influenced to respond in certain ways to issues presented in the media. There is no doubt that the media plays some role in international relations but the exact nature of this role is often debated. Is the media's role to negotiate the relationship between the major actors in international affairs? Or does the media play a more significant role as an international actor in its own right with the ability to influence and shape foreign policy and responses to international events and issues?

The chapter will familiarise students with some of the most well-known theories about the role and influence of the media on international relations. These theories range from those that claim the media has a decisive and substantial role in the formulation of foreign policy to those that argue that the media itself is influenced by political and market forces in order to maintain the status quo of power. Through some practical examples and case studies, students will be encouraged to critically examine these theories. Students will also learn how the media is a tool for different actors in international relations and how each of these actors uses the media in ways that can significantly influence their role in international affairs.

The chapter presents an overview of how the media is becoming one of the most valuable diplomatic tool for states but also how it is becoming a tool for individuals and groups to enter into and influence the international arena. While the role of the media in shaping international relations is still a subject that invites debate and arguments, the role of new media technologies has introduced another level of complexity to the debate. In particular, new media technologies allow for individual actors that are not connected to the state or to international media producers to create their own news and set the news agenda. In this chapter, students will learn how individuals and non-state actors use the media in ways that can also shape international relations and the ways in which governments respond to global events and issues.

Key Words: CNN Effect; Manufacturing Consent; Hegemony Theory; Media Frames; Silver Bullet Theory; Slacktivism.

Chapter 16

The Media and International Relations

ANNE ALY

INTRODUCTION

The world has seen many changes in the 350 or so years since the Peace of Westphalia. Modern international relations are characterised by developments such as the secularisation of politics, the development of international law, its principles and instruments and the development and progressive importance of international governmental organisations (IGOs), non-government organisations (NGOs) and other non-state actors as key players in international affairs. From a constructivist and structuralist point of view, today's key players in international relations are those entities that participate in and shape the discourse within the international system. Those players include states but also non-state actors: IGOs, NGOs, terrorist organisations, individuals, powerful heads of state, multi-national corporations and the media.

As a key player in international relations, it is worthwhile examining the relationship between the media and other key players. The media represents the world on a daily basis in ways that permeate how we think and how we behave. It is also a powerful tool of states through the use of propaganda messages about government domestic and foreign policies. Throughout history, governments have used the media to infiltrate the hearts and minds of their own people as well as people in other countries. Individuals and groups have also used the media to influence governments by amassing public opinion for or against a particular policy, action or issue. The media not only serves as a tool for actors to participate in international discourse, it can (and often does) also shape this discourse. As such the media cannot be discounted as one of the most significant and powerful players in international affairs.

Table 16.1 summarises the actors in the international system and their relationship to each other. The media is not only an actor in its own right but also functions to mediate the relationship between actors (see column 3). While the actors in the international relations arena use systemic tools to participate in the international system, the media plays an important role in influencing the effectiveness of these tools. There are still questions around the extent of media influence and its impact on government actions, however it is generally considered that the media's ability to influence public opinion through the ways in which represents international issues has a bearing on foreign policy.

This is known as the **CNN effect**. This theory suggests that international television and broadcasters, especially CNN, are a significant and governing factor in the formulation of foreign policy, this is explained in more detail in the next section of this chapter. Apart from this, the media is becoming one of the most valuable diplomatic tools for states. The evolution of e-diplomacy which uses new media platforms to achieve diplomatic objectives is examined later in this chapter. Non-state actors such as human rights NGOs

> **CNN Effect** – the theory that international television and broadcasters play a significant role in formulating foreign policy.

(Amnesty International, Human Rights Watch for example) use media campaigns to raise public awareness of issues and to 'name and shame' states at the international level. An example of this is the UN Commission on Human Rights 1235 procedure. Individual actors also use mass media to influence public opinion and in turn the actions of States. In short, the media's primary role in international relations is as a powerful influencer of public opinion. We should not dismiss how important public public opinion is to the machinations of the international system.

The United Nations Commission on Human Rights 1235 Procedure – Naming and Shaming the Violators

The UN Commission on Human Rights 1503 Procedure is a confidential procedure named after ECOSCO Resolution 1503. The procedure allows for the Commission to receive complaints about a consistent pattern or gross human rights violations such as genocide, apartheid, racial or ethnic discrimination, torture or forced migrations. When a 1503 procedure takes place, the Commission will investigate and take actions to stop the human rights violations. When this fails the Commission may then use the 1235 Procedure to hold an annual public debate about the human rights violations. If this also fails, the Commission can then resort to public condemnation of the violators and shame the leaders of the state.

Table 16.1   International actors and their media relations

Actors	Tools of International Relations	Media role
State to state	Regional alliances and treaties. Cooperation and diplomacy. State to state conflicts and war. Economic sanctions and/or benefits.	Communication of state values internally and to other states. States use media to communicate their economic, political and cultural interests. The CNN Effect.
State to transnational actors	States comply with international protocols set by IGOs. NGOs use 'naming and shaming' to influence state actions. States have policies on nationalisation that affect the operations of multinationals. Transnational entities act as spaces of expression for states.	Transnational entities use media campaigns to influence public opinion and put pressure on states. Media coverage of humanitarian issues and conflicts.
State to private actors	States comply with international protocols and norms of behaviour that impact on the actions of private actors. Private actors influence state policy and actions.	States use media as a vehicle of public diplomacy. States maintain status quos through media hegemony and dominant discourses. Media influences public opinion which can act as a constraint for intergovernmental cooperation and conflict. Censorship of private actors and state opposition.
Transnational organisations to private actors	IGOs set legal frameworks for international norms of behaviour. NGOs work to maintain human security and human rights.	NGOs use media campaigns to influence public opinion. IGOs publicly name and shame human rights violators.

THE CNN EFFECT AND MANUFACTURING CONSENT

With the advent of new technologies in the 1980s, world-changing events like the fall of the Berlin wall, Tiananmen Square, the First Gulf War and the 911 terrorist attacks have been broadcast to an international audience in real time. New technologies not only transformed the way in which the media reported international events, they also raised inevitable questions about the influence of the media on the process of foreign policy. It appeared that the streaming of international events live through television news media left little scope for a deliberate and thought-out foreign policy response as policymakers were forced to respond quickly to whatever issue journalists chose to focus on. Added to this was the end of the Cold War which many argued had created an ideological bond between policymakers and journalists. After the Cold War, it was assumed that the media would restore its claim to be the Fourth Estate as a defender of the public interest. Journalists, it was thought, would now be free to not only report on what they wanted but also to criticise government policy. The phrase CNN Effect was coined to refer to the notion that real-time news reporting could effectively influence foreign policy responses. It was first noted when extensive and emotional coverage of starving children in Somalia forced the US to send troops in Operation Restore Hope. In 1992, footage of a dead American soldier being dragged through the streets of Somalia prompted the withdrawal of US troops. Both of these actions are believed to be the result of media pressure.

The Somali intervention reignited a debate about the level of intrusion that the media can or should have in the formation of foreign policy. Policymakers saw Operation Restore Hope as media interference in the policy process. They argued that the media focus on the suffering of the Somali people had overtaken traditional policy processes forcing an immediate response in the form of an intervention. Critics of the Somali intervention called for the proper channels of policy-making to be restored and claimed that policy decisions made on the basis of highly emotional media reports were dangerous and risky. Even though Operation Restore Hope and the subsequent withdrawal of American troops in Somalia are often quoted in studies of the CNN Effect, there are other examples that highlight how the media can shape foreign policy by influencing public opinion.

International terrorist attacks have and will continue to attract intense media attention. In fact, the attention of the media is one of the main goals of terrorist organisations who seek to influence government policy as it provides them with an outlet to raise awareness of their cause and their demands. One of the major criticisms of media coverage of terrorism is that widespread and prolonged coverage of terrorist attacks in the international media plays into the hands of terrorists by giving them the attention they seek. In some cases media coverage of terrorism can have a strong influence on government decision-making.

In his book, *Inside Terrorism*, Bruce Hoffman (1998) describes the 1985 hijacking of a TWA flight by Hezbollah Shi'a terrorists. The hijackers demanded the release of 756 Shi'a prisoners held in Israeli prisons. They communicated their demands through a carefully planned media strategy that involved hijacking the flight and releasing all non-American hostages. The remaining 39 American citizens were kept as hostages ensuring that the hijackers would immediately capture the attention of the US media. The TWA hostage crisis became prime time news throughout the United States for two weeks. During that time media reports focused not only on the crisis itself but also on human interest stories with the hostages and their families. News reporters even spoke directly to the hijackers assuming the role of hostage negotiator. Ultimately, the Reagan administration was forced to pressure Israel into meeting the hijackers' demands to bring an end to the crisis. According to Hoffman, the TWA flight 847 incident demonstrated how influential the media can be in the government decision-making process.

Other analysts view media coverage of the TWA episode as problematic because the media leaked information that was used by the hijackers to avert security (Cohen-Almagor 2005). In the first 24 hours of the hostage crisis, the US planned to swap hostages for the release of the prisoners. When the international media broadcast reports that the US Army had dispatched its Delta Force anti-terrorist squad, the hijackers fled from Algeria to Beirut to avert an American rescue operation. The London *Times* reported a detailed account of US plans stating: 'The U.S. has reportedly sent a commando unit to the Mediterranean ready to storm the hijacked plane if necessary … The unit is said to be part of a crack anti-terrorist squad of several hundred men … The commandos, known as the Delta Unit, may have been sent to the aircraft carrier Enterprise which is currently in the western Mediterranean' (cited in Cohen-Almagor 2005).

Another, more recent example of the CNN Effect is the Australian government's policy on live trade. In one of its most notable episodes, the ABC's current affairs program *Four Corners* exposed the mistreatment of Australian cattle in Indonesia. The program showed graphic images of mistreatment that not only caused shockwaves among its Australian audience but also impacted on the live export trade. Public outrage was almost immediately followed by the Australian government ban on all live trade to Indonesia. The undeniable connection between the media reporting of the issue and the government policy response is a good example of the CNN effect.

At the opposite end of the CNN Effect is the **Manufacturing Consent** argument. Manufacturing consent is a term borrowed from a ground-breaking analysis of the relationship between policy makers and the media by Edward S Herman and Noam Chomsky (1988). While the CNN Effect argues that news media drives foreign policy, adherents of manufacturing consent argue that political and market forces drive the media in two

> **Manufacturing Consent** – the theory that political and market forces play a significant role in governing the media.

ways. Firstly, news media reports conform to official worldviews and mirror the official point of view on an issue or international event. This kind of consent manufacturing is obvious in newspaper reports of the 911 attacks which replicated the official line that the attacks were an act of war and effectively gained public support for a US military response. Secondly, news media reports conform to the interests of powerful political players. This kind of manufacturing consent promotes public support for a particular policy or agenda. In the next sections of this chapter we explore the complex relationship between the media, power and the state.

MEDIA AND HEGEMONY

Hegemony Theory was most famously developed by the Italian philosopher Antonio Gramsci (1891–1937) to explain how power works in modern capitalist societies. Gramsci, like other Marxists, was particularly interested in how one social class, the

> **Hegemony Theory** – a theory that explains how the dominant culture in a society maintains its dominant position.

ruling elite, could manipulate the moral fabric of society without resorting to force to maintain their bourgeois domination. Gramsci's theory of cultural hegemony considers Weltanschauung (or worldview) as an autonomous force in society. Weltanschauung is sometimes referred to as ideology and can be defined as the way in which individuals and societies view and make sense of the world around them using the themes, values, emotions and ethics at their disposal. How you view the world, and your place in the world, will ultimately be dictated by a number of factors: your gender, age, where you were brought up, how you were brought up and, most importantly the social norms and values of the society in which you live. These norms and values may appear to be transparent to us – we accept that there are boundaries of thought and behaviour that are considered 'normal' and we implicitly comply with these values and norms because we assume that they are natural and inevitable. However, these norms and values had to come from somewhere, and, according to Gramsci's theory of cultural hegemony, they are social constructs that are established and perpetuated by the social institutions we interact with on a daily basis. Cultural hegemony analyses the norms and values that are used by the ruling class to establish and maintain cultural dominance.

Cultural hegemony is particularly relevant for examining the role of the mass media for two reasons. Firstly, Gramsci's approach is based on the observation that any group that seeks to gain and hold political and cultural leadership must be able to appeal to the masses by demonstrating that it is committed to the common good (as opposed to its own agenda). To do this, the leadership group must communicate using shared symbols and values and must adopt the concerns of other groups into its agenda in order to gain the power it needs to impose its own worldview. Once in power, the dominant group must then continually face challenges from other groups by making their own values appear to be those of the masses. The cultural battles over values and norms are primarily fought in the arena of the mass media. One way of looking at the media is a social institution 'in which formally organised work takes place, directed towards the production of knowledge and culture' (McQuail 1983, 97). The media is therefore positioned as an institutional site of social control. By representing reality, the media creates discourses that are marked by rules and conditions for talking about social issues. The power of the media lies in its authority to produce truths by representing events, experiences and behaviours in ways that establish and maintain dominant ways of thinking. As a cultural industry the media is the domain where dominant interpretations of reality and cultural values become anchored in society through the media products consumed.

Secondly, cultural hegemony is also established by language and discourse. The term *lingua franca* refers to the common language used by diverse populations to communicate. Lingua franca is also an instrument of cultural hegemony when it represents the official source of information and ideas. Discourse is more than language. It describes the social boundaries that define the language and speech that are used around specific topics.

The French philosopher and social theorist Michel Foucault (1926–84) is probably best known for his influential writings on power, discourse and knowledge. Foucault's approach conceptualises discourse as the social construction of reality through language. Discourse allows us to experience reality and construct meaning by providing a set of rules about what can be said or done in relation to an experience. In a Foucauldian sense, discourses are inherently powerful because they define what is sayable and what is not. Discourses are created and perpetuated by those in power in order to establish and maintain cultural hegemony. Discourses are often contested and represent struggles for power. Some discourses ultimately become dominant discourses that are embedded in a society's worldview and ideology. A discourse has achieved dominance when it is no longer contested and when it is considered natural, normal or common sense. A relatively simple example of a dominant discourse is the 'war on terror'. When we consider the origins of this phrase and how it has become embedded in everyday language, we can start to understand how the media and political language establishes ways of speaking about issues that invite certain interpretations and reject others. At the end of this chapter you will find a question for reflection that asks you to consider this example in more depth.

By selecting particular messages to be communicated in particular ways to the populace through particular language and discourses, the ruling or dominant group can exert hegemony on the individuals and groups receiving the information. Mass media is the primary vehicle for transmitting information to the public. By limiting and manipulating how information is presented in the media, those in power can also influence what and how people think about their society and other societies. Mainstream political and moral values are not just reflected within the workings of the mass media; they are also sustained and promoted by them. What we understand to be credible information is dependent on the media's ability to present this information in ways that appeal to and correspond with our own embedded social values and popular ideas. Several media theorists have contributed to an understanding of how controversial issues and events are presented in the news and understood by the public. Some of these theories will be reviewed throughout the course of this chapter as we examine how media influences international affairs and global society.

Other scholars who have contributed to the concept of media and cultural hegemony, such as Edward Said (1979), contend that Western media coverage of foreign events and cultures reflect and perpetuate popular Western attitudes. Said refers specifically to United States popular media coverage of events and issues in the Middle East. His book, *Covering Islam: How the Media and the Experts Determine How We See the Rest of the World*, presents a comprehensive analysis of how Western media depictions of events and issues in the Middle East are culturally inaccurate representations founded on a tradition of imperialism. Said argues that such representations are not merely mistaken interpretations, but assertions of power and justifications for continued imperial ambitions.

There is a vast body of research that supports Said's interpretation that foreign news reporting sticks closely to dominant worldviews. One study conducted by the Centre for International and Security Studies looked at news reports on weapons of mass destruction (WMD) during May 1998, October 2002 and May 2003. This study highlighted misinformation and bias in news coverage of the issue (Moeller 2004). Part of the rationale for the imbalance in reporting was the fact that news conventions place greater emphasis on the official statements of political leaders and leave out any challenges to these statements. It is assumed that experts, intellectuals and scholars will provide a challenging commentary to the political statements. Effectively, this meant that news reports on WMD gave most weight to statements from the White House and therefore followed what the official statements had to say and the official language that was used to talk about this issue. What we can determine from studies such as these is that when the media covers significant international issues, the kinds of statements and the ways in which the issues will be presented will closely mirror the official language of key players – such as political leaders.

Few people will admit to the level of authority that the media has on their day-to-day lives. While you may think that the media has little, or even no control over what you think or how you behave, consider how and where you, and those around you, get your information about your world and acceptable behaviours in that world. News headlines and current affairs reports define the social issues of our time: crime; terrorism; drugs; street violence; shark attacks on Australian beaches; Nigerian scams; nasty neighbours; tenants from hell; ethnic criminal gangs; Hilary Clinton's hair and Kim Kardashian's waistline. Even if you dismiss media reports as sensationalism and resist media representations of certain groups as stereotypes, the media has still determined that these are social issues and packaged them as news.

Media frames refer to the organisation of news reports in ways that imply certain truths and represent certain realities while ignoring other viewpoints, truths or realities. Framing enables media writers to represent dominant meanings in their messages and define issues, events or experiences in ways that invite audiences to agree with certain interpretations. Media reports on the activities of the Ku Klux Klan, for example, can influence public opinion based on whether the activities of the white supremacist group are framed in terms of free speech or public safety. One study

> **Media Frames** – a concept that explains how the media organises and packages news reports in ways that represent some meanings and ignore others.

on the media representation of nuclear power identified several frames: progress; soft paths; runaway; devil's bargain; energy independence; and public accountability. How the issue of nuclear power is framed and how we interpret those frames will depend on a number of factors including the sociocultural context of the reports; global events such as Chernobyl and individual audience characteristics such as age or political beliefs (Gamson and Modigliani, 1989).

THE STATE AND THE MEDIA

The previous section of this chapter presented some of the concepts around media and power. It should be noted that there are debates about the power of the media and its ability to construct dominant discourses that influence international relations. Hammond (2003) acknowledges that today's media culture is characterised by a strong awareness of the ways in which news items manipulate images and construct reality. Popular films such as *The Truman Show*, *The Matrix* and *Wag the Dog* have developed public awareness of the role of the media in the construction of images and discourses that serve political purposes. Alongside this, the growing use of the internet as an alternative source of information has undermined the authority of the traditional news networks and mainstream news media. As Hammond argues, 'Even if most people still rely on TV for their news, the proliferation of sources of information and commentary means that we are less likely simply to accept the truthfulness of any single account' (2003, 30).

One of the earliest theories of media influence is the 'silver bullet' or 'hypodermic needle' model. The silver bullet theory of media effect evolved out of fear of wartime propaganda where it was assumed that enemy governments would be able to influence core values through the messages they broadcast. A simple definition of propaganda is information that is circulated with the aim of influencing an audience. The purpose of propaganda is to sway attitudes, opinions or behaviours using techniques such as distorting

> **Silver Bullet Theory** – also known as the hypodermic needle model, suggests that the media has a direct effect on people's ideas and behaviours.

information, utilising emotive language, using labels and stereotypes or omitting certain facts. Those who disagree with the message being communicated will often label it propaganda, while those who agree with it would consider it a factual and accurate representation of reality. Originally however, propaganda was considered to be a positive technique referring specifically to the spread of religion. It was not until the use of political propaganda during World War I that propaganda started to take on negative meanings. Since then, propaganda has been used as an apparatus of the state to gain public support for policies that would sometimes be met with opposition. In state-to-state conflicts, propaganda has been used to gain support for state participation in wars and to demonise the enemies of the state. During World War I, United States President Woodrow Wilson employed propaganda to influence public opinion in favour of the war. In Nazi Germany, the Ministry for Public Enlightenment and Propaganda effectively used propaganda to win national support for policies of Nazi Germany by demonising Jews and other minorities.

The Voice of America (VOA) is the US government's official external broadcasting association broadcasting on radio, television and the internet in 43 languages. As the official spokesperson of the American government, the VOA's charter is to represent American society and the policies of the United States' government. The VOA was created during the propaganda campaigns of World War II. Between 1942 and 1945 it was part of the Office of War Information. In February 1942 the VOA began live shortwave radio broadcasts to the enemy, Germany. By the end of the War, VOA was broadcasting in 40 languages throughout Europe, Asia and Africa.

At the end of World War II, the VOA discontinued many of its foreign language services, but as the Cold War presented a new enemy, the VOA became the most potent weapon in combating the propaganda forces of Russian Communism. In 1945, the VOA became part of the Department of State and integrated in US Foreign Policy. It started broadcasting in Russian to Soviet citizens in 1947. The very first broadcast in Russian stated that the VOA would give Soviet listeners an accurate representation of life in the United States in order to develop understanding and friendship between the peoples of the two countries. It was thought that broadcasts that represented the positive aspects of American life would be effective in countering the Soviet propaganda directed against America and her policies. Meanwhile, Radio Moscow, the Soviet Union's government-run radio station, broadcast its own brand of Marxist-Leninist propaganda.

New media technologies have also been embraced by states as forums for communicating with and informing publics. In more recent years, the term e-diplomacy has been coined to describe the use of the new information communication technologies to achieve diplomatic objectives. E-diplomacy is a relatively new concept but its basis lies in old ideas and traditions about using the media to communicate messages and influence foreign policy. The US State Department first established the Office of eDiplomacy in 2002. While its uptake has been slow, other foreign ministries have followed suit and the UK Foreign and Commonwealth Office established the Office of Digital Diplomacy. Worldwide, around 125 countries are making use of the new wave of e-diplomacy in varying capacities. One study on the use of Twiplomacy found 264 Twitter accounts for government institutions in 125 countries but that only 30 heads of state personally used their Twitter accounts. Jimmy Leach, Head of the UK's Digital Diplomacy at the Foreign and Commonwealth Office, describes how e-diplomacy works as both message and platform for the dissemination of messages. Importantly, Leach stresses that the digital platform allows for the dissemination of messages to segmented audiences in ways those audiences can relate:

> *It's not really about the platform, it's about the message – and the aim is to get messages which carry well across a variety of platforms and media … – it depends on getting the message and the platform right. We have our platform, of course, which is the right place for corporate-style communications, but for the distribution of messages, we need to tailor messages and platform to audience. Established social media platforms like YouTube and Facebook are handy (and cheap) but real breakthroughs can sometimes come with proper segmentation. (Hanson 2011)*

Like many innovations, the origins of e-diplomacy can be traced to a gap in communication that came to light in 1998. A Blue Ribbon Panel was set up to investigate the East Africa bombings – a series of bomb attacks on US Embassies in Tanzania and Kenya. The Panel concluded that the United States was not set up to effectively manage inter-agency communications. Today, e-diplomacy is most widely used for public diplomacy purposes although it also has applications for internet freedom and knowledge management. One of the leading champions of e-diplomacy, Fergus Hanson, argues that e-diplomacy also has applications for policy planning, consular affairs and citizen engagement.

Applications of e-Diplomacy

1. Knowledge management: to harness departmental and whole of government knowledge, so that it is retained, shared and its use optimised in pursuit of national interests abroad.
2. Public diplomacy: to maintain contact with audiences as they migrate online and to harness new communications tools to listen to and target important audiences with key messages and to influence major online influencers.
3. Information management: to help aggregate the overwhelming flow of information and to use this to better inform policy-making and to help anticipate and respond to emerging social and political movements.
4. Consular communications and response: to create direct, personal communications channels with citizens travelling overseas, with manageable communications in crisis situations.
5. Disaster response: to harness the power of connective technologies in disaster response situations.
6. Internet freedom: creation of technologies to keep the internet free and open. This has the related objectives of promoting freedom of speech and democracy as well as undermining authoritarian regimes.
7. External resources: creating digital mechanisms to draw on and harness external expertise to advance national goals.
8. Policy planning: to allow for effective oversight, coordination and planning of international policy across government, in response to the internationalisation of the bureaucracy. (Hanson 2012)

Hanson also argues that public diplomacy is more important but also more complex and challenging now than it has been since the beginning of the Cold War: this is because the public that diplomacy is trying to influence are not only greater in number and diversity largely due to new technologies and social media:

> *Just as the circumscribed court politics of the eighteenth century gave rise to the more complex diplomacy of the nation state in the nineteenth century, and the new dimensions of multilateral diplomacy were added in the twentieth century, in the twenty first century an additional dimension of public diplomacy is needed to address the publics which increasingly shape state behaviour. (Hanson 2012)*

Like most of the tools of the international system, public diplomacy is affected by the advent of new technologies. Opportunities exist for states to communicate directly with and in turn influence larger more geographically dispersed audiences. In this sense, e-diplomacy turns the state into a 'de facto media empire'. In particular, governments acquire a capacity which – at least in theory – should make it possible for them to counter some of the risks associated with the complexities of media communication. E-diplomacy also offers the opportunity for two-way, user-driven communication between states, state leaders and a more diverse public not limited to powerful individuals and elites. The new technologies embraced by E-diplomacy also allow states to enhance their capability to monitor and respond to issues of national significance and to promptly communicate their own worldview on these issues.

NON-STATE ACTORS AND THE MEDIA

One of the most far-reaching developments of the modern age has been new forms of communication. The print revolution gave individuals and groups access to a medium of communication that allowed them to spread their thoughts and ideologies to a broad audience. Non-state actors were able to broadcast their political agendas through the production of pamphlets, books and newspapers to challenge state hegemony. One of the first terrorist waves in modern history, the anarchist wave, appeared as a social movement in the late nineteenth and early twentieth centuries, beginning in Europe and spreading to America and Asia. The ideology of anarchy opposes all forms of social authority and visualises a classless and stateless society governed by the people with no formal authority. Between the 1840s and 1870s, anarchist journals featuring essays by prominent anarchist theorists appeared in Spain, France and Geneva. The trend continued into the late 1800s and early 1900s in America, Europe and the United Kingdom. The print media became the most effective vehicle for the spread of Anarchy throughout Europe, America and Asia.

Today's media environment is characterised by new media platforms that challenge the authority of traditional media sources of television, radio and newspapers. The internet and social media technologies such as Twitter are not only alternative sources of information, news or entertainment, they also allow us to produce and broadcast our own information, news and entertainment. Along with the exponential growth of new media technologies, there has been an expansion of media knowledge. Today's audience is much more media savvy than the audience of 1938 War of the Worlds broadcast. People today are much more likely to distrust or question organisational media news and seek out alternative sources of 'truth'. Young people in particular are much more aware of how news is formed and how media organisations construct certain issues to appeal to certain audiences and encourage certain viewpoints.

The internet offers a virtual marketplace of news, knowledge, information and ideas that allows us to pick and choose what is truth and what is not and to construct our own realities based on our own political, religious or cultural beliefs. Reports, opinion pieces and blogs about an issue, event or experience on the internet will often challenge details or opinions that are presented on television or in newspapers. We are now more empowered than ever to set our own news agendas, to form our own realities and to communicate with like-minded groups who share our worldviews.

In 2012, *Kony 2012* was one of the most globally viewed videos on YouTube amassing close to 100 million hits. The short film created by a group named Invisible Children aimed to raise awareness of and eventually capture Ugandan guerrilla leader Joseph Kony. Apart from becoming a massive hit on YouTube, the campaign was also shared by 8 million Facebook users and 1.6 million Twitter users. The makers of the video attempted to make Kony, a relatively obscure figure, into a household name through the magic of social media. Popularising Kony and amassing global support for his capture would then pressure governments to arrest him for the alleged atrocities of child enslavement and mass murders carried out by Kony's group the Lord Resistance Army (LRA). The Western media has been silent in its reporting of the atrocities committed by Kony and the LRA. It is safe to say that, unless you are a scholar or student of terrorism studies, you probably did not know that the LRA is a religious terrorist group seeking to establish a state based on the biblical Ten Commandments or that their deadly campaign resulted in the deaths of over 500 civilians in the Democratic Republic of the Congo in December 2008. In February 2008, long before the Kony campaign, LRA assailants attacked a Sudanese village burning residences, kidnapping villagers and killing civilians. In March 2009, almost 200 Congolese civilians were kidnapped by the LRA and in June 2009 the LRA was also responsible for kidnapping 150 civilians including 50 children.

The Kony 2012 video focuses on the LRA's forced recruitment of child soldiers. It begins with an ode to the power of social networking and introduces the film as a social experiment on the power of social media. The next 27 minutes feature the film-maker Jason Russell and his young son. Russell tells the story of meeting a young Ugandan named Jacob who witnessed his brother being killed by the LRA. The film is emotional and highly stylised, accompanied by moving music and a passionate promise from Russell to Jacob to stop the LRA. Russell delivers his message through a conversation with his son. We are never told what Russell actually does in Africa (he claims he works there) but his son tells us that he 'stops the bad guys'. Through the innocent eyes of Russell's son, the conflict in Uganda is reduced to a simple case of the good guys versus the bad guys. Eleven minutes into the film, we are introduced to Kony and his atrocities. The film claims that the problem is that 99 per cent of the population do not know who Kony is and, if they did, Kony would be stopped. It then documents the achievements of *Invisible Children* in raising awareness of Kony, culminating in a decision by the US government to deploy troops to central Africa to assist the Ugandan army in stopping the LRA. According to the video, it was the first time in history that the United States government took action because the people demanded it and not for self- defence. Kony 2012 is meant to appeal to the youth who are attracted to and familiar with social media. It presents the Kony 2012 campaign as a way for social media savvy youths to shape world affairs through the simple click of a mouse.

Despite the initial success of the Kony 2012 campaign in attracting millions of views as well as support from high-profile celebrities, the campaign quickly became embroiled in controversy and the movement lost public support. Criticisms of the campaign point out that Kony and the LRA have not been active in Uganda since 2006. The film's representation of Uganda as a country in the midst of a guerrilla war led the Ugandan prime minister to launch his own YouTube video in response to the film to correct the inaccuracies. The film was also criticised within Uganda and elsewhere for focusing too much on the film-makers and Kony and ignoring the victims of the conflict. Further criticism claimed that the film oversimplified a complex issue and that it promoted **Slacktivism** – the act of donating or taking an action that makes you feel good but has little effect. The film-makers and the organisation also came under fire when it was revealed that Invisible Children is an evangelical fundamentalist Christian movement and for spending a significant portion of donations on making films to promote their cause (rather than the actual cause).

Regardless of whether you agree with those who think that Kony 2012 was a catalyst for positive change or you think that the campaign

> **Slacktivism** – a term that describes taking an action in response to a social problem that has little effect but makes you feel good. An example is hitting the 'like' button on a Facebook post or reposting an item. These kinds of actions actually do nothing to improve the situation they claim to represent, but they do make us feel as if we have done something.

was irresponsible and ineffective, the case of Kony 2012 demonstrates the power of the media in influencing international affairs, foreign and domestic policies. Kony 2012 was not the first time that individuals and groups used the media to influence or change government policy. Because the media is such an important vehicle in shaping our ideas and beliefs, it has been used and manipulated by those who want to influence governments and their policies. In the 1970s, groups fighting for the Palestinian cause recognised the power and influence of the international media and took to the international stage by hijacking international airlines and capturing the attention of the world media. In democratic nations where politicians are answerable to their people, how the media represents government policy will have a significant impact on political decisions. People will formulate their opinions about a government policy or action based on how the media portrays those policies and actions and politicians who are keen to keep their electorate happy will be swayed by public opinion.

We should not be surprised that the internet has also appealed to non-state actors, including extremist groups with a political, ideological or social cause. These groups have traditionally had very little political influence. In some cases this is because the groups may be oppressed by the group in power. In other cases, it is because these groups are seen to operate on the fringe of society and are marginalised by the dominant group. Above all these groups have had very little, if any, access to the mainstream media and are often portrayed negatively in the media. In previous sections of this chapter we examined how the media maintains hegemony by reflecting dominant group values and norms. In this way, the media functions to effectively marginalise groups with values and norms that are considered to be outside the boundaries of the dominant groups' values and norms. When the media is an apparatus of the state, the state may use the media to demonise oppositional groups by labelling them extremist or to censure the groups' messages and effectively silencing them.

The internet offers extremist and marginalised groups access to an audience to which they can disseminate their own messages but also challenge the dominant values and norms. Examples of extremist groups that have taken to the internet to spread their message include white supremacist groups, religious 'cults', anarchists, radical feminists and anti-abortion groups. It also offers such groups the opportunity to mobilise their audiences in ways that circumvent the state apparatus to build alliances and organise strategies not only within borders but also across borders. In modern history, the arrival of the 'information age', marked by the onset of the digital revolution, transformed the global economy. Global transformations associated with the information age include the spread of global Capitalism and a subsequent decline of the social-welfare state as states became more preoccupied with security and managing the transnational flow of goods and people.

In line with these global trends, the diffusion of primarily Western cultural values through the international consumption of Western media products has also transformed the international landscape. Marmura (2010, 2) describes the impact of the digital revolution and the concurrent transformations in the global economy as having a significant impact on international relations: 'All of these developments have been implicated in a global resurgence of identity-based politics, the transformation of civil society in liberal democracies, and the establishment of new forms of social solidarity in which the state is no longer paramount'.

Marmura also reminds us that the internet remains a form of alternative media that allows access to minority groups with opposing worldviews. He argues that the widespread use of the internet by minority groups actually reinforces their minority status. This argument invites us to question how the internet as a marketplace of opposing ideas, worldviews, ideologies and 'truths' impacts on media hegemony and the ability of the elite or dominant group in a society to maintain the *status quo*.

One answer is that the Web acts as an equaliser by giving marginalised groups representation that they cannot find in the traditional mass media. Another answer is that the Web operates primarily as a marketplace of competing ideas and that individuals will search for and accept those ideas that most closely mirror their own cultural, political and social values while discounting those that do not. In this sense, the traditional mass media still maintains a level of hegemony in so far as it sets the agenda of news content not only for the media consumer but also for those groups using the Web to voice alternative views.

This second answer is perhaps best demonstrated by examining how terrorist or dissident groups use the internet. Since the first modern wave of anarchist terrorism, terrorist groups have embraced the media as a way of communicating their cause to a broad population. The term 'propaganda by the deed' was first coined to describe the use of violence as a means to draw attention to social inequality and to motivate others to perform acts of terrorism against governments. In the 1970s, terrorist groups recognised the immense value of attracting worldwide media attention to their cause by staging terrorist attacks on the 'international stage'. It was during this time that international airline hijackings became a popular tactic of choice for groups with an opposition message. Today's terrorists still recognise the value of international news. Major terrorist incidents are staged to attract international attention through traditional media coverage. At the same time, terrorist groups such as al-Qaeda have an internet presence to propagate their message and attract sympathisers. The internet also serves operational and tactical purposes allowing them to communicate with members around the world. It could be said that the internet serves as a secondary medium for terrorist groups but that access to traditional mass media remains their main goal.

There are also several examples of citizen-based groups successfully using the internet to lobby government and change particular policies. Gloor (2006) defines a Collaborative Innovation Network (CoIN) as 'a cyberteam of self-motivated people with a collective vision, enabled by the Web to collaborate in achieving a common goal by sharing ideas, information, and work' (Gloor 2006, 11). Bimber (1998) offers several examples of how such groups effectively used the internet to influence local and foreign policies of states in the absence of any widespread media attention.

CONCLUSION

This chapter explored the role of the media in international relations. The media plays an important role not just as an actor in its own right but also as a mediator of the relationship between states, transnational organisations (such as NGOs and IGOs) and individuals. The reach and influence of the media on individuals, states and the international discourse is often contested and has been the subject of years of research and debate. While we still have no definite answers about just how much the media influences us and how much we influence the media, we cannot deny that the media is an important aspect of our everyday lives as well as the global affairs that impact on our lives. The uptake of new technologies of communication has added a complex dimension to debates about media hegemony. Both state and non-state actors have embraced technology for different uses but with the same purpose of influencing the international discourse.

QUESTIONS FOR REFLECTION

1. How is the media a key player in international relations? Do you consider that the media's role is limited to influencing public opinion or does it have a greater role to play in international discourse?
2. Think about the phrase 'war on terror'. How does this phrase determine what we can and cannot say about terrorism? How has this phrase become part of our everyday language and how does this reflect a political agenda?
3. Should states censor the internet? If so, how would such moves impact on the international discourse?
4. To what extent has the information age transformed international relations? How effective is the internet in equalising the discourse?
5. Consider how states and non-state actors use the media. Do they use the media for the same things? How are they the same and/or different?

REVISION QUIZ

1. Non-state actors are key players in international relations according to which theoretical position?

    a. Constructivist
    b. Structuralist
    c. Realist
    d. Constructivist and structuralist

2. The theory that international television has a significant effect on foreign policy is known as:

   a. The BBC effect
   b. The ABC syndrome
   c. The CNN effect
   d. Media hegemony.

3. The notion that news media conforms to political and market forces is a key concept of:

   a. The CNN effect
   b. Media hegemony
   c. Manufacturing concept
   d. All of the above

4. Your world view is dictated by:

   a. Your age and gender
   b. Your parents
   c. The social norms of where you live
   d. All of the above

5. Weltanschauung refers to:

   a. Ideology and worldview
   b. News and information
   c. Culture and traditions
   d. Family and society

6. Media hegemony is best described as:

   a. The monopoly of international news corporations
   b. The power of the media to influence and maintain dominant ways of thinking
   c. The superiority of television news over print media
   d. The use of media by governments to influence election results

7. Propaganda is:

   a. Information used to influence an audience
   b. A political tool to limit opposition
   c. Positive or negative depending on its source
   d. All of the above

8. E-diplomacy is mostly used for:

   a. Policy planning
   b. Disaster response
   c. Public diplomacy
   d. Internet freedom

9. The media is used to influence foreign policy by:

    a. States
    b. Non-government organisations
    c. Terrorist groups
    d. All of the above

10. Non-government organisations use the internet:

    a. To promote Western cultural values
    b. To influence state policy by naming and shaming
    c. To develop their cells
    d. Instead of traditional mass media

Answers: 1: d; 2: c; 3: c; 4: d; 5: a; 6: b; 7: d; 8: c; 9: d; 10: b.

BIBLIOGRAPHY

Bimber, B (1998) 'The internet and political transformation: Populism, community, and accelerated pluralism', *Polity* 31(1), 133–61.

Gamson, W.A. and Modigliani, A. (1989) 'Media discourse and public opinion on nuclear power: A constructionist approach', *American Journal of Sociology* 95(1), 1–37.

Cohen-Almagor, R. (2005) 'Media Coverage of Acts of Terrorism: Troubling Episodes and Suggested Guidelines', *Canadian Journal of Communication* 30(3).

Gloor, P. (2006) *Swarm Creativity: Competitive Advantage Through Collaborative Innovation Networks* (Oxford, NY: Oxford University Press).

Hammond, P. (2003) 'The media war on terrorism', *Journal for Crime, Conflict and the Media* 1(1), 23–36.

Hanson, F. (2011) 'E-diplomacy in action: Interview with the UK's Head of Digital Diplomacy by Fergus Hanson', The Lowy Interpreter 24 May, viewed 24 February 2012. Available at: <http://www.lowyinterpreter.org/post/2011/05/24/Ediplomacy-in-action-Interview-with-the-UKs-Head-of-Digital-Diplomacy.aspx>.

Hanson, F. (2012) 'Revolution @State: The Spread of Ediplomacy', The Lowy Institute, March, viewed 24 February 2012. Available at: <http://www.lowyinstitute.org/publications/revolutionstate-spread-ediplomacy>.

Hoffman, B. (1998) *Inside Terrorism* (New York, Columbia University Press).

Marmura, S.M.E. (2010) *Hegemony in the Digital Age: The Arab/Israeli Conflict Online* (Plymouth, Lexington Books).

McQuail, D. (1983) *Mass Communication Theory* (London, Sage Publications).

Moeller, S.D. (2004) Media Coverage of Weapons of Mass Destruction, Centre for International and Security Studies at Maryland, 3 September, viewed 24 February 2012. Available at: <http://www.cissm.umd.edu/papers/display.php?id=32>.

Said, E. (1979) *Orientalism* (New York, Vintage Books).

Chapter 17
Global Governance

SANDRA POPIDEN

This chapter begins by defining the concept and practices of global governance. In this way, it provides students with an overview of the many governance challenges competing for attention on the international agenda. The chapter illustrates how the efforts to address global concerns such as international terrorism, international crime, asymmetrical war, weapons of mass destruction and climate change are all made more difficult by the financial constraints imposed by the global recession 2008–12 and the problems of compliance gaps in weak states. After discussing the numerous competing items on governance agendas, we then turn to the evolution of the international security and economic governance architecture. Despite the rise of regional organizations and non-state actors such as multinational corporations and non-governmental organizations, this chapter highlights that the international organizations created after World War II remain central to the global governance architecture. The chapter concludes with a discussion of the rise of new global powers such as China, Brazil and India and their efforts to alter decision-making procedures in order to increase the organizations' accountability and perceived legitimacy. One of the most significant challenges facing the international community is how to innovate or adapt international organizations to include new state members and non-state actors without significantly harming the effectiveness of the organization and their ability to make decisions needed to address diverse governance challenges.

Key Words: Global Governance, International Regimes, Intergovernmental Organizations, Regional Organizations, Millennium Development Goals, Supra-national Organizations, Intergovernmental Organizations, Responsibility to Protect.

Chapter 17

Global Governance

SANDRA POPIDEN

*Global governance institutions have adapted to some degree as new issues have emerged,
but the adaptations have not necessarily been intentional or substantial enough to keep up
with growing demand. Rather, they have been spurred as much by outside forces as by the
institutions themselves ... Multiple and diverse governance frameworks, however flexible,
probably are not going to be sufficient to keep pace with the looming number of transnational
and global challenges absent extensive institutional reforms and innovations. (US National
Intelligence Council Report 2010)*

WHAT IS GLOBAL GOVERNANCE?

Global governance is a complex and amorphous term that refers to humanity's efforts
'to provide security, prosperity, coherence, order, and continuity to the system' (King and
Schneider 1991, 181–2). Throughout much of history, this term referred to balance of power
politics and a rather limited conception of international diplomacy between sovereign states.
As economic interdependence rose over the last 200 years, the weaknesses of the state system
led states to establish more extensive norms and rules governing the interaction with other
states and regions. This included multilateral meetings of the European great powers in the
Concert of Europe, conferences that led to The Hague System conventions for war-fighting and
the establishment of international organizations
to solve functional problems (Karns and
Mingst 2010, 66–7). In the current era, **global
governance** involves relationships between
actors who establish transnational rules and
norms to manage coordination, collaboration and
distribution problems.

> **Global Governance** – the ways that global
> affairs are managed. This involves relationships
> between actors who establish transnational
> rules and norms to manage coordination,
> collaboration and distribution problems.

However, the collective means of monitoring, managing or enforcing rules at the international
level is not the same as a global government. The system is anarchic and policy coordination has
historically been decentralized and lacking formalized structure. There is no one government
or overarching political authority that is responsible for drafting or enforcing rules for the
world. Instead, global governance refers to purposive behaviour, goal-oriented activities and
systems of rule and norms that go beyond the level of the state (Koch 2011, 198). It is comprised
of international principles, norms, laws, **international regimes** and **intergovernmental
organizations** that impact relations and behaviour in areas including security, economic,
human rights or environmental policies. Unlike the domestic level, international laws often lack
enforcement mechanisms and depend on voluntary state ratification and compliance.

States have increasingly chosen to join over 240 intergovernmental organizations and **regional organizations** because they face problems that cannot be managed unilaterally. These offer states forums to increase their access to information, reduce transaction costs, institutionalize interaction and develop issue-linkages (Keohane 1984). These factors can promote norms of reciprocity and reputation-building while discouraging, shaming or sanctioning cheaters. Formal institutions and informal processes can help to coordinate problem-solving efforts and steer international collective action, as well as at times constraining

International Regimes – norms, principles, rules and decision-making procedures around which actors' expectations converge.

Intergovernmental Organizations – an organization consisting primarily of sovereign states whose members develop charters and international treaties involving international security, socio-economic and political issues. Examples include the UN, World Bank, IMF and WTO.

Regional Organizations – organizations formed by states within a particular region, focusing on managing economic, security or political issues. Examples include the European Union, African Union and NATO.

the behaviour of international actors. Members decide whether or not to ratify international laws and comply with international regimes based on moral suasion, the perceived costs and benefits of cooperation versus non-participation and the likelihood of penalties for non-compliance.

Arthur A. Stein argues that 'we live in a world of weak confederalism precisely because states find independent decision making inadequate to their needs; they thus prefer forms of joint decision making and governance, yet they are unprepared to relinquish core elements of their autonomy and independence' (Stein 2008, 75). Thus, there are unremitting tensions in the international system between sovereign states' interests and global governance initiatives that are present in all international institutions. Global governance efforts are messy, complex and are often, but not always, led by states or by the international organizations that states create. Increasingly, contemporary governance efforts involve multiple actors including governments, markets, international organizations, regional organizations, non-governmental organizations, firms and transnational advocacy groups who operate within three domains – the political, economic and sociocultural (UNDP 1997, 14–18).

Table 17.1   Actors in global governance

☐ States
☐ Sub-national jurisdictions
☐ Multinational corporations
☐ Intergovernmental Organizations
☐ Nongovernmental Organizations
☐ Transnational Advocacy Networks
☐ Foundations and Experts

Unprecedented improvements in transportation and communications technologies have led to the rising importance of non-state actors. Large multinational corporations, hedge funds and banks have all risen as significant players in the international political economy. For example, in 1998, there were approximately 53,000 multinational corporations with 45, 0000 subsidiaries spread throughout the world with global sales of $9.5 trillion (Held et al. 1999, 236). Similarly, according to the Bank for International Settlements, in 2010 the average daily turnover in foreign exchange currency markets rose from $1.53 trillion in 1998 to $3.98 trillion a day. To put this into perspective, the value of all merchandise exports in 2011 was $18.2 trillion dollars. Capital flows and international investments have brought about unprecedented wealth, but they have also led to devastating episodic periods of crisis, illustrating the wide jurisdictional gaps between the degree of interdependence and international regulations.

Table 17.2   World's 15 largest multinational corporations vs. 15 weakest states

Rank	Company	Revenues ($Billions)	Profits ($Billions)	Rank	Failed State Index	GDP ($Billions)
1	Exxon Mobil	$452,926	$41,060	1	Somalia	$2,37
2	Wal-Mart Stores	$446,950	$15,699	2	DRC	$15,46
3	Chevron	$245,621	$26,895	3	Sudan	$62,97
4	ConocoPhillips	$237,272	$12,436	4	Chad	$9,195
5	General Motors	$150,276	$9,190	5	Zimbabwe	$9,307
6	General Electric	$147,616	$14,151	6	Afghanistan	$18,02
7	Berkshire Hathaway	$143,688	$10,254	7	Haiti	$7,27
8	Fannie Mae	$137,451	$-16,855	8	Yemen	$33,22
9	Ford Motor	$136,264	$20,213	9	Iraq	$112,4
10	Hewlett-Packard	$127,245	$7,074	10	Central African Republic	$2,16
11	AT&T	$126,723	$3,944	11	Ivory Coast	$23,71
12	Valero Energy	$125,095	$2,090	12	Guinea	$5,087
13	Bank of America Corp.	$115,074	$1,446	13	Pakistan	$206,9
14	McKesson	$112,084	$1,202	14	Nigeria	$240,1
15	Verizon Communications	$110,875	$2,404	15	Guinea-Bissau	$953,5 (*million)

Sources: Fortune 500 Magazine's Annual Ranking of Largest 100 Companies (2012); State Failure Task Force Rankings (2012); CIA World Factbook GDP: Official Exchange Rate (2011).

Although **nongovernmental organizations** have traditionally lacked the financial capabilities of states, IGOs or **multinational corporations**, they have become increasingly important in transnational advocacy networks that contribute to norm creation. They are active in human rights, economic development, humanitarian aid, environmental and corporate social responsibility campaigns (Keck and Sikkink 2000). For example, the Bill and Melinda Gates Foundation is actually the single largest donor to international health projects and in 2010 they committed ten billion US dollars over ten years to fight disease (Koch 2011, 202). Again, for comparison, the World Health Organization's annual budget is approximately two

Nongovernmental Organizations – a diverse set of non-profit organizations participating in a wide variety of actions at local, national or international levels. They are often civic organizations that are not part of a government or a traditional business.

Multinational Corporations – for-profit organizations that operate outside the boundaries of any one state, involving production, services or sales in home and host countries. MNCS are also known as transnational corporations.

billion dollars. Thus, while the world's 7,500 international NGOs and millions of domestic NGOs (ibid. 2011, 230) have largely not been granted a formal seat at policy-making tables, their advocacy, monitoring and collaborative efforts help to form an emergent pillar of global governance (Muldoon 2003, 9).

From the perspective of neorealist scholars, there is a general skepticism that states can evolve from an anarchical system based on self-help and national interest. This is argued to be particularly unlikely when security issues are concerned. They are also far less likely to see IGOs as effective or enduring and challenge claims that non-state actors have independent agency or can bring about a shift beyond the traditional state-centric models of global governance. In comparison, social-constructivist and neoliberal theorists hold more room for optimism that the international community has the potential to collectively innovate and devise new global governance ideas and institutions. For constructivists, the emphasis is on identities, repeated interaction and the potential for the creation of **intersubjective consensus**. For neoliberal scholars, the focus is on reducing miscalculations, reforming international institutions and strengthening international laws. While states can no longer monopolize global governance, efforts to reform multilateral institutions are complicated by the sheer number and diversity of preferences and capabilities held by state and non-state actors. Humanity is facing a period of rapid changes and

Inter-Subjective Consensus – the social construction of shared meaning, values, beliefs, practices and social behaviour (often held by cultural groups).

challenges that are varied, complex and formidable. Innovative thinking and institutions are needed if the international system is to adapt 'from a multilateral system at the service of national interests to a true system of world governance' (de Kerckhove 2008, 204). At present, fluidity rules the day and the emergent system of global governance is dynamic and in flux. The ultimate outcome of the reform debates and the ultimate shape of the traditional pillars of global governance architecture are not yet fully determined.

This chapter begins with an evaluation of the array of the new **trans-sovereign** challenges that often require local, national and international collective action. Although regional organizations and private sources of authority are becoming increasingly important, the second section focuses on the evolution of the core elements of intergovernmental organizations at the centre of multilateral efforts on security and economic policy-making. It also emphasizes the

Trans-Sovereign Challenges – problems that no one state is responsible for, which cross state boundaries and which cannot be solved by any one state alone.

rising demand for global governance reforms of the permanent rules-based United Nations and Bretton Woods economic institutions. The third section examines emerging trends, such as changes in the relative distribution of economic power from West to East, periodic shocks to the system and the rise of non-state actors that all contributed to pressures for reform of the central pillars of the global governance architecture. Traditional governance mechanisms have proven insufficient to deal with complex interdependence and the proliferation of threats to life on earth. The final section asserts that the fundamental challenge of the twenty-first century is for state and non-state actors to devise new mechanisms and innovative reforms of existing patchwork of global institutions to more effectively manage the global crises and existential threats to our collective survival.

AN OVERVIEW OF GLOBAL GOVERNANCE CHALLENGES

Humanity currently faces a formidable array of **trans-sovereign** security, economic, developmental and environmental **challenges**. The good news in the global security environment is that nuclear deterrence and the long-term trends of rising tide of democratic regimes, levels of economic interdependence and UN peacemaking initiatives have reduced interstate wars (Mack et al. 2010). Economic development, international trade, foreign direct investment and peacekeeping efforts have also helped to reduce the number of civil wars (Fearon and Laitin 2003; Barbieri and Reuveny 2005; Doyle and Sambanis 2006). Although 1.5 billion people continue to live in countries affected by intra-state violence, the dominant form of violence in the post-World War II era has been reduced from its peak in the mid-1990s. The absolute or extreme poverty rate, (people living on less than $1.25 per day) has also been cut in half to 22 per cent of humanity over the last 20 years. Significant progress has also been made on other *Millennium Development Goals* (MDGs), such as promoting equal access for girls to primary education, improving health conditions, child survival rates and clean drinking water by 2015. However, large regional inequities remain with 3 billion people living on less than $2 dollars a day and at least 80 per cent of the developing world living on less than $10 dollars per day (Ravallion et al. 2008, 3).

Table 17.3   Global governance issues on UN agenda

Africa	Health
Aging	Human Rights
AIDS	Human Settlements
Atomic Energy	Humanitarian Assistance
Children	International Law
Climate Change	Oceans/ Law of the Seas
Decolonization	Peace and Security
Demining	Persons with Disabilities
Democracy	Population
Development	Refugees
Disarmament	Terrorism
Environment	Volunteerism
Family	Water
Food	Women
Governance	

Source: UN Global Issues http://www.un.org/en/globalissues/index.shtml.

Table 17.4   Millennium development goals (2000–15)

1)	Eradicate extreme poverty & hunger
2)	Achieve universal primary education
3)	Promote gender equality & empower women
4)	Reduce child mortality
5)	Improve maternal healt
6)	Combat HIV and other diseases
7)	Ensure environmental sustainability
8)	Develop a global partnership for development

Source: United Nations Development Program (2012)
http://www.undp.org/content/undp/en/home/mdgoverview.html.

However, the cautious optimism stemming from the decline in the incidence of high intensity great power and civil wars is now threatened. Dangers posed by weak states, international terrorist and criminal networks, nuclear proliferation and outlier regimes, cyber attacks and global pandemics all do not respect sovereign borders. In 2009, US President Obama also stressed that climate change and the theft of loose nuclear materials are new security challenges that impact the prospects for peace and prosperity of every nation. The World Bank President Jim Yong Kim also called upon G20 finance ministers to recognize that climate change poses an escalating 'real and present danger', stressing that the damages from natural disasters are reversing years of progress in economic development (Kim 2013).

The Global Recession (2008–12)

In this era of global interdependence, markets and global problems are progressing at a faster rate than the institutional or conceptual responses can adapt (Love M. 2007, 320). Meeting these challenges has been made even more difficult because, in the last five years, we have also witnessed the most devastating economic crises since the Great Depression. The 2008 financial crisis, which began due to highly speculative business ventures and practices of overleveraging in subprime mortgage-backed securities, led to the economic meltdown of investment banks and financial institutions at the centre of global finance. With the bursting of the property asset bubble in the United States, approximately $50 trillion in assets was destroyed in the world economy (Zakaria 2007). Bank failures triggered a global recession with high levels of market uncertainty, millions of jobs losses, a liquidity crisis and a sizable reduction in remittances. A recent inquiry found that this was an 'avoidable' crisis caused by 'widespread failures in government regulation, corporate mismanagement and heedless risk-taking by Wall Street' that quickly spread to other industrialized economies and contributed to the European sovereign debt crisis (Chan 2011).

As a consequence of market interdependence, the financial meltdown in the US spread, creating a loss of investor confidence in the economic sustainability of countries with mountainous debt burdens. This increased countries' borrowing costs and threatened the existence of the Euro. In fact, intelligence assessments warned of dire consequences of an unruly

Greek exit from the 17-member eurozone currency union that could have caused 'eight times the collateral damage as the Lehman Brothers bankruptcy' (National Intelligence Council 2012, xi). In response, governments have undertaken unprecedented levels of bailouts, nationalization of businesses and fiscal stimulus packages. The US Federal Reserve and the EU Central Bank also increased their coordination on monetary policy, lowered interest rates, employed quantitative easing and acted as lenders of last resort to struggling financial institutions. In 2012, the EU also created the European Stability Mechanism (ESM), with a lending capacity of up to $500 billion Euros, to act as a more permanent crisis resolution mechanism to avoid future crises (European Commission 2012, 3).

The global recession and widespread youth unemployment have also had a significant security impact by breeding political instability and increasing the risk of violence in under-developed countries, particularly in developing countries that lack the capability to employ adequate fiscal and monetary interventions. Increased market uncertainty, paired with scarcity of vital resources, youth bulges and populations are exacerbating existing problems of high rates of unemployment and hunger around the world. According to intelligence estimates, due to the economic slowdown, roughly a quarter of the countries in the world have already experienced low-level instability such as government changes and the risk of regime threatening instability remains likely (Blair 2009, 2). The slowdown of economic growth in emerging economies along with rising fuel and food prices also pushed an additional 100 million people around the globe into the undernourished category that contains over one billion people (FAO 2009, 8). Rising food prices also contributed to the mobilization of protests and riots across the globe that were more likely to become violent in poor countries with weak governments.

Weak States and Compliance Gaps

One of the most significant underlying problems in world politics is that approximately one-third of states are weak with limited capabilities to mitigate these shocks to the system. In a globalized world, the lack of capacity in failed states contributes to the permissive conditions for transnational problems, including the proliferation of weapons of mass destruction and loose nuclear materials, international terrorism, criminal networks and insurgencies that undermine both international and human security. The fact that more than 50 states are *weak* or failing underscores the challenges of contemporary multilateralism and the overall fragility of the international system (de Kerckhove 2008, 204).

Weapons of Mass Destruction

For 20 years, the father of the Pakistani nuclear bomb A.Q. Khan has posed major challenges to the non-proliferation regime by supplying nuclear materials to weak states such as North Korea, Libya and Iran. Other non-state actors, such as al-Qaeda and Chechen terrorist organizations, have also demonstrated a commitment over the last 15 years to purchase, steal or create WMD in order to fulfil their goal of killing millions (Mowatt-Larssen 2010, 2). The inability of the Nuclear Non-Proliferation Treaty to combat the combination of weak nuclear states and the potential for such materials to get into the hands of international terrorist organizations has reduced confidence in containment and deterrence. It also led to the creation of more aggressive interdiction efforts under the Proliferation Security Initiative, a preventive war against Iraq and the potential for future actions against Iran or North Korea.

International Terrorism

Shocking events such as September 11, 2001 have led to academics and policymakers to recognize the potential for weak states to pose an acute risk to global security. The 9/11 terrorist attacks alone led to approximately 3,000 deaths from over 90 countries and direct financial losses between $80 to $90 billion (Sandler and Enders 2008, 7). The subsequent wars fought in Afghanistan, Iraq and Pakistan led to 310,000 battle deaths, 965,000 indirect deaths and a financial cost of between $3 and $4 trillion (Costs of War Project 2012). While and deaths from terrorist attacks have declined and support for violence in the Islamic world has fallen since 2007, five of the world's deadliest conflicts – in Iraq, Afghanistan, Pakistan and Somalia – all involve Islamist insurgencies and have proven intractable (Mack et al. 2010).

Immediately after the most devastating single terrorist attack in recent history, the international community participated in an unprecedented level of cooperation in ratifying UN Resolutions 1368, 1373 and 1540. While many of the top leadership in al-Qaeda have been killed or detained, difficulties in implementing and enforcing the anti-terrorism regime remain. Such problems stem from the lack of an overarching consensus on a basic definition of terrorism, disputes over priorities and a lack of state compliance capabilities. Efforts to counter non-state terrorist networks have largely focused on prohibiting particular acts and targeting terrorist financing.

After 9/11, there were initial spectacular successes in targeting terrorist financing, however in recent years progress 'has now slowed and almost faltered' (Acharya 2009, 134). For example, as of 2007, only around 80 countries ratified all 16 international conventions and protocols against terrorism and ratification is not a sufficient condition for changing domestic law or increasing enforcement (Rosand, Millar and Ipe 2007, 7). Compliance limitations include border security, control of territory, monitoring financial transactions, freezing assets and preventing money laundering. States where the most terrorist attacks and deaths occur (Iraq, Pakistan, Afghanistan, Yemen and Somalia) also have some of the weakest enforcement capabilities. In 2014, President Obama proposed a $5 billion fund to support such counterterrorism capabilities in weak states on the frontlines of combating terrorism.

Illicit Criminal Activities

Fragile states are also attractive locations for drug cartels and international criminal networks. For example, Afghanistan's farmers harvest about 80 per cent of the world supply of the raw material for heroin and much of these funds are used to fund the ongoing insurgency (UNODC 2012a, 30). Over the last decade, there has been a significant growth in transnational organized criminal networks and the illicit trafficking of people, natural resources and firearms. Participation, capability and implementation gaps also impact the effectiveness of Conventions on Corruption (UNCAC) and Transnational Organized Crime (UNOTC) and protocols on human trafficking or trafficking firearms. These gaps are evident in current value of criminal money laundering, which 'have amounted so some 3.6 per cent of GDP (2.3–5.5 per cent) or around $2.1 trillion in 2009' with only .2 per cent of criminal funds being seized or frozen (UNODC 2011, 5). These illicit activities harm efforts to break poverty traps and promote the achievement of the Millennium Development Goals.

Insurgencies and Civil War

Weak states also create conditions favourable for insurgencies that often destabilize regions by lowering economic growth and leading to cross-border movements of militias, violence and refugees. According to the Human Security Report (2010), the number of internal armed conflicts increased by 25 per cent, reversing previous declines heralded in the HSR 2005 report, and inter-communal conflicts increased more than 100 per cent between 2003 and 2008. Low-income countries are the most likely to fall into these conflict traps. These involve repeated episodes of violence that worsen poverty rates and destroy economies, political institutions and social capital (Collier et al. 2003, 91). Civil wars lead a process of development in reverse and create of a culture of impunity with long-lasting consequences that increase a state's chances of experiencing the return to violence even a decade after the violence ends (ibid. 2003, 14). Countries in conflict are also the least likely to have met any of the MDG goals. However, a formidable obstacle that impacts the ability of the international community to address threats to international security and to protect human security is that the United Nations was not designed or intended to address such intra-state matters.

Due to principle of non-intervention in domestic affairs of member states, which remains the bedrock of international relations, the challenges posed by ongoing civil wars have proven notoriously difficult for the international community to address. Only in recent decades has the norm of sovereignty being contingent on respect for human rights been asserted. The failures of the international community to act, or offer a fitting mandate and funding of operations in Bosnia, Rwanda or Syria illustrate the continuing gap between normative capabilities and incentive capabilities (Stein 2008, 64). Improving economic development, domestic capacity-building and international coordination efforts are all critical to reducing human suffering and promoting positive peace-building efforts.

Climate Change

Severe weather events also have illustrated their ability to overwhelm countries' infrastructure and response systems. In 2012, super storm Hurricane Sandy hit the East Coast and led to damages of $65 billion, while 295 separate natural disasters around the globe causing economic losses of $200 billion (Aon Benfield 2012, 77). The International Panel on Climate Change (IGCC) reports provide evidence that rising CO_2 levels are associated with trends such as the disruption of seasons, changing rainfall patterns, the hottest years on record, increases in droughts, wildfires, melting polar ice caps, rising sea levels and coastal flooding. While the detrimental impacts of such losses are mitigated by insurance in developed countries, these mechanisms are largely lacking in developing countries. For example, in 2011, conflict and climate change contributed to drought and famine in the horn of Africa (Williams and Funk 2011, 2421), creating the world's worst humanitarian crisis (Garvelink and Tahir 2011).

Without intervention, temperatures are expected to continue to rise by more than '4 degrees Celsius by the end of the century, leading to widespread crop failures, malnutrition, loss of bio-diversity and dislocation large numbers of people from land inundated by rising seas' (Schneider 2012): 780 million people already lack access to clean water (UNICEF 2013) and that freshwater is increasingly becoming a strategic commodity (UNITF 2004). Despite these events and dire predictions, international prevention and management have been rather weak. For example, the Kyoto Protocol on industrial greenhouse gas emissions only covers about 15 per cent of the world's carbon output, with the US, China and India not participating (Eilperin 2012). Recent summits in Copenhagen (2009) and Cancun (2010) and Doha (2012) illustrate the difficulties in achieving a universal and legally binding climate treaty. To date, the proposal for a Green Climate Fund of $100 billion per year from industrial countries to developing countries to help them to respond and adapt to climate change has been approved but is not yet funded.

As these diverse threats to international and human security illustrate, there are a wide range of global governance gaps. According to Antonio Gueterres (2012), head of the UN refugee agency, the world presently faces a global humanitarian crisis at unprecedented levels, and refugee crises 'unmatched in recent history'. In fact, James Muldoon (2003) argues that the international system established in the wake of World War II is coming undone. He refers to the cornerstones of twentieth-century international relations such as the Westphalian state system, non-interference in domestic affairs, the inviolability of state borders and Wilsonian principles of collective security as being undermined by the forces of globalization and fragmentation that characterize the post-Cold War world.

THE EVOLUTION OF GLOBAL GOVERNANCE ARCHITECTURE

The United Nations System's Central Role in Global Governance

In 1945, in the midst of World War II and the bloodiest century in human history, 51 sovereign states met in San Francisco to sign the Charter of the United Nations. These states agreed that it was in their interest to create a series of intergovernmental organizations and international institutions intended to prevent the recurrence of another devastating great power war and Great Depression. The central aim of the United Nations was to maintain international peace and security through international law, the prevention or settlement of disputes or collective action to counter threats to peace. Members also committed to the development of friendly relations based on the principle of equal rights among states; to multilateral cooperation in solving international economic, social, cultural or humanitarian problems; and to respect universal human rights.

With the establishment of the UN, the founding member states intended to move beyond the limitations of balance of power politics and to replace the League of Nations that previously failed to combat aggression or deliver on the promise of collective security. Article 51 of the UN Charter enshrined that states can legally pursue individual or collective self-defense when faced with aggressive states. Perhaps the most significant change in the UN has been the dramatic rise in membership of states possessing varying degrees of strength and viability. Indeed, when the UN was created in 1945, 'some 80 per cent of the human population did not even exist yet as independent entities' (Zweifel 2006, 179). By the turn of the twentieth century, the UN had grown into a near universal and multi-dimensional intergovernmental

> **R2P** – a resolution supported by the UN in 2005 that established the norm of sovereignty as entailing responsibilities for the state and that the international communities have a responsibility to prevent mass atrocities.

organization with nearly 200 member states. Only recently have the long-standing principles of de jure state sovereignty and non-interference in the internal affairs of other states enshrined in the UN Charter begun to be challenged by norms such as the Responsibility to Protect (R2P) and notions of conditional sovereignty. According to the UN Charter, the UN Security Council was imbued with authority to manage threats to international peace. This means that they can issue resolutions implementing sanctions, international interventions or refer cases to the newly established International Criminal Court for prosecution of gross human rights violations.

Far from being monolithic, the United Nations is actually an intricate system involving six different principle organs and 19 independent specialized agencies. This complex system of UN organs includes the UN Security Council, the General Assembly, the Economic and Social Council (ECOSOC), the Secretariat, the International Court of Justice and the now defunct Trusteeship Council. The organs are located in New York, with the exception of the ICJ, which is located at The Hague in the Netherlands.

Table 17.5   The Responsibility to Protect norm

The R2P rests on three pillars:

☐ A state has a responsibility to protect its population from mass atrocities;

☐ The international community has a responsibility to assist the state to fulfil its primary responsibility;

☐ If the state fails to protect its citizens from mass atrocities and peaceful measures have failed, the international community has the responsibility to intervene through coercive measures such as economic sanctions. Military intervention is considered the last resort.

Source: UN Office of the Special Adviser on the Prevention of Genocide http://www.un.org/en/preventgenocide/adviser/responsibility.shtml.

Throughout the Cold War, East-West ideological divisions and great power constraints were high and this significantly impacted the ability of the organization to act. For example, following the collapse of the Soviet Union in 1991, the number of peacekeeping operations aimed at conflict management dramatically increased and there are now 14 operations with over 100,000 serving personnel and a budget of $7.33 billion (UNDPK 2013).

During the Cold War, the Secretariat also struggled to maintain the perceived neutrality of the UN to ensure continued monetary support for the organization. Likewise, the International Court of Justice largely remained underutilized by states and few contentious cases were brought to the world court during that period. With the end of the bipolar system's constraints, the Security Council also expanded their interpretation of threats to international security to include genocide and other systematic abuses of human rights, as well as the spread of infectious diseases.

UN Security Council

Like the League of Nations before it, there are five permanent members (P-5) in the Security Council – the United States, France, the United Kingdom, Russia and the People's Republic of China. In order to pass resolutions and respond to international crises all P-5 members must also vote in favour or abstain and four of ten non-permanent members must vote in favour of a resolution. Although the P-5 states make up less than 10 per cent of all UN members, they have the effective ability to capture the international agenda and block international action. Countries like Japan, Brazil, and India and South Africa continue to call for reforms of the UNSC to more accurately reflect changes in the current distribution of power and their increased share of membership contributions.

In the General Assembly, UNSC reforms are commonly proposed, but 'while there is general recognition of the need to reform and to enlarge the Council, opinions diverge when it comes to … the category of new members, their number, their geographic distribution and the Council's working methods' (Deiss 2011). Methods for increasing the legitimacy, representativeness, accountability and efficiency of the UN are all frequently discussed, but the volume of debate has yet to be matched with concerted action. The P-5 members have consistently resisted proposals to reduce their own power in the Security Council by either increasing the number of permanent members or by creating a new mechanism to elect countries. Thus, the current prospects for P-5 Security Council reforms are rather unlikely.

UN General Assembly

Another organ of the UN, the General Assembly (GA) consists of all UN member states and it lies at the centre of global multilateral deliberation. Members throughout the world work to advance their interests and peacefully manage international relations based on the principle of the sovereign equality of all members. However, the UNGA is not an international parliament that passes laws for the world. Instead, states generally pass non-binding resolutions that serve as expressions of global opinion and symbolic recommendations for action. This lack of enforceable of resolutions and conventions has led to the marginalization of this organ, with authority shifting 'to the Security Council and Secretariat, much to the dismay of the South' (Karns and Mingst 2010, 109).

One innovative idea for reform is to create another chamber to represent people rather than states, however any such proposals would require the support of the United States in particular (Franck 1998, 81). Based on the US Senate's record of asserting the sovereignty of American law and unwillingness to ratify human rights conventions, the feasibility of implementing dramatic change in the near term is remote. Moreover, critics maintain that the United States has lost its monopoly of influence and 'can no longer claim to be part of the majority within the Assembly' on a wide range of issues (Zweifel 2006, 74).

Table 17.6 Organizational structure of the UN

Organ	Function	Decision-making	Authority
(1) Security Council	An elite pact established the P-5 great powers in 1945 as the foremost authority in identifying and addressing threats to international security.	Passage of UNSC resolutions requires supportive votes of all P-5 members. P-5 states can abstain, but one veto means resolution is not adopted. Of the ten non-permanent members, support of four is needed to approve UNSC resolutions. Non-permanent members are elected by the GA by region for non-successive two-year terms.	According to Article 27 of the UN Charter collective action on threats to peace require the support of the permanent members. Authorization established in Chapter Six ('Pacific Settlement of Disputes') and Seven ('Action with Respect to Threats to Peace'). UNSC has the ability to legitimize the use of force and humanitarian intervention.
(2) General Assembly	Chief forum for multilateral deliberations, policymaking, and representation for 193 members of UN. GA can initiate studies and make recommendations to promote the codification of international law, cooperation on human rights and international collaboration in socio-economic and humanitarian areas.	Votes are based on a one state – one vote principle of sovereign equality. Many issues require a simple majority of the 193 member states. Decisions regarding the UN budget or peacekeeping budget, admission or suspension of members, elections or matters of peace and security require a two-thirds majority.	Make recommendations on issues of concern to the Charter. Recommendations on security issues can be made only if the UNSC is not discussing the threat. Conventions or resolutions lack enforceability; states cannot be forced to comply. Elects the non-P-5 members of the Security Council and other UN councils and organs and, on the recommendation of the Security Council, appoint the Secretary-General.
(3) Economic and Social Council	Forum for economic and social matters. ECOSOC's work currently accounts for 70% of the UN's budget.	54 members elected by GA for three years. Seats are based on geographical representation with 14 seats allocated for Africa, 11 to Asia, ten to Latin American and the Caribbean, six to Eastern Europe, and 13 to Western Europe and other areas.	ECOSOC makes recommendations and non-binding resolutions based on consensus or simple majority vote. The GA member states must also approve resolutions. Much of the word is done through nine functional committees.
(4) Secretariat	Executive organ Chief administrative officer, UN diplomat and advocate, civil servants serving members.	Impartial civil servants are led by UN Secretary General Ban Ki-Moon. Secretary General is recommended by UNSC and appointed by GA.	Drafts UN budget and reports. Conducts studies upon request. Raises threat to security to UNSC.
(5) International Court of Justice	Judicial organ	15 judges elected by GA for nine years. Majority Vote System	Lacks compulsory jurisdiction and enforcement mechanism. States in dispute can request a legally binding decision or a non-compulsory advisory opinion.
(6) Trusteeship Council	Established to supervise former colonies progress to self-determination	Inactive	Non-operational organ that no longer functions or meets.

Source: Charter of the United Nations.

Table 17.7   UNGA international human rights treaties US has not ratified

Convention on the Elimination of All Forms of Discrimination against Women (CEDAW)

Convention on the Rights of Persons with Disabilities (CRPD)

Convention on the Rights of the Child (CRC)

Convention against Enforced Disappearance (CED)

Land Mine Ban Treaty (MBT)

Convention on Cluster Munitions

Source: Human Rights Watch (2009). http://www.hrw.org/news/2009/07/24/united-states-ratification-international-human-rights-treaties.

You Make the Call – Does UN Inaction in Syria Mean the Security Council Needs Reform?

In 2011, demonstrations erupted throughout the Middle East and North Africa as people called for economic opportunity, freedom and dignity. Libya's dictator, Muammar Gaddafi, responded to protests with military force leading to a civil war. The UNSC responded by freezing Gaddafi's assets and referring the matter to the International Criminal Court for an investigation of war crimes. They also passed resolution 1970, calling for the enforcement of a 'no-fly' zone to protect civilians, which passed unanimously 10-0, with five abstentions. The UNSC delegated the intervention to NATO and after seven months of bombing missions and enforcing a naval blockade, the tide ultimately turned against the regime and he was captured and killed by Libyan militants. Libyans, along with Tunisians and Egyptians are all currently attempting to navigate into uncharted waters and move from Arab Spring revolutions to meaningful transitions to democratic regimes.

However, in Syria, an even bloodier civil war continues to rage. In this case, the Responsibility to Protect civilians norm has not proven a compelling impetus for UN action. The Security Council is divided with Russia providing support for the Syrian regime and refusing to vote for any resolution because the Libyan 'no-fly' zone intervention toppled the regime. Russia and China have vetoed UN resolutions calling for an end to the violence or solutions to the war. They also refuse to authorize any use of force, economic sanctions or arms embargo. The Bashar al-Assad regime continues to fire scud-ballistic missiles at rebels within its borders. Human Rights Watch accuses the regime of using internationally prohibited cluster munitions and President Obama recently threatened military intervention after the embattled regime unleashed chemical weapons on civilians.

The UNSC is currently hamstrung by internal divisions and is unable to stop the violence or effectively address the threats emanating from a geo-strategically important region. The record of member states' willingness and ability to intervene to protect civilians from extreme violence remains mixed. Turkey's Prime Minister Erdogan expressed frustration at the stalemate in the UNSC and said that the fate of the world 'cannot be left to what comes out of the mouth of the five permanent members'. His solution calls for ending the distinction between permanent and non-permanent members. You make the call, would this increase or decrease the ability of the UN to quickly and efficiently respond to international crises? How do you anticipate that different countries or theories might view these issues involving the UN and intervention?

UN Economic and Social Council

ECOSOC is the most complex of the UN subsidiary bodies. It serves as the central forum for matters of an economic, social, environmental or humanitarian nature. The economic and social programs conducted by ECOSOC usually account for 60–70 per cent of the UN budget, which was $5.15 billion US in 2012. These fellowships and grants provide people with training, supplies and technology to get the skills needed to increase countries' level of economic development. Unlike the World Bank and IMF, which have far greater resources, these are grants and aid, not loans. The 54 Council members work on the basis of recommendation decisions and non-binding resolutions based on consensus or simple majority vote.

ECOSOC has also been tasked by the General Assembly with assessing the progress toward achieving the eight Millennium Development Goals. The Annual Ministerial Review monitors progress and aims to assist vulnerable populations in achieving the MDG targets. ECOSOC has also created a biennial Development Cooperation Forum, which is a multi-stakeholder platform that includes civil society and the private sector. To date, more than 2,500 NGOs have been granted consultative status and they contribute to the quantity and quality of information on issues of development cooperation. In addition to these efforts, UN-sponsored global summits and conferences are also important components of global governance. To date, the six organs of the UN and the 19 independent specialized agencies that work with the UN have amassed a number of considerable achievements. However, the Security Council in particular faces substantial pressures, largely yet unmet, to undergo governance reforms to be able to more effectively respond to new threats and reflect the shifting power among actors in the twenty-first century.

ECONOMIC GOVERNANCE ARCHITECTURE: THE BRETTON WOODS INSTITUTIONS

The victorious coalition of allies in World War II also decided not to repeat the earlier pattern the economic protectionism that ran rampant during the earlier interwar period. The United States, acting as the economic hegemon, helped to pay the costs needed to cultivate and sustain an open global economic system. At a conference held in New Hampshire in 1944, delegates from 44 countries negotiated the establishment a series of international institutions intended to foster economic cooperation collectively known as the Bretton Woods order. The first of these pillars at the centre of governing the international political economy was the International Monetary Fund, whose position of influence in the international financial system has varied considerably over the last 60 years.

The International Monetary Fund

The IMF's original mandate was to promote international monetary cooperation and support the creation of a stable monetary system based on a fixed exchange rate and capital controls. The Bretton Woods system, based on trade liberalization and a monetary framework aimed at promoting exchange rate and price stability, brought about the greatest period of global economic growth to that point in the human history (Rodrik 2011). However, in 1971, President Nixon suspended the convertibility of the US dollar to gold and allowed the dollar to float. With the collapse of the fixed exchange rate system, the IMF shifted mandates and increasingly became the lender of last resort for developing countries. The IMF now aims to promote global growth and macroeconomic stability, monitor macroeconomic indicators of the financial health of economies and provide conditional loans if its 188 member states experience short-term balance of payments difficulties.

The breakdown of the cornerstones of the Bretton Woods system gave rise of trillions of dollars worth of capital flowing around the world daily, and this more interdependent global financial system has experienced both rapid growth and repeated episodes of balance of payment and debt crises. After decades of providing loans to indebted developing countries, the IMF has also acquired numerous critics and is experiencing a decline in legitimacy. Loan packages have traditionally included Washington Consensus policies including structural adjustment reforms, austerity, deregulation, privatization and liberalization of trade and capital markets. One of the Fund's most prestigious critics is former chief economist for the World Bank Joseph Stiglitz (2003), who characterizes the IMF's policies of imposed conditionality in some 80 countries as free market fundamentalism.

Criticisms of the IMF mounted in response to their handling of debt crises and the East Asian financial crisis in 1997. For example, tens of thousands of protestors took to the streets at IMF and World Bank meetings in Prague (2000), Washington, DC (2001) and Genoa (2001). Protestors levy charges that the IMF allows creditors to infringe on state sovereignty and they employ a one-size-fits-all set of loan conditions that harm the most vulnerable in debtor states. Another one of the most cited criticisms of the Bretton Woods institutions is that by long-standing convention the head of the IMF is a European and the head of the World Bank is an American. Thus, there are calls, from outside and even within the Fund, to create a merit-based system (especially for the top leadership positions) and greater representation in the decision-making procedures.

Indeed, only five years ago Helleiner and Momani (2008) wrote that the IMF was in crisis and might 'slip into obscurity' due to the decreased use of IMF loans by middle-income borrowers (ibid., 353). They argued that the Fund's financial difficulties stem from three sources: dissatisfaction of borrowers with conditionality, the rise of alternative private and regional lending alternatives and the critical view of policymakers under the Bush administration. The reduction in countries' use of IMF loans affects the influence, legitimacy and viability of the organization as the Fund's operating costs are paid by the interest fees from their lending operation (ibid. 2008, 355). However, since the global economic crisis the IMF has a renewed purpose as the demand for loans have increased with the contraction in the availability of private lending.

The IMF has responded to the crisis by streamlining conditions and quadrupling concessional lending. Over $300 billion in loans has been committed and in 2009 a Flexible Credit Line (FLC) was created as a form of crisis prevention for countries with strong fundamentals that do not require policy conditions (IMF 2012). The Fund has also responded to demands of the Jubilee 2000 campaign and promoted debt relief for some two dozen countries under the Heavily Indebted Poor Countries Initiative (HIPC). However, while the IMF's crisis of purpose may have waned, the crisis of legitimacy has not. Anti-austerity protests against the IMF's policies have continued, most recently in Greece, Portugal and Spain, with a common critique that the imposed conditionality is too narrowly focused on economics. Members in the developing world are also increasingly demanding quota and governance reforms including greater representation on the Executive Board. A host of proposals have been put forth to strengthen the accountability, transparency of decision-making and input into the top leadership positions at the Fund.

In 2008, the Fund's Independent Evaluation Office (IEO) issued a report on IMF governance stating that reforms to improve governance practices were 'a critical element in enhancing the Fund's relevance, legitimacy, and effectiveness'. In order to respond to the increased demand for loans from cash-strapped member states, the IMF required additional funds. The IMF sought a 100 per cent increase in their resources (Special Drawing Rights) to about US$720 billion. Countries such as China and Brazil responded that funding increases would require changes in IMF governance to reflect the rising economic importance of the dynamic emerging economies and developing countries. Leaders of the G20 economies met in Seoul in 2010 and pledged support for the doubling of member quotas and major realignment reforms, with more than a 6 per cent quota shift to emerging market and under-represented developing countries (IMF 2012).

If approved by the leading shareholders, the US (which alone can block any such motion) and three-fifths of the Fund's 188 members having 85 per cent of the Fund's total voting power, the quota changes passed by the IMF Governors would make China the third largest voting member. It would also reduce the overrepresented European vote share. When G20 countries met again in Tokyo in 2012 they also discussed the proposed amendment to transition to a more representative and democratically elected 24-member Executive Board. This amendment was passed by the IMF Governors and also awaits the approval by states. However, the IMF Executive Director for Brazil and several other Latin American and Caribbean countries, Paulo Batista, criticizes the Fund for being dominated by the North Atlantic and asserts that reform efforts 'are running up against a lot of institutional inertia' (Biron 2012).

At this point, the process of following through with the historic IMF governance reform deal, to give emerging market contributors greater voice and power in the IMF, remains stalled (Wroughton 2012). One key hurdle in which the Board has yet to agree is on the formula for determining voting shares. Europe has advocated for more weight to be placed on economic and financial openness based measures that would favour smaller European countries in representation. Besides economic size, there have also been discussions of altering the weight given to foreign exchange reserves or variability, or possibly including population or members' contributions. Thus, while the IMF has made improvements in increasing participation, monitoring and the organization's independence, it remains plagued by the **democracy deficit**. The crisis-prone nature of modern financial markets and the need for increased IMF funds to manage these instabilities have given emerging economy members additional impetus to demand a more ambitious set of reforms. The ultimate outcome on other proposals concerning appointment issues,

> **Democracy Deficit** – a situation in which intergovernmental or other organizations are lacking in democratic accountability and decision-making procedures.

Washington Consensus conditionality, demands for greater transparency of proceedings, mechanisms of checks and balances or divorcing the IMF's evaluation department from its lending all remain to be determined. As of yet, the funding members of the IMF are yet to ratify even their agreed upon reforms. These pressures for reform, if not addressed, will likely continue to escalate, due to shifting trends in relative economic power over the next half century.

The World Bank

The second pillar of the international economy established at Bretton Woods was the International Bank for Reconstruction and Development, with the mandate to reconstruct war-devastated Western Europe. It is now referred to as the World Bank Group, and includes institutions such as the original IBRD, the International Development Association (IDA), the International Finance

Corporation (IFC) and the Multilateral Investment Guarantee Agency (MIGA). The Bank's mandate has evolved to include fighting poverty and improving the standard of living across the globe by offering low-interest loans, interest-free credit, grants and technical assistance.

Loans are provided for economic and human development projects or policy reforms in low- and middle-income countries. In response to the global economic crises, the Bank has also increased their lending commitment to $52.6 billion in 2012 to help promote pro-poor economic growth and economic enterprise (World Bank 2011). Until recently, the World Bank focused on financing large infrastructure projects and did not systematically address issues such as corruption in member states. However, the Bank now emphasizes good governance practices in developing states, youth employment and small business assistance. They have also worked to empower women and to enhance the voice and participation of the poor in development projects.

Like the IMF, the World Bank plays an important role as a lending institution, as a gate-keeper to private lending and aid flows, and as a source of knowledge on a wide variety of economic issues. In comparison to the IMF, the World Bank has received fewer criticisms due to its greater focus on promoting pro-poor economic growth and development projects. It also does a better job of explaining the reasons for its decisions, and cooperates more extensively with other multilateral institutions and non-state actors. The Bank is publically promoting their efforts to encourage inclusiveness, innovation, efficiency, effectiveness and accountability.

However, both IGOs have been criticized for being dominated by creditor nations and for the practices of adopting strict lending conditionality due to their impact on vulnerable populations. Calls for reform have taken place both within the Bank and from elements of civil society and including increasing accountability to all stakeholders, greater efficiency, transparency and a more open and democratic decision-making process (Zweifel 2006, 85). Other governance reform proposals such as creating inclusive appointment procedures or creating mechanisms of overrule for decision-making are far more difficult to achieve because they are opposed by lending countries. This has traditionally been the case for proposals to increase developing countries' voting share (to at least 50 per cent over time). Some proposals, such as strengthening the Bank's Inspection Panel, are opposed by borrowing countries who favour sovereignty over accountability (Zweifel 2006, 97). In the near term, the economic crisis and the decline of private investments has confirmed the World Bank's central role in economic development funding. As the crisis wanes, however, the ultimate outcome of these reform efforts will determine the perceived legitimacy, future funding and relevance of the organization.

The World Trade Organization

The third institution proposed at Bretton Woods called for the creation of an International Trade Organization. However, this IGO was rejected and instead a series of rounds of multilateral trade liberalization agreements were developed under the General Agreement on Tariffs and Trade (GATT). In 1995, after eight GATT 'Rounds' states agreed to create the World Trade Organization, which is the only international organization focused on world trade. The WTO was the result of reform efforts to create a stronger regulatory mechanism for international trade and investment. In comparison with GATT, the 'new trade regime represents a quantum leap in global regulation' (Weiss 2005, 725). As a result of rounds of multilateral negotiations impediments to trade such as regulations, tariffs and other trade barriers, limitations are currently at their lowest rates in history. Moreover, WTO membership offers states (such as China) the opportunity to participate in bargaining and learning of the rules and norms of the global trading system that depends on perceived legitimacy (Wolfe 2008, 340).

Although the WTO has a relatively small budget and staff, there are at least two exceptional characteristics of the forum. The first is that decisions are made based on consensus among all 155 members. Secondly, they have imbued the international organization with an unprecedented and robust Dispute Settlement Body. To date, states have brought some 455 trade dispute cases before the DSB's binding arbitration panels to determine if there have been violations of the WTO agreements. If the panel finds evidence supporting the trade complaint, the WTO can authorize compensation or retaliatory measures to be enacted if the state refuses to comply. Unlike the other two economic pillars of the global economy, the WTO has the exceptional ability to act as an adjudicator and impact the behaviour of even the most powerful states. The IMF and World Bank only have such influence over developing countries that cannot afford to access private capital sources and choose to accept the loan packages. Although the WTO does not have **supra-national** enforcement power itself, the newfound ability of developing countries to challenge the trade-distorting policies of developed countries is evident in cases such as the following complaint: (DS267) Brazil vs. the US over American cotton subsidies. The WTO found the US subsidies in violations of WTO agreements, and when the US failed to comply, the panel authorized Brazil to impose $800 million in retaliatory measures on US exports. This threat of retaliation led to a negotiated agreement in which the US compensated Brazilian cotton farmers by paying them $147 million a year (Joffe-Walt 2010). Although low-income developing countries may lack the monetary capabilities to attend WTO meetings in Geneva or use the dispute resolution mechanism, there are more developing countries utilizing such opportunities than ever before. Reform proposals could also potentially compensate a victorious state for the costs of having to take the case to the resolution panel. However, even if compensation reforms were implemented, this would not alter fundamental differences in states' economic size or vulnerabilities. States with small economies that win their cases are likely to be less able to use the retaliatory measures in a meaningful way to affect policy changes in larger economies.

> **Supra-National** – a method of decision-making in which powers or influence have been delegated to an authority or an organization that transcends the boundaries of its member states. Supra-nationalism thus entails a loss of state sovereignty, as a state may be compelled to act in ways contrary to its preferences. For example, WTO dispute resolution panels are binding on member states, although it does not enforce the ruling directly. Similarly, the European Union is the most advanced example of a supra-national regional union, in which political integration has meant that EU policies can supersede the domestic laws of the 28 member states.
>
> **Intergovernmental Organizations** – states remain the primary actors and cooperate when they find it in their common interest. States control the degree of their participation and retain state sovereignty.

Overall, the trading regime based on multilateral WTO agreements has successfully removed or reduced obstacles to international trade. It has also promoted systematic commitments to economic openness among members that, as of yet, have proven resilient in the face of protectionist pressures arising in the global economic recession. These consensus-based agreements, based on principles of non-discrimination and transparency, have helped to generate higher levels of economic growth, employment, intra-industry trade, confidence among members and reductions in the cost of living. In contrast to the diffuse benefits of international trade for consumers and exporters, the costs of job losses in uncompetitive industries hurt by trade imports are concentrated and far easier to see. Although multilateral agreements largely result in more equitable agreements than the alternatives of bilateral or segmented regional trading blocs, the WTO remains controversial. In 1999, 50,000 people assembled at a WTO meeting, and at the 'battle in Seattle', a grand coalition of 'Teamsters and Turtles', criticized the trading system for promoting inequality and for prioritizing corporate profits before people, democracy or the environment (Derber 2003, 4).

Although the WTO is not a development organization, in 2001, for the first time, member states launched the Development Doha Round. This round of trade negotiations focused explicitly on agriculture which is central to the economies of 75 per cent of WTO members that are developing countries. Previous WTO trade agreements centred on manufactured goods, and more recently on intellectual property and services. However, ten years after the launch of the DDR, negotiations have broken down. Member states have failed to reach a consensus deal on issues including the right to food, agricultural subsidies, industrial tariffs, trade-in-services and other non-tariff barriers. The World Bank in 2003 estimated value of DDR negotiations on agriculture are estimated to be worth up to $350 billion for the global South by 2015 (Hawkes and Plahe 2013, 22).

Some analysts, who view the deadlocked Doha Round as a failure, recommend the alteration of the WTO's consensus-based principle to increase the organization's efficiency. However, others maintain that this would significantly undermine global governance in international trade, as the consensus-based rules allow for the process and any potential outcomes to have greater effectiveness and perceived legitimacy (Wolfe 2008, 343). Simply put, not all deals are the same. At this point, no deal may be better than a one-sided deal that promotes free trade in agriculture for developing countries while leaving unaltered the developed countries policies of heavy subsidization. Under the current consensus based decision-making, countries whose economies are dependent on international agriculture have the ability to protect their interests, including food security.

Moreover, the idea of food as a human right subject to international human rights law, not just trade law, remains another important and contested issue. The failure of the Doha Round takes place in a context of global food crises in 2008 and 2012, and where one in seven humans live in hunger (Hawkes and Plahe 2013, 22). Despite the deadlock on the Agreement on Agriculture (AoA) and the proliferation of Free Trading Agreements that severely undermine the principle of non-discrimination (Bhagwati 2008), the WTO offers countries in the Global South far greater opportunities than bilateral negotiations would to establish a more level playing field. Other WTO initiatives, such as Aid for Trade funds, help diversify the least developing countries' economies in order to achieve the Millennium Development Goals. For example, in 2007, aid to the LDCs to build their supply-side capacity and infrastructure to take advantage of increased market access reached $31 billion, which was a 62 per cent increase over the 2002–05 baseline average (WTO 2013).

In sum, other than the WTO, the IGOs at the centre of global governance efforts have decision-making procedures that remain largely as they were over 60 years ago. While the US and the EU have the ability to act to block international action and are fundamentally important to reform efforts, as a rule the IGOs are now 'power incongruent' (Alexandroff 2008, 8). That is, there is a mismatch between the distribution of power in the IGOs and in the international system.

The world has changed enormously with market interdependence, and diverse threats and economic crises are no longer limited by international borders. In addition, economic power has been dispersed, and new actors have risen in importance. The potential for the return of geopolitical divisions further complicate reforms efforts. The eventual outcomes of these negotiations aimed at increasing the flexibility of IGOs to balance among demands, including greater representation, accountability, efficiency and legitimacy, are yet to be determined.

NEW PLAYERS, NEW RULES? RISING GLOBAL POWERS

According to the US National Intelligence Council (2008), over the next 15 years China and India, the two most populous countries in the world, will continue their rise as the new global economic juggernauts. In the period from 2000 to 2010, the world's three leading emerging economies – Brazil, China and India's share of global GDP doubled and 'their share of world trade almost tripled' (Thakur 2011). Moreover, Goldman Sachs analysts also project that the four BRIC economies (Brazil, Russia, India and China) will have a combined GDP larger than that of the G7 countries by 2027.

While the US is currently the global hegemon accounting for approximately 25 per cent of world economic output and 40 per cent of world military expenditures, numerous sources assess that the United States has begun to gradually lose its global economic primacy, while China and India with nearly 40 per cent of humanity increase their strength as global competitors. Indeed, analysts such as Fareed Zakaria argue that the financial meltdown and global recession have already begun to usher in a 'post-American' world order (2009, 43). What remains unclear is how these monumental shifts in the distribution of power in the international system will realign the influence and practices of international institutions.

In addition, in 2008, the risk of an economic depression prompted a shift in economic coordination from the G8 to the G20. This *ad hoc* body now stands at the forefront of efforts to promote effective crisis management. Over seven G20 Summit meetings, ministers, heads of states and heads of governments have all strategized on how to coordinate their macro-economic policies, structural reforms and fiscal measures to stimulate demand. They also agreed to tackle the problem of banks that are 'too big to fail' and pledged to reform the Financial Stability Board (FSB) to increase its ability to coordinate and monitor their financial regulation agenda. In 2010, they also committed to refraining from increasing or imposing new barriers to trade and investment for three years. In the face of a weak economic recovery, G20 states also committed to buttressing the capabilities of existing multilateral development banks and established a broad commitment to undertake governance reforms of the international financial institutions. Finally, they also pledged $1.1 trillion in support for efforts to restore credit, growth, stability and youth employment.

The question of the G20's long-term relevance as a permanent steering organization for the world economy remains uncertain because it is a rather weak *ad hoc* body. Summit meetings lack clear and transparent decision-making rules or dispute resolution mechanisms. While some analysts criticize the group for being too large to be effective, others claim that it needs to do a better job of integrating the preferences of the world's smaller states. Moreover, like many other international institutions, it ultimately faces the problem of creating binding commitments among sovereign states. Immediately after the financial crisis, emerging economies had increased leverage to negotiate a framework of systemic reforms of existing global governance architecture. However, the ability to move from statements supporting reforms to specific binding agreements and implementable changes remains to be seen.

Table 17.8   Group of Seven (G7) and Group of Twenty (G20) countries

G7	G20
France	France
Germany	Germany
Italy	Italy
Japan	Japan
United Kingdom	United Kingdom
United States	United States
Canada	Canada
Russia	Russia
	+
	Argentina
	Australia
	Brazil
	China
	India
	Indonesia
	Italy
	Mexico
	Saudi Arabia
	South Africa
	South Korea
	European Union

Over the next 40 years, the unprecedented shift in economic growth, wealth and the distribution of economic power is expected to continue to shift from the West to East. The Western world faces aging populations and the developing countries, while particularly in Asia and Africa, they face population booms. According to the European Union's Institute for Security Studies (EUISS) 2010 report, efforts aimed at 'matching the new distribution of power with new rules and institutions will be critical to preserving international peace and stability' (NIC 2010, 9) Thus, global governance is a work in progress. One of the primary challenges is how to create or adapt existing intergovernmental organizations to include the interests of rising state powers and non-state actors in the context of decision-making rules that largely favour the preferences of the 1940s great powers.

CONCLUSION

Systemic reforms of multilateral institutions are needed to achieve any of the four pillars of America's international policy agenda, which include: 'non-proliferation and disarmament; the promotion of peace and security; the preservation of our planet; and a global economy that advances opportunity for all people' (Obama 2009). To date, progress on these 'pillars' of international cooperation has been uneven. The greatest gaps are evident in the environmental regime and the international community's checkered record regarding the Responsibility to Protect. In contrast to the well-developed international trading regime and the sizable emphasis placed on nuclear proliferation, until recently efforts to regulate international financial flows or address climate change have been far more incremental and *ad hoc*.

In general, on trans-sovereign issues ranging from security threats to finance or climate change, the international community has had a difficult time coordinating frameworks for action or preventative measures. Instead, multilateral efforts have largely focused on responding to individual international crises. Virtually all existing international regimes, from international trade, investment and developing countries' debt to security, human rights and the environment all face the challenge of reconciling the policy preferences of a diverse set of state and non-state actors (Fogarty 2012). Although global governance has developed to promote order, stability and even international justice, the gaps in the development of global rule-making and governance are wide.

With regard to the future of global governance, in many ways there are more questions than answers. Three main questions remain with regard to the debated reforms of the multilateral governance architecture. Will greater multipolarity lead to increased systemic volatility or resiliency? Likewise, will governments and international institutions be able to adapt and keep up with the rapid pace of change and shifts in power? Finally, will they prove willing and able to work with non-state actors in order to mend the cracks or create new global governance frameworks more appropriate for the twenty-first century? What is needed is leadership and innovative visions for creating mechanisms that balance efficiency with inclusivity. Such efforts are essential to increasing the effectiveness and legitimacy of efforts to govern the globe. Innovative multi-stakeholder models do exist, such as the development of the Millennium Development Goals framework or Kofi Annan's Global Compact on Corporate Responsibility's principles regarding forced and child labour standards. There is much more work to be done to create public-private partnerships and to improve the integration of local, national, regional and international efforts to prevent and manage trans-sovereign problems.

QUESTIONS FOR REFLECTION

1. What is meant by the democracy deficit and can international organizations overcome it? If so, what would this entail? How might this be accomplished?
2. What does a state-centric or a multi-lateral centric analysis overlook? How important have transnational corporations, non-governmental organizations and civil society become?
3. Who are IGOs, MNCs and NGOs accountable to?
4. What are the areas of progress in global governance?

5. What are the various global governance challenges and how do alternative theoretical perspectives approach managing them?
6. How would the IMF or World Bank operations be affected by different vote weighting systems? How would the effectiveness, accountability and legitimacy be impacted by voting rules based on population, one-state one-vote, GDP, size of contribution or by democracies?
7. How might the UN Security Council or UN General Assembly be reformed?
8. Will the outcomes of proposed global governance reforms be determined largely by the distribution of power or by efficacy and legitimacy?
9. Can China peacefully be engaged and brought into a concert of stakeholder rule-making countries? What theoretical perspective or lens do favour?
10. Do states have an obligation to protect basic human rights? If so, how?
11. What can or should the UN do to help fragile states to become viable? Are neo-trustee proposals Neo-colonialism? Why or why not?
12. What will be the consequences of the global population increasing from 7 billion to 9 billion by 2050, with the majority of births in developing countries?
13. Will the economic crisis continue to unite countries for reforms, or push countries toward protectionism?
14. Why do countries generally oppose preventive efforts and strategies, and instead prefer responding to crises?
15. Will the IMF, World Bank and UN remain relevant?

REVISION QUIZ

1. Global governance refers to:

    a. World government
    b. Transnational rules and norms to manage global problems
    c. Domestic responses to global problems
    d. Unilateral actions

2. Which of the following is not included in the Millennium Development Goals?

    a. Halving extreme poverty
    b. Promoting gender equality
    c. Universal primary education
    d. Universal youth employment

3 The Responsibility to Protect is an international:

    a. Norm
    b. Law
    c. Regime
    d. Organization

4. The International Monetary Fund is primarily responsible for:

    a. International trade
    b. International peace and security
    c. Monetary stability and international lending
    d. Economic development

5. Which of the following is not a United Nations organ?

    a. The General Assembly
    b. The Secretariat
    c. The International Board of Governors
    d. The Security Council

6. The World Bank was originally focused on:

    a. Loans for reconstruction in Europe
    b. Loans for the poorest countries
    c. Macro-economic stability
    d. Providing development grants

7   Who were the Teamsters and Turtles protesting against?

    a. The UN
    b. The IMF
    c. The World Bank
    d. The WTO

8. The WTO's primary focus is on:

    a. International trade
    b. International peace and security
    c. Monetary stability and international lending
    d. Economic development

9. Which of the following is not in the remit of the WTO's Dispute Resolution Mechanism?

    a. Issue binding verdicts
    b. Authorize compensation
    c. Enforce economic sanctions
    d. Authorize retaliatory measures

10. Other than the European Union, most regional and international organizations are based on:

    a. The principle of one-state one-vote
    b. Intergovernmental authority

c. Supra-national authority

d. Consensus decision-making principles

11 The percentage of people living in absolute poverty (less than $1.25 per day is):

a. 5 per cent

b. 22 per cent

c. 33 per cent

d. 55 per cent

12. Which of the following has not undermined the logic of nuclear deterrence?

a. The A.Q. Khan nuclear proliferation network

b. Terrorists' pursuit of weapons of mass destruction

c. The Start Treaty

d. Weak states and the possibility of loose nukes

13. Trends in international terrorism since 2007 have:

a. Increased

b. Decreased

c. Stayed the same

d. Shown the end of the terrorist threat

14. Which of the following does not refer to weak states?

a. Lack of ability to control borders

b. Lack of democracy

c. Lack of autonomy

d. Lack of capabilities to provide basic services and public goods

15. Which of the following is not included in the G20?

a. Argentina

b. Brazil

c. Taiwan

d. India

Answers: 1: b; 2: d; 3: a; 4: c; 5: c; 6: a; 7: d; 8: a; 9: c; 10: b; 11: b; 12: c; 13: b; 14: b; 15: c.

BIBLIOGRAPHY

Acharya A. (2009) *Targeting Terrorist Financing: International Cooperation and New Regimes* (London: Routledge Press), 134.

Adetunji, J. (2012) 'Turkey Calls for UN Security Council Reform Over Failure to Pressure Syria', *The Guardian* [Online] (13 October 2012). Available at: <http://www.guardian.co.uk/world/2012/oct/13/turkey-un-security-council-reform-syria> [Accessed 7 December 2012].

Albright, D. and Hinderstein, C. (2005) 'Unraveling the A.Q. Khan and Future Proliferation Networks', *The Washington Quarterly* 28(2) Spring Edition, 111–28.

Alexandroff, A. ed. (2008) *Can the World Be Governed? Possibilities for Effective Multilateralism* (Canada: Wilfrid Laurier University Press).

Allison, G. (September/October 2004) 'Nuclear Terrorism: How Serious a Threat to Russia?. Russia in Global Affairs'. Available at: <http://belfercenter.hks.harvard.edu/publication/660/nuclear_terrorism.html> [Accessed 7 December 2012].

Al-Nasser, N. (2012) 'United Nations Thematic Debate of the 66th Session of the United Nations General Assembly on Drugs and Crime as a Threat to Development' [Online] (26 June 2012). New York: United Nations. Available at: <http://www.un.org/en/ga/president/66/Issues/drugs/drugs-crime.shtml> [Accessed 7 December 2012].

Aon B. (2012) 'Annual Global Climate and Catastrophe Report' [Online] London. Available at: <http://thoughtleadership.aonbenfield.com/Documents/20130124_if_annual_global_climate_catastrophe_report.pdf> [Accessed 1 February 2013].

Bank for International Settlements (2010) 'Triennial Central Bank Survey of Foreign Exchange and Derivatives Market Activity in 2010 – Final result' [Online] (December 2010). Available at: <http://www.bis.org/publ/rpfxf10t.htm> [Accessed 12 January 2013].

Barbieri, K. and Reuveny R. (2005) 'Economic Globalization and Civil War', *Journal of Politics* 67(4), 1228–47.

Bhagwati, J. (2008) *Termites in the Trading System: How Preferential Agreements Undermine Free Trade* (Oxford: Oxford University Press).

Biron, C. (2012) 'Brazil Frustrated with European "Backtracking" on IMF Reforms. Inter Press Service News Agency' [Online] (19 October 2012). Available at: <http://www.ipsnews.net/2012/10/brazil-frustrated-with-european-backtracking-on-imf-reforms/ > [Accessed 7 December 2012].

Blair, D. (2009) 'Annual Threat Assessment of the Intelligence Community for the Senate Select Committee on Intelligence', US Office of the Director of National Intelligence [Online] (12 February 2009), 2. Available at: <http://intelligence.senate.gov/090212/blair.pdf> [Accessed 7 December 2012].

Boll, S, Sauga, M, and Seith A. (2012) 'Draghi's Pledge: ECB Divided over Efforts to Save Euro', *Spiegel Online* [Online] (30 July 2012). Available at: <http://www.spiegel.de/international/business/mario-draghi-s-new-euro-rescue-plans-sow-strife-in-ecb-council-a-847129.html> [Accessed 13 January 2013].

Chan, S. (2011) 'Financial Crisis Was Avoidable Inquiry Finds', *New York Times* [Online] (25 January 2011). Available at: <http://www.nytimes.com/2011/01/26/business/economy/26inquiry.html?_r=0'[>[Accessed 5 January 2013].

CIA World Factbook (2011) 'Countries' GSP (Official Exchange Rates)' [Online]. Available at: <https://www.cia.gov/library/publications/the-world-factbook/geos/xx.html> [Accessed 29 November 2012].

Collier, P., Elliott, V., Hegre, H., Hoeffler, A., Reynal-Querol, M. and Sambanis, N. (2003) *Breaking the Conflict Trap: Civil War and Development Policy* (Washington, DC: World Bank and Oxford University Press).

Costs of War Project (2011) Eisenhower Study Group Report, Watson Institute for International Studies, Brown University [Online]. Available at: <http://costsofwar.org/ > [Accessed 15 January 2013].

Davies, J.B., Sandstrom, S., Shorrocks, A. and Wolff, E.N. (2006) *The World Distribution of Household Wealth* (Helsinki: United Nations University, World Institute for Development Economics and Research).

Deiss, J. (2011) 'President of the 65th Session, UN General Assembly's Opening Remarks at the Conference on "Global Governance and Security Council Reform"'. Rome, Italy: United Nations [Online] (16 May 2011). Available at: <http://www.un.org/en/ga/president/65/statements/globalgovandscref160511.shtml> [Accessed 18 January 2013].

de Kerckhove, F. (2008). 'Multilateralism on Trial: From the 2005 UN Summit to Today's Reality'. In A. Alexandroff (ed.), *Can the World Be Governed? Possibilities for Effective Multilateralism* (Canada: Wilfrid Laurier University Press), 196–240.

Derber, C. (2003) *People Before Profit: The New Globalization in an Age of Terror, Big Money, and Globalization* (New York: St Martin's Press), 4.

Doyle, M. and Sambanis, N. (2006) *In Making War and Building Peace : United Nations Peace Operations*. Princeton Paperbacks (Princeton, NJ: Princeton University Press).

Eilperin, J. (2012) 'Kyoto Protocol Extended in Contentious UN Climate Talks', *The Washington Post* [Online] (8 December 2012). Available at: <http://www.washingtonpost.com/national/health-science/kyoto-protocol-extended-in-contentious-un-climate-talks/2012/12/08/f64a51c0–4178–11e2-ae43-cf491b837f7b_story.html> [Accessed 10 December 2012].

European Commission (2012) 'EU Economic Governance: Stronger Economic Rules to Manage the Euro and Economic Monetary Union'. European Union Economic and Financial Affairs (Belgium: European Union Publications Office).

FAO (October 2009) 'The State of Food Insecurity in the World: Economic Crises-Impacts and Lessons Learned'. Food and Agriculture Organization of the United Nations [Online]. Rome: United Nations Publications. Available at: <http://www.fao.org/docrep/012/i0876e/i0876e00.htm> [Accessed 20 January 2013].

Fearon, J. and Laitin, D. (2003) 'Ethnicity, Insurgency, and Civil War', *American Political Science Review* 97(1), 75–90.

Fortune 500 Magazine (2012) 'Annual Ranking of Largest 100 Companies' [Online] Available at: <http://money.cnn.com/magazines/fortune/fortune500/2012/full_list/> [Accessed 1 January 2013].

Franck, T.M. (1998) *Fairness and International Law and Institutions* (Oxford: Clarendon Press).

Fogarty, E. (2012) *States, Non-State Actors, and Global Governance* (London: Routledge Taylor and Francis Group).

Garvelink, W.J. and Tahir, F. (2011) 'Somalia Remains the Worst Humanitarian Crisis in the World', Press release, Center for Strategic and International Studies (CSIS), 16 December 2011.

Gnesotto, G. and Grevi, G. (2006) 'The New Global Puzzle. What World for the EU in 2025?' European Union's Institute for Security Studies (EUISS). Paris: European Union [Online] Available at: <http://www.iss.europa.eu/uploads/media/NGP_01.pdf> [Accessed on 15 February 2013].

Gueterres, A. (October 2012) 'Global Humanitarian Crisis at Unprecedented Levels, says UNHCR', Press Release, High Commissioner's Opening Statement to the 63rd Session of ExCom Palais de Nations, Geneva, 1 [Online]. Available at: <http://www.unhcr.org/506987c99.html> [Accessed 7 December 2012].

Hawkes, S. and Plahe J.K. (2013) 'Worlds Apart: The WTO's Agreement on Agriculture and the Right to Food in Developing Countries', *International Political Science Review* 34(1), 22–38.

Held, D., McGrew, A., Goldblat D., and Perraton, J. (1999) *Global Transformations: Politics, Economics and Culture* (Stanford, CA. Stanford University Press).

Helleiner, E. and Momani, B. (2008) 'Slipping into Obscurity: Crisis and Institutional Reform at the IMF'. In A. Alexandroff (ed.), *Can the World Be Governed? Possibilities for Effective Multilateralism* (Canada: Wilfrid Laurier University Press), 353–88.

Human Development Report (1997) 'Human Development to Eradicate Poverty. United Nations Development Program Report' [Online]. Available at: <http://hdr.undp.org/en/reports/global/hdr1997/> [Accessed on 17 January 2013].

International Monetary Fund (2008) 'IMF Board of Governors Adopts Quota and Voice Reforms by Large Margin', Press Release [Online] (29 April 2008). Available at: <http://www.imf.org/external/np/sec/pr/2008/pr0893.htm> [Accessed 15 December 2012].

International Monetary Fund (2012a) 'IMF Quota and Governance Publications' [Online] 9 October 2012. Available at: <http://www.imf.org/external/np/fin/quotas/pubs/index.htm> [Accessed 15 December 2012].

International Monetary Fund (2012b) 'IMF's Response to the Global Economic Crisis' [Online] (10 September 2012). Available at: <http://www.imf.org/external/np/exr/facts/changing.htm> [Accessed 15 December 2012].

Joffe-Walt, C. (2010) W'hy U.S. Taxpayers are Paying Brazilian Cotton Growers, National Public Radio: All Things Considered' (9 November 2010). Available at: <http://www.npr.org/blogs/money/2011/01/26/131192182/cotton> [Accessed 7 December 2012].

Karns, M. and Mingst, K. (2010) *International Organizations: The Politics and Processes of Global Governance*, 3rd edition (Boulder, CO: Lynne Rienner).

Keck, M. and Sikkink, K. (2000) *Activists Without Borders*, 2nd edition (New York: Cornell University Press).

Keohane, R. (1984) *After Hegemony: Cooperation and Discord in the World Political Economy* (New Jersey: Princeton University Press).

Kim, J. (2013) 'World Bank President Jim Kim at G20 Meeting: Climate Change Represents Real, Present Danger', World Bank Speech Transcript (16 February 2013). Available at: <http://www.worldbank.org/en/news/speech/2013/02/16/world-bank-president-jim-kim-at-g20-meeting-climate-change-represents-real-present-danger> [Accessed 20 December 2012].

King, A. and Schneider, B. (1991) *The First Global Revolution* (New York: Simon & Schuster).

Koch, M. (2011) 'Non-State Actors in Global Governance'. In B. Reinalda, ed., *The Ashgate Research Companion to Non-State Actors* (Farnham, England), 202.

Love, M. (2007) 'Global Problems, Global Solutions'. In M. Love (ed.), *Beyond Sovereignty: Issues for a Global Agenda* (Belmont, CA: Thomson and Wadsworth), 34.

Love, R. (2007) 'Combating the Proliferation of Weapons of Mass Destruction'. In M. Love, (ed.), *Beyond Sovereignty: Issues for a Global Agenda* (Belmont, CA: Thomson and Wadsworth), 279.

Mack, A. et al. (2010) 'Human Security Report 2009/2010: The Causes of Peace and the Shrinking Costs of War', Human Security Report Project [Online], 157. Available at: <http://www.hsrgroup.org/human-security-reports/20092010/text.aspx> [Accessed 1 December 2012].

Mowatt-Larssen, R. (January 2010) 'Al Qaeda Weapons of Mass Destruction Threat: Hype or Reality?' Paper, Belfer Center for Science and International Affairs [Online]. Available at: <http://belfercenter.ksg.harvard.edu/files/al-qaeda-wmd-threat.pdf> [Accessed 7 December 2012].

Muldoon, J.P. (2003) *The Architecture of Global Governance* (Boulder, CO: Westview Press).

National Intelligence Council (2008) 'Global Trends 2025: A Transformed World', Office of the Director of National Intelligence, NIC [Online]. Available at: <http://www.dni.gov/nic/PDF_2025/2025_Global_Trends_Final_Report.pdf> [Accessed 1 December 2012].

National Intelligence Council (September 2010) 'Global Governance 2025: At a Critical Juncture', Office of the Director of National Intelligence, NIC [Online], 7. Available at: <http://www.acus.org/files/publication_pdfs/403/Global_Governance_2025.pdf> [Accessed 7 December 2012].

National Intelligence Council (2012) 'Global Trends 2030: Alternative Worlds', Office of the Director of National Intelligence, [Online] (NIC December 2012, ii). Available at: <http://www.dni.gov/files/documents/GlobalTrends_2030.pdf> [Accessed 7 December 2012].

Nye, J. (July/August 2009) 'Get Smart: Combine Hard and Soft Power', Foreign Affairs [Online]. Available at: <http://www.foreignaffairs.com/articles/65163/joseph-s-nye-jr/get-smart> [Accessed 7 December 2012].

Nye, J. (November/December 2010) 'The Future of American Power Foreign Affairs'. Available at: <http://www.foreignaffairs.com/articles/66796/joseph-s-nye-jr/the-future-of-american-power>[Accessed 7 December 2012].

Obama, B. (2009) 'Obama's Speech at UN General Assembly', *New York Times* Transcript. [Online] (23 September 2009). Available at: <http://www.nytimes.com/2009/09/24/us/politics/24prexy.text.html?pagewanted=all&_r=0> [Accessed 7 December 2012].

Ravallion, M., Chen, S. and Sangraula, P. (2008) 'Dollar a Day Revisited', World Bank Policy Research Working Paper Series [Online] (1 May 2008). Available at: <SSRN: http://ssrn.com/abstract=1149123>[Accessed 25 November 2012].

Rodrik, D. (2011). *The Globalization Paradox: Democracy and the Future of the World Economy* (New York: W.W. Norton & Company).

Rosand, E., Millar A., and Ipe, J. (2007) 'The UN Security Council's Counterterrorism Program: What Lies Ahead?'. International Peace Academy [Online] (October 2007, 7). Available at: <www.ipacademy.org/asset/file/207/cter.pdf> [Accessed 7 December 2012].

Sandler, T. and Enders, W. (2008) 'Economic Consequences of Terrorism in Developed and Developing Countries: An Overview'. In P. Keefer and N. Loayza (eds), *Terrorism, Economic Development and Political Openness* (Cambridge: Cambridge University Press), 17–47.

Schneider, H. (2012) 'World Bank Warns of "4-degree" Threshold of Global Temperature Increase', Washington Post [Online]. (19 November 2012). Available at: <http://articles.washingtonpost.com/2012-11-19/business/35506100_1_celsius-climate-change-temperature> [Accessed 7 December 2012].

Sinclair, T. (2012) *Global Governance* (Cambridge: Polity Press).

State Failure Index (2012) 'US Fund For Peace and Foreign Policy Magazine' [Online]. Available at: <http://www.fundforpeace.org/global/library/cfsir1210-failedstatesindex2012-06p.pdf> [Accessed on 1 January 2013].

Stein, A. (2008) 'Incentive Compatibility and Global Governance: Existential Multilateralism, a Weakly Confederal World, and Hegemony'. In A. Alexandroff (ed.), *Can the World Be Governed: Possibilities for Effective Multilateralism* (Canada: Wilfrid Laurier University Press), 17–84.

Stigtitz, J. (2003) *Globalization and Its Discontents* (New York: W.W. Norton and Company).

Thakur, R. (2011) 'The United Nations in Global Governance: Rebalancing Organized Multilateralism for Current and Future Challenges', United Nations General Assembly 65th Session Thematic Debate on the United Nations in Global Governance, New York: UN Headquarters, June 2011. Available at: <http://www.un.org/en/ga/president/65/initiatives/GlobalGovernance/Thakur_GA_Thematic_Debate_on_UN_in_GG.pdf> [Accessed 7 December 2012].

UNDPK (2013) 'Current Peacekeeping Operations', United Nations Department of Peacekeeping Operations [Online]. Available at: <http://www.un.org/en/peacekeeping/operations/current.shtml> [Accessed 15 January 2013].

UNICEF (2013) 'Water, Sanitation, and Hygiene', United Nations Children's Fund [Online]. Available at: <http://www.unicef.org/wash/> [Accessed on 1 February 2013].

UNITF (2004) 'A Gendered Perspective on Water Reserves and Sanitation', United Nations Interagency Task Force on Gender and Water: United Nations Department of Economic and Social Affairs (New York: United Nations Publications).

UNODC (2011) 'Estimating the Illicit Financial Flows Resulting From Drug Trafficking and Other Transnational Organized Crimes', United Nations Office on Drugs and Crime Report [Online]. New York: United Nations Publications. Available at: <http://www.unodc.org/documents/data-and-analysis/Studies/Illicit_financial_flows_2011_web.pdf> [Accessed 7 December 2012].

UNODC (2012a) 'Afghanistan Opium Survey', United Nations Office on Drugs and Crime Report [Online]. New York: United Nations Publications. Available at: <http://www.unodc.org/documents/crop-monitoring/Afghanistan/ORAS_report_2012.pdf > [Accessed 7 December 2012].

UNODC (2012b) 'World Drug Report 2012', United Nations Office on Drugs and Crime Report [Online]. New York: United Nations Publications. Available at: <https://www.unodc.org/unodc/en/data-and-analysis/WDR-2012.html> [Accessed 17 December 2012].

United Nations Report (2012) 'Thematic Debate of the 66th session of the United Nations General Assembly on Drugs and Crime as a Threat to Development', New York: United Nations. [Online] (26 June 2012). Available at: <http://www.un.org/en/ga/president/66/Issues/drugs/drugs-crime.shtml> [Accessed 7 December 2012].

Weiss, L. (2005) 'Global Governance, National Strategies: How Industrialized States Make Room to Move under the WTO', *Review of International Political Economy* (Abingdon: Taylor & Francis), 12, 723–49.

Williams, P. and Funk, C. (December 2011) 'A Westward Expansion of the Warm Pool Leads to a Westward Expansion of the Walker Circulation, Drying East Africa', *Climate Dynamics*, 37(11–12), 2417–35.

Wolfe, R. (2008) 'Can the Trading System Be Governed? Institutional Implications of the WTO's Suspended Animation'. In A. Alexandroff (ed.), *Can the World Be Governed? Possibilities for Effective Multilateralism* (Canada: Wilfrid Laurier University Press), 289–352.

World Bank (2011) 'World Bank Group Support to Promote Growth and Overcome Poverty in Developing Countries Hits Nearly $53 Billion in 2012', Press Release [Online] (29 June 2012). Available at:< http://www.worldbank.org/en/news/2012/06/29/world-bank-group-support-promote-growth-overcome-poverty-developing-countries-hits-nearly-billion-2012> [Accessed 7 December 2012].

World Bank (2012) 'Projects and Operations' [Online]. Available at: <http://web.worldbank.org/WBSITE/EXTERNAL/PROJECTS/0,contentMDK:20264002~menuPK:572065~pagePK:41367~piPK:279616~theSitePK:40941,00.html#4> [Accessed 7 December 2012].

World Trade Organization (2013) 'Millennium Development Goals: Aid for Trade' [Online]. Available at: <http://www.wto.org/english/thewto_e/coher_e/mdg_e/a4t_e.htm> [Accessed 2 February 2013].

Wroughton, L. (2012) 'IMF Reforms Bogged Down by Delays, Deadlock', *Reuters* [Online] (8 October 2012), Available at: <http://www.reuters.com/article/2012/10/08/us-imf-governance-idUSBRE8970B120121008> [Accessed 7 December 2012].

Zakaria, F. (2007) *The Post American World*, 2nd edition (New York: W.W. Norton and Company, Inc.).

Zweifel, T. (2006) *International Organizations and Democracy* (Boulder, CO: Lynne Rienner).

Chapter 18
Religion and International Relations

NILAY SAIYA

This chapter introduces students to the topic of religion and international relations. The chapter covers three general issues. First, it discusses why the field of international relations has been slow to recognize the importance of religion until recently. Specifically, we will look at how the international system evolved in a highly secular fashion after the great wars of religion in the seventeenth century and how these secularizing events were expressed in the academic study of international relations in the form of the secularization thesis – the idea that religion is becoming less important in the world. As it turned out, however, the secularization thesis proved to be entirely incorrect. Religion was not becoming a dormant force in the world as predicted by the proponents of secularization; it was never completely divorced for global politics. The second part of this chapter examines the reasons behind religion's resurgence in the second half of the twentieth century and surveys specific manifestations of religion's renewed impact on international relations. Finally, we will look at five ways in which religion helps shape modern world politics: as a source of international norms, a source of foreign policy, a source of Nationalism, a source of violence and a source of peace. This section also introduces the important concept of the 'ambivalence of the sacred' – the idea that religion's role in international relations is not one-dimensional but has been used as both a motive for war and an instrument of peace. Throughout this chapter, students will become familiarized with important concepts like the global resurgence of religion, religious fundamentalism, religious terrorism and religious peacebuilding.

Key Words: Religion, Religious Actors, Secularization Thesis, Global Resurgence of Religion, Islamic Fundamentalism, Religious Terrorism, Religious Peacebuilding, Ambivalence of the Sacred.

Chapter 18

Religion and International Relations

NILAY SAIYA

INTRODUCTION

Religion has long been an important component of international relations. The Hebrew Scriptures chronicle several bloody battles between God's 'chosen people', the Israelites, and surrounding nations. Written against the backdrop of the Roman sack of Jerusalem, the Apocalypse of John predicts a time when Jesus Christ will reign over a coming Golden Age of peace between nations known as the 'Millennium' – a vision that

> **Religion** – sets of beliefs, practices, or rituals that seek knowledge of and harmonize with transcendent (non-material) realities.

has inspired both faith-based violence and peace efforts through the centuries. The Crusades from the eighth to thirteenth centuries were a series of military religious campaigns aimed at recapturing the Holy Land for Christianity and laid the groundwork for medieval Christian society. Inspired by divine revelation, Joan of Arc led French troops in a number of battles against England. In early modern Europe, warring Catholic and Protestant states fought against each other for centuries. Religion's influence also extends to more recent times – the rise in religious terrorism being only the most obvious example. Other illustrations of how religious beliefs have had widespread implications for international politics include the overthrow of the Shah of Iran in 1979 and the subsequent Islamic resurgence in the Middle East, the assassinations of Egyptian President Anwar Sadat in 1981 and Israeli Prime Minister Yitzak Rabin in 1995 by religious militants and the emergence of transnational, religiously oriented human rights groups. Yet the field of international relations has been slow to recognize religion's importance, and, until recently, tended to ignore it altogether.

Religion matters in international relations, however, because it is one of the basic forces of the world, an integral part of human identity, and involves all of life. Because religion is such a fundamentally important concept, it is inevitable that religion will exert an influence on international relations. Religion today matters in issues of key importance for global politics such as US-Iranian relations, Turkey's bid to join the European Union, the Israeli-Palestinian conflict, human rights and transnational terrorism. Perhaps no contemporary event illustrates the importance of religion in international relations more than the wave of democratic uprisings that have taken place across the Middle East and North Africa over the last few years, collectively known as the **Arab Spring**. These rebellions have touched virtually every country in the region and have had serious political ramifications. Sectarian

> **Arab Spring** – a series of anti-government protests and revolts that have spread across the Arab world since 2011.

tensions have broken out in Egypt and Libya along religious lines. Syria has descended into a full-blown religious civil war. The revolutions have also highlighted issues of religious terrorism and religious liberty for faith communities.

The goal of this chapter is to highlight the importance of **religious actors** in international relations. To this end, this chapter discusses religion's historical and theoretical sidelining in the

> **Religious Actors** – faith-based believers who are active politically.

field of international relations, reasons for its comeback and five ways in which religion matters in shaping international relations today. These include it being a source of norms, Nationalism, foreign policy, violence and peace.

RELIGION'S MARGINALIZED STATUS IN INTERNATIONAL RELATIONS

Because religion is a comprehensive belief system, it often exerts influence outside of the spiritual domain to include social and political matters, including international relations. Yet, until very recently, many scholars of international relations shared a common 'allergy to religion'. Writing in the wake of the tragedy of September 11, 2001, political scientist Robert Keohane (2002, 72) remarked that the attacks revealed how 'all mainstream theories of world politics are relentlessly secular with respect to motivation'. Political philosopher Timothy Samuel Shah also notes this striking puzzle as well: 'religion has become one of the most influential factors in world affairs in the last generation but remains one of the least examined factors in the professional study and practice of world affairs' (Shah 2012, 3). There are intertwining historical and theoretical reasons that explain why religion remained marginal in the study of international relations for so long.

Historically, religion's sidelining can be traced to the **Peace of Westphalia** (1648). The Peace of Westphalia ended the Thirty Years' War (1618–48), one of the longest and most devastating of the great wars over religion, fought between warring Protestant and Catholic states. It was agreed

> **Peace of Westphalia** – the treaties establishing the modern international system.

to at Westphalia that religion had a largely divisive, discordant and pernicious influence on politics and that it should be excluded from the new international system. The Peace signalled the rise of the modern nation-state and transferred temporal ruling prerogatives away from religious institutions and ideas (that is, the Catholic Church and the **divine right of kings**) toward secular sources of political legitimacy, resulting in a diminution of religious influence in

> **Divine Right of Kings** – the belief that kings derived their political authority from God.

the political realm and also of the ability of religious rulers to coerce adherence to a particular dogma. This marked the end of an international system under the control of the pope known as **Christendom**, which had existed for 1,000 years before the signing of the Westphalian Peace. In one fell swoop, international relations had become a secular enterprise. From that point

> **Christendom** – the Christian world during the medieval and early modern period.

on, authority was centralized in the hands of sovereign, secular and independent states, with individual rulers exercising complete control over their own territories.

The Secularism inherent in these historical realities made its way into the major theories of international relations: Realism and Liberalism. In these traditions, Secularism arises from their founders' engagement with – and rejection of – religion. Machiavelli and Hobbes (representing

Realism) and Locke and Kant (representing Liberalism) wrote at a time when the international system was being formed through the secularizing set of events in early modern and Enlightenment Europe described above. These thinkers both applauded this Secularism and built it into their explanation of the behaviour of states, focusing on explicitly secular factors like power and trade. Importantly, a treatise by Hugo Grotius called the *The Laws of War and Peace* – which helped to lay the normative foundations of the sovereign state system – was based on the notion that many of Europe's conflicts would not have occurred had it not been for religion's perilous influence. This Secularism has endured in these theories and explains why they have not performed well in describing the resurgence of religion.

Thus, international relations developed in a highly secularized fashion. Guided by the **secularization thesis**, the study of international relations became primarily concerned with secular actors (particularly states). Secular ideas increasingly motivated real-world politics as well. The secular ideals of the French Revolution in the nineteenth century, for example, gave rise to other secular forms of Nationalism. In the twentieth century, the appeal of Communism, Fascism and other forms secular Nationalism held sway in Europe and large parts of the Third World. Secularism's dominance in the academy was reflected in the writings of scholars like Max Weber, Emile Durkheim and Karl Marx, all of whom believed that religion was destined to fade with the advance of technology, science, rationalism, urbanization, mass literacy, popular mobility and industrialization. These thinkers also celebrated religion's demise in a normative sense. Skepticism about religion became engrained in the discipline of political science in the twentieth century. The result has been that a secularized field has been slow to understand the role of religion in international relations.

The Secularization Thesis and International Relations

The marginalization of religion in the field of international relations can be attributed to the dominance of the secularization thesis. This thesis maintained that religion would fade in importance and influence over time. Believers in the theory generally welcomed religion's demise, believing that religion was irrational, divisive, prone to violence and largely detrimental to human progress. The thesis predicts that as states modernize, they simultaneously become more secular and reduce the role that religion plays in politics. Many (primarily Western) scholars anticipated that through the process of modernization, people would begin to transfer their allegiances from primordial loyalties like ethnicity and religion to the nation-state of which they were a part. They expected that people would lead progressively secular lives and that religion's influence in society would eventually disappear. In short, the secularist assumptions as part and parcel of secularization theory became the conventional wisdom in international relations and still dominates the thinking of many social scientists.

RELIGION'S COMEBACK

International relations evolved in a highly secular manner from the Peace of Westphalia to the latter half of the twentieth century. During this time, few scholars of international relations took religion seriously. In the 1960s, for instance, mainstream social scientists took it as an article of faith that the world was becoming more secular. Consider the words of the eminent sociologist Peter Berger: 'In the twenty-first century, religious believers are likely to be found only in small sects, huddled together to resist a worldwide secular culture' (quoted in Stark and

Finke 2000, 58). By 1999, Berger had come full circle, writing that 'The assumption that we live in a secularized world is false: The world today, with some exceptions ... is as furiously religious as it ever was, and in some places more so than ever' (Berger 1999, 2). Much recent scholarship has corroborated Berger's conclusion, showing that religion is actually gaining in strength worldwide and is more politically engaged today than it has ever been. The secularization thesis, it turns out, was dead wrong. But what accounts for the **global resurgence of religion**?

> **Global Resurgence of Religion** – the increasing role of religion in shaping politics, culture and society around the world.

The first explanation points to trends like globalization and modernization – the very processes that the secularization thesis predicted would kill off religion – that have allowed the major world religions to experience a new-found relevance. Faced with the constant uncertainties inherent in globalization processes, many in the developing world retreated to the safety of those things with which they were most familiar. Religion, in particular, became a renewed source of identity against the homogenizing forces of globalization and the materialism, corruption

> **Secularization Thesis** – the idea that religion is becoming less important in the world.

and immorality that came with it. On the other hand, the same forces lashing out against globalization have embraced many aspects of modernity to convey their message. The free flow of migrant workers and refugees – often hailing from places in the Third World marred by internal strife and suffering – coupled with advances in modern communications technologies making possible the global proliferation of ideas, information and technology – cellular phones, satellite television and the internet – have contributed to the impressive global reach of religious movements. At times, religious actors have used the communications revolution to demand important rights like religious liberty. In other cases, propaganda disseminated through these vehicles has served to radicalize certain local religious communities at home and their Diasporas abroad. For example, beginning in 2010, the Yemen-based terrorist organization, al-Qaeda in the Arabian Peninsula, began publishing an online English language magazine titled *Inspire* as a means to distribute its extremist propaganda to Westerners. The publication routinely carried translated messages from Osama bin Laden that encouraged American and British readers to engage in subversive activities against their governments.

A second reason for religion's resurgence has to do with the utter failures of secular ideologies like Fascism and Communism, which led to extreme cruelty and millions of deaths (Juergensmeyer 1993). The galvanizing event marking the downfall of international Communism involved the collapse of the Soviet Union in 1991, when the ideology of atheistic Communism lost its appeal and support for Marxist revolutionary groups and socialist governments declined precipitously. The end of the Cold War and collapse of the Soviet Union portended a major structural move in global politics from international to internal conflicts, unleashed a wave of religious and ethnic struggles and permitted a new and more dangerous form of religion to emerge, the threat of which would capture the attention of the global community after the terrorist strikes of September 11, 2001. Today, the vast majority of the world's conflicts exhibit an ethnic and/or religious dimension.

Another secular ideology, **Arab Nationalism**, had also experienced a crisis of legitimacy years before the Soviet Union fell. Arab Nationalism

> **Arab Nationalism** – an ideology emphasizing Arab unity in the face of colonialism.

took root in many countries in the Middle East and North Africa in the twentieth century as a way to combat colonial powers. Arab nationalist regimes, however, often implemented bad ideas that had ruinous results. National Socialism in places like Egypt produced bureaucracy and torpor rather than economic growth, even as these countries experienced massive youth bulges. Perhaps the biggest setback for Arab Nationalism was Israel's routing of Arab armies in the disastrous **Six-Day War** of 1967 – an event that many Arabs interpreted as divine retribution for their governments' abandoning

> **Six Day War** – a war in which Israel captured several key pieces of territory after soundly defeating Egypt, Jordan and Syria.

of Islam. To make matters worse, regional oil wealth produced a new class of fantastically rich, Western-supported sheiks who used their rents to buy off large segments of the population or repress parts of the population that they feared. Ultimately these countries degenerated into callous, corrupt and deeply unpopular dictatorships. As the levels of freedom and standards of living declined in the Arab world, the appeal of **Islamic Fundamentalism** gained in strength by providing people with a sense of meaning and purpose and became the only vehicle

> **Islamic Fundamentalism** – a strict adherence to orthodox Islamic doctrines.

available to oppose the state. Religious believers decried the destruction of values believed to derive from religious principles, and sought to replace corrupt and self-serving secular political orders with new ones having spiritual underpinnings that conformed to religious texts and principles. Such patterns could be seen in Egypt, Algeria and Saudi Arabia. The power of Islamic Fundamentalism was also demonstrated in non-Arab Islamic countries as seen in the 1979 **Iranian Revolution** and the successful **mujahidin** resistance to the Soviet invasion of Afghanistan. Such movements aimed to combat in their own countries the Secularism that had become the basis for global politics in the first half of the twentieth century.

> **Iranian Revolution** – an event referring to the overthrow of the Shah of Iran in 1979 and the establishment of an Islamic government.

> **Mujahidin** – Muslim guerilla fighters.

As the twentieth century progressed, the world witnessed a long list of other international events in which religion played a significant role. Perhaps the most well known of these were the terrorist strikes against the United States 2001 by **al-Qaeda** in which 19 terrorists hijacked four passenger airliners and flew them into buildings in New York City and Washington DC, killing nearly 3,000 people. Yet these attacks were only one manifestation of religion's comeback in global politics. Other examples included the

> **al-Qaeda** – an international militant Muslim terrorist network founded by Osama bin Laden in 1988.

resurgence of Shi'ism (a minority version of Islam) against the dominant Sunnism throughout the Middle East; the so-called 'Arab Spring' which toppled long-standing secular regimes in Tunisia, Libya and in Egypt, and brought Islamist parties into the political sphere; the rise of right-wing religious political movements like the Hindu nationalist Bharatiya Janata Party in India and the Christian right in the United States; the resurgence of religious Nationalism in countries such as Turkey and Russia; the upsurge in Pentecostalism's political influence and participation in many

Latin American and African countries; and finally, a host of religiously motivated civil wars that broke out in last 20 years in the former Yugoslavia, Iraq and Syria.

In sum, real-world events since the turn of the century have forced a rethinking of the secularization thesis, particularly the near-global resurgence of religion and the ability of religious actors to impact international relations. This realization has given rise to a new wave of scholarship that has sought to understand religion and its global influence. Unlike the work of proponents of the secularization thesis, this new scholarship acknowledges the staying power of religion and its pervasiveness in political life. These scholars seek to understand how religion shapes political life, including fundamental aspects of international relations. Importantly, though, even today, the field generally remains highly secular and has been slow to incorporate religious ideas and actors into its frameworks.

HOW RELIGIOUS ACTORS SHAPE INTERNATIONAL POLITICS

Given the growing influence of religion on politics, understanding how religion matters in global affairs is an important endeavour for a comprehensive understanding of international relations. There has been a growing appreciation in many academic and policy circles that religion needs to be taken seriously. This has largely been in acknowledgement of empirical realities. This section discusses five ways in which religion helps shape outcomes in international relations: as a source of international norms, source of foreign policy, source of Nationalism, source of violence and source of peace. We will look at each of these in turn. Before continuing, it is necessary to state that the ways in which religion effects global politics examined here are not necessarily mutually exclusive, static categories. For example, religious Nationalism can lead to religious violence; people of faith can use foreign policy channels to influence international norms; religiously inspired international norms, in turn, can be used in peacebuilding efforts by faith-based practitioners. Indeed, religion often shapes political outcomes in highly complex ways. That being said, none of the interactions mentioned above is a foregone conclusion, and for that reason, each religious foundation will be examined separately.

Source of International Norms

First, religion has contributed to the moral and legal norms that characterize the international system. These ideas about the world, rooted in religion, inspire like-minded people in different countries to work together towards a common goal. These networks are joined together not by material self-interest but by shared normative beliefs regarding the rightness of certain moral causes. Historically, religion propelled key historical shifts that have given form to modern international relations; the rise of **Erastianism** (state control of religion) after the religious wars, the origins of the nation-state and the genesis of

> **Erastianism** – a political theory holding that the state should be superior to the church in ecclesiastical matters.

the United Nations system of the mid-twentieth century were all inspired, at least in part, by religion. Today, religious transnational groups seek to inspire change on issues as diverse as debt relief, religious persecution, democracy and development. Many contemporary religious leaders invoke their faith in the cause of making their societies more just. Globally shared values that may appear both secular and taken for granted often have behind them the shaping hand of religion.

The influence of religion on international norms can be seen specifically in areas like the morality of war and the ethic of global humanitarianism. The writings of Christian intellectuals like Augustine of Hippo and Thomas Aquinas were paramount in developing **just war theory**. Augustine and Aquinas rejected the idea that violence should be carried out on the behalf of Christ's will for humanity and instead believed that war should be undertaken only if a specific set of conditions were met. The resulting just war theory recognized that war was a great travesty and argued that it should be engaged in only when necessary to prevent a greater evil. Importantly, the concept of just war delegitimized 'unjust' wars of aggression, plunder, territorial expansion and religious conversion.

> **Just War Theory** – a doctrine that set out criteria for going to war and conduct in war.

With respect to the ethic of humanitarianism, faith-based individuals and organizations have been among the world's most ardent supporters of the idea that every human being is equally entitled to a certain set of basic immunities, protections and goods. An array of important international institutions – such as the Universal Declaration of Human Rights, the International Covenant on Civil and Political Rights, the International Committee of the Red Cross, the International Court of Justice and numerous others – would be inconceivable in their present form without the influence of religion. For example, Eleanor Roosevelt, chair of the Human Rights Commission which drafted the Universal Declaration on Human Rights in 1948, grounded her efforts in her Protestant faith.

Religious actors typically seek to affect norms in international relations through their application of **soft power**. This can be illustrated in how the Vatican has exercised influence in its ability to shape the thinking of millions of Catholics. The Second Vatican Council (1962) set into motion forces of progress that challenged authoritarian regimes around the world. In the 1980s, Pope John Paul II used his position of prominence to successfully confront communist governments in Eastern Europe by providing locals with a different vision of governance grounded in religious precepts. The Pope's use of soft power proved to be influential in the people of these countries non-violently confronting the Soviet Union and eventually bringing down international Communism. Subsequently, the Catholic Church used its position of prominence in support of democratization processes, human rights, conflict resolution and development throughout Latin America, Asia and Africa.

> **Soft Power** – the ability to attract others to one's cause rather than through the use of force.

In the United States, **evangelical Christians** have used their soft power influence to shape international norms related to human rights. In the late 1990s, American evangelicals spearheaded a massive effort to bring attention to the condition of worldwide religious freedom. In response, the Clinton administration established the Advisory Committee on Religious Freedom Abroad in 1996, and in 1998, signed the International Religious Freedom Act (IRFA). Conservative

> **Evangelical Christians** – Protestants who believe human beings are saved by personal faith in Christ's atonement and in the importance of missionary activity.

Christians have used the act as a basis for demanding countries with poor human rights records accord religious freedoms to their citizens. The Office of International Religious Freedom publishes annually an International Religious Freedom Report which identifies countries with particularly egregious violations of religious freedoms.

Sometimes these norms are not so oriented toward peace, however. As a case in point, consider al-Qaeda's use of **Salafi-Jihadism** as a tool to unite Sunni Muslims in attempt to recapture the grandeur of Islam's past, return to the ancient religious faith and practices of the Prophet Muhammad and his companions

> **Salafi-Jihadism** – a radical form of Sunni Islam which condones the use of violence as a means of creating a purified Islamic world.

and establish an Islamic caliphate over as large a territory as possible. In contrast to the groups mentioned above, the norms of al-Qaeda are not benevolent but rather conflictual and violent. Such groups seek to destroy the existing system of international norms (particularly the system of independent nation-states) and replace them with Islamically inspired ones.

Source of Foreign Policy

The second way religious actors exercise influence in international relations is through a state's foreign policy. To be sure, religion is never the sole consideration in the formulation of foreign policy, and only a few states base their foreign policies explicitly in religious precepts. Nevertheless, there are numerous examples of religion influencing foreign policy decision-making processes and outcomes.

Perhaps the most obvious linkage between religion and foreign policy is found in so-called **theocracies**. The governments of countries like Iran and Saudi Arabia derive their popular legitimacy from their perceived faithfulness to a particular religious ideology. This means, in

> **Theocracies** – countries ruled by religious leaders.

effect, that in such countries religion necessarily plays a role (even if an inconsistent one) in foreign policy. The Saudi regime has at times defined its foreign policy objectives through a religious lens: opposition to the Jewish state of Israel, antipathy towards the atheistic Soviet Union and support for the promotion of Islam internationally via its role in the **Organization of the Islamic Conference**. Iran too has at times embraced an explicitly religious foreign policy. In the wake of its Revolution in 1979, Tehran adopted an official policy of exporting its revolution abroad. Its activities included funding radical Islamist movements like Hamas and Hezbollah, confronting the West (particularly

> **Organization of the Islamic Conference** – A group of 56 Islamic-majority states that seeks to promote transnational Islamic solidarity

the United States), and, more recently, using its influence to help Shi'ites (the form of Islam dominant in Iran) gain a dominant position in neighbouring Iraq after the US-led overthrow of its dictator Saddam Hussein.

Religion can also have an effect on foreign policy in democratic states. In democracies, religious actors can lobby elected officials, make campaign contributions, shape public opinion and vote for candidates who support their causes. Consider the United States. Reflecting its Protestant heritage, Christianity has figured prominently in how Americans perceive themselves and the world. Since the country's founding, American politicians and publics have routinely expressed the view that America plays a special role in the international system because of the undeniably religious belief God has chosen the country to be an instrument for his purposes in the world. References by American presidents to the US as a 'shining city', 'redeemer nation' or 'chosen people' have framed the way in which Americans understand both domestic and international politics. From George Washington to Barack Obama, abolition to prohibition, suffrage to civil rights, the Revolutionary War to the Second Persian Gulf War, religion has played an important role in the American political scene, in both domestic and foreign affairs.

One of the most important religious actors in the US is the **American Christian Right**, which helped mold foreign policy thanks to its relationships with presidents, key members of Congress and the media. The Christian Right, along with other religious groups, inspired Cold War movements such as the campaign for Soviet Jewry. More recently, they have rallied behind legislative efforts for international religious freedom and against human trafficking such

> **American Christian Right** – a grouping of conservative Christian political factions active in the United States who advocate for socially conservative policies.

as the International Religious Freedom Act (1998), the Trafficking Victims Protection Act (2000) and the North Korea Human Rights Act (2004) (Haynes 2008a). During the administration of George W. Bush – a self-professed evangelical Christian – the Christian Right also lent strong support to the American military and the idea that America is the leader of the free world. Their positions included a strong preference for American unilateralism and cynicism of international/transnational bodies and treaties; a vigorous defense of the state of Israel; the overthrow of regimes hostile to the US; and support for the American military and the war against terror.

Faith, George W. Bush and Foreign Policy

One of the most outspoken American leaders concerning his religious beliefs was the country's 43rd president, George W. Bush. Many have suggested that Bush's personal faith played an important role in shaping his views on international relations. Though it is impossible to suggest with any degree of certainty whether theology played a role in Bush's decision to invade Iraq in 2003, when asked if his father would support the war, Bush responded, 'You know, he is the wrong father to appeal to in terms of strength. There is a higher father I appeal to' (Saiya 2012, 198). The Israeli newspaper *Al Haaretz* reported that in a conversation with Palestinian Prime Minister Mahmoud Abbas, Bush defended his Middle East policy by declaring, 'God told me to strike al Qaeda and I struck them, and then he instructed me to strike at Saddam, which I did' (Saiya 2012, 198). These religiously based statements indicate that the president believed he was doing the will of God with respect to his foreign policy choices.

Religion's influence on foreign policy can be seen in other democracies as well. In India, Hindu nationalists have attempted to steer the direction of both domestic and foreign policy. The coming to power of the Bharatiya Janata Party (BJP) in 1998 – a Hindu nationalist party that sought to integrate religion and politics at both the national and state levels – marked a heightened role for religion in Indian foreign policy until the BJP was defeated in 2004 by the secular Congress Party. During that time, dedicated Hindu nationalists in government devoted renewed attention and resources to confrontation with its neighbour Pakistan over its support for religious terrorism against India and were moved less by the economic concerns, secular orientation, multilateralism, pragmatism and official non-alignment policy of their Congress predecessors. Hindu Right politicians, including Deputy Prime Minister Lal Krishna Advani, spoke about the need to create an 'axis of virtue' between the United States, Israel and India in their mutual fight against Islamist terrorism and its sources in the Muslim world (Haynes 2008b: 156). India thus adopted a more aggressive nationalistic foreign policy vis-à-vis Pakistan and its own Muslim minority. The 2014 election of Narendra Modi – the new leader of the BJP – to the post of Prime Minister might signal a renewed role for religion in Indian foreign policy going forward.

Source of Nationalism

The third way in which religion matters in international relations is as a source of national identity. Nations are communities of people who comprise a common culture, share the same history and believe they have a common destiny. **Nationalism** – the belief that these nations should have their own states – is one of the most important forces in international relations, shaping politics both between and within states. After the Peace of Westphalia, secular Nationalism became the primary

> **Nationalism** – an ideology that prescribes political independence or self-governance to a group of individuals who define themselves in common terms of ethnicity, language, religion or historical narrative.

way that states organized themselves in Europe. Over time, however, just as religion began to influence other areas of international relations as part of its global resurgence, it also began to exert an influence on the growth and practice of Nationalism.

Religion and Nationalism interact in a variety of ways. Religion, for instance, can shape one's devotion to a particular piece of territory as a 'holy land' or 'sacred space'. It is hard, for example, to understand the violent conflicts that have surrounded the city of Jerusalem for millennia without taking religious factors into account. In places like Iraq and the Palestinian territories, religious Nationalism often operated as a rallying point among indigenous resistance movements against the regimes of their occupiers.

Religion can also shape and reinforce nationalist identities, defining a nation in terms of shared religion, that is, Russian Orthodoxy, Tibetan Buddhism and Jewish Zionism. Religious Nationalism was further a crucial component in the state-building of explicitly theocratic states like Iran, Saudi Arabia and Afghanistan under the Taliban – cases where religion and Nationalism were inseparable. At other times, religion worked in conjunction with other forms of identity like race, culture, or language in the development of Nationalism as seen in places as diverse as India, Egypt and Zimbabwe. Even today, religious Nationalism continues to inform contemporary nation-building projects in Israel, Northern Ireland, Sri Lanka and Ukraine.

Sometimes religiously based nations live in peace and tranquility. At other times, religious Nationalism leads to domestic or even international strife. This can happen when a healthy form of patriotic Nationalism (pride in the uniqueness of one's nation) over time is replaced with jingoism, xenophobia and hyper-Nationalism – when a nation views itself as superior to other nations and is convinced that these other nations are not only inferior but threatening and must be dealt with punitively. Religious hyper-Nationalism took root in the Balkans in the 1990s, when Christian Serbs and Muslim Bosnians, who had previously lived together peacefully, became embroiled in a brutal conflict that led to the fragmentation of Yugoslavia. Religious Nationalism has also shaped conflicts between adjacent states of different faiths. Take, for example, India and Pakistan. Ever since the two countries were partitioned in 1947, a conflict has raged between them over the over the disputed territory of Kashmir. Whether Kashmiri Muslims should be part of Hindu India or Muslim Pakistan lies at the heart of the conflict.

At the same time that religion often contributes to Nationalism, it must also be said that sometimes the transnational nature of religion works against Nationalism. This is because religion and not the nation still holds peoples' primary loyalty. Most religions span state borders. For example, when religious differences exist within the same nation-state, these distinctions can serve to tear countries apart as seen in Iraq, Ireland and Sudan. This point notwithstanding, a comprehensive understanding of Nationalism in today's world must take into account the religious factor.

Source of Violence

Since the terrorist attacks of September 11, 2001, religion's relationship to violence – the fourth way in which religion helps shape international relations – has seen a substantial increase in scholarship, primarily focusing on transnational Islamist groups and terrorism. The rise in religious conflicts has made it difficult to ignore the fact that religious dynamics matter a great deal in many civil wars and separatist struggles. Today, the majority of these conflicts have a religious dimension. Different theories attempt to account for this phenomenon. Perhaps the most famous of these theories, Samuel Huntington's **clash of civilizations,** posited that the end of the Cold War, with its rigid alliance system rooted in secular, Western ideologies, unleashed a wave of identity-based conflicts between and within the world's

> **Clash of Civilizations** – Samuel Huntington's claim that the future of global politics will be characterized by conflict between civilizations whose defining feature is a common religion.

religiously demarcated civilizations (Huntington 1993). A second explanation by sociologist Mark Juergensmeyer (2003) argued that a crisis of legitimacy in secular ideologies brought on by their failure to deliver the prosperity and social wellbeing they promised led to people in the Third World turning to indigenous ideologies like religion as a way to combat the foreign, corrupt and ineffective Western imports. A third account points to **political theology** as the key explanation (Toft, Philpott and Shah 2011). In this view, religious violence is a product of groups and individuals who hold an ideology that either espouses or condones the use of violence. This logic holds that religious

> **Political Theology** – the ideas a religious group holds about the proper relationship between religion and politics.

communities turn to aggression when they interpret their central scriptures, doctrines and rituals in such a way that calls for their religion to become the officially established religion of the state and others to be suppressed or when they believe they are engaged in a sacred duty to defend their faith.

The Clash of Civilizations

Initially published in the fall edition of *Foreign Affairs* in 1993, Samuel P. Huntington's provocative *Clash of Civilizations* has greatly informed the post-Cold War debate regarding the nature and future of international relations. In the wake of the attacks of September 11, 2001, Huntington's ideas regained the spotlight once more as scholars, policymakers, and journalists sought to make sense of the tragedy. The post-9/11 'clash of civilizations' discourse also influenced the scope and course of American foreign policy in the coming years, particularly relating to the idea of the 'West versus the rest'.

Huntington's landmark article attempted to offer a new paradigm of international relations by arguing that the future of international conflict would be marked along primarily religious or cultural lines, in sharp contrast to the ideological struggle of the Cold War between the US and the Soviet Union. Writing in response to those who believed that liberal democracy and free-market capitalism would flourish with the end of the Cold War, Huntington argued that the 'the principal conflicts of global politics will occur between nations and groups of different civilizations' (22). In Huntington's view, this is particularly true of relations between Muslims and non-Muslims. Huntington believed that Christianity and Islam are likely to clash insofar as both are missionary faiths that seek to convert people of other religions; both are universalistic faiths, emphasizing the truth claims of their particular religions; and both are teleological religions whose innate values symbolize the purpose of existence. Huntington wrote that the differences between civilizations stem from divergences in social and political values. Of the seven or eight major civilizations he describes, Huntington believed the greatest conflict to emerge will be between the Western and Islamic worlds. Huntington's thesis necessarily calls for the West to assert and maintain its dominance vis-à-vis other civilizations and maintain Western unity by promoting cooperation between the US and Europe, retaining its technological and military superiority, limiting the expansion of Chinese and Islamic military and economic power, advancing American identity by restricting immigration and repudiating multiculturalism and resisting the temptation to remake the world in the American image.

Whatever the reasons for the increase in religious friction, it is probable that religion's deep roots in society will mean that these kinds of conflicts will continue well into the future. This has important ramifications for international relations. Sometimes civil wars can spill across borders and become regional conflagrations. They also have a tendency to pull in external actors who vie for influence within the country. Furthermore, the demands by religious actors for self-determination could lead to new states based on religious identity like Israel and Pakistan.

Perhaps the most obvious example of religious conflict in the modern world is the phenomenon of **religious terrorism**. Scholarly interest in the study of religious terrorism has increased markedly since the attacks of September 11, 2001, though, in fact, religious terrorism had been steadily increasing worldwide since the 1980s. Until 1980, virtually all terrorism was secular in nature, encompassed in three types of organizations: (1) independence movements struggling against colonial occupiers as in Algeria and Kenya; (2) separatist groups seeking territorial autonomy or national sovereignty as in Ireland and

> **Religious Terrorism** – political violence motivated by religious belief against non-combatants.

Spain; and (3) socio-economic revolutionaries fighting for their version of justice in places like Latin America, Italy and West Germany (Fine 2008). What tied all these movements together was that they grounded their actions in secular ideals – Marxism, anti-colonialism, social justice – rather than in religious motivations.

Things began to change after the Iranian Revolution of 1979, which served as a catalyst for religious terrorism worldwide. As the aforementioned secular ideologies – class conflict, anti-colonial liberation and secular Nationalism – began to lose their appeal, religious terrorism experienced a relative upsurge. Whereas in 1968 – the year marking the advent of modern, international terrorism – when there were no active international religious terrorist organizations, that number rose to two in 1980; 11 in 1992; 16 in 1994; 26 in 1995; and 52 (or roughly half) in 2004 (Hoffman 2006, 81–130). This increase in religious terrorism has also been met with a marked decrease in the number of purely separatist/ethno-nationalist terrorist groups. According to former American Secretary of State Warren Christopher, religious terrorism has become 'one of the most important security challenges we face in the wake of the Cold War' (Juergensmeyer 2003, 6).

Today, religious violence, especially religious terrorism, has made its way onto the radar as a major national security issue, occupying the attention of policymakers around the world. For example, the current turmoil in the Middle East and North Africa raises important questions about whether Western powers should support or oppose democracy in the region if that means the ascension to power of religious political parties. In Sudan, religion has played an important role in fomenting violence against Christians at the hands of the Islamist government. Fears abound that a power vacuum in Libya may result in that country becoming a safe haven for al-Qaeda-inspired terrorists. Should it develop nuclear weapons, can a theocratic Iran be trusted to abide by the logic of deterrence theory? Understanding how religion influences politics can help us better understand and respond to these current dilemmas in which religion is a salient feature.

Source of Peace

At the same time that religion can contribute to violence in various ways, it can also help in resolving conflicts and building peace – the fifth way in which religion influences international relations. How can one explain this paradox? Many social scientists who study religion have noted that the world's religions are 'ambivalent' when it comes to their role in conflict and peace. Historian of religion, R. Scott Appleby, terms this paradoxical duality of religion the **ambivalence of the sacred**. Ambivalence in this context means that religions inherently neither support nor oppose violence or peace, conflict or cooperation, autocracy or democracy. Rather, whether or not

> **Ambivalence of the Sacred** – religion's ability to inspire both violence and peace.

a religion is congenial to peace depends in large part on how and by whom it is interpreted. Indeed, the Islamic and Christian scriptures, for example, contain numerous passages that seem to espouse authoritarianism, divinely appointed government, slavery or patriarchy in the home and in society at large, while at the same time containing passages emphasizing the qualities of love, tolerance, goodwill and patience. All great faiths are multi-vocal and contain within them numerous doctrinal currents. Just as religion sometimes causes conflict, it is also capable of playing a salubrious, even indispensable, role in peacemaking and reconciliation efforts.

Those emphasizing the productive role religion could potentially play in international diplomacy and conflict resolution aver that that conflict resolution, peacemaking and reconciliation are central to all of the world's religions. Furthermore, most religions share a broadly similar array of spiritual values that can bolster attempts at inter-faith cooperation. Religious leaders in particular have a moral obligation to help resolve conflicts and facilitate peacebuilding and are uniquely positioned to accomplish these goals. Many believe that religious peacebuilding is not only possible but necessary in helping end some of the world's long-standing conflicts, especially where these conflicts themselves involve issues of religion.

Religious organizations and leaders can play a positive role in fostering peace because of the moral authority, community stature, credibility, trust, moral standing and empathetic neutrality they often bring. Unlike many secular peace practitioners, faith-based peacemakers bring a unique dimension to their activities insofar as they are embedded in the very communities in which they wish to help establish peace. Their membership in the local community means that they are intimately aware of the complex dynamics that accompany many disputes, often in ways that outside peacemakers are not. They understand the importance of indigenous belief systems, religious symbols and rituals. Religious peacemakers can also offer spiritual healing to war-torn communities, activate their constituencies for peace and combine these strengths with the proven techniques of secular social justice workers – dialogue, facilitation skills and active listening – in providing a dynamic and effective method of pursuing peace.

Religious peacebuilding is not a new idea. Representatives of faith-based organizations have been influential in mediating civil conflict for years, and such efforts are increasing. In various parts of the world, religious peacemakers have engaged in an array of activities. Political scientist Daniel Philpott mentions several roles that religious actors have played in countries like Guatemala, South Africa and East Timor.

> **Religious Peacebuilding** – the pursuit of peace through faith-based initiatives.

These include mediation, foreign cooperation, building zones of peace, training individuals in conflict resolution, performing rituals of reconciliation, building friendships, imparting moral vision, healing victims, promoting forgiveness and conducting advocacy. Philpott also believes that one of the most effective vehicles whereby religious actors can achieve these goals is the establishment of a **truth and reconciliation commission**, pointing to the examples of truth commissions chaired by Archbishop Desmond Tutu in South Africa and Bishop Juan Gerardi in Guatemala. In addition to these countries, in Peru, East Timor and Sierra Leone, religious communities contributed

> **Truth and Reconciliation Commission** – national mechanisms designed to document the truth about past societal injustices.

logistical support to their countries' truth commissions, assisting in organizing and carrying out hearings, finding and encouraging victims and witnesses and providing counselling once hearings were over (Philpott 2012, 100). In such ways religion can be used as a means of conflict transformation, conflict management and conflict resolution. As peace facilitators, religious actors possess a number of peace-making instruments not as available to secular/outside agents of peace.

CONCLUSION

This chapter has provided a brief introduction to the topic of religion and international relations by highlighting three issues: (1) the reasons for religion's marginalization in the study and practice of international relations; (2) the reasons behind religion's comeback; and (3) five ways in which religion shapes contemporary international relations. In today's world, global religion is experiencing resurgence unparalleled in modern history. As a universal phenomenon pursued for ultimate reasons, religion has always mattered in international relations, and it always will.

This does not mean that the dominant actors in international relations will ever act solely on the basis of religion, define their identities and goals in purely religious terms or interpret the global landscape through purely religious optics, given that such actors are highly complex and motivated by a variety of aspirations. Yet, in a world that is becoming more religious, faith will continue to inform global politics in a host of ways. As this chapter has shown, the forces of religion have become powerful enough now that they can no longer be ignored by scholars or practitioners of international relations. Whether one believes that, on balance, religion is generally a malevolent or benevolent force in the world, one thing is clear: religion's influence on politics is not going away anytime soon; the twenty-first century truly is 'God's century' (Toft, Philpott and Shah 2011).

QUESTIONS FOR REFLECTION

1. What historical factors account for religion's marginalization in the study of international relations?
2. How has globalization contributed to religion's influence on international relations?
3. How has religion shaped the moral and legal norms of the international system?
4. Why has religion been influential in the making of American foreign policy?
5. What does the 'ambivalence of the sacred' mean in the context of international relations outcomes?

REVISION QUIZ

1. The Thirty Years' War ended with the signing of which treaty?

   a. Peace of Westphalia
   b. Treaty of Madrid
   c. Treaty of Paris
   d. Peace of Pressburg

2. Which political philosopher wrote *The Laws of War and Peace*?

   a. Machiavelli
   b. Grotius
   c. Kant
   d. Hobbes

3. What secular ideology guided the Soviet Union until it collapsed in 1991?

   a. Fascism
   b. Communism

c. Arab Nationalism
d. Nazism

4. Which country won the Six-Day War of 1967?

a. Israel
b. Egypt
c. Syria
d. Jordan

5. An Islamic revolution took place in which country in 1979?

a. Pakistan
b. Egypt
c. Iran
d. Iraq

6. In which country has the Bharatiya Janata Party been active?

a. India
b. Pakistan
c. Nepal
d. Bangladesh

7. Which Pope used his position of prominence to challenge international Communism during the 1980s?

a. Paul VI
b. John Paul II
c. John XXIII
d. Benedict XVI

8. Who founded al-Qaeda in 1988?

a. Ruholla Khoemeni
b. Abdul Aziz Rantisi
c. Osama bin Laden
d. Hassan Nasrallah

9. Who wrote about the 'clash of civilizations?'

a. Samuel Huntington
b. George W. Bush
c. Immanuel Kant
d. Francis Fukuyama

10. What is the term used to describe religiously-motivated political violence against civilians?

   a. Religious Fundamentalism
   b. Religious Nationalism
   c. Clash of Civilizations
   d. Religious Terrorism

Answers: 1: a; 2: b; 3: b; 4: a; 5: c; 6: a; 7: b; 8: c; 9: a; 10: d.

BIBLIOGRAPHY

Berger, P.L. (1999) *The Desecularization of the World: Resurgent Religion and World Politics* (Grand Rapids: Eerdmans Publishing).

Fine, J. (2008) 'Contrasting Secular and Religious Terrorism'. *Middle East Quarterly* 15(1), 59–69.

Hoffman, B. (2006) *Inside Terrorism* (New York, Columbia University Press).

Haynes, J. (2008a) 'Religion and a human rights culture in America', *The Review of Faith & International Affairs* 6(2), 73–82.

Haynes, J. (2008b) 'Religion and Foreign Policy Making in the USA, India and Iran: Towards a research agenda', *Third World Quarterly* 29(1), 143–65.

Huntington, S.P. (1993) 'The Clash of Civilizations?', *Foreign Affairs* 72(3), 22–49.

Juergensmeyer, M. (1993) *The New Cold War?: Religious Nationalism Confronts the Secular State* (Berkeley, CA: University of California Press).

Juergensmeyer, M. (2003) *Terror in the Mind of God: The Global Rise of Religious Violence* (Berkeley, CA: University of California Press).

Keohane, R. (2002) 'The Globalization of Informal Violence, Theories of World Politics, and "The Liberalism of Fear"'. In C. Calhoun, P. Price and A. Timmer (eds), *Understanding September 11* (New York: New Press).

Norris, P. and Inglehart, R. (2004) *Sacred and Secular: Religion and Politics Worldwide* (Cambridge: Cambridge University Press).

Philpott, D. (2012) *Just and Unjust Peace: An Ethic of Political Reconciliation* (Oxford: Oxford University Press).

Saiya, N. (2012) 'Onward Christian Soldiers: American Dispensationalists, George W. Bush and the Middle East', *Holy Land Studies* 11(2), 175–204.

Shah, T.S. (2012) 'Introduction: Religion and World Affairs: Blurring the Boundaries'. In T.S. Shah, A. Stepan M.D. Toft (eds), *Rethinking Religion and World Affairs* (New York, Oxford University Press).

Stark, R. and Finke, R. (2000) *Acts of Faith* (Berkeley, CA: University of California Press).

Toft, M.D., Philpott, D. and Shah, T.S. (2011) *God's Century: Resurgent Religion and Global Politics* (New York: W. W. Norton).

Epilogue
What Next for the Study and Practice of World Affairs?

EMILIAN KAVALSKI

*And so he [the student of world politics] embarks on a search for certainty, only to find
that it lies in such phrases as 'apparently', 'presumably', and 'it would seem as if'.*
James N. Rosenau (1960, 21)

The American military historian Roger Beaumont (1994, 145) has quipped that there is something quite paradoxical implicit in any attempt to 'conclude' the encounters with the world affairs. According to him, the sequential unfolding of the uncertainties, dilemmas and contingencies of a dynamic, complex and constantly moving target such as global politics works against focusing analysis and drawing neat conclusions. In short, our encounters with world politics do not cease. Beaumont's sentiment echoes the chagrin of the American International Relations (IR) scholar, James Rosenau. that both scholars and students expect edited collections to have a concluding chapter 'that ends on an upbeat note, celebrates the realization of common themes, ties all the contributions into a coherent whole and thus demonstrates the wisdom of collecting the essays between the same covers'. As Rosenau put it, 'to write an Epilogue is to strain for what may be a misleading sense of closure. It amounts to having the last word, just like superpowers do' (Rosenau et al. 1993, 127–8). Sharing Rosenau's repulsion towards the privilege of editorial 'superpower', this epilogue drafts a hesitant outline of some of the themes zigzagging across the analyses of the preceding chapters. The following remarks, therefore, are not *the* authoritative version of a 'concluding chapter that ties all the contributions into a coherent whole', but just one of many possible versions that can assist you in making sense of the possible trajectories that your own encounters with world affairs can take. Thus, rather than 'impose an outlook', this concluding chapter illustrates *a* perspective on the preceding discussions.

To begin with, the hope is that this textbook has made it clear that neither the study nor the practice of international relations is an 'exact science'. During the 1960s a number of IR scholars have tried to develop 'not merely a "science", but a powerful, parsimonious, and perhaps even elegant science of international politics' (Rogowski 1968, 418). As a result, more often than not, the IR mainstream has tended to propound explanations premised on assumptions of predictability rooted in the conviction that international life is a closed system, changing in a gradual manner and following linear trajectories, which can be elicited through discrete assessments of dependent and independent variables. What IR intends to produce in this way is a nearly mechanistic model of international politics that is perceived to be as rigorous and robust as the one of the natural sciences.

'Apparently', to use Jim Rosenau's suggestion in the epigraph, uncertainty has always been a defining feature of world affairs. So why then are policymakers, International Relations

(IR) scholars, and we – the news-thirsty publics – so surprised when the world turns out to be unpredictable? After all, depending on how far back one is willing to look, the discipline (at least in its 'Eurocentric' form) has gone a long way since the first department of international politics opened its doors at Aberystwyth or since Thucydides scripted his account of the Peloponnesian wars. In either case, the veritable age of IR should have 'presumably' provided it with enough experience to expect – if not necessarily be prepared for – the unexpected. Yet, as Rosenau (1980) reminds us, IR is anything but prepared for uncertainty (and has been so for a while). According to him, 'it would seem as if' the mainstream has lost its 'playfulness'. Thus, instead of allowing 'one's mind to run freely, to be playful, to toy around with what might seem absurd, to posit seemingly unrealistic circumstances and speculate what would follow if they ever were to come to pass', the IR mainstream has sidelined its mischievous nature in favour of stiff parsimonious models simplifying the contingent nature of most that passes in world affairs. For Rosenau, therefore, it is no wonder that IR has consistently failed to 'imagine the unimaginable' (Rosenau 1980, 19–31).

Thus, in the vein of 'imagining the unimaginable', how can we answer the question what does the future hold for the study and dynamics of world affairs? Perhaps, it would be useful to recollect a psychological experiment conducted at the University of Maine (USA) on a group of freshmen during the 1930–31 academic year. The experiment investigated students' 'wishes for improbable future events' – that is, what developments these students would like to happen in the future while fully aware that these things will never happen. As you can expect, the answers varied from the mundane (19.1 per cent wanted to 'become rich') and the concerns of the day

---

Imagining the year 2000

Do you think these predictions got it right?

Some see us drifting toward the all-powerful state, lulled by the sweet sound of 'security'. Some see a need to curb our freedom lest it be used to shield those who plot against us … More importantly, a new world unifying power – the United States – will have taken its place in the center of international affairs; forging a new 'empire', different from Britain's, different from Rome's, indeed not an empire at all in the old sense, but nevertheless a new core, a new catalytic force.

The Associated Press (27 December 1950)

This is preliminary to hypothesizing that in the year 2000 the American world system that has been developed in the last twenty years will be in a state of disintegration and decay. Just as American influence has replaced European influence during the current period, so also during the last quarter of this century American power will begin to wane and other countries will move in to fill in the gap. Among those that will play a prominent role in this respect will be China on mainland Asia, Indonesia in Southeast Asia, Brazil in Latin America, and I do not know what in the Middle East and Africa.

Samuel P. Huntington (1967, 316)

[T]he governments of developed states could ally themselves with authoritarian or totalitarian oligarchies in the poor world, with regimes that are able, with extant and yet-to-be-developed instruments of surveillance and control, to keep the lid on their domestic politics. The price would be privileges for the governing elite of these countries, a sharing in the benefits of 2000AD material culture that could never be paid to the masses. These oligarchies might continue to mouth the ideologies of development and ultimate prosperity for their citizens, and even provide, with outside assistance, the basis for modest improvement in their peoples' physical condition. Yet they would maintain the ability to control change and suppress dissent, acting in part as agents of the rich world.

Bruce M. Russett (1968, 188)

How to study the future of world politics?

Consider which of the following suggestions do you find most convincing and why

'The future', the Nobel Prize winning physicist and philosopher Percy W. Bridgman once said, 'is a program'. What did he mean by that? Every scientific prediction is based on the extrapolation of some earlier events or observations. We derive our guesses about the future by projecting ahead some time-series of events and experiences from the past. But there are many such series: they may run parallel, or converge or diverge; they may cross over so as to make relatively small what once was big, and to make what was small in the past big in the future. We do not want to project, then, single time-series of data and events in their changing patterns of interactions and proportions. As a strategist may try to read the future positions and capabilities of an army from the present deployment of its troops, so we can try to estimate at least some of the expectable patterns of the future of the world's populations, needs, resources, hopes, and efforts. It is in this sense that the world trends of today in their joint configuration add up to a program that can suggest to us something of the probable shape of things to come. Even then we cannot foresee the future with any certainty. It involves too many probabilities, singly and in combination. But though we cannot foresee precisely or reliably, we can try to provide some plans, preparations, and resources for some of the most likely risks, constraints, and opportunities for at least a limited span of time ahead.

Karl W. Deutsch (1968, 277)

One implication of the notion of 'modernization' is that the present is different from the past and the future will likely be different from the present. Successive eras may differ in 'evolutionary' ways – in which case, if we understand the mechanism of development, it may be possible to anticipate, perhaps even predict, the future. On the other hand, perhaps 'revolutionary' change is what international history is really about. Here, we probably can know a good deal more about the causes of revolutions, which are patterned and recurrent, than about their effects, which are manifold and varied. Regarding revolutions, therefore, it will always be easier to reflect than to project... It is always possible, of course, that changes in the course of international history are both non-recurrent and random, which would render the study of change most perplexing and attempts at theoretical understanding most frustrating.

Donald J. Puchala (2003, 3)

Point prediction in international relations is impossible. A more useful approach may be the development of scenarios, or narratives with plot lines that map a set of causes and trends in future time... Scenarios are not predictions or forecasts, where probabilities are assigned to outcomes; rather, they start from the assumption that the future is unpredictable, and tell alternative stories of how the future may unfold. Scenarios are generally constructed by distinguishing what we believe is relatively certain from what we think is uncertain. The most important 'certainties' are generally common to all scenarios that address the same problem or trend, while the most important 'uncertainties' differentiate one scenario from another... By constructing scenarios, or plausible stories of paths to the future, we can identify different driving forces (in lieu of independent variables, since it implies a force pushing in a certain direction rather than what is known on one side of an 'equals' sign) and then attempt to combine these forces in logical chains that generate a range of outcomes, rather than single futures. Scenarios... reinsert a sensible notion of contingency into theoretical arguments that would otherwise tend towards determinism... by raising the possibility and plausibility of multiple futures.

Richard Ned Lebow (2007, 429–30)

(19.9 per cent wanted 'smoking privileges for women' on campus) to the idealistic (53.3 per cent indicated that they wished for 'no wars') (Israeli 1932). While it is difficult to know how many of those taking part in the experiment thought of themselves as having become rich after graduation, we now know that the University of Maine permitted women to smoke in public in 1934 – just a few years after the experiment was conducted (and perhaps before many of the students taking part in the experiment had graduated). We also know that in 2011 the university proudly joined a growing cohort of tobacco-free campuses across the United States. These developments tell us how fickle our expectations are – it might seem strange to us that just three or four years before it was permitted, students at the University of Maine could not imagine a future in which women would be allowed to smoke on campus. It is interesting, however, the idea that at some point in the future undergraduate students would entertain, let alone support, the idea of a tobacco-free campus never crossed their minds. At the same time, wars are still part of the daily patterns of international affairs. In fact, most commentators tend to agree with the observation of the British IR scholar Edward H. Carr that 'war lurks in the background of international politics' (1981, 109). In fact, some such as the French philosopher Raymond Aron went as far as suggesting that IR is 'the science of peace and war' (1966, 6). However, while wars still form a part of international life, the nature of war has changed so radically that it is doubtful whether the participants in the 1930–31 University of Maine experiment will recognize the majority of contemporary conflicts as 'wars'. For them, the label applied to conflict between two or more countries; yet, interstate conflicts are extremely rare today. Instead, most of present-day wars are intra-state – involving different ethnic, religious, linguistic or other communities (this does not mean that such conflicts cannot spill into neighbouring countries, but that they pit against each other particular identity-based groups rather than states, *per se*).

In this respect, the 1930–31 University of Maine psychological experiment helps illustrate the futility of prediction – especially, prediction in world politics. As the American IR scholar, Robert Jervis has emphasized, 'history usually makes a mockery of our hopes or our expectations. The events of 1989, perhaps more welcome than any events since 1945, were unforeseen' (Jervis 1991/1992, 39). For the Canadian IR scholar Robert W. Cox this suggests that in the study of international relations 'practical knowledge (that which can be put to work through action) is always partial or fragmentary' – thus, even the smallest changes in practice reveal the 'arbitrary' nature of the discipline and often confuse, if not undermine, its 'conceptual unity' (Cox 1981, 126). According to the American IR scholar, Donald J. Puchala, the inherent fragility of the study of world affairs reflects its preoccupation with 'unobservable wholes' – such as international interdependence, security communities and so on – which reveal 'considerable uncertainty about whether the parts observed are actually elements of the wholes inferred' (Puchala 2003, 21–2).

In this respect, already in the distant 1942, Frederick S. Dunn, an American practitioner and scholar of IR (and founder of the influential journal *World Politics*) has suggested that the 'great difference between foreign affairs in books and foreign affairs in action lies in this, that foreign affairs in action consists largely of doubts and confusion, of difficult choices based on insufficient knowledge and dimly perceived objectives, followed by the same thing all over again, whereas foreign affairs in books commonly appear as definite, orderly, and rational' (cited in Fox 1962, 1). Therefore, many scholars have suggested that 'due to the changing conditions and human reflection, the openness of social systems, and the complexity of the interaction among stipulated causes make the likelihood of predictive theory [in IR] – even of a probabilistic kind – extraordinarily low' (Lebow 2010, 265). Echoing these sentiments Robert Jervis (1991/1992, 42) insists that:

> When elements are tightly interconnected, as they are in international politics, changes in one part of the system produce ramifications in other elements and feedback loops. Thus international politics is characterized by unintended consequences, interaction effects, and patterns that cannot be understood by breaking the system into bilateral relations ... With complex interaction and feedback, not only can small causes have large effects, but prediction is inherently problematic as the multiple pathways through which the system will respond to a stimulus are difficult to trace after the fact, let alone estimate ahead of time.

Is post-Western IR possible?

Consider the following statements and discuss what would the likely concerns of non-/ post-Western IR are likely to be

What makes [IR] Eurocentric is the assumption that the West self-generates through its own endogenous 'logic of immanence', before projecting its global will-to-power outwards through a one-way diffusionism so as to remake the world in its own image. I call this pervading white mythology of IR, the Westphilian narrative (twinned with its accompanying Eastphobian narrative). Indeed, the main problem with IR is not simply that it is constrained within a 'Westphalian straitjacket', but more that it is constrained within a 'Westphilian straitjacket' that at once renders racist hierarchy and racism invisible in the world while simultaneously issuing racist explanatory models of the world. Most significantly, the uncomfortable implication of this is that the extent to which … IR theorists reiterate the Westphilian narrative means that their analyses are for the White West and for Western imperialism in various senses. First is the assumption that self-generating Western agency and power in the world is 'the only game in town' which, when coupled with the dismissal of Eastern agency, unwittingly naturalises Western civilisation and Western imperialism. Second, it deserves emphasising that the representational leitmotif of imperialism was the very notion of White Western supremacy and Black Eastern inferiority, which served to demoralise the colonised Other in order to portray resistance as futile … Prior to, and even during much of, the eighteenth century, Europeans often recognised that East and West were interlinked. But the emergence of Eurocentrism led to the construction of an imaginary line of civilizational apartheid that fundamentally separated or split East from West. Having split these mutual civilisation into 'distinct entities', Eurocentric thinkers then elevated the Western Self and demoted the Eastern Other. The West was imbued with exclusively progressive characteristics – including rationality and liberalism – which ensured that the West would not only make political and economic modernity single-handedly but would also be the torch-bearer of political/economic development in the world. By contrast, the Eastern Other was imbued with all manner of regressive and antithetical properties – including Oriental despotism and irrationality – which ensured that slavery and stagnation would be its lot.

John M. Hobson (2007, 93–4)

'Europe' cannot after all be provincialized within the institutional site of the university whose knowledge protocols will always take us back to the terrain where all contours follow that of hyperreal Europe – the project of provincializing Europe must realize within itself its own impossibility. It therefore looks to a history that embodies this politics of despair. It will have been clear by now that this is not a call for cultural relativism or for atavistic, nativist histories. Nor is this a program for a mere rejection of modernity which would be, in many situations, politically suicidal. I ask for a history that deliberately makes visible within the very structure of its narrative forms, its own repressive strategies and practices, the part it plays in collusion with the narratives of citizenship in assimilating to the projects of the modern state all other possibilities of solidarity. The politics of despair would require of such history that it lay bare to its reasons why such a predicament is necessarily inescapable.

Dipesh Chakrabarty (2000, 45)

A seemingly noble ideal rationalizes hegemony in world politics today. It claims that justice among nations and peoples requires a universal standard upheld by a universal power, i.e. the US-West. How else could we live in a fair and equal world? The US-West offers our best hope for an 'open, rule-based' liberal world order. It alone has the right set of norms, institutions, and practices to forestall anarchy in the international system. I call this version of world politics Westphalia World. It assumes hegemony ensures not just global prosperity but also global peace. All states, societies, and peoples benefit. Westphalia World, I contend, perpetrates a profound violence. It abuses what I call Multiple Worlds: that is, the hybrid legacies produced by subalterns to serve, and thereby survive, generations of foreign occupation by colonizing powers now replaced by multinational corporations. Subalterns navigate nimbly among the Multiple Worlds of tradition and modernity, the sacred and the secular, native and foreign, not to mention several languages, on a daily basis. Yet subalterns rarely receive formal recognition for their critical role in making world politics. Theories of International Relations threat world politics as if Multiple Worlds neither existed nor mattered.

L.H.M. Ling (2014, 1)

Normatively speaking, therefore, the study of global politics should strive to develop relevant knowledge about the minimal conditions for resilient and sustainable living. In fact, a similar claim has been made by the American IR Scholar, Raymond Garfield Gettell as far back as 1922 when he insisted that 'the realization of the complexity of world politics should, however, make for a more tolerant and broad minded attitude in foreign relations' (Gettell 1922, 330). According to him the recognition of the complexity of global life infers not only the contingency of world politics, but also the ambiguity of our knowledge about its dynamics. In this respect, Gettell (1922) has argued that rather than striving to foretell the future by attempting to predict what the likely patterns of relations between various international actors would be, our energies will be expended better on tracing the trajectories of the ten key factors in world affairs:

- History
- Natural environment
- Race and nationality
- Population/demographics
- Government and diplomacy
- Military strength
- Economic power
- Political ideals
- Religion
- Significant individuals

According to Gettell, the interaction between these ten factors would shape the direction of world affairs during the twentieth century. The chapters included in this textbook suggest that the patterns of international politics will still continue to be influenced by the feedback and dynamics spurred by the complex exchanges between these ten factors – even though the meaning and content of some of them would have changed radically since Gettell's time. Yet, it is through observation of these ten factors that one can begin to sense the possible trends in world affairs. More significantly, accepting uncertainty and unpredictability as a normal part of international politics, this textbook aims to spur its readers to demand and contribute to political action capable of continually imagining global life other than what it currently is. In this respect, rather than ignoring, reducing or seeking to control the complexity of politics, the study and practice of IR can focus on developing adaptive capacities for tolerating and working with change. Hopefully, this textbook has provided you with the confidence and skills to observe thoughtfully and encounter meaningfully world politics.

BIBLIOGRAPHY

Aron, R. (1966) *Peace and War: A Theory of International Relations* (London: Weidenfield and Nicolson).

Beaumont, R (1994) *War, Chaos, and History* (Westport, CT: Praeger).

Carr, E.H. (1981) *The Twenty Years' Crisis, 1919–1939: An Introduction to the Study of International Relations* (London: Macmillan).

Chakrabarty, D. (2000) *Provincializing Europe: Postcolonial Thought and Historical Difference* (Princeton, NJ: Princeton University Press).

Cox, R.W. (1981) 'Social Forces, States, and World Orders: Beyond IR Theory', *Millennium* 10(2), 126–55.

Deutsch, K.W. (1968) *The Analysis of International Relations* (Englewood Cliffs, NJ: Prentice Hall).

Fox, W.T.R. (1962) 'Frederick Sherwood Dunn and the American Study of International Relations', *World Politics* 15(1), 1–19.

Gettell, R.G. (1922) 'Influences on World Politics', *The Journal of International Relations* 12(3), 320–330.

Hobson, J.M. (2007) 'Is critical theory always *for* the White West and *for* Western imperialism? Beyond Westphilian towards a post-racist critical IR', *Review of International Studies* 33.S1: 91–116.

Huntington, S.P. (1967) 'Political Development and the Decline of the American System'. In D. Bell and S.R. Graubard (eds) *Towards the Year 2000: Work in Progress* (Cambridge, MA: MIT Press).

Israeli, N. (1932) 'Wishes Concerning Improbable Future Events: Reactions to the Future', *Journal of Applied Psychology* 16(5), 584–8.

Jervis, R. (1991/1992) 'The Future of World Politics: Will It Resemble the Past?', *International Security* 16(3), 39–73.

Lebow, R.N. (2007) *Coercion, Cooperation, and Ethics in International Relations* (London: Routledge).

Lebow, R.N. (2010). *Forbidden Fruit: Counterfactuals and International Relations* (Princeton, NJ: Princeton University Press).

Ling, L.H.M. (2014). *The Dao of World Politics: Towards a Post-Westphalian Worldist International Relations* (London: Routledge).

Puchala, D.J. (2003) *Theory and History in International Relations* (London: Routledge).

Rogowski, R. (1968) 'International Politics: The Past as Science', *International Studies Quarterly* 12(2), 394–418.

Rosenau, J.N. (1960) 'The Birth of a Political Scientist', *American Behavioral Scientist* 3(1), 19–21.

Rosenau, J.N. (1980) *The Scientific Study of Foreign Policy* (London: Frances Pinter).

Rosenau, J.N., Der Derian, J., Elshtain, J, Smith, S. and Sylvester, C. (1993) *Global Voices: Dialogues in International Relations* (Boulder, CO: Westview Press).

Russett, B.M. (1968) 'Rich and Poor in 2000AD: The Great Gulf', *Virginia Quarterly Review* 44(2), 182–98.

The Associate Press (1950) 'How the Experts Think We'll Live in 2000AD', 27 December.

Index

Printed in Great Britain
by Amazon